SPECIAL STUDIES

Case Studies in the Achievement of

Superiority

Benjamin Franklin Cooling
Editor

**Center for
Air Force
History**

Washington, D.C.

1994

Library of Congress Cataloging-in-Publication Data

Case studies in the achievement of air superiority / edited by Benjamin
Franklin Cooling.
      632 p. cm.—(Special studies)
      Includes bibliographical references and index.
      ISBN 0–912799–63–3
      1. Air warfare—Case studies. I. Cooling, B. Franklin.
II. United States. Air Force. Center for Air Force History.
III. Series: Special studies (United States. Air Force. Center for
Air Force History)
UG630.C277 1991
358.4'14—dc20

90–29998
CIP

For sale by the Superintendent of Documents, U.S. Government Printing Office
Washington, D.C. 20402

Foreword

Writing in 1978, General William W. Momyer, former Commander of the Tactical Air Command and a distinguished veteran fighter pilot, stated that:

> The contest for air superiority is the most important contest of all, for no other operations can be sustained if this battle is lost. To win it, we must have the best equipment, the best tactics, the freedom to use them, and the best pilots.

Certainly, the wide-ranging case studies examined in this book confirm this message, as do more contemporary experiences from the Falklands War, the Bekaa Valley, and, most recently, the Gulf War of 1991.

The historical roots of air superiority date to the First World War, which marked the emergence of the fighter airplane, offensive and defensive fighter doctrine, and the trained fighter pilot. By the end of the war, the Imperial German Air Service had been decisively outfought, and though occasional bitter air combat still occurred, the Allied air arms were free to harass and attack German ground forces wherever and whenever they chose. After the war, there were defense commentators who injudiciously predicted—not for the last time—that the era of dogfighting was over; higher aircraft speeds would make maneuvering air combat a thing of the past. Instead, the lesson of the importance of air superiority was rediscovered in the skies over Spain, and confirmed again throughout the Second World War. Having tenaciously wrested air superiority from the Luftwaffe, the Allies in 1941 went on to achieve genuine air supremacy, a situation acknowledged by General Dwight Eisenhower, who, riding through Normandy after D-Day, remarked to his son: "If I didn't have air supremacy, I wouldn't be here."

Sadly, many of these lessons were lost in the post-Second World War era, when technology advances—supersonic design theory, nuclear weapons, and "robot" aircraft—seemed to signal an end to the traditional air-to-air fighter—even though the experience of the Korean War demonstrated that transonic jet combat was not merely possible, but the new normative form of air warfare. Indeed, the fighter airplane underwent a dramatic transformation into a nuclear-armed strike aircraft, now that popular wisdom held that surface-to-air and air-to-air missiles foreshadowed the end of the era of "classic" air combat. That prediction collapsed in the face of the Vietnam war and the experiences of the Middle East. The 1970s witnessed both a revolution in fighter aircraft design (spawned by the technology advances of the 1960s and 1970s) and a return to basics in both design fundamentals and the training of fighter pilots. Operations in the Falklands war, over the Bekaa Valley, and most recently, during DESERT STORM confirmed not only the benefits of this revolution and rediscovery, but also the enduring importance of air superiority.

During DESERT STORM (which occurred while this book was in press) the airmen of the United States Air Force established air superiority over Iraq and occupied Kuwait from the outset of the war, defeating the Iraqi air force both in the air and on the ground. By so doing, they created the conditions essential for decisive air war. Strike and support aircraft and helicopters could go about their duties without fear of molestation from enemy aircraft. Iraq's forces, pinned in place, were denied any respite from punishing air attack. Because of coalition air supremacy, coalition land operations could be undertaken with an assurance, speed, and rapidity of pace never before seen in warfare. Bluntly stated, the Gulf war demonstrated that with air superiority, General Norman Schwarzkopf could undertake his famed "Hail Mary" play. Lacking air superiority, Iraq paid dearly. Its III Corps became vulnerable to air attack—stuck in a traffic jam out of Kuwait City on the "Highway of Death."

Air superiority, like democracy itself, must be constantly secured and renewed. In recognition of this, the United States Air Force is developing the F–22 Advanced Tactical Fighter to ensure that America retains its technological edge well into the 21st century. The case studies in this volume, encompassing several major air-to-air battles, eloquently demonstrate why the quest for air superiority remains critically important for today's Air Force.

RICHARD P. HALLION
Air Force Historian

United States Air Force
Historical Advisory Committee

Acknowledgments

The essays in this anthology of air superiority campaigns were written by some of the nation's foremost military and air historians. Individuals who participated in the review of the entire manuscript included Gen. William W. Momyer, USAF (Ret.); Dr. Richard H. Kohn, Chief of the Office of Air Force History; Dr. Alfred Goldberg, Office of the Secretary of Defense; Dr. Dennis Showalter of Colorado College; and Col. Fred Shiner, Herman S. Wolk, and Bernard Nalty from the Center for Air Force History. Dr. Benjamin Franklin Cooling served as general editor of the volume.

Laura Dahljelm of Center for Air Force History edited the manuscript and gathered the photographs and artwork, and Anne E. Johnson shepherded the book through the publications process. Financial support was provided by Col. John A. Warden III of the Office of the Air Force Deputy Chief of Staff for Plans and Operations.

Photographs appearing in this volume are primarily from the collections at the Department of Defense Still Media Records Center, the National Air and Space Museum, the Library of Congress, and the National Archives. Those sources of illustrations outside official U.S. government repositories are noted.

"MiG Sweep," by renowned aviation artist Keith Ferris, is reproduced on the cover and dustjacket, courtesy of the USAF Art Collection. Lori Crane of Headquarters Air Force Graphics designed the cover, and Kathy Jones supplied the art for reproduction.

Contents

Maps

Photographs

Introduction

To military aviators, "air superiority" is an unquestioned prerequisite for effective aerial operations. Stripped to its barest essentials, it has a deceptively simple definition. As the authoritative Department of Defense *Dictionary of Military and Associatied Terms* (Joint Chiefs of Staff Publication 1) declares: air superiority is "that degree of dominance in the air battle of one force over another which permits the conduct of operations by the former and its related land, sea, and air forces at a given time and place without prohibitive interference by the opposing force." Not only is this the accepted definition for the United States Air Force, but it has been accepted by officials of the North Atlantic Treaty Organization (NATO), Southeast Asia Treaty Organization (SEATO), Central Treaty Organization (CENTO), and the Inter-American Defense Board (IADB). Presumably, other nations and signatories to similar defense treaties, like the Warsaw Pact countries, have equal pronouncements on this central issue of modern warfare.[1]

Airpower thinkers have now elevated the question of air superiority to the aerospace operational medium. Of course, traditionally, military operational superiority of one sort or another has formed a major theme of warfare. Naval professionals have long held to a concept called "command of the sea," while land disciples of Clausewitz have formulated like principles. Authors of air doctrine have further refined the concept of air superiority, although sometimes confusing it with other terms such as "absolute" air superiority, "defensive" air superiority, or "local" air superiority, for example.[2] While many operators have little time to differentiate the subtitles of the terms, it seems widely recognized that air superiority is crucial to effective, sustained combat operations.

Once the dictionary has been left behind, the student of air power must confront the issues of air superiority: how to gain it, how to maintain it, and what is required of an air force and its commanders in the waging of campaigns under various circumstances. As British official historians Sir Charles Webster and Noble Frankland emphasized in their *Strategic Air*

Offensive Against Germany, air superiority is a term that has been in constant, but generally unclear and often conflicting, use almost since the first employment of military aircraft. Some observers have interpreted air superiority as the possession of a larger air force, or one which has greater destructive power. Others have seen it as the ability to drive the enemy air force onto the defensive and thus deny the opposition the means of carrying out counteroffensive operations. Yet to still others, said Webster and Frankland, "It is purely a question of air communications, and means simply the ability to fly at will over enemy territory, and to some extent prevent the enemy from doing the same." To these eminent historians, such ideas merely provided "aspects of air superiority." They felt it was not a question of being able to use an air force, but rather "a question of being able to use it effectively."[3]

Effectiveness, of course, means more than merely breaching an opponent's air defense. It is a question of breaking through and doing critical damage. Webster and Frankland applied this point to strategic bombardment, reconnaissance, close air support of ground and naval operations, as well as other missions of air power. Their definition was the extent to which it is possible for one combatant (or impossible for the other, conversely) to conduct constant and effective naval, land, and air operations in spite of any opposition. Thus, as seen in the chapters of this volume, air superiority constitutes both an ability to deny the enemy air superiority as well as asserting friendly air superiority over him. It was obvious to Webster and Frankland that air superiority can rarely be absolute. It is merely a means to an end: the unhindered use of the air for military purposes. It must be the product of various factors, ranging from ground antiaircraft fire, counterair action, geography, and weather, to communications, intelligence, organization, command and control, interservice and inter-allied cooperation, industrial capacity, national will and morale, and technology. The authors in this volume have tried to incorporate such factors where relevant to their particular discussions of air superiority.

The essays in this volume address some of the most important campaigns of air superiority ever fought in the twentieth century. They focus upon combat experience since such episodes provide the basis for doctrine. The thorny question of doctrinal development in peacetime, the overwhelming emphasis on strategic bombardment to the detriment of tactical air power (which includes reconnaissance or observation, pursuit/interception, and interdiction, for example), and the elusive factors of geopolitics and economics as they pertain to airpower doctrine, become apparent in the first essay. The authors of some essays suggest the absence of any unifying and universally accepted principle for achieving air superiority. Prior to World War II, as one American flyer remembered, "I think during that period, we really didn't know what we were trying to do. We were doing it but not defining it." Thus, to Lt. Gen. Elwood R. "Pete" Quesada, "the fighter business in those days was a bunch of guys going up and fighting another bunch of guys without a known objective."[4]

Quesada was only a major in July 1941, but he discerned that the concept of air superiority was "really defined after the Second World War started." This conclusion has been confirmed in the essays as the authors have examined how different peacetime doctrinal interpretations changed under the pressures of war. In fact, a major theme of this anthology suggests a difference between theory and practice in the management of air conflict. Tactical airpower leaders in the United States today define their mission as sixfold: counterair (defensive and offensive), air support of ground operations, interdiction, special operations, "support" to include reconnaissance and electronic combat, and theater nuclear warfare. Obviously, nearly all are extremely difficult to carry out without air superiority. This fundamental fact is no different today than it was seventy years ago and promises no drastic redirection in the future. Only the means of achievement may shift, as the historians in this volume have suggested from their studies of the past. This anthology represents, then, a corpus of thought by professional historians based on original research, intensive analysis, and collegial discussion of major issues of air superiority. The purpose is to illuminate continuing professional issues by employing historical experience.

Notes

1. U.S. Joint Chiefs of Staff, Department of Defense, *Dictionary of Military and Associated Terms—JCS Pub 1* (Washington, Government Printing Office, Sept 3, 1974), p 20.
2. Woodford Agee Heflin, ed, *The United States Air Force Dictionary* (Maxwell AFB, Ala., 1956), pp 2, 4, 37, 133, 158, 229, 303.
3. Sir Charles Webster and Noble Frankland, *The Strategic Air Offensive Against Germany, 1939–1945* [United Kingdom History of the Second World War] (London, 1961), pp 20–23.
4. Richard H. Kohn and Joseph P. Harahan, eds, *Air Superiority in World War II and Korea* [USAF Warrior Studies] (Washington: Office of Air Force History, 1983), p 18.

1

Developments and Lessons before World War II

Leonard Baker and B. F. Cooling

Air superiority doctrine came slowly to the air forces of the world. Like most other forms of air doctrine, it had its origins in World War I. Major military powers saw aviation primarily as an adjunct to ground operations. Prior to the war, however, aviation had been viewed as providing communication, observation, and reconnaissance support to ground troops. True, Count Ferdinand von Zeppelin had informed the German Imperial General Staff in the 1890s that his rigid airships or dirigibles could assault fortifications and troop concentrations with bombs, as well as transport soldiers. Even the early writers of specific aviation studies projected a violent, even apocalyptic potential, for aircraft. Futurists like H. G. Wells warned in 1908 that bombardment of cities and other combat roles for aircraft could be anticipated in the future. Yet, the primitive flying machines in 1914 proved too short-ranged, underpowered, and hardly worthy of combat. If aviators and inventors envisioned an offensive role in war for such craft, conventional soldiers could not.[1]

Peacetime experiments with bombsights and machineguns fired from aircraft in flight led to the use of airplanes in the Italo-Turkish war of 1911–12 and the Balkan wars of the following year. Lt. Benjamin Foulois (later Maj. Gen. and Chief of the U.S. Army Air Corps in the 1930s) recalled of his own flying experiences at San Diego, California, in 1914 and 1915: "We had ideas about using the airplanes as an offensive weapon, which was contrary, of course, to military policy. But, we were out there dropping oranges, dropping sacks of flour, and doing all sorts of work of that kind; . . . with the idea of developing it for that type of work." Thus,

1

aviators had begun to think about what military policymakers had not yet fully understood: i.e., the combat uses of air power.[2]

The developing state of aviation and the tightly prescribed organizational arrangements for aviation, as part of land and sea forces at the time, precluded doctrinal breakthroughs before World War I. The fact that few soldiers, sailors, or airmen then visualized an enemy contesting the use of air space over the battle, and thus elevating combat on land or sea into a fight for command of the air, may seem incredible. But, airmen were too busy learning how to fly and operate their machines. The whole question of achieving air superiority hardly affected battleship admirals or cavalry generals predisposed to shaping the course of battle through their own particular mode of warfare. Only combat itself would dictate otherwise. Speculation upon the various roles for air power and the doctrine necessary for implementing those roles became one of the most important results of the use of aviation in the First World War.

The Catalyst of World War I

The origins of air superiority doctrine lay not in theory, but in experience gained over the Western Front in France. Air superiority doctrine derived from the crucible of World War I. Yet, even then, ground action largely shaped its early concepts. The realities of the battlefield lay on the ground where infantry, artillery, machineguns, barbed wire, poison gas, and later tanks, dominated tactics. The Western Front became stabilized by Christmas 1914, and the war became a protracted fight in which manpower and industrial mobilization, logistics, organization, and psychological adjustment to life in the trenches became as important to operations as the tactics of infantry or cavalry. This kind of conflict became a backdrop for airmen to consider their own role in modern warfare. They began to formulate doctrine for defining this role. However, the process took place only over time—those drawn-out months of stalemate when total war of mass dictated procurement of large quantities of men and materiel to be poured onto a rather limited section of terrain. In such an environment, doctrine became inevitably linked to the actual experience of combat.

Observation aviators soon began contesting air space with one another. Ground commanders demanded that enemy observation be kept away from friendly lines. At first, the observation airmen merely shot at one another with handguns or used other weapons of opportunity. Later, they introduced machineguns, until finally, lessons from this inconclusive sparring led to an inevitable spiral of newer aircraft and armament designed to wrest control of the air from the prying eyes of enemy reconnaissance. Before long, this escalation continued on yet a second plane as airmen began bombing targets on the ground. As Maj. Gen. Hugh Trenchard, General

Officer Commanding the Royal Flying Corps in the field for the British Expeditionary Force (BEF), explained to Lt. Col. William Mitchell, an American observer in June 1917: "When the airplanes began to attack each other and drop bombs, the troops on the ground yelled for protection and brought the air forces to task for not keeping all enemy airplanes out of the air near them." Thus began the contest for air superiority.[3]

Historians have observed that the side in the conflict that possessed the best aircraft momentarily commanded the sky. Indeed, part of the story of air superiority was that of technological superiority. While the story of individual aircraft types and designs, or the generational sequence from Fokkers to Spads to Nieuports and Sopwith aircraft lies beyond the scope of this essay, the technical edge remains important to understanding this gestation period for air superiority doctrine. For example, the last part of 1915 and the first months of 1916 were dominated by what Allied pilots termed the "Fokker scourge." German aircraft manufacturer Anthony Fokker (actually a transplanted Dutchman) produced his famous *Eindecker* monoplanes, which mounted a novel synchronized machinegun mechanism for firing through the propeller, thus affording flyers a relatively stable aerial gun platform. This aircraft dominated the air for a time. Then, Allied aviators recaptured technological superiority with their Bristol, Sopwith Camel, Salamander, and Spad fighters, only to lose it once more when the Germans came up with their Albatros and Halberstadt airplanes in 1917. Such was the ebb and flow of aviation technology; the advantage became as much a factor of superior aircraft designers and manufacturers by the middle of the war as tactics and individual flying skill. At the time of Verdun and the Somme in 1916, air superiority depended on factors all the way from industry through ministries of defense, right to the frontline aviators at aerodromes in France.[4]

Of course, aviators concerned with the air battle focused primarily upon air fighting techniques, formation flying, increased training, and proper command, control and coordination arrangements, as these factored into the air superiority equation. Everyone worked to send the best prepared flyers into battle, although the heavy attrition rate of men and machines for both sides often lowered qualitative and quantitative levels below the satisfactory point. Individual squadron commanders like Capt. Oswald Boelcke of the German Military Aviation Service particularly recognized the virtue of vigorously training pilots in fighter techniques before taking them into combat. Boelcke's pupils, such as Baron Manfred von Richthofen, proved the value of such precombat training by combining superior aircraft with superior pilot skills to win many air battles over the Western Front. Here was the true cutting edge of air superiority in actual combat—the wedding of man and machine. As one student of the air war has concluded, the large number of inexperienced replacements, combined with curtailment of training due to shortages of materiel, lubricants, gaso-

Sopwith Camel.

line, and other supplies, resulted in a marked decline of German frontline pilot proficiency by 1918. This downturn contrasted with a rejuvenated Allied pilot training program and superior fourth-generation fighter aircraft at a particularly pivotal moment in the war.[5]

Air superiority for the Allies, at least, also depended upon how well air leaders used their combat strength. Early on, Trenchard and his French counterpart, Commandant Jean du Peuty, learned the merits of Allied command cooperation. In moments of crisis when German offensives threatened one or the other's sector, they exchanged men and aircraft freely. Entry of American aviators into the war in 1917 extended this strong interallied cooperation. Both the Royal Flying Corps and the *Aviation Militaire* trained and supplied the American Air Service of the American Expeditionary Forces (AEF), thereby enhancing the overall air superiority edge for the Allies. In a sense, the Americans both on land and in the air provided additional manpower, while the Allies provided material aid and standardized procedures, training, and weapons. Of nearly 1,500 American Air Service combat pilots, about one-half trained in French, British, and Italian schools, while more than 20,000 ground support personnel did likewise. American training programs usually copied or modified European guidelines, and the manual of pursuit aviation given to all American flyers was a translation of the French air ace Albert Deullin's notes. Such methods minimized normal interoperability problems for this Allied force.[6]

The interchange of ideas and experience led naturally to some early efforts at codifying airpower doctrine. Both German and Allied combatants learned over the course of the conflict that there were two abiding principles—concentration of force and the priority of counterair operations. However, the daily demands of combat prevented emergence of a single architect of doctrine at this time. Achievement of air superiority *over* the battlefield was obviously an extension of superiority *on* the battlefield. Senior leaders saw attainment of both through offensive massing of firepower, weaponry, and men at the principal point of engagement. Aviators, like their ground superiors, therefore favored concentration of military striking power, rather than parceling out assets among smaller organizational elements. Trenchard, for example, mirrored Field Marshal Douglas Haig's principle of the massed offensive; only in Trenchard's case, the mass would be of aircraft in the air. Consequently, both generals earned the label of "butcher" by those subordinate to them. Yet, Haig and Trenchard represented a generation of military leaders who remained disciples of the offensive and sought to use any new tool such as the airplane to underpin this faith.[7]

Trenchard's Royal Flying Corps became the benchmark for Allied air efforts by 1916 and 1917. French air assets had been decimated during costly land battles, thus relinquishing primacy of effort to their British comrades. German aviators also suffered from the same attritional struggles in the air, struggles as bloody and debilitating as those incurred in the trench fighting on the ground. But Trenchard clung tenaciously to his tenets of careful preparation for combat: training in rear areas before initiation to

Fokker Eindecker.

5

battle, followed by relentless pursuit of the tactical air offensive to win and maintain air superiority. He used this offensive to clear the skies of enemy fighters and then to attack the enemy's trenches, staging areas, supply dumps, and logistical network. Trenchard's advocacy of aggressive air warfare reflected the growing interest among senior war leaders on both sides that airplanes might offer a war-winning weapon.[8] After witnessing a German aerial bombardment of London in mid-1917, the perceptive South African senior statesman and member of Great Britain's Imperial War Cabinet, Gen. (later Field Marshal) Jan Smuts declared that air power could be used as an independent means of war operations. "As far as can at present be foreseen," he proclaimed, "there is absolutely no limit to the scale of its future independent war use."[9]

Implicit in such conclusions about the strategic virtue of air power was the notion that bombardment of an enemy's homeland industries and war production would have an effect on the tactical stalemate in France. Yet, the needs of ground generals prevented switching the principal emphasis of air operations to strategic attacks beyond the battlefield. A given fact of World War I remained that aviation (as part of essentially what was a ground war) had to remain at the call of the soldier. Airmen had to formulate their doctrine and mission in light of that consideration. As late as September 11, 1918, merely two months before the Armistice, Brig. Gen. William "Billy" Mitchell, now the Chief of the American Air Service for First Army, issued his Battle Orders Number 1, citing in italics: "Our air service will take the offensive at all points with the object of destroying the enemy's air service, attacking his troops on the ground and protecting our own air and ground troops."[10]

American entry into the war coincided with growing concern about doctrinal codification of air operations. The American aviators, for example, sought to collect experience and lessons upon which to base their own air contribution. Mitchell in 1917 posited tenets that very much reflected conventional military thought of the period. Only ground arms could win the ultimate victory, he acknowledged, and the Air Service was a supporting arm of land warfare. But, within aviation itself, there existed two general types, he claimed. "Tactical" aviation operated in the immediate vicinity of surface forces; and "strategical" aviation worked far in advance of the other arms and had an independent mission. Tactical aviation would comprise observation, pursuit, and tactical bombardment. Strategical aviation also included pursuit, as well as day and night bombardment. Pursuit aviation, uniquely, would work both the strategic and tactical mission areas. Its object, declared Mitchell, was to attain "mastery of the air" through air battles. Mitchell's differentiation of aviation types paralleled the thinking of other Air Service officers such as Maj. Marlborough Churchill and Maj. Frank Parker. Both were members of an AEF board studying the role of aviation, and Churchill, at least, referred openly to "superiority in the air" and may well have been the actual author of this term. In any event, other aviators, including Americans, dared to reach out for more independent airpower alternatives to ground support, as even Mitchell himself did later on.[11]

Everyone seemed admittedly clearer about types of aviation than doctrinal subtleties. It may have been Maj. (later Lt. Col.) Edgar S. Gorrell who first introduced Italian bombardment doctrine into the American camp to supplement British theory. Gorrell served as the first Chief of the AEF's Air Service Technical Section in Paris, where he fell under the influence of Count Gianni Caproni di Taliedo, a wealthy Italian aircraft manufacturer and aviation enthusiast. Caproni also introduced Gorrell to the persuasive ideas of a controversial Italian aviator, Giulio Douhet. Caproni had developed a heavy bombardment airplane which he wanted to sell to the Americans. Douhet sought to gain adherents to air power as a viable alternative to the bloody land stalemate of the war. Gorrell became the willing American apostle for what Maj. Gen. Laurence S. Kuter of the subsequent United States Army Air Forces would call in 1943, the "earliest, clearest, and least known statement of the American conception of the employment of air power."[12]

Gorrell took Douhet's theory and the promise of Caproni's bombers, as they both existed in 1917, and formulated a strategic offensive plan that carried the concept of air superiority far beyond the battlefield. Basically, all aviation thinkers until this point reflected an age in which war had become total. Since domestic industry had become the underpinning for conflict, some method was needed to negate this factor. Aerial bombardment of homefront industries, demoralization of war workers, and interdiction of logistical lifelines would remove the tools of war from armies and end the conflict. Here was something more than just another tactical device to achieve local air superiority. Strategic bombardment offered geopolitical options, although Gorrell, like Trenchard, Douhet, and Mitchell, probably considered mostly the immediate impact on the battlefield. "Apparently," noted Gorrell in his plan, "both the Allies and the Germans have begun at the same time to conceive of the immense importance of aerial bombing, and we find in all countries, both Allied and German, the conception of the immensity of such a problem and the beginning of a preparation for a bombing campaign."[13]

Gorrell's plan could not be tested. Aircraft production problems, lack of approval from the War Department General Staff in Washington, Allied disunity as to implementation, and the onset of the Armistice relegated strategic bombardment to the realm of hope but not fulfillment. Still, military aviation emerged from the war with a fairly clear view of itself. As Mitchell explained in a position paper on the tactical application of military aeronautics in 1919, the principal mission "is to destroy the aeronautical force of the enemy, and after this to attack his formations, both tactical and

7

Italian aircraft manufacturer Count Gianni Caproni di Taliedo.

strategical, on the ground or on the water." He felt that secondary employment of aeronautics pertained to "their use as an auxiliary to troops on the ground for enhancing their effort against hostile troops." He defined four elements of military aviation: pursuit, bombardment, attack, and observation. Pursuit aviation, claimed Mitchell, was "designed to take and hold the offensive in the air against all hostile aircraft," adding that "it is with this branch of Aviation that air supremacy is sought and obtained." Mitchell noted further that bombardment's mission was to attack enemy concentration points distant from their front lines. He viewed bombardment's role at the beginning of the war as hitting the enemy's "great nerve centers" so as to paralyze them to the greatest possible extent. Within the theater of operations of an army, bombardment would be used against supply points of all sorts, including airdromes, railroad stations, roads, and communications, "and last against troops and trains on the roads."[14]

Mitchell included two other important forms of military aviation, in addition to pursuit and bombardment. Attack aviation, he said, was the "last specialization in aviation which occurred on the Western Front in Europe just as the war ended." It was designed for direct assault with cannon, machineguns, and bombs upon hostile ground forces, tanks, antiaircraft artillery, airdromes, supply convoys, and railroad trains in the combat area. Finally, Mitchell also concluded that observation aviation would remain important to air support of ground operations. Indeed, Mitchell spoke from experience. He and his aviators had participated in all these functional areas during the battles of St. Mihiel and the Meuse-Argonne in

1918. If the war had lasted longer, they claimed later, then verification of the effectiveness of such massive, centralized air offensives might have resulted in the independent decisiveness of air power itself. As it was, the Armistice had robbed them of resolution.[15]

Evaluation Between the Wars

Air superiority as it emerged from the World War had a somewhat limited meaning. Truly, it signified control of the skies over the land battlefield as well as the area through which armies conveyed men and materiel to the fighting. Given the range and carrying limitations of aircraft as well as the limited destructive power of aerial ordnance, it could not have been otherwise. French and German aviators concentrated upon close air support of ground operations through observation, artillery fire-control, and tactical employment of fighters and bombers. Gotha bombers and Zeppelin raids had spread terror throughout England during the war, but caused only limited damage. British, Italian, and American airmen began looking beyond tactical air operations to the war-winning potential of strategic bombardment in the air superiority matrix. However, only the future could resolve doctrinal boundaries of a "battlefield," since modern warfare now included not only the area of immediate combat and logistical support, but the entire country that provided arms and soldiers for the contest. The question of air superiority doctrine after the war had to consider both dimensions.[16]

Limited military budgets, demilitarization of the defeated Central Powers (Germany and Austria-Hungary), the disintegration of Russia through revolution, the false promises of the League of Nations, and profound war weariness all pervaded Europe after the World War. The Treaty of Versailles forced Germany to relinquish her air service, although the treaty army of the Weimar Republic maintained a small technical office responsible for at least collecting and studying aeronautical information in the absence of an air force. Russian aviation, which had lacked strength even before the 1917 revolution, struggled in a short war with Poland before emerging with fresh vigor under Soviet Communist sponsorship. British, French, Italian, and American aviators returned to peacetime chores of training and maintenance, as well as the increasingly debilitating battles with army and navy rivals over organizational control of air forces. In a world tired of conflict and anxious for disarmament, aviators everywhere faced fiscal constraint, large inventories of obsolescent aircraft, and little prospect of immediate improvement.

However, none of this dampened confidence in the future. Aviators speculated about independent, strategic air power as the answer in modern war. While military aviation and national defense meant something differ-

9

ent in each country, the aviation community found universal accord on that one tenet. Their principal enemy was military reactionism. Warriors like France's venerable Marshal Ferdinand Foch held that "no more than Artillery, the armored cars, etc., can the air service by itself constitute an army. If it is developed to an inordinate extent, this must, in view of the necessarily limited resources, inevitably be to the detriment of the other arms, and in particular of the infantry, still of paramount importance, and so reduce the value of the whole Army." Aviation to men like Foch had to remain auxiliary to the ground army. Battles over roles and missions as well as doctrine would be fought as tenaciously within ministries of defense after the World War as the great attritional land battles of that conflict had been fought in the mud of Flanders.[17]

Naturally, spokesmen for air power sought independence from army and navy control. This became fundamental to air activity of the decade. Everyone looked to the Royal Air Force (RAF) of Great Britain and the Italian air service as models of independence, failing to realize how bitter struggles continued in both countries to retain such independence. Still, an independent air ministry coequal with admiralty and war office meant that theorists like the RAF Chief, Air Marshal Sir Hugh Trenchard, or the controversial Italian brigadier, Giulio Douhet, could pursue their doctrinal arguments without the trammels of parent service control. Trenchard still had to battle the Royal Navy and British Army for RAF survival, but he was not subordinate to either of them. He could use his office to speak out openly for the cause of air power. Douhet, who was judged "to have a difficult temper and to be a unilateral polemic," faced similar bureaucratic battles within military circles. He finally resigned to continue his crusade in the journalistic arena. The third major theorist of the period, Billy Mitchell, proved just as thorny to his service colleagues as Douhet. His criticism of superiors within the Army, where the American Air Service remained firmly implanted, finally drove him to civilian life as well. In fact, Mitchell's efforts pointed as much toward winning air independence from the Army as to providing intellectual underpinnings to military aviation.[18]

All three of these theorists devoted their efforts in the 1920s to advancing the future potential of air power. Trenchard was the least vocal, perhaps, confining his work to internal government channels. His most familiar statements appeared in a 1928 or 1929 paper, "The War Object of an Air Force." Therein he outlined his thesis that the object of all three military services was to defeat the enemy nation, not merely its armed forces. The air force would concentrate upon the production centers and arteries of transportation and communication. Its aim, he felt, "is to break down the enemy's means of resistance by attacks on objectives selected as most likely to achieve this end." While an air force might have to battle the enemy's own air units at the beginning for control of the air, the only true objective should remain the enemy homefront. Trenchard saw nothing wrong in bombing cities as long as the targets remained military ones. Civilian workers in war industries remained legitimate targets since he foresaw a "moral" effect of creating panic among them and dispersing their contribution to the war effort.[19]

Douhet's theories received wider scrutiny, largely because of his numerous publications. His pivotal work, *Il Dominio Dell'Aria (The Command of the Air)* appeared in 1921. Its theme applied equally to a continental nation such as Italy, as well as to maritime powers like Great Britain. The book especially appealed to younger aviators committed to Douhet's dictum that "the control of the air allows us to stop the enemy from flying and to keep his faculty for ourselves." Moreover, Douhet looked beyond the limits of a land battlefield. Underlying his theories were twin assumptions that 1) aircraft are instruments of offense against which no effective defense can be foreseen; and 2) civilian morale can be shattered by bombardment of population centers. Douhet's main tenets and scenarios for future war flowed from these assumptions.[20]

Douhet stated bluntly that to insure an adequate national defense, it was necessary to be in a position to "conquer" the command of the air in the event of war. Like Trenchard, he saw the primary objectives of an aerial attack as industrial and population centers. He rejected the idea that an enemy air force should be fought in the air, but rather "by destroying the collection points, the supplying and the manufacturing centers of the enemy aviation." Like the RAF chief, Douhet thought that the role of armies should be purely defensive, containing an enemy advance while the strategic aerial offensive proceeded with the destruction of the enemy's warmaking capability and morale. He also rejected the notion of specialized fighters to defend against enemy bombers, preferring instead to devote all air resources to "battle planes" which would carry out bombardment, and yet would also be self-defending. Inherent survivability of such aircraft would obviate the need for friendly pursuit escort, since they would always get through and thus prevent the enemy from ever mounting its own air offensive. As another prominent French soldier of the era, Marshal Henri Pétain suggested, Douhet provided "an inexhaustible source for reflection."[21]

Douhet and Trenchard ultimately proved far less controversial than Mitchell. As Assistant Chief of the Air Service in the United States Army, this zealous crusader gathered around him a coterie of American airpower enthusiasts. However, his major problem was the questioning of War Department authority to make air policy. The issue became highly politicized as Army staff officers studied various peacetime reorganization schemes and rejected any thought that an air service should exist separate from the ground forces. For a time, even Mitchell embraced that position. However, his thinking gradually changed between the end of the war and the mid-twenties. His publicity ploys such as bombing an old German bat-tleship off the Virginia Capes to demonstrate the power of bombardment and continuous criticism of land-bound Army leaders embroiled Mitchell in endless debate. As even his friend Trenchard observed, "He's a man after my own heart. If only he can break his habit of trying to convert opponents by killing them, he'll go far." But Mitchell could not alter his maverick style. Eventually court-martialed, he left the service unrepentent in 1926. His voice could not be silenced even then, and there was more to his contribution than mere controversy.[22]

Mitchell moved even beyond Trenchard and Douhet in thinking about air power. Noting in *Our Air Force* (1921) that "as a prelude to any engage-ment of military or naval forces, a contest must take place for control of the air," he contended that the first battles of any future war would be air battles. The nation winning them, he claimed, would be practically certain of ultimate victory because its air arm could operate and increase without

Maj. Gen. Hugh Trenchard.

12

Imperial War Museum

Left: **Giulio Douhet:** *Below:*
Brig. Gen. William Mitchell.

hindrance. Two years later, in a little known manual that he published privately, Mitchell suggested that pursuit and bombardment had to work together to achieve such goals. "Each must understand the methods, powers, and limitations of the other, because regardless of which side has aerial supremacy, our bombardment will force a concentration of enemy pursuit at a time and place selected for an attack." Mitchell argued for a modernized American air service of some 5,000 aircraft, comprising 60 percent pursuit, 20 percent bombardment, and 20 percent attack (or ground support aircraft).[23]

Gradually, however, Mitchell became better known for more sweeping views of the potential for air power in gaining strategic air superiority. His best known work, and one quoted extensively at his court-martial, was *Winged Defense*. Here he propounded the unprecedented power of airplanes for changing the rules for the conduct of war and the formulation of strategy. "The advent of air power, which can go straight to the vital centers and either neutralize or destroy them," he proclaimed, "has put a completely new complexion on the old system of making war." Mitchell seemed to be paraphrasing Douhet and Trenchard on this point. Yet, he diverged from the Italian, at least, with his contention that "the only effective defense against aerial attack is to whip the enemy's air forces in air battles." Furthermore, Mitchell would not accept Douhet's concept of an all-purpose battle plane.[24]

The American had been a pilot-commander; the Italian had served mainly in a staff capacity, and this fact conditioned their respective approaches to air power. Then too, both men reflected different national perspectives. Douhet formed his theories based on the geographical and political realities of Italy. His focus remained continental and limited to potential European enemies. He admitted that if he were considering issues of possible confrontation between Japan and the United States, then his conclusions would be different. Mitchell reflected the strategic needs of the United States, a nation with continental defense as well as overseas maritime interests. Thus, Mitchell was the first theorist to expand the application of aviation to global terms. His tours of Europe and the Far East in the early 1920s increased his appreciation of wider issues. He suggested in several *Saturday Evening Post* articles in the winter of 1925–26 that while the United States could act defensively from its home bases, to defeat a future enemy it would have to operate offensively via island-stepping routes to Europe or Asia. Nevertheless, Mitchell felt that American bombers could go unscathed to "any target if the United States had control of the air.'[25]

Naturally, there were those who differed with Douhet and Mitchell. Gens. Amedeo Mecozzi and Italo Balbo, prominent Italian aviators, attacked many of Douhet's tenets on both practical and moral grounds. They argued for confining bombardment to purely military targets and keeping air power more closely aligned with naval and ground force needs. In America, Maj. William C. Sherman, the Air Service instructor at the Army's Command and General Staff College, took a more pragmatic stance than Mitchell. He prepared a War Department pamphlet in 1926 concerning fundamental principles for Air Service employment and published his thoughts commercially in a book entitled *Air Warfare*. "The organization and training of all air units is based on the fundamental doctrine that their mission is to aid the ground forces to gain decisive success," he noted in the War Department pamphlet. Privately, he expanded upon Mitchell's theories by suggesting that the idea of unescorted bombers reaching their targets unscathed was fallacious, and that pursuit aviation "is in fact, the very backbone of the air force." He advocated long-range pursuit escort of bombers beyond Mitchell's initial air superiority battle. Such diversity of thinking reflected fruitful debate in air training schools around the world and especially at the U.S. Army Air Service Field Officers' School (subsequently called the Air Corps Tactical School).[26]

The theorists focused upon the future. But the present realities of air power in the 1920s were something quite different. The Chief of the U.S. Army Air Service, for example, noted in 1923 that while the British might have 5,000 aircraft, the French some 3,000, and even the Italians about 1,000 machines, most of them were war relics. Including some 267 "aircraft of modern design" delivered to the U.S. Army and Navy since 1922, he anticipated that American aviators could realistically expect no more than 289 serviceable aircraft for the two services by mid-1926. This might be less than 20 percent of the requirement, he admitted, but neither cost-conscious legislators nor suspicious Army and Navy officers would approve any more than that. Army leadership, at least, permitted the Air Service to attain comparable status with infantry, cavalry, and artillery branches in the 1926 Air Corps Act. But, in the opinion of Lt. Laurence S. Kuter, the service's squadrons at this time "were more flying clubs or training units than combat organizations."[27]

The primacy of pursuit over bombardment aviation remained constant until the mid-twenties. This was due in part to pursuit planes being more advanced technologically. However, it did not prevent aviators from speculating about the future of strategic air power. They began to distinguish between basic functions of an "air force" as compared to an "air service." Capt. Carl Spatz (later, Spaatz) told one civilian correspondent in 1926 that "air service" formed that part of aviation that worked directly with and in conjunction with ground troops, and he cited observation as his example. An "air force" was that part of aviation capable of independent action without regard to the land battle and included pursuit, bombardment, and attack aviation. "These branches of aviation strike independently at enemy centers such as cities, factories, railroad yards, docks, etc.," he explained, "without regard to location or operation of ground troops." In other words, declared Spatz, "it is a 'Force' within itself." As he told a Marine Corps School audience at Quantico, Virginia, in November 1927: "Missions of pursuit is [sic] to secure the air superiority necessary for operations of our bombardment, attack, and observation units, and to prevent hostile aircraft from operating effectively."[28]

The conflict between dreams and reality could be found in presentations by Air Corps Maj. Earl L. Naiden before an audience at the Army War College in 1929. He presented statistics contrasting American military aviation with other air forces of the world. In the event of war, the Army Air Corps had barely 671 aircraft available to tactical units, after subtracting obsolete, training, and cargo aircraft. All told, Naiden cited inventories of 209 pursuit, 68 bombardment, 68 attack, as well as 531 observation aircraft for the land service, with an additional naval air strength of 223 pursuit, 141 torpedo and bombardment, 291 observation, and 32 patrol planes. Even then, the combined American military aviation establishment hardly approached the "balance" envisioned by Mitchell a decade before, and observation aircraft continued to dominate the inventories. Of course, Naiden's lecture also suggested that other nations took a different approach to the question of balance.[29]

Naiden demonstrated how the different aviation powers envisioned the proper mixture of aircraft types to secure balance. He did not explain that such balances reflected different strategic or tactical priorities, however. (See Tables 1–1 and 1–2)

Naiden's figures showed that at the end of the immediate postwar decade, only Great Britain had embraced strategic air power in fact as well as in theory. The United States alone had incorporated attack aviation (or ground support aviation) as a distinct class for its inventory of missions and aircraft. Only Japan lagged far behind in priority accorded pursuit aviation. Virtually all nations still flew open cockpit biplanes of World War I vintage. As one perceptive future United States Air Force leader of research and development after the Second World War commented, "we hadn't advanced a hell of a lot over where we were in World War I."[30]

Advances in military aviation would occur more rapidly in the 1930s. At first, the Great Crash of 1929 and deepening worldwide economic depression affected governments everywhere. Military spending was cut to the bone. Only the rise of totalitarian regimes in Germany, Italy, and Japan and their threat to international peace stimulated rearmament. When a new cycle of wars began after 1931, military affairs once more assumed major attention around the world. Air power became the new tip-weight on the scales of power. True, as French aviation writer Camille Rougeron concluded in 1937, military professionals such as those who formulated the strategy and doctrine of air warfare had been deprived of the "rigorous daily testing of their ideas" by an enemy fighter force for nearly twenty

TABLE 1–1
Comparative Squadron Strengths, 1929

Country		Bombardment	Observation	Pursuit	Other
Great Britain		32	11	12	1 torpedo/ bombing
France	(Army)	31	69	32	
	(Navy)	9	5	5	
Italy	(Army)	24.2	26.2	26	
	(Navy)	3	13.2	6	
Japan	(Army)	3.5	10.5	10.5	
	(Navy)				

TABLE 1–2
Balanced Air Forces Percentage Projection, 1929

Country		Bombardment	Observation	Pursuit	Attack
Great Britain		51	26	23	0
France		25	49	26	0
Italy		32	39	39	0
Japan		29	60	11	0
United States					
	(Army)	27	40	27	6
	(Navy)	25	51	25	0

years. But suddenly, conflicts in Spain, the Far East, and ultimately in Europe itself at the end of the decade thrust aviators into a position of having to rethink and refashion air superiority issues. It becomes necessary, therefore, to understand the individual progress made by the major air powers of the world in the 1930s. Identification of the peculiar approaches taken by each nation to the air superiority question can be identified and used to clarify that nation's approach to air power as it entered the Second World War.[31]

Italy

Given the importance of Douhet, it might have been expected that his native Italy would have stood at the forefront of military aviation during this period. In fact, political and economic problems plagued that nation until Benito Mussolini seized power in 1922. The dictator embraced Douhet's theories insofar as he could use them for political purposes. He slowly built a domestic Italian aviation industry and an independent air force. He encouraged competition for aircraft designs and stimulated public displays of the new Italian aircraft such as the crossing of the North Atlantic from Rome to Chicago and back by a squadron of 24 seaplanes in 1933. By the end of the decade, *Il Duce* could boast about 29 firms building aircraft and 6 making engines. In short, Mussolini's regime converted the Italian air arm *(Regia Aeronautica)* from an aging 1,000-airplane force in 1922 to a powerful combat arm numbering 2,600 aircraft in 1939. Of course, there were also accompanying problems to the rise of Italian air strength.[32]

On the one hand, Mussolini's air force followed the Douhet theory of organizational independence. The *Regia Aeronautica* comprised four branches: an independent air force, an army cooperation contingent, a naval air service, and a colonial air force. Air officers studied Douhet's theories, but in practice, the *Aeronautica* was more heavily involved in army cooperation and tactical employment than strategic bombing. This became evident in Ethiopia during 1935–36 and during the Spanish Civil War. Ethiopia was too primitive a land to really test Douhet's theory of strategic bombardment, but Italian aviators gained experience in the use of various types of projectiles and in air-dropping ammunition, food, and water to Italian soldiers. Spain also provided mainly tactical experience, even though Italian air units, based on the Balearic Islands, Sardinia, and mainland Italy, claimed to have accomplished successful independent strategic bombardment missions against cities and harbors at heights of 16,000 to 18,000 feet. Italian air leaders maintained that they paralyzed Barcelona, particularly over a 30-day bombardment campaign; however, the weakness of Loyalist counterair may have been more a factor than Italian air power. Still, *Aeronautica* officers never departed from the view that war would be short and decisively influenced by air power applied against the population and economy of an enemy. If, as one commentator thought, "the force began its descent from the fairly respectable reputation which it had held among the air forces of the leading world powers" by the late 1930s, the reasons related less to doctrine and tactics than to factors beyond the control of the Italians.[33]

Italy lacked adequate raw materials to develop the air armada demanded by Douhet. In 1940, the *Aeronautica* requested 7,200 aircraft, but industry could provide only 45 percent of that figure. "We are convinced of the necessity of working toward standardization of material, that is, of reducing to a minimum the number of standard planes, engines, arms, equipment," said one Air Ministry official in 1939. Italy could not support the concept of a long war, and her answer lay with an air superiority force-in-being. It could help suppress dissident tribesmen in Africa and deter aggression from northern neighbors. First-line aircraft like the Fiat CR–32 fighter and the Savoia-Marchetti SM–79 and SM–81 bombers provided the means, even if none of them quite epitomized Douhet's battleplane. In 1940, the *Aeronautica* consisted of skilled and brave pilots and adequate but aging aircraft. Acceptance of Douhet's thinking by *Aeronautica* leaders produced inadequate cooperation with the Army and Navy in the long run, and even Mussolini displayed no further interest in aviation other than for propaganda purposes. Still, given the short-war mentality, the economic weaknesses of the Fascist state, and the clear limits to aircraft industrial expansion by the end of the decade, the *Regia Aeronautica* probably pro-

Savoia-Marchetti SM–79.

19

vided an adequate air superiority force for the nation (short of any general war on the scale of 1914–18), only if truly integrated into armed forces kept strictly for homeland defense.[34]

France

France emerged from the World War with a strong military air corps as part of its army. For a time, the Breguet 19 bomber and the Potez 25 army cooperation plane numbered among the best aircraft in the world. One Breguet 19 flew across the Atlantic in 1927, and a group of thirty Potez 25s circumnavigated Africa in 1933. An independent air ministry was formed in 1928, and a government decree in April 1933 introduced a new and independent air force, *L'Armée de l'Air*. However, continued subordination to the national image of the army as the first line of defense, shrinkage of air force budgets, rapid turnover in political administrations, and internal military feuding doomed hopes of French supremacy in European military aviation. The country's general exhaustion after the war, and particularly that of her military leadership, must also be cited. As Marshal Ferdinand Pétain told a parliamentary inquiry later: "After the war of 1914–18, it was finished for me. My military mind was closed. When I saw the introduction of other tools, other instruments, other methods, I must say they didn't interest me."[35]

Disdain for the role of air power could be found in declarations by senior army generals of the period. The venerable Pétain decreed, "Direct action of air forces in the battle is illusory," and his younger protégé, General Maurice Gamelin, pronounced solemnly, "There is no such thing as the aerial battle. There is only the battle on the ground." The 1921 Army manual suggested the role of air power in one sentence: "By day it scouts, by night it bombards." While 15 years later, manuals devoted a scant 3 pages out of 177 to aviation, pointing to a reconnaissance role for fighter aircraft and a bombardment mission for bombers against enemy airfields and troop concentrations. In short, for most of the interwar period, military aviation in French military minds was tied to the land battle. While the young air force leaders fought for a strategic mission, they and their civilian chiefs in the air ministry couched their quest for parity with the other two services in vaguely defined roles, styled aerial operations, aerial defense, and auxiliary service for the Army and Navy. The result was a legacy of interservice rivalry and "stunted dialogue" which, as one observer has declared, steadily matured into a "mutual indifference."[36]

Because of the harsh economic realities of the decade and their own particular political disequilibrium, the French were slow to modernize their military. Only the ominous rearmament of Nazi Germany dictated the need for a French response by 1935. Despite the nationalization of selected armaments firms and Air Ministry expropriation of 28 firms in 1936, as well as dislocation resulting from dispersal of engine and airframe factories from the Paris region to Southwest France out of German range, annual aircraft production surged beyond the 2,000 mark by 1940. Some 32,000 aircraft workers in 1935 increased to 82,000 by 1939. Despite the fluctuations in politically charged rearmament programs of Air Ministers Pierre Cot and his successor Guy la Chambre, and the criticism that all programs took place with too little too late, at least one historian has concluded that by the summer of 1940, when France and Germany once more locked in deadly land and air battle, the French had sufficient combat aircraft to command the air over the country against a numerically inferior German Luftwaffe.[37]

The actual French aircraft inventory underwent transition typical of all air forces of the world in the interwar period. But, a crisis in technical capabilities surfaced by 1936, (in effect awarding air materiel superiority to Germany and Great Britain). French airplanes continued to display disturbing weaknesses in engine compression and lack of motorcannon, retractable landing gear, night-flying instruments, and radio-equipped cockpits. A rush to catch up with foreign competition led to some improvement by the end of the decade. Still, the bomber force consisted of what one commentator has termed "aesthetic monstrosities" for the most part and reflected indecision as to the spectrum of duties required of it, from tactical to strategic in nature. The cumbersome Farman 220 (often called the world's first four-engine bomber) and aging Breguet 19s, Amiot 143s, Potez 540s, and Lioré et Olivier 20s were supplemented by newer medium aircraft, including Martin and Douglas bombers from the United States. More promising, perhaps, were French pursuit or fighter aircraft including the Bloch MB–152, Dewoitine D–500 series, Morane-Saulnier MS–406, and American import Curtiss Hawk 72A series. Whether or not the French aircraft industry could properly surge in production to meet battle losses or even opening day requirements for war remained unclear.[38]

Effectiveness of the French air arm as an air superiority force hinged largely upon the issue of employment, not technology or doctrine. The political and psychological atmosphere in which the Armée de l'Air evolved in the interwar years affected its ability to actually achieve air superiority in 1939–40. The Air Force was part of a century-old struggle between the military and government in France, as well as typical interservice rivalries. Army generals retained so much power that, at the time of the independence of the French Air Force, they literally retained operational control of some 118 of 134 combat squadrons. While both services came closer together in thinking about utilization of combat aviation during the next five years, the Air Ministry dismantled its strategic strike force, which it had laboriously developed, and parceled it out once more among the infantry divisions. Frankly, these internecine battles in government circles sapped the focus and strength of Air Force leaders when they needed to prepare their service to fulfill its varied missions in modern war.[39]

Actually, many of the French aviators retained an affection for ground support, with which they were familiar from the World War and colonial campaigns against Rif rebels in Morocco. Gradually, however, a separate group of strategic enthusiasts emerged as Douhet's theories were translated into French. Only these strategic proponents were forced by circumstances to differentiate between the earliest days of a war, when the Air Force's strategic power could be employed against an enemy homeland, and subsequent stages of combat, when even strategic aircraft would have to return to more traditional direct support of the ground fighting. At best, only a week's duration would be allowed for massive bombing assaults against an enemy communication and transportation network, munitions depots, military installations, and industrial facilities. This was hardly Douhet's envisioned cumulative blow from the air. The French version of strategic air war was more a preliminary strike to cripple the speed and efficiency of enemy preparation for a ground offensive. Even here, the ascendancy of such a school in any one political administration might be quickly reversed when that regime was voted out of office. In the end, the French Air Force spent so much time emphasizing a strategic offensive to establish institutional presence and independence, that it neglected clear indicators that Germany's doctrine of air superiority supported ground armies in the attack.[40]

The Dewoitine D–500 series of aircraft were added to the French fighter inventory during the 1930s.

Formation of the twin-engine all-metal Amiot 143 bombers.

French Air Force fascination with strategic bombardment came at the very time when French Army leaders finally began to appreciate the greater need for aviation in their own planning. Attaché reports emphasized German experience with air-ground teamwork in Spain as well as during their own maneuvers. French Army and Air Force leaders agreed to the requirement for more focus upon defensive fighter forces and air coverage over the land battle, but apparently only in principle. The French air staff spent little time with key issues like adequate ground communication systems, command and control arrangements, and development of a ground observer corps for the defensive battle. Airfields were poorly positioned for air defense, and French cities and industrial sites lacked adequate warning and antiaircraft batteries to work with the fighters. By focusing so much upon strategic aviation, *Armée de l'Air* leaders distanced themselves from their own political superiors who by 1939-40 rejected such strategy for fear of German reprisal and wanted the air superiority battles linked more closely with combat on the ground. Ignoring governmental policies, possibly circumventing both the civilian air minister and parliament, the French air leadership pursued its more narrowly focused service interest. It approached a major European conflagration with inadequate ground structure, insufficient personnel for its slowly rearming air fleet, and a doctrine apparently so different from that of the ground forces that the two services appeared to be preparing to fight largely independent campaigns.[41]

The French faced an additional dimension to the air superiority issue—that of psychological ascendancy. This element became part of achieving air superiority in the same fashion that technical or quantitative superiority could be factored in. The German-French confrontation after 1936 added this unique but elusive dimension to the whole European situation. The French nation found itself literally beaten in the air long before the opening battles of 1940. When French observers toured German aircraft facilities they came away shocked and dutifully reported to Paris on the Luftwaffe's superiority in planes, manpower, and capabilities. They did not realize that it was a massive Nazi bluff. French air chief Gen. Joseph Vuillemin told the French ambassador in Berlin in 1936, "if war comes this autumn, as you fear, there will not be one French plane left after fifteen days," a figure he still cited two years later. Such fears led to a disjointed, unbalanced French air rearmament effort that fell so strikingly short by 1939 that even Gen. Maurice Gamelin, supreme commander of the armed forces, declared just a month before Germany invaded Poland in September, "The Air Force will not play in the next war the role which certain military commentators foresee. It will burn itself out in a flash." Gamelin attempted to correct various command-and-control arrangements to improve air-land battle planning, but his fatalism and the lateness of the hour prevailed. The French government attempted an eleventh-hour surge of aircraft production in 1939–40, and as one French air leader entitled his postwar memoirs, the sky was not empty when the Germans invaded the West in May 1940. At least one historian contends that by the outset of the campaign, France had produced sufficient aircraft (4,360) to outnumber the German air strike force, which counted only about 3,270 aircraft. Fighter forces alone counted over 2,900 aircraft, most of which had been fabricated within the past 18 months. French pilots were among the best trained in Europe. However, the French nation was ill-prepared for battle. Defeatism and fatigue pervaded the period between the wars, while pacificism, spawned in part by fears of German bombardment of civilian targets, contributed to a national malaise. The overall unpreparedness of the French military establishment for the speed and intricacies of modern combat was not yet discernable, for France retained its reputation as the strongest military power in Western Europe. Yet, military leaders continued to prepare to fight any new war in the mold of that just past.[42]

German conquest of Western Europe took only a few months in the spring and summer of 1940; France fell in six weeks. Part of this stunning victory could be attributed to air power, applied in connection with ground operations, as well as misapplication of Western air forces in the air superiority battle. Since Dutch, Belgian, and Scandinavian air forces proved negligible, the story hinged upon the air power of the Anglo-French alliance, and cooperation of the *Armée de l'Air* and the Royal Air Force of Great Britain. Together, Western powers actually arrayed only 1,610 aircraft against the Luftwaffe on the decisive northeastern front, suggesting a severe numerical inferiority that quickly led to seizure of the air initiative by the Germans. The French alone had only 119 of their 210 squadrons available for action in this sector, despite 8 months of combat inactivity during the so-called "Phoney War," plus the obvious fact that here lay the predominant threat. France retained the other squadrons in the colonies, positioned to counter an Italian attack, or being reequipped in the rear. Despite numerical inferiority, the Allied Air Forces in May and June contributed to a 40 percent loss rate which nearly exhausted Luftwaffe capabilities.[43]

The French Air Force lacked neither valor nor skill in the Battle of France. Yet, one interpreter suggests that scarcely 20 percent of the fighter force was ever deployed against the enemy, with an operational rate of only .09 French sorties compared to 4 German sorties per aircraft per day. Similarly low statistics existed for the French bomber force (.25 sorties per aircraft per day) and the reconnaissance units, which averaged only one mission every three days. Battle losses may have led to this conservative deployment, at least in the minds of the Air Staff, which necessarily looked to a longer war and was unsure at this stage of production rates for aircraft and crews versus attrition. Unaware of the weakening power of the Luftwaffe by mid-June, French air leaders reacted to the ground disasters and withdrew their first-line squadrons to the safety of North Africa. Explanation of this action suggests a political choice to insure survival of the French air institution after a lost war. Still, this apparent breakdown of will or perhaps desire to save lives and equipment may have caused French leaders to miss that moment when air superiority might have been wrested back from the enemy.[44]

Problems surfaced quickly even where French fighters and bombers were thrown into the battle. Pronounced failures developed less from counterair combat than from misperception of the new warfare of movement on the ground. The campaigns in the West were part of an air-land battle and, at this stage of the war, were less affected by strategic bombardment than by close cooperation between the Army and the Air Force. The long interwar fight for independence, which had left so much resentment between Air Force officers and the civilian governments, now impeded air-ground teamwork. The French Air Force Staff focus upon carrying the war to Germany (a focus shared with RAF Bomber Command, and now denied both organizations by inadequacy of equipment and tacit agreement of all protagonists in the war for fear this would expand the conflict beyond military targeting to the civilian community) poorly served the needs of a French Army staggering under the pounding of German blitzkrieg (or lightning war). At the same time, the years of Army condescension toward the Air Force left French land generals unprepared to properly enunciate their needs to aviators in combat. Antitank missions flown by Air Force pilots failed because of the lack of armor-piercing ammunition, while French bombardment squadrons were thrown piecemeal into interdiction and deep-strike strategic military missions without proper massing of aircraft

25

or resolution of rendezvous issues with fighter commands. The pace of missions seemed frozen at the level of World War I experience, failing to recognize the speed of a modern war of movement. On the other hand, even an innovative soldier like Col. Charles de Gaulle failed to inform Air Force leaders of the time and direction of his armor counterattacks against the German juggernaut, which might have insured the best possible use of tactical air strikes in direct support of his operation. The record suggests possibly less that the Luftwaffe controlled the skies around the clock, and more that the French and British air-land battle lacked the cohesiveness that characterized German operations.[45]

A modern commentator has declared that the French air effort in 1940 was one of gallant and competent individual performances that had no appreciable impact upon the actual battle. Perhaps the same could be said for their land counterparts. Once the Germans breached static French positions on the Meuse River at Sedan, neither land nor air reaction proved responsive to the crisis of the moment. The issue of air superiority blended quickly with other doctrinal requirements such as close air support, while collapse of will and the floodtide of defeat swept Allied air and land elements past the point where the *Armée de l'Air* and the RAF could have seized command of the air in mid-June, even though Luftwaffe losses may have made that possible.[46]

Russia

The situation in Russia provided a unique aspect of the interwar air superiority story. Military aviation had never been a strong part of the Czar's army, despite some notable pioneers in the field of aeronautics like Igor Sikorsky. Russian aviators hardly distinguished themselves in the ill-fated campaigns against Germany and Austria-Hungary on the Eastern Front during the World War. Knocked from the conflict by revolution, Russia faced years of domestic rebuilding and rehabilitation before it could regain a position of influence in European affairs. The new Soviet leadership in the early 1920s realized that aviation would be vital to future national defense. Therefore, it established a large army air force called *Voennyo-Vozdush-nye Sily* or VVS, as well as a smaller naval air arm. The VVS was designed specifically to support Red Army operations. It was not a unified service since its units remained subordinate to army commands mobilized for war, and its staff was simply a division of the Red Army staff. Military district commanders retained authority over air regiments in peacetime, while VVS units became part of corps, armies, and fronts (army groups) during wartime. All of this was done to insure utmost cooperation between land and air contingents. Doctrinally, the task of the VVS included securing air superiority, supporting army ground forces, and performing air reconnaissance. The air superiority mission remained paramount.[47]

While the theories of Douhet never captivated Soviet leadership, brief flirtations with strategic bombardment enamored Soviet theorist A. N. Lapchinsky in the 1920s and resulted in construction of the world's largest four-engine bomber force in the early and mid-1930s. But the Spanish Civil War discredited strategic bombardment as an effective weapon in Soviet minds and reaffirmed the more traditional emphasis on tactical air operations. For the most part, Soviet authorities faced three principal problems in building air power after the revolution: construction of aircraft plants, recruitment of pilots from the newly liberated Russian proletariat, and research and development of engines and airframes.[48]

At first, the majority of Soviet aircraft came from foreign sources, either abandoned or captured during foreign interventions at the end of the World War, or purchased in the West. Special arrangements with postwar German leaders for research and development yielded promising results. Yet, servicing the resultant menagerie of aircraft proved to be a problem for Soviet air officials. This stimulated a long period of work toward self-sufficiency. By 1930, Soviet aviation included respected models like the all-metal Tupolev ANT–3 reconnaissance plane, various models of general purpose R–5 aircraft, Polikarpov I–3, I–4, and later, I–15 and I–16 models of fighter aircraft, and the long-range Tupolov TB–1 and TB–3, and the SB–2 bombardment planes. In the official Soviet propaganda view: "In the years of the prewar five-year plans a powerful aircraft industry was created in the Soviet Union thanks to the unstinting efforts of the Party, the government and all the people."[49]

As the future Soviet Marshall Georgii Zhukov noted in his memoirs: "In two years implementation of an organizational plan for the Red Army's air force began in which tactical, operational, and strategic problems were considered from the viewpoint of national defense in the event of aggression." Still, the Soviet Union experienced severe setbacks during the dictatorship of Premier Josef Stalin. While figures vary, among millions of Russians sent to prison or execution chambers at least 35,000 officers of the armed forces lost their lives, including 3 successive chiefs of staff of the VVS and a large part of the air arm's junior officers in 1938–39 alone. Moreover, the purges removed the cream of senior military, political, scientific, and administrative leaders in the country. Predictably, replacements were younger and inexperienced but loyal followers of Stalin. This loss of talent and professional expertise definitely affected the Soviet Union's ability to wage war. Conformity replaced ingenuity. If earlier Soviet military leadership had come close to resolving technical problems of the VVS through modernized equipment and provision of an industrial base, the new Soviet leaders lost that sharp edge so necessary for doctrinal development and implementation. Political intimidation sapped the strength of military leadership in the Soviet Union and affected how the best minds in that nation would resolve strategic problems for a land with vast, virtually indefensible borders.[50]

Russian leaders sent volunteers to test their technical skills and equipment in the Spanish Civil War, and 3 years later, employed them against Japanese aviators in the skies over Manchuria and the Mongolian People's Republic. Russian pilots and 1,500 ground personnel went to aid the Spanish Loyalists in 1936. They participated in numerous tactical operations, though not always in cooperation with the Spanish. Employing standard doctrinal practices of the time for achieving air superiority through counterair battles, the Russian aviators faced a stern test from similarly voluntary contingents of German and Italian airmen helping the opposition side of Francisco Franco. The Russians proved generally inferior in all categories of equipment, tactics, training, and personnel. As the Loyalists began to lose ground to Franco's forces, Soviet leaders lost interest in the expedition and gradually withdrew their volunteers. Heavy equipment losses to superior German aircraft and the lack of replacement parts for grounded Russian machines served as lessons to VVS leaders. In addition, Spain turned the Soviets away from strategic bombardment because of inconclusive results and the primitive equipment involved in the effort.[51]

More useful results emerged from the Russo-Japanese conflict between May and September 1939 during the little known Nomonhan or Kahlhkingol incident. The Japanese were quite successful against raw Russian pilots in early air superiority battles. But, Zhukov's insertion of Soviet veterans from Spain reversed the tide. They trained the younger pilots, and while Russian equipment losses exceeded those of the Japanese, the Russian airmen acquitted themselves well toward the end of the fighting. Newer Russian aircraft promised a brighter future, but Zhukov noted: "Unfortunately, [Russia's] economy was not sufficiently equipped at the time to launch mass production of these splendid models.[52]

The outbreak of a new European war in September 1939 found the Soviet Union as precariously placed for action against Nazi Germany as was France or Great Britain. Ideologically, the U.S.S.R. could not align itself with those western democracies despite a shared fear of German aggression. Thus, Premier Stalin sought to buy time through a nonaggression pact with German Chancellor Adolf Hitler. The Russians had numerous plans and programs on paper for improving their military establishment. Yet, few had been fully implemented. Despite the experience in Spain and the Far East, the Soviet military was not combat ready for a major conflict. Newer aircraft had begun to appear in VVS inventories including the Ilyushin Il–4, Petlyakov Pe–8 bombers; Petlyakov Pe–2 and Ilyushin Il–2 attack planes; and the Lavochkin LaGG–3, Mikoyan MiG–3, and Yakolev Yak–1 fighter aircraft. Still, the main problem was production.

According to Soviet sources, total aircraft output in 1940 numbered only 64 Yak–1 fighters, 20 MiG–3 fighters, and 2 Pe–2 dive bombers, while that of the first half of 1941 reflected an increase to 1,946 fighters, 458 bombers, and 349 attack planes. Soviet statistics remain suspect, but the irrefutable fact seemed to be that the main air forces available to the Soviet Union on the eve of World War II consisted principally of outdated models, many of which had already proven inadequate in Spain and the Far East. With an imperfectly mobilized defense establishment, peacetime airfields crowded with storage facilities, flight lines virtually inviting attack, and the absence of a modern air warning network on the western frontier, the Soviet air arm in 1939 was quite unprepared for war.[53]

Moreover, Soviet military leadership, caught in the purges, could not quickly incorporate the lessons of Spain and the Far East into doctrine. A draft Red Army Field Manual of 1939 stated simply: "Aviation is linked strategically and tactically to the ground forces, it performs independent air operations against objectives deep in the enemy rear area, and it fights enemy aviation securing air supremacy." The VVS would perform combat missions to "attain air supremacy, support ground troops in penetration of enemy tactical defenses, cover troops and rear facilities from air strikes, carry out strikes against operational and strategic reserves and targets in the enemy rear area, support the commitment of an exploitation echelon to a breakthrough, support the latter's combat actions in the operational depth of the enemy defenses, support airborne landing parties, support friendly forces by air, and perform air reconnaissance." The first of these missions—gaining air superiority—was an essential prerequisite for the success of the others, and that theme echoed implicitly but not explicitly through both official field manuals and what passed for theoretical treatises on employment of aviation.[54]

Soviet leaders could not agree on the means of attaining air superiority. A conference of high-ranking commanders in December 1940 issued a report entitled, "The Air Force in an Offensive Operation and in the Struggle for Air Supremacy." The title expressed Stalin's unswerving zeal for offensive rather than defensive operations. The authors of this report suggested that air supremacy would make it possible to prepare an army group's offensive, provide air cover to troops being brought up to the front (especially cavalry and mechanized forces), quickly and systematically penetrate an enemy's fortified zone, and exploit a success in depth. "Attainment of air supremacy," declared the authors, "requires destruction of the enemy's aviation on his airfields, coupled with a simultaneous strike against aviation rear services." A minority of conference attendees, however, doubted such conclusions. This equally persuasive group argued that aviation had to be divided into Army Aviation intended for close support of ground forces, and Frontal Aviation operating in accordance with an Army Front or Group. Further, this group downplayed the German surprise assault on Poland and subsequent victory over the French, boasting instead of Russian successes in Spain, Manchuria, and even the Winter War of 1939–40 against Finland. Obviously, portions of the conference group remained out of touch with lessons of air power unfolding around them. They reflected a Soviet military leadership split between realists, who recognized their country's unpreparedness for modern warfare, and optimists who had not yet learned that well-organized and coordinated defense based on pursuit planes, an air warning network, and ground antiaircraft guns might be indispensable for defeating an enemy air force in the initial air superiority battles at the beginning of an invasion.[55]

Germany

By the late 1930s, Nazi Germany was the perceived enemy throughout Europe. The phenomenal growth of German military power had shocked the world. The Treaty of Versailles at the end of the World War had effectively stripped a defeated Germany of even the most rudimentary military aviation. Only a thinly disguised planning staff within the small army of the Weimar Republic, a modest production capacity for civil aviation, and the clandestine research and development arrangements with the Soviet Union marked German air efforts in the 1920s. Then with the assumption of power by Hitler in 1933, German rearmament proceeded rapidly. Hitler provided for a Ministry of Aviation under one of his political cronies, the former wartime air ace, Hermann Goering, thereby insuring that the new German Air Force, or Luftwaffe, had an early political base. Similar sponsorship of a highly subsidized civilian airline, Lufthansa, provided a camouflaged training facility for pilots, navigators, and even officials in the Air Ministry. The ever-present German scientific excellence provided the technological underpinnings for rearmament; German design teams produced important aircraft prototypes in Spain, Sweden, and Switzerland as well as in Russia; and Hitler's courtship of the business community gave the regime the necessary industrial base for a healthy armaments program. The military's own assessments of the lessons from the previous war also contributed to the German resurgence. It was against this backdrop that German interpretation of the doctrine of air superiority took place.[56]

Above all, German military professionals of the Weimar era thought they knew why the Fatherland had lost the war. Numerous commissions, inquiry boards, and the clandestine General Staff all concluded that Germany could never again fight a prolonged, multi-front war against a coalition of enemies. The only answer lay with a short, decisive fight leading to German victory—the essence of the German word *blitzkrieg*. While the land army undoubtedly was the nation's first line of defense because of geography, it became evident by the 1930s that a reemergent German air

30

arm could play a prominent role in achieving blitzkrieg victory. At the same moment, however, this did not mean that the Luftwaffe would act simply as handmaiden to the Army. The new Luftwaffe leadership wrestled with questions of strategic bombardment versus traditional army support tasks like their counterparts in other nations. Gen. Walther Wever, the Air Force Chief of Staff before his death in 1936, produced a paper entitled "Conduct of the Air War," in which he advocated that Luftwaffe employment should reflect the general dimensions of national grand strategy. The air arm's particular role in doing so would include attainment and maintenance of air superiority, support of both army and navy, attacks on enemy industry, and interdiction of enemy logistics between battlefield and homefront.[57]

Wever stressed in his 1935 paper that achievement of air superiority preceded all other missions for the Air Force. But he noted the transitory and elusive nature of air superiority. The changing technical capability of aircraft, new production, and combat losses would cause air superiority to pass back and forth in battle between Germany and an enemy. Striking the enemy homeland's industries and civil population, suggested Wever, might actually prolong a war past that propitious moment for attaining quick victory because it would involve the use of those precious air resources needed to affect the land battle. Thus, for Wever, the role of strategic bom-

Bundesarchiv-Militärarchiv

Walther Wever, Germany's Air Force Chief of Staff.

bardment as a part of a general air superiority campaign should occur only when 1) an opportunity existed to effect quickly the course of the war; 2) land and naval preparations had opened this opportunity; 3) a stalemate had occurred; or 4) a decisive effect could be achieved through the destruction of the enemy's sources of power.[58]

Wever clearly reflected traditional German fears of being surrounded by continental enemies. Land and sea borders demanded priority defense by traditional ground and naval forces. Professionals in those services naturally wished to have aviation employed in a subsidiary role. However, Wever and other figures of the period, such as Air Secretary Erhard Milch and Dr. Robert Knauss (sometime Lufthansa and Air Ministry executive as well as instructor at the German Air War College) proved equally strident about an independent role for air power. Knauss suggested that the Luftwaffe offered vast potential for affecting the European military balance, even more than army divisions or capital ships of the navy. Thus, the same arguments swirled through German military circles about the role of air power that attended national defense discussions in other countries. The fundamental issue always seemed to be the emphasis on strategic or tactical employment of aviation, and which one offered the best potential for achieving air superiority. In Germany, as elsewhere, the matter hinged largely on aircraft production, provision of trained manpower, and the overall economic strength of the nation.[59]

In January 1933 when Hitler took power, 3,200 workers could produce no more than 33 aircraft annually. Only a full-scale government bailout could rescue the industry and accomplish the aviation programs envisioned by Goering, Milch, and other Nazi officials. Three years later, this same industry employed 124,878 people and produced over 5,000 military and commercial aircraft annually, according to the influential journal *The Economist*. By 1939, production rates approached 500 to 600 aircraft per month, and 170,000 men worked shifts exceeding 60 hours a week on occasion. This was unprecedented anywhere in the world at the time, and it may be fairly stated that Nazi Germany possessed an aviation industry second to none. Old established firms such as Junkers, Dornier, and Heinkel were tied to the Nazi cause, and the true miracle of German rearmament could be found largely in its focus upon the aviation sector. In many eyes, German aircraft production methods resembled mass production more closely than those in Great Britain, France, or the United States.[60]

The German government-industrial team produced a variety of formidable aircraft by 1939, reflecting the German emphasis on air superiority as a prelude to other air operations. In a most rapid fashion, German aviation had moved from the early models of Arado Ar–68 and Heinkel He–51 fighter aircraft, the Heinkel He–70 bomber-reconnaissance craft (originally designed as a fast passenger and mail transport), the Henschel Hs–123 dive bomber, close-support aircraft, and the distinctive Junkers Ju–52 transport, to more sophisticated and familiar planes which would remain first-line for the 1940s. While the Ju–52 remained a work-horse in the Luftwaffe, by 1938–39 newer fighters like the Messerschmitt Bf–109 and Bf–110, the Junkers Ju–87 dive bomber and Ju–88 multi-purpose aircraft, the Dornier Do–17, Do–215, and Do–217, as well as the Heinkel He–111 and Junkers Ju–86 bombers all provided Nazi Germany with an enviable array of aerial weaponry. Such achievements, which shocked the French when they saw them, disguised certain structural weaknesses in a program that would have long-term consequences. But, such weaknesses also tended to reflect German geopolitical and strategic bias for employing Luftwaffe power.[61]

Despite the quasi-public ownership of the aviation industry of Nazi Germany, the government never installed the production controls that might have been anticipated from a totalitarian regime. Thus, each aircraft maker tried to build a full panoply of airplanes, from small trainer to multi-engine bomber. German designers refused to concentrate on a smaller number of aircraft types. Even within the Air Ministry, competing personalities and bureaucratic goals produced chaos. The Luftwaffe's technical office failed to establish priorities and specifications that might have led to consistent programs and better use of engineering skills, materials, and available time. In fact, the low level of engine development resulted from this confusion and thwarted production of a viable four-engine bomber. Then too, shortages in skilled labor, factory capacity, and raw materials suggested that the Luftwaffe had to focus on achieving air superiority in a short war, or at the very beginning of the fighting. There could be no slow buildup to a desired level later in the conflict. All of this underscored the short war strategy and, in turn, worked to Hitler's advantage as he could use a superior force-in-being diplomatically in attempting to expand the *Reich*.[62]

If the Nazi regime ever entertained intentions of the Luftwaffe's emerging as a long-range strategic force, then a series of events and decisions in the late 1930s effectively modified that goal. The Luftwaffe, in fact, became primarily a tactical weapon, with missions closely aligned with ground force strategy. Early manning of the new air arm with former army officers, Germany's European position, and the inherent weakness of production all contributed to this end. The question of whether the major cause was technical weakness of the four-engine bomber program, or Hitler's own particular employment of air power as a diplomatic, not a war-fighting tool at this stage, remains unclear. The fact is, however, the German air arm did not plan to attain air superiority through strategic bombing operations, due in part to lessons from the Spanish Civil War.[63]

Hitler, like Mussolini, saw the Spanish conflict as an opportunity both to thwart the spread of Communism as well as to test his military machine. "With the permission of the Fuehrer," stated Goering later, "I sent a large part of my transport fleet and a large number of experimental fighter units, bombers, and antiaircraft guns" so as to test the material and the personnel under actual combat conditions. These so-called volunteers of the famous Kondor Legion engaged in all types of air operations during the two-year involvement. Bombardment of coastal ports and interior cities from Madrid to Guernica, interdiction of supply routes, air superiority dogfights, as well as traditional ground support missions, gave Luftwaffe volunteer aviators invaluable lessons with which to improve their air arm. Infamous instances of bombing effectiveness like Guernica, which killed or maimed 2,000 defenseless civilians in 3 hours, provided Hitler and his propaganda ministry the tools with which to intimidate governments elsewhere in Europe. However, some lessons that emerged from the Spanish Civil War altered the direction of German air superiority thinking and weapon development, with great portents for the future.[64]

Kondor Legion veterans such as Lt. Col. Wolfram von Richthofen, a cousin to the World War ace and the last commander of the German contingents in Spain, returned home with new ideas about employment of air power. His experiences convinced him that aviation was more than a mere substitute for artillery when properly applied to the land battle. He convinced Luftwaffe officials that organization of close-support formations of bombers and fighters working with armored columns could effect a breakthrough on the ground. By the time the Spanish involvement ended in the spring of 1939, both veterans and home officials emphasized the Luftwaffe's role in the air-land battle rather than strategic bombing operations. But, winning a quick land victory first required gaining use of the air space.

The Ju–88 bomber.

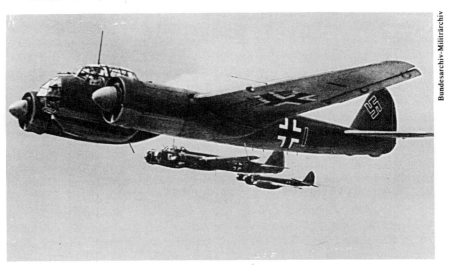

Bundesarchiv-Militärarchiv

The Heinkel He–111 bomber.

Much of this thought remained internal to military circles, as Hitler and his political leaders saw a different use for the Luftwaffe in the diplomatic arena outside of war.[65]

From the German reoccupation of the Rhineland in 1936 through the Munich agreement to dismember Czechoslovakia two years later, Hitler's deft use of the Luftwaffe's potential to reduce Europe's great cities to rubble and kill large numbers of civilians quieted foreign opposition to a whimper. Germany's rumored air strength became a vital partner in Nazi diplomatic initiatives. Most of it was bluff, but it worked. Despite two years of warning from French military attachés in Berlin, senior French air officials drew conclusions from personal observation at maneuvers and visits to German factories. Their view was based not on statistics, but visual proof of superior German aviation technology. Yet, as one German general admitted years later:

> In addition to the systematic bluff at top levels, there was also the willing self-deception of the foreign air observers, who simply refused to believe what their eyes saw and insisted on assuming that there was still more hidden behind it. They had no way of knowing that many of the gigantic hangers they were shown were either completely empty or filled with ancient, dust-covered aircraft.[66]

In general, a pacifistic West believed the chimera of Hitler's air armada largely because of its own psychological and material unpreparedness to do otherwise. In a strange twist to post-World War II deterrence, the Luftwaffe of the late 1930s effectively countered any Anglo-French notions of a preemptive strike to destroy Nazi power before it was too late. The propaganda value of the Kondor Legion in Spanish skies and the roar of massed Luftwaffe formations above Nazi party rallies at home gave a certain poignant meaning to air superiority in Hitler's policy. Whether it was a general aversion to war, the fear of wholesale civilian slaughter à la Guernica and the public press, the inadequate air and civil defenses (including shortages of hospital beds and gas masks in London and Paris), or simply a calculated government policy to buy time for rearmament, the western democracies appeased Germany largely because of perceived Luftwaffe superiority. Perhaps only the inner circle of foreign intelligence analysts knew of structural weaknesses in German rearmament programs such as the Luftwaffe Technical Office's admission that in order to realize Nazi goals should war result from diplomatic miscalculation, eighty-five percent of the world's oil output would be needed to supply aviation fuel for the air arm.[67]

Great Britain

The counterpoise to Nazi intentions came from Great Britain's Royal Air Force. In August 1914, British Foreign Minister Sir Edward Grey declared solemnly: "If Germany dominated the Continent it would be disagreeable to us as well as to others, for we should be isolated." Great Britain had no intention of letting this occur even in the 1930s. Yet, her military power was allowed to decline after the end of the World War. The government bound itself to a "Ten Year Rule," which, when formulated in 1919, assumed for planning purposes that there would be no major war in Europe for a decade. However probable that may have seemed at that point, the rule's annual extension up to 1932 held the British armed forces captive, notwithstanding changing international circumstances. In this same period, Air Marshal Trenchard and military theorists like Maj. Gen. J. F. C. Fuller and Capt. B. H. Liddell Hart predicted a dominant role for air power in any future conflict. All three saw bombardment as a humane alternative to the trench bloodbath on the Western Front. True, both Fuller and Liddell Hart painted a gory picture of civilian casualties and devastated English cities during the first month of an air war. Others, such as Brigadier P. R. C. Groves, observed: "Great Britain is probably the most vulnerable nation in Europe. From the point of view of aerial defense her insular position is a disadvantage, for the seas which surround her favor surprise attack by aircraft and render it difficult to observe their lines of retreat. . . ." By the 1930s, British defense planners had become notably concerned with a so-called "bolt from the blue" or "knock-out blow" inflicted from the air using the very surprise that worried Graves and others.[68]

The British decision to rearm in 1934 (because of the rise of Nazi Germany) came against a backdrop of an aging RAF inventory of aircraft better suited to imperial police chores than European deterrence. The RAF naturally preferred twice as many bombers as fighter planes under rearmament schemes, which generally allocated one-third of each year's defense budget to air matters. This reflected Trenchard's contention that strategic bombardment could win a war. Still, a residue of obsolete biplanes remained on-line until the end of the decade. Westland Wapiti, Hawker Hart, Fairey III, and Vickers Wildbeast bombers sufficed for controlling the Northwest Indian frontier, perhaps, but their payloads would contribute little to a European battle. Even the Vickers Vimy and Virginia as well as Handley Page heavy bombers, designed for continental fighting, hardly equated with emerging monoplanes across the English channel. RAF fighter aircraft were no better, although biplanes like the Armstrong Whitworth Siskin, Bristol Bulldog, Fairey Fox, Gloster Grebe/Gamecock, and Gloster Gauntlet, as well as Hawker Fury, wore sleek aluminum paint schemes of peacetime. Newer twin-engine monoplane bombers began to enter RAF service by the mid- thirties in the form of the interim Fairey Hendon night bomber, and the Armstrong Whitworth Whitley, Bristol Blenheim and Type 152 Beaufort, Fairey Battle, Handley Page Hamden, Vickers Wellesley, and Vickers Armstrong Wellington. The decision to produce four-engine heavy bombardment aircraft followed, although it would be the Wellington (1,200-mile range, 4,500-pound payload, and 235 miles-per-hour speed) and her twin-engine counterparts which would have to carry Trenchardist theory to German skies if war were to develop in the late thirties. RAF officials decided by 1938 that research and development would proceed on a long-range, four-engine aircraft but admitted that rollout could not begin before 1942.[69]

Ironically, it would not be so much bombardment as a tactical air defense for defending Great Britain that pushed that nation into developing forces for air superiority. Soon after the 1935 plan (or "scheme" as the British called it), which aimed at doubling the existing strength of the so-called Metropolitan Air Force, Air Ministry officials decided that the defensive as well as the offensive nature of British air policy dictated reorganization along more functional lines. This led to establishment in 1936 of Bomber, Fighter, and Coastal Commands, supported by Training Command and Maintenance Group (later Command), with subsequent additions including commands for Balloon, Reserve, and Army Cooperation. Overseas commands remained area rather than function oriented, and essentially multi-functional in composition. This move insured that commanders would not be overburdened with a multiplicity of responsibilities in Great Britain, and that no arm would be slighted in budgetary allocations. Although the Fleet Air Arm was lost to the Admiralty in 1937 (land-based air remained under RAF control), the "First Article of the Air Staff Creed" had triumphed in the form of a unified Air Force. Even formulation of an Advanced Air Striking Force (AASF) as part of the British Expeditionary

Force commitment to the continent by 1939 did not fundamentally change this integrity. The AASF followed the pattern of multifunctional overseas commands, though its primary mission was to bombard German industrial targets in the Ruhr as part of general air support for the Anglo-French ground forces.[70]

Low aircraft production levels before 1938 added a note of both urgency and unreality to all RAF doctrinal planning. The Munich crisis found the RAF unable to field more than 666 aircraft, only 93 of which were the new eight-gun Hawker Hurricane fighter planes. Civilian members of the defense community increasingly questioned the RAF's principal commitment to bombardment in the face of low production figures and the evident threat of Nazi air attack. They sought to strengthen Great Britain's home island capacity to prevent the knock-out blow by Luftwaffe bombers. More and more people embraced Brigadier Groves's notion that no inland city in Great Britain lay any more than 20 or 30 minutes from the coast, which meant that German bombers could sweep in from the English Channel against London or from the North Sea against the Midland industrial cities, cross the coastline, and strike their targets beofore RAF interceptors could stop them. Traditional air patrols and ground spotters were neither economical or efficient. Therefore British authorities applied science and technology to the problem and developed Radio Direction Finding or RDF equipment (what the Americans later styled *Radar*), as well as fast fighter or pursuit planes to destroy enemy aircraft in the air (rather than on the ground as envisioned by Bomber Command). Thus emerged a tactical defensive air superiority force and doctrine, beyond the capabilities of most other air forces of the world at that time.[71]

A secret research program begun in 1934, produced by 1939 a chain of twenty RDF stations in Great Britain and three overseas locations to detect incoming aircraft before the planes had left the continent. Douhet, Trenchard, and Mitchell had not anticipated this scientific breakthrough for the defense in their claims earlier that the bomber would always get through to the target. Technology could now help neutralize the offensive power of military aviation. With a sound ground communication system and anti-aircraft artillery, as well as two superior fighter aircraft—the Hawker Hurricane (8 machineguns, 325–342 mile-per-hour speed, and 34,000–35,000-foot ceiling) and the Supermarine Spitfire (8 machineguns, 355–370 mile-per-hour speed, 34,000–35,000-foot ceiling)—the British had a formidable force for defending the home islands.[72]

Perhaps the RAF's greatest weakness in the late 1930s was quantitative in nature. Despite 5-year expansion programs, first-line aircraft had increased only from 732 in 1934 to 1,911 by 1939. Personnel expansion had accompanied the technical improvements from a base of 41,000 in 1934 to 176,000 by 1939. But, whereas the RAF increase could be counted in multiples of 3 or 4, her primary enemy, the Luftwaffe, had jumped 10-fold in

The premier RAF fighters were the Hawker Hurricanes *(above)* **and Supermarine Spitfires** *(below)*.

39

the same period. Over 4,000 aircraft and 500,000 personnel provided an enemy challenge to RAF planners. RAF air superiority lay with that unproven intangible—morale—coupled with superior technology. One American military attaché, Maj. S. A. Greenwell, viewed an RAF airfield in May 1939 and wrote home about the Spitfires, Hurricanes, Gladiators, and Furies, as well as the ground facilities. He told superiors:

> There is one observation I believe I am qualifid to make. It is about the tremendous change in outlook among the officers of the Northold Command, now that they are getting ships and equipment which will enable them to do what will be expected of them in the event of war. Instead of what may be described as a do or die feeling about the ships with which they would have been forced to fight during the past fall and winter, they are now filled with enthusiasm over their equipmemt and what they can do with it

The British and their Royal Air Force alone among the opponents of Nazi Germany held a psychological edge when it came to countering the threat from the Luftwaffe.[73]

Japan

On the opposite side of the world, Imperial Japan emerged in this period as the air power of the Far East. Long compared with Great Britain because of its geographical similarity as an island nation, Japan faced problems in the air that were more like those of Germany than England. Japan, too, lacked raw materials for her industries and by the mid-1930s had embarked upon expansionism on the Asian mainland. But in addition to an inadequate resource base, she had to rely upon foreign sources for systems design and finished productions, especially in aviation. Japan welcomed European advisers and their aircraft in the 1920s, so that her military leaders could acquire the latest equipment and techniques for their services. In 1924, the Japanese Army Air Force (IJAAF) numbered twenty-four squadrons, with all of their aircraft built abroad. Eleven years later this force numbered thirty-seven squadrons, with all planes manufactured in Japan, though still of foreign design. By the end of the 1930s, nationalist stirrings had carried Japan toward complete independence of foreign sources. The Japanese simply hid such development from foreign observers. They projected a continuing foreign dependency, a primitive state of design and production, and isolation from the general aviation developments elsewhere. Whether or not Japan's burgeoning industrial base could provide adequate support in any but the shortest war remained unclear. Nonetheless, this nation posed a distinct threat to peace in the Far East, and her air forces enjoyed air superiority in areas of influence close to home.[74]

There was no major air power in the Far East to challenge Japan. Still, any discussion of the Japanese approach to air superiority must address four critical issues before 1941: 1) the development of the indigenous air-craft industry; 2) combat experience in China and Manchuria/Mongolia; 3) aviator training; and 4) the psychological edge derived from foreign ignorance and condescension toward the Japanese military. Again, Japan's experience paralleled that of Nazi Germany; air forces-in-being were prepared for short war, and Japan intimidated less powerful neighbors with such air power. There was little evidence to suggest that Japanese officials in the 1920s and 1930s emphasized the strategic importance of air superiority in Douhet's sense, or in an attritional air war against their own home islands.[75]

Japan launched her rearmament program in 1919, strengthening fleet and land air arms for narrow, tactical missions. Aircraft such as the Fiat BR-20 bomber (which became the IJAAF's type I) and the Heinkel HE-111B-0 and Seversky 2 PA-83 fighters were acquired through either purchase of manufacturing rights or importation of the actual airplane. Among those foreign countries supplying aviation equipment were Great Britain (aircraft), Germany (engines, propellers), and the United States (airframes, engines, parts). The Japanese sent young students to American universities and aircraft plants to prepare for eventual self-sufficiency. By the mid-1930s, Japanese firms like Mitsubishi, Nakajima, and Kawasaki had become large concerns, with smaller shops such as Aichi, Kawanishi, and Hitachi all producing modern, all-metal, low-wing monoplanes, which ranked with foreign aircraft in capability and quality. The government protected and partially subsidized the domestic aviation industry, which turned to full military production only in 1939. Cooperation among the Japanese manufacturers proved nonexistent, however, and duplication of effort could not be prevented. Total annual military aircraft production rose from 445 in 1930 to 1,181 in 1936, and 4,768 by 1940.[76]

Japanese aircraft of the period definitely reflected the type of missions projected by the Army and Navy and experienced during campaigns on the mainland. The Japanese Navy Air Force (IJNAF) focused on aircraft such as the Aichi D3A carrier dive bomber, Kawanishi H6K and H8K flying boats, Mitsubishi A5M fighter, Mitsubishi F1M observation biplane, Nakajima B5N and B6N carrier torpedo bombers, and the most famous of all Japanese aircraft, the Mitsubishi A6M Zero-Sen carrier fighter. Japanese Army Air Force (IJAAF) aircraft included the Kawasaki Ki-45 Toryu two-engine, heavy fighter; the Mitsubishi Ki-15 and Ki-30 light bombers; Ki-46 strategic reconnaissance aircraft; and J1N1 reconnaissance/night fighter. Both air arms gave attention to the development of a heavy bombardment airplane. Mitsubishi produced the Ki-21, and Nakajima manufactured the Ki-49 Donryu—both aircraft achieving 1,300–1,600 mile ranges. By 1939, the impending possibility of war with the United States led IJNAF officials to seek a long-range naval torpedo bomber. Mitsubishi suggested its G4M aircraft with a range of 2,262 miles, though weak in armor and armament. As was the case in Germany, the Japanese did not develop a 4-engine bomber, although Mitsubishi executives urged the Navy to incorporate that principle into the G4M aircraft. In general, maneuverability and speed characterized Japanese fighters, while durability attended the various types of carrier and light bombardment aircraft. If Japanese military aviation was the best in the Far East at the end of the 1930s, its problem was the strength of the defense industrial base as part of the quest to maintain overall air superiority in that region.[77]

The Japanese tested many of these airplanes against the Chinese and the Russians between 1937 and 1941. The Japanese flyers enjoyed air superiority against the Chinese from the beginning. The IJAAF practiced close air support of ground operations and tactical interdiction strikes, while both Army and Navy air arms carried out bombing raids against virtually unprotected Chinese cities. Shanghai and Nanking hardly provided the type of strategic target envisioned by European theorists such as Douhet. If the Chinese populace seemed terrorized by the rain of aerial bombardment, the size and rural character of Chinese society neutralized the political impact of such tactics. The Republic of China under Chiang Kai-shek did not succumb, although large portions of the country passed under Japanese control. Such footholds on the mainland led to engagements with the Russians by 1939, and in particular, to the little-known Nonmonhan incident where Soviet aviation provided a sterner test for Japanese pilots and their aircraft. In fact, initial Japanese success in gaining air superiority gradually evaporated as Soviet Marshal Zhukov introduced veterans from the Spanish Civil War to train and fight with the inexperienced Russian aviators initially positioned on the Manchurian front. Neither of the Japanese air arms learned much about air superiority from the Asian experience. They basically practiced the type of war that they had been prepared to fight in the first place. Support of land operations, tactical bombardment, training of pilots, and testing material were the chief activities. China for the Japanese, like Spain for the Germans, Italians, and Russians basically taught air forces the tactical lessons necessary for waging intensive air-ground campaigns. The Japanese did not confirm or deny the long-range strategic tenets of Douhet, Trenchard, or Mitchell. But then, Japan, like the others, simply lacked the technological tools to wage strategic air war in the 1930s and probably did not sense any great need to do so.[78]

What these limited war experiences of the 1930s taught the various participants was the lesson of superior aircrew training. If the short, intensive air campaign remained the goal of Japanese air strategists (as it did their German and Italian counterparts), then provision of top quality pilots and crews became a prime requisite for success. Both IJAAF and IJNAF training schools provided 300 hours flying time during training before assignment to a tactical component. By comparison, American military aviators of the period received only 200 hours. Since both Japanese air arms sacrificed safety factors in aircraft so as to secure high performance, they demanded highly skilled aviators to operate the equipment. The IJAAF emphasized pilot training while the naval arm also stressed bombardier, gunner, and navigator training. One Japanese naval ace, Saburo Sakai, recalled the rigorous training pilots would undergo in the search for proficiency: "Our instructors constantly impressed us with the fact that a fighter plane seen from a distance of several thousand yards often is no easier to identify than a star in daylight," noted Sakai. "And the pilot who first discovers his enemy and maneuvers into the most advantageous attack position can gain an invincible superiority," he added. The instructors had the students practice snapping their eyes away ninety degrees and back again seeking to locate the target star. "Of such things are fighter pilots made," boasted Sakai. Foreign observers later would admit that Japanese fighter pilots might be fewer in number than their opponents, but they still were among the best in the world.[79]

Few foreign observers would have thought so in the 1930s, however. Not only was most of the world ignorant of Japanese military prowess and the outstanding quality of aircraft because of Japanese secrecy, but such ignorance combined with complacency, chauvinism, and arrogance on the part of most westerners. Borrowed technology, copied aircraft designs, and the obsequious personal style of the Japanese (as well as myths of Japanese physical weaknesses) were used to lull the West into thinking the Japanese aviators were inferior. Not long before the Japanese victory at Pearl Harbor in December 1941, one aviation writer in the United States noted that "Japan if engaged in a great war would crumble like a house of cards, dragging after itself the myth of her military prowess and the carefully cultivated daydream of Pacific hegemony and complete world domination." He suggested low training figures (only 1,000 new pilots a year) and production rates (less than 3,000 workable aircraft of all types on-line), and the high incidence of accidents as proof. He declared the Japanese copying of foreign design made all Japanese aircraft at least 3 years out of date. "While the leading designers in other parts of the world are introducing in their national air forces 2,000 horsepower engines, the Japanese are still to produce their first 1,000 horsepower motor," he observed. In his view, American aviation circles would not have to take a second look at the leading Japanese military aircraft types "to decide that most of them are obsolete or obsolescent."[80]

Japanese air power in the late 1930s suffered from several deficiencies like that of Nazi Germany. Both countries lacked crucial raw materials for aviation, including oil and lubricants. Japanese air doctrine was narrow and uncoordinated between the two service aviation programs. Students of the period also noted weak air-ground communications, inadequate aircraft range, poor levels of air defense technology and organization, and relatively low production rates for both aircrews and aircraft. In 1941, for example, Japan produced only about one-half the total number of German military aircraft, and one-quarter that of the United States. Aircrew training rates (both army and navy) that year stood only at 6,000, while that of the United States totaled 11,000. Yet, Japan—like Germany—stood as the superior air power in its particular part of the world. Both countries thought in terms of short war on the favorable terms of air, sea, and land superiority. Their major dependence would be placed on the element of surprise and on a limited number of well-trained airmen in high performance aircraft executing skillfully laid-out geo-political plans. Confident of early victory (provided at least partially through air superiority in the theater of operations), Japan like Germany overlooked the latent strength of her most potential enemy and what that portended in terms of maintaining air superiority long enough to achieve ultimate political victory.[81]

United States

Japan's potential enemy was the United States, although European colonial powers such as Great Britain, the Netherlands, and France also blocked Japanese plans for expansion in Southeast Asia. Lying behind protective oceans, yet intimately involved with the Pacific and Asian spheres since the nineteenth century, America was a sleeping giant both politically and militarily in the 1930s. Beset like the rest of the world by the Great Depression, the United States also faced the same antiwar manifestations and budgetary strictures for military spending as the other western democracies. The United States Navy provided the traditional "first line of defense" while smaller land-air garrisons guarded frontier possessions from Alaska to Panama, and from Hawaii to the Philippines. America was a maritime nation like Japan and Great Britain. Like the other two, U.S. military planners had to think more expansively about the strategic implications of distance and national security than the continental European powers. The 2,400-mile distance from the west coast to Hawaii, for example, held vast importance for military professionals grappling with problems of air and sea power. Thus, military leaders divided their air assets between Army and Navy (like Japan). U.S. Navy and Marine Corps air missions hinged upon their tactical roles as fleet air auxiliaries. But, the U.S. Army Air Corps remained organizationally part of the land service (with attendant missions), yet searching for independence from ground force control like Great Britain's RAF.[82]

Doctrinal struggles between the U.S. Army air and ground components essentially focused upon three major mission areas: ground support, strategic bombardment, and coast defense. The Air Corps developed a doctrine for strategic bombardment, while fully accepting a role in coast defense as a method for gaining funding for bombers and the support for independence. But the ground-dominated War Department General Staff fought to keep the Air Corps focused on the ground support function, while the Navy naturally opposed any Air Corps aspirations to assume primacy in coast defense. Overlooked was the fact that the Air Corps simply could not fulfill most of its promises given the limitations of technology and money. The Air Corps, like the Army as a whole, was a Mobilization Day force during peacetime; its regulars formed a cadre to test and train, develop elaborate paper plans, and prepare for wartime expansion. Meanwhile, it produced doctrine and maintained a small force-in-being of increasingly obsolescent aircraft while constantly seeking force modernization and a wider institutional role. Arguments between the armed services over budget, roles, and missions, as well as internal service squabbling among the Army's arms, branches, commands, bureaus, and field headquarters (of which the Air Corps was but one element), hampered the progress of American air power development.[83]

Capture of the Air Corps Tactical School (ACTS) faculty by strategic bombardment enthusiasts and the developing ascendancy of bombardment over pursuit aviation characterized Air Corps doctrinal development at this time. Equipping line units with a succession of superior bombers like the Boeing B–9, Martin B–10, and Douglas B–18, together with the appearance of the Norden bombsight, promised the type of high-speed, high-altitude, precision bombing long sought by Mitchell's disciples. No pursuit or fighter aircraft in the American inventory could blight the bomber's promise. Impassioned debate might attend faculty meetings at ACTS, but the proven superiority of bombardment over pursuit during maneuvers and tests simply reinforced an overall Air Corps conclusion that bombardment could first neutralize an enemy air force at its bases (whether on land or afloat), before proceeding to destroy the enemy's industrial base. As Maj. Gen. Henry H. Arnold, Chief of Staff of the Air Corps in 1938, observed, the notion that "unescorted bombers might be able to outrun defending fighters, temporarily existed." But for most of this period, as Lt. Gen. James H. Doolittle commented sagely in 1945: "Basically, the trouble was we had to talk about air power in terms of promise and prophecy instead of in terms of demonstration and experience."[84]

In 1935, the Army Air Corps established an independent striking force called the General Headquarters or GHQ Air Force, developed the B–17 four-engine bomber in conjunction with the Boeing Company, and published a new doctrinal statement. GHQ Air Force incorporated the Trenchard-Douhet-Mitchell notion of a centrally controlled mass (pursuit, attack, and bombardment units), functioning as an offensive striking force and not tied to ground operations. This force could deploy quickly to protect not only

Among the bombers in the Air Corps inventory during the 1930s were the
Martin B–10 *(above)* and the Boeing B–17 *(below)*.

American coastlines, but also overseas possessions. The development of the four-engine Boeing B–17 held promise with its average speed of 232 miles per hour, carrying capacity of 4,800 pounds, and proven durability during a 2,100-mile flight from the Boeing plant in Seattle, Washington, to the Air Corps test facility at Dayton, Ohio. The airplane convinced Air Corps leaders that here was the device for implementing Army Training Regulation TR 440–15, which stated that aerial coast defense operations would be based on joint action of the army and navy. The B–17 was an adequate instrument for distant destruction of an enemy fleet as well as for strategic bombardment.[85]

Bombardment aviators in the American service acquired even greater confidence than before. Col. Hugh J. Knerr, the Chief of Staff for GHQ Air Force, told the Army War College class of 1935–36 upon the occasion of their visit to Langley Field in June 1936:

> The bombardment aircraft of the GHQ Air Force will never be expected to rest comfortably within its hangars awaiting an air attack after the declaration of war, but will be employed so as to *prevent* the launching of an air attack against our country, the massing of ground forces within striking distance of our frontiers, or the approach of enemy carriers and other elements of a hostile fleet to a point from which attacks may be launched against us.

Here was an American Air Corps doctrine for achieving air superiority through an air offensive. True, some leaders, like "Hap" Arnold and GHQ Air Force Commander Brig. Gen. Delos Emmons, worried that unprotected bombers could not reach their targets. Others, however, debunked the notion of a resurgent pursuit aviation, contending that "it lacks range for employment in the air offense, and is required for antiaircraft defense." Even then, as one Air Corps lecturer at the Army War College pointed out in 1936: "too much reliance should not be placed upon interception since the speeds of modern bombers had become so high and the handicaps of weather conditions so great that an interception under war conditions is nothing more or less than intelligence luck." Nobody yet had surmounted the range-speed problem for American offensive pursuit aviation or the defensive weaknesses of inadequate early ground warning to overcome slow interception. "We in the United States," noted Arnold in his memoirs, "were still debating the need for fighter escorts for bombers."[86]

The U.S. Army Air Corps talked about a "balanced air force" by the end of the 1930s, but the proportions were different from those of 1929. Now, its leaders wanted 40 percent bombardment, 25 percent pursuit, 20 percent attack aviation for ground support, and 15 percent observation. Doctrine for this distribution was more or less in place; the proper materiel was not. In fact, the major thrust of the American aviation program in the late 1930s centered on production of appropriate new models for each part of the envisioned inventory. The vaunted B–17 heavy bomber formed but one part of the program. Also important were those pursuit aircraft, and the Air Corps sought to develop two distinct types. One would be a small, high performance "flying machinegun" with a performance radius measured "in time in the air at full power that is about an hour" with speeds in excess of 300 miles per hour. This would be the defensive force used against enemy bombers escaping the American bombardment offensive by GHQ Air Force. A second type of pursuit wanted by the Air Corps would be an offensive "air battle cruiser" to accompany the bombers. This aircraft could be a multi-seat fighter, with an operating range up to 1,000 miles as well as greater speed than the bombers so as to "accompany or rendezvous with bombardment when the support of additional fire power is required by the latter." Since it sometimes took 5 years to evolve new aircraft, Arnold once noted, constant experimental and interim models might be required.[87]

This search for modernized materiel forms something of an unsung chapter in America's involvement with air superiority. While remaining detached from Europe's internal feuding, and even from involvement during the initial years of a Second World War, the United States profited from watching foreign technical developments in aircraft. A second heavy bomber appeared during this period of neutrality, styled the B–24 Liberator (after rejection of experimental B–15 and B–19 models). The twin-engine attack bombers like the Douglas A–20 (or DB–7), North American B–25, and B–26, as well as the Navy's single-engine Douglas torpedo and dive bombers also emerged. Most important were Army and Navy attempts to secure improved pursuit or fighter aircraft for their services. The Navy found its solution among the Brewster F2A Buffalo and Grumman 4F4 Wildcat aircraft. The Air Corps settled upon the Republic P–35 and subsequent variants of the famous Curtiss "Hawk" family which ranged from the P–36 to P–40. All of these models reflected the trend toward all-metal, low-wing monoplanes with speed and range to meet service requirements. Other promising Army aircraft on the drawing boards at this time included the twin-engine Lockheed P–38 and the Bell P–39, though none could equal first-line European or Japanese counterparts.[88]

Interestingly enough, the Munich settlement in September 1938 provided what Arnold later styled the Army Air Corps' "real Magna Charta" of independence because it caused President Franklin D. Roosevelt to actively pursue rearmament and particularly to emphasize aviation in that rearmament. Roosevelt and his close civilian advisers probably knew or cared little about the semantic nuances of doctrinal debate within the Air Corps. They thought in terms of quantity and quality of aircraft with which to counter threats to national security. Put in simple terms, the American approach to the concept of air superiority at highest government levels was typically concerned less with concept and more with production of overwhelming quantities of what it thought American industry could provide. American faith in the inherent greatness of its industrial capacity promised to overcome the qualitative and numerical deficiencies of an Army Air

Corps that numbered less than 2,500 airplanes of all types when war clouds once more engulfed Europe in 1939. Roosevelt saw the task in terms of mass production. Arnold realized, however, that "the strength of an Air Force cannot be measured in terms of airplanes only. Other things are essential—productive capacity of airplanes, of pilots, of mechanics, and bases from which to operate." The issue after 1938 was not doctrinal to either man. The U.S. Army Air Corps had wedded its air superiority doctrine to offensive, strategic bombardment. What was needed then was upgraded materiel, quantity production, and the procurement of trained manpower from a nation then unprepared for war. By December 1941 rearmament had begun to pay off. (See Table 1–3) Air superiority would come not from a small force-in-being, but a massive air armada fabricated for a war of longer duration and manned by expertly trained airmen.[89]

Conclusions

The world's major air powers balanced on a series of precarious "ifs" at the start of the Second World War. Aviators everywhere had promised results they were frankly incapable of achieving at this stage of aviation development. If Germany, Italy, or Japan began a war, they needed to win quickly and conclusively, allowing themselves time to reconstitute battle losses from a very limited pool of economic resources. There would be no question of gaining air superiority over the course of time during prolonged warfare. Their national strategies hinged on immediate attainment and maintenance of air superiority from the beginning of a conflict. For Great Britain, France, the Soviet Union, or the United States, however, survival depended upon limited forces-in-being that could buy time for rearmament and aerial counterattack to win air superiority. The French *Armée de l'Air* could not win air superiority on its own, except, perhaps, in a very limited sense of time and air space. Rather, it depended upon a cooperative operation with the British RAF. For the British and the Russians, at least, survival depended upon defensive pursuit winning the air superiority battle over the homeland. For the British and the Americans—both of whom thought principally in offensive bombardment terms—time would be needed to build the force capable of eliminating enemy air resources on the ground. The British, at least, admitted the need for fighter production, but it took the Americans a long time to decide as to how much priority should be accorded pursuit aviation.

Actually, the nature of warfare, and by implication air superiority, had changed by 1939. Destruction of an enemy's armed forces in battle had been the goal of the 1914–18 war, despite desultory attempts to affect the

TABLE 1–3

AAF Airplane Inventory, 1939–1941

End of Month	Total	Heavy Bombers	Medium Bombers	Light Bombers	Fighters	Reconn- aissance	Trans- ports	Trainers	Communi- cations
1939									
Jul	2,402	16	400	276	494	356	118	735	7
Aug	2,440	18	414	276	492	359	129	745	7
Sep	2,474	22	428	278	489	359	136	754	7
Oct	2,507	27	446	277	490	365	137	758	7
Nov	2,536	32	458	275	498	375	136	755	7
Dec	2,546	39	464	274	492	378	131	761	7
1940									
Jan	2,588	45	466	271	464	409	128	798	7
Feb	2,658	49	470	271	458	415	128	860	7
Mar	2,709	54	468	267	453	415	125	920	7
Apr	2,806	54	468	263	451	416	125	1,022	7
May	2,906	54	470	259	459	410	124	1,123	7
Jun	2,966	54	478	166	477	414	127	1,243	7
Jul	3,102	56	483	161	500	410	128	1,357	7
Aug	3,295	65	485	158	539	407	128	1,506	8
Sep	3,451	72	484	157	568	404	128	1,630	8
Oct	3,642	87	483	154	581	408	127	1,794	8
Nov	3,862	93	483	153	613	404	125	1,983	8
Dec	3,961	92	481	158	625	404	124	2,069	8
1941									
Jan	4,219	92	478	165	630	403	122	2,326	3
Feb	4,479	103	484	195	647	401	131	2,513	5
Mar	4,975	108	494	240	775	397	133	2,814	14
Apr	5,604	112	522	276	939	394	133	3,199	29
May	6,102	112	554	279	969	389	132	3,630	37
Jun	6,777	120	611	292	1,018	415	144	4,124	53
Jul	7,423	121	642	323	1,101	434	159	4,568	75
Aug	8,242	121	696	339	1,374	458	174	4,979	101
Sep	9,063	126	722	350	1,513	482	187	5,544	139
Oct	9,964	137	751	356	1,696	473	206	6,199	146
Nov	10,329	157	685	350	1,618	495	216	6,594	214
Dec	12,297	288	745	799	2,170	475	254	7,340	226

Source: Headquarters, U.S. Army Air Forces, Office of Statistical Control, *The Army Air Forces Statistical Digest (World War II)* (Washington, 1945), p. 135.

homefront through aerial bombardment. By 1939, however, this earlier goal became subordinated in some countries to a vision of war in the air almost exclusively directed against enemy production and the will of the populace, following suppression of an enemy's air force. Aviation as a handmaiden to ground forces had become anathema to most airmen, despite the respectable tactical performance of aviation in World War I. The central thread running through interwar military aviation was strategic air power. And, by the destruction of an enemy's resources, strategic air power could bring air superiority to build and field air forces. Unfortunately, by 1939, subtle nuances governed implementation of that doctrine.

In peacetime, air superiority could be seen as something different than in wartime. It was more a game of numbers and production base, as well as psychological intimidation in anticipation of war. When war came, the notion of a floating pocket of air superiority surrounding the independent strategic offensive seemed possible. Even general or overall air superiority throughout a war zone or theater of operations for a longer duration than just a single sortie or mission also had to be considered. Of course, air superiority impinged upon those unavoidable missions like close air support of ground combat operations, interdiction campaigns, and use of aircraft in resupply. Also, there remained hope for a defensive means to win air superiority through interception of enemy aircraft escaping the bombardment offensive. All of these facets of air superiority would undergo the test of practical experience in a Second World War.

The cauldron of actual combat would resolve fundamental air superiority questions beyond the "given" that it was absolutely indispensable to any and every air operation. German, Italian, Russian, and Japanese airmen received tactical lessons and experience in the little wars of the 1930s which provided them with some answers. But, mere observer reports from those conflicts could not substitute for actual combat experience among the western democracies that sat on and watched from the sidelines the conflicts in Spain, Ethiopia, China, and Manchuria. This fact created a doctrinal vacuum in peacetime. It stunted the growth of air superiority doctrines in Great Britain, France, and the United States.

The true impetus for doctrinal adjustment emerged from the first two pivotal years of the Second World War, 1939 and 1940. Whether or not Japan learned anything from the aerial campaigns over western and eastern Europe in this period is not clear. Even the Americans seemed not to derive definite air superiority lessons from the battles for France and Great Britain. U.S. airmen did learn lessons about the value of interception through radar, ground control networks, and superior pursuit as they affected defensive counterair operations. These factors enabled American writers of FM 1–15, *Tactics and Techniques of Air Fighting* (September 1940 edition), to suggest that pursuit had the priority mission of denying "the hostile air force freedom of the air." But American aviators generally remained committed to the viability of long-range offensive bombardment striking power as the means for gaining overall air superiority and ending a war with victory.[90]

Nowhere were the incongruities of air superiority definition more apparent than in the contrasting doctrinal statements of the RAF and the U.S. Army Air Corps (after June 20, 1941, the Army Air Forces). Whereas the U.S. Army's Field Service Regulations had been clear in 1923 concerning the primacy of pursuit aviation, declaring that its general mission was "to establish and maintain aerial supremacy" by "seeking out and defeating the hostile aviation" (as close to a definition of air superiority as one might find), the situation was less clear by 1939–40. No such distinct definition of air supremacy (or air control or air superiority) could be found in the Tentative Field Service Regulations FM 100–5 of the American Army, or in the Air Corps Field Manual FM 1–5, *Employment of Aviation of the Army*. FM 100–5 talked about dividing pursuit aviation into interceptor and fighter segments and the indecisive nature of "air fighting," but nowhere could the reader find a clear and succinct definition of "air superiority." No one in American military circles established the parameters of air superiority as clearly as manual writers in Great Britain.[91]

The British War Office document, *The Employment of the Air Forces with the Army in the Field* (1938), devoted a major section to air superiority. The document's writers declared that air superiority "is a state of moral and material superiority which enables its possessor to conduct air operations against an enemy and at the same time deprives the enemy of the ability to interfere effectively by the use of his own air forces." In terms of army cooperation, air superiority implied to the British that their reconnaissance and bomber aircraft could carry out their assigned tasks effectively, as well as insure that the army would suffer "the minimum of interference" from enemy bombers and reconnaissance. The authors readily admitted the transitory nature of air superiority and concluded that the struggle for it would begin as soon as opposing air forces came within range of one another and would even continue for the duration of a campaign. Air superiority could be transferred from one side to the other with varying rapidity by the advent of superior numbers of aircraft, of new and better models, of fresh tactics, and of new commanders of outstanding personality. Eschewing "purely defensive measures" to accomplish this task, RAF authorities suggested that while affected by questions of superior equipment and organization, air superiority was "even more dependent on superior morale and it can be obtained only by the combined offensive action of bomber and fighter aircraft."[92]

Few aviators anywhere understood the complicated and perplexing questions of air superiority until entering the actual cauldron of combat. What one modern author terms "the problem of friction in war" eventually blotted out most of the prewar theorizing and agonizing arguments over pursuit and bombardment as the means for achieving air superiority. The peacetime context of small, M-day air forces provided inadequate testing laboratories, and even the minor conflicts of the interwar period shed only the dimmest light upon possible future directions for this principle. "Everything in war is simple, but the simplest thing is difficult," wrote the great Prussian philosopher of war, Carl von Clausewitz. "The difficulties accumulate and end by producing a kind of friction that is inconceivable unless one has experienced war." It would not be until the middle and later years of the Second World War that satisfactory doctrinal answers could be worked out concerning air superiority. It would await the return of peace for those lessons to be codified and incorporated into preparations for the next war.[93]

Notes

1. On early predictions on the future of air warfare, see H. G. Wells, *War in the Air* (New York, 1908), especially pp 167–208; R. P. Hearne, *Aerial Warfare* (London and New York, 1909), pp 136–37, 169; and Claude Grahame-White and Harry Harper, *The Aeroplane in War* (London, 1912), pp 208–09. Zepplin quoted in Lee Kennett, *A History of Strategic Bombing* (New York, 1982), p 9.

2. Chronology of Air Force History to 1939, drawn principally from "Outline of the Development of Military Aviation in the United States," RG 18, MMB, NA; Historical Documentation of Major General Benjamin D. Foulois, K 239.05122–766 (3–926–38), p 44, U.S. Air Force Historical Research Center, Maxwell AFB, Ala. (AFHRC).

3. Trenchard quoted in William Mitchell, *Memoirs of World War I* (New York, 1960 ed), p 105; Walter Raleigh and H. A. Jones, *The War in the Air* (London, 1922–1936), vol 2, pp 235–36; C. H. Hildreth and Bernard C. Nalty, *1001 Questions Answered About Aviation History* (New York, 1969), p 109; Charles D. Bright, "Air Power in World War I: Sideshow or Decisive Factor?" *Aerospace Historian* 18 (Jun 1971), pp 58–62.

4. Technology, doctrine, and weapons development can be explored in Richard P. Hallion, *Rise of the Fighter Aircraft, 1914–1918* (Annapolis, 1984), chaps II, VI, IX; I. B. Holley, Jr., *Ideas and Weapons* (Washington, 1983 ed), esp part II; John H. Morrow, Jr., *German Air Power in World War I* (London, 1982), chap 3.

5. Hallion, *Fighter Aircraft,* chap IV.

6. Geoffrey Rossano, "The Apprenticeship: How the Allies Trained the American Air Service," *Journal of American Aviation Historical Society* 28 (Spring 1983), pp 22–31, esp p 30.

7. Cyril Falls, *The Great War* (New York, 1959), pp 181–82, 264–65; R. A. Mason, "The British Dimension," in Alfred F. Hurley and Robert C. Ehrhart, eds, *Air Power and Warfare: The Proceedings of the Eighth Military History Symposium, United States Air Force Academy, 18–20 October 1978* (Washington, 1979), p 29.

8. Raleigh and Jones, *War in the Air,* I, pp 6, 418–19, 473; Andrew Boyle, *Trenchard* (New York, 1962), pp 184–89, 219; Sir Charles Webster and Noble Frankland, *The Strategic Air Offensive Against Germany, 1939–1945* [History of the Second World War] (London, 1961), pp 37–38, 40.

9. Smuts quoted in Dudley Saward, *Bomber Harris: The Story of Sir Arthur Harris, Marshal of the Royal Air Force* (Garden City, 1985), pp 18–19.

10. Maurer Maurer, ed, *The U.S. Air Service in World War I* (Washington, 1978), vol I, append A, p 343.

11. On Mitchell, see his paper, "General Principles Underlying the Use of the Air Service in the Zone of the Advance A.E.F.," *Bulletin of the Information Section, Air Service AEF* 3, (April 30, 1918), p 132; Churchill, Parker, and the corporate board thinking can be followed in Maurer, ed, *Air Service,* vol II, pp 107–23.

12. Lawrence Kuter, "Air Power—The American Concept" (c. 1943), photostat of typescript, 167.6–50, AFHRC; Gorrell's plan in Maurer, ed, *Air Service,* vol II, pp 141–57; see also Robert Frank Futrell, *Ideas, Concepts, Doctrine: A History of Basic Thinking in the*

United States Air Force, 1907–1964, (Maxwell AFB, 1974 ed), pp 12–14; also Thomas H. Greer, *The Development of Air Doctrine in the American Air Army, 1917–1941* (Maxwell AFB, Sept 1955), pp 4–13, 35–36.

13. Maurer, *Air Service,* vol II, p 141.

14. William Mitchell, "Tactical Application of Military Aeronautics," Jan 5, 1919, File 97–10, Army War College Curricular Files, U.S. Army Military History Institute, Carlisle Barracks, Pa. (MHI).

15. William Mitchell, "Air Service at the Meuse-Argonne," *World's Work,* XXXVIII (Sept 1919), pp 555–58, 559; L. H. Brereton, "Difficulties Encountered in the Recent Offensive," n.d., Mitchell Collection, Box 6, Library of Congress (LC); Report of Committee 5, G–3 Course, Army War College Curriculum 1930–1931, "Employment and Organization of Army Aviation and Anti-aircraft Defense," Sept 27, 1930, pp 1–3; Army War College Curricular Files, MHI; General Headquarters, AEF, Summaries of Air Information, March–April–May, June–September, October–November, all 1918, File 51000300, Library, National Air and Space Museum, Washington, DC, (LNASM).

16. Holley, *Ideas and Weapons,* chap X; James T. Hudson, *Hostile Skies: A Combat History of the American Air Service in World War I* (Syracuse, NY, 1968), p 51.

17. Ferdinand Foch, "Memorandum on the Subject of an Independent Air Force," Sept 14, 1918, in *Air Power Historian* III (July 1956), p 161; Greer, *Air Doctrine,* pp 31, 36–37.

18. On Trenchard, see Boyle, *Trenchard,* 350–53, also Brian Bond, *British Military Policy Between the Two World Wars* (Oxford, 1980), pp 72, 74, 78, 85–86, 108, 109, 144, 222, 251, 321, 323; on Mitchell, see Alfred F. Hurley, *Billy Mitchell: Crusader for Air Power* (Bloomington, 1975 ed), chaps 5 and 6; on Douhet, see Giorgio Rochet, "Douhet and the Italian Military Thought, 1919–1930," in Claude Carlier, ed, *Colloque International: Colloque Air 1984* (Paris, 1984), pp 19–30.

19. Trenchard's memorandum, "The War Object of an Air Force," May 2, 1928, quoted in Saward, *Bomber Harris,* pp 33–34; Kennett, *Strategic Bombing,* pp 75–76; Henry A. Probert, "The Independence of the Royal Air Force (1918–1945)," in Carlier, *Colloque,* esp p 117.

20. Edward Warner, "Douhet, Mitchell, Seversky: Theories of Air Warfare," in Edward M. Earle, ed, *Makers of Modern Strategy* (Princeton, 1944), pp 485–497, summarizes the theorists' impact at this time, while Douhet's ideas can be read in the translation by Dino Ferrari of *The Command of the Air* (New York, 1942; reprint, Office of Air Force History, 1983), esp pp vii–x, 5–6, 28, 47–48, 57–58, 67, 337, 374–89; a recent critique of Douhet appears in Barry D. Watts, *The Foundations of U.S. Air Doctrine: The Problem of Friction in War* (Maxwell AFB, 1984), esp chap 2.

21. Quoted in P. Vauthier, *La Doctrine de Guerre du General Douhet* (Paris, 1935), intro; Rochet, "Douhet," p 20.

22. A recent study of the Mitchell era can be found in John F. Shiner, *Foulois and the U.S. Army Air Corps, 1931–1935* (Washington, 1983), pp 11–28, while Trenchard's comment can be found in Boyle, *Trenchard,* p 299.

23. William P. Mitchell, *Our Air Force: The Keystone of National Defense* (New York, 1919), pp xix, 200–01.

24. William Mitchell, "Notes on the Multi-Motored Bombardment Group—Day and Night," pp 70, 97–107, quoted in Hurley, *Mitchell,* p 83; also William Mitchell, *Winged Defense: The Development and Possibilities of Modern Air Power* (New York, 1925), pp 19, 139, 199.

25. Warner, "Douhet, Mitchell, Seversky," pp 499–500; Hurley, *Mitchell,* p 94.

26. William C. Sherman, *Air Warfare* (New York, 1926), chap V, esp p 128.

27. Intvw, Hugh N. Ahmann and Tom Sturm with Gen Laurence S. Kuter, Sep 30–Oct 3, 1974, pp 62, 67, 79–80, 108–09, U.S. Air Force Oral History Program, K239.0512–810, AFHRC; Mason M. Patrick, "The Development of Military Aeronautics in the U.S. as compared with that in France, Great Britain, Japan, Italy, and Russia," Nov 27, 1923, G–3 Course 15, File 1–20, vol III, Army War College Course 1923–24, AWC Curricular Archives, MHI; Memo, Patrick-Adjutant General, Dec 19, 1924, Box 10, and Mar 27, 1925, Box 11, both William Mitchell Collection, LC.

28. Ltr, Capt Carl Spaatz to Gerald Garard, Jan 29, 1926, Folder Jan 2–Apr 27, 1926, Box 4, Spaatz Collection, LC; Spaatz Lecture, "Bombardment and Pursuit Aviation," Quantico, Va., Nov 4, 1927, File 51000400, LNASM.

29. Maj Earl L. Naiden, Sept 17, 1929, to G–3 Course 6, Army War College, File 363–A–6, Army War College Curricular Files, MHI; Kuter intvw, pp 5, 7, 9, 10, 14.

30. Intvw, Dr. Richard H. Kohn and Hugh N. Ahmann with Gen Bernard A. Schriever, Jun 14, 1985, p 5, as part of Senior Statesmen Conference Intvw, AFCHO Draft Mss.

31. Camille Rougeron, *L'aviation de bombardment*, (Paris, 1937 ed), vol I, p 117; also, Hurley and Ehrhart, eds, *Air Power and Warfare*, sect II.

32. On the Italian air force in the Mussolini era, see Giorgio Apostolo and Andrea Curami, "The Italian Air Force, 1919 to 1923," pp 257–68; Andrea Curami and Giorgio Apostolo, "The Italian Aviation from 1923 to 1933," pp 269–80; and Giancarlo Garello, "The Air Force During the Italian Fascism," pp 281–92, all Carlier, ed, *Colloque 1984*. An important recent discussion appears in James J. Sadkovich, "The Development of the Italian Air Force Prior to World War II," *Military Affairs* 51, (July 1987), pp 128–36.

33. U.S. Army Air Forces Historical Office, *Comparative History of Research and Development Policies Affecting Air Materiel, 1915–1944*, [AAF Historical Study 20], (Washington, 1945), pp 154–56, 162–63; Wesley Frank Craven and James Lee Cate, eds, *The Army Air Forces in World War II*, Vol I: *Plans and Early Operations* (Chicago, 1949; reprint, Office of Air Force History, 1983), pp 82–85.

34. U.S. Air Force Historical Study 20, pp 162, 163; Segre, "Douhet in Italy," pp 78–79; William L. Shirer, *The Collapse of the Third Republic* (New York, 1969), p 376; Basil Collier, *A History of Air Power* (New York, 1974), p 92.

35. Pétain quoted in Shirer, *Collapse*, p 174.

36. Robert J. Young, "The Strategic Dream: French Air Doctrine in the Inter-War Period, 1919–39," *Journal of Contemporary History* 9 (Oct 1974), pp 63–64; General D'Astier de la Vigerie, *Le ciel n'était pas vide, 1940* (Paris, 1952), p 23; Shirer, *Collapse*, pp 174, 179, 274, 389; M. Ribet, *Le Proces de Riom* (Paris, 1945), p 461; AAF Historical Office, *History of Research and Development Policies*, pp 175–78; Anthony Robinson, ed, *Aerial Warfare* (London, 1982), p 152.

37. Faris R. Kirkland, "The French Air Force in 1940: Was it Defeated by the Luftwaffe or by Politics?" *Air University Review* XXXVI (Sept–Oct 1985), pp 102–03; Claude Carlier, *Le Development de l' Aeronautique Militaire Française de 1958 à 1970*, (Vincennes, May 1976), p 6; Martin Alexander, "Force de Frappé ou Feu de Paillé? Maurice Gamelin's Appraisal of Military Aviation Before the Blitzkrieg of 1940," in Carlier, ed, *Colloque 1984*, pp 65–80; Young, "French Air Doctrine," pp 67–75.

38. Kirkland, "French Air Force," pp 102–07; Bill Gunston, *The Encyclopedia of the World's Combat Aircraft* (New York, 1976), pp 12, 22, 31, 46–47, 129, 143, 167, 181; John Batchelor and Bryan Cooper, *Fighter: A History of Fighter Aircraft* (New York, 1973), p 71.

39. Kirkland, "French Air Force," pp 103–05.

40. *Ibid.*, pp 105, 108; also Alexander, "Force de Frappé," pp 67–68.

41. Kirkland, "French Air Force," p 108.

42. D'Astier de la Vigerie, *Le ciel n'était pas vide, 1940;* Kirkland "French Air Force," pp 102–03; see also General Christienne, "L'industrie aeronautique française de septembre 1939 à juin 1940," pp 141–65; P. Buffotot, "Le moral dans l'Armée de l'Air française (de septembre 1939 à juin 1940)," pp 167–95; and P. Buffotot and J. Ogier, "L'Armée de l'Air pendant la bataille de France (du 10 mai à l'armistice): Essai de bilan numerique d'une bataille aerienne," pp 197–226, all in Service Historique de l'Armée de l'Air, *Recueil d'articles et études (1974–75)* (Vincennes, 1977).

43. Kirkland, "French Air Force," p 116.

44. *Ibid.*

45. *Ibid.*, pp 109–15.

46. In addition to *Ibid.*, 115, see R. J. Overy, *The Air War 1939–1945* (London, 1980), pp 26–30.

47. S. A. Tyushkevich, *The Soviet Armed Forces: A History of their Organizational Development* (Moscow, 1978), pt. II; Neil M. Heyman, "NEP and the Industrialization to 1928," Kenneth R. Whiting, "Soviet Aviation and Air Power under Stalin, 1928–1941," and John T. Greenwood, "The Great Patriotic War, 1941–1945," in Robin Higham and Jacob Kipp, eds, *Soviet Aviation and Air Power: A Historical View* (Boulder, Col., 1977), chaps 3, 4, 5.

48. A. S. Yakovlev, *Fifty Years of Soviet Aircraft Construction* (Moscow, 1970), p 4;

Kenneth R. Whiting, "Soviet Air Power in World War II," in Hurley and Ehrhart, eds, *Air Power and Warfare*, pp 98–101; and Neil M. Heyman, "NEP and the Industrialization to 1928," pp 41–42, as well as Greenwood, "Patriotic War," in Higham and Kipp, *Soviet Aviation*, p 70.

49. Yakovlev, *Fifty Years*, chap 2, p 8 esp; also, Robert Jackson, *The Red Falcons: The Soviet Air Force in Action, 1919–1969* (New York, 1970), chap 2.

50. Georgii Zhukov, *The Memoirs of Marshal Zhukov* (London, 1971), p 109; Colin Munro, *Soviet Air Forces* (New York, 1972), pp 24, 26–36.

51. Munro, *Soviet Air Forces*, pp 37–38; Yakovlev, *Fifty Years*, paints a different picture, pp 18–19.

52. Zhukov, *Memoirs*, pp 140, 150, 154; Craven and Cate, *AAF in World War II*, Vol I: *Plans and Early Operations*, pp 79–80.

53. Yakovlev, *Fifty Years*, chap 4, p 46 esp; Gunston, *Combat Aircraft*, pp 120, 128, 151, 180, 223.

54. M. N. Kozhevnikov, *The Command and Staff of the Soviet Army Air Force in the Great Patriotic War, 1941–1945* (Moscow, 1977 and trans by AAF), pp 26–29, cites the following relevant works: A. N. Lapchinsky, *Vozdushnaya armiya* [The Air Army] (Moscow, 1939); S. A. Mezheninov, *Vozdushnyye sily v vonvyne i operatsii* [The Air Force in War and in an Operation] (Moscow, 1927); A. S. Algazin, *Obespecheniye vozdushnykh operatsiy* [Support of Air Operations] (Moscow, 1928); A. V. Sergeyev, *Strategiya i taktika Krasnogo Vozdushnogo Flota* [Strategy and Tactics of the Red Air Fleet] (Moscow, 1935); P. P. Ionov, *Obshchaya taktika Voyenno-Vozdushnykh Sil* [Air Force General Tactics] (Moscow, 1934).

55. Kozhevnikov, *Command and Staff*, pp 28-92.

56. Williamson Murray, *Strategy for Defeat: The Luftwaffe, 1933–1945* (Maxwell AFB, 1983), pp 3–8; Hermann Hauptmann, *The Luftwaffe: Its Rise and Fall* (New York, 1943), p 91; Horst H. Boog, *Die deutsche Luftwaffenführung, 1935–1945: Führungsprobleme, Spitzengliederung, Generalstabsausbildung* (Stuttgart, 1982), the main thrust of which appeared in English as "Higher Command and Leadership in the German Luftwaffe, 1935–1945," in Hurley and Ehrhart, eds, *Air Power and Warfare*, pp 128-58.

57. Murray, *Strategy for Defeat*, p 8; for a larger discussion of the role of "blitzkrieg" in German military thought see Larry H. Addington, *The Blitzkrieg Era and the German General Staff, 1865–1941* (New Brunswick, 1971), esp chap 1, 2.

58. Hermann, *Luftwaffe*, p 143; Murray, *Strategy for Defeat*, pp 5-6; Gunston, *Combat Aircraft*, p 12.

59. Murray, *Strategy for Defeat*, pp 8-9.

60. "The German Air Force," *The Economist*, April 15, 1939; Edward L. Homze, *Arming the Luftwaffe: the Reich Air Ministry and the German Aircraft Industry, 1919–1939* (Lincoln, 1976), provides a detailed study of the military-industrial team that forged the Nazi air arm.

61. Gunston, *Combat Aircraft*, pp 22, 62–63, 79, 113–17, 122–25, 146–49.

62. Homze, *Arming the Luftwaffe*, chap 9; Horst A. Boog, "The Luftwaffe and Technology," *Aerospace Historian* 30 (Fall–Sept 1983), pp 200–06; Memo, Engineers at Rechlin Aircraft Experimental Station to S. S. and S. H. A., German Air Force Policy During the Second World War, Aug 15, 1944, trans, Air Historical Branch, Air Ministry (GB), Apr 1956, Roll K 5003 K 512.621 – VII/155, AFHRC.

63. Boog, "Luftwaffe and Technology," in Hurley and Ehrhart, eds, *Air Power and Warfare*, pp 147–49.

64. On Kondor Legion experiences, see William L. Shirer, *Rise and Fall of the Third Reich* (New York, 1960), pp 297, 300n; Hermann, *Luftwaffe*, p 180; Jackson, The Red Falcons, pp 54–55; Goering's statement appears in *International Military Tribunal, Trial of the Major War Criminals before the International Military Tribunal: Proceedings and Documents* (Nuremburg, 1947–1949), vol 9, pp 280–81.

65. Murray, *Strategy for Defeat*, pp 16–17.

66. *Ibid.*, pp 18–19; Heinz J. Rieckhoff, *Trumpf oder Bluff? 12 Jahre Deutsche Luftwaffe* (Geneva, 1945), pp 157–158; Collier, *Air Power*, pp 114–16.

67. Shirer, *Rise and Fall*, pp 310–11, 488–89, 571; Sir Charles Webster and Noble Frankland, *The Strategic Air Offensive Against Germany, 1939–1945* [History of the Second World War] (London, 1961), pp 45–46; United States Strategic Bombing Survey, "Oil Division

Final Report," (Jan 1947), pp 14, 15, 60; Richard Suchenwirth, *The Development of the German Air Force, 1919–1939* [USAF Historical Study 160] (Maxwell AFB, 1968), p 128.

68. Brigadier P. R. C. Groves, "For France to Answer," *The Atlantic Monthly,* Feb 1924, p 150; Lord Grey quoted in Grey, Viscount of Fallodon, *Twenty-Five Years* (London, 1925), vol I, p 299; Kennett, Strategic Bombing, pp 39–40, 96.

69. Kennett, *Strategic Bombing,* pp 76–77; Gunston, Combat Aircraft, pp 14, 34–35, 73–74, 92, 102, 104–05, 212–13, 215, 218.

70. Denis Richards, *The Fight At Odds* [History of the Royal Air Force, 1929–1945] (London, 1974), vol I, pp 19–20, 31; Overy, *The Air War,* pp 12–14; Charles Messenger, *"Bomber" Harris and The Strategic Bombing Offensive, 1939–1945* (New York, 1984), pp 13–19; Bond, *Military Policy,* pp 197–98, 207–08, 210–11, 285, 287, 294, 309, 326, 328.

71. Richards, *Fight at Odds,* pp 20, 25–26, 31; Overy, *The Air War,* pp 14–16.

72. Derek Wood and Derek Dempster, *The Narrow Margin: The Battle of Britain and the Rise of Air Power, 1930–1940* (New York, 1961), esp chaps 3–10; Gunston, *Combat Aircraft,* pp 106–07, 206–07, Batchelor and Cooper, *Fighter,* pp 75–76.

73. Rept, Maj S. A. Greenwell—G–2, May 25, 1939, File 165/2060–1230–75, Case 40171, RG 165, MRB, NARS; Richards, *Fight at Odds,* p 18.

74. AAFHC, *Research and Development Policies,* pp 182–188; Alvin D. Coox, "The Rise and Fall of the Imperial Japanese Air Forces," *Aerospace Historian* 27 (June 1980), pp 75–78; Katus Kohri, et al., *The Fifty Years of Japanese Aviation, 1910–1960* (Tokyo, 1961), book 2, chap 3, pp 92–112.

75. Craven and Cate, *AAF in World War II,* Vol I: *Plans and Early Operations,* p 81.

76. Coox, "Japanese Air Forces," pp 80–81; Warren M. Bodie, "Secrets for Sale," *Airpower* 15 (November 1985), pp 10–23, 40–55.

77. Coox, "Japanese Air Forces," pp 80–81, 84; Gunston, *Combat Aircraft,* pp 9, 126–27, 160–63, 167–69.

78. Coox, "Japanese Air Forces," pp 76, 78, 84; AAFHC, *Research and Development Policies,* pp 182–88; Lucien Zacharoff, "Japanese Air Power," *Aviation Magazine,* September 1941, pp 48–49, 146–47, 150. For the most recent scholarship on the Russo-Japanese controversy, see Coox, *Nomonhan; Japan Against Russia, 1939* (Stanford, 1985).

79. Coox, "Japanese Air Forces," pp 75, 78.

80. Zacharoff, "Japanese Air Power," p 49, 146; Coox, "Japanese Air Forces," pp 75, 79, 81; Craven and Cate, *AAF in World War II,* Vol I: *Plans and Early Operations,* p 81.

81. Alvin D. Coox, "The Rise and Fall of the Imperial Japanese Air Forces," in Hurley and Ehrhart, eds, *Airpower and Warfare,* p 91.

82. Mark S. Watson, *The War Department; Chief of Staff; Prewar Plans and Preparations* [United States Army in World War II] (Washington, 1950), esp chaps I–V; Craven and Cate, *AAF in World War II,* Vol I: *Plans and Early Operations,* chap 2; Eugene Emme, "The American Dimension," in Hurley and Ehrhart, eds, *Air Power and Warfare,* pp 69–79.

83. Shiner, *Foulois,* esp chaps II, IX, XI.

84. Doolittle's comments appear in Hearing before the Committee on Appropriations, Senate, *Department of Armed Forces, Department of Military Security,* 79th Cong, 1st sess (Washington, 1945), pp 283–284; Maj Follett Bradley, "Peacetime Composition of Air Force," Student Memorandum 387–7, Feb 24, 1932, AWC Curricular Files, MHI; Henry H. Arnold, *Global Mission* (New York, 1949), p 149; Robert T. Finney, *History of Air Corps Tactical School, 1920–1955* [USAF Historical Study 100] (Maxwell AFB, Mar 1955), chap IV.

85. Shiner, Foulois, pp 227–29; Craven and Cate, *AAF in World War II,* Vol I: *Plans and Early Operations,* pp 64–69.

86. Bernard Boylan, *Development of the Long-Range Escort Fighter* [USAF Historical Study 136] (Maxwell AFB, 1955), pp 18–21; Col H. J. Knerr, Lecture for War College Class of 1935–36 upon the occasion of their visit to Langley Field, Jun 12, 1936, Case 3–10, and Memo, Department of Large Airplanes, n.d., Box 1, Hugh J. Knerr Collection; Frank M. Andrews, "The GHQ Air Force," unpub. article for *The Reserve Officer,* June 1935, Box 9, F. M. Andrews Collection, both MD, LC; US War Department, *Final Report of War Department Special Committee on Army Air Corps,* July 18, 1934 (Washington, 1934), pp 12–15 esp.; also Air Corps Tactical School, *Air Force Air Operations: Counter Air Force* (Maxwell Field, May 5, 1937), pars. 2g and 3a–d; Memo, Adj. Gen.—Chief of Staff, Doctrines for

Employment of the GHQ Air Force, Aug 11, 1938, Case 97–77; Lecture, Maj Gen. Oscar Westover, "Air Armament," Sept 26, 1938, pp 35–46, G–3 Course 7, 1938–39; and Lect., Maj Gen Frank M. Andrews, "General Headquarters Air Force," Oct 1, 1938, pp 13–14, G–3 Course 12, 1938–1939, all AWC Curricular Files, all MHI.

87. Arnold, *Global Mission,* pp 178–79; Knerr, Lecture, Jun 12, 1936, pp 6–7.

88. Gunston, *Combat Aircraft,* pp 20, 24–25, 32, 42–43, 45–47, 64–65, 66, 93, 130, 143, 144, 171.

89. Arnold, *Global Mission,* p 178, also 157–183 inter alia; Boylan, *Long-Range Escort Fighter,* pp 23–29; Martin P. Claussen, *Material Research and Development in the Army Air Arm, 1914–1945* [USAF Historical Study 50] (Maxwell Field, 1946), pp 32–34.

90. For lessons learned by AAF from battles of 1939–40, see "Unpub. Diary of Brig Gen Carl Spaatz on tour of duty in England," entries Jun 2 and 16, Aug 9 and 27, Sept 12, all 1940, Diary Box, Spaatz Collection, MD, LC; Rept, Brig Gen B. K. Yount, "Report as Air Observer in England," Mar 11, 1941, Case 39–611; Brig Gen James E. Chaney, "Observations on Trip to England, Final Report," both in AWC Curricular Archives, MHI; Boylan, *Long-Range Escort Fighter,* pp 35–38; Kuter, "Air Power—The American Concept," cited in Greer, *Air Doctrine,* p 23; Futrell, *Ideas, Concepts, Doctrine,* pp 57–59.

91. U.S. War Department, Office of Chief of Staff, *Tentative Field Service Regulations, United States Army,* 1923 (Washington, 1924), p 22; U.S. War Department, Office of Chief of Staff, *FM 100–5, Tentative Field Service Regulations, Operations* (Washington, 1939), p 18; U.S. War Department, Office of Chief of Staff, *FM 1–5, Air Corps Field Manual, Employment of Aviation of the Army* (Washington, 1940), p 9.

92. United Kingdom, War Office, *The Employment of the Air Forces with the Army in the Field* (London, 1938), pp 30–32.

94. Clausewitz quoted in Barry D. Watts, *The Foundations of U.S. Air Doctrine: The Problem of Friction in War* (Maxwell AFB, Dec 1984), p 17.

Bibliographical Essay

It may be traditional to begin a bibliographic essay with notice of various collections of primary documents. Indeed, the serious student of air superiority could probe for years in the archives of those countries mentioned in this chapter and yet never fully discover the documents which satisfactorily explain World War I and interwar approaches to the elusive subject of "air superiority." The whole study of doctrinal development for the primary aviation powers of the period has hardly been started and could profitably expand upon the model set by Robert Frank Futrell, *Ideas, Concepts, Doctrine: A History of Basic Thinking in the United States Air Force, 1907–1964* (Maxwell AFB, Alabama: Air University, 1974). In the absence of such a comprehensive study, one must resort to a national approach via published works mentioned below.

Among the basic works on military aviation and war, Anthony Robinson, ed., *Aerial Warfare* (London: Orbis, 1982); Basil Collier, *A History of Air Power* (New York: Macmillan, 1974); and C. H. Hildreth and Bernard C. Nalty, *1001 Questions Answered about Aviation History* (New York: Dodd, Mead, 1969) will all prove useful. Likewise, on specifics of aircraft, see Bryan Cooper and John Batchelor, *Fighter: A History of Fighter Aircraft* (New York: Scribners, 1973); and Bill Gunston, *The Encyclopedia of the World's Combat Aircraft* (New York: Chartwell, 1976). Lee Kennett, *A History of Strategic Bombarding* (New York: Scribners, 1982) traces the rise of bombardment aviation and its relationship to winning air superiority. Indeed, the classic Sir Charles Webster and Noble Frankland, *The Stra-*

tegic Air Offensive Against Germany, 1939–1945 [History of the Second World War]
(London: Her Majesty's Stationery Office, 1961) contributes to the discussion. Two
useful symposia proceedings should also be consulted: Claude Carlier, ed., *Colloque
International, Colloque Air, 1984* (Paris: Foundation Par Les Etudes de Defense
Nationale, 1975); and Alfred F. Hurley and Robert C. Ehrhart, eds., *Air Power and
Warfare: The Proceedings of the Eighth Military History Symposium, United States
Air Force Academy, 18–20 October 1978* (Washington: Office of Air Force History,
1979).

On early predictions about the future use of aviation in war, see H. G. Wells,
War in the Air and Particularly How Mr. Bert Smallways Fared While It Lasted
(New York: Macmillan, 1908); R. P. Hearne, *Aerial Warfare* (London and New York:
John Lane, 1909); and Claude Grahame-White and Harry Harper, *The Aeroplane in
War* (London: T. Werner Laurie, 1912). World War I experience may be approached
through the following examples, starting with Cyril Falls, *The Great War* (New
York: G. P. Putnams, 1959). John H. Morrow, Jr., *German Air Power in World War I*
(Lincoln: University of Nebraska Press, 1982); and Richard P. Hallion, *Rise of the
Fighter Aircraft, 1914–1918* (Annapolis: The Nautical and Aviation Publishing Com-
pany, 1984) offer an international view of major air superiority issues. For the Amer-
ican side, start with James Hudson, *Hostile Skies: A Combat History of the
American Air Service in World War I* (Syracuse: Syracuse University Press, 1968);
and the useful documents compilation, Maurer Maurer, ed., *The U.S. Air Service in
World War I* (Washington: Office of Air Force History, 1978), 4 vols. See also
Charles D. Bright, "Air Power in World War I: Sideshow or Decisive Factor?" *Aer-
ospace Historian* 18 (1971); Geoffrey Rossano, "The Apprenticeship: How the
Allies Trained the American Air Service," *Journal of American Aviation Historical
Society* 28 (1983); as well as William Mitchell, "Air Service at St. Mihiel," *World's
Work*, XXXVIII (1919), and William Mitchell, "General Principles Underlying the
Use of the Air Service in the Zone of the Advance A.E.F.," *Bulletin of the Informa-
tion Section, Air Service AEF*, 3 (1918). Also informative is the reprinted Ferdinand
Foch, "Memorandum on the Subject of an Independent Air Force, 14 Sept. 1918,"
Air Power Historian III (1956). See also I. B. Holley, Jr., *Ideas and Weapons:
Exploitation of the Aerial Weapon by the United States During World War I: A Study
in the Relationship of Technological Advance, Military Doctrine, and the Develop-
ment of Weapons* (Washington: Office of Air Force History, 1983 reprint).

Published sources on foreign experiences remain essential to understanding the
interwar period. Taken in order of appearance in this chapter, start with the Italian
story and Douhet's influence. Dino Ferrari's translation of Douhet's *The Command
of the Air* (New York: Coward-McCann, 1942) has been reprinted by the U.S. Air
Force, Office of Air Force History (1983) with a new introduction, and a stimulating
modern synthesis appears in John F. Shiner, "Reflections on Douhet," *Air University
Review* XXXVII (1986), pp 93–95. Claudio G. Segre, "Douhet in Italy: Prophet
Without Honor?" *Aerospace Historian* 26, (1979) provides a rare English language
evaluation of Italian military aviation, while Edward Mead Earle, ed., *Makers of
Modern Strategy: Military Thought from Machiavelli to Hitler* (Princeton: Prince-
ton University Press, 1941), remains valuable although dated. See also P. Vauthier,
La Doctrine de Guerre du General Douhet (Paris: 1935).

France's interwar story can be followed via traditional accounts like William L.
Shirer, *The Collapse of the Third Republic* (New York: Simon and Shuster, 1961);
Maurice Ribet, *Le Proces de Riom* (Paris: Flammarion, 1945), and Camille Rougeron, *L'Aviation de bombardment* (Paris: Berger' Levraurl, 1937). Newer viewpoints
on that experience can be found in General P. Christienne, "L'industrie aeronautique
française de septembre 1939 à juin 1940," pp 141–65; P. Buffotot, "Le moral dans

l'Armée de l'Air française (de septembre 1939 à juin 1940)," pp 167–195; and P. Buffotot and J. Ogier, "L'Armée de l'Air pendant la bataille de France (du 10 mai à l'armistice): Essai de bilan numerique d'une bataille aerienne," pp 197–226, all in Service Historique de l'Armée de l'Air, *Recueil d'articles et études (1974–1975),* (Vincennes, 1977); and Faris R. Kirkland, "The French Air Force in 1940: Was it defeated by the Luftwaffe or by Politics?" *Air University Review* XXXVI (1985), pp 101–18.

On Italian military aviation, in addition to the essays by Goergio Apostolo, Andrea Curami, and Ciancarlo Garello in Carlier, *Colloque 1984,* another short work will prove indispensable. See James J. Sadkovich, "The Development of the Italian Air Force Prior to World War II," *Military Affairs* 51 (July 1987), pp 128–136, for a non-Italian evaluation.

The story of Soviet military aviation development can be followed both in translation of Russian studies as well as original works in English. The former include S. A. Tyuskevich, *The Soviet Armed Forces: A History of Their Organizational Development* (Moscow, 1978), published for the United States Air Force by the Government Printing office, n.d.; and A. S. Yakovlev, *Fifty Years of Soviet Aircraft Construction* (Moscow, 1968), published in English in Jerusalem by Israel Program for Scientific Translation, 1976. Publications in English, for example, include Colin Munro, *Soviet Air Forces* (New York: Sports Car Press, 1972); Robert Jackson, *The Red Falcons: The Soviet Air Force in Action, 1919–1939* (London: Clifton House, 1970); and Robin Higham and Jacob Kipp, eds., *Soviet Aviation and Air Power: A Historical View* (Boulder, Col.: Westview Press, 1977).

Obviously more coverage has been given German experiences. In addition to what can be pieced together from International Military Tribunal, *Trial of the Major War Criminals Before the International Tribunal, Proceedings and Documents* (Nuremberg, 1947–49), 42 vols., one should commence with Williamson Murray, *Strategy For Defeat; The Luftwaffe, 1933–1945* (Maxwell Air Force Base: Air University Press, 1983). Edward L. Homze, *Arming the Luftwaffe: The Reich Air Ministry and the Germany Aircraft Industry, 1919–39* (Lincoln: University of Nebraska Press, 1976) suggests the importance of military-industrial linkages and winning technological air superiority. West German historian Horst A. Boog must be consulted for a mildly revisionistic portrayal of the Luftwaffe in "The Luftwaffe and Technology," *Aerospace Historian* 30 (1983); and *Die deutsche Luftwaffenführung, 1935–1945: Führungsprobleme, Spitzengliederung, Generalstabsausbilden* [Beiträge zur Militär—und Kriegsgeschichte[(Stuttgart: Deutsche Verlags-Amstalt, für Militärgeschichtliches Forschungsamt, 1982). Still useful are Hermann Hauptmann, *The Luftwaffe: Its Rise and Fall* (New York: Putnams, 1943); Heinz Joachim Rieckhoff, *Trumpf oder Bluff? 12 Jahre Deutsche Luftwaffe* (Geneva: Verlag Inter-Avia, 1945); and Richard Suchenwirth, *The Development of the German Air Force, 1919–1939* [USAF Historical Study 160] (Maxwell AFB: USAF Historical Division, Aerospace Studies Institute, Air University, June 1968). Larry H. Addington integrates air and ground tactics properly into the discussion of "blitzkrieg" in his *The Blitzkrieg Era and the German General Staff, 1865–1941* (New Brunswick: Rutgers University Press, 1971).

Most readers will be more familiar with the British story. Thus, British sources include Denis Richard, *The Fight at Odds,* [Royal Air Force, 1929-1945] (London: Her Majesty's Stationary office, 1974); Brian Bond, *British Military Policy Between the Two World Wars* (Oxford: Clarendon, 1980); and H. Montgomery Hyde, *British Air Policy Between the Wars, 1918–1939* (London: Heinemann, 1976). Useful theoretical pieces include Brigadier P. R. C. Groves, "For France to Answer," *The Atlantic Monthly* CXXXIII (1924); B. H. Liddell Hart, *Paris or the Future of War* (New

York: E. P. Dutton, 1925); and War Office (Great Britain), *The Employment of the Air Forces with the Army in the Field* (London: War Office, 1938). Derek Wood and Derek Dempster, *The Narrow Margin; The Battle of Britain and the Rise of Air Power, 1930–1940* (New York: MacGraw-Hill, 1961); and Uri Bialer, "The Danger of Bombardment from the Air and the Making of British Air Disarmament Policy, 1932–34," in Brian Bond and Ian Roy, eds., *War and Society: A Yearbook of Military History* (London: Croom Helm, 1975) suggest various additional factors of air superiority including the technical and psychological dimensions.

Japanese air experience suffers from the same problems as the Soviet story: lack of adequate coverage in English. Katsu Kohri, *et al.*, *The Fifty Years of Japanese Aviation, 1910–1960* (Tokyo: Kantoska, 1961) illustrates fundamental problems in translation of Japanese-language material. However, at least one American scholar, Alvin D. Coox, has plumbed both Japanese and English-language sources to provide very useful accounts in "The Rise and Fall of the Imperial Japanese Air Forces," *Aerospace Historian* 27 (1980); and his majestic two-volume *Nomonham: Japan Against Russia, 1939* (Stanford: Stanford University Press, 1985) promises many invaluable insights about Japanese combat preparation. Suggestive of the wide range of possible research opportunities is Warren M. Bodie, "Secrets For Sale: The Amazing, Documented Story of How America's Prewar Aviation Industry Gave Japan Vital Information in Building Both the Zero and Oscar Fighters," *Airpower* 15 (1985).

Naturally, the American story remains of greatest interest. Original source collections can be consulted in three principal locations: Washington, D.C., Maxwell AFB, Alabama, and Carlisle Barracks, Pennsylvania. No serious researcher of the period can overlook the official documentation in Record Group 18, Records of the Army Air Forces, especially with ancillary record holdings for the Army's Chief of Staff, Chief Signal Officer, General and Special Staffs, as well as joint boards and other agencies, all of which are in the National Archives. The Manuscript Division of the Library of Congress holds personal paper collections for Army Air Service/ Air Corps figures such as Carl A. Spaatz, Ira C. Eaker, Henry H. Arnold, Hugh J. Knerr, George S. Simonds, Frank M. Andrews, William Mitchell, and Benjamin D. Foulois. A short diversion to the Office of Air Force History at nearby Bolling Air Force Base will uncover the papers of George C. Kenney as well as microfilmed holdings from the U.S. Air Force Historical Research Center, Maxwell AFB, Alabama. Of course, a visit to the latter facility may uncover materials not covered by microfilm. The curricular archives of the Army War College and other personal papers and oral history holdings at the U.S. Army Military History Institute, Carlisle Barracks, Pennsylvania parallel Maxwell in terms of interest for students of the American military air experience before World War II.

Specialized topics concerning the American doctrinal experience include Thomas H. Greer, *The Development of Air Doctrine in the Army Air Arm, 1917–1941* [USAF Historical Studies Number 89] (Maxwell AFB, Alabama: USAF Historical Division, Research Studies Institute, Air University, September 1955). Wesley Frank Craven and James Lea Cate, eds., *The Army Air Forces in World War II,* Volume I: *Plans and Early Operations* (Washington: Office of Air Force History, 1983 reprint), and an encapsulated piece by Cate, "Development of Air Doctrine, 1917–41," *Air University Review* I (1947) should also be consulted. Barry D. Watts, *The Foundations of U.S. Air Doctrine: The Problem of Friction in War* (Maxwell Air Force Base: Air University Press, December 1984), suggests revisionist trends at work in air power history research. The best overall study of the interwar United States Army (which included the Air Corps) remains Mark Skinner Watson, *The War Department; Chief of Staff: Prewar Plans and Preparations* [United States

Army in World War II] (Washington: Historical Division United States Army, 1950). The initial chapters of DeWitt S. Copp, *Forged in Fire: Strategy and Decisions in the Air War over Europe, 1940–1945* (Garden City: Doubleday, 1982) are indispensable to understanding the U.S. Army Air Corps/Air Force transition to World War II.

A taste of Air Force thinking can be gleaned from the following: U.S. Congress, Senate Committee on Appropriations, *Department of the Armed Forces, Department of Military Security,* 79th Congress, 1st session, 1945 (Washington: Government Printing Office, 1945); U.S. War Department, Office of the Chief of Staff, *Tentative Field Service Regulations, United States Army, 1923* (Washington: War Department, 1924); U.S. War Department, *Final Report of War Department Special Committee on Army Air Corps, July 18, 1934* (Washington: Government Printing Office, 1934); U.S. Army Air Corps Tactical School, *Air Force Air Operations: Counter Air Force* (Maxwell Field, Alabama, May 1937); United States War Department, Office of the Chief of Staff, *Tentative Field Service Regulations, Operations, 100–5* (Washington: War Department, 1939); and U.S. War Department, Office of Chief of Staff, *FM 1–5, Air Corps Field Manual; Employment of Aviation of the Army* (Washington: War Department, 1940).

Among U.S. Air Force Historical Studies monographs of utility to the subject of this essay are Robert T. Finney, *History of the Air Corps Tactical School, 1920–1940* [Number 100] (Maxwell AFB: USAF Historical Division, Research Studies Institute, Air University, March 1955); Martin P. Claussen, *Materiel Research and Development in the Army Air Arm, 1914–1945* [Number 50] (Washington: Headquarters, Army Air Forces, Historical Office, 1946); and Bernard Boylan, *Development of the Long-Range Escort Fighter* [Number 136] (Maxwell AFB: USAF Historical Division, Research Studies Institute, Air University, September 1955). Fundamental to the context of U.S. Army-Air Corps/Army Air Forces relations are Christopher R. Gabel, *The U.S. Army GHQ Manuevers of 1941* (Ann Arbor: University Microfilms, 1981); and Garrett Underhill, "Air Corps Learned Plenty on Maneuver; But Did the Ground Troops?" *Aviation* 40 (1941).

Finally, the biographical approach to the study of any period always yields information, for example, Georgii Zhukov, *The Memoirs of Marshal Zhukov* (London: Jonathan Cape, 1971); Gray, Viscount of Fallodon, *Twenty-Five Years* (London: Hodder and Stoughton, 1925); Andrew Boyle, *Trenchard* (New York: W. W. Norton, 1962); Leonard Mosley, *The Reich Marshal: A Biography of Hermann Goering* (New York: Doubleday, 1974); Harold Nicolson, *Diaries and Letters, 1930–1939* (London: Collins, 1966); Charles Messenger, *"Bomber" Harris and the Strategic Bombing Offensive, 1939–1945* (New York: St. Martins, 1984); and Dudley Saward, *Bomber Harris: The Story of Sir Arthur Harris, Marshal of the Royal Air Force* (Garden City: Doubleday, 1985). For American biographies, see H. H. Arnold, *Global Mission* (New York: Harper, 1949); Benjamin D. Foulois with C. V. Glines, *From the Wright Brothers to the Astronauts—The Memoirs of Major General Benjamin D. Foulois* (New York: McGraw-Hill, 1968); John F. Shiner, *Foulois and the U.S. Army Air Corps 1931–1935* (Washington: Office of Air Force History, 1983); Alfred F. Hurley, *Billy Mitchell: Crusader For Air Power* (Bloomington: Indiana University Press, 1975); and John J. Pershing, *My Experiences in the World War* (New York: Frederick A. Stokes, Co., 1931). Most assuredly, students of the American air experience must begin with the early chapters of DeWitt S. Copp, *Forged in Fire: Strategy and Decisions in the Air War over Europe, 1940–1945* (Garden City: Doubleday, 1982).

A formation of Henschel Hs–123s, armed with small 50-kg bombs, takes off on a support mission during Hitler's offensive against Poland.

2

The Luftwaffe Against Poland and the West

Williamson Murray

When World War II began on September 1, 1939, the generally held assumption among airmen was that strategic bombing would be the mode in which air forces would fight the coming war. The Germans held similar assumptions to beliefs that were prevalent in the U.S. Army Air Forces (AAF) and the Royal Air Force (RAF). But they were also open to a wider strategic view on the employment of air power: that the destruction of the enemy air force and the achievement of air superiority, and the support for the army's efforts on the ground (particularly interdiction), were equally worthwhile tasks. As a result, the Luftwaffe was the best prepared of all the world's air forces in 1939 to fight a realistic campaign to support overall military objectives. This essay attempts to lay out the general framework within which the Luftwaffe approached the problem of air superiority before and during the first campaigns of the Second World War. It aims to give the reader an understanding of the strengths as well as the weaknesses of the German approach to air superiority and how those strengths and weaknesses contributed to the campaigns of 1939 and 1940.

Lessons of World War I

When World War I ended in November 1918, there was little clarity about the role of air power in modern war except that it represented a dimension that no major nation could safely ignore. If the full employment potential of aircraft was somewhat uncertain, nevertheless the warring powers had employed aircraft in virtually all the roles in which they have appeared through to the present: air superiority, strategic bombing, close air support, interdiction, and photo reconnaissance all played their parts (only air transport did not receive significant attention). However, the lack of clarity over the lessons of World War I, unfortunately, led many interwar theorists to emphasize the theoretical and to ignore the practical realities of air power.

One lesson should not have been ambiguous: the fundamental principle on which all World War I air operations rested was the need for air superiority. Without that basic attribute, photo reconnaissance aircraft did not return with intelligence; tactical bombers on close air support or interdiction strikes suffered shattering casualties; and strategic bombers suffered prohibitive losses that soon ended bombing campaigns. On the other hand, bombers and reconnaissance aircraft, sheltered by air superiority, could carry out their missions without prohibitive losses. The achievement of air superiority, however, posed a difficult and costly challenge. Even when air forces gained local superiority, whether through quantitative or qualitative advantages, that superiority usually proved transitory. The enemy could master numerical inferiority by reinforcing contested sectors. In the case of qualitative inferiority, he could redress technological imbalances by advances of his own. This resulted in an air war with shifting balances and heavy casualties. Ironically, the lesson on the importance of air superiority and the difficulties inherent in achieving it did not strike a responsive chord among interwar airpower theorists.

The seeming paucity of "lessons" on other aspects of aircraft employment failed to inhibit evolution of theories arguing that the aircraft would be *the* dominant weapon of *the* next war. Two major threads in such thinking evolved: the ancestors of the modern schools of "counterforce" and "countervalue" nuclear strategies. British theorists placed primary emphasis on direct attacks on enemy population centers (particularly the working class), while American theorists stressed the vulnerability of enemy economic systems to precision bombing attacks directed at nodal points in the industrial structure. As the future Air Marshal Sir John Slessor suggested in 1936, a nation could gain and maintain air superiority only through a "resolute bombing offensive" against enemy cities and industries.[1] A more general, but certainly representative, discussion on air power in a future conflict appeared in an RAF Air Staff memorandum of 1924 arguing that air forces

> can either bomb military objectives in populated areas from the beginning of the war, with the objective of obtaining a decision by moral(e) effect which such attacks will produce, and by the serious dislocation of the normal life of the country, or, alternatively, they can be used in the first instance to attack enemy aerodromes with a view to gaining some measure of air superiority and, when this has been gained, can be changed over to the direct attack on the nation. The latter alternative is the

method which the lessons of military history seem to recommend, but the Air Staff are convinced that the former is the correct one.[2]

Thus, a major theme in interwar thinking was that the traditional strategic factors would not bind air power. In other words, aircraft had negated the principles of war.[3]

While a few airmen like Brig. Gen. William "Billy" Mitchell addressed the problems of gaining and maintaining air superiority, other prewar theorists denigrated not only defensive air war but also strikes against enemy air power. In fact, many airmen regarded such strategies as a waste of effort. There was, of course, evidence supporting the belief that "the bomber will always get through"; most notably bombers evolved more quickly than fighters in the 1930s and consequently, it proved difficult to envision a successful interception of enemy air fleets. Nonetheless, a minimizing of the possibility of fighters or bombers attacking enemy air forces or air bases also reflected ideological beliefs that strategic bombing was the only proper employment for aircraft. As Sir Hugh Trenchard somewhat crudely stated while discussing a possible air war with France:

> I would like to make this point again. I feel that although there would be an outcry, the French would probably squeal before we did (in an air war between France and Great Britain). That was really the first thing. The nation that would stand being bombed longest would win in the end.[4]

Luftwaffe Development

The general historical view has tended to place the Luftwaffe outside the mainstream of the interwar airpower theories. It suggests that the many German Army officers transferring to the new service in 1933 brought with them only narrow, land-war oriented concerns.[5] Thus, supposedly, the Luftwaffe became closely tied to the army's coattail with neither interest in nor understanding of strategic bombing. Reinforcing this view has been a historical construct, the so-called "blitzkrieg" strategy, that argues along the following lines: the Nazi leadership, faced with certain economic and political preconceptions, evolved a grand strategy suited to Germany's peculiar needs. This strategy, the argument continues, did not include rearmament in depth, but created an elite panzer force, supported by the Luftwaffe, to fight short, quick campaigns to avoid a long, drawn-out war.[6]

Unfortunately, this generally accepted view now appears erroneous. German grand strategy and its air component did not follow an obvious or consistent path. Rather there existed at the highest level an almost complete lack of strategic planning. Admittedly, Hitler possessed a clear sense of his long-range goals: to destroy the European constellation of power and to establish in its place a Europe under German control entirely free of Jews and "Jewish-influences." While the destruction of the diplomatic balance from 1933 to 1936 proved surprisingly easy,[7] a combination of massive rearmament, foreign exchange difficulties, and other problems caused political and economic crises after 1936 that the outward thrust of German policy had obscured.[8] Those difficulties prevented the Germans, including Hitler, from framing a coherent national defense policy. The Führer, of course, maintained a firm sense of the ultimate objective toward which he was driving both state and military; nevertheless, he worried little over the means available, while his generals, with the possible exception of the Army's Chief of the General Staff, Gen. Ludwig Beck, never worried overly about strategic questions. In truth there seemed to be chaos in German defense policy. What is especially surprising, given the current reputation that Germans enjoy in military affairs, is 1) the lack of centralized control or even generally accepted goals among the military, and 2) the cavalier disdain that the services showed towards economic realities throughout the rearmament process.[9]

Within a sea of contending forces, the Luftwaffe found its interests well protected by Hermann Goering's position in the Nazi political structure. Nevertheless, in its formative years others, beside its commander in chief, chartered the Luftwaffe's course. The two most important individuals were the State Secretary, Erhard Milch, and the first Chief of Staff, Gen. Walther Wever. Early on, the Luftwaffe's leaders considered an all-strategic bombing force structure[10]—a theme that struck a responsive chord in the Luftwaffe throughout the prewar period.[11] But Milch and Goering rejected the proposal, not because strategic bombing was foreign to their Weltanschauung (world view), but rather because Germany's industrial, technological, and geographic situation made a strategic bombing force unrealistic for the immediate future.[12]

Wever largely cast the Luftwaffe's strategic framework in the 1930s. While Milch handled the economic and administrative tasks of creating the new military service and Goering took care of politics, Wever established the intellectual and strategic patterns within which the Luftwaffe grew. Despite a lack of aircraft experience, he had received his appointment as the Luftwaffe's first Chief of Staff.[13] In the short period before his death in 1936, Wever exercised an extraordinary influence over the Luftwaffe's basic doctrine.

Two documents spelled out his thinking on the question of air power: a speech to the *Luftkriegsakademie* (Air War College) in November 1935, and the Luftwaffe's basic doctrinal manual, *Die Luftkriegführung* (The Conduct of Air War), published in late 1935.[14] Wever argued for a more broadly based approach to air power than did most other theorists in this period. He was never an unabashed champion of strategic bombing, but rather suggested that a variety of factors would determine the Luftwaffe's role in any future war: the overall strategic situation, the weather, national objectives, and the nature of enemy forces among others. In particular, one

Prominent Luftwaffe leaders
included Hermann Goer-
ing, Commander in Chief,
(*left*) and Erhard Milch, the
State Secretary (*below*).

could not easily separate the struggle against enemy air forces from the support that the Luftwaffe would have to provide the Army and Navy. Even though its flexibility of employment gave it advantages over ground and naval forces, its primary opponent would be the enemy air force. Wever argued that gaining air superiority, whether local or general, represented a most difficult goal. Changing technology, new aircraft types and replacement by new production, and freshly trained crews would allow an enemy air force to return and fight again.[15] Air superiority would demand an unremitting commitment. Nonetheless, like most interwar airpower theorists, he believed that the bomber would be the decisive weapon of aerial warfare.[16] While one could and should rely on active as well as passive defensive measures, the best method of defeating the enemy in the air, he contended, was to strike at the basis of his air power: in particular at his bomber fleet on the ground and at the industrial support that allowed the enemy to make good his losses.[17] The Luftwaffe's doctrinal manual made it clear that the enemy's *air force* was the primary target at the beginning of war.

> One must attack the enemy's air force from the beginning of war. Its defeat will weaken the enemy's armed forces, while protecting one's own air force to carry out other missions important to the war effort. The struggle aims preeminently at the enemy's bomber strength. First of all mobile units must be destroyed. Surprise strikes of one's own bombers at the beginning of war can succeed in hitting the enemy's bombing power at peace time bases.[18]

Between Wever's death and the outbreak of war, the Luftwaffe developed into a formidable instrument. That expansion from a nonexistent force in 1933 to the most powerful air force in the world in 1939, with over 4,161 aircraft (including 1,179 fighters and 1,180 bombers)[19] imposed a considerable strain on the national economy. The Germans not only faced the task of acquiring the technical and operational expertise necessary for such a force,[20] but within the space of 6 years they virtually had to replace that force with a new generation of aircraft.[21]

The prewar development of German operational concepts was considerably influenced not only by theory but by Germany's exposed strategic situation, the megalomaniacal goals of her leader, and actual combat experience in Spain. War games conducted as early as 1934 suggested that direct attacks on an enemy's air force and bases would not entirely eliminate his bombing capability. Therefore, the Germans concluded that they needed fighter defenses and antiaircraft artillery to protect their airpower resources and industry.[22] The Spanish Civil War underlined the fact that fighter aircraft would play a crucial role in gaining air superiority. The lessons were strong enough to cause Ernst Udet, in charge of production by the late 1930s, to change the projected long-range goal for the Luftwaffe's force structure from a ratio between fighters and bombers of 1 to 3 to a ratio of 1 to 2.[23]

In retrospect, Germany's continental position exercised the greatest influence over her air strategy. Unlike British and American airmen, the Germans *had* to think in terms of land conflict. From the onset of any conflict, the *Reich* faced a major struggle on the ground, a reality that the Luftwaffe's leaders could not ignore. It was fine to talk about bombing factories and population centers, but if Germany lost the frontier battles, she would lose provinces like Silesia or the Rhineland. Such defeats would end the struggle. Thus, air superiority was more than a means to defeat enemy air forces or to attack his factories and cities. It would also enable the Luftwaffe to help the army with close air support[24] and to interdict enemy supply lines to the front.[25]

Germany's geographic position also explains another substantive difference between the Luftwaffe on the one hand and the U.S. Army Air Forces and the RAF on the other. At the war's outbreak, the Germans believed that the Luftwaffe's structure could dominate the skies over their frontiers. In a sense, they were correct. The Luftwaffe did possess sufficient aircraft to achieve air superiority within the limited geographic framework of Central Europe. In another sense, that geographical frame of reference placed severe intellectual limitations on the ability of the Luftwaffe's leaders to conceptualize the problems associated with an air war on a continental scale. American and British airmen, the former familiar with the continental distances of the United States, the latter with those of the Empire, thought within a wider framework. Consequently, when the Germans pushed beyond their frontiers, north to Norway, west to France and the Atlantic, south to North Africa and the Mediterranean, and east into the depths of Russia, they discovered themselves out of their depth. What had been sufficient quantitatively and qualitatively for gaining air superiority around their frontier proved insufficient to handle the problems associated with a continental air war. In the vast spaces of Europe, the Luftwaffe of 1941 and 1942, which possessed virtually the same force structure that it had possessed in 1939 and 1940, found it virtually impossible to establish anything more than local air superiority. By the time the Germans had realized the full dimension of their error it was too late.

Admittedly, the Luftwaffe was working in the late 1930s to produce a "continental" bomber (one with the load and range of British and American four-engine aircraft).[26] Moreover, the Luftwaffe also developed a long-range fighter, the Bf–110, to support its bomber formations deep in enemy territory. That two-engine aircraft, however, proved inadequate for the mission (even to the extent of being unable to protect itself) against first-class enemy fighters. On the other hand, the Bf–109, one of the two best air superiority fighters in the world at the end of the 1930s (the other being the British Spitfire), was a very short-range aircraft. And the Germans fell into the same trap as British and American airmen in believing that no single-engine air superiority fighter could achieve sufficient range to accompany deep penetrating bomber formations.[27] Surprisingly, the Luftwaffe did experiment successfully with drop tanks to extend fighter combat radius during air operations in Spain. That success apparently had no impact on the engineering and operational establishment back home, and in the early years of the war the Bf–109 fought with severely restricted range.[28] This error resulted from an inherent belief that bomber formations could defend themselves (common to all air forces before the war), as well as from an unwarranted confidence in the anticipated capabilities of the Bf–110.

Training Ground in Spain

German participation on the Nationalist side of the Spanish Civil War provided the Luftwaffe with valuable experience and lessons on future aerial combat. Nevertheless, the size of the German commitment and the nature of the war itself largely confined that experience to the tactical and technical spheres.[29] To begin with, Hitler was unwilling to commit more than a small force (the Kondor Legion) to Franco's aid. As he explained in late 1936, it was to Germany's advantage that the Nationalists not win quickly and that Spain continue to divert Europe's attention from the *Reich's* growing power.[30] Consequently, German air support to Franco

The Bf–109 proved to be the Luftwaffe's premier air superiority fighter.

72

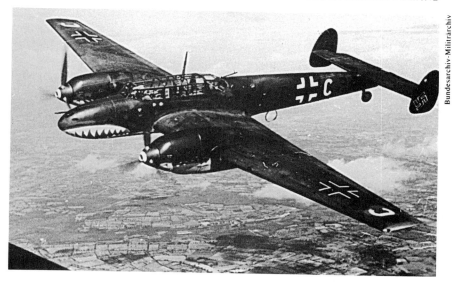

The twin-engine Bf–110 had numerous shortcomings.

remained at a relatively low level throughout the struggle (6,000 men in 1937). At its peak in 1937 the Kondor Legion contained no more than 40 He–111s, 5 Do–17s, 3 Ju–87s, 45 Bf–109s, 4 He–45s, and 8 He–54s.[31] But the Germans were able to learn a good deal from the experiences of the small force. First of all, in 1936 they recognized from combat how technologically deficient were the first generation of German aircraft sent to Spain. Not only did the Germans rapidly replace those aircraft with newer models such as the Bf–109, but the experiences in Spain sped the process of reequipping the Luftwaffe back home with a new generation of fighters and bombers. With respect to air superiority, the lessons learned from air-to-air combat proved equally valuable. Like the RAF, the Luftwaffe before the Spanish Civil War had evolved a set of fighter tactics based on close formations of three aircraft.

Combat experiences in Spain, however, underscored the vulnerability of such tactics. The future World War II ace, Werner Mölders, established a looser combat formation based on the finger formation of four aircraft with two sections of two aircraft. The German tactics were later copied by nearly all the world's air forces. Mölders, after his return from Spain, wrote a lengthy report on his experiences, and that report formed the basis for German air-to-air doctrine at the outbreak of the war.[32] It was to give the Germans an important initial advantage over their opponents.

The "finger-four" tactics proved to be the basic building block of World War II air-to-air combat. They provided not only better visual coverage, but also direct defensive coverage for those fighters carrying out attacks on enemy aircraft. Equally important was the fact that the Luftwaffe was able to shuttle a considerable number of its senior and particularly its middle-level commanders through Spain so that combat experience gained in the Civil War could be passed as widely as possible through the rapidly expanding Luftwaffe.[33] Nevertheless, one should not overestimate the Spanish learning experience and its impact on the German military. On the ground and in the air the commitment of German forces remained limited; military operations in terms of the equipment and tactics were at best primitive; and the air war particularly remained almost entirely out of contact with the rapid development of technology (such as radar) in the advanced industrialized nations.

German plans and preparations in 1938 for *Fall Grün*, the invasion of Czechoslovakia, established a pattern that the Luftwaffe repeated in the next two military confrontations: *Fall Weiss* (invasion of Poland in 1939) and *Fall Gelb* (the offensive of May 1940 into France and the Low Countries). The *Wehrmacht* was so weak in 1938 that German planners had to concentrate nearly all its forces, including the Luftwaffe, on the destruction of the Czech Republic.[34] Virtually nothing remained in the West (five divisions and a smattering of air units) to protect against a possible French reaction.[35] Two air forces (*Luftflotten*, or airfleets, equivalent to numbered air forces in American terminology), the First and the Third, received the task of destroying the Czech Air Force and supporting the invasion. The Luftwaffe's plans called for strikes against

Werner Mölders (*right*), **father of "finger-four" tactics, talking with Hermann Goering.**

Czech airfields to destroy the opposing enemy air force and its infrastructure at the outset.[36] Thus, the first goal was to establish air superiority over Bohemia and Moravia; destruction of Czech bases and airfields would also prevent Soviet air reinforcements from reaching the Czechs. After achieving air superiority, the Luftwaffe would then support the army's effort with interdiction and close-air-support strikes as well as attacks on armament industries.

German documents suggest that even the relatively limited military assets of Czechoslovakia presented a considerable problem to the Luftwaffe. First of all, the Luftwaffe was significantly weaker in 1938 than in September 1939 or May 1940. The numerical change between September 1938 and May 1940 was substantial; the qualitative improvement was also notable. In 1938 the Luftwaffe was still introducing a new generation of aircraft and as late as August was having severe difficulties in maintaining an "operationally ready rate" over fifty percent.[37] Moreover, aircrew transition from obsolete biplane fighters, such as the Arado Ar–68, into the Bf–109, had proved to be hazardous, for the high performance and narrow undercarriage of the –109 were difficult to handle. The result was a high accident rate in the fighter force throughout 1937 and 1938.

Luftwaffe staff officers felt that Germany had been lucky in avoiding a war over Czechoslovakia during 1938. As a study in the fall of 1938 pointed out:

> In the last months the following special measures have had to be carried through at the same time: 1) the provision of organizational equipment to many new units; 2) the reequipment of numerous units with new aircraft; 3) the early overhaul of about 60 percent of the frontline aircraft; 4) the replacement of spare parts in squadrons reequipping with new aircraft; 5) rebuilding of numerous aircraft in the supply depots; 6) rearmament of many aircraft with new weapons; 7) accelerated introduction of overhauled motor models . . . ; 8) establishment of four new air groups and one new airfield . . . ; 9) preparation and resupply of mobilization supplies, corresponding to the newly established units, rearmed units, and transferred units . . . The compression of these tasks into a very short time span has once more and in clear fashion pointed out the known lack of readiness in maintenance of flying equipment as well as in technical personnel.[38]

If there were problems in maintaining the Luftwaffe in 1938, prospects on the operational side were equally gloomy. German plans detailed most of the Luftwaffe for operations against Czechoslovakia and left little to defend western airspace or to cover the minuscule deployment of ground forces on the *Westwall* (the German fortification on the French frontier). Even the Czech air defense system posed a substantial challenge. Third Air Force claimed that its air campaign could have crippled Czech air power, but admitted that a combination of inexperienced air crews and bad weather would almost certainly have caused debilitating losses through ground accidents, crashes, and mid-air collisions.[39] First Air Force, deployed in Saxony and Silesia, reported that while the Luftwaffe enjoyed considerable superiority in aircraft, its airfields had been vulnerable to counterair operations.[40] Moreover, the Germans feared that the strong anti-aircraft defenses around the fortified zones and industrial centers in Bohemia and Moravia could have inflicted serious losses on German aircraft over Czech targets, especially as low-level strikes (vulnerable to anti-aircraft fire) would have formed the basis for most mission profiles during bad weather.[41]

For the Luftwaffe, Hitler's decision not to push the Czech crisis over the brink came as an enormous relief. It avoided war with Great Britain and France—a war that the *Reich* would have fought at considerable disadvantage.[42] Unfortunately for the Allies, the Germans used the eleven months between Munich and the outbreak of war far better than their future opponents. By the late summer of 1939, the Luftwaffe was in considerably better shape than it had been in 1938. This time Hitler refused to be cheated of an opportunity to wage a limited conflict.

Poland

Luftwaffe planning for the Polish campaign began in April 1939. Reacting to a British guarantee to Poland, Hitler announced to his entourage that they would "cook the British a stew on which they would choke."[43] He also demanded that the military begin preparations for an attack on Poland at the end of August 1939. Poland presented an easier problem to German planners than had Czechoslovakia in 1938. Not only was the *Wehrmacht* in better shape,[44] but Poland's strategic situation was even more hopeless than Czechoslovakia's. Hostile territory surrounded the Poles; they possessed no natural defenses; their military forces were less well equipped than the Czechs'; and Polish terrain proved an ideal place to test the army's mechanized and motorized formations.

Within the strategic context of the decision to conquer Poland, the Luftwaffe cast its plans. The initial target of air operations would be the Polish Air Force in a move to gain general air superiority. That would enable the Germans to attack the mobilization and deployment of the Polish Army as well as its logistical system.[45] The Germans also planned a massive aerial assault on Warsaw to destroy military and industrial targets, and thereby paralyze the Polish government at the beginning of hostilities. Bad weather around Warsaw in the early morning of September 1, however, prevented the Germans from launching such a blow and limited the initial efforts to attacks on the Polish air and ground forces. Once the weather had cleared, air operations against the Polish military were going so well that the German Air Force commanders hesitated to shift the emphasis of their attacks to strategic targets.[46]

Despite obsolete aircraft, the Poles proved themselves surprisingly tenacious opponents in the air. Undoubtedly, a high skill level among their pilots made them dangerous opponents.[47] The Poles had deployed a substantial portion of their fighters and bombers to satellite fields before the war broke out. Thus, the initial German strikes did not substantially affect the Polish force structure.[48] Combat, however, against Luftwaffe formations that possessed qualitative and numerical superiority in aircraft soon shredded the Polish Air Force. Given the German superiority, the results were never in question. By the end of the first day, the Germans had gained general air superiority; by the end of the second day, little remained of the Polish Air Force support structure.[49] Having gained air superiority, the Luftwaffe finished off the Polish fighter force and shifted its attention to deep interdiction attacks on the enemy's transportation system and to direct support of the ground offensive.

Air superiority allowed the Luftwaffe to accomplish a number of important missions. On the ground the combination of rapidly advancing mechanized units and air strikes against the Polish Army proved devastatingly effective. Interdiction missions made it impossible for the Poles to patch together a new line of resistance once German armored forces had broken out into the open. Along the Bzura River, the Luftwaffe caught large Polish formations attempting to fight their way through German encirclements in order to reform along the Vistula. These air attacks so demoralized the Poles that some troops even threw away their weapons.[50] German losses against the Poles were not light. By the time the campaign was over the Luftwaffe had lost 47 Bf–109s (5.6 percent of the force structure), 81 bombers (6.5 percent), 50 close-air-support aircraft (13.2 percent), and a total of 261 of all types (7.2 percent). Losses on the Western Front to the French and British in September spoke volumes for the complete lack of activity by Allied air forces. The Germans lost 13 aircraft in combat and 18 aircraft through noncombat causes in the west for the entire month of September.[51]

The German ability to maintain the thrust of mechanized units and to push fighter and close-air-support coverage forward rested on an effective air transport system. Airlift squadrons, equipped with Ju–52s, resupplied the army as mechanized forces outstripped the ground-based logistics system. At the same time, Bf–109 squadrons established themselves on forward airfields within conquered territory and received supplies of fuel, ammunition, and parts through airlift.[52] This operational concept, established before the war, played a crucial role in helping the Luftwaffe's fighter force keep up with the Army's thrusts during both the French campaign and the invasion of Russia as well as in Poland; such a system, however, had no utility in circumstances where no forward movement occurred and where opposing air forces grappled independently of ground operations.

The German victory over Poland represented only a limited operational success, however. The entrance of Britain and France into the war (ironically, after the Luftwaffe had destroyed most of the Polish Air Force) placed Germany in a dangerous strategic situation. Hitler had, in fact, underestimated the *Reich's* economic and strategic vulnerability, while hoping that the Soviet Union could make up whatever shortages an Allied blockade caused.[53] As a result of serious economic difficulties, Hitler pushed for an immediate offensive against the West; the Army, unhappy with the performance of its troops in Poland, argued strongly against offensive operations before spring. Generally, the Luftwaffe seconded these Army efforts, but for different reasons. First, it preferred to wait out the bad weather. Second, a rest period after Poland allowed it to make good its losses, as well as to build up fighter and bomber strength, quantitatively and qualitatively (in the latter case with the introduction of the Ju–88 into the bomber force). In any case, bad weather and the unwillingness of Anglo-French strategists and politicians to put *any* pressure on the *Reich* allowed the Germans to postpone the western offensive until the spring of 1940.[54]

Scandinavia

During the winter the German Navy and Hitler began to worry about the economic and strategic vulnerability of Scandinavia, particularly the ore traffic along the Norwegian coast during the winter and spring. The *Altmark* affair in February 1940 (in which British destroyers cornered a German supply ship in Norwegian coastal waters and freed Allied merchant sailors on board) convinced the Führer that if he did not act soon, the British would block the transshipment of iron ore. Therefore, he ordered the *Wehrmacht* to plan an invasion of Denmark and Norway *(Weserübung)*. For one of the few times in the war there was a modicum of interservice cooperation in Germany under the *OKW (Oberkommando der Wehrmacht,* Armed Forces High Command).

For the Luftwaffe, as with the other services, Denmark presented little problem. Norway, however, was another matter. Her long coast and ready accessibility to British sea power made military operations against her hazardous. In retrospect, the Luftwaffe played *the* critical role in operations against Norway. At the start, the Germans faced a vacuum in terms of Norwegian air defenses. Facing no opposing air force, the Luftwaffe's success in establishing air superiority depended upon whether the Germans could gain and hold the Norwegian airfields. If they could not do so, and if the Norwegians held on, then the RAF could move into Norway and, together with the Royal Navy, isolate German forces that had landed in the ports.

The seaborne landings went according to plan with one important exception. German naval forces, moving up the Oslo fjord, ran into significant resistance and lost the heavy cruiser *Blücher* and with it not only the landing force but also much of the administrative structure assigned to the occupation. Had the Norwegians acted with dispatch, they could have mobilized, protected Oslo's main airport with reservists, and denied the Germans access into the heart of their country. They did not. Informed by the German operations officer in charge of the invasion (who was then in Oslo to threaten the Norwegian government) of the difficulties encountered by the Navy during the move up the Oslo fjord, the Luftwaffe had aircraft over Oslo harbor within an hour. By 0900 hours, a small element of German paratroopers had seized the airfield. Troops flown in by Luftwaffe Ju–52s seized the capital by early afternoon.[55] On Norway's Atlantic coast, German airborne troops seized the Stavanger/Sola airfield and by the end of the day 180 German aircraft had landed (including bombers, twin-engine fighters, and Stukas). Luftwaffe transport squadrons delivered not only fuel, ammunition, and maintenance personnel but light flak units as well. By the next day, other Norwegian airfields as far north as Trondheim had fallen into German hands.[56]

The rapid establishment of German air power in the vacuum of central and southern Norway won the campaign. From its new bases, the Luftwaffe dominated the land and prevented naval battles. Not only did it protect German forces from the RAF, but it prevented a timely and effective intervention by Allied sea power.[57] The speed with which the Germans had seized the airfields and then turned them into operational bases, capable of supporting significant air operations, was one of the nastiest surprises of the campaign. Once the Luftwaffe had the fields in operating condition, it was able to isolate the battlefield, to support the ground forces in breaking up what was left of the Norwegian Army or what the Allies managed to land, and to supply German units throughout the theater.[58] The results were then never in doubt.

The Low Countries and France

After the opening move in Scandinavia, the *Wehrmacht* launched its massive spring assault on Western Europe. Two great German air forces (the Second and the Third) covered the movement of 3 army groups, 7 armies, and 136 divisions (10 of them panzer).[59] Altogether the Luftwaffe deployed over 3,500 aircraft out of a frontline strength of 4,500.[60] (The remainder supported Luftwaffe operations in Norway and the training establishment). In addition, a transport command of 475 Ju–52s (refitted after the Norwegian campaign) provided airlift for extensive airborne operations against the Dutch and Belgians. In the long run the Ju–52s formed the logistical backbone for the rapid forward deployment of air

Above: **Junkers Ju–52s formed the logistical backbone for the Luftwaffe's movement of air units into Western Europe;** *below:* **Ju–87 Stuka dive bombers.**

units, particularly the short-range Bf–109s, as the battle surged deeper into Allied territory.

At the start of the campaign the Luftwaffe aimed to 1) achieve air superiority over the battlefield by attacking Allied air bases and aircraft, 2) provide airborne drops on Dutch and Belgian forts and bridges, and 3) support the army along the main axis of its advance through the Ardennes across the Meuse and on toward the English Channel. The Luftwaffe executed the second of these objectives with dispatch, though not without heavy casualties. The glider and paratrooper assaults on Fort Eben Emael and Dutch bridges, along with the hammering advance of the infantry in Army Group B, fixed Allied attention on the north and the seeming replay of the 1914 Schlieffen Plan. All the while, German armored and motorized forces rolled through the dark forests of the Ardennes on their way to Sedan and other points along the Meuse.

Meanwhile, the Luftwaffe launched a series of blows at Allied air bases to disrupt and destroy the infrastructure of Allied air power. Unsupported bomber formations mounted those attacks and, as was the case throughout the war, they paid a heavy price.[61] Luckily for the Germans, the French Air Force, although performing substantially better than most historians have acknowledged, faced insurmountable problems. As with the Luftwaffe in 1937 and 1938, and the RAF in 1938 and 1939, the French in 1940 were moving into a new generation of aircraft. As a result, many French fighter squadrons in early 1940 were running operational ready rates of barely forty percent. The pressures of combat operations only exacerbated these difficulties.[62] Thus, while new fighter aircraft possessed considerable potential, they did not provide the operational performance (in terms of sorties) of the Spitfire, Hurricane, and Bf–109.

Massive German bomber and fighter strikes rocked Allied air forces and placed them in a defensive posture from which they never recovered on the continent. Because they enjoyed the initiative, the Germans were able to gain a considerable measure of surprise. It was not that those in the West (politicians as well as military men) did not expect a German attack; but rather that the intensity and ferocity of the assault, coming as it did on military organizations that, whatever their expectations, were existing in a peacetime environment, caused the dislocation and surprise.

German airborne drops on the Dutch airfields, while they did not succeed in gaining immediate operational control of the bases, in effect, rendered the Dutch Air Force *hors de combat* at the outset. Luftwaffe attacks on Belgian airfields destroyed approximately half of the Belgian aircraft on the ground and damaged the support structure. The Germans also managed to inflict substantial damage on some British and French airfields. At Conde Vraux, the base of the RAF's 114 Squadron, Luftwaffe bombers destroyed 6 of 18 aircraft and damaged the remainder severely enough to render them unserviceable. Attacks on other British airfields were not as successful.[63]

81

Nevertheless, the outset of hostilities proved anything but favorable to Allied air operations.

Substantially adding to Anglo-French difficulties was the fact that the command and control system failed to function on May 10th. Not until eleven in the morning on that day did Allied air commanders receive authority to attack German columns and airfields and then with the admonition that they were "at all cost to avoid bombing built up areas."[64] The delay in releasing the air forces to attack even military targets reflected the failure of Allied political leadership to act decisively even when confronted with the terrible reality of German opening moves. By and large, the RAF's forces in France confined themselves to flying cover for the British Expeditionary Force (BEF) as it moved into Belgium. It saw little of the Luftwaffe, largely because the Germans had no intention of interfering with a move that so obviously played into their hands.

Unfortunately, virtually all of the Luftwaffe's operational records were destroyed at the end of the war. Consequently, it is impossible to determine exactly how the Germans allocated their air resources for the campaign in the west. Nonetheless, the overall conduct of the first weeks of the campaign do suggest a general pattern to German air operations. The first strategic objective of Luftwaffe operations was to destroy or at least severely impair the Allied air base structure, thus rendering it difficult for the enemy air forces to intervene against the movement forward of the German Army. These German bomber and long-range fighter attacks *do not* seem to have received substantial support from the Bf–109 force. Rather, the German single-engine fighter force seems to have been engaged largely in screening and protecting the movement forward of the armored force through the Ardennes. Some of the fighter force also engaged in straight out air-to-air missions to seek out and destroy enemy fighters and bombers.[65] Neither the fighters nor the twin-engine bomber force engaged in close-air-support missions for the Army. Only the Stuka force flew that mission profile and then largely in support of the breakthrough along the Meuse on May 13. After the breakthough at Sedan, the Stuka force reverted to the air interdiction mission, as it possessed very limited capability in 1940 to perform close air support in a mobile environment.[66]

At the same time that the Luftwaffe's bombers and fighters were striking Allied airfields and the support structure, Bf–109s were making an intense effort to sweep the skies over the Ardennes of Allied reconnaissance aircraft and bombers that might give away the main direction of the *Schwerpunkt* emphasis. Only the RAF appears to have made a sustained effort in the Ardennes region, and strong Luftwaffe forces in the area inflicted crippling casualties on the British. On May 10, four waves of Battle bombers covered by six Hurricanes attempted to strike German columns in the Ardennes. Of thirty-two Battles, the Germans managed to shoot down thirteen and damage the remaining nineteen. On the 11th, eight Battles again attacked the Germans in the Ardennes. Of the attacking aircraft, only one returned badly damaged; the remainder had all been lost.[67]

It is worth underlining the fact that its massive air operations cost the Luftwaffe heavily. On May 10 the Germans lost eighty-four aircraft (including forty-seven bombers and twenty-five fighters)—more aircraft than it would lose on any day of the Battle of Britain. On the following day, the Germans lost a further forty-two aircraft (including twenty-two bombers, eight dive bombers, and ten fighters).[68] Allied losses were no less severe,[69] but of course the Germans enjoyed a considerable quantitative advantage over both opposing air forces (which was magnified by the fact that a substantial portion of the RAF had remained in the British Isles for air defense purposes and was consequently not involved in the battle for air superiority over the Western Front).

On May 12, Guderian's panzer divisions began crossing the Semois River. Allied air attacks, especially by Battle bombers, caused the Germans considerable difficulties, including forcing Guderian to move his headquarters. Defending German fighters and antiaircraft guns inflicted heavy casualties on RAF bombers, shooting down eighteen of the fifty aircraft. But the French were able to inflict some painful casualties on the Luftwaffe. Five Curtiss fighters caught twelve Stukas returning unescorted from a raid and shot all of them down.[70] Unfortunately, the general air superiority that the Germans enjoyed over the Ardennes made such incidents the exception.

By May 13 German armored forces had come up on the Meuse between Dinant and Sedan. By the 14th Guderian had his infantry, supported by artillery and Stukas, across the river and busily engaged in punching through French defenses. Even more important was the fact that the Germans had managed to bridge the Meuse and began moving armored forces across the river. The threat posed by this German thrust and the collapse of French units produced by the Luftwaffe's Stukas and German infantry finally awoke the French high command to the danger. Desperate calls from the French led the RAF to throw its bomber forces against the growing German penetration. Their effort aimed at destroying the bridges thrown across the Meuse by German combat engineers and at attacking German columns moving up to and across the river. The results were a disaster for the RAF. Luftwaffe fighters and antiaircraft savaged attacking formations. The official history records the RAF's losses as thirty-five out of sixty-three Battle bombers dispatched and five out of eight Blenheim bombers dispatched (or forty out of seventy-one aircraft—a loss rate of fifty-six percent of the attacking force).[71]

Still, these operations caused the Germans serious difficulties. The war diary of XIX Panzer Corps (Guderian's force) noted that "the completion of the military bridge at Donchery had not yet been carried out owing to heavy flanking artillery fire and long bombing attacks on the bridging point. ... Throughout the day all three divisions have had to endure constant air attack—especially at the crossing and bridging points. Our fighter cover is inadequate. Requests (for increased fighter protection) are still unsuccessful."[72] Luftwaffe reports also indicated the pressure that Allied air attacks were exerting in the Ardennes: "vigorous enemy fighter activity through which our close reconnaissance in particular is severely impeded."[73] Nevertheless, while Guderian's war diary exhibited dismay over inadequacies in the fighter cover, German air defenses had been most successful against RAF bombers. No air force could support a fifty-six percent level of attrition, and on the next day the Germans noted a significant decrease in the intensity of RAF air attacks along the perimeter of the breakthrough.

Once German armored formations had broken through French defenses along the Meuse, the campaign was over. The French Army, frozen in a doctrinal rigidity of its own making, was incapable of replying to the German thrust. Exploitation of the breakthrough now proceeded with dispatch. Behind surging columns of armored and motorized units, the Luftwaffe pushed its operating bases forward so that Bf–109 and dive bomber units could remain in contact with the ground forces that were rapidly pushing ahead and in danger of passing out of the range of effective air cover. On May 17, within twenty-four hours of its abandonment by the French, German fighter squadrons had established themselves at Charleville, west of the Meuse. Because the Army's logistical system was choking the Meuse bridges, Ju–52 transports flew in everything—from maintenance personnel to fuel and munitions. So short of POL was the forward operating base that aircraft returning from Charleville to rear area bases had all but the minimum fuel load pumped out of their tanks.[74]

Once in the open, the Germans found a noticeable slackening in the Allied air resistance. Anglo-French air units scrambled pell mell to the south as the German Army chewed through their frontline bases. Ground crews, supplies, and maintenance equipment all had to move south of the Somme with little warning, and the process of sorting out ground organizations in the wreckage of defeat represented an impossible task, given the available time. In addition to problems posed by the rapid move to the south, German air attacks placed considerable pressure on the Allied support structure as well as on fighting strength. The one group of Dewoitine 520s (the newest and best French fighter aircraft, close in performance to the Bf–109s and Spitfires) put up a respectable showing in air-to-air combat with the Luftwaffe, but by May 21 had lost half of its aircraft on the ground through German attacks on its bases.[75]

The Luftwaffe met its first setback over Dunkirk. There the Germans faced an enemy who possessed first-class equipment and whose base structure across the channel remained intact and invulnerable to ground operations. RAF Fighter Command had not committed any of its limited number of Spitfires to the defense of France. Thus, while the Hurricanes and Dewoitine 520s had put up a respectable showing in air-to-air combat, only now over Dunkirk did the Luftwaffe run into aircraft fully the equal of the Bf–109. Moreover, British bases on the other side of the channel lay closer to evacuation beaches than did even such German forward operating bases as Charleville. Consequently, British fighters possessed more loiter time in the combat zone than did the Bf–109s. Given German numbers, the result was a furious air battle in which RAF Fighter Command thwarted Goering's promise that the Luftwaffe, by itself, could destroy the trapped Allied ground forces.[76] With the 109s at the outer limit of their range and with the bomber force still flying from bases in western Germany, the coordination of the two was a formidable task. By May 26 Fighter Command was providing almost continuous cover over Dunkirk. Standing patrols of squadron strength (10-plus fighters) were taking off from British airfields approximately every 50 minutes. While some German bomber formations received fighter escort, others did not. On the 26th the British lost only 6 fighters while the Luftwaffe lost 37 aircraft on that day, the great majority in the Dunkirk area.[77]

May 27 told a similar story. Sixteen squadrons of Fighter Command covered the Dunkirk area with pilots flying 2 to 3 missions each day.[78] *Fliegerkorps* II, engulfed in the fighting over Dunkirk, reported that it had lost more aircraft on the 27th than in the previous 10 days of the campaign.[79] The battle for air superiority in the skies over Dunkirk was costly to both sides. From May 26 through June 3, the RAF lost 177 aircraft destroyed or damaged; the Germans lost 240.[80] Yet the air battle was by itself inconclusive; neither side had won a clear-cut victory. Nevertheless, strategically, Fighter Command was able to contest successfully with the Luftwaffe and thwart the Germans from bringing the full weight of their air power to bear on the evacuation. In that sense, "the miracle of Dunkirk" was as much Fighter Command's victory as it was the victory of the Royal Navy and the little boats.

Dunkirk, as the fighter ace Adolf Galland suggested in his memoirs, should have alerted the German high command to the inherent weaknesses in the Luftwaffe's force structure.[81] The Germans possessed the range and striking power to gain air superiority, provided air operations were within a limited space, where the army forward thrusts could extend aircraft range by seizing bases for further operations. Whether the Luftwaffe could defeat an air force whose bases were not threatened by ground operations, and who possessed a level of production equal to if not superior to it in some categories was another matter.

The current conception of the defeat of France is that it cost the Germans relatively little. The German victory in France often serves as the paradigm for the mobile, flexible operations advanced by many of the current critics of the American defense establishment. The cost, therefore, is worth noting. During a campaign in which heavy fighting occurred over less than a period of a month, German and Allied casualties added up to over half a million (not including prisoners of war). German panzer forces, moreover, lost nearly 30 percent of their tanks (753 out of 2,574) during the furious advance.[82] The Luftwaffe suffered equally. In May alone it lost 27.4 percent of its bomber force, 12.3 percent of its fighter force, and 20.2 percent of its total force structure.[83] (See Table 2–1)

German losses suggest, as do ground casualties, that the French put up a more respectable showing than historians have allowed. The losses also suggest that the defeat of 1940 was due less to national rot than to gross incompetence of France's military leadership.[84] The RAF's fighter losses during the French campaign amounted to 474 aircraft—more than half the number of fighters with which it had begun operations on May 10 (in England as well as in France).[85] German pilot losses among Bf–109 forces were not disastrous but do suggest the intensity of the fighting. Records indicate that Luftwaffe losses for the campaign included 15.2 percent of the fighter pilots on active service at the onset of operations in the West.[86]

TABLE 2–1
German Aircraft Losses, May–June 1940
Destroyed on Operations

Aircraft Type	Strength 4.5.40.	Due to Enemy Action	Not Due to Enemy Action	Total	Destroyed Not on Operations	Total Destroyed	Losses as Percentage Of Initial
Lose Recce	345	67	5	72	6	78	23%
Long-Range Reece	321	68	18	86	2	88	27
Single-Engine Fighters	1,369	169	66	235	22	257	19
Twin-Engine Fighters	367	90	16	106	4	110	30
Bombers	1,758	438	53	491	30	521	30
Dive Bomber	417	89	24	113	9	122	30
Transport	531	188	18	206	7	213	40
Coastal	421	20	16	36	3	39	16
Total	5,349	1,129	216	1,345	83	1,428	28%

Source: This table was drawn from two major compilations of the Air Historical Branch: AHB, Translation, VII//107, "Luftwaffe Strength and Serviceability Tables, August 1938-April 1945;" and Translation VII/83, "German Aircraft Losses, September 1933-December 1940." These tables, in turn, were compiled from the German quartermaster records then in the hands of the AHB.

The campaign in France brings out several interesting points. The German effort in the air and on the ground generally saw a close integration and cooperation at all levels. The sum of that cooperative effort resulted in a devastating military victory over Allied military power in the West. The Luftwaffe did not gain complete air superiority over its opponents at the outset of the campaign. However, the pressure that it placed on the opposing air forces beginning May 10, on the ground and in the air, allowed it to carry out its mission objectives, while generally preventing its opponents from executing theirs. The value that general air superiority contributed to the German victory is best represented by events along the Meuse between May 13th and the 15th. From the outset the Luftwaffe was able to shield its close-air-support attacks on French troops on the left bank of the Meuse from Allied interference. The one incident, mentioned above, when five Curtiss fighters of the French Air Force intercepted twelve Stukas and shot down all twelve suggests what stronger Allied fighter forces might have been able to do. The result of such Allied weakness was that the German Stuka forces laid down a devastating pattern of support, materially contributing to the collapse of French troops along the Meuse, especially at Sedan, in front of Guderian's XIX Panzer Corps. Then, when the Germans had broken through, Allied air power attempted to cut the Meuse bridges with a sustained bombing effort. Allied fighters, inferior in numbers, were never able to give their bombers adequate support. The result was an aerial massacre. While Allied bombing attacks did cause the Germans severe discomfort, they were not sustainable; there was little left after the 15th to carry out further heavy attacks.

Once in the open, German armored forces cut a wide swath through the rear area of northern France and forced Allied air forces to abandon their bases. That hurried retreat resulted in the loss of spare aircraft parts, ammunition, and fuel, all of which were in short supply on new and unprepared airstrips. The German ground advance also thoroughly disrupted the command and control system (which had never worked particularly well from the point of view of air commanders). From that point on, the Allied air effort against the Germans in France rapidly diminished.

The air battle over Dunkirk represented a different story. There the German army had outrun its air support, and Luftwaffe efforts to dominate the battle area faced insurmountable obstacles. Even with the forward movement of Luftwaffe fighters behind surging army spearheads, the Bf–109, heart of the air superiority force, remained far from the evacuation beaches. On the other side of the channel, RAF Fighter Command, flying from secure bases and not under the threat of ground operations, was able to disrupt the Luftwaffe's effort to halt the evacuation. The escape of the British army, in effect, made the strategic defense of Great Britain that summer a viable possibility. In that sense the RAF won an important victory by preventing unhindered use of the Luftwaffe's capability.

Allied air forces were insufficient to thwart the combined German effort on the ground and in the air. Nevertheless, the historian leaves the French campaign with the sense of how closely the whole German campaign had balanced on the edge of defeat. One can argue that the decision that lost the air battle and perhaps the campaign was taken in October and November 1938. Under great pressure from both the House of Commons and the public to repair the glaring deficiencies in British defenses, the government of Neville Chamberlain announced major increases in its purchasing plans for fighter aircraft. However, it was all a sham move by a government determined not to spend *any* more on national defense. What Chamberlain and his advisers did was to extend the contracts for Hurricanes and Spitfires without increasing monthly production totals. Therefore, there was no net gain over what was already planned. The production performance of the British aircraft industry from late 1938 through summer 1940 clearly indicates that monthly production figures could have been substantially increased; but they were not.[87] As a result, Allied air forces were quantitatively and qualitatively inferior in May 1940. What Allied air forces with 300 to 400 more Spitfires and Hurricanes might have achieved is obvious. Not only would they have been able to contest air superiority with the Luftwaffe for a longer period of time, but they could have protected their own bases better and provided significantly more support for bomber sorties. Further, the long line of vehicles curling up toward the Meuse or the traffic jams of vehicles waiting to cross provided wonderful targets. The 56 percent loss of British bombers on May 15, however, rendered the strike force *hors de combat* after one mission and the movement forward of the panzers safe from enemy air interference. The result was disastrous defeat for British and French military forces.

As surprised as others by the completeness of the French collapse, the Germans believed they won the war. With the armistice, Germany's leaders went on vacation. Hitler spent time visiting Paris and World War I battlefields as well as enjoying picnics along the Rhine.[88] His military advisers did not work much harder. Gen. Alfred Jodl, number two on the *OKW* staff, suggested at the end of June that "the final victory of Germany over England is only a question of time."[89] Hitler himself hoped right to the end of July that Great Britain, recognizing her hopeless position, would sue for peace. As early as May 20 he had suggested that England could have peace for the asking.[90]

Battle of Britain

Considering the abject performance of British policymaking in the late 1930s,[91] one can excuse the Germans for their belief that Britain would surrender. What Germany missed was that the British mood had substantially changed. Churchill's oratory was not mere rhetoric; it indicated a first-class strategic mind—with the ruthlessness and toughness of spirit needed to back it up. On July 5, 1940, after fruitless negotiations, the Royal Navy destroyed much of the French fleet in its North African base at Mers-el-Kebir to keep it from serving the Germans.[92] That action signaled that the British were in for the duration. Yet, two weeks later, Hitler still extended the olive branch to Great Britain as he promoted his admirals and generals with great ceremony in Berlin.

The strategic problem posed by British resistance represented a whole new dimension of strategy to the *Wehrmacht's "Weltanschauung"*. The *Reich's* military forces were not only ill-equipped to solve the strategic problem, they possessed none of the intellectual and professional background that an amphibious assault on the English coast demanded. In fact, one can wonder how seriously the Germans took the proposed invasion, code-named Operation SEA LION. The Army willfully disregarded the Navy's logistical capabilities in presenting plans for a seventy-mile invasion front. Operations off the North Cape in early June best represented the Navy's attitude. Despite earlier discussions between Hitler and his naval commander in chief, Grand Admiral Erich Raeder, over a possible landing in the British Isles, the naval high command committed Germany's only two battle cruisers, the *Gneisenau* and the *Scharnhorst,* to operations off the Norwegian coast, more to influence planned postwar budget debates than for strategic reasons. As a result, both were so damaged that neither was ready for operations until December. Thus, Germany had at her disposal only one heavy cruiser, two light cruisers, and four destroyers at the end of June.[93]

Because the Navy and Army had neither the inclination nor resources for combined operations, Germany possessed no suitable landing craft in 1940. Consequently, SEA LION rested its cross-channel logistical lift on Rhine river barges. With few escort vessels, the Germans had to count on the Luftwaffe to exclude the Royal Navy and the RAF from the channel. Summing up the general sloppiness of German strategic thinking in the summer was an *OKW* directive suggesting that the Luftwaffe substitute for the absence of naval power. With air superiority, the landings on the British coast would take the form of a powerful river crossing.[94]

Since the Royal Navy had stationed a large number of destroyers with cruiser support at Portsmouth and Harwich among other locations, one can seriously doubt whether SEA LION ever had a chance, even had the Luftwaffe beaten the RAF in September.[95] Only a few British destroyers in among such an invasion fleet would have been a disaster. It is difficult to see how the Luftwaffe could have intercepted even a bare majority of the thirty to forty destroyers and cruisers that the British had already deployed by mid-August to meet the invasion. Moving at speeds upwards of thirty knots, destroyers would have been an extraordinarily difficult target to hit.

Moreover, the Luftwaffe and the German Navy had done virtually no preparatory work to iron out how they would cooperate in protecting convoys against enemy surface attacks or how they would cooperate in a massive air-sea battle. It is worth noting that in 1941 in the waters off Crete, the Luftwaffe found it impossible to protect the German seaborne landings from the Royal Navy despite total air superiority and perfect weather conditions.[96] Thus, the Luftwaffe had little sense of the complex tasks that its air units would have faced in subduing the Royal Navy while supporting an invasion.[97] Interestingly, neither Hitler nor Churchill seemed to have fully believed that a cross-channel invasion was in the cards. The Prime Minister in September 1940 sent a sizeable percentage of Britain's armored strength to the Middle East—hardly the decision of a man who believed an invasion was imminent.[98] Hitler also appears to have been dubious about prospects for the invasion; from the beginning, the Führer, for the only time in the war, had little to do with the planning and conduct of operations preparing the way for SEA LION.

The Luftwaffe faced very different strategic problems in the summer of 1940 than it had dealt with in its three previous campaigns. Its opponent, the RAF, possessed relatively secure bases that would not be under ground attack unless it was first defeated. Consequently, the Luftwaffe ground support structure could not move forward behind the army's advance. Only air attacks could hope to disrupt RAF maintenance and supply. Nevertheless, with new bases in the Low Countries and northern France, German bombers could reach most of the important transportation, industrial, and population centers in Great Britain as well as RAF airfields. And unlike other air forces in 1940, the Luftwaffe had attempted to solve the long-range escort problem. Unfortunately for German prospects, the fighter explicitly designed for that role, the Bf–110, while possessing the range to accompany deep penetration missions, could not stand up against first-class, single-engine fighters. Against the Hurricane and Spitfire it lacked both speed and maneuverability—a deadly combination. Thus, the Bf–109 would have to protect not only the bombers but Bf–110 formations as well, and the range of the Bf–109 was such that even with the airfields in Pas de Calais it could barely reach London.

In a June 1940 memorandum, Jodl sketched out the strategic framework for victory over Britain.[99] For a direct strategy, he saw three approaches: 1) an air and naval offensive against British shipping along with attacks against industry; 2) terror attacks against major cities; and finally 3) landing operations to occupy an already prostrate England. The Luftwaffe, Jodl suggested, must gain air superiority; by destroying industrial plants, it would insure that the RAF could not recover. He also suggested that air superiority would prevent the RAF from striking the *Reich* and particularly the Ruhr. It is within this context that German attacks on Bomber Command's airfields must be seen: German air strategy during the

Battle of Britain aimed not only at Fighter Command's destruction, but also at the elimination of the bombing threat to Germany.

On the day that Jodl's memorandum surfaced, Goering issued general instructions to his forces.[100] After redeployment to airfields near Britain, the Luftwaffe would go after the RAF. Its targets would be Fighter Command and Bomber Command, ground support echelons, and the aircraft industry. Goering suggested "as long as the enemy air force is not destroyed, it is the basic principle of the conduct of an air war to attack the enemy air units at every possible opportunity—by day and night, in the air, and on the ground—without regard for other missions." Once the Luftwaffe had succeeded in gaining air superiority, it would assault British imports and stockpiles. The heavy losses of the French campaign had indeed made an impact on the *Reichsmarschall*. He urged his commanders to conserve the Luftwaffe's fighting strength as much as possible and not allow overcommitments of either personnel or materiel.

To destroy the RAF and gain air superiority, the Luftwaffe deployed Second and Third Air Forces in France and the Low Countries and Fifth Air Force in Norway. The former two components controlled over 2,600 aircraft, while the latter possessed nearly 300 more. (See Table 2–2) The redeployment of such large air units from bases in Germany required considerable time and effort. In addition, the Luftwaffe faced difficulties in making good the losses suffered in France. Thus the two-month hiatus between victory over France and the beginning of the air campaign against the British Isles reflected the above factors, as well as German overconfidence.

German prospects were not helped by their intelligence services. Col. Joseph "Beppo" Schmid provided the basic survey of the RAF on July 16.[101] Like succeeding intelligence work, Schmid's study was arrogantly overconfident of Luftwaffe capabilities and generally ignorant about the British defense system. Schmid only came close to the mark in the quantitative counters: his estimate calculated that with 50 squadrons the RAF possessed approximately 900 fighters (675 in commission). (In fact, the RAF possessed 871 fighters of which 644 were operationally ready.[102]) Schmid also got the ratio between Spitfire and Hurricanes generally correct (suggesting a 40–60 ratio). (In the operational squadrons the RAF possessed 279 Spitfires, and 462 Hurricanes, a 38–62 ratio.[103])

From there, Schmid's estimate went downhill. Schmid characterized both the Hurricane and Spitfire as inferior to the Bf–109, while only a "skillfully handled" Spitfire was superior to the Bf–110. He calculated that British fighter production lay somewhere between 180 and 300 machines per month (actual production for the month of July reached 496, 476 for August, and 467 for September)[104], but argued that production would soon go down due to reorganization, vulnerability to air attack, and raw material greatest errors in evaluating the higher levels of British command and con-

TABLE 2–2
German Air Strength: July 20, 1940

Aircraft Type	Second and Third Air Forces			Fifth Air Force			Luftwaffe		
	Strength	In commission (N)	commission (%)	Strength	In (N)	commission (%)	Strength	In (N)	commission (%)
Long-Range Bombers	1,131	769	68%	129	95	74%	1,401	903	64%
Dive Bombers	316	248		-	-	-	449	332	74
Single-Engine Fighters	809	656	81	84	69	82	1,060	865	82
Twin-Engine Fighters	246	168	68	34	32	94	398	293	74
Long-Range Recce	67	48	72	48	33	69	280	189	74
Short-Range Recce	90	?	-	-	-	-	250	178	71
Total	2,659	1,889	74%*	295	229	78%*	3,838	2,750	72%

*Includes only those aircraft categories for which in commission numbers are available.

Source: Table 2–2 represents a compendium of Luftwaffe strengths from Air Ministry, *The Rise and Fall of the German Air Force, 1933–1945,* p.76, "Luftwaffe Strength and Serviceability Tables, August 1938–April 1945," Air Historical Branch, Translation No. VII/107; and Francis J. Mason, *Battle over Britain* (London, 1968), p. 186

trol. A short paragraph dismissed Fighter Command's ability to control its units effectively: "The Command at high level is inflexible in its organization and strategy. As formations are rigidly attached to their home bases, command at medium level suffers mainly from operations being controlled in most cases by officers no longer accustomed to flying. . . . Command at low level is generally energetic but lacks tactical skill."[105] Finally, Schmid never mentioned the British radar system and its implications for the attacking German forces. The intelligence estimate ended in the confident assertion that

> the Luftwaffe is clearly superior to the RAF as regards strength, equipment, training, command and location of bases. In the event of an intensification of air warfare the Luftwaffe, unlike the RAF, will be in a position in every respect to achieve a decisive effect this year if the time for the start of large scale operations is set early enough to allow advantage to be taken of the months with relatively favorable weather conditions (July to the beginning of October).[106]

Schmid's memorandum is important not only for the gross overconfidence it reflected, but also because such intelligence errors would plague the Germans throughout the war.[107]

A second point needs to be made about the failure to see the implications of the British radar system. While the Germans were somewhat behind the British in technical developments, they did possess radar. However, considering the nature of the war that Germany had prepared to fight (and thus far had fought—a continental air and land war in which their forces were on the offensive), the Germans missed an oportunity to use radar for offensive air operations. Had the *Jagdführer (Jafü)*—the Second and Third Air Force officers responsible for fighter operations—possessed radar plots of air operations over Great Britain, they might have played a more significant role. Particularly in the early phases of operations, they could have reacted to Fighter Command's responses as their own attacking forces built up behind Pas de Calais. However, with little active or passive intelligence, the *Jafüs* faced a dismal summer trying to make sense of what returning pilots said. Even disregarding the advantages that such a system would have given, German radar on Pas de Calais could at least have allowed the Luftwaffe to observe British responses to raids and to understand better the British defensive system.

In fact, the Luftwaffe faced a far more tenacious opponent than it supposed. The British air defense system, led by its commander in chief, Air

Bundesarchiv-Militärarchiv

Joseph ''Beppo'' Schmid, chief of Luftwaffe intelligence.

Marshal Sir Hugh Dowding, was well-equipped and well-prepared.* The cutting edge of the defenses was Fighter Command, disposing of somewhere around 600 serviceable Spitfires and Hurricanes (approximately 800, altogether).[108] While the RAF had suffered heavy losses in May and June (509 Spitfires and Hurricanes), the number of fighters available was never a serious problem.[109] Under the direction of Britain's Minister for Aircraft Production, Lord Beaverbrook, British fighter production had already overtaken Germany's. Under Lord Beaverbrook's demanding pressure the ratio between national figures would be nearly 2–1 in favor of the British by late summer.[110] The greatest problem was not lack of aircraft but lack of pilots. The RAF had lost nearly 300 pilots in France, and at the beginning of July out of an establishment of 1,450 pilots in the Table of Organization, Fighter Command possessed only 1,253. Moreover, most pilots lost in France had been experienced; their replacements were straight out of the OTUs (Operational Training Units).[111]

In microcosm, the strategic problem confronting the Germans in the summer was similar to that facing Allied air forces in 1943, particularly in terms of the daylight offensive. Because of the Bf–109's limited range, German bombers could only strike targets during the day in southern England, where fighter protection could hold losses to acceptable levels. This situation allowed the RAF a substantial portion of Great Britain as a sanctuary. Within that area, relatively free from the threat of air attack, the RAF could establish and control an air reserve and protect a substantial portion of Britain's industrial production, particularly in the Birmingham-Liverpool area. Should the Germans attempt to attack targets behind London, the RAF could impose an unacceptable level of attrition on the unescorted bombers.

Moreover, the limited range of German fighter cover allowed the British one option that they never had to exercise. Should pressure on Fighter Command become too great, it could withdraw north of London to refit and reorganize; then if the Germans launched SEA LION it could return to the struggle with full force. Consequently, the Luftwaffe could only impose on Fighter Command a rate of attrition that its commander would accept. The Germans were never in a position to attack the RAF over the full extent of its domains. Similarly, in the 1943 daylight air battles, American escort fighters could only protect the B–17s and B–24s on a line running roughly along the western bank of the Rhine. Beyond that protective curtain, the Luftwaffe's fighters imposed an unacceptable attrition rate on the Americans. Not until Eighth Air Force possessed escort fighters of sufficient range to reach over the length and breadth of the *Reich* were Allied air

---

*Organizations of the United Kingdom Air Defenses in the summer of 1940 can be found in the succeeding chapter, page 122.

forces able to break the Luftwaffe and win a general air superiority over the European continent.

The pause after the fall of France reflected not only German overconfidence and the abiding certainty that Great Britain would recognize her hopeless situation, but also the organizational and logistical difficulties of shifting to new bases along the channel. Moreover, the Germans had to make good those aircraft losses suffered in the spring and integrate new crews into active units. Yet a pervasive mood of overconfidence marked the German approach to the battle. Operational estimates forecast that only four days of major operations over southern England would break Fighter Command. The Luftwaffe would then need only four weeks to eliminate the remainder of the RAF and destroy the factories on which British air strength rested. Then, the Luftwaffe, savaging British cities by day and night, could protect the SEA LION landings, if required to give, as Jodl characterized the operation, a final "death blow."[112]

By the end of July, Luftwaffe thinking for the coming air battle had crystalized. On July 21, Goering suggested to senior commanders that besides the RAF, the British aircraft industry represented a critical target for winning air superiority. Above all, the *Reichsmarschall* argued that the fighter forces should possess maximum operational latitude in protecting bomber formations. Thus, Luftwaffe bomber raids would bring up the RAF's fighters, and fighter sweeps would seek out and attack the Spitfire and Hurricanes wherever they could be found: on the ground, taking off, climbing to fighting altitude, or attacking German bombers. And the Bf–109s would enjoy the advantage of the initiative, since they were not tied exclusively to protecting the bombers. Such a strategy would maximize fighter speed and maneuverability.[113]

Three days later *Fliegerkorps I* mapped out four basic missions for the Luftwaffe in the upcoming campaign. The foremost task was to gain air superiority through attacks on the RAF and its supporting aircraft factories, particularly those producing engines. Second, the Luftwaffe would support the future invasion with attacks on the enemy bomber force and fleet and eventually, when the invasion began, against enemy ground forces. Third, German air units would attack British ports and imports; and finally, independent of the first three tasks, the Luftwaffe would launch ruthless retaliatory terror raids against major British cities (in retaliation for the present or future attacks of Bomber Command on Germany).[114]

Goering's remarks made good sense. In retrospect, Fighter Command was indeed the heart of the British defensive system. What the staff study by *Fliegerkorps I* suggests, however, is that Goering's subordinates, including his air force commanders, held other goals, which no matter how worthwhile, served to distract German strategy from the fundamental aim— destruction of Fighter Command. German decisionmaking during the battle reflected this confusion, and the Germans proved all too willing to move from one strategy to another.

The Luftwaffe did not officially begin its offensive until mid-August with the launching of "Eagle Day" on August 13, 1940. The battle in fact began earlier than that: the British date the beginning as the 10th of July. The period between July 10 and August 13 indicates an escalation level of Luftwaffe operations as the Germans probed their opponents over the channel and southern British ports. The overall purpose seems to have been to wear Fighter Command down before the beginning of the main battle and to close the channel to British maritime and naval shipping. Thus, the focal points of early air battles were the convoys along the southern coast. In retrospect, the German strategy was in serious error. It allowed the British air defense system to gain extensive experience with German operational methods. On the radar side, the British worked flaws out of the existing system, and the slow increase in the tempo of German operations gave British radar operators confidence in their abilities to estimate size and to predict the course of raids.[115] There were some major errors in the first days, such as on the 11th of July when the radar system scrambled six Hurricanes to meet what was supposedly a lone raider making for Lyme Bay. In fact, the Hurricanes ran into a major raid of fifteen dive bombers, escorted by thirty or forty twin-engine fighters.[116] Such nasty experiences occurred with lessening frequency as the battle proceeded.

The opening phase came at considerable cost to both sides in aircraft and air crews. By the second week of August, Fighter Command had lost 148 aircraft, compared to 286 for the Luftwaffe (105 Bf–109s).[117] Yet, the cost to Fighter Command in pilots was serious. In July, the loss of Spitfire and Hurricane pilots along the channel was well in excess of the Bf–109 pilot losses in the Luftwaffe (84 pilots, 10 percent, versus 45 pilots, 4.1 percent).[118] Higher British losses, of course, reflected British tactics, which were still inferior to those used by Bf–109 pilots in air-to-air combat. Greater British fighter pilot losses were compensated for by the fact that British fighter squadrons inflicted heavy damage on the bomber formations. The upshot of the preliminary phase was a stand-off. The Luftwaffe forced the Royal Navy to close down the channel convoys that had formed the focus of July air battles. But Fighter Command and its support structure had gained invaluable experience and confidence.

The weaknesses in British air-to-air fighter tactics in France and at the beginning stages of the Battle of Britain reflected the prewar dogmatism of an Air Staff that had argued categorically that dogfights would not take place in the next war. Consequently, RAF fighters flew in very close formations called "vics," which not only gave far less visual coverage and thus warning of a German fighter attack but also made it easy for Bf–109s, bouncing such a formation, to shoot down more than one of the British fighters. As combat experience spread throughout Fighter Command, the British quickly adapted their tactics to fit the realities of the situation. The lesson, however, was a costly one.

In retrospect, the prospects on the German side were less bright. Not only had the Luftwaffe tipped its hand, but nothing had yet broken the overconfidence clouding the minds of German commanders. They had in fact learned little about the workings of the British air defense system. An early August intelligence estimate announced:

> As the British fighters were controlled from the ground by R/T their forces are tied to their respective ground stations and are thereby restricted in mobility, even taking into consideration the possibility that the ground stations are partly mobile. Consequently, the assembly of strong fighter forces at determined points and at short notice is not to be expected. A massed German attack on a target area can therefore count on the same conditions of light fighter opposition as in attacks on widely scattered targets. It can, indeed, be assumed that considerable confusion in the defensive networks will be unavoidable during mass attacks, and that the effectiveness of the defenses may thereby be reduced.[119]

Thus, as planning for the assault on the British air defenses neared fruition, the Germans had as little idea of their opponent and his tactics as they had enjoyed at the beginning of July.

Eagle Day was to begin on August 10, but bad weather delayed the start to the 13th. On that day the Germans again postponed operations—to the afternoon—but too late to recall bombers, which insured that most bomber strikes in the morning possessed no fighter cover. As the Germans muddled their way into battle, the British felt a clear change in tempo beginning on August 11. On that day German fighter sweeps, in combination with a large raid on southern ports, resulted in a furious dogfight over the channel that cost No. 11 Group dearly. By the end of the day the British had twenty Hurricane pilots killed with two wounded and five Spitfire pilots killed (over seven percent of No. 11 Group's pilots in one day). German losses were also heavy, and while losing only twelve Bf–109 pilots, the Luftwaffe lost twenty-five other aircraft and two more Bf–109s from which the pilots escaped unharmed.[120]

The fighting on August 11 heralded the start of massive air battles lasting for the next week. On the afternoon of the 13th the Germans began their attacks on the RAF and its support structure. Raids on airfields, sector stations, and aircraft factories now became the center of the Luftwaffe's attention. Ironically and almost inexplicably, German intelligence misidentified the parent factory for Spitfire production in Southampton as a bomber firm, and not until much later (and for the wrong reasons) did they hit this critical target.[121] Moreover, the Germans made a serious mistake in failing to follow up their August 12 attacks on radar sites that had damaged five out of the six stations and put the Ventnor station entirely off the air until August 23.[122]

On August 15, discouraged by the lack of results and the tenacity of the defenses, Goering called a meeting of senior commanders at Karinhall, his country estate near Berlin. While most senior commanders were absent from the battlefront, the Luftwaffe launched a series of major blows. It is doubtful whether the absence of senior commanders had much of an impact. Nevertheless, the conduct of these raids does not suggest that the Luftwaffe was absorbing and learning from its combat experience. Concurrently, Fifth Air Force for the first and last time launched its aircraft against northern England in daylight and suffered a serious setback that ended its participation in the daylight offensive. The raid suffered a 15.4 percent loss to British fighters (22 aircraft out of 143)—clear evidence that the British had deployed Fighter Command in depth and not in a thin shell protecting southern England. The savage air fighting on the 15th came as a terrible shock to Luftwaffe commanders, who lost 75 aircraft. That success had not come easy to the British—altogether Fighter Command lost 26 fighter pilots, killed, injured, or missing.[123]

While the British were savaging his force, Goering, far removed at Karinhall, berated his senior commanders. Not only did he criticize target selection (although failing to give substantive suggestions), but he removed radar stations from the Luftwaffe's target list.[124] Goering's decision seems to have been based partially on inaccurate damage estimates of what the raids on the 12th had achieved. An important influence on his decision would seem to have been the faulty estimate by Luftwaffe intelligence on the effectiveness of the British command and control system. On the following morning, German intelligence reported that heavy losses had reduced Fighter Command to 300 serviceable aircraft, but as raids over the following days still met opposition, doubts on intelligence estimates began to appear.[125]

Sustained bad weather beginning on the 19th brought a five-day lull. As both sides licked their wounds, the Luftwaffe's operations staff issued a new directive on August 20, which reemphasized that the RAF, and particularly Fighter Command, was the primary target. Furthermore, the directive advocated that along with efforts to destroy Fighter Command in the air, the air attacks should target the ground support organization, the aircraft industry, and aluminum smelting plants and rolling mills.[126] At the same time Goering finally recognized the Stuka's vulnerability to fighters and withdrew them from the battle. He also made the serious error of tying the Bf–109 fighters closely to the bomber formations. Goering's decision reflected the chorus of complaints from bomber units on the inadequacy of fighter cover and the heavy losses that bomber formations were taking from RAF attacks. It was a bad tactical mistake. Tied to the bomber formations, the Bf–109 force was not only less effective in its air-to-air operations against British fighters but no more capable of protecting the bombers. In addition, Goering ordered the Bf–109s to escort the Bf–110s. Finally, the *Reichsmarchall* redeployed Third Air Force single-engine fighters, which now concentrated behind Pas de Calais under the control of Kesselring's Second Air Force.127 While this decision provided greater support to the attacks on Fighter Command bases defending London, the decision effectively removed the Third Air Force from the daylight offensive and took the pressure off much of Southern England. The pressure of sustained operations was beginning to tell on both sides. Neither fighter force was in a position to take such losses on a sustained basis. (See Table 2–3)

The bad weather ended on August 24; three weeks of intensive operations then began. For the first two weeks, the Luftwaffe's target remained Fighter Command and its support structure. The Germans placed enormous pressure on the defense system. And while they did not inflict daily losses as high as they had in mid-August, they did push the British fighter forces to the limit. Luftwaffe bomber formations thoroughly devastated Fighter Command's frontline airfields and seriously stressed not just British pilots but also the command and control system and the maintenance support force. Reserves of pilots on both sides were running out. But if the British were under extraordinary pressure, the Germans saw no relaxing in the defenses. Fighter Command's resistance proved as tenacious as ever.

TABLE 2–3
Fighter Pilot Losses:
RAF Fighter Command and Luftwaffe

	RAF Fighter Command (Hurricanes and Spitfires)		Luftwaffe (Bf–109 force)	
	Total Losses all causes	Percent* Losses of Pilots	Total losses all causes	Percent† Losses of Pilots
July	84	10%	124†	11%
Aug	237	26%	168	15%
Sept	276	28%	229	23.1%

*based on # of pilots available at the beginning of the month
† may include some late returns from the Battle of France

Source: The figures for British losses are based on the combat loss tables for July, August and September in Mason, *Battle over Britain* and on the tables he provides on Fighter Command's establishment for July 1, August 1, and September 1. The Luftwaffe figures are based on the tables available in BA/MA, RL 707, 708 Gen. Qu.6 Abt. (1), Ubersicht uber Soll, Istbestand, Einsatzbereitschaft, Verluste und Reserven der fliegenden Verbande. It is worth noting that the combat loss results available in Mason places the Luftwaffe fighter pilot losses at a significantly lower level: they would be July, 45 pilots, 4 percent; August 175; 15.7 percent; and September 177, 17.8 percent. Only the figures for July are wildly at variance and may reflect late returns from the Battle of France in the BA/MA RL 700 series.

Early in September the Germans made their final mistake. Discouraged that the current strategy did not seem to be pressuring Fighter Command sufficiently, Hitler and Goering switched the Luftwaffe's approach from an air superiority strategy to a daylight strategic bombing offensive against London. The change reflected two basic attitudes. On the one hand, the German leadership was furious at the British temerity in bombing the *Reich's* cities. On the other hand, the Führer was undoubtedly delighted to have an opportunity to see whether ruthless "terror" bombing attacks on the "soft" British plutocracy might not lead to the collapse of the war effort. The change, of course, fit in nicely with the theories of Trenchard and Douhet, which had argued that air power had negated the classic strategic lessons of history. The change did find favor in the Luftwaffe's high command. Kesselring pushed for the new strategy because he, like many in the Luftwaffe's intelligence service, believed that the RAF was on its last legs. He argued that a series of great raids on London would bring what was left of Fighter Command within reach of his fighters.

The shift in bombing strategy came with startling suddenness. On September 7, the pressure on Fighter Command's throat entirely relaxed. Late in the afternoon, Kesselring launched 348 bombers and 617 fighters, nearly 1,000 aircraft, against London.[128] The change caught No. 11 Group so much by surprise that the response was most uneven; controllers initially reacted as if the massive raid was targeting the sector fields and the controlling network.[129] Consequently, British fighters did not reach the German bombers until most had dropped their loads. In swirling dogfights south of London, Fighter Command lost 22 more Hurricane and Spitfire pilots, but inflicted the loss of 40 aircraft, including bombers. More importantly, the Luftwaffe lost 22 Bf–109 pilots.[130]

The damage the Luftwaffe dealt out to London was terrible, but the respite that followed proved invaluable to hard-pressed defenders, ground support as well as aircrew. One week later, Kesselring's forces returned for a repeat performance. Aircrews, assured that the RAF was through, discovered what some Luftwaffe commanders had sensed at the end of August: Fighter Command was an extraordinarily resilient instrument. Air-to-air combat on the 15th worked out to a rough equivalency in fighter pilot losses. There were twenty British pilots to seventeen German fighter pilots, yet the Hurricanes and Spitfires had savaged the German bomber formations. Besides Bf–109 losses, the Germans lost a further forty-one aircraft. While those losses were not, in and of themselves, at catastrophic levels, the Luftwaffe's bomber crews had reached the breaking point: many, at the first appearance of British fighters broke and, dumping their bomb loads, ran for the coast.[131] Even though heavy daylight air operations continued into October, the Battle of Britain was over. The Luftwaffe had indeed failed to gain anything approximating air superiority.

The Battle of Britain was one of the most uplifting victories in human history. "The few" had indeed triumphed, but they had triumphed because of outstanding leadership on their side and sloppy, careless execution on the German side. The foremost factor in the Luftwaffe's failure lay in the overwhelming overconfidence with which it had approached the problem of defeating the RAF. That task alone represented an altogether new strategic problem, entirely beyond that with which the Germans had hitherto grappled. A cavalierly incompetent intelligence service reinforced the mood of overconfidence. Confident in its abilities and hopeful that the British would sue for peace, the Luftwaffe dallied from mid-August. And in desperation the RAF, inspired by the threat to national existence, rallied its forces. Not only did the Luftwaffe dally, but by engaging in largely irrelevant operations over the channel for nearly two months, it also built up the confidence as well as the expertise of Fighter Command. The muddled execution of Eagle Day and succeeding days was a fitting anticlimax to the bad beginning. With a commander in chief far removed from the battle, with its air fleet commanders ensconsed in comfortable mansions, the Luftwaffe moved from one strategic conception to another with no clear idea of an overall strategy. Blinded by its own intelligence as to the importance of the radar system, and misguided as to the location of fighter factories in Britain, the Luftwaffe was still capable of inflicting excruciating pain on Fighter Command. But that pain, without the discipline of a strategic concept, could not gain a decisive victory.

From the invasion of Scandinavia in April 1940 the Luftwaffe was involved in massive air operations spanning nearly all of Western Europe. Its losses, in terms of aircraft alone, were staggering. And the cumulative pressures reaching back to April finally broke the morale of some units, particularly bomber squadrons, which had been engaged more or less continuously ever since their brilliant and devastating intervention in the battles that had led to the fall of France. (See Tables 2–4, 2–5, 2–6)

In fact, the Luftwaffe was the only air force in the world in 1940 that thought in terms of an air superiority strategy over the *enemy's territory.* Admittedly it had cast that strategy very much within a Central European *Weltanschauung* (world view). And where Luftwaffe operations worked together with the Army to remove Germany's continental neighbors that strategy was impressively effective. Air superiority, once gained by massive strikes against enemy air forces, allowed the Luftwaffe to support, protect, and supply the Army's rush into the enemy's heartland. Where the enemy did not possess the time, the resources, or the space to avoid the heart thrust, death by paralysis soon followed. With Great Britain, the Luftwaffe faced a very different problem. The Germans did possess a strategy of air superiority, but the strategic framework of the Battle of Britain

101

TABLE 2–4
Fighter Pilot Availability and Losses, 1940
(Bf–109 Squadrons)

	Pilots available at beginning of month	Pilots operationally ready at beginning of month	Percentage ready out of total available (%)	Pilot losses during month	Percentage of Pilot losses (%)
May	1110	1010	91 %	76	6.8%
June	1199	839	79	93	7.8%
July	1126	906	80.5	124	11
Aug	1118	869	77.7	168	15
Sept	990	735	74.2	229	23.1

Source: Based on the figures in BA/MA, RL 2 11/707, 708, Gen. Qu.6.Abt. (1), Ubersicht uber Soll, Istbestand Verluste Einsatzbereitschaft, und Reserven der fliegenden Verbande.

TABLE 2–5
Luftwaffe Aircraft Losses, July–September 1940
(Destroyed on Operations)

Type Aircraft	Strength 29.6.40	Due to Enemy Action	Not Due to Enemy Action	Total	Destroyed Not on Operations	Total Destroyed	Total Destroyed as percent of Initial Strength (%)
Close Recce	312	1	2	3	5	8	3%
Long-Range Recce	257	47	14	61	9	70	27
Single-Engine Fighters	1,107	398	79	477	41	518	47
Twin-Engine Fighters	357	214	9	233	12	235	66
Bomber	1,380	424	127	551	70	621	45
Dive Bomber	428	59	10	69	19	88	21
Transport	408	3	1	4	11	15	4
Coastal	233	38	29	67	14	81	35
Total	4,482	1,184	271	1,455	181	1,636	37%

Source: Based on the figures in AHB, Translation VII/83, "German Aircraft Losses, September 1939–December 1940."

TABLE 2–6
Luftwaffe Aircraft Losses, May–September 1940
Destroyed on Operations

Type Aircraft	Strength 29.6.40	Due to Enemy Action	Not Due to Enemy Action	Total	Destroyed Not on Operations	Total Destroyed	Total Destroyed as percent of Initial Strength (%)
Close Recce	345	68	7	75	11	86	25%
Long-Range Recce	321	115	32	147	11	158	49
Single-Engine Fighters	1,369	567	145	712	63	775	57
Twin-Engine Fighters	367	304	25	329	16	345	94
Bomber	1,758	862	180	1,042	100	1,142	65
Dive Bomber	417	148	34	182	28	210	50
Transport	531	191	19	210	18	228	43
Coastal	241	58	45	103	17	120	50
Total	5,349	2,313	487	2,800	264	3,064	57%

Source: Based on the figures in AHB, Translation VII/83, "German Aircraft Losses, September 1939–December 1940."

was so radically different from their experience that they never properly grasped the issues. This was particularly so, since they had wasted so many assets in the waiting period of July and early August. When the Luftwaffe began its major effort in mid-August, it was already too late. British production and sage leadership were enough to keep Fighter Command in the struggle through to the period of bad weather. It is sobering to note, however, that Fighter Command's pilot losses in August and September were both worse than the Luftwaffe's worst month in the January–May 1944 air battles over Germany—air battles that finally broke the Luftwaffe's back and irrevocably won air superiority over the continent for Allied air forces.[132]

There has been a condescending tendency among Anglo-American commentators on the Battle of Britain to point to the Luftwaffe's "extraordinary" mistakes. It is worth noting, however, that neither the RAF nor the American Army Air Forces possessed an air superiority strategy in 1943 in the air battles over Germany, and both paid a fearful price in terms of the lives of their aircrews. In 1944 the appearance of the P–51, almost by accident, enabled the American Army Air Forces in Europe to wage a successful campaign of air superiority. The immense cost of that victory underscores the price of winning and maintaining air superiority over an opponent with the resources and depth to fight an independent air war. In 1940, even the Luftwaffe did not have the resources in aircrew and aircraft to wage such a battle through to victory.

Notes

1. Sir John Slessor, *Airpower and Armies* (London, 1936), p 68.
2. Public Record Office, Air 20/40, Air Staff Memorandum No. 11A, March 1924.
3. For a fuller discussion of the development of air power theories in the interwar period, see Appendix I of Williamson Murray, *Strategy for Defeat, The Luftwaffe, 1933–1944* (Maxwell AFB, Ala., 1983). For other works on the development of prewar air doctrine and airpower theories and their incessant themes that air war would no longer be bound by the principles of war, see Sir Charles Webster and Noble Frankland, *The Strategic Air Offensive Against Germany,* Vol I: *Preparation* (London, 1961); Anthony Verrier, *The Bomber Offensive* (London, 1968); Max Hastings, *Bomber Command* (London, 1979); John Terrain, *The Right of the Line* (London, 1985); Thomas H. Greer, *The Development of Air Doctrine in the Army Air Arms, 1917–1941* (Maxwell AFB, Ala., 1955); Thomas Fabyanic, "A Critique of United States Air War Planning, 1941–1944," St. Louis University dissertation, 1973; and Barry Watts, *Foundation of U.S. Air Doctrine: The Problem of Friction in War* (Maxwell AFB, Ala., 1983).
4. Sir Charles Webster and Noble Frankland, *The Strategic Air Offensive Against Germany,* vol IV, appendix I, Minutes of a Conference Held in The Room of the Chief of the Air Staff, Air Ministry on Jul 19, 1923.
5. For this view see Dennis Richards, *The Royal Air Force, 1939–1945* (London, 1953), p 29; Asher Lee, *The German Air Force* (New York, 1946), pp 16–17; and even Webster and Frankland, *The Strategic Air Offensive Against Germany,* Vol I: *Preparation,* p 125. For the weaknesses in this view, see Williamson Murray, "The Luftwaffe Before the Second World War: A Mission, A Strategy?" in the *Journal of Strategic Studies,* Sept 1981.
6. For the theory of blitzkrieg strategy, see Larry Addington, *The Blitzkrieg Era and the German Staff* (New Brunswick, NJ, 1971); Alan Milward, *The German Economy at War* (London, 1965); Burton Klein, *Germany's Economic Preparations for War* (Cambridge, Mass, 1959); and most recently F. H. Hinsley, *British Intelligence in the Second World War Influence on Strategy and Operations,* vol I (London, 1979). For a strategic analysis of why this theory is largely erroneous, see Williamson Murray, "Force Structure, Blitzkrieg Strategy and Economic Difficulties: Nazi Grand Strategy in the 1930s," *Journal of the Royal United Services Institute,* Apr 1983.
7. For an outstanding discussion of how easily Hitler was able to overthrow the European diplomatic balance of power, see Gerhard Weinberg, *The Foreign Policy of Hitler's Germany, 1933–1936,* vol I (Chicago, 1970).
8. For the relationship between Germany's economic difficulties and her strategic policies, see Williamson Murray, *The Change in the European Balance of Power, 1938–1939: The Path to Ruin* (Princeton, 1984), particularly Chap 1. See also Friedrich Forstmeier and Hans-Erich Volkmann, eds, *Wirtschaft und Rüstung am Vorabend des Zweiten Weltrieges* (Dusseldorf, 1975).
9. For the best current discussion of the German rearmament effort and the general unwillingness to face the strategic, economic, and financial consequences of the rearmament programs, see Wihelm Deist, Manfred Messerschmidt, Hans-Erich Volkmann, and Wolfram

Wette, *Des Deutsche Reich und der Zweite Weltkrieg,* Vol I: *Ursachen und Voraussetzungen der deutschen Kriegspolitik* (Stuttgart, 1979). For an excellent summation of this volume in English, see Wilhelm Deist, *The Wehrmacht and German Rearmament* (London, 1981).

10. Bernard Heimann and Joachim Schunke, "Eine geheime Denkschrift zur Luftkriegkonzeption Hitler-Deutschlands von Mai 1933," *Zeitschrift fur Militärgeschichte* III (1964).

11. For the reappraisal of the Luftwaffe's interest in strategic bombing, see Klaus A. Maier, Horst Rohde, Bernd Stegemann, and Hans Umbreit, *Das Deutsche Reich und der Zweite Weltkrieg,* Vol II: *Die Errichtung der Hegemonie auf dem Europäischen Kontinent* (Stuttgart, 1979); and also Williamson Murray, *Strategy for Defeat, The Luftwaffe, 1933–1945* (Maxwell AFB, 1983), and Murray, "The Luftwaffe before the Second World War: A Mission, A Strategy?" *Journal of Strategic Studies,* Sept 1981.

12. In 1933, Germany had no aircraft fully suitable for employment as a strategic bomber. The Ju–52 was pressed into service as an interim bomber, but the German air leadership had few illusions about its suitability for the mission. See Edward L. Homze, *Arming the Luftwaffe, The Reich Air Ministry and the German Aircraft Industry, 1919–1939* (Lincoln, 1976), chap IX.

13. Homze, *Arming the Luftwaffe,* p 60.

14. Walther Wever, "Vortrag des Generalmajors Wever bei Eröffnung der Luftkriegsakademie und Lufttechnischen Akademie in Berlin-Gatow am 1.November 1935," *Die Luftwaffe* (1936); and *Luftwaffe Direktive* 16, "Luftkreigführung," (Berlin, 1935). Copies of both of these documents were made available to me by Oberstleutnant Klaus Maier of the Militärgeschichtliches Forschungsamt, Freiburg, Federal Republic of Germany.

15. Paragraph 18, "Die "Luftkriegführung." See also paragraph 9.

16. "Vortag des Generalmajors Wever . . . ," p 7.

17. *Ibid.,* p 6, and Paragraph 17, "Die Luftkriegführung."

18. Paragraph 103, "Die Luftkriegführung."

19. Air Historical Branch, Air Ministry, VII Translations: Luftwaffe Strength and Serviceability Statistics, G302694/AR/9/51/50.

20. Given the rapidity of expansion as well as the Germans' own inclinations, they were not able to build an organization that fully integrated the technical and engineering side of the house with the operational world. For a discussion of the defects within the Luftwaffe, see Horst Boog's outstanding article, "Higher Command and Leadership in the German Luftwaffe, 1935-1945," *Air Power and Warfare, Proceedings of the Eighth Military History Symposium, USAF Academy,* ed by Colonel Alfred T. Hurley and Major Robert C. Ehrhart (Washington, 1979) and his ground-breaking book, *Die Deutsche Luftwaffenfuhrung, 1935–1945, Führungsprobleme, Spitzengliederung, Generalstabsausbildung* (Stuttgart, 1982).

21. The extraordinary difficulties that the Germans ran into in that process are discussed in a gloomy memorandum written shortly after the Munich crisis: Der Chef des Nachschubsamts, Nr. 3365/38, g. Kdos., 3.11.38.; Anlage L.7.Nr. 15.222/38, "Erfahrungsbericht uber die Spannungszeit," Milch Collection, Imperial War Museum, Reel 55, Vol 57, p 3270.

22. Karl-Heinz Volker, *Dokumente und Dokumentarfotos zur Geschichte der deutschen Luftwaffe* (Stuttgart, 1968), Doc. #184, p 429.

23. Homze, *Arming the Luftwaffe,* p 172.

24. It is worth noting that close air support did not receive a high priority in the Luftwaffe's allocation of resources. In fact, the tactics and command and control necessary for its implementation were largely developed in Spain by General Wolfram von Richthofen without much enthusiasm from the Air Ministry. Conversation with General Major A.D. Hans W. Asmus, Baden Baden, November 7 and 8, 1980, and letter from General Asmus, February 6, 1981. For more on Spain see "Lehren aus dem Feldzug in Spanien, Einsatz vom Schlachtfliegern," aus einer Studie der 8.Abt. des Generalstabes aus dem Jahre 1944; and Hans Herwig Freiherr von Beust, "Die deutsche Luftwaffe in spanischen Kreig," 2.10.56., p 162, U.S. Air Force Historical Research Center (AFHRC): K113.302.

25. Wever's doctrinal statement "Die Luftkriegführung" made clear that cooperation with the army could be a major role for the Luftwaffe depending on the wartime situation (see particularly paragraph 20). This of course was a very different attitude from that manifested by most other air forces at this time.

26. One of the persistent legends of airpower history is the argument that the Luftwaffe

had no interest in strategic bombing because it possessed no four-engine bombers on the outbreak of the war. In fact the Germans were hard at work attempting to make a suitable four-engine strategic bomber. See in particular Edward Homze's excellent article: "The Luftwaffe's Failure to Develop a Heavy Bomber Before World War II," *Aerospace Historian*, Mar 1977.

27. On the lack of interest in a long-range fighter in the U.S. Army Air Forces, see Thomas A. Fabyanic, "A Critique of United States Air War Planning, 1941–1944," St. Louis University Dissertation (1973) and Bernard Boylan, "The Development of the Long-Range Escort Fighter," unpublished manuscript (Maxwell AFB, 1955), AFHRC. The RAF attitude was quite similar: escort fighters of high performance and range simply could not be developed. See the lecture given by the future vice commander of Bomber Command R. H. N. S. Saundby to the RAF Staff College in May 1937, "Bombing Tactics," Public Record Office (PRO) AIR 5/1132, pp 10–15.

28. Adolf Galland, *The First and the Last* (New York, 1954), p 31.

29. *Ibid.*, p 63.

30. Gerhard Weinberg, *The Foreign Policy of Hitler's Germany* (Chicago, 1970), p 298.

31. Matthew Cooper, *The German Air Force, 1933–1945, An Anatomy of Failure* (New York, 1981), p 59.

32. Derek Wood and Derek Dempster, *The Narrow Margin: The Battle of Britain and the Rise of Air Power, 1930–1940* (New York, 1961), pp 49–50.

33. Air Ministry, *The Rise and Fall of the German Air Force, 1933–1945* (London, 1948), p 14.

34. For a more detailed examination of the military and strategic context within which the great powers were operating in the fall of 1938, see Murray, *The Change in the European Balance of Power, 1938–1939*, chap VII.

35. As in 1939 the French had no intention of carrying out any significant offensive operation against the German frontier. See particularly Gamelin's discussions with the British Chiefs of Staff in PRO CAB 21/595, 26.9.38, "Notes on a Meeting."

36. The after-action reports by the First and Third Air Forces are the basic documents for German air plans against Czechoslovakia. Both underline the *general* unpreparedness of the Luftwaffe for a military campaign against Czechoslovakia. See Bundesarchiv/Militärarchiv (BA.MA) RL7/67, Der Kommandierende General und Befehlshaber der Luftwaffengruppe 1., Ia Nr 197/38, 11.7.38., Betr: "Planstudie 'Grün' 1938"; BA/MA RL 7/164, Der kommandierende General und Befehlshaber de Luftwaffengruppe 3., Ia Nr. 7829/38, 1.12.38." Erfahrungsbericht über die Spannungzeit 1938 'Fall Grün,' Teil III"; and BA/MA RL 7/67, "Planstudie 1938, Hauptteil II, Teil A. Aufmarsch und Kampfanweisung 'Fall Grün,' zur Lw. Gruppenkommando 3., Führungsabteilung, Az Plst 38/Ia op, Nr. 525/38, 20.7.38."

37. "Luftwaffe Strength and Serviceability Tables, August 1938–April 1945," Air Historical Branch, Translation No. VII/107.

38. Chef des Nachsubsamts, Nr. 3365/g. Kdos. 3.11.28., Milch Collection, Imperial War Museum, Reel 55, Vol 57.

39. BA/MA RL 7/164, Der Kommandierende General und Befehlshaber der Luftwaffengruppe 3., Ia Nr. 7829/38, 1.12.38"; "Ehfahrungsbericht über die Spannungzeit 1938 'Fall Grün,' Teil III."

40. BA/MA RL 7/1, Der kommandierende General und Befehlshaber der Luftwaffengruppe 1., Ia Nr. 197/38., 11.7.38 Betr: "Planstudie 'Grün' 1938."

41. BA/MA RL 7/67, "Planstudie 1938, Hauptteil II, Teil A. "Aufmarsch und Kampfanweisung 'Fall Grün,' zur Lw. Gruppenkommando 3., Führungsabteilung, Az Plst 38/Ia op, Nr. 525/38, 20.7.38."

42. For a further examination of the military and strategic factors involved in the 1938 confrontation, see Murray, *The Change in the European Balance of Power, 1938–1939*, chap VII.

43. Alan Bullock, *Hitler: A Study in Tyranny* (New York, 1964), p 499.

44. Serious problems would still show up in the offensive against Poland, particularly in the army. See Williamson Murray, "German Response to Victory in Poland: A Case Study in Professionalism," *Armed Forces and Society*, Winter 1981.

45. Maier, et al., *Das Deutsche Reich und der Zweite Weltkrieg*, vol II, p 97.

46. "The Luftwaffe in Poland," a study produced by the Luftwaffe historical branch (8th Section), 11.7.44., AHB, Translation No. Y 11/33.

47. The Poles would of course show themselves to be outstanding pilots in the air defense of Great Britain in late summer 1940. For the performance of the Poles in the Battle of Britain, see Francis K. Mason, *Battle over Britain* (New York, 1969), pp 207–08.

48. Robert Jackson, *Fighter! The Story of Air Combat, 1936–1945* (New York, 1979), pp 27–28.

49. Air Ministry, *The Rise and Fall of the German Air Force, 1933–1945* (New York, 1983), p 54.

50. Maier, *et al., Das Deutsche Reich und der Zweite Weltkreig*, vol II, p 124.

51. BA/MA, RL 3/1025, Front-Flugzeug-Verluste im September 1939.

52. For the development of these operational concepts before the war, see Air Ministry, *The Rise and Fall of the German Air Force, 1933–1945*, p 48.

53. For a fuller examination of the strategic situation on the outbreak of the war, see Chapter X of Murray, *The Change in the European Balance of Power, 1938–1939.*

54. *Ibid.*, Chapters IX and X.

55. Telford Taylor, *The March of Conquest, The German Victories in Western Europe, 1940* (New York, 1958), pp 117–18.

56. Air Ministry, *The Rise and Fall of the German Air Force*, pp 60–61.

57. For a graphic description of the enormous difficulties under which Allied naval and land forces operated as well as the general strategic handicap resulting from German air superiority, see Martin Gilbert, *Winston Churchill*, vol VI.

58. For those who think that the contemporary world has little need for history, one might note that the contemporary situation in the Gulf states of the Middle East, with relatively ineffective air forces compared to the super powers, invites a similar use of air power: air strikes to soften up the indigenous opposition, airborne units to seize and hold the strategic airfields, and a rapid build up by airlift of both ground forces and ground support forces for air units (admittedly on a grander scale). Once such a force had achieved general air superiority there would be little hope of an effective counterstrike.

59. Taylor, *March of Conquest*, p 184.

60. Air Ministry, *The Rise and Fall of the German Air Force*, p 66.

61. See Table II, for the cost to the German bombers force in the Battle of France.

62. See in particular, Patrice Buffotot and Jacques Ogier, "L'armée de l'air française dans la campagne de France (10 mai–25 juin 1940)," *Revue historique des Armées*, Vol II, No 3, pp 88–117.

63. Major L. F. Ellis, T*he War in France and Flanders, 1939–1940* (London, 1953), p 37.

64. Alistair Horne, *To Lose a Battle, France 1940* (London, 1953), p 37.

65. See the discussion in Galland, *The First and the Last*, pp 2–5, which suggests that the missions that he was involved in during the first two weeks of the campaign were either screening missions to keep Allied aircraft away from German army units or direct free chase missions in which the Bf-109s aggressively sought out Allied aircraft.

66. See my contribution on the development of Luftwaffe close air support in the early war years in the Office of Air Force History's companion volume to this study.

67. Ellis, *The War in France and Flanders*, p 54.

68. "Der Einsatz der deutschen Luftwaffe während der ersten 11 Tage des Frankreichfeldzuges," Auszüge aus dem täglichen Lagemeldungen des Oberbefehlshabers der Luftwaffe, Abl. Ic., AFHRC: K 113.306–3, v 2. The German losses are attributable to a wide variety of causes: Allied antiaircraft artillery as well as fighters contributed to these losses.

69. See Ellis, *The War in France and Flanders*, p 53, for a general discussion of British losses.

70. Horne, *To Lose a Battle*, p 253.

71. Ellis, *The War in France and Flanders*, pp 55–56.

72. *Ibid.*, p 56.

73. *Ibid.*, p 56.

74. "Das Jagdgeschwader 27 des VII Flieger-Korps im Frankreichfeldzug, 1940," Generalmajor A. D. Max Ibel, 25.6.53., BA/MA, RL 10/591.

75. Jackson, *Fighter*, p 42.

76. Testimony of the former chief of German air intelligence Schmid on 18.6.54.,

AFHRC: K 13.306–3, v 3.

77. Ellis, *The War in France and Flanders*, pp 181–82.

78. *Ibid.*, p 184.

79. Einsatz des II. Fliegerkorps bei Dunkirchen am 27.5.40.: Schwerer Tag des II. Fliegerkorps," AFHRC: K 1113.306–3, v 3.

80. Ellis, *The War in France and Flanders*, p 246.

81. Galland, *The First and the Last*, p 7.

82. Heinz Guderian, *Panzer Leader* (New York, 1957), p 75 and Maier, *et al.*, *Das Deutsche Reich und der Zweite Weltkrieg*, vol II, p 294.

83. BA/MA RL 2 III/1025, gen. QU.6. Abt. (III A), "Front-Flugzeugverluste," figures for May 1940.

84. Two recent works have attempted to excuse the French performance in 1940 by arguing that the high command was not fully responsible due to circumstances beyond its control; see Robert J. Young, *In Command of France, French Policy and Military Planning* (Cambridge, Mass., 1978); and Jeffery Gunsburg, *Divided and Conquered, The French High Command and the Defeat of the West, 1940* (Westport, Conn, 1979). This view has been substantially refuted by the first American to secure full access to the French military documents for the 1920s and 1930s: Robert A. Doughty, "The Evolution of French Army Doctrine, 1919–1939," University of Kansas doctoral dissertation, 1979.

85. Ellis, *The War in France and Flanders*, pp 312–13.

86. BA/MA. RL 2 III/707, Gen. Qu.6.Abt. (I), Ubersicht uber Soll, Istbestand, Einsatzbereitschaft, Verluste und Reserven der fliegenden Verbände. These tables were usually about 5 days behind actual losses. Therefore there is some distortion and in fact the Germans clearly lost more pilots in May than in June (but many of the losses in May were not reported until June). What matters are the trends and the overall implication of those trends. The 15.2% figure suggests a fairly heavy attrition.

87. Murray, *The Change in the European Balance of Power, 1938–1939*, p 273.

88. Telford Taylor, *The Breaking Wave* (New York, 1967), pp 53–54.

89. Chef WFA, 30.6.40., "Die Weiterführung des Krieges gegen England," International Military Tribunal (IMT), *Trial of Major War Criminals (TMWC)*, vol XXVIII, pp 301–03.

90. Jodl diary entry for 20.5.40 in IMT, *TMWC*, vol XXVIII.

91. For aspects of this British failure see particularly chapters II, VI, VIII, IX, X and XI of Murray, *The Change in the European Balance of Power, 1938–1939*.

92. For a terse description of the Royal Navy's attack on its former ally, see Arthur Marder, *From the Dardanelles to Oran* (London, 1972), chap V.

93. Maier, *et al.*, *Das Deutsche Reich und der Zweite Weltkrieg*, vol II, pp 221–24.

94. Air Ministry, *The Rise and Fall of the German Air Force, 1933–1945*, p 75.

95. Stephen Roskill, *The War at Sea* (London, 1954), pp 248–49.

96. *Ibid.*, p 441.

97. *Ibid.*, pp 252–54.

98. Gilbert, *Winston Churchill*, vol VI, pp 719, 730–31.

99. Chef WFA, 30.6.40, "Die Weiterführung des Kreiges gegen England," IMT, *TMWC*, vol XXVIII, pp 301–03.

100. BA/MA RL 2 II/27, "Allgemeine Weisung für den Kampf der Luftwaffe gegen England," Obdl, Führungstab Ia Nr. 5835/40, 30.6.40.

101. For a translation of Schmid's intelligence estimate, see Mason, *Battle over Britain*, pp 612–13.

102. Richard Overy, *The Air War 1939–1945* (London, 1980), p 33.

103. Mason, *Battle Over Britain*, p 130.

104. Overy, *The Air War*, p 33.

105. *Ibid.*, p 613.

106. *Ibid.*, p 613.

107. For a devastating indictment of the Luftwaffe's intelligence service and for the basic causes of such faulty and careless work, see Boog, *Die Deutsche Luftwaffenführung*, pp 76–124.

108. J. R. M. Butler, *Grand Strategy*, vol II, Sept 1939–June 1941, (London, 1957), p 282.

109. Mason, *Battle over Britain*, p 121.

110. This ratio is based on the figures given in Mason, *Battle over Britain*, p 125, and the

United States Strategic Bombing Survey, *Final Report*, p 277.

111. Based on figures in Butler, *Grand Strategy*, vol II, p 282.

112. Air Ministry, *The Rise and Fall of the German Air Force*, p 79; Basil Collier, *The Defense of the United Kingdom* (London, 1951), p 160; for the Jodl characterization of SEA LION, see Chef WFA, 30.6.40, "Die Weiterführung des Krieges gegen England," IMT, *TMWC*, Vol XXVIII, pp 301–03.

113. BA/MA RL 2 II/30, "Besprechung Reichsmarschall am 21.7.40."

114. BA/MA RL 8/1, Generalkommando I. Fliegerkorps, Abt. Ia Nr. 10260/40, 24.7.40., "Gedanken über die Führung des Luftkrieges gegen England."

115. Collier, *The Defense of the United Kingdom*, pp 167–71.

116. *Ibid.*, pp 166–67.

117. *Ibid.*, p 171.

118. Based on the daily loss tables for July of the RAF and for the Luftwaffe available in Mason, *Battle over Britain*.

119. Quoted in Air Ministry, *The Rise and Fall of the German Air Force*, p 80.

120. Percentages based on the establishment of Fighter Command on August 1 in Mason, *Battle over Britain*, p 203.

121. Mason, *Battle over Britain*, p 237.

122. Collier, *The Defense of the United Kingdom*, p 184.

123. Based on loss tables in Mason, *Battle over Britain*, pp 261–64.

124. Collier, *The Defense of the United Kingdom*, pp 190–91.

125. *Ibid.*, pp 197–98.

126. Air Ministry, *The Rise and Fall of the German Air Force*, p 82.

127. Mason, *Battle over Britain*, pp 284–85, 289.

128. *Ibid.*, p 359.

129. Collier, *Defense of the United Kingdom*, p 236.

130. Mason, *Battle over Britain*, pp 365–69.

131. *Ibid.*, pp 386–95.

132. See Table LIV of Murray, *Luftwaffe*, p 228. The worst month for the Luftwaffe was May 1944, when the Germans lost 25 percent of the fighter pilots on duty at the month's beginning. (Based on calculations from the following documents: BA/MA 2 III/728–731, gen. Qu. 6. Abt (I), Übersicht über Soll, Istbestand, Einsatzbereitschaft, Verluste und Reserven der fliegenden Verbände.)

Bibliographical Essay

Original Sources

Unlike the case with the other German services, virtually all of the Luftwaffe's records were destroyed at the end of World War II. There are some materials available, but they are heavily weighted toward the supply and production side of the Luftwaffe, and few records remain that deal with operational units. Those few records that survived the war were captured by the victorious Anglo-American allies and have been returned to the Germans. They are now at the military archive at Freiburg in the Federal Republic of Germany. Microfilms of a portion of those records are in the National Archives in Washington and at the Imperial War Museum in London. In addition, the records of the team that worked on Luftwaffe histories for the United States Air Force in Karlsruhe in the 1950s are available at both the Militar/Archiv in Freiburg, Federal Republic of Germany and the USAF Historical Research Center at Maxwell Air Force Base, Alabama.

These archival sources can be fleshed out by reference to published documentary sources such as those dealing with the war crimes trials of the Nazi political and military leadership after the war. The most obvious and important is International Military Tribunal, *The Trial of Major War Criminals*. The collection of German diplomatic papers, published both in German and in translation *(Akten zur Deutschen auswärtigen Politik: Documents on German Foreign Policy)* contains many important military documents. On the *Luftwaffe*, Karl-Heinz Volker, *Dokumente und Dokumentarfotos zur Geschichte der Deutschen Luftwaffe* (Stuttgart: Deutsche Verlags, 1968) contains many important documents on the prewar developments of the German air force. On the overall conduct of German strategy and operations, see H. R. Trevor Roper, *Blitzkrieg to Defeat: Hitler's War Directives* (New York: Holt, Rinehart and Winston, 1965); Franz Halder, *Kriegstagebuch*, ed by Hans Adolf Jacobsen (Stuttgart; Deutsche Verlags, 1964). The statistical materials on German production are contained in the United States Strategic Bombing Survey, *The Effects of Strategic Bombing on the German War Economy* (Washington: Government Printing Office, 1945), and in Sir Charles Webster and Noble Frankland, *The Strategic Air Offensive Against Germany,* vol IV (London: HMSO, 1961) are also useful.

Memoir Sources

As with the other German military services, an extensive autobiographic collection of works exists on the Luftwaffe—some good, poor, and dreadful. At the highest level, Walter Warlimont's *Inside Hitler's Headquarters* (New York: Praeger, 1964) provides insights on the inner workings of the high command, while Nicholas von Below's *Als Hitlers Adjutant 1937–1945* V. (Mainz: Hase & Koehler, 1980) covers Hitler's working relations with the Luftwaffe. Of the direct war literature, Adolf Galland's *The First and the Last* (New York: Holt, 1954) is by far the best memoir on the fighter force. On the bomber side Werner Baumbach's *The Life and Death of the Luftwaffe* (New York: Coward-McCann, 1960) is the best.

Secondary Sources

The first years of the Second World War have come in for a general reevaluation over the past ten years, and a number of important works have appeared that have substantially added to our knowledge of the Luftwaffe. The first two volumes of the semi-official ongoing history of Germany's part in World War II have particular applicability to this study and have synthesized as well as expanded our knowledge of the 1933–40 period. They are Wilhelm Deist, Manfred Messerschmidt, Hans-Erich Volkmann, and Wolfram Wette, *Das Deutsche Reich und der Zweite Weltkrieg*, Vol. I: *Ursachen und Voraussetzung der deutschen Kriegspolitik* (Stuttgart: Deutsche Verlags, 1979); and Klaus Maier, Horst Rohde, Bernd Stegmann, and Hans Umbreit, *Das Deutsche Reich und der Zweite Weltkrieg*, Vol. II: *Die Errichtung der Hegemonie auf dem Europäischen Kontinent* (Stuttgart: Deutsche Verlags, 1979). Our understanding of the intellectual and organizational framework within which the Luftwaffe was born, organized, and died has been enormously expanded by Horst Boog's *Die Deutsche Luftwaffenführung, 1933–1945, Führungsprobleme, Spitzengliederung, Generalstabsausbildung* (Stuttgart: Deutsche Verlags, 1982). His views in condensed fashion appear in an article in English, "Higher Command and Leadership in the German Luftwaffe, 1935–1945," by Alfred F. Hurley and Robert C. Ehrhart, eds., *Airpower and Warfare, Proceedings of the*

Eighth Military History Symposium, USAF Academy, (Washington: Government Printing Office, 1979). Two recent works on the Luftwaffe from different perspectives have appeared in English and are important sources for their coverage of the early war years: Williamson Murray, *Strategy for Defeat, The Luftwaffe, 1933–1945* (Maxwell AFB: Air University Press, 1983); and Matthew Cooper, *The German Air Force, 1933–1945, An Anatomy of Failure* (New York: Jane's 1981). Richard Overy's *The Air War, 1939–1945* (London: Europa Publications, 1980) represents a significant departure point; while it contains several small errors, it puts the air war into a much larger perspective than is generally true of airpower histories. For a general background on the military, political, and strategic history of the late 1930s, see Williamson Murray, *The Change in the European Balance of Power, 1938–1939* (Princeton: University Press, 1984). On the development of German air doctrine before World War II, see Williamson Murray, "The Luftwaffe before the Second World War: A Mission, A Strategy?" *Journal of Strategic Studies,* September 1981. The most important work on the prewar plans and development of an industrial base is Edward L. Homze's *Arming the Luftwaffe, The Reich Air Ministry and the German Aircraft Industry, 1919–1939* (Lincoln: University of Nebraska Press, 1976). Homze's excellent article "The Luftwaffe's Failure to Develop a Heavy Bomber Before World War II," *Aerospace Historian,* March 1977, makes clear the technological and conceptual failure in the German attempt to design a four-engine bomber.

These are a number of historians whose works are still of considerable importance and have not been entirely dated by newer studies. The best general work on the air conflict during the Second World War is the brilliant and careful examination of Bomber Command's operations: Sir Charles Webster and Noble Frankland, *The Strategic Air Offensive Against Germany,* vols I–III (London: HMSO, 1981). While their story is obviously that of Bomber Command, their discussion of doctrinal, technological, and strategic issues is of enormous importance to any airpower historian. David Irving's *The Rise and Fall of the Luftwaffe, The Life of Field Marshal Erhard Milch* (Boston: Little, Brown and Company, 1973) is overly favorable to its subject but contains interesting points of view on the Luftwaffe. Denis Richards, *The Royal Air Force, 1939–1945* (London: HMSO, 1953) is somewhat dated but still useful. An early in-house study of the Luftwaffe by the RAF's Air Historical Branch, *The Rise and Fall of the German Air Force* (London: HMSO, 1948) has just been issued publicly by the AHB and is most valuable. Cajus Bekker, *Luftwaffe War Diaries* (London: MacDonald and Co., 1968) adds little to our understanding of the subject. Richard Suchenwirth's *Historical Turning Points in the German Air Force War Effort* [USAF Historical Study No. 189] (Maxwell AFB: Air University, USAF Historical Research Center, 1968) contains some interesting information as does that author's *Command and Leadership in the Air Force* [USAF Historical Study, No. 174] (Maxwell AFB: Air University, USAF Historical Research Center, 1969).

There are numerous works on the Luftwaffe's preparations for the coming war. The best of these in German are Karl Heinz Volker, "Die Entwicklung der militärischen Luftfahrt in Deutschland, 1920–1933," in *Beiträge zur Militär-und Kriegsqeschichte,* vol III (Stuttgart: Deutsch Verlags, 1962) and that author's *Die deutsche Luftwaffe, 1933–1939: Aufbau, Führung und Rüstung der Luftwaffe sowie die Entwicklung der deutschen Luftkriegsführung.* For the early development of the Nazi rearmament effort, see Edward W. Bennett's *German Rearmament and the West, 1932–1933* (Princeton: Princeton University Press, 1979). Wilhelm Deist's *The Wehrmacht and German Rearmament* (Toronto: University of Toronto Press, 1981) has an excellent section on the Luftwaffe's place in Germany's preparations for war. On early strategic thinking in the Luftwaffe see particularly: Bernard Heimann and Joachim Scunke, "Eine geheime Denkschrift zur Luftkriegskonzeption Hitler-

Deutschlands vom Mai 1933," *Zeitschrift fur Militärgeschichte,* vol III (1964). Richard Overy's "The German Pre-War Aircraft Production Plans: November 1936–April 1939," *English Historical Review,* 1975, is the best account of that topic.

A number of important works exist that deal with the Luftwaffe's role in the early campaigns of World War II. On the Polish campaign, Robert M. Kennedy's *The German Campaigns in Poland, 1939* (Washington: Government Printing Office, 1956) remains the best account of operations in English. On the western campaigns the most interesting and authoritative in English remains Telford Taylor, *The March of Conquest* (New York: Simon and Schuster, 1958). Alistair Horne's, *To Lose a Battle, France 1940* (London: Little Brown and Company, 1960) is of considerable importance. For obvious reasons these campaigns do not concentrate on the air battle and its significant losses but rather on the course of the decisive land conflict. Patrice Buffotat and Jacques Ogier, "L'armée de l'air française dans la campagne de france (10 Mai–25 Juin 1940)," *Revue historique des Armées,* Vol II, No 3, offers a unique look at the problems that the French air force faced in 1940 as well as its contributions. Maj. L. F. Ellis, *The War in France and Flanders, 1939–1940* (London: HMSO, 1953) contains invaluable information on air operations. On the Battle of Britain, the most authoritative work on the conduct of operations is Francis K. Mason's *Battle over Britain* (London: McWhirter Twins Ltd, 1968). Telford Taylor's *The Breaking Wave* (New York: Simon and Schuster, 1967) is outstanding on the strategic framework within which the battle was fought. The official history by Basil Collier, *The Defense of the United Kingdom* (London: HMSO, 1957) is also important on various aspects of the battle.

Bomb damage in London.

3

The Royal Air Force and the Battle of Britain

Robin Higham

Great Britain approached the Battle of Britain in the summer of 1940 from an entirely different position than did Germany. It was not merely that the British were conscious of being in a markedly inferior position and thus on the defensive, but it was also that they were still developing a grand strategy.[1] Only in 1938 had prewar military expansion begun to reflect the Air Staff's demand for reserves of both machines and manpower so that the Royal Air Force (RAF) could project a real measure of air power. The task was by no means complete when the Second World War opened in September 1939.

Moreover, the road to the battlefield was from 1934 constantly under reconstruction. First, there was the technological revolution, yielding aircraft changes over the next five years from wood, steel, and canvas biplanes to all-metal monoplanes with retractable undercarriages, variable-pitch propellers, and high-octane gasoline engines, as well as enclosed cockpits with radios. Soon radar was introduced. Second, there was the sudden switch in potential enemies for Great Britain, from France back to Germany, with the corresponding need to relocate the RAF from facing south to looking east and rethink operational needs. Third, the division of the Metropolitan Air Force at home into commands took place in 1936, at the same time the number of personnel was being dramatically expanded. However, it was not until 1938 that pilot training was seriously addressed. Fourth, the mobilization of industry and the economy was held in check until after Hitler invaded Austria in the spring of 1938, when business as usual was finally abandoned.

The RAF was directly affected by all these matters in several noteworthy ways. It was extremely short of trained staff officers and intelligence personnel. At the time of Munich in September 1938, the new Fighter Command, which was formed in 1936 and sought a defensive force of fifty squadrons, had in fact only five squadrons of modern all-metal Hurricanes and one of Spitfires, the aircraft with which it would fight the Battle of Britain in the summer of 1940. So desperate was the situation that several squadrons of Blenheim light bombers, which really did not fit into anyone's strategic plan, were refitted as fighters. In the meantime, the view was that Bomber Command would not be effective against Germany until mid-1942 when it would have a sufficient force of the new heavy four-engine bombers ordered in 1936. The RAF knew it was in no condition to fight the Luftwaffe.[2]

All during the period 1934–39 the public emphasis was on the fact that the RAF's first-line strength was approaching parity with Germany's, the idea being that this would act as a deterrent. Consequently, the focus was on producing aeroplanes regardless of type. Political and financial constraints of the depression era dictated the government's course. The British Air Staff remained wedded to the doctrine of bombardment and rejected alternatives that might waste money on projects yielding no immediate benefits. Internal disputes over air defense measures and the multi-place versus single-place fighter aircraft hampered development of a balanced RAF, with the promising Hurricane and Spitfire aircraft only emerging from the drawing boards late in the period.

Britain's situation was further complicated by the alliance with France, which required the dispatch in September 1939 of the British Expeditionary Force (BEF) to the Continent, and the need, therefore, to take its air component from Fighter Command and an Advanced Air Striking Force from Bomber Command. These planes were placed at hazard outside the new RDF (radio direction-finding, as radar was at first called) screen provided by the Chain Home stations, which were slowly being erected to shield the eastern and southern coasts of Great Britain. Combined with Fighter Command's sector-control system of plotting and voice-radio direction of fighters, the radar system gave protection against surprise and the advantage of economy of force in positioning defense forces. In the spring of 1940, the lightning German successes against neutral Norway, Denmark, Holland, and Belgium suddenly presented the British with the likelihood of attacks from far more points of the compass than they had ever suspected in any prewar worst-possible-case analysis. Even more unfortunate for the British was the disaster of May and June 1940 when French pleas for assistance sucked Air Chief Marshal Sir Hugh Dowding's Fighter Command below the safety level, while the upset at Dunkirk forced him to mount long-range patrols over water and at times over hostile territory.[3] Then, the complete collapse of France occurred, extending the string of enemy bases all the way to the far western end of the English Channel. Suddenly, Dowding and Fighter Command had to defend against, in effect, both Germany and France, with an organization that was not even adequate to defend against one.

In ways, however, these adverse circumstances put the RAF in its element. At this stage of the war, the RAF was an immobile, World War I-type air force. The units that it had sent to France possessed little transport of their own and were thus hopelessly at a disadvantage in a mobile war. But in the coming Battle of Britain, the RAF operated as in World War I, from behind an impenetrable barrier, the English Channel (not unlike the trenches of the Western Front), and from home fields. The British further had the advantage in their Fighter Command being led by two men, Air Chief Marshal Sir Hugh Dowding as Air Officer Commanding-in-Chief (AOC-in-C), and Air Vice-Marshal Keith Park as AOC of the critical No. 11 Group, who were both scientifically inclined fighter commanders from the previous war.[4] It was Dowding who had nurtured RDF, and it was Park who as chief of staff to Dowding at Fighter Command had created the sector control system, which enabled ground controllers by voice radio to vector airborne fighters onto enemy formations. This innovation eliminated standing patrols and conserved men and machines.

Given that the Air Staff regarded the RAF as being only about one-third the strength of the Luftwaffe, and in view of the fact that the scale of reserves was expected to be sufficient only for about four weeks, perhaps six, Dowding's whole concern was to conserve and to buy time. He would achieve victory—and thus retain air superiority—by keeping his force in being. That he won the daylight Battle of Britain was because of skill, luck, and German mistakes.

For the RAF, time was on its side. The longer the Germans delayed their onslaught, the stronger became the RAF and the closer came the autumn bad weather, when an invasion could not be launched and sustained. On the one hand, the Air Staff was still moving at a leisurely rate in solving its problems. Therefore, when Winston Churchill became Prime Minister in May, he created the Ministry of Aircraft Production and installed Lord Beaverbrook as czar. The latter did not so much increase production as organize the repair services so that by October they were beginning to return handsome dividends.[5] On the other hand, until March 1941, when an internal British inquiry forced a reappraisal, the Air Ministry completely overestimated the size of the Luftwaffe and the scale of attacks that it could launch to such an extent that the odds appeared about double what they actually were.[6]

On the German side, the Luftwaffe had to pause after the blitzkrieg across the Low Countries and France to re-equip. It had not prepared for a collapse of France occurred, extending the string of enemy bases all the

(*Left*) **Air Chief Marshal Sir Hugh Dowding; Air Vice-Marshal Keith Park** (*below*).

cross-Channel attack and a maritime war, and it had internal arguments that were not resolved when the battle started. Disagreement as to the correct strategy transpired, not only between Reichsmarshall Herman Goering, the Luftwaffe's leader, and his field commanders, but even between General Feldmarschalls Albert Kesselring of *Luftflotte* 3 and Hugo Sperrle of *Luftflotte* 2 and the higher commanders and fighter leaders, such as then Maj. Adolf Galland. Ironically, if the Germans had concentrated on coastal convoys and the ports, they might have brought Britain to her knees since Britain's endurance without imports was only about six weeks. The Germans could have had the advantage in fighter tactics in that their pairs and fingers of four were recently proven battle formations and much more flexible than the RAF's air-show style "vic" of three, which was cumbersome as well as a disadvantage for inexperienced pilots. The Luftwaffe did not have heavy bombers and so entered the battle with mediums intended for blitzkrieg support operations and with dive bombers, which were vulnerable in a hostile environment. This meant that the bombers had to be escorted, and their speed limited the Me–109's time over England to about twenty minutes in the combat area since the German pilots refused to use the leaky, wooden, long-range fuel tanks then available.[7]

It was a hard-fought struggle in which the number of sorties flown, as the charts showed, zoomed astronomically to about 5,000 weekly (versus

Field Marshal Albert Kesselring (*left*) **and Reich Marshal Hermann Goering** (*far right*).

Bundesarchiv-Militrärchiv

1,500 in normal operations), first in the assaults on coastal convoys, then in the attacks on airfields and aircraft factories, and finally in the daylight raids on London. (See Figure 3–1) The two-month struggle subsided as quickly as it arose. But it left behind some mysteries and myths, beginning with the Air Ministry's successful propaganda efforts after the battle and continuing for the next forty-odd years with the failure to ask some basic questions about the victory, including:

1. Was there really a shortage of pilots? If so, why?
2. Was there really a shortage of aircraft? If so, why?
3. What role did salvage, repair, and maintenance play in the battle?
4. Did the Air Staff have a grand strategic plan or was the whole conduct of the defensive battle left to Dowding?
   Why did not the light bombers play much of a role in the battle?
5. What role did luck play?
6. What role did personality play?
7. What part did experience contribute to success?
8. What medical factors were involved?

This chapter approaches the answers to these and other questions by first looking briefly at the battle itself and then by examining various issues which its conduct raises.

The Opening Phase

In the first phase of the battle, from July 7 to August 7, the Luftwaffe concentrated on coastal convoys to draw the RAF into the air. While these attacks were not serious and were soon abandoned, they hurt Fighter Command. It became evident that convoy patrols were wearing for aircrews and consumed too many of the limited hours available to each aircraft before maintenance work was required. Airmen shot down over the water had a poor chance of survival because the RAF at first provided neither individual dinghies nor an air-sea rescue service. (The Germans had both.)

When the battle started, the RAF nominally had fifty-two squadrons in Fighter Command, or two more than originally planned just before the war. (See Figure 3–2) Of these, twenty-nine were equipped with Hurricanes and nineteen with Spitfires, with some considerable variance between aircraft depending upon whether or not they had yet been fitted with the metal, three-bladed, constant-speed propellers or still carried the older two-bladed wooden airscrews. Both British fighters were generally the equal of the Me–109 except that they could not fly inverted or bunt (nose over suddenly) into a sharp dive without temporary fuel starvation. The remaining squadrons were two-seater Defiants and twin-engine Blenheims, which,

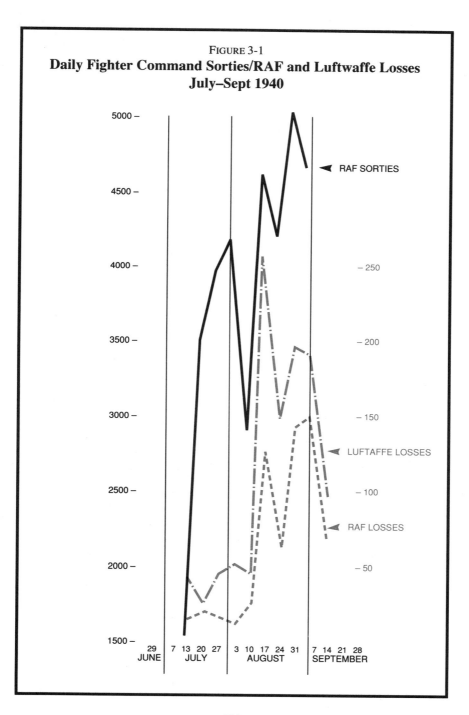

FIGURE 3-1
Daily Fighter Command Sorties/RAF and Luftwaffe Losses
July–Sept 1940

121

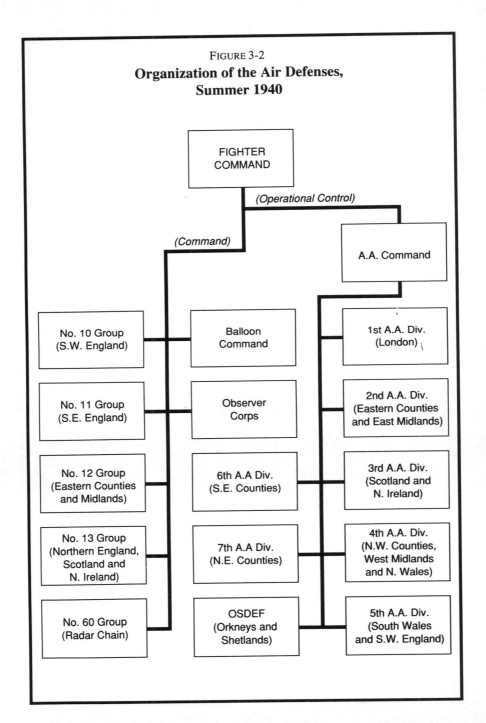

FIGURE 3-2
**Organization of the Air Defenses,
Summer 1940**

because they were no match for the German Me–109, have not been counted in this narrative.[8]

Dowding began the battle with 916 pilots in the Spitfire and Hurricane squadrons. This number rose to 924 on August 1 and 946 a month later. However, in the 3 months of the battle he lost 585, or 64 percent; therefore, to emerge from the fight as he did, he actually used 1,509 pilots. It can be argued that had he had a higher initial establishment, he might have suffered fewer casualties. Not only would more pilots per squadron have meant less combat fatigue, but it would also have insured the availability of more experienced pilots for training and leading newcomers, resulting in fewer novices thrown into combat too soon. Thus it can be argued that with 48 Hurricane and Spitfire squadrons averaging 12 serviceable aircraft each, Dowding should have been provided with an establishment of twice as many pilots as he had aircraft: that is, 1,512, or 588 more than he had on August 1. This would not have been an impossible figure to obtain if the worthless squadrons of Battles in Bomber Command, and Blenheim I biplanes, and possibly Defiants in Fighter Command, had been stripped of their pilots, as will be noted later. Experience, of course was another matter.

The AOC-in-C, Dowding, himself had wartime command experience, but was just over a week away from retirement on July 5 when the Secretary of State for Air, Sir Archibald Sinclair, asked him to stay on for another three months. It was, as Dowding pointed out to Sinclair, the fifth postponement. The repeated delays in granting retirement hardly bred confidence or good relations with the Air Ministry. And indeed, the manner of Dowding's retirement and subsequent treatment remained a subject of controversy. The truth was that no air marshal wished to fight a defensive fighter battle, especially since the Prime Minister had already in June 1940 made it clear publicly that it would be to save civilization.[9]

In July, as the Germans attacked the convoys, the British fighters were ordered to go for the bombers and to avoid melees with the enemy fighters, since only the bombers could do much damage to Great Britain.[10] In truth, the struggle over the sea was more wearing than effective, though the principles were correct on both sides. However, better targets were available if intelligence and tactics had permitted their exploitation. On the English side of the Channel Fighter Command had from sixteen to thirty-two aircraft on each of its forward airfields, while many of the aircraft factories upon which the RAF depended, and especially the Hawker Hurricane and Supermarine Spitfire factories, were well within German bomber range. Yet, these targets initially were ignored even though the Germans had photographed them before the war in clandestine high-altitude PRU (photo-intelligence) sweeps.[11] Conversely, on the German side of the Channel there were some fifty airfields within range, each with some fifty German aircraft packed onto them, against which the RAF could have sent low-level daylight strikes. That the RAF did not undertake such attacks was related to its doctrine, which concentrated on attacks on industrial targets, and on the fact that there was no proper doctrine for the light bombers in No. 2 Group, the Blenheims.[12]

On the other side, the Germans were careless because once the offensive proper started on August 12, they assumed at first that they could destroy the RAF in four days—after all, they had just walked over Poland, Norway, Holland, Belgium, and France. Beyond that there was a fundamental argument between Albert Kesselring, who was basically an Army officer, and Hugo Sperrle, who was a long-time flyer, as to whether or not London was the proper target. Hitler ruled out London until September, and it was finally agreed upon to go for RAF airfields and aircraft factories in order to make the RAF rise and fight, so they could be shot down. (A year later in Russia the Germans got it correct: they attacked at dawn and destroyed 1,200 Soviet aircraft on the ground and eliminated an enemy air force the easy way; however, the Russians did not have either the radar network, or the savvy of a Keith Park, with his World War I-style dawn patrols to guard against just such a surprise.)[13]

All in all, July was a boon to the British. It allowed Dowding to return to the line most of the 12 squadrons that had flown back unfit from France, to make good most of the 296 Hurricanes and 67 Spitfires lost there, and to replace most of the 340 pilots lost or wounded. On June 24 his squadrons had been 20 percent below their normal pilot establishment. In July 432 new Hurricanes and Spitfires and 121 repaired aircraft were added to the inventory. Newly joined pilots arrived at squadrons with 150 hours plus 10 at the new group pools, which were gradually becoming operational training units (OTU). At the OTUs new pilots mastered the Hurricane, the Spitfire, or a high-powered, dual-control trainer, the Miles Master, before joining their squadrons.[14]

The trouble was that, on the one hand, the RAF really needed the new loose tactics that the Germans had learned in the Spanish Civil War of 1936–39 instead of the unwieldy "vic," while on the other hand, the new pilots needed more gunnery practice. And, as Park and Dowding noted in their reports, the RAF also needed heavier guns than the First World War vintage .303s, even though 8 of them were now mounted in the wings of its new aircraft.[15] One other legacy of the 1918 war faced the new pilot. He was still expected largely to be trained in the squadron. However, when his unit got embroiled in the battle, leaders did not have the time to provide proper training, and so the new men were wasted.

As the battle began to unfold in the summer of 1940, the man upon whom the brunt of command fell on the British side was Keith Park, the former New Zealand artillery officer who had been at Gallipoli. As a member of the Royal Flying Corps, Park became a successful fighter pilot on the Western Front during World War I, ending as a 26-year-old squadron leader fully conversant with the wily ways of the German enemy. In addition to a career spent in fighters, he had worked at Bentley Priory as Dowding's chief of staff and fully understood what Dowding wanted. He also had a solid grasp of the operations of the new sector control system based upon radar. Park knew that this high-level radar reached out at 15,000 feet over the enemy coast from Cherbourg to the mouth of the Rhine. But he was also aware that this low-level radar had a range of only 25 miles and suffered from surface clutter in some areas. It was thus quite possible for enemy aircraft to sneak in underneath it and to evade the posts manned by the Royal Observer Corps who were responsible for visual sightings.

Park commanded No. 11 Group with the bulk of his airfields sited closely to the south of London, but with a few to the northeast. To his west was No. 10 Group under the South African Air Vice-Marshal (AVM), Sir Quentin Brand, with whom he had friendly relations, but to the north across the Midlands was No. 12 Group commanded by AVM Trafford Leigh-Mallory, no respector of either Park or Dowding. In the far north was AVM Richard Saul, another New Zealander, guarding Scotland. Owing to the very shortness of the warning time available to Park, being as close to the enemy as he was, his tactics were necessarily different than those of Leigh-Mallory whose headquarters was in the center of England. Dowding himself ultimately came under some criticism for his dispositions, but he could rightfully reply that he was suddenly faced with a totally unforeseen situation after the fall of both Norway and France and that, moreover, the RAF was woefully short of airfields. In 1934 the fighting area, as it was then called, occupied seven of the fifty-two airfields in the service, and they

Air Vice-Marshal Trafford Leigh-Mallory, Commander of No. 12 group.

were all grouped close to London. Although a building program had been undertaken, each new airfield took about three and one-half years to construct. Dowding's dispositions stemmed from both the paucity of fields available and the priority given to Bomber Command for many of them.

The Great German Offensive

For a variety of reasons, including bad weather, the Germans did not open their great offensive until August 13—*Adler Tag* (Eagle Day). Then they started out correctly. They breached the British radar defenses with attacks on a number of stations that were not only clearly sited, but also, as a result of hasty construction, had all their valuable hutments vulnerably clustered below their highly visible towers. Ventnor, on the Isle of Wight, was knocked out completely. However, before the Germans realized that they had breached the wall, a mobile unit was brought in and the station itself faked being in action.

By August 15th German attacks had destroyed a number of RAF planes, yet, this was in effect a wasted effort since most of the aircraft did not belong to Fighter Command, the prime target. Because of faulty intelligence, the Germans were attacking the wrong airfields. On the 13th, for instance, the Luftwaffe lost forty-six aircraft in destroying thirteen RAF fighters in combat and one on the ground: the other forty-six RAF aircraft destroyed that day were not part of Dowding's command. On the 15th, Goering called a conference of the *Luftflotten* commanders at Karinhall, his home near Berlin, because bad weather was predicted in France. This meeting concluded that the Luftwaffe suffered from the failure of the German bombers and fighters to join up prior to attacking and from poor communications between the two German aircraft types.

From Fighter Command's point of view, for a day in the life of the battle, August 15 can be selected at random. The day started with the pursuit of scattered German intruders first tracked on radar by the Observer Corps, and then in one case spotted among low clouds by Spitfires, which took 8,000 rounds to shoot down a Dornier floatplane. A Ju–88 was chased and lost in the same south-coast area, while another was driven off by anti-aircraft artillery fire over the Thames estuary. By 10 o'clock in the morning the plotting tables were clear, and all Chain Home radar stations were back on the air (six had been down for repair). As the skies now began to show evidence of clearing, one squadron of fighters in each sector was moved forward to No. 11 Group's satellite fields and one section in each brought to readiness. On the German side of the Channel, in spite of the absence of the five top leaders at Karinhall, the Chief of Staff of *Fliegerkorps* II, Paul Diechmann, ignoring the radar stations, prepared to launch a massive

126

assault against Fighter Command airfields. At mid-morning No. 11 Group had four Hurricane squadrons on patrol and one refueling. Seven Hurricane and Spitfire squadrons were "available," two were changing station, and two were released for the morning.

As massive raids began to build up on the plotting tables, controllers waited to see what direction they would take. Fortunately one of the more experienced controllers had just scrambled two squadrons that picked up a dive-bomber attack on their own airfield, only to be attacked by the German top cover. In the melee that followed, the Germans thought they had obliterated the airfield, and the RAF thought it had shot down ten dive bombers, while in fact it had lost four fighters. Damage to the airfield was minimal, though stray bombs knocked out power to radar elsewhere. The Germans lost two Stukas. Meanwhile, another raid, using fragmentation bombs, hit another forward airfield, but again there were no aircraft to destroy. As soon as these raids cleared the coast outbound, the controllers brought their fighters down to refuel and rearm as stray bombs had again knocked out several radar sites, and experience had taught them the necessity of returning aircraft to readiness as quickly as possible. Luckily, Manston was not being used, for it was hit at this time by a low-flying hit-and-run raid by Me–110s adapted for bomb-carrying.

While the south now fell quiet over the lunch hour, in the north *Luftflotte* 5 from Norway tried a feint and a two-pronged attack, but owing to poor navigation it had the effect of placing the defending fighters in exactly the right place at the right time to meet the real attack head-on. Moreover, the Germans, believing that all of Fighter Command was down south because of the intensity of the resistance, were unprepared for the fact that Dowding was doing what he had in the First World War: resting tired squadrons in the north while they rebuilt themselves. Thus, the incoming Germans were met by a squadron of Spitfires and two squadrons of Hurricanes hastily scrambled by the No. 13 Group controller who anticipated a major raid on Edinburgh. German losses were already approaching twenty percent when yet another independent, unescorted German raid came droning in over the coast near Hull only to be met by a hastily scrambled squadron of Spitfires and two flights of Hurricanes. It proceeded to attack the Bomber Command station at Driffield, where it did some damage before heading out to sea again, leaving ten destroyed Whitleys for a loss of ten Ju–88s.

At the same time, No. 11 Group plots began to thicken again with bombers taking off from the Low Countries and dog-legging and feinting while fighters from the Cap Gris-Nez area were rising to escort them. And while controllers waited to sort them out, a small force of Me–109s and –110s shot in at low level and put Martlesham Heath out of action for forty-eight hours just after its Hurricanes were airborne for convoy patrols. Three of the fighters vectored against this intrusion were shot down.

127

Now clear that they faced 88 Ju–88s with an escort of 190 fighters, No. 11 Group vectored in 3 airborne squadrons and scrambled 4 more, but they could not break through to the bombers, which even had the audacity to split into 2 streams and attack 2 different targets. Once again the targets struck were heavy bomber production facilities, not Fighter Command bases. Further raids fanned out across southern England and casualties among the defenders rose. But as the enemy bombers arrived in smaller groups with reduced escorts, so the defenders' scores rose, one of the most welcome being the shooting down near Croydon of the leader of the most effective hit-and-run force that had struck Martlesham Heath earlier in the day.

By the time the light began to fade and operations came to their natural conclusion for the day, the Germans had flown over 2,000 sorties, against which Fighter Command had put up 974. And for the effort Fighter Command claimed 182 German aircraft shot down—an understandable exaggeration in the heat of battle—at a cost of 34 RAF fighters. (These figures were later reduced to 50 Luftwaffe planes.) More important were that the Germans had not found any salient weaknesses in the defense, *Luftflotte* 5 was never again committed to a substantial assault on Britain, and the Germans had lost about 50 aircraft in raids against airfields that were largely irrelevant to the defense.

One reason that the Germans failed to do as well as they might have on August 15 was that the Luftwaffe made no attempt to catch the RAF down refueling (as the United States Navy would catch the Japanese carrier aircraft during the Battle of Midway in May 1942). The Germans did have

Junkers Ju–88A destroyed.

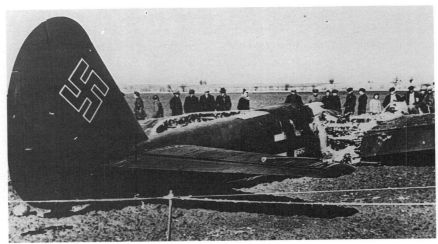

a small force, which engaged in hit-and-run raids using Me–110s and Me–109s as fighter-bombers, but it made very limited sorties. Both sides normally had at least twenty-five percent of their aircraft on the ground "unserviceable," and thus these were static targets in the open or in hangars. The temptation, of course, is to ask why the RAF itself did not try this tactic upon the Germans who were densely massed on Belgian and French airfields. The short answer is, of course, that both Dowding and Park argued that they could not afford to take the risk. However, the RAF could have carried out such attacks using the unemployed Blenheim light bombers, which would have forced the Germans to look to their own security.

On the 15th, the Germans had also undoubtedly discovered that they were no longer in a blitzkrieg situation. Neither the vaunted Messerschmitt 110 nor the Junkers 87 Stuka could fly over England without an escort. At the same time, though the Germans had their own Freya radar, they did not seem to have asked themselves what were radar's strengths and weaknesses. They never fully realized the pivotal role that radar played in the RAF's defense, nor did they ascertain how the RAF fighter-control system worked, though they could listen in to it. If they had analyzed British defenses, they would have destroyed the system.

On the 16th, the Luftwaffe hit the outer ring of Fighter Command airfields, but failed to aim at the center or discern the weakness of sector control stations: the operations rooms were above ground and vulnerable to bombing, as were their essential communications. The vital airfield at Tangmere could have been knocked out, but was not. It was the same the next day. A surprise attack in the afternoon, which eluded radar, was spotted by the Royal Observer Corps (ROC), and alert controllers scrambled the squadrons at Kenley and Biggin Hill just in time to avoid the coordinated high- and low-level bombs that ripped open the operations room at Kenley. However, the Germans did not realize their opportunity at Kenley, and quick work on the ground soon had an alternate center established in town. What Goering did learn from the raid was that he had lost ten Ju–88s in the low-level phase. Consequently, he stopped any more such raids. In part he was misled by his chief intelligence officer, "Beppo" Schmid, and by the claim of his pilots, into thinking that he had about broken the RAF. Perhaps this error was a legacy of the 1914–18 war, when claims were easily verifiable by the infantry. The optimistic reports may have combined in Goering's clouded, drugged mind with his desire to fight the great battle of his Richthofen Circus all over again. In other words, Schmid and Goering were misled by failing to take into account the natural tendency of airmen engaged in combat to provide duplicate accounts of their triumphs. Moreover, the Germans tended to hear what they wanted to believe because they were under pressure to produce results. The trouble was that, as the battle progressed, the British did not seem to have heard the same story and their resistance never crumbled before the Germans gave up.

British Air Defense

On the British side, Park lost control of No. 11 Group on the 18th for two hours, fortunately without drastic consequences, when telephone lines were bombed and strafed. Part of the difficulty was the misuse of the system and an inadequately trained staff, which was recruited straight from civilian life to the units and not given a training program until after the beginning of October 1940.[16]

On the 19th, Park ordered his controllers to keep the battle over land as much as possible, so that any pilots who bailed out could be rescued. He also tried to avoid losses by ordering his fighters not to attack enemy fighters. At this time, Dowding had ordered Leigh-Mallory's No. 12 Group, to the north of No. 11, to patrol over No. 11's airfields when all of the latter's squadrons were committed. This sowed the seeds of future ill will and led immediately to a dispute over the "big wing" concept of mass squadron formations.

Park, in tactical command of operations in the southeastern sector, had very little time to get his squadrons into the air. From the Pas de Calais to the center of London is 90 miles, and at 300 miles per hour that distance could be covered in 18 minutes. At 190 miles per hour it took the bombers 28½ minutes. Me–109s were shackled to the speed of the bombers, which meant that they used one hour's fuel to go to London and return. For all fighters in 1940, the rate of climb fell off above 12,000–15,000 feet. Park's fighters needed 6½ minutes to climb to 15,000 feet and 10 minutes to reach 20,000 feet, plus time to maneuver, if possible, to attack with the sun at their backs. With the delays while radar and ROC information was fed into the filter room and absorbed by the controller, the margin of time was often very narrow. Hurricanes and Spitfires were scrambled with specific roles: the Hurricanes were to wade into the bombers and disrupt them, often doing this by head-on attacks in formation, while Spitfires fended off the top cover of escorting Me–109s.

To make the most of his barely adequate warning time, Park had learned to dispatch his squadrons singly to meet incoming raiders as quickly as possible. Wing Commander Douglas Bader and AVM Leigh-Mallory advocated forming up 3 squadrons to make massive kills. However, out of 32 occasions when "big wings" formed, they found the enemy on a mere 7; only once did they get to the incoming aircraft first, ahead of the other defenders, and at that time they shot down 8 enemy aircraft, not the 57 claimed.[16] In his report of November 7, 1940, Park made very strong comments about the performance of the big wings or "Balbos" (named after

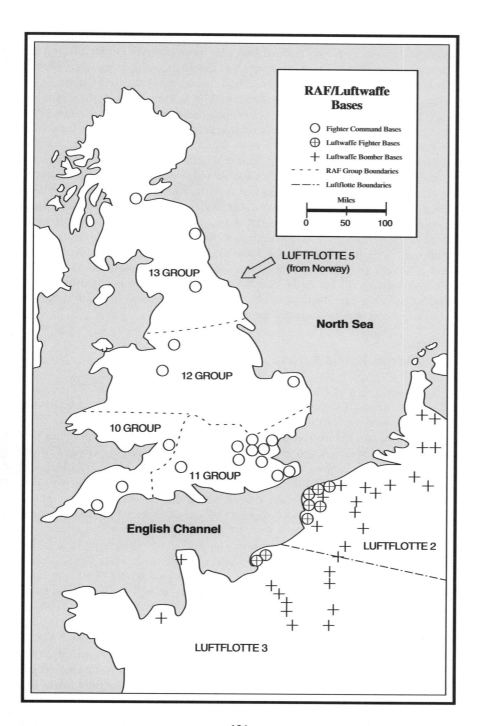

the Italian general who led mass formation flights in the 1930s). He reported that the big wings from Duxford had only shot down 1 enemy aircraft at the same time that his own squadron had destroyed or damaged 211. Moreover, even in October, the "Balbos" had taken an average of 56 minutes to arrive after being called and had remained on station no more than 24 minutes; the total result for 10 such operations had been 1 Me–109 shot down.

Park had every right to speak with asperity. In No. 11 Group, time was of the essence; the clock inexorable. Much farther to the north, Leigh-Mallory with his No. 12 Group in the Midlands had much more time to contemplate his actions. But he also thought with the slow deliberation of an Army Co-Operation Command type to whom time was not as vital. Even his strong supporter, Bader, the legless advocate of the big wing, complained that Leigh-Mallory failed to scramble his squadrons in time to cover it. This was a major cause of discord between Park and Leigh-Mallory. Vincent Orange, in his 1984 biography of Keith Park, has added that a further irritant was that when asked for replacement pilots, Leigh-Mallory "dumped" his duds into No. 11 Group. This was something that Park absolutely could not tolerate. He needed the best he could get. To send the worst was to sentence them to death.[18]

The Tide of Battle Turns

Several days of bad weather finally gave way on August 24 to clear skies and allowed renewed intensive air activity. In the meantime, both sides had used the lull to regroup their thoughts and their forces. The Germans had begun the concentration of their single-seat fighter forces in the Cap Gris-Nez area so as to give them greater endurance over Great Britain itself by basing them on airfields as close as possible to that country. In general, the new phase of the battle that opened on the 24th and lasted until September 6th is viewed as the one in which the Germans tried to smash their way through the British defenses and knock Fighter Command and its support system out of being.

Unfortunately for the Germans, the series of random night attacks made on the 24th on parts of London, while unintended, led to British retaliation on the night of the 25th with the bombing of Berlin. This long and confused clash that lasted some two months played out the way it did for a number of reasons. Clearly it was not merely a numbers game, for there were very human elements in the drama from top to bottom. Both Dowding and Park had an occasion to fight their battle with the Prime Minister sitting at their elbow. They were conscious that Churchill was a knowledgeable person who asked detailed questions, who was absolutely fascinated by war, and who had already on August 20th immortalized the pilots with his words, "Never in the field of human conflict was so much owed by so many to so few."[19] There was the tall slim Park, visiting his stations in a Hurricane while his wife was a cypher officer in his headquarters.[20] There was young Squadron Leader Peter Townsend, leading No. 85 Squadron and during those long hard hours of August 30–31 flying not only four daylight patrols in his Hurricane, but also a two-hour one in the middle of the night.[21] There was Wing Commander Douglas Bader, having the satisfaction of finally getting a big wing off the ground on the 30th to defend No. 11 Group's North Weald airfield. There were all the people on the ground and in the air who were learning a new reporting system to overcome the fact that both radar and the Royal Observer Corps were under-reporting the heights at which the enemy were flying. And there were all those postal and utility engineers who responded to emergencies such as bombing without warning places like Biggin Hill. Further, when the main and the trunk telephone lines were destroyed, a whole new sector control room had be be established on an emergency basis while the aircraft already airborne had to be handed off to nearby Hornchurch to control.

On the other side of the Channel, Adolf Galland and his fighter pilots were also getting increasingly fatigued. On August 20, Hitler, stung by the RAF raid on Berlin, officially opened London as a target. This was to prove a godsend to Fighter Command, now extremely hard-pressed, because the Germans dissipated their efforts further, adding this new target to their attacks on ports and nonessential airfields. At the same time, Goering and his advisers were watching the score, the "body count," on the RAF and believed that in their private war of attrition they were winning, having shot down 791 enemy aircraft for a loss of 353 of their own. Actually neither side had an accurate count, and though by September 2 the daily losses were about equal in aircraft, the RAF thought its position the more critical both in reserves of aircraft and trained pilots.

Yet the Germans had failed to win in either the four days they had originally estimated, or in the four weeks of actual combat. The latter was the magic time during which, according to the British Chief of the Air Staff's estimate in spring 1939, the RAF would begin to get its second wind after consuming its first aircraft reserves. New planes were now becoming available from production and newly trained aircrew were arriving from accelerated programs.[22] Fortunately for the RAF, the intra-Luftwaffe argument between Sperrle, who wanted to continue to attack the enemy airfields and Kesselring, who wanted to hit London, was won by the latter. The fateful decision was finally made that the whole weight of the Luftwaffe attack should be switched to London; thus, on Saturday, September 7, Fighter Command's airfields were saved. It was not a moment too soon. The day before, Dowding had finally divided his command into three types: Class A—all in No. 11 Group and those fit to reinforce it; Class B—squadrons in the other three Groups that could be called into No. 11 to replace exhausted squadrons; and Class C—all those with combat experience, but

Above: **RAF Squadron Leader Peter Townsend**; *right:* **Squadron Leader Douglas Bader**; *below:* **Luftwaffe fighter commander, General-major Adolf Galland.**

too weak to fight, and from whom experienced pilots would be drawn to reinforce the other two classes of squadrons.

The level of Hurricanes and Spitfires at maintenance units, produced and wasted by being shot-down or written off on September 7 is shown on Figure 3–3. This only in part supports the conclusions of the Air Historical Branch in February 1945, repeated in a different graphic form in the official history, *The Royal Air Force, 1939–45*. (See Figure 3–4) What is interesting is that production and wastage were about equal and do not account for the dramatic fall in stocks in storage.

No. 11 Group, which did most of the fighting, had only 19 squadrons in early July and only 23 when the battle really began in August. At the end of September, No. 11 had dropped to 20 squadrons. On August 10 the storage units had 160 Hurricanes and 129 Spitfires available for issue to all of Fighter Command, to replace a wastage for the previous week of 64. However, in the next 4 weeks, wastage averaged 240 per week; for the last 2 weeks of the 4-week period, 297 Hurricanes and 209 Spitfires were lost in battle or accident. On September 7 only 86 Hurricanes and 39 Spitfires were immediately available for issue. This period from August 25 to September 7 was the crisis of the battle as far as aircraft supply was concerned. Had the Germans continued their attacks at this time, they would have run Fighter Command out of aircraft.[23]

As it was, the last blow of the old offensive on September 4 almost destroyed Fighter Command. Park scrambled all his planes, but No. 12 Group to the north failed to get fighters over his naked airfields fast enough. What most infuriated Park was that his vital sector-control apparatus was smashed; and everything had to be moved to temporary quarters. He sensed that a switch in German strategy was coming, however, when yet another aircraft factory in his Group area was bombed. He consequently ordered special patrols over the Spitfire works at Southampton and the Hurricane works at Kingston-on-Thames. Also on the 4th, he sent up paired squadrons to take on incoming raids as soon as they reached the coast: the Spitfires were to tackle the escort, while the Hurricanes went for the bombers. Even so, on September 5th, 6 of the 7 sector airfields and 5 advanced landing grounds were seriously damaged. Losses in the last 2 weeks had been 200 more fighters than had been produced, and reserves were at an all-time low of 127. The loss of over 300 pilots in August, many of them "greenhorns," meant a deficit over training of 40. And of the original 1,000 pilots with which Fighter Command had started the war, only about 250 now remained in action.

Not unnaturally, worrisome situations demand consultation, and Park was at Fighter Command Headquarters at Bentley Priory on the evening of the 7th when the Germans made the anticipated switch in targeting and with no feint achieved surprise by flying straight into London. As he climbed his Hurricane away from Northolt in the soft September evening

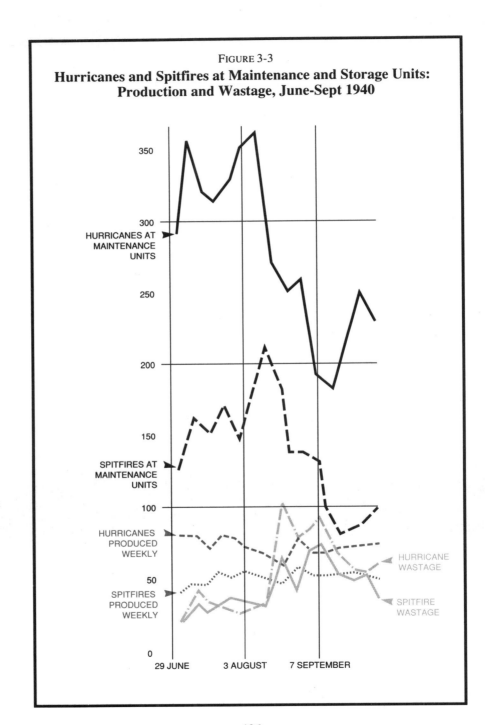

**Hurricanes and Spitfires at Maintenance and Storage Units:
Production and Wastage, June-Sept 1940**

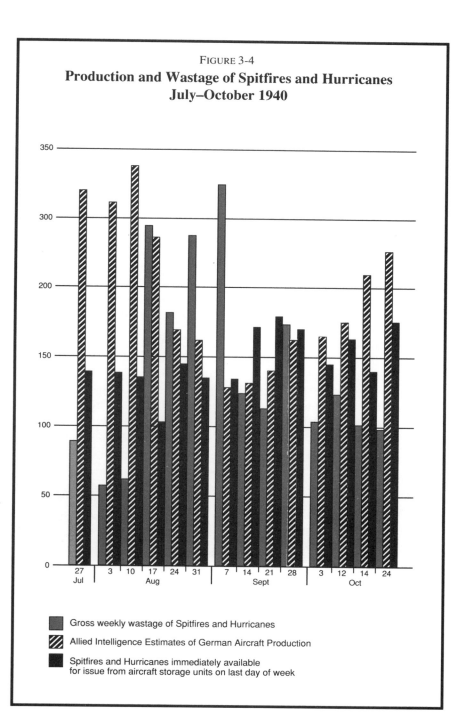

FIGURE 3-4

**Production and Wastage of Spitfires and Hurricanes
July–October 1940**

Gross weekly wastage of Spitfires and Hurricanes

Allied Intelligence Estimates of German Aircraft Production

Spitfires and Hurricanes immediately available
for issue from aircraft storage units on last day of week

light and looked down on the burning capital city, Park knew that Fighter Command was saved, just as Dowding had earlier known that England was saved when it was clear in June that France had collapsed and there would be no more fatal drain of Hurricanes to the Continent. On the other hand, although the battle strategy had changed, the attrition contest between the two fatigued air forces had not.

According to statistics worked out by Williamson Murray from the daily tabulations in Francis K. Mason's 1969 *Battle Over Britain,* the RAF lost 84 pilots in July from all causes, 237 in August, and 264 in September versus the Luftwaffe's 124, 168, and 229 respectively, or in terms of totals, the British lost 585 to the German's 520 fighter pilots. Over 58 percent of the casualties were British. So Dowding lost about 64 percent of his elite force. But like the Spartans at Thermopylae, it was a noble sacrifice with a very small loss of life, even though the British came off worse than their enemy.[24] How many of those casualties were the result of inexperience and lack of training cannot be known, but the Air Ministry itself had to accept the blame for the shortage of aircrew which Dowding endured because of their failure to start an expanded training scheme early enough to anticipate the wastage of intensive war operations.[25]

On Saturday the 7th, the members of the Air Council stood on the roof of the Air Ministry and watched the Germans flying up the Thames, until it became prudent to seek shelter below. It was quite a sight to watch 300 bombers escorted by 600 fighters.[26] Though his bombers set part of the East End afire, Goering underestimated the size of London. The Reichsmarschall perhaps never realized that its metropolitan area was already by then over 40 miles in diameter—the world's largest target. Nor did he know that 60 percent of the bombs would fall in open spaces.[27]

A Spitfire being rearmed.

Spitfires of 610 Squadron.

Given the respite of the shift away from his airfields and the time to reorganize his weary squadrons, Dowding reinforced No. 11 Group with fresher pilots where he could and one new Spitfire squadron. On Sunday the 8th, both sides took it relatively easy, except that in the evening London was hit again in what was to prove the beginning of fifty-seven consecutive nights of raids. From now on, Park's squadrons were briefed to scramble and fight in pairs. Over the next few days the tempo once again began to increase after another brief lull for bad weather on the 10th. On the 11th the Germans began one last attempt to achieve daylight air superiority—mastery of the air—and failed. Churchill in his somewhat overdramatic, but highly successful manner, called it the crux of the war. The attack reached its zenith on Sunday the 15th, Mrs. Park's birthday. When her husband apologized at breakfast for not having a present for her, she said a bag of Germans would do.[28]

For Park the day was further personalized by the arrival of the Prime Minister and his wife at No. 11 Group Headquarters. Down in "the Hole" as the plotting table began to fill with raids, Churchill chomped on a cold cigar, as Park had forbidden him to smoke because the air-conditioning system would not stand it. Park committed all his own twenty squadrons, asked Brand of No. 10 Group to the west for three, and requested three more from Dowding. Finally, the Prime Minister asked about reserves, and Park is said to have replied, "There are none." It may have been a shrewd gesture of defiance by Park, knowing he would have all his planes down, refueled, and rearmed before the Germans could be back again. And Churchill in telling the tale later knew exactly how to make the most of it.[29]

The story soon unfolded that the RAF had shot down 183 enemy aircraft for a loss of 41. After the war, the truth was found to be 56 Germans for 26 British. But, in September 1940, the crux of the matter for Goering was that the Luftwaffe had failed to gain air superiority. His boast had come to nought. Hitler postponed Operation SEA LION indefinitely. There would be no further blitzkrieg in the West, no invasion of Britain.

Recommendations Based on Experience

At the time he left No. 11 Group, after only seven months in command, Keith Park submitted to Dowding a number of important recommendations based on his experiences. Dowding endorsed many of these in forwarding the report to the Under Secretary of State for Air, Harold Balfour, on November 15, 1940. Among the conclusions reached by the two commanders were the following.

The more the enemy bombers were attacked, the more they were surrounded with fighters. It became increasingly difficult to distinguish in the early-warning stages between bombers and fighters. Moreover, as the incoming formations increased their altitudes, No. 11 Group's fighters had to be withdrawn from forward airfields in order to have more time to climb, so as not to be jumped at a disadvantage before they reached altitude. In spite of theory, radar proved inadequate for the higher altitudes, and in early October standing patrols had to be instituted of single, and then paired, Spitfires to provide extra warning time. Park noted that each time the RAF changed its procedures in such ways as these, the enemy's losses increased and No. 11 Group's decreased.[30]

Other apparently mundane arrangements were also important. After the bombing of the airfields, the aircraft were dispersed, but neither additional motor vehicles nor telephones were supplied quickly enough to handle the resulting decentralization. Another result of the increasing intensity of operations was the need to abandon the old system of training new pilots in squadrons. Squadrons in quiet sectors had to be combed for experienced pilots, and these people received no rest.

Perhaps the most important development for the future of RAF fighters lay in the adoption of the finger-four formation and the shift to a squadron organization of three flights of four machines. Park concluded that what was needed was a 400 mile-per-hour aircraft with 4 cannon and a service ceiling of 40,000 feet, and squadrons commanded by men under 24 years of age, as older men were less successful at withstanding the exhausting pressure. He recommended better training in defensive tactics, in flying formation through clouds, in gaining height in the presence of the enemy, and the like, as well as reduced continuous service time.

Dowding, who maintained that the Battle of Britain lasted through the fighter-bomber phase in October, concluded, among other things, that the fighter's primary duty was to shoot down bombers. Since the bombers could not rise above 43,000 feet because of the thinness of the air, only a few fighters, provided with exhaust-driven turbo-superchargers to achieve that height or more, were needed. Fighter Command suffered badly when enemy planes began to operate at such high altitudes that standing patrols were required in order for the RAF machines to get up high enough to meet them. If pilots were to be effective, the very high-altitude work required more attention than heretofore to the cockpit environment. The problem was that drafts from sloppily fitting canopies, lack of seals and insulation as well as the absence of electrically heated gloves, suits, and boots were all matters that became urgent as heights increased and winter arrived. (Some of these were things that had been known and ignored since the First World War. Others were a consequence of the rapid strides taken by the new technology, since modern aircraft had reached the squadrons starting only in the summer of 1938.) Another example of the problem was the major handicap caused by the lack of VHF (very high frequency) radio sets fitted in Fighter Command aircraft during the battle. The switch from conventional sets had started a year before, but slow production had created shortages, and thus only limited frequencies were available. As a result, transmissions could be both garbled or, as happened to the Poles on September 6, intercepted and false orders given.[31]

Dowding was not convinced that a new organization of squadrons into pairs and fours instead of flights of three aircraft was desirable, in part because this would disrupt long-established accommodations. It seems that his mind at times bogged down in tradition just as much as did others. On gunnery, he believed that harmonizing the guns at 250 yards worked best. Dowding thought the armament of the RAF was not one of its strongest points: rather than relying on the Army, the RAF should produce its own armament. Thus, it would neither be shackled to using the .303-inch machine-gun because there was plenty of ammunition for it nor would it be saddled with 20-mm guns that did not work in the air, both of which had been frustrations during the battle.

The political, as much as the military, aftermath of the victory must not be overlooked, for human nature was involved. Dowding and Park had shown that a defensive battle could be won, and they had become popular heroes as had the young flyers of Fighter Command. But when the Air Ministry published in the spring of 1941 what proved to be one of the first million-copy best-selling paperbacks in the world, it never mentioned any of the commanders by name. After reading *The Battle of Britain*, Churchill told the Air Ministry that it was admirable, but he protested to the Secretary of State for Air, his former adjutant in France in World War I, that the "jealousies and cliquism which have led to committing this offence are a discredit to the Air Ministry. . . [as if] the Admiralty had told the tale of Trafalgar and left Lord Nelson out of it!"[32]

141

Suffice it to say that the reason for these harsh words from the Prime Minister was not only the above, but also the fact that Dowding had been quickly relieved and sent on a mission to the United States. He then had to be recalled as unsuitable and ordered to write his formal report on the battle, which was critiqued and shelved, while he was forbidden to publish his memoirs. He was eventually ennobled, but no statue was ever erected to him in London.[33] Dowding was succeeded by Sholto Douglas, the Deputy Chief of the Air Staff, one of his adversaries during 1940. Park was sent to Training Command and his place taken by Leigh-Mallory at No. 11 Group. Park then held peripheral commands up until 1944 when Leigh-Mallory was killed on his way to India. Park was then sent to replace Leigh-Mallory as Air Officer Commanding-in-Chief under Mountbatten at South-East Asia Command.

Not until a decade after the publication of the official history, Basil Collier's *The Defence of the United Kingdom* in 1957, did the pendulum begin to swing the other way and try to place the roles of Dowding and Park in perspective and peel away the self-righteous airs that covered some of the key memoirs. Moreover, not until the 1980s, some forty-five years after the battle, have historians begun to consider whether the RAF as a whole played the role it should have in maintaining air superiority over the British Isles.

Historical Assessment

The battle over Britain in the summer of 1940 was the second time that the RAF had fought over its home bases. The patterns in World War II evolved more rapidly and the technology was more sophisticated than in World War I, yet they were also similar. Moreover, the earlier conflict was still recent enough that senior commanders had firsthand experience in it, and they were well aware of the importance of their own historical past.

The great changes associated with the technological revolution in aviation and the beginnings of the electronic age actually slowed the rate of change to new equipment, compared to that in 1914–18; by 1940, changes would not be ushered in and out in six-month cycles, as they had been earlier. A new fighter design now required up to four years. But technological development gave the defense new eyes and hands-on controls. What has been called the greatest air battle in history to that date was fought at a time of great transition by an elite coterie of fighter pilots personified as heroes in their beautiful, photogenic, elliptical-winged Spitfires, all of which has helped create a mythical aura about this first electronic conflict.

When Dowding penned his own secret report after the battle, he raised a number of technical points. He could not, as the AOC-in-C, Fighter Command, deal with the matter of grand strategy or even of RAF strategy. The result was that both he and the Air Staff focused, as have writers since, on shortages of pilot replacements, anti-aircraft weapons and personnel, repair parties for airfields, and ground troops to guard those aerodromes. A few of these factors require some explanation before an attempt is made to consider the even more important question of the relationship of grand strategy to air superiority in the summer of 1940.[34]

Pilot and Aircraft Resources

With all the concentration on the operational side of the Battle of Britain, little attention had been paid to the numerical factors which might have led on the one hand to the defeat of Fighter Command and on the other to an earlier stonewalling of the Germans.

Dowding's tactics were limited by the fact that he started the battle with squadrons that were not yet on a full footing in pilots, fitters and riggers, machines, and supplies. More than this, Churchill and the Battle of France had dangerously siphoned off his strength. Further, the RAF's lack of a grand strategy and of a Commander in Chief meant that resources were never properly allocated to fight the battle at hand rather than some mythical struggle in the future.

By the Air Staff's own calculations in 1937–38, a 16-aircraft fighter squadron should have had immediate reserves of 2 aircraft in the squadron and another 10 in maintenance for a total of 28, while the stored reserve in addition to that was to stand at 3 times that figure or 84 more.[34] Ideally, each of Dowding's 50 fighter squadrons should have been composed of 112 aircraft for a grand total of 5,600. When that calculation was made the Air Ministry had not yet come to grips with the durabilty, repairability, cost, and wartime salvage realities of modern aircraft, for in 1938 there was not a single repair depot in the RAF.

In 1934 the RAF began to address the pilot problem by forming the first 8 of the Royal Auxiliary Air Force squadrons and retaining the short-service personnel* in the service. But the latter action only aggravated the situation as it dried up the flow into the reserves. As a result, the RAF Volunteer Reserve (RAFVR) was started. However, as the Secretary of State for Air pointed out after Munich in a memorandum of October 25, 1938, by early 1940 the RAF would no longer be able to expand the number

---

*Short-service personnel gave five years' active service and then spent time in the Reserves.

of squadrons because of a shortage of aircrew. Sir Kingsley Wood decreed that the first call for new aircrew had to go for fighter pilots. By the outbreak of the war in September 1939, the RAFVR had produced 2,500 new pilots, but most were not fully trained and the slow pace of the Phoney War did not help accelerate the completion of their readiness; nor did one of the worst winters in European history.[36] Yet SD. 98, the secret *Table of Wastage,* which Dowding was expected to use for planning purposes, suggested that erosion would be at the rate of 15 per- cent per month for all RAF pilots and 3.5 percent per month of war establishment (or prescribed war strength which was never clearly defined down to 1939). In single-seater day fighters, Dowding could expect his 55 squadrons to fly 300 sorties a month, to lose 1,650 aircraft in 6 months or 275 a month, of which half (138) would be repairable. In addition, 1,073 pilots, 179 per month, could be expected to be killed, captured, injured, or unaccounted for.

One problem in assessing the pilot shortage is that the surviving figures do not tally. This may be explained in part by the fact that until September 1940 there was no Central Statistical Section at the Air Ministry. There seems to have been more pilots, especially NCO pilots, available than were for some time tallied. (Figure 3–5) Moreover, the RAF high command's belief in the bomber offensive constantly, in spite of policy statements and directives to the contrary, saw the impotent heavy bomber arm favored instead of Fighter Command.

In assessing the claim of a shortage of pilots, one can start at the battle-line and work backward to show that Fighter Command need not have been short of pilots. At the beginning of the battle, there were 1,200 pilots in Fighter Command. On July 1 there were 916 on duty in the Hurricane and Spitfire squadrons, 924 on August 1, and 946 on September 1. Losses in this period were 332 killed and 248 wounded on operations, and 150 killed and 181 wounded in accidents and air raids, for a total of 911.[37] In addition, a number of pilots were posted as instructors and others were sent overseas. By September 7, according to a later Air Historical Branch study, Fighter Command considered itself 201 below authorized strength, and many of those in the squadrons were inadequately trained. The average squadron was down, then, to 17 or 18 instead of 20 to 24 fully trained pilots.

There were several ways in which Dowding might have increased his supply of fighter pilots, but most of these alternatives needed the cooperation of the Air Staff, and some required more forethought than had been given to the matter. Dowding himself could have grounded the miscellaneous squadrons of Blenheims and Defiants and other aircraft that were unusable in the summer of 1940, netting perhaps 180 more pilots for the Hurricanes and Spitfires. Pilots would actually have been safer in single-seat Hurricanes and Spitfires, for all 4 Blenheim Is shot down during the

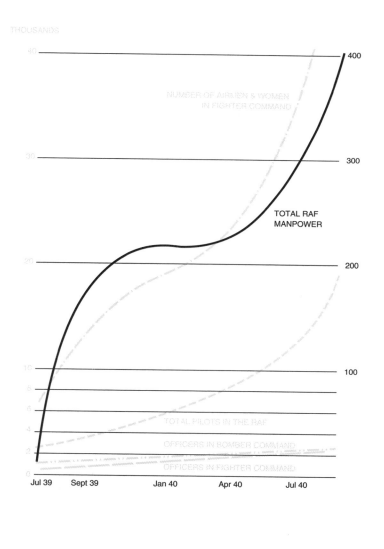

FIGURE 3-5
RAF Manpower

Battle of Britain were destroyed by Hurricanes that mistook them for Ju–88s.[38] Dowding, as well as Park, should have more strongly supported the idea of group pools—the Fighter Operational Training Units, or OTUs—at which new pilots received about 10 hours in modern operational aircraft before being sent to a squadron. Initially, he resisted OTUs because he was convinced, as was Park, that pilots should be trained in operational squadrons, a legacy of World War I. However, when the campaign broke out in France the squadrons were too busy and the casualties too great for them to undertake that work. New pilots posted to them languished for want of instruction or were quickly killed off; either way, the units began a spiral dive. When Dowding eventually accepted the idea of OTUs, he had to find instructors for them and work up a training program. The course lasted a minimum of 6 weeks, though Dowding and his advisers would have preferred more time.

On June 16 the 3 OTUs were plentifully equipped with 53 Hurricanes, 67 Spitfires, and perhaps 30 Miles Master high-speed two-seater trainers. Newly brevetted pilots were getting 15 hours on these, and judging by the author's own experience in March 1945 (a routine 19 hours in 18 days), 3 weeks would have been adequate. Since the serviceability rate at the OTUs was 60 percent, by August 14 (when there were 93 Hurricanes and 58 Spitfires at the 3 OTUs), 91 aircraft a day would have been available. With flight training for 6 hours a day, 7 days a week, the OTUs could have turned out 255 pilots weekly, or just over 1,000 monthly, assuming, of course, adequately trained pilots who only needed hours on fighter-type aircraft and perhaps some gunnery practice.

Sources within the RAF statistical records (available in 1985) differ as to how many pilots the service was producing at this time. One source shows a gain of 1,841 pilots in September 1940 alone.[39] If that is to be believed, there was an adequate supply; it was simply being mismanaged. However, it seems that even if the statistics from the training system, which show a lower annual output of 5,300 pilots in 1940, are accurate, what they indicate is complacency, obstinacy, and lack of foresight.

As early as November 1939, Lt. Col. R. Smith-Barry, the famous developer of the Gosport "patter" instructional system of the two world wars, had suggested that an intensive training system be developed, for he accurately foresaw a shortage of pilots. The May 1940 campaign in France made it painfully obvious that the RAF badly needed far more pilots than the training system, still geared to peacetime thinking, was turning out. The paucity of pilots was in part due to AOC-in-C Charles Portal of Bomber Command, who obtained consent to lengthen the training course by 25 per cent in December 1939; that decision, coupled with a very bad winter, led to an even lower than normal output. By some effort, the subsequent monthly rate of production had been raised to 442 pilots in

May, 533 in June, and 933 in July; and the order was finally given to fly all aircraft as much as possible. There were still difficulties: a shortage of spares, insufficient aircraft at some schools, and even worse, as the Inspector General noted, the use of skilled tradesmen and instructors in airfield defense and routine station duties. The appointment in July 1940 of an air marshal as Air Member for Training on the Air Council finally began to lead to some changes, but by then Goering was about to launch his offensive.

Nor are the above the only dimensions of the problem. Allocation of pilot trainees to bomber or fighter paths was made in such a way that the ratio of pupil enrollment in OTUs in the late summer of 1940 was 3.2:1 against Fighter Command. On October 1 there were 842 pupils at Bomber, Coastal, and Army-Cooperation Command OTUs, compared to only 263 at Fighter Command.[40] At that time, Portal had 19 heavy, 13 medium, and 6 light bomber squadrons—a total of 38—compared to Dowding, who had 52 day and 8 night fighter squadrons. In spite of the policy of defending the island arsenal first and then of launching a bomber offensive, the bomber gang still dominated. The RAF was still putting emphasis on Bomber Command manning despite a directive even from the Secretary of State for Air giving priority to fighter pilots.[41] And at this time a number of Bomber Command's aircraft, such as the Hampden, still only required one pilot. The vital center of the struggle was Fighter Command. The fate of Great Britain hung on the allocation of a few hundred men, but as in the First World War, internal politics interfered with beating the enemy.

That there was a pilot shortage was, then, largely due to parochialism and to the failure to plan ahead. Pilot training might, as Dowding suggested, take a year. It could not, therefore, be adjusted to meet the fluctuations of the war as they occurred. It is hard to explain by any other terms that misallocation of resources—the paucity of pilots alloted to Fighter Command at a time when it was fighting, in Churchill's words, *the* crucial battle to save Western civilization.

Serious as were pilot losses, another consideration, reaching back to the prewar years, was the matter of aircraft production and reserves. In this respect, Dowding was an excellent choice to lead Fighter Command. He was probably the most professional senior officer in the Royal Air Force of the day. The anti-aircraft artillery chief, Gen. Sir Frederick "Tim" Pile, who met with him daily during the Battle of Britain, said that Dowding could talk immense sense about air defense and many other technical matters for hours on end.[42] Yet he faced a constant struggle to acquire what he considered was sufficient aircraft for his command.

In the First World War, the air defense of Great Britain had shown that the defense could master the attack if it could inflict a steady loss on the attackers. Yet from 1918 on, the RAF had doctrinally placed itself into the grand-strategic-deterrent role. Ironically, after gaining its independence in 1917, the RAF was confirmed in the early 1920s as the only service that could defend the United Kingdom from air attack. It had proposed to do this with a force composed primarily of offensive bombers. However, in the long period governed by the Ten-Year Rule (a financial planning dictum that there would be no major war for the next decade), the RAF had ordered no such aircraft, and very few Home Defense fighters either. As a result, when Hitler came to power in 1933 and the existence of the Luftwaffe was publicly announced, Great Britain had neither a long-range deterrent bomber force that could reach Berlin nor the wherewithal to defend the home base. What followed then was a complex of decisions—taken in the face of an apparently strong public movement never to fight again—to develop new aircraft.

When rearmament began in 1934, various types of aircraft were being produced simply to keep a nucleus of firms active and to comply with annual appropriations. Rearmament coincided with the costly technological revolution. Moreover, it was hard for RAF officers rotated in and out of the Air Ministry to come to grips with the need to concentrate on a few types of aircraft for efficient production; this had hardly been the pattern either in the First World War—because of rapidly changing types—or in peacetime—because of the small number of orders. Thus by the time war broke out in 1939 the British aircraft industry was producing some 59 different designs, dissipating efforts, and wasting engines. Some types were already known to be obsolescent, like the Whitley heavy bomber, fitted with 2 Rolls-Royce Merlins; 1,445 of these were simply crated up and stacked on airfields for most of the war.[43] Even when Lord Beaverbrook was appointed the czar of the Ministry of Aircraft Production, manufacture of unusable types continued.

During the summer of 1940, the only aircraft that could be thrown against the German assault with any reasonable effectiveness and chance of survival were Hurricanes and Spitfires. Production of the Defiants, two-seaters fitted with a four-gun turret, and the Blenheims was already dwindling. The excellent Beaufighter was only in the testing stage, and the Whirlwind was as yet untested. The rest of the so-called fighters, which made up the figures for British fighter production, were aircraft such as the Gladiator—a four-gun biplane. To put it bluntly, all "fighter" aircraft manufactured, outside of the Hurricanes and Spitfires, did only two things— they added to the paper figures of numbers of aircraft produced, and they wasted resources of manpower and materiel, especially of the scarce Merlin engines. Such planes as the Whitleys, Defiants, Battle light bombers (so decimated in the earlier Battle of France), and Fulmars for the Fleet Air Arm squandered engines that were better used in single-seat fighters.

The RAF's Order of Battle remained remarkably stable over the period July 1–September 1. The total number of Hurricanes and Spitfires in the

Fighter Command squadrons rose only from 756 to 761 and then fell back to 759. The number of these planes that were serviceable rose from 548 on July 1 to 558 and stayed there, while the number unserviceable actually dropped over the summer from 208 to 201.[44]

Dowding, then, had to fight the Battle of Britain with a force that never exceeded 761 Hurricanes and Spitfires, while facing a Luftwaffe force of 980 fighters. Misinformed by his intelligence services, he thought he was at an even greater disadvantage than was actually the case.[45] While historians may today worry about accurate numbers of aircraft produced, lost, and damaged at the time, and pilots killed or wounded, it is important to remember that commanders are influenced by what they and their staffs believe or perceive to be the best information available. Thus, in the Battle of Britain, Dowding and Park were influenced by State Room nightly returns, which usually showed fewer Hurricanes and Spitfires ready for issue from the repair and storage units than were actually available, an anomaly that was not cleared up until after the war.

Apart from the government's reluctance to spend vast sums of money for rearmament in the immediate prewar years for fear of bankrupting the country, the biggest problem for the RAF, which had quickly begun to garner a large share of the defense budget, was determining the most rational procurement program. Decisions had to be made concerning which types of aircraft were really needed for war, and as in the First World War the supply of engines remained critical.

The government's hesitation was related, too, to its desire not to upset the economy, to maintain a "business as usual" stance during prewar rearmament. This attitude also put a damper on the matter of reserves. There were several alphabetical schemes for aircraft production, because totals varied according not only to the types and quantities ordered but also to the reserves allowed for, and how they were all to be counted.

The delay in coming to grips with the necessity for reserves, instead of pouring everything into frontline aircraft with the hope of deterring the Germans, can be seen in the following statistics that also indicate the way in which the RAF clung to the view that the best defense was a good offense, no matter what. The Air Ministry history of the expansion of the RAF points out that on October 1, 1938, Fighter Command had 29 squadrons with 406 first-line aircraft (of which 238 were obsolete), while on August 1, 1939, it had 36 squadrons with 576 aircraft. However, in neither case did it have any reserves. In contrast, Bomber Command had moved during the same time period from no reserves to 6 weeks reserves, though this had been achieved in the case of the medium [light] Blenheims by simply "rolling up" [folding] some of the squadrons so that instead of 31 there were now only 20. In addition, another 8 Blenheim squadrons had been converted into fighters.[46]

Two other changes of a technical nature were important. Not until the 1936–37 budget estimates did a sum appear for aircraft storage and then it was only £400,000. By 1939–40, £17,300,000 was included, and the total had risen to £32,000,000 as compared to £20,165,000 for the whole RAF estimates in 1934.[47] Not until "Scheme L" of March 1938 was "business as usual" abandoned and the cabinet agreed that the limits of peacetime finances would be removed and outside firms brought into the production picture.[48] Even so, it was only at this late date that Lord Nuffield's immense motor-car manufacturing organization was brought into Spitfire production. It has been reckoned that had the action been taken in 1936, Nuffield's shadow factory would have meant an extra 1,500 Spitfires by the Battle of Britain.[49] In view of the fact that wastage in the First World War had been at the rate of 66 percent per month, with metal aircraft (and with somewhat different bases of calculation), the fairly common suggestion in 1940 was for 225 percent reserves.[50]

On July 1, 1940, RAF Maintenance and Storage Units (MUs) had on hand 410 Hurricanes and Spitfires. With an initial establishment (the number of aircraft deemed essential, plus spares) in the squadrons of 756, the MUs should have had 1,701 to conform to the recommended 225 percent reserves on hand. In other words, they were short 1,291 new fighters, and in July they would receive only 394 from the factories. By August 1 they were 1,246 short, and a month later, 1,319. But if all fighter production had been switched after Munich to Hurricanes and Spitfires (which admittedly for various reasons was not realistic), and assuming that all aircraft were of equal difficulty to produce, the total of new Hurricanes and Spitfires arriving in the MUs in July would have been 1,050 instead of 394. By September 1st, 1,227 instead of 463 would have been added, cutting the gap from 1,319 to 97. The importance of these speculations can be seen in looking at the actual wastage rates.

According to the Air Ministry's figures the wastage rate for July was 128 Hurricanes and Spitfires (or 32 per week, well below new production of 98.5 per week); in August it was 436 (87.2 per week, still below production at 92.6); and in September it was 397 (or 99.25 per week, which was 106.4 percent of the weekly production of 93.25 aircraft).[51] These figures do not, then, lead the reader to expect the dramatic fall in stocks at the Maintenance and Storage Units, which is visible in graphing the figures provided.

Several factors caused this reserve to be drawn down rapidly during the heat of battle and to give the impression that by mid-September the RAF was almost out of spare aircraft: the increase in sizes of squadrons, the shunting aside of damaged aircraft and their replacement with new planes, and the increasing backlog of machines awaiting repair. All of these problems were related to expansion, modernization, and the failure to organize the staff.

In the week ending August 10, just before *Adler Tag,* stocks stood at an all-time high of 574 Hurricanes and Spitfires in various states from ready for immediate issue to awaiting modifications at MUs. In 5 weeks, by September 10, they had dropped to 254, or a drain from stocks that averaged 64 aircraft per week. Two things occurred that account for the drastic reduction. First, in July the decision was made to build up all Hurricane squadrons from an initial establishment of 16 aircraft with 2 reserves, to a level of 20 plus 2, which accounted for 116 machines to 29 squadrons. Second, as fighting intensified, new aircraft were issued from stores because maintenance needs went beyond what units could handle.[52]

It was the practice at the time to repair only bullet holes on the squadron bases; aircraft that were more badly damaged were flown to RAF repair and maintenance units or dismantled and taken by road. Not until after the battle were mobile teams organized to visit the stations and repair aircraft on the spot. The daily equipment reports show an accumulation of aircraft too badly damaged by the standards of the day to be repaired by the squadrons. It is not possible to tell from these records how many of these machines were being reported more than once, on subsequent days, but they indicate clearly that repairs were not keeping up with the demand. In June the daily figure for Hurricanes declared unserviceable ran at about eight, in July at about twelve, and in August at fifty-five; dropping back to thirty-three by the end of the month, it rose again in September to forty-eight and still stood at forty-nine in early October. The pattern for Spitfires was similar but reached into the lower fifties twice in September; it was still at thirty-eight in early October.

The daily equipment records also show that the backlog of machines held at squadron bases but awaiting repairs that would take more than twelve hours was at a low of thirty-five Hurricanes on June 14, rose to a sudden peak of seventy-seven on July 31, and then dropped back slightly to a plateau in the middle sixties until September 15, when it reached seventy-seven; it dropped again to fifty-seven in early October. The smaller number of Spitfire squadrons showed a more erratic rate, varying between the low thirties, with a high of seventy-one on July 21, the forties with a high of fifty-three on August 30, and about forty for the rest of the period.[53]

The Air Ministry's weekly casualty reports provided additional information, with the advantage of indicating whether the loss or damage was caused in action, although they did not indicate the degree of damage.[54] These reports show that the number of Hurricanes and Spitfires lost weekly from all causes totalled 75 in July, 237 in August, and 462 in September. In addition, the numbers damaged and needing to be repaired in July, August, and September, were 50, 133, and 270, respectively.

In the equipment reports, the category designated "struck-off strength" did not necessarily mean that the aircraft was a total loss. In peacetime, it had indeed meant that the squadron could happily get a new machine, and the old one would probably be put on the scrap heap. In wartime, especially after the arrival of the Beaverbrook organization, a machine was more apt to be sent for repairs, although listed as "struck-off"—no longer having to be accounted for by the squadron. By September the struck-off rate was running at around ten percent of the aircraft available in Fighter Command.

During this period, the production of new Hurricanes and Spitfires remained fairly constant: 394 in July, 463 in August, and 373 in September. But the number of repaired Hurricanes and Spitfires being returned to service climbed from 85 in June to 121 in July, 146 in August, and 166 in September. In October, as the pressure of intense fighting dropped off and the civilian repair organization of the Ministry of Aircraft Production (MAP) under Beaverbrook's direction really got underway, supplementing the RAF repair system, the number of repaired and returned machines rose to 255. (In October 1942, the number of Hurricanes and Spitfires returned to service was 815.) If the repair organization had been set up earlier, Dowding would have been under less tension. Until the Ministry of Aircraft Production repair records are located, it will not be possible to find out the fate of all of the aircraft officially struck off. Yet, evidently, many of them were rebuilt at MAP units. In the meantime, where did they go?

Some went to OTUs. But as a production expert confirmed when looking at the graphs, there has to be another explanation.[55] What seems likely is that, as in the case of the pilots, the figures were being kept in separate pigeonholes. The RAF was reporting on the aircraft on its official lists. During the summer, however, "struck off" machines were handed over to the MAP to be repaired. They did not offically come back until returned to No. 41 Group, and so it was only in October that the number of aircraft in storage began to rise satisfactorily. Once again, Dowding and Fighter Command were at a disadvantage, fighting a crucial battle with a less than fully mobilized machine.

As cumulative maintenance needs began to overwhelm the squadrons, fatigue affected the ground crews as well as the pilots. Accidents increased as pressures rose and living conditions proved inadequate.

It may well be that part of the problem of manpower management in 1940 was related to the common administrative failure to appreciate the rapid upward curve of compound growth. (See Table 3–1) Other factors were a shortage of staff officers of all sorts, and the fact that statistics was still a relatively new field. By peacetime standards Fighter Command had been expanded, but the Air Staff did not realize early enough that there were trained pilots and ground crew available, waiting to be allotted to fighting units as needed. Because of this, perhaps one-third of the RAF was unemployed at the end of September 1940.

TABLE 3–1

RAF Manpower

	Officers	NCOs	Total Pilots	Airmen (Fitters & Riggers)	Total RAF Personnel
Jul 31, 1940			2,432		
Jul 1, 1940			1,527		303,280
Aug 1, 1940			—		—
Sept 1, 1940	6,729	10,964	17,693	51,979	395,191
Oct 1, 1940	8,579	12,955	21,534	55,396	457,475

Note: See also Figure 3–4 on page 137.
Source: AIR 20/1966.64819 Report to Cabinet Office, 12/4/41, and AIR 22/312.70833, AIR 8/218.RC2942, and AIR 20/25.2937.

The Germans had the advantage of being on the offensive: they could choose the time and place of their actions. As noted in Samuel Stouffer's *The American Soldier,* under those circumstances fighter pilots reckoned in 1944 that they could fly up to about twenty-eight hours in every seven days without going over the threshold of combat fatigue. However, that was later, in a period of great élan. In 1940 even the German pilots, with their constant worry about fuel shortages and the likelihood of attack, were under increased pressure. And RAF defensive fighter pilots felt an even greater strain, in part because they lived in the midst of their own civilian population.[56]

They spent sixteen hours a day sitting at dispersal on their fields waiting for the telephone to ring or the Tannoy (public address system) to blare. They then had to run fully clothed to their aircraft, climb in, strap in, and with adrenalin pumping, take off and climb at full throttle. On an average they did this twice a day, which altogether totaled about one hundred minutes. And when they were released, there was little if any properly organized recreation. Their billets were on the station, which might be bombed, and they had little time for sleep.

In a sense, the problems of the pilots were the problems of a service that had never considered that it might be bombed on its home airfields. It was not until May 30, 1941, that the decision was made to abandon the peacetime plan for stations and to disperse living quarters. Until then, RAF stations were compactly designed so that all the buildings were within comfortable walking distance of one another. Even when the war started, the first protection provided was revetments for the aircraft; then some slit trenches were constructed; but only gradually were sick bays and other vital buildings sandbagged or provided with blast walls.

Apart from the lack of organized sports and adequate rest, Fighter Command pilots had no definite operational tour. It was not until after the Battle of Britain that a tour was fixed at 200 hours with a 6-month break between tours. Thus, pilots could see their comrades being shot down and count the odds on their own fingers. If they had not been perennial optimists, pilots would have been very depressed. And indeed some were haunted into fatigue and sleeplessness. Misjudgment of personnel requirements by senior men who had been trained in the 1914–18 war was evident in other arrangements; in 1920 it was assumed that no fighting would take place above 20,000 feet, so no work was done on oxygen equipment or on heated clothing. Only after the great victory of September 8 did the public realize what Fighter Command had been going through and swing around to back them unconditionally.[57]

Air Defense Systems

It was Dowding who was responsible for encouraging Henry Tizard and Robert Watson-Watt in the development of radar. As AOC-in-C of Fighter Command from 1936 on, Dowding managed to combine these new tools for air defense into a system.

The word "system" becomes important with the establishment of the command, control, and communications network into which the radar stations and the squadrons themselves had been integrated by Keith Park, as Dowding's prewar chief of staff. His plotting table and filter system were based on his own artillery experience, the targets now being in three rather than two dimensions. Naturally some adjustments were found to be necessary, but Park was always willing to make changes when the test of battle proved his arrangements wanting.

As it was, the system of Chain Home RDF (radar) stations was still being installed when the battle began.[58] At first, all the valuable hutments were grouped directly below the towers instead of being scattered or buried in bombproofs. This same failure to think through the impact of bombing and enemy air action was evident in the placing of sector stations, which were all sited on airfields (natural targets, easy to find by their standard RAF hangars). And communications lines were either laid above ground or sunk in shallow trenches, without duplicate back-up systems. That these things happened can be blamed on a shortage of money (which prevented the dispersed design of airfields until mid-1941), a too busy AOC-in-C and too few staff, the heavenward-glancing minds of airmen, and the British national character, which had already demonstrated its displeasure for digging trenches in Flanders in 1914–18. However, this time, the British lacked the tools to do it quickly, cheaply, and efficiently.[59]

When finished, the radar system provided a radical change. From a radar report of enemy activity plotted on the board in front of him, the controller would order one or more squadrons to scramble for an interception. The squadron would then be guided over R/T (voice radio) by its sector controller, who would, if he had time to maneuver the fighters into the ideal visual position for an attack, try to warn the squadron leader of additional enemies, and listen in to the leader giving orders to his pilots. In 1935, or even 1938, that had been impossible. Radar and sector control had at last penetrated the fog of war. Part of what made the whole system work was that the controllers were nearly all themselves former pilots. And when control was transferred from group to sector stations, the controllers lived among the pilots they directed, a move that allowed greater trust and feedback.

The airfields for Great Britain's air defense had been sited by force of circumstances so that they faced both the German and the French menaces. Politics and the location of important bases and factories had also ensured some spread of airfields throughout the country outside of East Anglia and the southeast and south. These factors combined well with the fact that Hurricanes and Spitfires were still grass-airfield machines; they could still use the established aerodromes and their satellite fields. And, as Dowding noted in his final report, it was the plethora of these airfields which made it hard to knock Fighter Command out on the ground. Yet peacetime parsimony had denied the AOC-in-C funds to build pens for individual fighters. Instead, he had been forced to make use of revetments that held three aircraft, with a corresponding greater danger of blast and splinters from bomb-bursts on the concrete hardstands.

The standard grass airfields had several advantages. They enabled aircraft to take off and land into the wind under most conditions, though some fields were roughly L-shaped. If the base was bombed, there was usually still room for the aircraft to use part of the field. But this was in the days before bulldozers and perforated steel planking, so aerodrome repair was a major task. The standard service approach of laying on a fatigue party to fill craters simply deprived the aircrews of trained maintenance, armament, and wireless airmen at a time when all were desperately needed. It was Churchill who saw that this was nonsense and "suggested" that squads of navvies (laborers) be organized instead. Park himself angered the Air Ministry by "contracting" directly with the Army for help.[60]

On each of Fighter Command's 43 grass airfields were stationed from 1 to 4 fighter squadrons in any mixture of Hurricanes, Spitfires, and Blenheims. Nine to 12 aircraft could take off in almost any direction in line abreast, as long as they could get airborne and clear a 50-foot obstacle with

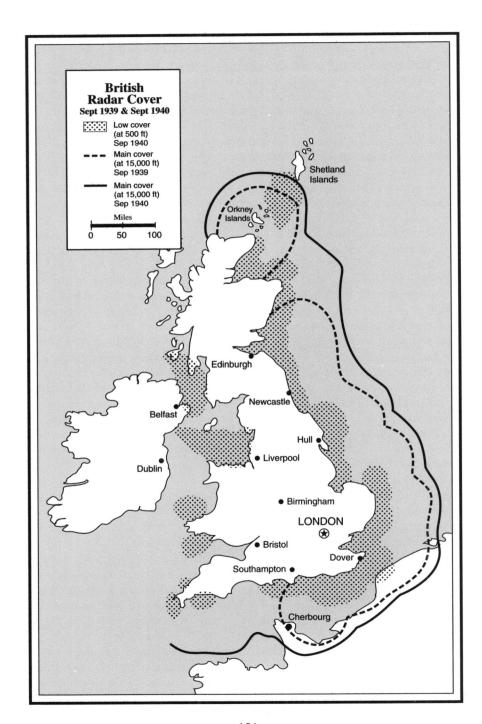

British
Radar Cover
Sept 1939 & Sept 1940

Low cover
(at 500 ft)
Sep 1940

Main cover
(at 15,000 ft)
Sep 1939

Main cover
(at 15,000 ft)
Sep 1940

Miles

0   50   100

Shetland
Islands

Orkney
Islands

Edinburgh

Newcastle

Belfast

Hull

Liverpool

Dublin

Birmingham

LONDON
⊛

Bristol

Dover

Southampton

Cherbourg

156

a run of less than 3,000 feet. For early World War II fighters half the distance was usually more than sufficient. The fully loaded Hawker Hurricane I fitted with a metal propeller weighed 6,600 pounds and had a wing loading of just under 26 pounds per square foot. The Supermarine Spitfire, fitted with the same 1,050-horsepower Merlin engine and metal propeller, was a smaller and lighter aircraft, at 5,784 pounds, with a wing loading of 23.9 pounds per square foot. Both aircraft took about the same 6½ minutes to climb to 15,000 feet, but the Hurricane was about 30 miles an hour slower than the 355-mile-per-hour Spitfire at that altitude. At full throttle, each had an endurance of 55 minutes. If the pilot got into a panic situation and pushed the throttle "through the gate" (broke through a wired-off slot at the upper end of the quadrant), then the engine had to be taken out of the aircraft, stripped, inspected, and perhaps rebuilt, since it was only guaranteed for 3 minutes at that boost.

Aviation lore is replete with ways that international linkages have affected its developments, and ultimately, its history. Having a direct bearing upon success and failure of the RAF in the Battle of Britain was the matter of guns. The Hurricane and the Spitfire were originally designed to specifications that required synchronized guns firing through the propeller arc and mounted in such a way that a pilot, as in the First World War, could clear stoppages from inside the cockpit. But in the course of development, the Birmingham Small Arms Company obtained a license to manufacture the American Colt Browning .303 machinegun, at the same time that RAF studies showed that a fighter pilot would have only two seconds in which to deliver a crippling blow. For a variety of reasons, the British insisted on sticking with .303 ammunition, of which there was an abundant supply. This indicated, then, that an extremely high rate of fire had to be delivered in order to do significant damage within the limited time available. So in both the Hurricane and the Spitfire eight guns became a necessity, and it was decided to mount them in the wings, outside the propeller arc, in order to achieve the highest rate of fire possible. But this solution, which had been developed in the days of wood and fabric-covered aircraft, was fast becoming ineffective because of two factors: the increasing toughness of the new all-metal machines fitted with armorplate and the inaccurate gunnery of wartime combat.

The effect of this revolution in aircraft technology, as Park and Dowding observed in their reports, was that aircraft had to be fitted with guns using .50-caliber bullets or 20-mm shells in order to make a kill in the short time that a vulnerable part of the enemy aircraft or its crew were in the line of fire. Even as the Battle of Britain was in progress, the British were struggling to introduce the 20-mm cannon, copies of which had been in the armament shops for some time before thewar. The early models jammed; in the meantime, difficulties of another sort arose as a shortage, ironically, of Browning .303 guns developed. Thus, in addition to the lack of personnel trained in gunnery, there was a growing weakness in the armament of the fighters themselves that eroded their effectiveness. Both the Hurricane and the Spitfire proved to be adaptable to heavier guns, and the Spitfire proved to be amenable to change throughout the war so that it remained a first-line machine with an armament equal to the tasks given it.[61]

Air Leadership

In September 1938 Prime Minister Neville Chamberlin had been forced to buy time by appeasing Hitler at Munich. He knew that Bomber Command's deterrent force could not reach Berlin and that Fighter Command was not adequately equipped. His decision as much as anything else cost him his position when France fell in May 1940. Chamberlain was succeeded by Winston Churchill, who was a former army officer with combat experience. Churchill had at one time or another been the minister responsible for each of the three services. He also was in charge during the opening phase of the first air Battle of Britain in 1915 and was a member of the War Cabinet during the second air battle in 1917–18. Determined to wage war successfully and energetically, he acted quickly to place his dynamic Canadian friend, Lord Beaverbrook, in charge of a new Ministry of Aircraft Production. For all that, he never fathomed all the problems of the air forces.

RAF leadership was reasonably homogeneous, although Dowding was one of a small group who represented the higher ranks left from twenty years earlier. Almost all the other top leaders had been commanders in 1918—for example, Park, who had been twenty-six at the time, ten years younger than Dowding. There were serious command problems in the RAF which needed to be faced in a wartime expansion.

1. When would Dowding finally retire from the post of AOC-in-C Fighter Command?

2. When would Great Britain, a year into the war, find its RAF high command for the conflict? In the next few months there would be a new Chief of the Air Staff and new AOC-in-C's at Bomber Command, Fighter Command, and in the Middle East.

3. How would the smoldering ill-will between Park and Leigh-Mallory that antedated the Big Wing controversy and concerned loyalty to Dowding be resolved?

4. Given the absence of doctrine in Fighter Command, the lack of an overall aerial strategy in the RAF (still wedded to an impossible deterrent doctrine), and the failure to work out an effective role for Bomber Command aircraft, would a doctrine be found for the light bombers of No. 2 Group?

5. How would the failure of the Chamberlain or Churchill governments

to work out a limit on the forces that could be sent to the Continent, considering those commitments would bring air defenses at home below a minimum level, be resolved?

Dowding's retirement had been postponed a number of times, primarily because of the difficulty of deciding upon a willing and suitable successor at such a critical time. Defense was not a sought-after command in the offensive-minded service. The matter was poorly handled by the Secretaries of State and the Air Ministry bureaucracy, and Dowding was justifiably upset. More than once he was left in doubt to within days of an expected retirement date; this occurred in early July 1940, and it must have been difficult for Dowding to give his full attention to the battle.

The hostility between Park and Leigh-Mallory should have been evident to Dowding, because it had been smoldering since 1938 when Leigh-Mallory was first posted to Fighter Command. Park, very much a gentleman, may have failed to inform Dowding that Leigh-Mallory did not agree with the way the command was run and was determined "to get" Dowding.[62]

The matter of doctrine is also important, but black-and-white statements of doctrine are not so much in the British constitutional manner as they are in the American. And in view of the essential hostility to defense and the lack of a precise statement of RAF offensive doctrine, it is not too surprising that there was no specific document on the conduct of fighter operations other than those issued in World World I. Fighter squadrons had spent a good deal of their time on colonial stations doing imperial policing. When at home they concentrated on fancy flying for the Hendon Air Pageant to keep the RAF in the public eye. Moreover, until the sudden advent of radar and modern fighter aircraft, World War I dogfight dogma would do. Beyond this, while there was a central flying school for instructors, there was no fighter establishment developing and teaching doctrine. All of this was done in the squadrons, and if there was unity in the RAF it was because the small core of officers who led the fighter squadrons knew each other personally.[63]

The grand-strategic-deterrent concept developed from 1918 on was like much else in its day, an untried theory which had never been practiced for lack of equipment. It was in fact ineffective against the blitzkrieg in the West. Thus by the end of June 1940 it was high time to reconsider the role Bomber Command was to play in the war, and certainly the part its light bombers might take.

Role of Bomber Command

It can well be argued that the proper use of Bomber Command during the Battle of Britain should have been in continuous attacks on the Luft-

Left to right: **Sir Charles Portal, Admiral Sir Dudley Pound, and Prime Minister Winston Churchill.**

waffe's airfields in France and the Low countries. Doctrine and lack of training prevented the RAF from using that part of its resources effectively in what could have been a devastating counteroffensive. While it is true that the Germans had their Freya radar, they did not have any better low-altitude coverage nor any better night-fighter defense than did the British. Germany would have had to deploy far more men in an active defensive role, and the wear and tear on their airfields as well as on their aircraft and personnel would have been well worth the cost to the RAF in aircraft shot down by the German defenders. Surprise dawn raids by the twin-engine Blenheim light bombers escorted by their clones, the Blenheim fighters, might also have made the Luftwaffe more edgy. The nearest Bomber Command came to helping, apart from occasional strikes, was attacking the assembly of invasion barges, but these barges would never have been used, anyway, unless the RAF had been defeated. It seems clear now that priority should have been given to knocking out the Luftwaffe, and seizing air superiority.

To achieve this goal, no fighter cover would have been needed. The Blenheim bombers (as shown in 1941) remained reasonably safe even from

Me–109s over enemy territory as long as they kept a tight "vic" of 3 and could range as far afield as Cologne. Moreover, consultation of the wastage tables would have shown that the expected loss rate for light bombers would be 1 aircraft every 11 sorties in the summer or a 9 percent rate. While that was generally not acceptable in the long run, these were desperate times and Blenheims appear to have been safer over the Continent than they were over England. Moreover, the Blenheims had the exceptional serviceability rate of 106 percent, meaning that even their reserve aircraft were ready for operations.

In truth, most of Bomber Command was, in the spring and summer of 1940, in no condition to go to war. The Vice Chief of the Air Staff, Air Marshal Sir Richard Peirse, supported by the Deputy Chief, AVM Sholto Douglas, was opposed to offensive action by the heavy bombers for fear of reprisals by the Germans. And there never had been any role for Bomber Command in trying to prevent air attacks upon the United Kingdom. Other than the deterrent idea, most British thinking had been devoted to what an enemy could do to the UK. Only in September 1938 had the RAF discovered that it was impotent as a deterrent.[64]

When on June 20, 1940, the Air Staff ordered the new AOC-in-C, Bomber Command, Charles Portal, to send his approximately 100 heavy bombers to attack the German aircraft industry, Portal's response was that it would be a waste of time since his crews could not find factories hidden in the woods. He suggested instead that they concentrate on the invasion ports, as these were targets that they might be able to find. His medium bombers, which had been ordered to attack enemy airfields, were now ordered to attack barges. And Churchill complained they could not hit them either![65] However, within a week the Air Staff changed its mind again and switched Bomber Command to more grand-strategic targets. London took the view that it was its job to determine policy, and the AOC's job to find the means to carry it out.

It is quite evident that the Air Staff did not have any practicable doctrine for the employment of their heavy bombers and that the crews were untrained. In Bomber Command and Coastal Command were a number of Blenheim IV squadrons equipped with a fast, light (medium) bomber. In addition to these fourteen squadrons evenly divided between the two Commands, Coastal had as well five squadrons of Hudson twin-engine medium bombers. These aircraft were perfectly capable of penetrating the German defenses in daylight (as they demonstrated as late as August 1941 in an attack on the power plants at Cologne and again in January 1942 on Schipol airfield in Holland). In other words, they were capable of low-level penetration and survival. So why were they not more fully employed in the Battle of Britain? Why was the life-or-death struggle left to a handful of pilots in Fighter Command?

The basic answer is that there was no doctrine for the employment of

Blenheims and Hudsons outside of Coastal Command. At the beginning of the revolutionary changes in aircraft and rearmament in 1934, the Blenheim had been thrust upon the RAF by the news baron, Lord Rothermere, a former Air Minister (1917–18). It had been an embarrassment. No. 2 Bomber Group, equipped with the Blenheims, hardly appears in the official histories, and the name of its AOC has yet to be found in either the Air Force List or in the privately produced history. But the equipment lists do tell a story.

In sharp contrast to the Hurricanes and Spitfires of Fighter Command with their steady 75 percent serviceability rate, the Blenheims of Bomber Command had more than 100 percent serviceability. For instance, on August 1 there were 186 planes out of 176 assigned (including spares) available, on September 15th, 218 out of 208, and on September 27th, 213 out of 208. In other words, these 7 squadrons must have had plenty of maintenance personnel and must have been doing very little flying: the maximum levels of 100 percent of establishment, plus spares, were maintained and available.

By refusing to use the Blenheims, the Air Staff was fighting the Battle of Britain with one hand tied behind its back. It was failing to use concentration, mobility, and surprise, as well as economy of force, to strike the enemy on his own airfields and throw him off balance. There are two explanations for why the RAF never used the Blenheims in this role. First, a pessimistic view persisted of the defeat in France that regarded the use of Blenheims and Battles there as sending lambs to the slaughter. But, as noted below, that was not a dispassionate analysis. Second, and much more basic, was the general RAF dislike of the Blenheim as an aircraft that had been thrust upon it, an embarrassment which interfered with the true role of Bomber Command. As a result, the AOC-in-C of that command had little interest in them and would later in the fall suggest that they were useless in the UK and should be transferred to the Middle East.

The real problem of the Blenheims was that there was a prejudice against them among senior officers; consequently, there was no doctrine for their use as light bombers. At the same time, paucity of theory and imagination caused them to be operated at maximum vulnerability rather than making use of their assets. Brought down from 12,000 feet to the deck, well routed and with the benefit of surprise, and tucked close for defensive purposes, they had the ability to be a useful offensive strike force. Or they could be used as twin-engine fighters on offensive operations. The point is that they were a feasible weapon that did not get a chance until late 1940 because of prejudices against them. What could have been done was demonstrated on August 7 when a squadron of RAF light medium bombers swept in over Haamstede in the Low Countries, catching Jagdgeschwader 54's Me–109s just scrambling and putting the *staffel* out of action for two weeks.[66]

It was not as if the Air Staff did not have access to experience. The AOC of Bomber Command's No. 2 Group, AVM Cuthbert MacLean (like Park, a New Zealander), had drawn lessons from the Battle of France immediately after that experience. He pointed out that while the Blenheims needed fighter cover in clear weather, up to three aircraft could operate with cloud cover against limited targets, and that their best protection against fighters was to fly a low, tight formation. By doing this and not splitting up at the target, No. 2's squadrons often took very low casualties and made raids to the edge of Paris and as far away as Kiel and Cologne.

Starting in June, No. 2 Group aircraft were ordered out singly to attack enemy targets; these were mostly oil refineries and other such targets, and the bombloads were too small to cause much grief. In the long run much more success was achieved with night intruder operations, which were begun on July 17/18 over Caen airfield. In July the Group lost thirty-one aircraft in action, three written off on landing, and four in flying accidents; it was about the same in August, with a total for the two months of twenty-eight officers and eighty-seven NCOs lost.[67]

Yet the bombers continued to be underutilized for airfield bombing. While in contrast the Luftwaffe made excellent use of bad weather for small hit-and-run raids by a very few aircraft. A British "vic" of three Blenheims could have operated favorably under the same circumstances over France and the Low Countries, where there was an average of fifty enemy machines per airfield. In August alone there were at least nine days of low clouds that would have been ideal for hit-and-run raids using cloud cover and map-reading navigation.

Bristol Blenheims of No. 604 Squadron.

As an example of what was possible, on August 16 two Ju–88s got into the circuit at Brize Norton, put their undercarriages down as though going to land, and were evidently mistaken for local aircraft, resulting in the destruction of forty-six British aircraft and the impairment of eleven. Not every raid would have had that sort of success, but in such a desperate struggle the British should have hazarded some losses.[68] In all fairness to Park it must be noted that in October 1940 he wished to start offensive operations, but Dowding said no.[69]

RAF in France

B. H. Liddell Hart, the British military historian who was one of the founders of the concept of armored blitzkrieg, had parted company with Trenchard in the mid-thirties over the question of putting defense of the home base before an offensive strategy. In 1939, he resigned from *The Times* of London to write *The Defence of Britain*. For deserting the establishment and telling the truth he was made the scapegoat for the defeat in France in 1940. Liddell Hart argued that the island arsenal had to be made safe before it could be used. How this was to be done was a puzzle that the powers in London had not solved when the Battle of Britain began.

The Germans had actually accomplished in May 1940 what they had set out to do in March 1918—break through the Allied lines. Now the full impact of having sent the RAF Advanced Air Striking Force to France without enough transport became appallingly clear. In days the force was on its way home, decimated by a loss of 959 aircraft and over 900 aircrew. Those squadrons that belonged to Fighter Command had at once, of course, to be rebuilt. But perhaps as critical was the question of reinforcements to the French.

When the British Expeditionary Force had left for France in Septmber 1939, it had been accompanied by four fighter squadrons with a further two earmarked to go. This had left Dowding with fewer than the minimum fifty-two squadrons, which it had been agreed he should have for Fighter Command. Two more were designated for Norwegian operations, and four were unready for service. When the German attack in the West began on May 10, the Army called for greater support, and the Air Ministry dispatched thirty-two more Hurricanes drawn from various squadrons. But the very next day the French asked for ten more squadrons to help them mount a critical counteroffensive. Dowding forcefully opposed sending any more until he had his full fifty-two squadrons; he was, in fact, unwilling to send *any* of his carefully honed forces to operate in France, where they would have neither the protection of the early-warning radar nor the effectiveness of the sector control system to guide them. In addition, he made it quite clear that given the wastage rate occurring in France, the supply of Hurricanes would soon be exhausted, no matter where their bases were.[70] The War Cabinet sided with Dowding and refused the ten squadrons requested. But the next day, the War Cabinet, believing that a lesser force might stave off the defeat of France, agreed to send eight half-squadrons—another thirty-two aircraft. That afternoon Churchill, then in Paris, asked for six more Hurricane squadrons. For practical reasons, this request was not granted in full. It prompted Dowding to write to the Minister of Defense (Churchill) and to the Air Council, asking for their decision on the minimum force that they believed could defend the United Kingdom if France were defeated. He pointed out that if his forces were reduced below that figure, then Great Britain would be allowing France to drag her down to defeat. On May 19 and 20, Churchill and the Cabinet finally ruled in Dowding's favor: no more fighter squadrons should leave Great Britain. At the same time, the situation in France proved so desperate that the squadrons there were withdrawn to England, leaving only three with the Advanced Air Striking Force.

Role of Intelligence

All of these moves took place only just in time for No. 11 Fighter Group to organize the air cover for the beaches at Dunkirk, where Fighter Command as such got its baptism of fire against major German formations. The British did in fact know a great deal about the Luftwaffe from their pre-war intelligence. However, because of their own orientation toward grand-strategic bombing, the RAF failed to see the Luftwaffe as basically a tactical air force attached to the German army for blitzkrieg purposes. The RAF high command underestimated the Luftwaffe's immediate battlefield effectiveness as well as its lack of long-range hitting power when deprived of the ground army to disrupt an opponent's airfields. Fighter Command had access to low-grade Luftwaffe signals intelligence and could decode ordinary operational signals in pretty short order. However, it did not have access to ULTRA, the intercepted top-secret German coded messages, in anything approaching the magnitude that has been recently imagined.[71] First, many of the German communications went by landline and could not be intercepted. Second, what was passed over the air in ENIGMA codes had to be broken into German and then translated, analyzed, and transmitted. In the summer of 1940 this was still very much a hit-or-miss proposition. While Dowding did get ULTRA as soon as it became available, almost nothing that he received was of immediate use for each day's countermoves, except Goering's signals from Karinhall. Much more important was how he, his staff, and his controllers judged the lessons of the previous days' activities, and how they reacted to what the radar and Observer Corps reports indicated the enemy was preparing to do. Having just been

165

in France and Belgium, the RAF knew where the airfields were, but in mid-1940 it still had a very limited number of aircraft available for photographic reconnaissance work. The development of the unarmed Photographic Reconnaissance Unit (PRU) Spitfires and similar aircraft was only just beginning, but would soon become a vital means of gathering information. In the meantime, the RAF was not as well off as the Germans, who already had begun to cover much of Europe with special high-flying aircraft fitted, ironically, with modified RAF cameras.[72]

Antiaircraft Command

Closely allied with the RAF in the defense of the United Kingdom was Antiaircraft Command, led by Sir Frederick Pile, the only British general to hold the same top operational command throughout the Second World War. Dowding, Pile's close friend and associate, expressed his opinion later that one of the most enduring lessons of the Battle of Britain was that the anti-aircraft organization set up before the war and perfected up until mid-1940 had worked well in partnership with the RAF. Because of the excellent aircraft-recognition training in Anti-Aircraft Command, there were very few incidents of friendly fire on RAF aircraft.

The effectiveness of anti-aircraft fire in daylight demonstrated the effects of experience. In July it took 344 rounds to knock down an enemy aircraft, but in August only 232 were needed. When the Germans started night operations in September and the batteries had to resort to barrages, it took 1,798 rounds per aircraft destroyed.

During the Battle of Britain, special attention was paid to the relationship of gunfire to the activities of the fighters, both in locating enemy aircraft by burst from the guns and in breaking up formations so that the Hurricanes could get among them. A point often overlooked is that it was estimated that ten percent of the aircraft brought down during the course of the struggle were the victims of light antiaircraft machinegun fire. This kind of defense was particularly important when so many attacks by roaming German aircraft took place below the heights at which heavy guns could be brought to bear effectively.[73]

Although the First World War had shown that both ground and air defenses could become effective against enemy raiders, for years after the war they were neglected. It was not until the Munich crisis of September 1938 that the public suddenly became nervous about antiaircraft defense, and the Air Staff agreed to a vast increase in its scale. But merely making the money available did not solve the problem. The Ideal Scheme, drawn up assuming no financial limitations, had envisaged a German attack by 1,700 bombers in March 1938. To defend against this, the scheme called for the number of searchlights to be increased from 2,547 to 4,500, and the gun defense increased to a 16-gun density over sensitive points and 4 guns elsewhere. What was needed were modern 3.7-inch and 4.5-inch heavy guns, and these were just becoming available in mid-1938. In addition, the Air Ministry, which had taken the attitude that the defense of airfields could be adequately accomplished by .303 or perhaps .5-inch machineguns, suddenly decided that it wanted 40-mm Bofors at a time when the Army was competing for them.

It was really the political fall-out resulting from the obvious lack of preparedness of the country that caused the Cabinet early in November 1938 to approve what was virtually the whole of the Ideal Scheme. By the spring of 1939 the War Office was demanding seventy-two-gun densities over vulnerable points. And on July 18, 1939, Pile was appointed to lead Antiaircraft Command, whose headquarters were adjacent to Dowding's Fighter Command headquarters at Stanmore. By the outbreak of hostilities, Pile's command had reached its full scale of seven divisions, though not by any means its full establishment of materiel nor even a fully-trained status. At the end of June 1940 the Antiaircraft Command was stiffened with gunners from the BEF, which was home from France (although they had lost all their guns and equipment). As the battle progressed, the increase in numbers proved to be a great asset, especially in the southeast corner around Dover, where the antiaircraft defenses had to be manned round-the-clock, requiring a full double complement for the guns on a shift basis.

By the end of June 1940 the RAF and Antiaircraft Command were recovering from the losses in France. The campaigns had been too swift and the circumstances were regarded as too unusual to have much impact upon the way the Battle of Britain was fought. What was important was that the top leaders at Stanmore and at Uxbridge were experienced commanders who had both fought in the First World War and who had spent considerable time in the interwar years becoming specialists in their field. What they desperately needed was time.

Neither Fighter Command nor Antiaircraft Command was fully equipped with modern weapons. In terms of the actual numbers of single-seat first-line fighters, the RAF was about equally matched with the Luftwaffe, although it did not think so. Antiaircraft Command was still badly under-equipped, plagued with shortages of guns, electric predictors, and radar. Much of the entire defensive system was highly vulnerable, having been hastily laid down under peacetime budgetary restrictions.

Conclusions

Although the Battle of Britain has been billed as the first great air battle in history, the leaders who fought it, the bases they used, and patterns they followed were closely tied to the experiences of the First World War, which had ended twenty-two years earlier. The legacy was the need for continuous planning and preparation, and especially of staff training. One important reason why the RAF did not know what it, let alone the Germans, really possessed in the way of people and equipment was that it had too few trained people to keep track of vital plans and programs as the rapid expansion took place. Even as good a mind as Dowding's, lost track of actual pilot and other resources available by September of 1940.

Winning air superiority is a complex business, which includes the recruitment and training of all personnel, from pilots to bomb-crater fillers; the design, development, and production of aircraft, as well as their issue, maintenance, repair, and replacement; and the provision of necessary manpower during a desperate battle. The RAF in mid-1940 was still on the rearmament slope of the production wave and would not be fully ready for war until 1942.[74] Squadrons were undermanned, with too few pilots and not enough ground crew, and the stations from which they operated had inadequate troops for manning the antiaircraft defenses or repairing damage.

Just as important was the failure of those at the top of the chain of command, and of their deputies, to understand the new fighter-control system and to recognize the shortcomings of the people using it, as well as its technical weaknesses. For example, Keith Park, aware from his experience in 1918 that headquarters would demand information promptly, had installed teletypes. Impatient aides, using the telephones instead of the teletypes, interfered with his command, control, and communications system just as much as did the enemy. The vulnerability of sector stations and communication lines, sited on airfields and above ground, were partly the side effects of peacetime parsimony, but partly the result of inaccurate foresight. Planners do have to consider that worst possible cases may be still more severe than they have envisaged.

Since a commander's success depends upon the quality of both his armed forces and his intelligence, he should be concerned that both elements are well trained. One of the major British weaknesses was that intelligence officers were recruited straight from civilian life and sent untrained to squadrons, where they were tolerated rather than welcomed. Not unexpectedly, as form-fillers instead of informed interviewers, many did not glean as much information as they should have. The Battle of Britain took place at a time of technological transition, and itself demanded the adoption of new procedures. As is usual, the older commanders took to the changes less easily than those who had to run the new systems. Part of the difficulty came, no doubt, from the fact that the RAF had senior officers who did not fly, and thus there was no way of giving them "hands on" experience with the evolving systems and an understanding of the acuteness of time.

Some of the attitudes necessary for command in a defensive battle become sharply evident in the study of the summer of 1940. Park correctly saw that his objective was to *prevent the enemy from bombing,* since his fighter aircraft lacked the range or the power to do a great deal of other kinds of damage. From his forward position between the enemy and British airfields, aircraft factories, and other vital targets, Park had to play a spoiling game, just as Dowding, well aware of his marked numerical inferiority, had no other choice but to fight a battle in which victory would be survival. At this stage of the war it was nonsense to talk of the RAF destroying the Luftwaffe. The British concern was first and foremost to survive to fight again another day under more favorable conditions. In these circumstances, then, Park used classic techniques linked with a new communication system. Responding to short warning times, he worked squadrons in pairs at the most. (The evidence from the Battle of Britain would seem to support Park's view that big wings were successful *only when* they had time to form up, but that they were also unwieldly). His pilots were not to concern themselves with high scores, but with survival, and the evidence shows that losses dropped as hours flown rose—at least until pilots reached the point of exhaustion. More and better training would have produced significant rewards for Fighter Command.

There were certainly other points to be considered. At least one might be posed as an ethical question for staff officers: Park's dilemma when Leigh-Mallory proved uncooperative and critical of Dowding. The failure of a tired and overworked AOC-in-C to deal with a personality clash between his subordinates reminds us that the greatest enemy is not always outside the gates. Another point that comes across clearly is that the Air Staff failed to see themselves as responsible for making grand strategy. The Air Staff apparently never worked out an overall grand strategy for the worst possible case, such as the total isolation of the United Kingdom that did actually occur in the summer of 1940, and how the resources should be allocated to deal with that scenario. Partly this was a legacy of the pre-radar maneuvers leaving the dictum that the bomber will always get through. In part it was a blindness caused by specialization into different flying missions, strengthened from 1936 when the RAF was compartment-alized into commands. Then Dowding and Fighter Command had the job of defending the United Kingdom, and the task was not considered to have an offensive component (except in terms of a bomber offensive, which even the AOC-in-C of Bomber Command said would not work). As a result, the Blenheim IV's of No. 2 Bomber Group were never effectively used in a coordinated campaign against Luftwaffe airfields.

Political aspects of the conduct of the air war, as well as military ones, were noteworthy, too. The government at the time of the Battle of Britain was a tight community. The Secretary of State for Air had been the Prime Minister's adjutant in the First World War, and the Under-Secretary had been a flight commander in the Deputy Chief of the Air Staff's squadron in 1917. Above all there was the intense personal interest displayed by the Prime Minister in the battle, once he had been persuaded not to give all the Fighter Command aircraft to France. If it is essential to see that the commander in chief, as any senior commander, is neither understaffed nor overburdened, then it is equally important to make sure that he or she is not isolated. If not the AOC, then someone has to question both assumptions and data.

The Battle of Britain showed that the normal establishment for antiaircraft units simply was inadequate and had to be doubled when they were placed in continuous action as at Dover. The same could be argued for fighter squadrons. In the Battle of Britain neither their pilots nor their repair echelons were sufficient to maintain the units at operational efficiency under the stress of four and five sorties a day. The statistics available also suggest that the pilot shortage of the Battle of Britain may be as controversial as the supposed *shell shortage* of 1915: was there or was there not one? Part of the difficulty of answering this question is that there was a gap in the statistics from July 1939 to September 1940. This suggests that no organization should be without its statistical section, but at the same time the RAF case also raises the specter that an analyst may not see the figures that are there because of a preconception. It is possible that when asked about pilots, the responsible authority at the Air Ministry only listed officers. This seems plausible since unrepaired aircraft also simply got lost in the system. As Justice Singleton's inquiry into the RAF's estimates of the Luftwaffe made evident, an independent outside audit is an essential tool from time to time.

The changes in technology that so abruptly shifted the RAF in 1936–38 from the wood and canvas biplane era into the metal monoplane threw off mobilization schedules and forecasts. On the one hand, it meant that much of the mobilization of RAF manpower shot ahead of the availability of aeroplanes, while on the other it resulted in the senior commanders' being overly cautious about the amount of training fledglings needed before being allowed to take the precious new weapons into combat.

In one sense the Battle of Britain may have been atypical in that it occurred in the midst of a major advance in technology when much had not yet been assimilated. Yet perhaps the same could also be said of the First World War in the air. If so, then those who fought the 1939–45 war failed to heed that experience of their youth which so much influenced them as mature commanders.

In another way the Battle of Britain in the summer of 1940 is a very useful lesson, for it emphasizes not only so many of the subtler human ingredients of victory or defeat while at the same time being a classic example of the type of exercise that many military men like to ignore. It was a victory for the defenders in a struggle in which their objective was not a battle of attrition to wear down and destroy their opponents, but their own survival until time could be brought to bear on their side. It was the classic response of a passive power against an aggressor. But the defense could have failed for lack of foresight in the lotus years of peace and during the gift months of the Phoney War when more time than had been expected was granted. Above all the Battle of Britain pointed to the need to keep clearly in mind the short-term objective so that the long-term would remain an option.

Notes

1. AIR 41/8.79031 Air Historical Branch narrative history of the expansion of the RAF, pp 71ff.

2. AIR 41/8.79031, p 74, "the front-line air force was but a facade."

3. The air side of the story 1939-40 is covered in the official volume by L. F. Ellis, *The War in France and Flanders, 1939–1940* (London, 1954).

4. On Dowding see Robert Wright, *The Man Who Won the Battle of Britain* (London, 1969), and on Park, see Vincent Orange, *A Biography of Air Chief Marshal Sir Keith Park, GCB, KBE, MC, DFC, DCL* (London, 1984).

5. The story of the Ministry of Aircraft Production is buried in a number of the "civilian" volumes of the United Kingdom History of the Second World War, for which see Robin Higham, *Official Histories* (Manhattan, Kans., 1970). The MAP records are in AVIA 10 at the Public Record Office in London.

6. Hinsley, *British Intelligence in Second World War*, vol I (London, 1979), pp 102, 177n, 299, 301, for the inquiry conducted by Justice Singleton. The tendency was for the Air Ministry to look upon the whole of the Luftwaffe as available for operations against England. This attitude, which was also evident in other countries' assessments of their enemies in the disarmament talks that finally collapsed in 1934, was coupled to a gross overestimate of the Luftwaffe at about 7,000 aircraft. Dowding himself actually viewed the numbers a little more realistically.

7. On German aircraft see William Green's *Warplanes of the Third Reich* (London, 1970), pp 541–42, 544–45. Me–109 endurance was 80 minutes, but the bombers took 57 minutes to fly from Cap Gris Nez on the French coast to London and back. Allowing for take-off, rendezvous, and landing time, this left the Me–109 about 10 minutes for fighting over England. Confirmed by Adolf Galland in BBC–TV's "The World at War," Chapter 12.

8. So many of Dowding's squadrons had been decimated in France and over Dunkirk that he actually had in June only 26 fully fit for action, and even some of these were partially fatigued. (AIR 20/5202; Dowding's dispatch of Aug 2, 1941, and the Air Ministry comments on it.)

9. On Dowding's retirement see E. B. Haslam, "How Lord Dowding Came to Leave Fighter Command," *Journal of Strategic Studies*, 1981, pp 175-86. Also AIR 19/572.

10. The most detailed account is to be found in Francis K. Mason, *The Battle Over Britain* (New York, 1969), which gives a diary of events. Other works consulted are listed in the select bibliography.

11. Colonel Roy M. Stanley, II, USAF, *World War II Photo Intelligence* (New York, 1981). The German negatives are in the National Archives in Washington, largely unexplored.

12. Michael J. F. Bowyer, *2 Group, R.A.F., A Complete History, 1939–1945* (London, 1974), pp 1–128.

13. John T. Greenwood, "The Great Patriotic War, 1941–1945," in Robin Higham and Jacob W. Kipp, *Soviet Aviation and Air Power* (Boulder, Colo., 1977), pp 76–77.

14. AIR 41/14.80081, p 150. In a note in Appendix 16 here Dowding noted that Hurricanes destroyed in France at the rate of 25 a day were lost, whereas those, especially the newly armored ones, brought down at the rate of 8 a day in UK were usually back in service in one to two days (AIR 41/14.80234).

15. On gun development see H. F. King, *Armaments of British Aircraft, 1909–1939* (London, 1971), and G. F. Wallace's *The Guns of the Royal Air Force* (London, 1972), among others. On the inability to shoot, see H. R. Allen, *Who Won the Battle of Britain?* (London, 1974), pp 63–70.

16. Park, in his report of Nov 7, 1940, (AIR 2/5246.66581) noted the weaknesses of radar and the Royal Observer Corps. He instituted high-flying standing patrols, and these aircraft were caught up in a German hoax: Park notes that some of them were shot down by a rare He–113 fighter. In fact, no such airplane existed in the Luftwaffe although photographs of a machine in German markings had been circulated to create the impression that it did. See William Green, *Airplanes of the Third Reich* (New York, 1970), p 336. Dowding's comments of Nov 15 are in the same AIR 2/5246.66581 file.

17. AIR 2/5246.66 81.

18. Laddie Lucas's *Flying Colours* (London, 1983), p 31, is a defense of Bader by one of his pilots.

19. General Lord Ismay, *The Memoirs of General Lord Ismay* (London, 1960), p 182.

20. Vincent Orange, *Sir Keith Park* (London, 1984).

21. Townsend, *Duel of Eagles*, p 384.

22. AIR 41/14.79062, pp 56ff.

23. Mason, *The Battle Over Britain*, pp 595 and 598, and is taken from AIR 22/293.64819, Part II.

24. Williamson Murray, *Luftwaffe* (Baltimore, 1985), p 53, which is based on Mason's tables.

25. AIR 41/14.79062, p 70n.

26. Maurice Dean, *The Royal Air Force and Two World Wars* (London, 1979), p 145.

27. Robin Higham, *The Military Intellectuals in Britain* (New Brunswick, NJ, 1966), p 181, quoting from C. L. Dunn, *Emergency Medical Services*, vol II, (London, 1953), pp 210–19.

28. Orange, *Park*, p 109.

29. *Ibid.*; Churchill, *Their Finest Hour*, pp 332–37.

30. AIR 2/5246.66 81.

31. Mason, *The Battle Over Britain*, p 355.

32. Martin Gilbert, *Winston Churchill*, vol IV (London, 1983), p 1060.

33. Letter from Miss M. H. C. Parks of the Air Historical Branch, MOD, to author, July 26, 1984. This chapter was accepted in 1985. A statue was erected in 1988.

34. See J. R. M. Butler, *Grand Strategy*, vol II (1957), pp 165–73, 251–58, 267–94.

35. AIR 41/14.790 2, p 69.

36. AIR 41/8.7923, pp 114ff.

37. AIR 16/609.63182, Apr 22, 1952.

38. See Owen Thetford, *Aircraft of the Royal Air Force Since 1918* (London, 1979); and Mason, *The Battle Over Britain*, pp 198, 344.

39. AIR 20/1966.64819. See also Robin Higham, unpublished history of BOAC (London: British Airways).

40. AIR 20/2037.64227.

41. AIR 41/8.79231, p 119, Oct 21, 1938. AIR 41/8.79031, p 133, notes that only on Aug 1, 1939, was the officer corps divided into GD (flying) (general duties types) and Technical Officers (Engineering, Armament and Signals) because it was finally realized a modern air force could not manage satisfactorily with these functions handled on a part-time basis.

42. Robert Wright, *The Man Who Won the Battle of Britain* (New York, 1969); Robin Higham, *The British Rigid Airship* (London, 1961); Robin Higham, *Armed Forces in Peacetime: Britain 1918–1939* (London, 1962); Great Britain, Air Ministry, *The Secret History of the RAF* (typescript, 1945); Sir Frederick Pile, *Ack-Ack* (London, 1956), p 96.

43. M. M. Postan, Denis Hay, J. D. Scott, *The Design and Development of Weapons* (London, 1964); Denis Richards and Hilary St. George Saunders, *The Royal Air Force, 1939–1945*, vol I (London, 1953–54), p 154.

44. The figures used hereafter are derived first from Mason's *The Battle Over Britain* and then from *After the Battle* magazine's *The Battle of Britain*, 2nd edition (London, 1982). These two works contain corrections not found in the official histories such as Basil Collier's *The Defence of the United Kingdom* (1957). Behind these published sources are the raw RAF

reports of the order of battle in the Public Record Office in AIR 20/ 835.64700; the daily returns of the Equipment Branch in AIR 16/943-945; and the returns on personnel (AIR 20/ 2037) and production (AIR 22/293.64819). Combat reports are in AIR 50/2. Richards and Saunders, *The Royal Air Force*, and Winston Churchill, *Their Finest Hour* (Boston, 1949) contain statistics and comments on production and pilots, as does also Sir Maurice Dean's *The Royal Air Force and Two World Wars*.

45. Collier, *The Defence of the United Kingdom*, p 112, notes the overestimate of the Luftwaffe; F. M. Hinsley in *British Intelligence in the Second World War*, vol I (Cambridge, 1979 to present), p 299, provides an account of the problem, its continued impact into early 1941, and its resolution with Justice Singleton's inquiry and report. Mason, *The Battle Over Britain*, p 128. See also Martin Gilbert, *Winston S. Churchill*, Vol VI: *1919–1941* (London, 1983), p 479.

46. AIR 41/8.79031, p 75.

47. AIR 41/8.7944, p 139.

48. AIR 41/8.80363, p 169, and AIR 41/8.79231, p 10.

49. Ian Colvin, *None So Blind* (London, 1965), p 138, quoting Viscount Swinton, Secretary of State for Air, 1935–1938.

50. Robin Higham, *Armed Forces in Peacetime* (Hamden, Conn., 1963), p 207. The 225 percent figure used here was developed just prior to World War II in Scheme M for more modern aircraft and seems more reasonable to use than the 96 reserve aircraft per squadron of 16 quoted earlier which was probably based upon World War I wastage rates.

51. For production, AIR 22/293.2.64819. According to this source and as quoted in Mason, *The Battle Over Britain*, p 59, the figures are as given. However, my chart is compiled from AIR 10/1835.64700, No. 41 Group's records, and it gives a rather different picture.

52. F. J. Adkin, *From the Ground Up* (Shrewsbury, 1983), pp 199-200. By custom each machine had a fitter and a rigger and they did all the work up to major inspections. But war showed this to be impossible. Fighter squadrons were the last to go over to the "garage" system.

53. AIR 16/943,9 4,945.

54. AIR 16/1037.R 2504.

55. Professor Frank Tillman, Head, Department of Industrial Engineering, Kansas State University.

56. S. C. Rexford-Welch, *Royal Air Force Medical Services*, vol II (London, 1954), pp 177–82. See also Samuel A. Stouffer, *et al.*, *Studies in Social Psychology In World War II* (Princeton, 1949), 4 vols.

57. See Mason, *The Battle Over Britain*, for Sept 8. A number of the public saw only the wild off-duty side of fighter pilots, and others had no way of telling that young men in blue uniforms were the elite defenders who had an hour or so before been fighting over their very heads. Too often it looked too pretty for war compared to the Army.

58. R.D.F. (Radio Direction Finding) was the decoy code name used to disguise early radar. See R. V. Jones, *The Wizard War* (New York, 1978).

59. The revolution in mechanization of construction was just around the corner, but bulldozers, trenchers, and the like were not yet available. Most such work was done by hand or by a slow steam shovel which was too big for laying deep landlines.

60. Orange, *Park*, p 103.

61. G. E. Wallace, *The Guns of the Royal Air Force, 1939–45* (London, 1972), pp 30–37, 54–68, 77–99.

62. Orange, *Park*, pp 75–81.

63. AVM Peter Wykeham, *Fighter Command: A Study in Air Defence, 1914–1960* (London, 1960). One of the curses of interwar procurement was that as few as one squadron of a type was bought, which meant lack of standardization. Moreover, as in the army regiment so in the RAF squadron, it was the unit that did the bulk of the training of its officers and airmen.

64. Sir Charles Webster and Noble Frankland, *The Strategic Air Offensive Against Germany*, vol I (London, 1961); Robert Wright, *The Man Who Won the Battle of Britain* (London, 1969), pp 68, 94; and Orange, *Park*, pp 75, 78, 81.

65. Churchill, *Their Finest Hour*, p 457.

66. Mason, *The Battle Over Britain*, p 212.

67. Michael J. F. Sawyer, *2 Group, RAF: A Complete History, 1936–1945* (London, 1974), pp 106–22.

68. Mason, *The Battle Over Britain*, p 270.

69. Orange, *Park*, p 115.

70. Dowding acted on the lesson of the Gallipoli inquiry, which had stressed that it was the duty of the military commander or adviser to speak out to the Cabinet if he disagreed with his political superior on a matter of vital national policy. (For the background and reasons for this, see returns on personnel [AIR 20/2037] and production [AIR 22/293.64819]. Combat reports are in AIR 50/2. Richards and Saunders, *The Royal Air Force*, and Winston Churchill, *Their Finest Hour* (Boston, 1949) contain statistics and comments on production and pilots, as does also Sir Maurice Dean's *The Royal Air Force and Two World Wars*.

71. Group Captain Winterbotham's sensational 1974 revelations in *The Ultra Secret* (New York) have to be read very carefully as to time and place, as does Ronald Lewin's *Ultra Goes to War* (New York, 1980) and similar volumes. The best is Hinsley's *British Intelligence in the Second World War*, a balanced treatment.

72. See note 11 above.

73. Collier, *Defence of the United Kingdom*, p 490, and General Sir Frederick Pile, *Ack-Ack* (London, 1956).

74. For the wave theory of increases and decreases in production and training, see Robin Higham, *Air Power: A Concise History* (Manhattan, Kans., 1984), p 3.

Bibliographical Essay

It is difficult to understand the role of the Royal Air Force in the Battle of Britain without knowing something of the service's history. Unfortunately, there is no reliable one- volume study to provide a general background. The two most recent volumes that attempt this are both rather thin on text: Chaz Bowyer, *History of the RAF* (New York: Crescent Books, 1977); and Michael Donne and Squadron Leader Cynthia Fowler, *Per Ardua ad Astra: Seventy Years of the RFC and the RAF* (London: Muller, 1982). Ranking really as a memoir by one who spent most of his life as an Air Ministry civil servant, Sir Maurice Dean's *The Royal Air Force and Two World Wars* (London: Cassell, 1979) has to be read with care. An older view of the interwar years is provided in Robin Higham's *Armed Forces in Peacetime: Britain, 1918–1939* (London: Foulis, 1963), and a detailed examination of the development of bombing doctrine appears in Higham, *The Military Intellectuals in Britain, 1918–1940* (New Brunswick, New Jersey: Rutgers University Press, 1966). For a more detailed examination of part of the subject, see H. Montgomery Hyde, *British Air Policy between the Wars, 1918–1939* (London: Heinemann, 1976); Hyde had the advantage of being able to use the documents in the Public Records Office opened up at the end of the sixties.

The most useful and provocative new work to appear in some time is John Terraine's study of the RAF in the European War, 1939–45. Written by an author with a strong background in the 1914–18 struggle, it provides a large base wedged upon the records and narrative official histories from which to proceed. In Britain it is entitled *The Right of the Line* and in the United States, *A Time for Courage* (New York: Macmillan, 1985).

The Air Ministry history, *The Rise and Fall of the German Air Force, 1933–1945*, first published in 1948, shows what the RAF thought it knew of the Germans. On more particular topics the RAF has been well served by the so-called Putnam series of books on British aircraft companies, which includes also the much revised and expanded Owen Thetford volume *Aircraft of the Royal Air Force Since 1918* (London: Putnam, seventh revised edition, 1979). The Royal Observer Corps is the subject of air correspondent Derek Wood's *Attack Warning Red* (London: Macdonald's and Jane's, 1976), a work which gives a pretty fair idea of the workings of the warning system during the Battle of Britain as well as details of its formation and subsequent career.

A good share of the burden in the fighting was undertaken by the Royal Auxiliary Air Force squadrons, almost entirely filled with officer pilots, and their story is covered by Leslie Hunt in *Twenty-one Squadrons: The History of the Royal Auxiliary Air Force, 1925–1957* (London: Garnstone Press, 1972). Operational Research was just beginning in the RAF, and Fighter Command was the leader in accepting it. The story is told in an official history published in 1963, *Operational Research* in the R.A.F.

The story of Fighter Command itself has been told by Air Vice Marshal Peter Wykeham in *Fighter Command: A Study in Air Defence, 1914–1960* (London: Putnam, 1960). Ronald W. Clark made his name originally with *The Rise of the Boffins* (London: Phoenix House, 1962) and followed that with the official biography of Sir Henry Tizard, *Tizard* (London: Methuen, 1965), which gives one side of the long, behind-the-scenes quarrel with Professor Lindemann (Lord Cherwell), whose biography is *The Prof in Two Worlds,* by Lord Birkenhead (London: Collins, 1961). Against this must be read C. P. Snow's *Science and Government* (Cambridge: Harvard University Press, 1962, in the revised edition). R. V. Jones, himself one of the pioneer scientists, has written *The Wizard War* (New York: Coward, McCann, 1978), which provides the sound technical story, but is perhaps less easy to follow than Brian Johnson's *The Secret War* (London: Methuen, 1978), developed by a BBC producer to help his audience understand the scientific side of the war. Two other aspects of the backroom can be traced in two books by Group Captain F. W. Winterbotham, who served in RAF intelligence and then at the cypher operation at Bletchley: *The Nazi Connection* (New York: Dell, 1978), which tells part of what the RAF knew or could have known about the Luftwaffe, and his 1974 lid-blower, *The Ultra Secret* (New York: Harper and Row), which for the first time revealed the existence of the British codebreakers' ultimate success. But in the latter book, as well as in Ronald Lewin's *Ultra Goes to War* (New York: Pocket Books, 1980), the reader must be wary of statements for the early years of the war.

A few other works that provide background deserve mention. The first of these is a fresh study of the 1914–18 war, Denis Winter's *The First of the Few: Fighter Pilots of the First World War* (Athens: University of Georgia Press, 1983), because of the insights it gives into several of the dramatis personae, especially Goering, Park, Douglas, and Harold Balfour, the British Under Secretary of State for Air. And if the whole point of piloting a fighter within range of an enemy aircraft is to knock the enemy down, armament is essential. Here three books tell various sides of that story. H. F. King in *Armaments of British Aircraft, 1909–1939* (London: Putnam, 1971) combines accurate research with the recollections of a former Flight correspondent. G. F. Wallace's *The Guns of the Royal Air Force, 1929–1934* (London: Kimber, 1972) was written by an armaments practitioner who was involved in the development of the Hispano 20-mm cannon so that it could be manufactured for British fighters. And the official history of the Birmingham Small Arms Company, usually known simply as BSA, *The Other Battle* (Birmingham, 1946), by Donovan Ward, tells the story of the importation and modification of the Colt Browning .303 machineguns.

A general introduction to the war economy and aircraft production can be found in R. J. Overy's recent *The Air War, 1939–1945* (New York: Stein and Day, 1981). Aspects of the subject are treated in the British official histories other than those specifically mentioned below, and they can be found either in Robin Higham's *A*

Guide to the Sources of British Military History (Berkeley: University of California Press, 1971) or in *Official Histories* (Manhattan, Kans.: Kansas State University Library, 1970). Engine development is the special subject of Robert Schlaifer and W. D. Heron, *The Development of Aircraft Engines and Fuels* (Boston: Harvard Business School, 1950) and of Herschel Smith's more recent *Aircraft Piston Engines* (New York: McGraw-Hill, 1981), while the Merlin itself is the subject of one volume of Ian Lloyd's *Rolls-Royce: The Merlin at War* (London: Macmillan, 1978). The first third of M. M. Postan, D. Hay, and J. D. Scott, *The Design and Development of Weapons* (London: HMSO, 1964) is devoted to aeronautical affairs as seen by three official historians.

A number of official volumes need to be consulted in a study of the Battle of Britain. Basic, of course, is Basil Collier's *The Defence of the United Kingdom* (London: HMSO, 1957) and J. R. M. Butler, *Grand Strategy,* vol II (London: HMSO, 1957), both of which set the battle in the wider scene. L. F. Ellis, *The War in France and Flanders, 1939–1940* (London: HMSO, 1953), deals with the air components sent to France as part of a tri-service campaign history. The general history of the Air Force during the war has been told by Denis Richards and Hilary St. George Saunders; only the first volume of *The Royal Air Force, 1939–1945: The Fight at Odds* (London: HMSO, 1953) is pertinent here. The Air Ministry's own original paperback, *The Battle of Britain,* first published in the United States by Doubleday in 1941 is now a piece of history in itself. Of the other official works, the first volume of Sir Charles Webster's and Noble Frankland's *The Strategic Air Offensive against Germany, 1939–1945: Preparation* (London: HMSO, 1961) is most revealing. As a result of the ULTRA revelations, F. H. Hinsley, et al., have begun publishing *British Intelligence in the Second World War* (Cambridge: Cambridge University Press, 1979–), of which the first volume covers the Battle of Britain period. The last piece of official history is the more recent volume by F. J. Hatch, which indicates how the Battle of Britain affected Canada: *Aerodrome of Democracy: Canada and the British Air Commonwealth Air Training Plan, 1939–1945* (Ottawa: Directorate of History, Department of National Defense, 1983).

The next nearest thing to an official history are Sir Winston Churchill's memoirs, many sections of which are based upon official narratives or papers. The second volume of *The Second World War, Their Finest Hour* (Boston: Houghton Mifflin, 1949) is the appropriate one here. The mammoth biography and papers by Martin Gilbert handles this period in volume VI (London: Heinemann, 1983). Another autobiography having a direct bearing on the air war is by the Deputy Chief of the Air Staff, Sholto Douglas (Lord Douglas of Kirtleside): *Combat and Command* (New York: Simon and Schuster, 1966); it was largely written by Robert Wright. Also important is General Sir Frederick Pile's *Ack-Ack* (London: Panther, 1956). Sir Maurice Dean has been mentioned above. Also playing a role was Harold Balfour (later Lord Inchrye), whose memoirs are entitled *An Airman Marches* (London: Hutchinson, 1933) and *Wings Over Westminster* (London: Hutchinson, 1973).

Apart from a few single-volume studies currently in print, the two most useful words on the Battle of Britain for details are Francis K. Mason's *Battle over Britain* (New York: Doubleday, 1969) and *After the Battle* Magazine's *The Battle of Britain Then and Now. Mark II* (London, 1982). A history by a participant is Peter Townsend's *Duel of Eagles* (New York: Pocket Books, 1972); Laddie Lucas's *Flying Colours* (London: Granada, 1983) is the story of Douglas Bader by one of his pilots; J. R. D. Braham in *Night Fighter* (New York: Bantam, 1984) tells what it was like in that specialty; and H. R. "Dizzy" Allen, another squadron leader in 1940, has both analyzed the battle in a straightforward way in his three memoirs and attacked its tactical conduct in *Who Won the Battle of Britain?* (London: Casse 11, 1972).

A much older study which caused something of a sensation when it first came out is Derek Wood and Derek Dempster, *The Narrow Margin* (London: Hutchinson, 1961), by two young journalists who were boys at the time of the battle. Norman Franks has recently written *The Air Battle of Dunkirk* (London: Kimber, 1983) based on PRO records and interviews with survivors.

There is as yet no biography of Leigh-Mallory. The original standard authorized biography of Dowding was Basil Collier's *Leader of the Few* (London: Jarrolds, 1957). But after the Sholto Douglas memoirs appeared, that terribly correct and reticent commander, Lord Dowding, decided that he needed to say something, and he asked Robert Wright, who had been his personal assistant during the battle, to produce a new book. The result was *The Man Who Won the Battle of Britain* (New York: Scribners, 1969). But Park never wrote his memoirs, and his story was not told until after his death when a fellow New Zealander, Vincent Orange, who had access to the records, wrote *Sir Keith Park* (London: Methuen, 1984), at last giving him his due.

Other works exist, and more will no doubt appear. Books besides those listed here are referred to in the chapter footnotes. It remains, however, to comment briefly on the documentary resources. While some materials are available at the RAF's beautiful Battle of Britain Museum complex at Hendon, the bulk of the documents are housed at the Public Records Office at Kew, and the photographs are at the Imperial War Museum at Lambeth (both in London). The place to start for the PRO is the paperback *The Second World War: A Guide to Documents in the Public Record Office* (1972), for which there is supplement No. 16, "Information on Operational Records of the Royal Air Force." The papers are divided into blocks, such as AIR 16 for Fighter Command. The problem, then, is to know how the records were accumulated. The Form 540 provides in one part a log of squadron activities and, in another, details of all flying activities. Useful material lurks here if time can be spared to study the records. For this chapter, Dowding's dispatch and his comments upon it, orders of battle (issued daily), returns from the Equipment Officer (also daily), which give detailed information as to the serviceability of aircraft, personnel reports, and the like were consulted, as is indicated in the notes. These were obtained through a continuous exchange of ideas and information with a former RAF officer who is now a professional researcher and who was, therefore, also able to offer considerable guidance to the materials containing the items I believed would be useful. As historians break into new areas, discovering the nomenclature of the documentation becomes part of the puzzle to be solved. In this case both Dowding and Park wrote very full accounts and memoranda, and there is a recently declassified multivolume history of the Air Ministry, but as yet, there is no history of the Air Staff.

4

The Soviet Air Force
Against Germany and Japan

Kenneth R. Whiting

When the Luftwaffe attacked the U.S.S.R. in June 1941, the Soviet Air Forces came close to being knocked out of the war completely in the early weeks of the conflict. The German aircraft roamed the skies over Russia at will; they were in complete control of the air. Four years later, the pitiful remnants of the once mighty German Air Force were unable to put together even a token opposition against the thousands of Soviet planes swarming over Berlin. The question arises, naturally, as to why the Luftwaffe was able to attain air superiority so easily in June 1941 and lose it so completely in the last part of the war.

Evolution of Soviet Air Forces

Before discussing in some detail the Russo-German contest for control of the air in the 1941-45 period, it would seem appropriate to describe briefly the evolution of the Soviet Air Forces, or VVS [*Voenno-vozdushny sily*], prior to World War II and summarize what it brought into the war in the way of equipment, combat experience, and doctrine. In other words, exactly how did the Soviet VVS evolve from a mixed bag of foreign aircraft in 1917 into a modern air force by 1941?

Until Stalin's Five-Year Plans for industrialization at a forced tempo began to produce results in the early 1930s, aviation made up only a tiny portion of the Red Army and as late as 1929 consisted of "a thousand combat aircraft of old construction."[1] There could be little improvement until

179

Soviet industry could support a modern aviation industry. During the First Five-Year Plan (1928–32), however, there was a vigorous expansion of the aircraft industry; old plants were expanded and modernized and new ones constructed. Between 1928 and 1932, the labor force in the aviation industry increased by 750 percent and the number of engineers and technicians by 1,000 percent.[2] As a result, during the Second Five-Year Plan (1933–37), the output of aircraft quadrupled from 860 in 1933 to 3,578 in 1937.[3] Although many specifics are either lacking or are dubious, the overall evidence indicates a rapid expansion of the Soviet aircraft industry during the 1930s.

In that same period, Soviet aircraft designers were under intense pressure to overcome the nation's dependence upon foreign aircraft. N. N. Polikarpov got the jump on the decade with his R–5 reconnaissance plane in 1929. Although primarily a reconnaissance aircraft, later versions were used as fighters and dive bombers, and it was in action during the Great Patriotic War* up to 1944. In 1933 he really came to the fore as the preeminent Soviet designer of fighters when he produced the I–15 and the I–16 in the same year. The former had a top speed of 230 miles per hour and the latter a speed of 220 miles per hour.[4] The Polikarpov aircraft were by far the best Soviet fighters in the late 1930s. Another outstanding designer, A. N. Tupolev, produced a heavy bomber, the TB–3 [tyazhelyy bombardirovshchik] in 1930 and a light bomber, the SB–2 [skorostnoy bombardirovshchik], or fast bomber, in 1934. Tupolev's bombers and Polikarpov's R–5, R–15, and R–16 were the main Soviet stable of aircraft for subsequent adventures in Spain, China, and the Soviet Far East in the late 1930s.

As the planes poured off the assembly lines in the later 1930s, the demand for pilots and technicians needed to keep the planes operational resulted in the VVS becoming a great technical training institution with academies and flying schools mushrooming up all over the country. In addition, the voluntary Society for the Promotion of Defense Aviation and Chemical Warfare, called *Osoaviakhim* in its Russian acronym, taught thousands of young people the various technical skills needed for aircraft maintenance as well as training many to fly. According to a German observer, "by the end of 1940 the clubs had almost achieved their target of 100,000 trained pilots."[5] Thus, it was not too surprising that the Soviets were able to maintain a steady flow of replacement pilots during the Russo-German war, a capability that played no small part in the eventual attainment of air superiority.

---

*The Soviets divided World War II into two periods: the war prior to the German invasion of Russia on June 22, 1941, is called the "imperialist" war, and the German-Soviet phase is entitled the Great Patriotic War (*Velikaya otechestvennaya voyna*).

Stalin's forced industrialization and the resulting "semi-isolationist" foreign policy in the early 1930s were ideal for building up the Soviet military-industrial complex. Nevertheless, Japanese expansion and the rise of Hitler meant that the Soviets faced potential enemies in both the East and the West, the perennial nightmare of Russian strategists, Tsarist or Communist. In 1935 Stalin felt it advisable to shift to a "united front" policy, i.e., cooperation with any anti-fascist party, whatever its leanings otherwise. Hardly had he opted for his new policy when the Spanish Civil War put him in a dilemma: either let down his allies in the popular fronts, especially in France, or support the Republicans in Spain against Franco, a move that might frighten the French and British governments. In October 1936 he began to ship, as cautiously as possible, aircraft, tanks, and artillery to Spain along with the people to operate the weapons.

In aircraft, the Soviet assistance was approximately 1,500 machines, although in any one month not more than a third of that number was operational. Of the thousand or so fighter aircraft, around 500 to 600 were I–15As or I–15Bs and the rest were I–16s. There were over 200 SB–2 bombers, and the rest were R–5 reconnaissance planes. Soviet aircraft made up over 90 percent of the Republican air force by early 1937, and the Republicans had air superiority until early 1938, when the Nazis equipped the Kondor Legion in Spain with Messerschmitt Bf–109 fighters, superior to the Soviet I–15s and I–16s in every way. The obvious inability of the Soviet fighters to oppose the Germans led Stalin to begin phasing out the Soviet Air Force in Spain in mid-1938 so that by the end of the year all Soviet aircraft had left the country.

Although Soviet fliers gained valuable combat experience in Spain, the concepts derived were mostly negative. For example, the VVS came to the conclusion that strategic high-level bombing was an ineffective use of fliers and machines, a conclusion the Germans also drew from their Spanish experience. In retrospect, considering the modesty of the bombing effort in both cases, plus the rather primitive equipment involved in that effort, it is not surprising that neither the Luftwaffe nor the VVS was impressed with the results obtained in the Spanish adventure. The Soviet pilots were also made painfully aware of the inferiority of their machines in combat with the German Bf–109s. All in all, the Soviet involvement in the Spanish Civil War, especially in the air war, was far from successful.

The VVS, while still engaged in Spain, was also getting bloodied in the Far East. In July 1937, the Japanese began an all-out assault on China,

---

*The I–16 had many nicknames applied to it during the Spanish Civil War. It was called *Rata* (Rat) by the Franco forces, *Mosca* (Fly) by the Loyalists, while the Soviet fliers referred to it as *Ishak* (Donkey). With its short, barrel-like configuration it was an easy plane to identify, and everyone in Spain got to know it.

Two mainstay bombers during the 1930s were the TB-3 (*above*) and the
SB-2bis (*below*), both built by the designer A. N. Tupolev.

and Stalin saw much to be gained in helping the Chinese, thereby keeping the Japanese so busy in China that they would not be tempted to make any incursions into Soviet territory. The Russians delivered aircraft, set up repair facilities, and provided "volunteer" Russian pilots. The aircraft used in China were the best the Soviets had at that time—the I–15, I–16, SB–2, and TB–3—and the Soviet fighter planes did much better against the Japanese machines than they had against the Messerschmitt Bf–109s in Spain. It was also in the Chinese adventure that the Soviet pilots realized that the 7.62-mm machinegun was a very inadequate weapon for downing bombers, and as a result the installation of the 12.7-mm gun was begun.

While the Soviets were engaging the Japanese indirectly in China, they found themselves in direct confrontation with them on 2 occasions: at Lake Khasan in 1938 and at Khalkhin-Gol in Outer Mongolia in 1939. In the latter confrontation, really a mini-war that lasted about 4 months (May–September 1939), Georgi K. Zhukov got his career off to a flying start. He insisted on very close air-ground cooperation, and it was his successful employment of some 500 aircraft that went a long way toward insuring victory, especially in inhibiting the enemy reinforcement of the battlefield.[6]

During the 1936–39 period, simultaneously with the use of the VVS in Spain and the Far East, Stalin was ruthlessly purging his senior military leaders, a senseless blood purge that wiped out four-fifths of the top commanders of the Red Army. No military force could stand a blood-letting of that magnitude without suffering pernicious anemia in its command system.[7] Soviet aviation was especially hard hit as seventy-five percent of the senior officers in the VVS were eliminated by the end of 1939, including its commander, Ya. I. Alksnis, and his deputy, V. V. Khripin. The purge also extended to the aircraft industry and the design bureaus—Petlyakov and Tupolev were both under arrest for some time. There can be little doubt that the poor showing of the VVS in the Winter War with Finland and the early period of the Great Patriotic War can be partially attributed to Stalin's blood lust in the late 1930s.[8]

The euphoria engendered by the victory at Khalkhin-Gol and the easy task of acquiring part of Poland in late 1939 with Hitler's acquiescence, was chilled in the 1939–40 Winter War. The Finnish campaign was not the VVS's finest hour. Although operating with a 15–to–1 advantage over the Finns with their 145 obsolete aircraft, the VVS's air-to-air combat record was dismal, its coordination with the ground forces was extremely poor and its bombing accuracy mediocre. Stalin, shaken by the Finnish fiasco, began to overhaul his armed forces, including the VVS. In January 1940, A. I. Shakurin was made head of the aviation industry, and the aircraft designer, A. S. Yakovlev, became his deputy. Output was significantly increased, and new designs were tested and put into serial production; in short, Soviet aviation production was put on a crash program.[9]

The main thrust of the aircraft procurement plan was to acquire a stable of fighters capable of a decent showing against the Luftwaffe's Bf–109, a task well beyond the abilities of the I–15 and I–16. In 1940 two new fighters went into serial production, the MiG–3, a product of the Mikoyan-Gurevich design bureau, or OKB, and the Yak–1 from the Yakovlev OKB. The MiG–3 had a top speed of 400 miles per hour and was a match for the Bf–109 above 16,000 feet. The Yak–1, whose design was influenced by the British Spitfire and the Bf–109, was a low-wing monoplane with a top speed of 400 miles per hour at 20,000 feet. In 1941, another fighter was put in production, the LaGG–3, the product of the OKB of Lavochkin, Gorbunov, and Gadkov. It was largely of wooden construction and was rather heavy, which made its rate of climb somewhat slow. Of the three, the Yak–1 was the best. It handled well, was easy to maintain under austere conditions, and was the favorite of the pilots in the crucial early years of the war.[10]

Unfortunately for the VVS, the bulk of the planes it received in the two and a half years before the German attack were obsolescent since the new types did not begin to flow into combat units until early 1941. Even the new planes that were acquired were not effectively used when the attack did come, since their pilots were not yet fully trained in their use and, as Marshal Zhukov noted, only fifteen percent of the pilots were trained for night flying.[11] Of course, inasmuch as the overwhelming number of Soviet planes destroyed by the Luftwaffe in the first days of the war were sitting on the ground, a larger number of new types in the inventory would not have helped much.

Soviet Air Organization

In 1934 the People's Commissariat of Defense [*Narkomat Oborony*], or NKO, was formed with the objective of centralizing control of the military, but in 1937 a further step in that direction led to the creation of a single organ, the Committee of Defense of the U.S.S.R. Later in that same year, however, the Navy got its own People's Commissariat [*Narkomat VMF*]. Even before the German attack, in May 1941, Stalin assumed the chairmanship of *Sovnarkom* [Council of People's Commissars], the executive arm of the government, thus combining control of both party and government in his own hands. A week after the Nazis struck, the Politburo created a new institution, the State Committee for Defense [*Gosudarstvenniy Komitet*

OKB stands for Opytnoe Konstruktorskoe byuro, or Bureau of Experimental Design; the plane produced by a bureau carried the initial letters of the designer's name, e.g., Yak for Yakovlev or Tu for Tupolev, etc.

Oborony], or GKO, to replace the *Sovnarkom*; under the chairmanship of Stalin, the GKO was designed to keep control of both government and military in a synchronized war effort.[12] GKO administered military matters through *Stavka* of the High Command [*Verkhovnogo Glavnokomandovaniya*], or to use its customary title, *Stavka* VGK, headed by Stalin as Supreme Commander in Chief [*Verkhovnyy Glavnokomanduyushchiy*]. Stalin, thus garbed in several hats, namely chairman of GKO, Supreme Commander in Chief, Commissar of Defense, and head of *Stavka* VGK, was centralization epitomized in one man.[13] Directly subordinate to *Stavka* was the General Staff which provided information and detailed plans of operations for Stavka consideration.

The dozen or so top military leaders who manned *Stavka* advised Stalin and developed strategic plans—Garthoff calls this Stalin's "military Politburo."[14] Below *Stavka,* at the operational level were the *Fronts,* made up of several armies plus air components and supporting artillery and armor. Late in the war, an active *Front* could total a million men and encompass an area of 100 to 150 miles wide and 50 to 100 miles deep.[15] *Stavka* came up with the strategies, the *Fronts* carried them out (operational), and smaller formations (armies, divisions, etc.) executed their tactical implementation.

On the eve of the war the Soviet Air Force was made up of five components: 1) Long-range Bomber Aviation, or DBA [*dal'nebombardirovochnaya aviatsiaya*]; 2) Frontal Aviation [*VVS fronta*]; 3) Army Aviation [*VVS armii*]; 4) Corps Aviation [*korpusnye aviaeskadril'i*] and 5) Reserve Aviation [*aviatsionnie armii reserva*]. DBA was controlled by the High Command, Frontal Aviation was attached to various *Fronts,* and Army Aviation operated under the ground force commanders. Both Corps and Reserve Aviation were directly under the High Command and could be shifted about as needed. Furthermore, each of the four naval fleets had its own aviation, and the air defense forces, or PVO *Strany,* had a respectable number of interceptors.

In the period between the Winter War and the Nazi onslaught, the Red Army, including the VVS, was being drastically overhauled and was still in the midst of the resultant confusion when the Germans struck. The territories that accrued to the Russians as a result of the Soviet-Nazi Pact of August 1939, namely eastern Poland, the three Baltic states, and Rumanian Bessarabia, moved the Soviet border much farther west. New airfields had to be constructed and old ones lengthened to accommodate the new types of planes coming into the inventory. The construction was scheduled to reach its peak in July-September 1941. Furthermore, the NKVD, which was in charge of the work, insisted on carrying out the construction of the majority of the airfields simultaneously with the result that most of the

**Fighter planes in Soviet inventory at the time of the German assault in 1941
included (*from top to bottom*) the MiG–3, Yak–1, and LaGG–3.**

airfields were either partially or completely out of use in June 1941. Soviet fighters were crowded together on those fields possessing operational runways, thus depriving them of maneuverability, camouflage, or dispersal, i.e., sitting ducks all in a row awaiting the Luftwaffe.[16]

Soviet Prewar Air Doctrine

The leaders of the VVS, like those of many other air forces in the 1930s, were to some degree attracted to the Douhet doctrine on the role of the strategic bomber—the smashing and terrorizing of the enemy by massive air attacks on his industry and cities. A. N. Lapchinsky, an outstanding theorist of the 1930s, although conceding an important place for independent bomber strikes, nevertheless, held to the Soviet teaching of the "interaction of all arms," i.e., not to put all emphasis on the strategic bomber. In addition, the adventure in Spain led Soviet airmen to downgrade the effectiveness of high-level strategic bombing, to perceive the dive bomber as capable of far greater accuracy, and to see the main role of air power as close-support for the ground forces. For example, the Field Regulations put out in June 1941 stated that the basic task of aviation was to assist the ground forces in combat operations and to insure control of the air. VVS was specifically given the following missions: to attain control of the air, to assist the ground forces, to provide cover for the troops achieving breakthrough by striking targets deep in the enemy rear, and to conduct air reconnaissance.[17] In cooperating with the ground forces, the air forces were split into *Front* and Army Aviation, a division that did not work out in practice since it fragmented the air support and made the concentration of forces difficult and centralization of control nearly impossible.

In a sense, air supremacy was considered one of the most important missions of the VVS, as successful close support was dependent upon control of the air. The Soviets held that attainment of air supremacy would only be possible through the combined efforts of the air assets of several *Fronts* plus the aviation of the High Command and the air defense forces. The struggle for control of the air would be carried out in two ways: destruction of the enemy aircraft on the ground and by attrition in air combat. The experience in Spain, however, led the Soviets to favor air combat as the best method, a concept that meant giving the main role to fighter aviation. In the *Combat Regulations for Fighter Aviation, 1940,* it was clearly stated that fighter aviation was the chief means in the struggle with the enemy for control of the air and had as its basic task the destruction of the enemy aircraft on the ground and in the air.[18]

Although the fighters were to be the main element in attaining air supremacy, medium- and long-range bombers were scheduled to carry out deep penetration strikes on enemy airfields, training centers, fuel and munitions dumps, and other facilities supporting enemy aviation.[19] In addition, independent bomber operations were to destroy military and administrative centers, disrupt transport, and hit naval facilities—operations directly controlled by the High Command.

As the authors of the standard work on the Great Patriotic War put it, Soviet military art in the prewar years worked out correctly the fundamental theoretical problems likely to face the VVS. But, as they add somewhat pathetically, the theory did not take into account the possibility that it might be the enemy who had the control of the air.[20] In short, Soviet air doctrine in early 1941 assumed that any German attack would come after the VVS had absorbed its new types of planes and had completed its network of airfields in the newly acquired regions. The theory was predicated on the Soviets having the offensive edge and gave little thought to defense.

German Air Superiority in the Early Days of the War

Hitler's Operation BARBAROSSA, the plan for the invasion of the Soviet Union, called for pursuing the Russians to " . . . a line . . . from which the Russian Air Force can no longer attack German territory" and that the "effective operation of the Russian Air Force is to be prevented from the beginning of the attack by powerful blows."[21] By late June 1941, the Germans had deployed the forces needed to execute BARBAROSSA. The main offensive was to be a 3-pronged advance in the directions of Leningrad, Moscow, and Kiev carried out by Army Groups North, Center, and South respectively. Each of the 3 army groups was allotted an air fleet [*Luftflotte*], and the total number of aircraft committed came to 1,940 plus 60 planes attached to Army Command Norway, for a total of 2,000 combat aircraft.[22] In addition, the Germans had 1,270 transport and liaison planes and some 1,000 Finnish and Rumanian aircraft for a grand total of 4,270 aircraft along the Soviet border. This is not far from the official Soviet estimate of "nearly 5,000 aircraft, including about 1,000 Finnish and Rumanian planes, on the western frontier of the U.S.S.R."[23]

The strength of the Soviet Air Force in the western regions is even harder to ascertain than that of the Luftwaffe. Before the attack, the German estimate of the number of Soviet aircraft facing them in the region about to be attacked was 5,700. In *Soviet Military Doctrine*, scholar Raymond Garthoff pointed out that as early as October 5, 1941, an alternate member of the Politburo admitted in *Pravda* that Soviet air losses came to 5,316.[24] Making some shrewd guesses, Garthoff concluded that Soviet aircraft losses in the summer of 1941 probably totaled around 8,000 since they had some 2,500 planes still flying at the end of the year and they had 10,000 aircraft in their inventory on the western frontiers on June 22, 1941.[25] According to one more or less authoritative Russian account, only 22 percent of their planes were new type fighters, although fighter aircraft constituted 64 percent of the combat machines facing the Germans.[26]

The combat experience of the Luftwaffe pilots gave them a distinct edge against the Russian fliers. It was not only the slowness of the transitioning of Soviet pilots in the new types of aircraft, but also the lack of flying time of pilots in general that reduced their ability to face their German counterparts. For example, for the first three months of 1941, the fliers of the Baltic Special Military District were in the air on an average of just over fifteen hours, in the Western Military District, nine hours, and in the Kiev Military District, just four hours[27]—hardly enough to sharpen the skills of fliers about to contend with combat-experienced pilots in Messerschmitt Bf-109s.

Early on the morning of June 22, 1941, the first wave of 637 bombers and 231 fighters hit the Soviet airfields, and the carnage was almost unbelievable.[28] The few Soviet planes that managed to get airborne were immediately shot down. Luftwaffe bombers flew up to 6 missions a day, while dive bombers and fighters flew up to 8. One Soviet account states that on the first day the Luftwaffe attacked 66 airfields along the frontier on which were parked the newest types of Soviet fighters, and some 1,500 aircraft were destroyed either on the ground or in the air.[29] The Soviet and German figures for kills and losses on the ground throughout the entire war were unreliable at best, with discrepancies sometimes bordering on the ludicrous. However, even the Soviets admitted the unbelievable havoc wrought by the Luftwaffe in the opening days of the German offensive.

The VVS was caught sound asleep, totally unprepared for the devastating surprise attack. In addition, a poorly organized antiaircraft defense, inferior planes, inexperienced pilots, and utter confusion in the upper echelons of command all combined to make the Soviet efforts to counter the Nazi onslaught an exercise in futility. Within a few days the German airmen had torn the guts out of the Soviet Air Force. Field Marshal Alfred Kesselring, Commander of the Second Air Fleet, claimed that the German pilots achieved "air superiority" two days after the opening of hostilities.[30] Gen. V. Gorbachev had the Soviet pilots holding out a little longer, but admitted that by early July control of the air passed to the enemy for a long time. But, he argued, the Germans did not accomplish their objective—the destruction of the Soviet Air Force.[31] The very fact that so many Soviet aircraft were destroyed on the ground meant that the pilots were alive and able to fly the new machines being turned out by the Soviet aviation industry. As one historian put it: whenever it was essential the Germans could always achieve air superiority over any sector of the Eastern Front they

189

chose; superiority over all sectors simultaneously eluded them only for the lack of aircraft.[32]

The Soviets claim that their aviation did better against the Germans in the struggle for Kiev and the Black Sea area, flying over 26,000 sorties during the August-September fighting.[33] The magnitude of the German victory, however, would seem to demonstrate the ineffectiveness of the numerous sorties claimed. What little was left of the VVS during the summer and fall of 1941 was used mostly for assistance to the faltering ground forces. The situation was so desperate that some Soviet fliers resorted to ramming German aircraft, or like Captain Gastello, flying their planes into trains or troop concentrations[34]—heroic deeds much celebrated by Soviet air historians, who have little to extol in that period, but hardly likely to have affected the outcome of the air war.

Achieving air supremacy by deep penetration strikes against German airfields, fuel and ammunition dumps, as well as transport in general—one of the objectives set forth in the 1940 regulations and part of the accepted doctrine—turned out to be a catastrophic failure. Soviet medium bombers as they arrived over German targets at regular intervals were shot down with ridiculous ease by German fighters or antiaircraft fire. Long-range bombers of DBA were no more effective. The awful losses suffered in the first few weeks of the war crippled the Soviet bomber effort for much of the war.[35] The combination of heavy losses in carrying out strikes against the German rear, strikes flown without fighter escort, and the dire straits of the ground forces resulted in some corps and divisions of DBA being transferred to the operational control of *Front* commanders for use in close-support.[36] In describing the ineptness of Soviet bombing, Rotmistrov put it succinctly that the experience in Spain resulted in "a limitation of air operations to a tactical framework over the battlefield."[37]

The Luftwaffe was so confident in its air supremacy by the end of June that the bulk of its planes was shifted to close-support for the ground forces. Some sixty percent of sorties were in direct support with a concomitant reduction of indirect support missions. Thus the Ju-88s, He-111s, and Do-17s, designed for attacking objectives behind the front lines, were used over the battlefield itself.[38]

It was this Luftwaffe concentration on the battlefield that allowed the Soviets to accomplish one of the operations that would eventually enable the VVS to contest the German air supremacy, namely the movement of those airframe and engine factories from the vulnerable areas in the west to safer eastern regions well out of range of German bombers. This transfer of plants, personnel and all, began soon after the German attack and, according to an official account, 1,360 large plants and 10,000,000 workers, a total of 1,500,000 tons, had been moved by the end of December.[39] By early 1942, the transplanted aircraft factories were turning out Yak-1s, Il-2

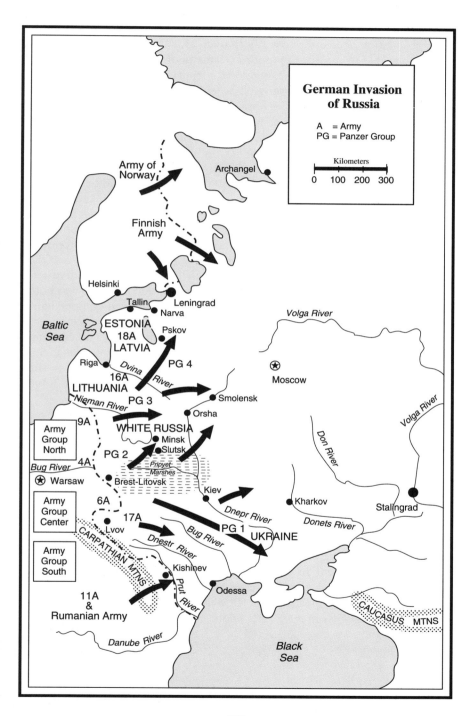

German Invasion of Russia

A = Army
PG = Panzer Group

Kilometers

0 100 200 300

Army of Norway

Archangel

Finnish Army

Helsinki

Tallin
Narva
Leningrad

ESTONIA
18A
Pskov

Baltic Sea

LATVIA

Riga
Dvina River
PG 4

Moscow

Volga River

16A

LITHUANIA
Nieman River
PG 3

Smolensk

9A

WHITE RUSSIA

Orsha

Army Group North

PG 2

Minsk
Slutsk

Volga River

Don River

Bug River
4A
Warsaw

Pripyet Marshes

Brest-Litovsk

Kiev

Army Group Center

6A

17A
Lvov

Dnepr River

Kharkov

Stalingrad

Donets River

CARPATHIAN MTNS.
Dnestr River
Bug River
PG 1
UKRAINE

Army Group South

Kishinev

11A
&
Rumanian Army

Prut River

Odessa

CAUCASUS MTNS

Danube River

Black Sea

191

Shturmoviks, MiG–3s, Pe–2s, and Tu–2s—some 3,600 in the first 3 months. Then production accelerated swiftly to over 25,000 aircraft in 1942.[40] This was comparable to the 1942 output in Germany of over 27,000 planes, but the Germans were fighting on 2 other major fronts.[41]

The German drive on Moscow, slowed down near Smolensk in August and September because of the diversion of Guderian's Panzer Group to the south to help in the Ukrainian campaign, got rolling again in good weather, became bottomless bogs in the rainy season, or as the Russians style it, the infamous rasputitsa (season of mud). Tanks and trucks were immobilized, aircraft, operating from primitive airstrips, were forced to stand down.[42] It was not until mid-November that the drive on Moscow could be resumed, a drive that reached some 50 miles from the city. Again nature intervened, this time with freezing cold and snow, and the non-winterized Luftwaffe became a semi-immobile force of frozen planes. The Soviet Air Force had two advantages in the battle for Moscow: accustomed to cold-weather operations, its planes were prepared for the freezing temperatures, and the rapid German advance served to extend logistics and only primitive airstrips were available, while the Soviet retreat meant that the VVS was both shortening its supply lines and falling back on relatively well-equipped airfields. In addition, the considerable assets of Moscow's PVO aviation were merged with Frontal and Long-Range Bomber Aviation in a unified command under the control of the head of the Red Army Air Force, thus facilitating economy of effort and enhanced flexibility. According to the Russians, the VVS flew over 15,000 sorties to the Luftwaffe's 3,500 between mid-November and December 5.[43]

The Soviets under Zhukov's plan for counterattack by all 3 Russian *Fronts* in the Moscow area got off the mark on December 5, and by the 25th the German threat to Moscow had been eliminated. Zhukov's Western *Front* was supported by Frontal, PVO and Long-Range Aviation, the latter a misnomer for a force that "bombed and strafed his [German] infantry marching formations, tank and truck columns."[44] The other two fronts were also ably assisted by their air components. The Soviets had marshalled around 1,200 aircraft to half that number for the Luftwaffe. The combination of withdrawing aircraft from the Eastern Front to aid in the Mediterranean theater and the severe losses incurred in using bomber-type planes (Bf–110s, He–111s, and Ju–88s) for close-support reduced the number of aircraft available drastically. In December 1941, the VVS finally attained air superiority in some localities, which went a long way in restoring a modicum of aggressiveness in the Soviet pilots.

Organizational Changes

Although Lt. Gen. Pavel F. Zhigarev was named Commander of the Red Army Air Forces [*Komanduyushchi VVS–RKKA*] almost immediately after the initiation of BARBAROSSA, his new designation gave him little authority to coordinate the various air forces into a cohoerent whole. The disastrous defeats of the first six months of the war, however, made it mandatory that something be done to get some unity into the application of air power. Because the VVS was shredded into a number of semi-autonomous forces under diverse commands, it was impossible during the early months of the war to organize massive air strikes in critical situations. According to the official Soviet account, the unified control of Army, Frontal, Long-Range, and PVO Aviation in the battle for Moscow paved the way for a more centralized Red air force.[45]

In April 1942, Gen. Aleksandr Novikov, the air commander on the Leningrad *Front*, was brought in to replace Zhigarev as head of the Red Army Air Force, a job he was to hold for the rest of the war. It was obvious to Novikov, as well as to his bosses in *Stavka*, that with Army Aviation under ground command, Frontal Aviation under the *Front* commander, Long-Range Aviation under *Stavka*, naval aviation under fleet admirals, and, in extreme cases, air squadrons under separate army corps, operational unity was not just difficult to achieve—it was impossible. On May 5, 1942, therefore, an order from the Commissariat of Defense instituted some changes. It was pointed out that in order to augment the striking power of the air force so that it could be used in massive attacks, the air forces of the Western Front were to be united in the First Air Army.[46] Army Aviation was completely abolished as a separate entity, ADD* was left under the direct control of *Stavka*, and PVO Aviation remained somewhat autonomous. Most of the air assets, however, began to be grouped into air armies. The new organization proved to be so effective that by 1945 there were 17 air armies with a total of 175 air divisions under their control.[47] An 18th Air Army was formed in December 1944, but it was merely a new designation for ADD.

Another problem was the scarcity of air reserves available to *Stavka* for bolstering air support on tottering fronts. The main reserve in 1941 was Long-Range Aviation (then called DBA) along with air units in the interior of the country. Such a paucity of air units handicapped *Stavka* in attempts to show some flexibility in shifting units about. Finally, in August 1942, *Stavka* reserves were greatly enlarged by the creation of ten air corps,

---

*The designation DBA for Long-Range Aviation was changed to ADD [*aviatsiia dal'nego deistviaa*] in March 1942, at which time it was under the command of Gen. A. E. Golovanov.

each corps consisting of two or more air divisions mostly equipped with new and better planes.[48] By mid-November, on the eve of the Stalingrad counteroffensive, *Stavka* Reserves amounted to over thirty-two percent of the total aircraft of all the fronts.[49] These reserves enabled *Stavka* to be much more flexible in shifting air power to where, and at what time, it was most needed. The air armies reinforced by *Stavka* Reserve air corps were able to deliver the massive air attacks so lacking in the first period of the war.

On the lower level, the divisions of Frontal Aviation, mostly composite, were made into homogeneous fighter, bomber, or ground-attack divisions. Their regiments in turn were standardized. For example, a fighter regiment now had around thirty-six aircraft divided into two squadrons each with four four-fighter flights plus the squadron leader's pair. The number of planes per division varied with the type of regiment. A bomber regiment had twenty-seven aircraft, a ground-attack one had twenty-two aircraft.[50]

Central control and coordination within the VVS were helped greatly by the dispatching of *Stavka* representatives for aviation to the various theaters. These were senior air commanders representing the authority of the Supreme Command. The representative had an operational staff of five officers with him, and the team studied the situation on maps, prepared orders for the commanders of the air armies, defined ADD's missions, and coordinated all air operations with the front commanders.[51] During the battle for Stalingrad, Novikov himself went to the area to coordinate the efforts of the air armies of the several fronts involved and to bring ADD and PVO aviation into the synchronized effort. He was in control of the 2d, 16th, 17th, and 8th Air Armies plus the two air corps and seven divisions sent to the battle zone by *Stavka* from its reserves. He was also a member of the group of *Stavka* representatives, headed by Marshal Zhukov, that planned and carried out the counteroffensive (November 19, 1942, through February 2, 1943).[52] As the Soviet offensive operations widened after Stalingrad, *Stavka* representatives for aviation increased in number to accommodate the growing number of *Fronts*. For example, immediately after the victory at Stalingrad, Gen. F. Ya. Falaleyev was sent out to coordinate the operations of the air armies of the Southern and Southwestern *Fronts* and was later to do the same for the VVS forces of the Voronezh and the Southwest *Fronts*. To list the names of the Stavka representatives for aviation over the last three years of the war is to call the roll of the top air commanders of the Red air force in World War II. These people carried clout when they arrived on the scene.

Development of Air Tactics

Despite Soviet protestations to the contrary, the Luftwaffe fighter pilots outclassed their Russian counterparts decisively in the first year and a half of the war. The Russians were faced with the catastrophic loss of planes in 1941–42, the German advantage in battle-hardened fliers in better machines, the inflexibility of the average Soviet flier, and a reluctance to engage in air combat with the enemy. Pilot desperation even manifested itself in the ramming [taran] of German aircraft, a maneuver in which the Russian flier, his ammunition exhausted, would fly his plane into his opponent's, usually trying to cut up the empennage with his prop. If done skillfully, or with luck, the Russian pilot might be able to land his damaged plane or succeed in bailing out. In the early years of the war the exchange of an obsolescent I–16 for a German bomber with a two- or three-man crew was a good swap from the point of view of the VVS, but by 1943 most Soviet fighters were modern enough to make it a poor trade for obsolescent German bombers. Consequently, the taran maneuver fell out of favor.[53]

By 1943, as was shown in air combat over the Kuban River area in the North Caucasus, and in the mass engagement at Kursk, the Soviet pilots were displaying more aggressiveness and much more flying skill. They had acquired extensive combat experience, were equipped with much better machines, and were the products of better training. Local air superiority at widely separated locations, such as the defense of Moscow in December 1941 and the battle of Stalingrad a year later, was transformed into air superiority along most of the Soviet-German front by late 1943. It was the Luftwaffe that was reduced to the role of striving for temporary air superiority at crucial points along the front after the Battle of Kursk.

By late 1942, Soviet fliers were using different and more flexible tactics. The basic flight unit was by then the pair, or para, and the flight of two pairs, the zveno, was in vogue in place of the former flight of three aircraft in a tight V, or "Vic" formation, forced to stick close together because of the lack of on-board radios. Continuous combat against the German Rotte, a loose pair, or the Schwarm, a flight of two pairs, convinced the best Russian pilots that emulation was in order. The Rotte and Schwarm, as one author put it, "was never bettered . . . and was adopted by all the major air forces."[54] A larger German formation consisting of three Schwarme, the Staffel, was also duplicated in the Soviet gruppa, a formation of three or four pairs. The great advantage of the para was that it enabled each pilot to cover the other's blind spots; in other words it was "the classic fighting pair, the leader and his wingman to cover him."[55] In the numerous dogfights over the Kuban in the spring of 1943, the para and the zveno of four aircraft became the standard fighter units.[56]

195

The Soviet fighter pilots by 1943 no longer flew horizontally all the time. The new tendency was for the formations to be echeloned upwards. Aleksandr A. Pokryshkin, who became Russia's second leading flier in the number of kills, came up with the dictum in 1943 that altitude was the primary objective in air combat because it enabled the pilot to dive at his opponent with the consequent increase in speed and maneuverability.[57] The Pokryshkin formula was "altitude-speed-maneuver-fire."[58] The formula, however, was easier to chant than to comply with effectively. But as more and better fighters became available, and machines more comparable to the German Bf–109s and Focke-Wulf 190s, more Russian pilots followed Pokryshkin's guidelines in air combat. The use of vertical tactics became more widespread as the pilots mastered their new planes, especially the La–5s and Yak–7Bs.

The euphoria engendered by the victory at Stalingrad and the excellent showing over the Kuban resulted in an increased aggressiveness on the part of the Soviet pilots. They began to attack their opponents with more confidence. It was also early in the spring of 1943 that the so-called "free hunters," or *Okhotniki*, began to operate effectively. The *Okhotniki* were volunteers accepted from among the best and most battle-hardened fliers in the air divisions and regiments. A "free hunting" unit was usually a *para* or *zveno* of fighters or fighter-bombers whose mission was to seek out targets of opportunity and carry out reconnaissance simultaneously. The *Okhotniki* were very effective in tightening the air blockade around the Stalingrad pocket.

Lack of radar made air defense a difficult chore, and it was not until the late autumn of 1942 that there was any wide use of radio for fighter control. The Soviets claimed that at that time the 16th Air Army was equipped with a radio network for fighter control. It consisted of a central station at 16th Air Army headquarters, radio stations at divisional and regimental levels, plus stations along the front for target control. Twenty-five commanders of reserve regiments were brought in as forward controllers, and even a manual on directing fighters by radio appeared in September 1942.[59]

Training of Flying Personnel

One of the main causes for the Soviet victory on the Eastern Front was the Luftwaffe's ever-increasing shortages in both aircraft and aircrews as the war wore on. At the outset of the war there was no doubt about the superiority of the German pilots and their equipment. The Soviet fliers, lacking the extensive combat experience of the Luftwaffe pilots and flying inferior aircraft, took a bad beating in the opening months of the war, an

196

experience that gave them an inferiority complex for some time. Soviet air tactics were also behind those of the Luftwaffe, and it was not until well into 1942 that the Soviets emulated the looser and more flexible tactics of their opponents.

In spite of the June catastrophe, however, the Soviets managed to keep an air force in being and by late 1941 and early 1942 had received enough replacement aircraft to make creditable showings at Leningrad and Moscow. Although many Soviet aircraft were destroyed on the ground in the opening days of the war, many pilots escaped disaster and were available to man the new aircraft being produced. Nevertheless, losses in aircrews were high enough to induce substantial cutbacks in training programs. By 1943, the situation in planes and manpower had improved enough to allow the old regimen to be reinstituted.

During the war the importance of the Voluntary Society for the Promotion of Defense, Aviation, and Chemical Warfare [*Osoaviakhim*] in preparing aircrews, especially pilots, declined, and most pilots began their training in primary flying schools. One German account reports that there were 130 of them by the latter part of the war. The trainees spent 9 to 12 months in primary flying schools before going to service schools for advanced training in their specialty. There were 60 for fighter pilots, 30 for bomber types, 30 for ground-attack fliers, and 8 for long-range aviation. The entire training program lasted from 12 to 14 months. The student load at the different schools varied widely, from 200 to 2,000, with the average fighter school having 750 trainees.[60] Since the Soviet Union had no manpower problems, the production of pilots exceeded the output of aircraft, a situation quite contrary to that prevailing in Germany.

The Luftwaffe, despite its easy triumphs in the initial months of the war, did suffer a steady drain in men and planes as it expended its energies in close support of the ground forces. Furthermore, as early as 1942, the Germans began to raid their training program for emergency operations on the Eastern and Mediterranean Fronts. Both training aircraft and instructors were siphoned off to meet these situations. For example, a German force of around 100,000 men was surrounded by the Soviets in early January 1942 at Demyansk, and the Luftwaffe was ordered to supply the entrapped force by air. For 3 months (February 20 to May 18) the German Ju–52 transports delivered an average of 276 tons a day to the beleaguered troops, while enduring the worst possible weather and overflying hostile territory. But the loss of 265 transports with their crews was a high price to pay. Furthermore, as a German writer points out, it set a precedent that led to a disastrous loss of pilots and transports—the ill-fated airlift designed to supply Paulus's Sixth Army trapped at Stalingrad.[61] Later in 1942, some 320 Ju–52s were sent to the Mediterranean theater to aid the faltering German campaign in North Africa, and 164 of them were lost. That, combined with the 495 transports expended in the Stalingrad fiasco, made a total of 659 transports and aircrews, many of them from the training schools, lost by the Luftwaffe. One writer quotes a captured German officer as saying that they had no crews since the instructor crews were shot down with the Junkers.[62]

This was only one element in the manifold woes besetting the Luftwaffe in the latter part of the war, but it was a very important one. There was no single cause for the shortage of pilots, but rather a conglomeration. The cavalier attitude of Goering and his staff toward training programs, the fuel crisis that necessitated the curtailment of student flying, the shortage of operational aircraft for student training, and the accelerating loss rates in three different theaters (Eastern, Mediterranean, and the *Reich* itself), all resulted in shorter and shorter training time for the Luftwaffe aircrews. In 1943 an intense effort, somewhat belated, led to a doubling of the number of fighter pilots, but the increase barely covered the losses. By 1944, the experience and skill levels of Luftwaffe fighter pilots began to plummet. This declining ability of the pilots increased the losses, which in turn forced further shortening of training time, a vicious circle that proved fatal.[63]

The Russians, however, with an ever-increasing output of both planes and pilots, could afford to lengthen their training times in order to sharpen flying skills. The pilots upon leaving the service schools went to replacement regiments and received further advanced instruction. Throughout most of the war the flying crews were then sent to air training regiments attached to air armies from which they were gradually introduced into combat units. As Maj. Gen. Walther Schabedissen put it, the Soviet training program was well organized with adequate time for thorough preparation for entry into combat.[64]

The Aircraft

It was not until the fall of 1942 that the Russians acquired a sufficient number of new types of planes to give the Germans a real fight. The temporary air superiority won in the defense of Leningrad and Moscow in the winter of 1941–42 owed more to the weather than to the quality of Russian aircraft or their pilots. During 1941 and most of 1942, Soviet fighters were inferior to the German Bf–109. The MiG–3 was less than adequate at lower altitudes where, of course, the fighting was; the LaGG–3 was more dangerous for its pilots than was the enemy; and only the Yak–1 lived up to expectations. By the summer of 1942, almost a third of the frontline fighter regiments were equipped with Yak–1s.[65]

Two new fighters came into the VVS inventory in time for the Battle of Stalingrad—the La–5 and the Yak–9. The La–5 was a radical adaptation of the LaGG–3, the new aircraft having an air-cooled radial engine in place of the LaGG–3's liquid-cooled power plant. The La–5 went into production in

July 1942, and by the end of 1942 a total of 1,129 had been delivered.[66] A regiment of La–5s, manned by factory pilots, was rushed into the Stalingrad battle where it performed astonishingly well. The plane was very maneuverable at low-to-medium altitudes, handled well, and was a pilot's delight. By the time production ceased in late 1944, a total of 10,000 La–5s had been delivered. Later developments by the Lavochkin OKB included the La–7, which went into series production in the second half of 1944, some 5,733 being built in the last year of the war. It had a maximum speed of well over 400 miles per hour and was designed to intercept the German FW–190A–8.[67]

The Yak–9 went into production in the latter part of 1942 and made its debut at the Battle of Stalingrad in the winter of 1942–43. The plane was used both as an interceptor and as a fighter-bomber. Also in 1943, the Yak–3 came into the inventory. The production of Yakovlev fighters during the war came to a total of 36,732, including 8,721 Yak–1s, 6,399 Yak–7s, 16,769 Yak–9s, and 4,484 Yak–3s.[68] The later Yakovlev planes were excellent fighters, able to fly fast, maneuver at all altitudes, handle well, and were, in short, worthy opponents for the Bf–109s and FW–190s in dog fights.

The Messerschmitt Bf–109 was one of the best fighters in World War II and certainly better than anything the VVS could put against it during the first year and a half of combat on the Eastern Front. Designed by Professor Willi Messerschmitt in 1935 and picked as the Luftwaffe's standard single-

The Yak–3, with its high speed and maneuverability at all altitudes, proved a formidable opponent to the Luftwaffe's fighters.

199

seat fighter, it kept its ascendency throughout most of World War II. Some preproduction models were sent to Spain in December 1936 for evaluation under combat conditions, and they came to dominate the Spanish skies by late 1937. The new fighter entered Luftwaffe service in early 1937. The backbone of the Luftwaffe's fighter force on the Eastern Front on the eve of the launching of BARBAROSSA was the Bf–109E and Bf–109F, the EMILS and FRIEDRICHS. The latter was the finest version of the many models of the Bf–109, although succeeded in late 1942 by the Bf-109G, the GUSTAV. The Bf–109F had a maximum speed of 388 miles per hour, a range of over 500 miles, and a service ceiling of nearly 40,000 feet. The Messerschmitt fighter accounted for over two-thirds of Germany's output of single-seat fighters, a total of over 33,000 aircraft.[69]

The other German premier fighter of World War II was the Focke-Wulf FW–190, an aircraft "regarded by many as the Luftwaffe's finest piston-engined fighter of the war."[70] First flown in mid-1939, it entered service in mid-1941. It had an air-cooled radial engine, unique among German fighters, a maximum speed of just over 400 miles per hour and a range of 500 miles. By the end of 1942, some 2,000 FW–190s had been produced, and by the end of the war output totaled 19,500. In the hands of a skilled Luftwaffe pilot, the FW–190 was a formidable weapon system.

In close support aircraft the two sides were fairly evenly matched after the first disastrous year. The German Ju–87 Stuka dive bomber, which wreaked such havoc in Spain, Poland, the Low Countries, and France in 1939–40, was already obsolescent by the time of the Battle of Britain when it met the Hurricanes and Spitfires, but was able to play a major role in Russia so long as the Luftwaffe maintained air superiority. By 1943, however, the Stuka was taking heavy losses unless it had fighter cover. With a maximum speed of only 255 miles per hour, it could not outrun Soviet interceptors and was very vulnerable when coming out of a dive.

Another German dive bomber, the Ju–88, came into service in August 1940. A twin-engine multi-place aircraft, it served in many capacities during the war. It became, with minor modifications, a bomber, a dive bomber, a ground-attack plane, and a *Zerstorer,* or heavy fighter. With a full bomb load it could only travel at a slow 258 miles per hour, however, which made it an easy target for fast pursuit planes. Nevertheless, the Ju–88 in its various guises was the most numerous of the twin-engine German aircraft produced during the war—over 15,000 of them.[71]

Its Soviet competitor, the famous Il–2 *Shturmovik,* designed by Yakovlev between 1938 and 1940, entered service in limited numbers in July 1941. The original single-seat version was extremely vulnerable to attack from the rear, but in 1942 a second seat was installed to accommodate a rear gunner. Heavily armed and armored, the Il–2 became one of the most celebrated Soviet aircraft in the Great Patriotic War and a tank destroyer par excellence. Another Soviet dive bomber, the Pe–2, was an effective close-support aircraft. Designed by Vladimir M. Petlyakov's OKB, the Pe–2 was a two-seat monoplane powered by two 1,000-horsepower engines equipped with superchargers and went into series production in 1940. Over the next 5 years, the Soviet aircraft industry turned out 11,426 Pe–2s. The plane carried 5 machineguns and a 3,300-pound bomb load and had a top speed of 335 miles per hour.[72]

Until at least 1944, the erosion of German technological superiority vis-à-vis the gradual improvement of Soviet aircraft and equipment was offset by the skill of the German pilot. But that advantage diminished as the Luftwaffe's loss of aircrews led to an infusion of skimpily trained fliers. Furthermore, most of the German planes on the Eastern Front were at best modified versions of the 1935–39 generation, while many Soviet aircraft were designed after the onset of the war, as for instance the later Yakovlev and Lavochkin fighters and the two-seat Il–2.

Aircraft Production Ratios

As World War II ground on into 1943 and 1944, it became evident that pilot skill, superior or at least equal equipment, and tactical know-how could offset some numerical disadvantages only to a certain point; and the Luftwaffe had reached that point. The Germans were being out-produced in aircraft not only by the British and Americans, but even by the Russians, and the numbers game was looming ever larger as a decisive factor in the air war. Even in 1941 the Soviet aviation industry turned out more planes than did its German rival and in the following year exceeded German production by 10,000 aircraft. It was not until 1944 that the *Reich* came abreast of the U.S.S.R. in output. By then, however, the Luftwaffe had additional problems—the defense of the homeland from Anglo-American strategic bombardment, the horrendous loss in aircrews, and a serious fuel shortage. Ironically, just when the German industry reached a crescendo, other factors reduced the value of its effort drastically.

Soviet historians downplay the Allied role in the defeat of Germany and are especially contemptuous of the Anglo-American strategic bombing as a factor in the undoing of the Luftwaffe. To the Western observer, the diversion of the best German aircraft to the Mediterranean Theater and to the defense of the *Reich,* and the resultant heavy attrition of the Luftwaffe first-line planes and aircrews, would seem to be very important factors indeed in the defeat of German air power. The Luftwaffe had chosen to use its best fighters to defend against the onslaught of Allied bombers and could spare fewer and fewer first-line fighters for the Eastern Front. The Soviets, however, counter by pointing out that the VVS had gained air superiority in the late summer of 1943 at Kursk before the bombardment of the *Reich* had reached an effective stage.

The Soviet aviation industry had several advantages over its German counterpart. Where the Nazi leadership tended to be a conglomeration of independent fiefdoms, especially Goering's jealously guarded Luftwaffe, the Soviet war effort was definitely in the hands of one man, Stalin. He kept a close watch on the activities of the head of his aviation industry, Shakurin, and his deputy Yakovlev, and their directives had the backing of the commander in chief himself. The Luftwaffe high command, on the other hand, was a maze of competing careerists busily engaged in intrigues, all possible because of Goering's notorious indolence and Hitler's on-and-off attitude toward air power. Thus, no one person exercised overall supervision in the matching of aircraft procurement to present and future strategic needs.[73] Moreover, lulled into overweening confidence early in the war that victory was assured and that there was no need to put the nation on an all-out war effort, the German aircraft industry tended to coast along until well into 1943. As one writer points out: "Unfortunately for the Luftwaffe, in the production of aircraft, the training of men, and the development of new equipment, its high command was sadly deficient."[74]

The Luftwaffe, furthermore, was simultaneously facing even more productive enemies than the Russians. For example, in 1943, when the Luftwaffe was in serious trouble in the Mediterranean Theater and on the Eastern Front, and at a time when Allied strategic bombing was beginning to exact a toll on German industry, the German aviation industry produced only 22 percent of the Anglo-American output in aircraft and only 16.8 percent if one adds in the Russian production, in other words, 24,800 planes versus 146,900. In 1944 a tremendous surge in the production of fighters brought the German output in aircraft up to 39,800, but that all-out effort seemed slight in comparison with the 163,000 planes turned out by her 3 main enemies. In short, the German aviation industry was delivering only 24 percent as many aircraft. Even a comparison of German and Russian aircraft production shows the Germans lagging badly in 1943, just about even in 1944, about 34,000 to 24,000 in the former year, and 40,300 to 39,800 in the latter.[75]

It is possible that if the German planes had been far superior to those of its enemies, the adverse ratios just described might not have been so injurious to the life expectancy of the Luftwaffe. Yet, most of the aircraft the Germans were turning out in 1943 and 1944 were slightly modified versions of those produced in the preceding three years, planes that had been in series production even before the war. By early 1943, 80 percent of the Luftwaffe's combat aircraft consisted of six types: Ju–87, Ju–88, He–111, Bf–109, Bf–110, and FW–190; and the He–111, Ju–87, and Bf–110 were obsolete.[76] Attempts to produce new types for the replacement of the obsolete ones were often unsuccessful as the intended successor did not live up to expectations. For instance, the intended replacement for the He–111, the He–177, turned out to have serious design difficulties and never reached mass production. To add to the Luftwaffe's list of woes, in 1943, and even more so in 1944, the intense pressure on the aviation industry for increased output, especially in fighters, plus the necessity to disperse the industry widely because of the Allied bombing, did quality control no good.[77]

Like the Germans, the Soviets did not innovate much in the production of aircraft during the war. Heavy attrition throughout the war, especially in the 1941–42 period, made the Soviets very cautious about interrupting production lines to introduce new types of planes and engines. Thus, only one basically new aircraft went into production during the war, the Tu–2 twin-engine medium bomber that came into service in early 1944. The rest were further developments of planes already on the line when the war came or shortly thereafter. In engine production, the "nothing-new" concept was extremely rigid. For example, by 1942 Klimov had improved his M–105

The Ilyushin Il–2 *Shturmovik*, a two-seat ground attack plane, was one of the Soviet Union's most effective weapons in the war against Germany.

The Petlyakov Pe–2 proved to be an outstanding dive bomber, and together with the Il–2, accounted for the bulk of Russian bomber production in World War II.

engine considerably, but the new engine, the M–107, was not put into series production until 1944 because the demand for engines was so great that interruptions to retool or delays by assembly-line changeover were certain to get a resounding *"nyet"* from Stalin and his GKO.[78]

Radio-Radar Capabilities

Throughout the war the Soviets lagged behind both the Germans and the Allies in the use of radio and radar. As of June 22, 1941, the VNOS [*vosdushnoe nablyudenie, opoveschenie i suyaz'*], or Air Detection, Warning, and Communications Service, was all the Soviets had for early warning and alerting the air units of approaching attacks. VNOS deployed a regiment and nineteen separate battalions along the western frontier from the Baltic to the Black Sea, and only one battalion and three separate companies were in the radio business, the rest being restricted to visual observation.[79] With an unsophisticated system as thin as that, it is little wonder that Soviet air units were constantly being surprised, both on the ground and in the air. Unlike the separate Air Signal Corps of the Luftwaffe, Soviet signal officers were assigned to the air forces from the Red Army signal organization. According to German General Schwabedissen's description of the situation in 1941, the signal officers assigned to armies or *Fronts* in turn controlled the signal personnel in division, regiments, or lower level units at the mobile air bases. The personnel in the mobile air base units operated the wire and radio communications within their assigned airfield systems.[80] Former German airmen are nearly unanimous in their observation that Soviet radio transmissions were often in the clear, proof positive (in their opinion) of poor radio discipline.

By late 1941 Soviet ground-air communications in control of airborne fighter and ground-attack units were becoming much more frequent. But on the whole, adequate utilization of radio as an air-control tool was hindered by the shortage of equipment, the lack of trained personnel, and poor radio discipline.[81] During the defense of Stalingrad, VVS commander Gen. A. A. Novikov ordered the creation of a radio network for the 16th Air Army, a system consisting of a central station near the Air Army's headquarters, substations on the airfields of divisions and regiments, and transmitters along the front for direct communications with the fighters. The radio control stations, according to the Soviets, had the following tasks: "inform fliers in the air concerning the situation in the air; warning about enemy aircraft that might appear; summoning fighter planes from airfields and reassigning them to new targets."[82] The major method of air control in the counteroffensive was by radio.[83] In the area of reconnaissance, radio communications were widely used for the first time in the summer of 1942, but even then the reconnaissance was mostly tactical.[84]

Soviet radar, or RLS [*radiolakatsionnaya stantsiya*] in its Russian acronym, was relatively primitive when the war began for Russia. Soviet sources attribute an important role to it in the defense of Leningrad and Moscow in 1941 and claim that by the end of the war, RLS had become the chief means of detecting enemy aircraft and for vectoring Russian aircraft to their targets. Thus after 1943 "visual observation posts had virtually lost their importance as a means of detection for the PVO."[85] And according to Chief Marshal of Aviation P. Kutakhov, "with the acquisition of radar by the VVS (from September 1943) there began a wider use of the more economical method of operations—interception of enemy aircraft from the position of 'alert on the airfields.' "[86]

Progress in radio transmission improved considerably by 1943, and in the air operations over the Kuban in May, all the Russian fighters had radios aboard and along with the ground-attack aircraft "were systematically and consistently directed by radio control stations established along advance positions at the points of main effort."[87] By that time the VVS had much more control over its communications, and in 1944 radio-radar-telephonic communications in the VVS were made a separate command responsible to the Red Army Air Forces commander.

By the spring of 1944 the Russians were using radar quite extensively for detection and for guidance of their own aircraft in interception. Just how good their radar was and how well they used it is difficult to ascertain with any accuracy. For example, Schwabedissen in a passage that would have amazed contemporary Soviet authorities, claimed later that all the radars in Russia, as late as the autumn of 1944, "were ground-based instruments of British manufacture or instruments copied in the Soviet Union from British models."[88] Airborne interceptor radar was either lacking or was poorly used, which is no surprise since one of the weaknesses of the Communist air defense system in the Korean War (1950–53) was the absence of airborne interceptor radar on the night fighters.[89]

Most evaluations by Western historians seem in agreement that the Soviets improved their radio and radar capabilities considerably over the course of the war—somewhat hit or miss on occasion, but well enough organized on the whole to serve the VVS adequately.[90] There was a very mixed picture prior to early 1943, but from the May 1943 battle over the Kuban to the overwhelming of the Luftwaffe in 1945, the evidence indicates that communications in general steadily improved. However, even those who agree on the vast improvement in Soviet radio-radar services also agree that the Soviets' electronic systems were not up to those of the Germans or the Allies by quite a wide margin.[91]

Denouement in Europe, 1944 and 1945

The year of 1943, the *annus mirabilis* ("year of wonders") in Soviet military fortunes, was one in which the VVS wrested air superiority from the Luftwaffe. By the end of the year, the Germans, in obedience to Hitler's orders, were trying to hold a defensive line from near Leningrad to the Black Sea. By early 1944, with manpower stretched exceedingly thin, the German army commanders were clamoring for air support to supplement their inferior ground forces, but the Luftwaffe was stretched even thinner. German air power, which two and a half years earlier had been an overpowering offensive weapon on the Eastern Front, was now reduced to a defensive force rushing about like a fire brigade trying to put out fires all along the front.

While the Luftwaffe struggled to overcome a lack of good aircraft and, even more important, a shortage of skilled pilots, the VVS, supplied with an ever-increasing flow of excellent planes and good pilots, was dominating the air through sheer numbers. According to the Soviets, the Red Army only increased by 11 percent in manpower during 1943, but increased 80 percent in guns, 33 percent in tanks, and 100 percent in aircraft.[92] Russian industry proved itself more than adequate to fulfill the needs of the armed forces. Although Soviet statistics cannot be checked for accuracy, the following would seem to serve as rough indicators of the growing Soviet might in the air: the VVS had 1,200 aircraft in the Moscow counteroffensive, 5,000 during the battle for Kursk, 6,000 during the liberation of Byelorussia, and 7,500 at Berlin, and by then was able to coordinate the actions of 600 to 700 planes in a single operation. At the battle of Moscow, Soviet planes flew 16,000 combat sorties, 36,000 at Stalingrad, 90,000 at Kursk, and 153,000 sorties in the Byelorussian operation.[93] Making some allowance for the propensity of the then current commander in chief of the VVS to boast a bit, the difference between 16,000 sorties at Moscow in 1941 and 153,000 sorties in the Byelorussian operation in 1944 was not only impressive, but also tells the story of the Luftwaffe's loss of air superiority on the Eastern Front.

By March 1944, the Red Army, ably assisted by the VVS, pushed its frontline in the Ukraine to the Bug River, with a salient along the Black Sea that encompassed Odessa. In the north, the Baltic and the three Byelorussian *Fronts* took to the offensive on June 22 in commemoration of the Nazi attack in 1941. The four *Fronts* had a combined total of 6,000 aircraft.[94] By July, Minsk had fallen and the Soviets had torn a 250-mile hole in the German lines, thus opening the path to Poland and Lithuania. In the south, the Ukrainian *Fronts,* four of them, tore into Rumania, helped by the Rumanian Army's turning on its erstwhile German ally. By the fall of 1944 the various Ukrainian *Fronts* had fanned out over the Balkans.

The VVS was not only getting more planes, but also getting better ones. The Yak–9, which made its first appearance over Stalingrad in the winter of 1942–43, was being used in 1944 not only as an interceptor, but also as a ground attack plane and a fighter-bomber. In mid-1943 Yakovlev increased its fuel capacity giving the Yak–9D (*dal'niy,* long-range) a range of 870 miles. Its range was extended even further in 1944 as the Yak–9DD (*dal'nyy deystiya,* long-range operations) could get from the Ukraine to Italy, a distance of 1,120 miles. This plane was used as an escort for the American B–24 and B–17 bombers in their shuttle-bombing runs. It had a top speed of about 380 miles per hour.[95] The Petlyakov Pe–2 underwent improvements throughout the war. When the new German Bf–109G appeared on the Russian Front in early 1943, the Pe–2 was enhanced with a M–105PF engine which could develop over 1,200 horsepower.[96]

By 1944 the German bombers had to confine their activities to night operations since they had practically no fighter cover for daytime activities. The Yak–3 (replacing the Yak–1 on the production lines in the summer of 1943) poured into the VVS inventory in 1944. A 400 mile-per-hour fighter, it was a match for the Bf–109G and the Focke-Wulf FW–190. The Lavochkin La–7, which went into series production in the summer of 1944, had a top speed of 420 miles per hour and was especially designed to cope with the FW–190.[97]

By early 1945 the Russians were poised to administer the *coup de grace* to their Nazi foes. On the Soviet-German front they had 11 air armies with a total of nearly 15,000 combat aircraft against the Luftwaffe's 1,875 planes, the Russian inventory having nearly doubled in a year.[98] The VVS's overwhelming edge over the Luftwaffe was dramatically illustrated when Col. Gen. S. I. Rudenko's 16th Air Army was increased to over 2,500 air-

The ubiquitous Yak–9 fighter served across the entire Eastern front.

craft in January 1945, giving Rudenko a more than 20–to–1 superiority over his opponent, while Krasovsky's 2d Air Army was increased to 2,588 aircraft.[99] In January 1945 the Red Army smashed into Poland and began its march on Berlin at the rate of 12 to 14 miles a day. Finally, in the attack on Berlin in April 1945, the VVS was able to concentrate 7,500 of its 15,540 combat aircraft against the pitiful remnants of the once proud Luftwaffe. The Soviet claim of 1,132 German planes shot down in the battle for Berlin may be dubious, but there can be no doubt about who controlled the air over that city.[100]

Soviet-Japanese War in the Far East

Once Germany had surrendered, the Soviets were free to enter the conflict against Japan. Until the Yalta Conference in February 1945, Stalin wanted no part of a two-front war since the Russo-Japanese Neutrality Pact of April 13, 1941, allowed him to concentrate his forces in the west and draw down on forces in the east. With Germany on the ropes, however, Stalin at Yalta agreed "that in two or three months after Germany has surrendered and the war in Europe has terminated the Soviet Union shall enter the war against Japan. . . ."[101] The buildup of the Soviet forces in the Far East began soon after the Yalta meeting. According to Japanese intelligence, by June, a daily average of 10 troop trains and 5 munition trains arrived in the Far East. The Japanese estimated that between April and the end of July, the Soviets increased their strength in the Far East from 850,000 to 1,600,000 troops, 1,300 to 4,500 tanks, and 3,500 to 6,500 aircraft.[102] Gen. John R. Deane gives slightly different figures: 1,500,000 men, 3,000 tanks, and 5,000 aircraft,[103] while the Soviet figures for their forces in that area on August 5, 1945, were 1,577,725 troops, 3,704 tanks, and 5,368 aircraft, of which 4,807 were combat planes.[104] These forces faced a total Japanese opposition in Manchuria, Inner Mongolia, Korea, and the Kurile Islands of about 1,000,000 men, 1,215 tanks, 1,800 aircraft, and 6,700 guns and mortars.[105] The Japanese and their Mongolian and Manchukuoan allies were the residue left behind when the Japanese high command finished pulling out the best cadres to send to other fronts.

Marshal A. M. Vasilevsky directed the operations against the Japanese, and he had 3 *Fronts* under his command: the 1st Far Eastern *Front* under Marshal K. A. Meretskov was deployed from Vladivostok to Bikin and included the 9th Air Army; the 2d Far Eastern *Front* under General M. A. Purkayev stretched from Bikin to where the Amur turns south toward Mongolia, and he was in charge of the 10th Air Army; and, finally, the Trans-Baikal *Front*, with the 12th Air Army, commanded by Marshal R.

Ya. Malinovsky, was strung out along some 1,300 miles of Mongolian-Manchurian border. The offensive, which began on August 9, called for all 3 *Fronts* to push into Manchuria, but the main punch to be delivered by Malinovsky's Trans-Baikal *Front* plunging through the Great Khingan Mountains toward Changchun and Mukden. Malinovsky's tanks penetrated some 250 miles into Manchuria by August 15, and his greatest problem was not Japanese resistance, but supplying his machines with fuel. By August 19 the Japanese Kwantung Army had arranged surrender terms with Vasilevsky.

Air operations played a minor role in the August campaign in the Far East. The VVS flew only 14,030 combat sorties and 7,427 noncombat missions, partly because of the inclement weather between August 11 and 20. About a fourth of the sorties were reconnaissance, but the most important contribution of the Air Force to the campaign was the hauling of supplies and men. The transports carried 2,777 tons of POL, 16,497 men, and 2,000 tons of munitions and other materiel.[106]

Gaining air superiority was an easy task for the battle-hardened VVS. The Japanese planes were obsolete, the best having been siphoned off to oppose the American drive across the Pacific. The Japanese fighters, Type 97 and Type 1 (Nakajima fighters NATE and OSCAR) were 60 to 100 miles per hour slower than the Soviet Yak–9s and La–7s, while the Mitsubishi bombers were 100 miles per hour slower than the Russian Pe–2s and Tu–2s.[107] In addition, the Soviets were fighting a disheartened Japanese Army—the atomic bombs hit Hiroshima on August 6 and Nagasaki on the 9th. On August 10, the Emperor told the Imperial Council that the war must end. All in all, this was not the milieu in which troops could give their all in a do-or-die effort.

Despite the fact that the Red Army was attacking a badly demoralized Kwantung Army, in some respects a Soviet "mopping-up operation," the speed with which the armored and motorized forces, in close synchronization with the VVS, carried out the campaign testified to lessons well-learned on the Eastern (German) Front over four years of hard campaigning. A comparison between the smoothly coordinated air operations in Manchuria, northern China, Korea, and the Kuriles in August 1945 and the bewildered Red Army and its air forces in the summer of 1941 was a vivid demonstration of how well the Soviet commanders had been trained in the murderously effective school of combat.

How the VVS Achieved Air Superiority

It would seem that the main reason for the Soviet victory in the air war on the Eastern Front was the overwhelming numerical superiority in both aircraft and manpower. The German and Soviet historians are at variance in their evaluations of how well or how poorly the VVS and the Luftwaffe fought the air war, and their statistics are very often far apart. Yet, they do agree that the VVS had a vast superiority in aircraft and aircrews in 1944 and 1945.

Although the VVS took a murderous licking in the summer and fall of 1941, probably losing around 10,000 planes, a high percentage of them were destroyed on the ground and thus did not entail the loss of pilots and navigators. This factor was to loom largely in favor of the Soviets when aircraft did become available in respectable numbers in 1942, since it was easier to replace a plane than a trained pilot. By the spring of 1942 the Soviet aviation industry was rolling out enough aircraft to put the VVS back in business. In addition, by November 1942 the Allies had delivered 3,000 planes to the Russians.[108]

During the Great Patriotic War, the Soviet aircraft industry turned out 125,000 planes, while the Germans produced only 100,000 between 1941 and the middle of 1945. The Soviets, however, had only 1 front to supply while the Germans were using large numbers of their aircraft in the Mediterranean Theater and in defending the *Reich* against the British and American bombers. By 1943 the Luftwaffe was drawing down on its aircraft in Russia to supply the needs of the Mediterranean and home fronts. This left the Eastern Front with a relative scarcity of planes and many of those obsolete at that. The Germans, because of the Luftwaffe's muddled leadership and Hitler's misconceptions concerning the role of air power, were late in putting the aircraft industry on a full-time basis. That they could have done much better in the production of aircraft, especially fighters, is borne out by the output figures for 1943 and 1944. In 1941 and 1942, when the German aircraft industry was relatively secure from Allied bombing, the industry produced only 11,776 and 15,409 planes, respectively, for a total of 27,185 versus the Soviet total of 41,171 for those same two years. Yet in 1944, when the *Reich* was being plastered by Allied bombers, the German aviation industry turned out 39,807 aircraft, almost the same as the Russian production for that year.[109] By then, however, the vast majority of those aircraft were needed to defend the homeland, and only a relatively sparse allotment could be spared to bolster the Eastern Front.

The same disparity existed in available aircrews—the Russians had enough to fill all available cockpits and the time to train them adequately. For reasons previously mentioned, the Germans were caught in a vicious circle. As early as the airlift rescue of the troops trapped in the Demyansk pocket in early 1942, the Luftwaffe had to call on both planes and instructors in some of its flying schools, a reinforcement that was costly in both training aircraft and pilot-instructors. As flying training courses in Germany were shortened, the pilots entered combat insufficiently trained and casualties rose rapidly. For example, German fighter losses in the July–December 1941 period came to 447 in combat and 378 from noncombat causes, while in the January–June 1944 period, losses stood at 2,855 in combat and 1,345 noncombat-related, losses far greater than any increase in the inventory would seem to warrant.[110] The increased casualty rate led to further slighting of pilot training with concomitantly still higher pilot losses.

Any evaluation of the Allied role in weakening Luftwaffe fighting capabilities on the Eastern Front immediately runs into an almost hysterical Soviet denigration of the Allied contribution to the air war. As the official history of the VVS in World War II has it: "Bourgeois falsifiers of World War II history attempt by any means at their disposal to minimize the role of the Soviet Air Force in the defeat of the Luftwaffe."[111] Their argument is that the Luftwaffe was already losing the air war over Russia by 1943, which was prior to any effective Allied bombing of the German homeland, and the increased German output of aircraft in 1944 and 1945 at the height of the Allied bombing amply demonstrates its ineffectiveness. There is little mention in Soviet accounts of the withdrawal of German aircraft from the Eastern Front between 1943 and 1945 for operations in the Mediterranean Theater and for defense of the homeland. Nor is there any acknowledgment, except in a derogatory form, of the contribution of Lend-Lease aircraft. But to the non-Russian it would seem obvious that the absence from the Russian front of large numbers of the Luftwaffe's best planes and most skilled pilots must have provided a great assist to the VVS.

Other contributing factors in the Soviet air victory were the qualitative improvements in aircraft, equipment, and tactics as the war wore on. By 1944, the Yak–9 and La–7 were worthy matches for the Bf–109G and the FW–190. Improved radio communications and increased use of radar by late 1943 were of enormous importance in command and control. The emulation of German fighter tactics, although learned somewhat slowly, helped the Soviet pilot immensely. As Pokryshkin points out, the working out of new combat procedures under substantially new conditions "was a complicated process."[112] Complex or not, by 1943 the Soviet fighters were flying in pairs, thinking in terms of altitude and vertical attack, and learning not to expend their ammunition while far from their target.

Finally, some of the blame for the German defeat in the air must be laid on Adolf Hitler. Hitler was ground-forces oriented and until late in the war left aviation pretty much to the commander in chief of the Luftwaffe, Reich Marshal Hermann Goering. Goering in turn, because of his "supinity" and "frivolous insouciance," left most of the direction of the air force to successive chiefs of staff, especially Hans Jeschonnek, who held that job between February 1939 and his suicide in August 1943.[113] Jeschonnek was incapable of questioning an order by Hitler, however potentially dangerous it might be. As Goering's stock with Hitler declined, the more readily Jeschonnek acquiesced in carrying out even ridiculous directives and in promising more than he could deliver, the ill-fated Stalingrad airlift being a case in point.

Stalin, however, was an aviation buff, taking an intense interest in design and production even before the war. He took a keen interest in the VVS's command structure, the procurement of its machines, and one of his outstanding designers, Yakovlev, gave Stalin high marks in knowledgeability of things aeronautical. Like his top commanders, Stalin learned during the war, and although prone to botch things up in 1941 and early 1942, he eventually assembled a capable staff in *Stavka,* a staff he listened to before making decisions. Despite Khrushchev's claim that Stalin plotted strategical operations on a schoolboy's globe, most of the testimony of those close to him on the *Stavka* portray him as keenly interested in, and knowledgeable about, the military situation at the front. It is hard to visualize Stalin as relying on his "intuition" or consulting an astrologer.

At least one historian, Von Hardesty, has likened the experience of the Soviet Air Force in World War II to that of a phoenix, rising from the ashes of defeat in 1941.[114] "The qualitative transformation of Soviet air power, telescoped in the time frame of 1942–43," he declared, "remains one of the most remarkable turnabouts of World War II."[115] Certainly one result of such transformation was the achievement of air superiority over the Luftwaffe, although the Russian experience emphasized purely localized achievement, and thus differed from the western Allied quest for theater-wide air superiority. The Soviet Union parleyed its vast geographical distances, tactics of attrition, the achievements of a redeployed and protected aviation industry east of the Urals, and brutish use of men and machines to achieve victory. Moreover, Soviet air leaders like Alexsandr Novikov tied air power to Red Army ground operations in a way unrepeated in the West. The VVS was not used as a separate strategic weapon. Localized air superiority was achieved through massing of aircraft to provide air cover for other distinctive Soviet tactics styled by Von Hardesty, "air offensive" (application of enormous firepower of armor, artillery, rockets, and aircraft for land breakthroughs) or "air blockade" (similar applications of aircraft to isolate enemy operations such as at Stalingrad). The vast extent of the war in Russia simply would not permit a goal of achieving overall air superiority for extended periods. Ironically, the Soviet Air Force never devoted prolonged operations to destroying the Luftwaffe as a fighting force in the manner of RAF and AAF strategic bombardment. Also, the VVS and the Luftwaffe never tangled one-on-one in a climactic struggle for air supremacy over the Eastern Front. The picture of the war in the East emerges then as two antagonists vying for air superiority only in the sense of aiding a combined arms operation. What matured for the VVS over the course of four, hard-fought years was teamwork with the Red Army. This union eventually steamrolled a steadily weakening German enemy, plagued by realization of her abiding prewar fears of fighting a multi-front war against a coalition of enemies.

Notes

1. *Istoriya Velikoy Otechestvennoy Voyna Sovetskogo Soyuza 1941–1945. [The History of the Great Fatherland War of the Soviet Union, 1941–1945]* (Moscow: *Voennoe Izdatel'stvo Ministerstva Oborony Soyuza* SSR, 1960), vol I, p 90. This is a six-volume cooperative effort published between 1960 and 1965. Referred to hereafter as *Ist. Velik. Otech. Voyn.*

2. *Aviatstroitel'*, No. 6 (June 1933), pp 1–2, as cited in *The Soviet Aircraft Industry*, Institute for Research in Social Science (Chapel Hill, N.C., 1955), p 6.

3. *Ist. Velik. Otech. Voyn.*, vol I, p 65.

4. *Aviatsiya i kosmonavtika* [Aviation and Cosmonautics], No. 1 (January 1974), p 23. The letter "I" in the I–15 stands for the Russian word *istrebitel'*, or "fighter," and the "R" for *razvedka*, or "reconnaissance." On the eve of the Great Patriotic War, the letter designation was changed to indicate the name of the designer of the aircraft.

5. W. Schwabedissen, Generalleutnant, *The Russian Air Force in the Eyes of German Commanders* (Maxwell AFB, Ala., 1960), p 26.

6. The Japanese refer to the conflict as the "Nomonhan Incident," while the Soviets call it the "Kalkhin-Gol Incident." The best account representing the Japanese point of view is in the two-volume work: *Japanese Studies in Manchuria*, vol XI, part 3, books A and B, "Small Wars and Border Problems: The Nomonhan Incident" (Washington, 1956). This work also includes an English translation of a Soviet account: S. N. Shishkin, *Kalkin-Gol* (Moscow: Military Publishing House, 1954). A Soviet account can be found in *Ist. Velik. Otech. Voyn*, vol I, pp 236–45. Also see John Erickson, *The Soviet High Command* (New York, 1962), pp 517–23 and 532–37.

7. Erickson, *Soviet High Command*, pp 505–06.

8. *Ibid.*, pp 500–01.

9. A. I. Shakurin, "Aviatsonnaya Promyshlennost' Nakanane Velikoy Otechestvennoy Voyny [The Aviation Industry on the Eve of the Great Fatherland War], *Voprosy Istorii*, 2 (1974), pp 81–99. A. S. Yakovlev, *Tel' zhizni* [The Aim of a Lifetime] (Moscow, 1966), p 183.

10. Jean Alexander, *Russian Aircraft Since 1940* (London, 1975), pp 193–95 and 421–24; A. S. Yakovlev, *Fifty Years of Soviet Aircraft Construction* (translated for NASA by the Israeli Program for Scientific Translations) (Washington, n.d.), p 55; *Aviatsiya i kosmonavtika*, 11 (November 1974), pp 24–25.

11. According to Zhukov, the Red Army received 17,745 combat planes, including 3,719 new types, between January 1939 and June 22, 1941, a little over 7,000 aircraft a year. *The Memoirs of Marshal Zhukov* (New York, 1971), pp 201–03.

12. G. Mikhaylovskiy and I. Vyrodov, "Vysshchiye organy rukovodstva voyny" [The Highest Organs in the Direction of the War], *Voennoistoricheskiy zhurnal*, 4 (April 1978), p 24.

13. *Ibid.*

14. Raymond Garthoff, *Soviet Military Doctrine* (Glencoe, Ill., 1953), p 196.

15. *Ibid.*, pp 209–10.

16. *Ist. Velik. Otech. Voyn.*, vol I, pp 476–77; V. Gorbachev, "Primenenie Sovetskikh VVS v nachal'nom periode Velikoy Otechestvennoy voyny" [Employment of the Soviet

VVS in the Initial Period of the Great Patriotic War], *Voenno- istoricheskiy zhurnal*, 11 (November 1983), p 31. Lt Gen Gorbachev also points out that the size of the regiment in that period (60 to 64 planes) made it necessary in some cases to occupy more than one airfield or to crowd them excessively on one field.

17. *Polevoy ustav Krasnoy Armii (proekt 1941 g*. [Field Regulations of the Red Army (projected for 1941)] (Moscow: Voenizdat', 1941), p 17 as cited in *Ist. Velik. Otech. Voyn.*, vol I, p 448.

18. *Boevoy ustav istrebitel'noy aviatsii 1940 g*. [Combat Regulations for Fighter Aviation 1940] (Moscow: Voenizdat', 1940), p 5, as cited in *Ist. Velik. Otech, Voyn.*, vol I, p 449.

19. *Boevoy ustav bombardirovochnoy aviatsii 1940 g*. [Combat Regulations for Bomber Aviation 1940] (Moscow, Voenizdat', 1940), pp 8–9, as cited in *Ist Velik. Otech. Voyn.*, vol I, p 449.

20. *Ist. Velik. Otech. Voyn.*, vol I, p 449.

21. Text of "Case Barbarossa" in H. R. Trevor-Roper, ed, *Blitzkrieg to Defeat: Hitler's War Directives, 1934–1945* (New York, 1964), pp 49–52.

22. H. Plocher, *The German Air Force Versus Russia, 1941*, ed. H. R. Fletcher (Maxwell AFB, Ala., 1965), pp 30–35.

23. *The Soviet Air Force in World War II*, ed. by Ray Wagner and trans. by L. Fetzer (New York, 1973), p 26; P. A. Rotmistrov, in his *Istoriya Voennogo Iskusstva* [A History of Military Art], 2 vols, (Moscow: Voennoe Izdatel'stvo Ministerstva Oborony SSR, 1963), vol II, p 43, gives a much higher figure for the German air strength. He has a total of 4,940 aircraft with the three main army groups, including the Rumanian contribution, plus the Finns with 900 planes for a grand total of 4,940 aircraft; Gorbachev, *Voenno-istoricheskiy zhurnal*, p 25, gives a figure very close to Rotmistrov's, viz. 4,980.

24. Garthoff, *Soviet Military Doctrine*, p 503.

25. *Ibid.*, p 429.

26. *Ist. Velik. Otech. Voyn.*, vol I, p 476.

27. *Ibid.*

28. Plocher, *German Air Force Versus Russia, 1941*, p 41.

29. *Ist. Velik. Otech. Voyn.*, vol II, p 16; Erickson, *Soviet High Command*, p 593, reports 2,000 Soviet aircraft destroyed in the first 48 hours.

30. Plocher, *German Air Force Versus Russia, 1941*, p 42.

31. Gorbachev, *Voenno-istoricheskiy zhurnal*, p 28.

32. Matthew Cooper, *The German Air Force 1933–1945: An Anatomy of Failure* (London, 1981), p 224.

33. *The Soviet Air Force in World War II*, pp 60–63.

34. *Ibid.*, p 44.

35. Up to March 1942, the Soviet long-range bombing force was called *Dal'nyaya bombardirovochnaya aviatsiya* or DBA. From March 1942 until December 1944 it was named *Aviatsiya dal'nego deystviya*, or ADD, and for the rest of the war was called the Eighteenth Air Army. Under any of the above designations, the "long-range" was a relative term since the inventory had more medium- and short-range bombers than really long-range ones. See A. Tyskin, "Taktika dal'ney bombardirovshnoy aviatsii v letne-osenney kampanni (1941 goda)" [Tactics of Long-range Bombardment Aviation in the Summer and Fall Campaign (1941)] *Voenno-istoricheskiy zhurnal*, 12 (December 1971), p 65.

36. V. Reshetnikov, "Primenenie aviatsiya dal'nego deystviya" [Employment of Long-range Aviation], *Voenno-istoricheskiy zhurnal*, 2 (February 1978), p 36.

37. Rotmistrov, *Istoriya Voennogo Iskusstva*, vol II, p 49.

38. Cooper, *The German Air Force*, pp 225–26.

39. *Ist. Veliki. Otech. Voyn.*, vol 6, pp 45–46.

40. *Ibid.*, pp. 45–48; Alexander, *Russian Aircraft*, pp 1–4.

41. Cooper, *The German Air Force*, p 262.

42. Albert Seaton, *The Battle for Moscow* (New York, 1971), chap 4.

43. *Soviet Air Force in World War II*, pp 78–79.

44. *Memoirs of Marshal Zhukov*, p 350.

45. *Soviet Air Force in World War II*, p 79.

46. *SVE*, vol 2, p 292; See M. Kozhevnikov, "Rozhdenie vozdushnykh armiy" [Birth of the Air Armies], *Voenno-istoricheskiy zhurnal*, 9 (September 1972), pp 68-72, for details. A

translation of this article by James Waddell can be found in *Aerospace Historian*, June 1975, pp 73–76.

47. Kozhevnikov, "Birth of the Air Armies," p 69.

48. *Ibid.*, p 70.

49. *Soviet Air Forces in World War II*, p 115.

50. Alexander Boyd, *The Soviet Air Force Since 1918* (New York, 1977), pp 144–45.

51. M. Kozhevnikov., "Koordinatsiya deystsviy VVS predstavitelyami Stavki VGK po aviatsii" [The Coordination of VVS Operations by Stavka VGK Representatives for Aviation], *Voenno-istoricheskiy zhurnal*, 2 (February 1974), pp 34–35.

52. *Ibid.*; Zhukov in his memoirs as quoted in the Kozhevnikov article lists the top Stavka representatives at Stalingrad, in addition to himself and Novikov; they included Golovanov, chief of ADD, Voronov, head of artillery, and Fedorenko, armored forces chief. Obviously, Stavka sent only its best as representatives.

53. Hardesty, *Red Phoenix*, pp 28–29; the authors of *Soviet Air Force in World War II*, pp 106–07, have only paeans of praise for the ramming (*taran*) tactic and the roll call of *taran* heroes at Stalingrad almost equals that bestowed on Captain Gastello of earlier fame.

54. Mike Spick, *Fighter Pilot Tactics* (New York, 1983), pp 43–44.

55. According to Spick (p 43) the loose pair, or *Rotte*, was developed in Spain in 1937 when the Germans had too few of the new Bf 109s to stick to the conventional vic formation of three aircraft. The Russian experience against the *Rotte* of the Condor Legion in Spain impressed some fliers, but the concept was slow in being adopted in the VVS.

56. Hardesty, *Red Phoenix*, p 141; the authors of the official history, *The Soviet Air Force in World War II*, p 111, claim that the *zveno* of four aircraft, that is two *para*, became the basic tactical unit as early as the early fall of 1942.

57. *SVE*, vol 3, p 641; John T. Greenwood, "The Great Patriotic War, 1941–1945," in R. Higham and J. Kipp, eds, *Soviet Aviation and Air Power* (Boulder, Colo., 1977), p 84; V. Babieh, "Vliyarnie razvitiya aviatsionnoy tekhniki i oruzhiya na taktiku frontovoy aviatsii" [The Influence of the Development of Aviation Equipment and Armament on the Tactics of Frontal Aviation], *Voenno-istoricheskiy zhurnal*, 8 (August 1983), p 22.

58. Hardesty, *Red Phoenix*, p 143.

59. *Soviet Air Force in World War II*, p 103.

60. Maj Gen Walther Schwabedissen, *The Russian Air Force in the Eyes of German Commanders* (Maxwell AFB, Ala., 1960), p 378.

61. Cajus Bekker, *The Luftwaffe Diaries* (New York, 1968), p 277.

62. Williamson Murray, *Strategy for Defeat: The Luftwaffe 1933–1945* (Maxwell AFB, Ala., 1983), pp 160–63.

63. *Ibid.*, pp 254–55.

64. Schwabedissen, *Russian Air Force in the Eyes of German Commanders*, p 379.

65. William Green and Gordon Swanborough, *Soviet Air Force Fighters*, part 2, (New York, 1977), p 57.

66. *Ibid.*, part 1, p 25.

67. Alexander, *Russian Aircraft Since 1940*, pp 173–74.

68. *Ibid.*, p 436.

69. Kenneth Munson, *German Aircraft of World War 2 in Color* (Dorset, UK, 1978), p 122; Martin Windrow, *German Air Force Fighters of World War II*, vol I (New York, 1968), pp 17–18.

70. Munson, *German Aircraft of World War 2*, p 60.

71. Cooper, *The German Air Force*, p 51.

72. Alexander, *Russian Aircraft Since 1940*, pp 295–304; *Aviatsiya i Kosmonavtika*, 10 (October 1974), p 27.

73. Cooper, *The German Air Force*, p 268.

74. *Ibid.*, p 259.

75. Data for the calculations was derived from *Ist. Velik. Otech. Voyn.*, vol 6, pp 45–48 and Overy, *The Air War*, p 150.

76. Cooper, *The German Air Force*, pp 266–67.

77. Murray, *Strategy for Defeat*, p 318.

78. Alexander, *Russian Aircraft Since 1940*, p 4 and 7.

79. *SVE*, vol 2, p 163.

80. *Russian Air Force in the Eyes of German Commanders*, p 31.

81. *Ibid.*, pp 154–55.

82. *Soviet Air Force in World War II*, p 103.

83. *Ibid.*, p 147.

84. *Ibid.*, p 125.

85. *SVE*, vol 2, p 164; Soviet backwardness in the field of radar during the war is a sore point with their historians. For example, a Lt Gen (reserve) M. Lobanov, in an article entitled "K voprosu voznikoveniya i razvitiya otechestvennoy radiolokatsii [Concerning the Origin and Development of Indigenous Radar], *Voenno-istoricheskiy zhurnal*, 8 (August 1962), pp 13–29, laments that for too long it has been assumed in the West and even in the Soviet Union that radar came to the Russians via Lend-Lease. He then goes on at great length to show how radar was developed indigenously in the USSR from the early 1930s. According to Lobanov (p 20), the "RUS–1" radar went into series production in 1939 in time for use in the Winter War, and by the beginning of the Soviet-German war the radio industry had produced 45 complete "RUS–1" sets and was replacing it with the "RUS–2."

86. Chief Marshal of Aviation Pavel Kutakhov, "Voenno-vozhdushnye sily" [The Air Forces], *Voenno-istoricheskiy zhurnal*, 10 (October 1977), pp 36–43.

87. Schwabedissen, *Russian Air Force in the Eyes of German Commanders*, p 255; *Soviet Air Force in World War II*, p 163.

88. *Ibid.*, p 376.

89. Robert F. Futrell, *The United States Air Force in Korea, 1950–1953* (New York, 1961), p 571.

90. Lt Gen Klaus Uebe, *Russian Reaction to German Airpower in World War II* (Maxwell AFB, Ala., 1964), pp 99–100.

91. Schwabedissen, *Russian Air Force in the Eyes of German Commanders*, p 377; Overy, *The Air War*, p 200.

92. *Ist. Velik. Otech. Voyn.*, vol 5, p 467.

93. Kutakhov, "Voenno-vozdushnye sily," p 37.

94. *Ist. Velik. Otech. Voyn.*, vol 4, p 16.

95. Alexander, *Russian Aircraft Since 1940*, pp 426–29.

96. *Ibid.*, pp 299–300.

97. *Ibid.*, pp 430–33 and 172–73.

98. Greenwood, "The Great Patriotic War," pp 118–19.

99. *Ibid.*, p 119.

100. *Soviet Air Force in World War II*, p 361.

101. Text of the "Agreement Concerning the Entry of the Soviet Union into the War Against Japan, signed at Yalta February 11, 1945," in Max Beloff, *Soviet Policy in the Far East, 1944–1951* (London, 1953), p 25.

102. *Japanese Special Studies on Manchuria*, Vol XIII: *Study of Strategical and Tactical Peculiarities of Far Eastern Russia and the Soviet Far Eastern Forces* (Washington, 1955), pp 111–12.

103. John R. Deane, *The Strange Alliance* (New York, 1947), p 248.

104. Raymond Garthoff, "Soviet Intervention in Manchuria, 1945–1946," Orbis, Vol X, No 2 (Summer 1966), p 527.

105. *Ibid.*; *Ist. Velik. Otech. Voyn.*, vol 5, p 548.

106. Garthof, "Soviet Intervention in Manchuria," p 531.

107. *Soviet Air Force in World War II*, p 368.

108. Robert A. Kilmarx, *A History of Soviet Air Power* (New York, 1962), p 184. Soviet historians tend to downgrade U.S. Lend-Lease in general and aircraft in particular. During the Great Patriotic War, the U.S. delivered 14,018 aircraft to the USSR. See also Robert H. Jones, *The Roads to Russia: United States Lend-Lease to the Soviet Union* (Norman, Okla., 1969), appendix A, table II.

109. Overy, *The Air War*, p 150.

110. Murray, *Strategy for Defeat*, table LXIV, p 306.

111. *Soviet Air Force in World War II*, p 382.

112. A. Pokryshkin, *Kryl'ya Istrebitelya* [Fighter Wings] (Moscow: Voenno Izdatel'stvo Ministerstva Vooruzhennykh Sil Soyuza SSR, 1948), p 22.

113. Oleg Hoeffding, *German Air Attacks Against Industry and Railroads in Russia, 1941–1945* (Santa Monica, Calif., 1970), p 8; Cooper, *The German Air Force*, pp 317–18.

114. Von Hardesty, *Red Phoenix; The Rise of Soviet Air Power, 1941–1945* (Washington, 1982), chap 8.

115. *Ibid.*, p 222.

Bibliographical Essay

In trying to trace the Soviet struggle to attain and maintain air superiority during what the Russians refer to as the Great Patriotic War (1941–45), the historian has to rely to a large extent upon the accounts presented by the major participants in that struggle, Germany and the Soviet Union. Neutral observers caught only peripheral views of the four-year war between the two antagonists. The account of the air war on the Eastern Front as written by the German participants and later historians often seems more prone to find a scapegoat for the Luftwaffe's defeat than an exercise in historical understanding. The defeat is variously blamed on the Russian climate, Hitler's strategic peculiarities, partisan interference with logistics, and, above all, Hermann Goering's inadequacies as head of the Luftwaffe. The Soviet writers, on the contrary, seem to suffer from a severe case of braggadocio; statistics of German losses are prominent in Soviet accounts and usually exaggerated, while their own are either ridiculously low or not even mentioned. The net result for the outsider trying to understand what happened is a never-never land of conflicting claims and assertions.

Bibliographies specifically devoted to the air war on the Eastern Front are scarce, and the researcher-writer has to make do with pertinent sections of works dealing with the Luftwaffe on all fronts or the VVS's role as a relatively minor part of the Great Patriotic War in general. Michael Parrish's *The USSR in World War II: An Annotated Bibliography of Books Published in the Soviet Union, 1945–1975*, 2 vols (New York: Garland Publishing, 1981); Myron J. Smith, Jr.'s *The Soviet Air and Strategic Rocket Forces, 1949–80: A Guide to Sources in English* (Santa Barbara, Calif.: ABC-Clio, 1981); the extensive bibliography in Von Hardesty's *Red Phoenix: The Rise of Soviet Air Power, 1941–1945* (Washington: Smithsonian Institution Press, 1982); and the excellent bibliography of works available on the Luftwaffe in World War II to be found in Williamson Murray's *Strategy for Defeat: The Luftwaffe 1933–1945* (Maxwell AFB: Air University Press, 1983) are some of the more valuable bibliographical sources.

The German side of the conflict is copiously, if not entirely satisfactorily, covered in a series of monographs written by senior German officers who participated in the war, a project conceived and developed by the Air Force Historical Division at the Air University. This German Air Force Historical Project, which got underway in 1953, enlisted the aid of many of the Luftwaffe's generals and some historians who were able to refresh their memories (and one hopes, check them) through the use of a collection of Luftwaffe documents known as the Karlsruhe Document Collection. Some of the outstanding products of the project, to name just a few, were General Paul Deichman's *German Air Force Operations in Support of the Army*, General Plocher's three volumes entitled *The German Air Force versus Russia*, General Walther Schwabediessen's *The Russian Air Force in the Eyes of German*

Commanders, General Klaus Uebe's *Russian Reactions to German Airpower in World War II,* and Richard Suchenwirth's *Historical Turning Points in the German Air Force War Effort.* All of these were published by the USAF Historical Division Research Studies Institute, Air University, in the 1950s and early 1960s. There are a few eyewitness accounts written by German pilots, for instance, fighter-pilot Adolf Galland's *The First and Last* (New York: Ballantine, 1957); Hans Rudel's *Stuka Pilot* (New York: Ballantine, 1958); and bomber-pilot Werner Baumbach's *Broken Swastika: The Defeat of the Luftwaffe* (London: Robert Hale, 1960), all of which give the reader some insight into the details of Luftwaffe operations, but, perforce, are only "tunnel-visions" of the war as a whole. All in all, spotty as the German accounts may be, there are enough solid works to help counter-balance the unbridled Soviet outpouring of histories, memoirs, and analyses, a veritable deluge of literature concerning the Soviet Air Force in World War II.

In spite of that "deluge" there are still practically no original sources open to Westerners. Foreign scholars, therefore, have to do the best they can with secondary works (histories and memoirs), many of which are studded with references to archival materials, but impossible to check for accuracy and context. Fortunately for those stubborn enough to try to get a fairly accurate picture of the Soviet performance in the air war, the war has become "big business" in the U.S.S.R. Every anniversary of an important battle, and some not so important, elicits a torrent of speeches, articles, and books depicting the event, usually with an admixture of patriotic exhortations. Of course, the Soviet military historian has to tailor his recitation to conform with whatever political line is in the ascendancy, but this is not surprising since custom-made history has been *de rigeur* ever since Stalin achieved political control in the 1930s. Nevertheless, much of the story may be good history. Descriptions of the VVS's activities in the war are less likely to run athwart the censor than such larger questions as Stalin's role as supreme commander.

Major sources, in lieu of access to documentary collections, are the official histories of the Second World War. The *Istoriya Velikoy Otechestvennoy Voyny Sovetskogo Soyuza, 1941–1945 gg* [History of the Great Patriotic War of the Soviet Union], a six-volume work edited by a staff headed by P. N. Pospelov, is rich in detail, but the VVS gets rather sparse coverage. This work has been dwarfed recently by the *Istoriya Vtoroy Mirovoy Voyny, 1939–1945 gg* [History of the Second World War], a twelve-volume history published between 1973 and 1982. It was a joint effort by several institutes under the direction of an editorial commission headed first by Marshal of the Soviet Union and Minister of Defense A. A. Grechko and upon his death, by Marshal of the Soviet Union and Minister of Defense D. F. Ustinov. The official history of the air war, *Sovetskie Voenno-Vazdushnye Sily v Velikoy Otechestvennoy Voyne, 1941–1945 gg* [The Soviet Air Forces in the Great Patriotic War] (Moscow: Voyenizdat, 1968) is an especially blatant one-sided version and a relatively useless piece of self-serving writing. It has been translated by Leland Fetzer and edited by Ray Wagner under the title of *The Soviet Air Force in World War II* (New York: Doubleday, 1973).

The best source for studying the Soviet activities in World War II including the air war is the output of periodical articles, especially those in the *Voenno-istoricheskiy zhurnal* [Military Historical Journal], one of the Ministry of Defense's more prestigious journals. The articles in this journal cover a wide spectrum, from detailed descriptions of specific actions to broad analyses of extensive periods of the war. Since it has been published continuously since January 1959, just about every senior commander who survived the conflict, and some not so senior, has published his perceptions of some aspect of the struggle. John Erickson's *The Road to Berlin* (Boulder, Colo.: Westview Press, 1983) lists all the articles devoted to World War II on pp. 816–22 in his superlative 200-page bibliography. Fugitive pieces pertaining to the fortunes of the VVS in World War II occur in a number of other military journals: for example, the Air Force's own journal, *Aviatsiya i kosmonavtika* [Aviation and Astronautics], *Kryl'ya rodina* [Wings of the Motherland], *Morskoy sbornik* [Naval collection], *Kommunist vooruzhennykh sil* [Communist of the Armed Forces], and *Voprosy istorii* [Problems of History]. There also are some interesting sketches and articles in the Ministry of Defense's daily newspaper, *Krasnaya zvezda* [Red Star]. A judicious reading of this voluminous output in periodicals and newspapers is probably the best way of getting an approximate picture of the Great Patriotic War and the VVS's role in it.

Some major Soviet books dealing with the Great Patriotic War have been translated into English. Among these are the *Memoirs of Marshal Zhukov* (New York: Delacorte Press, 1971); V. I. Chuikov, *The Battle for Stalingrad* and his *The Fall of Berlin* (New York: Holt, Rinehart, and Winston, 1968); S. M. Shtemenko, *The Soviet General Staff at War, 1941–1945* (Moscow: Progress Publishers, 1975); and his *The Last Six Months* (New York: Doubleday, 1977). There is, however, a paucity of information about aviation's role in these books—the authors seem to have kept their eyes firmly on the ground. Aleksandr S. Yakovlev, designer of the famous Yak fighters and also the Deputy Minister of the Aviation Industry during the war, has written rather extensively about both planes and his part in the arcane goings on in the Kremlin in his *The Aim of a Lifetime* (Moscow: Progress Publishers, 1972), and *Fifty Years of Soviet Aircraft Construction* (Washington: NASA, 1970). A good sampling of memoir literature apropos the war can be found in Seweryn Bialer, ed., *Stalin and His Generals* (New York: Pegasus, 1969), and an overall analysis of the conflict in V.D. Sokolovsky, ed., *Soviet Military Strategy* (New York: Crane, Russak, 1975), pp 136–166, in the third edition edited by Harriet Scott.

Finally, mention should be made of books written by American and British air historians of the VVS's role in World War II. Surprisingly enough there are relatively few good ones, especially in view of the voluminous output devoted to air combat in the ETO, North African, and Pacific theaters. Probably the definitive work in English on the Great Patriotic War is John Erickson's two volumes: *The Road to Stalingrad* (New York: Harper & Row, 1975), and *The Road to Berlin* (Boulder, Colo.: Westview Press, 1983). Alexander Boyd's *The Soviet Air Force Since 1918* (New York: Stein and Day, 1977), in spite of its title, concentrates primarily on World War II. Von Hardesty, *Red Phoenix: The Rise of Soviet Air Power, 1941–1945* (Washington: Smithsonian Institution Press, 1982) is devoted to World War II and has a very extensive bibliography. John T. Greenwood's chapter entitled "The Great Patriotic War, 1941–1945," in Robin Higham and Jacob Kipp, eds., *Soviet Aviation and Air Power* (Boulder, Colo.: Westview Press, 1977), is a good summary of the air war over Russia. Raymond Garthoff's *Soviet Military Doctrine* (Glencoe, Ill.: Free Press, 1953) has stood the test of time and is still one of the best analyses of how Russia fought the war, while R. J. Overy, *The Air War, 1939–1945* (New York: Stein and Day, 1981) has some very perceptive things to say about the air war in general and the Soviet participation in particular.

And lest we forget that essential ingredient of air warfare, the aircraft, let us note a few of the better works: Jean Alexander, *Russian Aircraft Since 1940* (London: Putnam, 1975), Henry Nowarra and G. Duval, *Russian Civil and Military Aircraft, 1884–1969* (London: Fountain Press, 1971), and William Green and Gordon Swanborough, *Soviet Air Force Fighters*, 2 parts (New York: Arco, 1978). The Soviet journal *Aviatsiya i kosmonavtika* has over the years published numerous articles about both the Soviet aircraft in the war as well as information on the designers of both aircraft and engines.

B–17 Flying Fortresses over northern Tunisia.

5

Northwest Africa, 1942–1943

David Syrett

American and British forces landed in French North Africa on November 8, 1942, and quickly seized Algeria and Morocco from the Vichy French regime. By the narrowest of margins, however, they failed to secure Tunisia before it was occupied by Axis forces. What followed was a protracted campaign to clear the enemy from all of North Africa, which became the first major offensive operation against German and Italian forces by the western Allies in World War II.

Allied victory in Tunisia eventually resulted from the ability of American, British, and Free French forces to conduct both combined and joint operations with minimal interallied and interservice friction. Solutions worked out during the Tunisian campaign concerning problems of command and control, logistics, tactics, doctrine, and the use of air power served as the basis for future campaigns from Sicily to Northwest Europe. The principles of command, control, and doctrine learned in Northwest Africa became part of United States Army Air Forces (AAF) field regulations underpinning how aviators viewed the acquisition and preservation of air superiority as well as other missions.

When the Allies invaded Northwest Africa, they were unprepared to achieve the air superiority required to destroy Axis strongholds that had already arisen in Tunisia. Lack of advanced planning and experience led to almost insurmountable difficulties. Allied ineffectiveness resulted from the absence of all-weather airfields for a winter campaign; a shortage of aircraft, trained crews, fuel, spare parts, and munitions; poorly coordinated employment of bombardment, ground support, and air defense aviation; dispersal of air assets due to subordination of aviation to ground force requirements; as well as inadequate air-ground and interallied air cooperation. Personality conflicts between air and ground commanders also hampered development of operational teamwork. Before the Allies could carry out the destruction of the Axis enemy, crises of command and control, air organization, and the lack of aerial resources had to be resolved. Further, an effective doctrine for the use of air power in support of ground operations had to be clearly delineated. The acquisition of air superiority in North Africa was dependent upon all of this.

Background to the Campaign

The late autumn of 1942 in North Africa was a time of great hope and bitter disappointment to the Allies. British forces in the Western Desert began the offensive that would carry them from the Suez Canal to Tunisia after smashing Field Marshal Erwin Rommel's Axis forces at the second battle of El Alamein (October 23–November 4). Four days later, American and British forces landed in French Northwest Africa on an arc running from Casablanca to Algiers. Vichy French resistance soon ended, and the Allies raced eastward towards Bizerta and Tunis in Tunisia. For a brief moment, it appeared that the Allies would overrun Tunisia, trap Rommel's army in Libya (where the British Eighth Army would crush it), and quickly clear North Africa of the enemy. However, the prospect passed quickly. At the end of November, the Allied advance from the west stalled on the outskirts of Djedeida.

The Allies might have taken Tunisia shortly after landing in Northwest Africa had it been possible to quickly mount a strong ground and air attack. However, problems stemming from consolidation of the beachhead and the buildup of requisite forces and supplies for the race to Tunis prevented rapid exploitation of such an opportunity. Questions arose over priorities and enemy intentions; the vast geographical distances engendered by operations in Northwest Africa as well as the inexperience of the composite Allied force all played a role. A variety of missions occupied Allied air units like the U.S. Twelfth Air Force, which had nothing to do with Tunisia but were vital to overall Allied success in the Mediterranean. Escorting Allied convoys and insuring against possible Spanish or combined Axis-Spanish intervention from Spain or Spanish Morocco against the flank of the invasion force numbered among such missions.[1] This threat passed quickly, but because a large part of the Allied forces was diverted from a quick thrust to Tunisia, and the landings themselves in Morocco and western Algeria had been so far from the main Axis enemy, the full weight of Allied military power in this sector or theater could not be deployed quickly to carry out a pincer operation with the westward moving British Eighth Army. This enabled the enemy to build a stronghold in Tunisia, to which Rommel's army and other Axis forces retired by winter.

The failure of the Allies to capture Tunisia in November, before the Axis forces arrived in strength, forced the Allies to fight a winter campaign in the mountainous region of western Tunisia. The Luftwaffe quickly developed a number of all-weather airfields and ground support facilities on the coastal plain of eastern Tunisia. The enemy was thus "in the remarkable position of fighting on an equality, if not actually possessing tactical air superiority, since Allied ground organization was faced by immeasurably greater problems, which were only gradually overcome," stated one Royal Air Force (RAF) observer.[2] The lack of Allied all-weather airfields within operational range of eastern Tunisia permitted the enemy to have *de facto* aerial superiority over all of Tunisia.[3] The first Allied air objective, therefore, was to gain air superiority over Tunisia and the central Mediterranean by destroying Axis aircraft either on the ground or in the air. Accomplishing this proved difficult.

Allied Air Force Problems with Doctrine

The AAF's Twelfth Air Force and the RAF's Eastern Air Command were not prepared in terms of doctrine or command and control to fight a prolonged campaign in Tunisia. Committed primarily to a strategy of strategic bombardment, the AAF and RAF had given too little thought before the war to requirements for a campaign such as the one in Tunisia. In such a campaign, aircraft would have to be used not only for strategic bombardment, but also for maritime missions, interdiction, close air support of ground forces, and, most importantly, for gaining and maintaining air superiority throughout an area that embraced not just Tunisia proper, but also the whole central Mediterranean region. The RAF had gained invaluable experience in this vein since the inception of aerial operations in the Middle East in 1940. However, competition for men and resources with other sectors of a worldwide conflict hampered internal codification of various lessons learned. The AAF had virtually no similar experience to draw upon.

The AAF, being part of the U.S. Army at the time, had doctrine imposed on it by senior officers who knew little about the actual employment of air power in modern warfare. Field manuals, setting forth air doctrine, largely reflected the thinking of Army ground officers. As a result, such missions as close air support, air superiority, and maritime operations were addressed imprecisely. For example, FM 1–5, *Employment of Aviation of the Army,* issued on April 15, 1940, failed to clarify such topics. Nor did such manuals as FM 1–10, *Tactics and Techniques of Air Attack* (1942) address in realistic terms such subjects as escort of bombers, close air support of ground troops, or maritime operations. FM 31–35, *Aviation in*

225

Support of Ground Forces, issued on April 9, 1942, did attempt to formulate a doctrine for support of land operations. The manual called for establishing air support commands that would attack ground targets in support of ground forces. FM 31–35 placed air support commands under the control of the ground force commander, while the commander of the air support command was to act as an air adviser to the ground commander.

AAF actions prior to the invasion of North Africa gave a much clearer view of the situation than the words of the field manuals. In virtually all of the prewar maneuvers of 1940–41, the air elements displayed weaknesses in direct support of ground operations. The failure resulted from the aviators' commitment to strategic bombardment, rapid expansion of forces, and a shortage of proper pursuit and attack aircraft. During the large maneuvers held in Louisiana and the Carolinas, the AAF, Navy, and Marine Corps all deployed numbers of aircraft, but most of the missions had little to do with direct close air support of the maneuver forces, or the winning of air superiority. They focused more upon interdiction. As a result, when the United States entered the war in December 1941, a number of ground officers believed that the AAF would be unable to carry out assigned missions in direct support of the ground forces.[4]

Another reason for lack of sound doctrine and proper means for achieving air superiority in Northwest Africa was the manner and speed in which the Twelfth Air Force was assembled, which precluded much thought being given to essentially intellectual problems of command, control, and doctrine. Most importantly, the Twelfth Air Force had never trained or operated together as a unified force before entry into the theater of operations. Activated at Bolling Field near Washington, D.C., and sent to Great Britain on September 12, 1942, it was assigned to support part of the Allied force scheduled to invade Northwest Africa in Operation TORCH on November 8. In most cases, the air and ground support units, personnel, and equipment for the Twelfth Air Force were obtained either directly from the United States or in Great Britain from the Eighth Air Force. Most of the units went to the new Twelfth Air Force in no particular order, but rather in bits and pieces—a standard operating procedure throughout the rapidly expanding air force overseas. Furthermore, because of the pace of operations in Northwest Africa once the forces had landed, little thought was given to problems of command, control, and doctrine, which might be encountered in any protracted battle for Tunisia.

The RAF's experience proved quite similar. Most of the Eastern Air Command consisted of units drawn from the United Kingdom, and the British experienced similar command, control, and doctrinal problems. Following the battle of France and withdrawal from Dunkirk in June 1940, a huge fight developed in British military circles as to the role of the RAF in any future British Army operation. The disagreement called into question the role of the Army in the war and raised fundamental questions of doctrine, command, and control of aircraft deployed in support of British forces should they return to the European continent. At various times, the RAF established units, such as the Army Cooperation Command, to furnish direct air support to ground operations. But these units never were very strong because Bomber, Coastal, and Fighter Commands claimed priority on men and equipment, especially during the Battle of Britain in 1940. Furthermore, like senior counterparts in the U.S. Army Air Forces, RAF commanders thought that victory could best be achieved by strategic bombardment of Germany, thereby making support of ground forces quite academic. The Air Ministry took the position that when and if the British Army ever took to the field in Northwest Europe again, then the RAF would assign aircraft to support it from Bomber, Coastal, and Fighter Commands. Naturally, the soldiers took a different approach, believing firmly that unless the Army controlled the ground support aircraft, the RAF would most likely withdraw them for other missions.[5]

The controversy had not been resolved when the RAF's Eastern Air Command began operations in Northwest Africa. Furthermore, the command's leadership had at best only fragmentary knowledge of the experiences of the Western Desert Air Force in Egypt because it was simply too soon for transmittal of "lessons learned" back to staff and training commands in Great Britain. Thus, at the beginning of this pivotal Northwest Africa campaign, the RAF units on the scene had little doctrine or training for supporting ground forces and did not know what kind of relations to develop with the Twelfth Air Force and Allied ground forces.

Operational Issues during the Race for Tunisia

The invasion of Northwest Africa (Operation TORCH) found no less than five separate air elements providing cover for the initial landings. Still, two primary components committed to the operation were the U.S. Twelfth Air Force (1,244 aircraft) and the RAF Eastern Air Command (454 aircraft). Allied planners anticipated no problem in gaining air superiority over French air units stationed in the Vichy French colonies, and it was hoped that diplomacy might eliminate any resistance to Anglo-American landings. Under the leadership of Brig. Gen. John K. Cannon, XII Air Support Command accompanied the Western Task Force to Casablanca. The remainder of the Twelfth Air Force under Maj. Gen. James Doolittle operated with the Central Task Force at Oran, and the RAF Eastern Air Command led by Air Marshal William Welsh supported the Eastern Task Force at Algiers. Both the American and British air contingents reported to Lt. Gen. Dwight D. Eisenhower, Allied Commander in Chief, Northwest Africa. (See Figure 5–1) In addition, U.S. carrier-based naval air and the British Fleet Air Arm covered the landings.

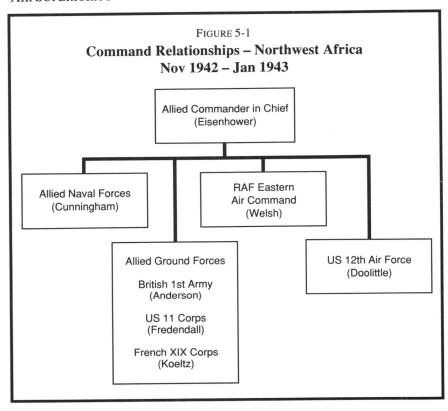

FIGURE 5-1

Command Relationships – Northwest Africa
Nov 1942 – Jan 1943

Allied Commander in Chief
(Eisenhower)

Allied Naval Forces
(Cunningham)

RAF Eastern
Air Command
(Welsh)

Allied Ground Forces

British 1st Army
(Anderson)

US 11 Corps
(Fredendall)

French XIX Corps
(Koeltz)

US 12th Air Force
(Doolittle)

After the Allies had subdued token French air opposition and helped ground forces consolidate their foothold ashore, the air-ground team was to race to capture Tunisia and deny the region to the enemy. The Twelfth Air Force would begin its buildup on local French airfields to guard the line of communications to the Mediterranean against possible Spanish or Axis-Spanish intervention, while preparing an offensive air striking force for strategic bombardment of Axis targets in Europe. At first, it was assumed that the RAF Eastern Command would handle air cover for ground force operations toward Tunisia. Soon, however, both Allied air contingents discovered their resources were inadequate for what became the principal task—defeat of the remaining Axis forces in North Africa. Neither ally could deploy enough men and aircraft, nor develop sufficient forward base strength to secure the immediate and permanent air superiority necessary to accomplish this mission.[6]

Initial attempts to restrict the operations of Axis air forces via a series of raids on airfields (to destroy the enemy's frontline air superiority as the

228

land forces tangled on the Tunisian battlefields) gave way by early winter to increased Allied air assaults mainly on enemy port facilities and eventually the shipping lanes from Italy and Sicily. The Eastern Air Command conducted 4,165 sorties during the month of December at a cost of 50 aircraft, while the Twelfth Air Force dispatched 1,243 sorties 'n this same period, with a loss of 35 aircraft. Neither German-Italian 'and forces nor their air components seemed daunted by Allied air operations. The Luftwaffe mounted some 1,030 sorties (losing 40 aircraft) of its own during this period. It bombed Allied port facilities at Algiers from Sardinia and Italy with impunity, since Allied air forces apparently lacked night aerial interception equipment. Both Italian and German air forces constantly harassed Allied ground operations to the discomfort and annoyance of senior Allied leaders.[7]

The prelude to Tunisia from the west developed into what Eisenhower termed a logistical marathon between Axis and Allied forces. One major difficulty was that the Allies operated at the end of an exceedingly long supply line that stretched back to the United States and Great Britain. Even the arrival of supplies in Northwest Africa promised no end to logistical headaches. Northwest Africa was a large theater of operations. It is, for example, 560 miles by road from Algiers to Tunis. The roads themselves were dirt, and only a single-track railroad served the region. The Axis powers, in contrast, depended upon a much shorter supply line by sea and air from Italy via Sicily. Eventually, Allied air commanders determined that here was the choke point for strangling the enemy via an intense interdiction campaign. However, like everything else in this theater, such a campaign could not take place in strength until the air forces had closed within striking range of targets.

In addition, rain and mud caused untold problems for the Allies by December. Lt. Gen. K. A. N. Anderson, Commander of the First British Army, thought like most people that North Africa was "a dry country." He experienced a very unpleasant surprise, for the "rains began in early December and continued until early April. March was the wettest month. Rain, mist, and a peculiar glutinous mud formed the background to all our operations during this period."[8] The RAF's airfield at Souk el Arba "was liable to become unserviceable at very short notice after heavy rain," and U.S. Twelfth Air Force units fared no better.[9] When they got to western Tunisia, one American general noted in December that all Allied airfields were the same; if there were two hard surfaced runways, one would be used as an aircraft parking ramp. "The rest of the landscape was ankle-deep mud." Since the Allies captured only 5 all-weather airstrips when they landed in Northwest Africa, it was not unusual for scores of Allied aircraft to be "mudbound." One night in November, some 285 Allied aircraft were stuck in the mud at Tafaraoui airfield. Without sufficient all-weather facilities, the Allied air forces simply could not attain air superiority. By con-

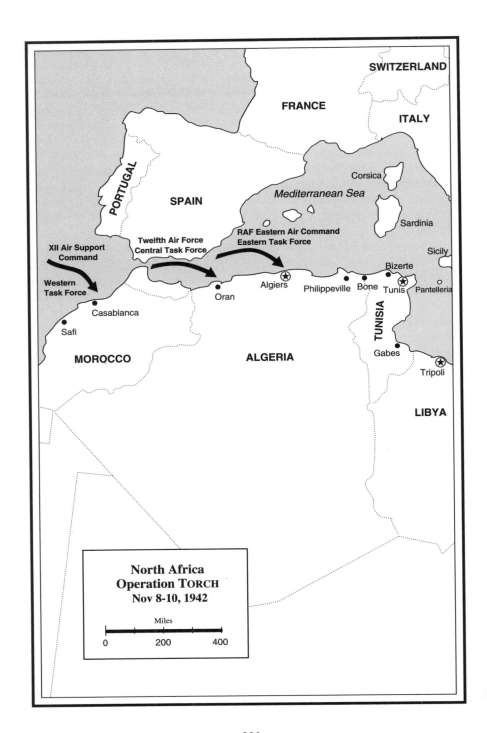

SWITZERLAND

FRANCE

ITALY

PORTUGAL

SPAIN

Corsica

Mediterranean Sea

Sardinia

RAF Eastern Air Command
Eastern Task Force

Sicily

Twelfth Air Force
Central Task Force

Bizerte

XII Air Support
Command

Algiers

Philippeville

Bone

Tunis

Pantelleria

Western
Task Force

Oran

TUNISIA

Casablanca

Safi

MOROCCO

ALGERIA

Gabes

Tripoli

LIBYA

North Africa
Operation Torch
Nov 8-10, 1942

Miles

0   200   400

trast, their opponents operated from secure, all-weather bases in Sicily and Sardinia, as well as from airfields with hard-surfaced runways at Sidi Ahmed, El Aouina, Sfax, Sousse, and Gabes in North Africa.[10]

By the end of the Tunisian campaign, some 9,000 AAF aviation engineers had constructed more than 100 additional airfields, but this was accomplished in the face of immense obstacles. Most of the engineers lacked proper training, and because of poor planning very little of the equipment required to build airfields was available for several months. Only by the beginning of March 1943 had enough heavy construction machinery arrived so that the engineers could construct facilities with increasing skill and speed. The Allied command greatly assisted this effort by issuing a realistic set of specifications for the construction. In forward areas, airfields would consist of one runway with loop taxiways and dispersed hard-stands for aircraft parking. There would be no buildings constructed, and munitions and fuel dumps would be located just off existing roads. These simple specifications and the ruthless use of large numbers of heavy construction machines enabled the AAF aviation engineers to build the airfields required to support the rapid movements of Allied ground forces in the final weeks of the campaign.[11]

Of course, the lack of all-weather airfields was merely one facet of the logistical and administrative obstacle confronting the Allies at the beginning of the Tunisian campaign. At the American airfield at Thelepte, for instance, the lack of spare parts led to cannibalization of wrecked aircraft. Tin from five-gallon British army issue gasoline cans served to patch holes in aircraft because of the lack of aluminum. Propeller blades were interchanged, handpumps were used to refuel aircraft, and jerry-rigged tanks on the back of ordinary cargo haulers served in place of regulation fuel trucks.[12] Even then the attritional struggle for air superiority continued inconclusively because the Allies could not bring to bear sufficient aircraft despite a virtual two-to-one superiority in numbers over the course of the campaign. The Allies' "magic circle" or aircraft operating radius remained too far removed from the principal battle area of Tunisia until the hard-working engineers could complete their runway construction. Allied air units worked from Bone, 120 miles from the front, and Youks as well as Souk-el-Arba, 150 and 70 miles respectively, behind the frontlines—distances prohibitive for early acquisition and maintenance of air superiority over the battle area. For the inexperienced American and British air units, Operation TORCH had fallen short of its goal by Christmas 1942, because Allied land and air leaders lacked the means for the *coup de grace* before Rommel completed his retirement from the East into Tunisia.[13]

Meanwhile, Field Marshal Bernard Law Montgomery's Eighth Army advanced in hot pursuit of Rommel. Weather and desert logistics also plagued British Empire land and air forces, as Air Marshal Arthur Tedder,

Maj. Gen. James Doolittle,
Commander of the Twelfth
Air Force in North Africa.

the Air-Officer-in-Charge (AOC), RAF Middle East, found his own aircraft of the Western Desert Air Force tied to Egyptian bases as the army advanced beyond his operating radius. Yet, the British and Axis forces were now passing once more over ground they had fought for during the past two and one-half years. During this operation, the RAF and British Army displayed superb army-air cooperation which became a model for Anglo-American efforts in the winter campaign and beyond. RAF fighters and fighter-bombers leap-frogged in the Eighth Army's train, while landing sites were well known to the British from previous passage over the ground. Rommel shepherded his forces out of direct contact with the British, and the Luftwaffe and RAF engaged in few air superiority clashes, most air activity being confined to operations against German and Italian land forces. Attached to RAF Middle East Command was the U.S. Army Middle East Air Force (the Ninth Air Force after November 12), which conducted simultaneous operations against Axis ports and base facilities both in Tunisia and Sicily-Italy, as well as the first air strikes on oil fields in central Europe. Eventually, Montgomery and the Eighth Army also were stopped by the tightly constricted Axis ground and air defense perimeter in Tunisia. Before both the eastern and western pincers of the Allies could mount their final blow, fundamental command and organizational changes became necessary that altered the complexion of air operations for the future. These changes developed from the merging of the Middle East and Northwest African theaters of operation.[14]

Command Crisis

Eisenhower knew by the end of November 1942 that the Allied air forces were not conducting the war effectively in the air. He recognized that the rush to secure Tunisia had resulted in a "waste of equipment," especially aircraft, since no defense of bases and lines of communication had been possible. Furthermore, the Allied Commander in Chief realized that there was not only almost no communication between Twelfth Air Force Commander Doolittle and Air Marshal Welsh, the Commander of the Eastern Air Command, but in addition, neither officer had any "overall picture" of what was happening.[15] Lack of teamwork or coordination in the air meant that acquisition of air superiority would be difficult, if not impossible. The problem in its simplest form was that at the beginning of the Allied campaign in Northwest Africa, the RAF and AAF components were two separate but equal air forces under the direct command of Eisenhower; there was no air leader assigned to command both air forces. Consistent with U.S. Army doctrine, Eisenhower had directed that Allied air units be subordinated to the ground commanders leading the drive on Tunisia. In turn, these soldiers dispersed the American air effort in widely scattered missions, the ineffectiveness of which was even attested to by the Germans.[16]

When Tedder met with Eisenhower on November 27, he was appalled by what he had found in Algiers. He informed the American that his own investigations confirmed the uncoordinated command arrangements, with Doolittle virtually running his own private air war from a headquarters in Algiers, while Welsh's command post lay some distance outside the city. To make matters worse, Adm. Sir Andrew Cunningham, the commander of Allied naval forces in the Western Mediterranean, maintained his headquarters aboard ship because it had the only good communications between Algiers and the rest of the world. After the meeting, Tedder cabled Air Chief Marshal Sir Charles Portal, the Chief of the Air Staff, in London that he was concerned about the command, control, and communications situation in Algiers.[17]

Tedder was one RAF officer who spoke with authority in 1942 concerning the subject of waging war in the air. He had commanded the air force that had smashed the Axis air arm in the Western Desert. He had created and implemented all the measures required for a theater air force commander to work successfully with ground and naval forces. Tedder believed that the entire Mediterranean and Middle East was one theater in which a single officer should command all Allied air forces. This unity of command would produce better results than several separate air commands, which might work at cross purposes. Furthermore, in Tedder's mind, it was essential that the headquarters of the air force commander be located next to the headquarters of the commander of the largest ground formation in the thea-

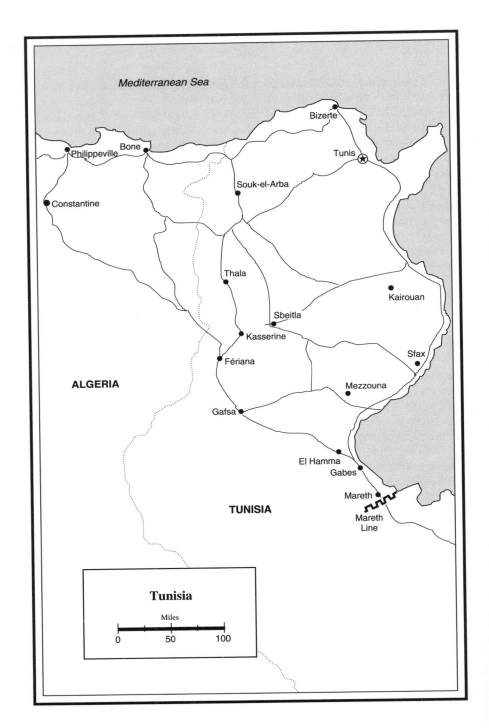

Mediterranean Sea

Bizerte

Bone
Philippeville
Tunis

Constantine

Souk-el-Arba

Thala

Kairouan

Sbeitla

Kasserine

Sfax

Fériana

ALGERIA

Mezzouna

Gafsa

El Hamma
Gabes

TUNISIA

Mareth

Mareth
Line

Tunisia

Miles

0   50   100

ter. Portal agreed with Tedder, whose thinking pointed not merely to changing details, but to a total overhaul of the entire command structure of Allied air forces in the Mediterranean.[18]

After meeting with Tedder, Eisenhower wanted him assigned as an adviser "on questions of air, ground and naval cooperation, deployment of air forces in conditions of meager facilities, and the selection of targets in amphibious operations." But Tedder declined, believing that "advice without authority and responsibility is useless," and eventually the British Chiefs of Staff disapproved Eisenhower's request, noting that the American general might have Tedder's services as commander of all Allied air forces in the Mediterranean, but not as an adviser. Eisenhower was not prepared for this step since he thought it impossible for one man to command two air forces separated by hundreds of miles of Axis-controlled territory. He agreed in principle that this might be the best ultimate solution, but for the moment, Eisenhower decided to appoint Maj. Gen. Carl Spaatz (then commanding Eighth Air Force in Great Britain) as Acting Deputy Commander in Chief for Air—in the capacity of an adviser and not a commander.[19]

Part of the effectiveness problem with the Allied air effort in Northwest Africa stemmed from Eisenhower's two senior air leaders. Doolittle, Commander of Twelfth Air Force, thought the Allies had to "abandon our present 100% botched up organization, stop trying to win the Tunisian War in a day . . . ." According to Doolittle, the only way to win in Tunisia was for the Allied ground forces as well as the RAF to go on the defensive while the Twelfth Air Force was given first priority on everything in order to break the enemy in Tunisia by a sustained American air offensive.[20] Obviously, Doolittle's path to victory in Tunisia not only over-simplified the logistical, strategic, and administrative problems confronting the Allies in Northwest Africa, but his plan underestimated or at least misjudged what would be required to defeat the enemy in Tunisia. Most importantly, Doolittle did not understand the requirements of waging a war in conjunction with Allies and with land and naval forces. The Twelfth Air Force was not operating in a vacuum, and the conduct of the war in Tunisia could not just be turned over to Doolittle's Twelfth Air Force by shoving the U.S. Army and the British to the sidelines.

Eisenhower's other senior air leader in Northwest Africa was Welsh, Commander of Eastern Air Command, who thought that the Americans were putting some aspects of Doolittle's plan into effect. Although he knew how important it was to the war effort "to keep the peace with the Americans," this British officer believed that the Americans were systematically cutting the RAF out of policymaking and eventually wanted to push the RAF out of Northwest Africa as soon as possible. Also, if there were to be a single air force commander in Eisenhower's command, Welsh thought that the Americans would demand that he be a AAF officer. Welsh further contended that Cunningham, the commander of the Allied naval forces in the Western Mediterranean, was a British officer who wanted to disband the RAF and divide it up between the British Army and Navy. And if that was not enough, Welsh contended that Anderson, Commander of the British First Army, was "almost as impossible as he could be to work with."[21] Clearly, the attitudes and beliefs of Doolittle and Welsh plus their inability to work together most likely played a role in Eisenhower's decision to change the command structure of the Allied air forces in Northwest Africa.

At the end of 1942, Eisenhower cabled Gen. George C. Marshall, Chief of Staff of the U.S. Army, outlining all the problems encountered in the attempt to achieve coordination between the Twelfth Air Force and the Eastern Air Command since the Allied landings in November. He noted that a single air commander was needed, and that Spaatz should be appointed to command the Allied air forces in Northwest Africa. He wanted Marshall's concurrence before presenting the case to the Anglo-American Combined Chiefs of Staff (CCS). Eisenhower still supported the concept of a single air commander for the whole Mediterranean, but "not as long as the Allies were physically separated by the presence of the Germans." Marshall replied that Army and air officers in Washington supported Eisenhower but that "it might be well to press for a single air commander throughout the Mediterranean even before unified control of the TORCH air forces under Spaatz had been demonstrated a success." When all of this was presented to the British, they expressed misgivings about Spaatz's lack of experience "in command and administration of a mixed Air Force in the field," but they reasoned that "any system of unified air command in TORCH was better than the present chaos," and that Eisenhower should be allowed to choose his own subordinates.[22]

In agreeing to Spaatz's appointment as TORCH air commander, the British stipulated that his chief of staff must be an RAF officer; Doolittle should command all long-range bombardment aviation; and Welsh should take over all aircraft employed in ground support operations. They also insisted that an RAF officer be appointed under Spaatz to command fighter planes employed to protect Northwest African ports and all aircraft used for maritime operations. Further, a senior RAF officer had to be appointed to Spaatz's staff "with special experience of Air Force maintenance and supply." The British also told the Americans they were convinced "that unified air command throughout the Mediterranean Theaters is the right answer...."[23]

By placing several RAF officers in key command and staff positions under Spaatz, the British figured that the air forces under Eisenhower's command would not get too far out of control before the question of the command structure of all Allied air forces in the Mediterranean could be resolved at the forthcoming Chiefs of State meeting in Casablanca. The

Lt. Gen. Carl Spaatz, Commander of the Northwest African Air Forces, receives the Legion of Merit Medal from Allied Commander in Chief Gen. Dwight D. Eisenhower at a ceremony held in North Africa.

Commanders in the Northwest African campaigns included (*from left to right*) Air Vice Marshal Harry Broadhurst, Air Vice Marshal Sir Arthur Coningham, Gen. Bernard Montgomery, Gen. Sir Harold Alexander, Air Chief Marshal Sir Arthur Tedder, and Brig. Gen. Laurence Kuter.

British conceived of Spaatz as commander of an air force divided into three major units by function, not by nationality, namely one command for strategic bombardment, a second for support of ground forces, and a third for maritime missions and the protection of North African ports. The problem was that Eisenhower, and most likely Spaatz as well, did not agree with this type of command structure, or perhaps he did not fully understand the British position. On January 4, Eisenhower cabled London that Spaatz's new command would consist of the Twelfth Air Force, whose missions were strategic bombardment and the provision of support to American ground forces in central Tunisia; while the Eastern Air Command's missions were to provide air support to the British First Army, the protection of North African ports, and various maritime activities.[24] On the following day, Eisenhower's headquarters issued the order activating Spaatz's Allied Air Force. When the Assistant Chief of the Air Staff for Plans in London read Eisenhower's cable of January 4, setting forth the missions of the Twelfth Air Force and the Eastern Air Command in the new Allied Air Force being setup in Northwest Africa, he thought that the scheme "will in fact merely perpetuate the chaos now existing."[25] However, it did resolve—on paper—the thorny question of ground control of air assets.

In late January, the Combined Chiefs of Staff met during the Casablanca conference and approved a unified command for all Allied air forces in the Mediterranean, as well as other sweeping command changes. (See Figure 5–2) Tedder was named to head the command, while Spaatz became commander of the all-important Northwest African Air Forces (NWAAF), which were to operate over Tunisia and the Central Mediterranean. Spaatz particularly embraced the idea of an integrated headquarters so as to provide "greater scope for mutual understanding and pooling of ideas and techniques." While squabbles could be anticipated about relative ranks, duties, and approaches to problem-solving between the Allies, unanimity of purpose among the top commanders predictably would lead to uniformity of effort down the chain of command. When the Northwest African Air Forces came into existence on February 18, the mission of this new element was clear. It was to destroy the enemy air forces' support of land operations, to attack enemy ships, ports, air bases, and road nets "with the object of interfering to the maximum extent possible with enemy sea, land, and air communications. . . ." By consolidating administratively diverse units of the AAF Twelfth Air Force, the RAF Western Desert Air Force, and the RAF Eastern Air Command, Allied leaders hoped to resolve the organizational arrangement needed to secure permanent air superiority in all corners of the theater.[26]

The Allied Air Force and Axis Counterattacks of Winter

Heavy fighting accompanied arrival of Rommel's forces in Tunisia, as well as the reorganization of the Axis defense. Rommel's famed *Afrika Korps* (now styled the First Italian Army) faced Montgomery's British Eighth Army, while in the west, Eisenhower's Allied forces were confronted by Hans-Jurgen von Arnim's Fifth Panzer Army. Under a January reorganization, Axis armed forces now came under overall command of Field Marshal Albert Kesselring. *Luftflotte* 2 had the continuing task not only of helping maintain the logistical lifeline between Italy-Sicily and Tunisia through provision of air cover and transport aircraft, but also forward-based tactical bombardment and fighter support via *Fliegerkorps* Tunis. Seven principal airdromes from Bizerta to Kairouan, six near Gabes, and others at Mezzouna, Sfax, and La Fauconnerie, served as forward bases from which the 53d and 77th Fighter Wings, for example, could operate. Axis losses of 201 aircrews and 340 aircraft (out of a strength of 877), incurred from stopping the Allied advance toward Tunis, were more than offset by the Luftwaffe and Italian Air Force's ability to draw upon resources in Sardinia, Italy, and Sicily in order to continue maintenance of local air superiority at crucial points in the campaign.[27]

The question of attaining air superiority loomed paramount to both sides, mainly because it held the key to continued Axis presence in North Africa. By this period, the Allies had finally begun to muster sufficient quantities of aircraft and to overcome forward airbase shortages so as to better contest the air space over the battle area as well as interdict the Axis logistical lifeline. In a sense, all air activities (whether reconnaissance, interdiction, strategic bombardment, counterair, or ground support) were indissolubly linked to the air superiority issue. But air power in itself remained unquestionably tied to the ground force effort to eradicate the Axis bridgehead in Tunisia.

In January and February, the Axis forces launched a series of limited counteroffensives designed to enlarge their constricted bridgehead and disrupt Allied plans before final arrival of Montgomery's army from Egypt and Libya. Near disasters like Kasserine Pass (February 14–23) only confirmed the immaturity of Free French and American ground units, as well as the continuing lack of close coordination between air and ground operations. Virtually daily disagreement between Allied airmen and ground generals clouded the picture and reflected Tedder's contention that aircraft in Northwest Africa, at least, were being "frittered away in penny packets" by "attacking targets all on the orders of local Army Commanders."[28] Air Marshal Sir Arthur Coningham, Commander of the Western Desert Air Force, echoed such sentiment, suggesting that lack of realistic training and the

FIGURE 5-2

Allied Command Relationships in the Mediterranean

March 1943

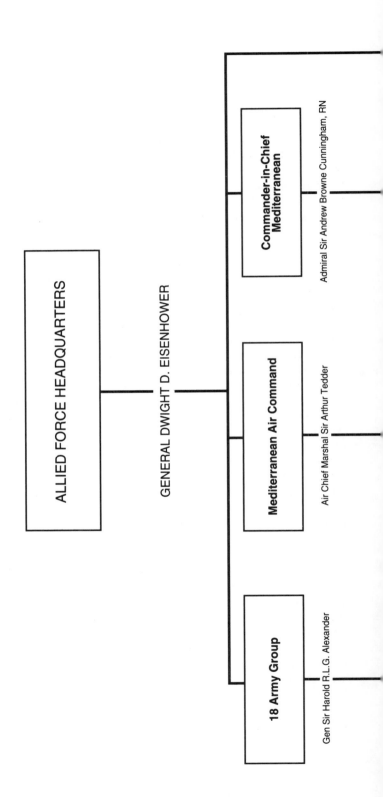

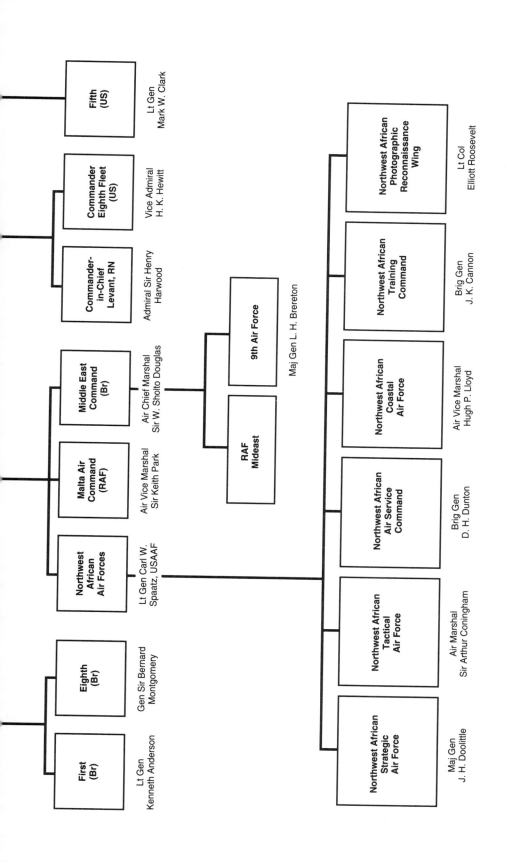

First
(Br)

Lt Gen
Kenneth Anderson

Eighth
(Br)

Gen Sir Bernard
Montgomery

Northwest
African
Air Forces

Lt Gen Carl W.
Spaatz, USAAF

Malta Air
Command
(RAF)

Air Vice Marshal
Sir Keith Park

Middle East
Command
(Br)

Air Chief Marshal
Sir W. Sholto Douglas

Commander-
in-Chief
Levant, RN

Admiral Sir Henry
Harwood

Commander
Eighth Fleet
(US)

Vice Admiral
H. K. Hewitt

Fifth
(US)

Lt Gen
Mark W. Clark

RAF
Mideast

9th Air Force

Maj Gen L. H. Brereton

Northwest African
Strategic
Air Force

Maj Gen
J. H. Doolittle

Northwest African
Tactical
Air Force

Air Marshal
Sir Arthur Coningham

Northwest African
Air Service
Command

Brig Gen
D. H. Dunton

Northwest African
Coastal
Air Force

Air Vice Marshal
Hugh P. Lloyd

Northwest African
Training
Command

Brig Gen
J. K. Cannon

Northwest African
Photographic
Reconnaissance
Wing

Lt Col
Elliott Roosevelt

failure to heed lessons from the Western Desert air war lay at the root of such problems.[29] Americans such as Spaatz quite agreed.

Eisenhower and Spaatz had met on January 21 to attempt to bring about some degree of cooperation and coordination between various Allied armies and air forces to blunt and then halt the German attack on the French XIX Corps in central Tunisia. Eisenhower told Spaatz that he had selected Anderson as his deputy, with command over all Allied ground forces, and requested that Spaatz establish an army support command headquarters at Anderson's headquarters to coordinate the actions of Allied Air Force with those of the Allied ground forces. Spaatz directed Brig. Gen. Laurence S. Kuter to establish the Allied Support Command, consisting of the XII Air Support Command and the RAF's 242 Group, with the mission of supporting the Allied ground forces.[30] Even before the formal establishment of the Allied Support Command, aircraft of the XII Air Support Command and 242 Group were attacking enemy targets in front of the British II and French XIX Corps.[31]

Spaatz, by setting up the Allied Air Support Command under the command of Kuter, achieved centralized command and control of all Allied aircraft used to support Allied ground forces in Tunisia. The American general, however, concluded that the AAF in Tunisia was employing the wrong tactics to win air superiority while supporting ground forces. Spaatz thought that attacks should be mounted with the greatest possible force and constantly changing targets to prevent the enemy from massing against the Allied Air Force. Another tactic was to attack enemy aircraft on the ground in an effort to destroy the Axis air forces. Above all, Spaatz thought that it was a mistake to engage in indecisive operations, contending that the role of an air force was to hit the enemy's "soft parts . . . and in return protect the soft part of one's own force. . . ."[32]

During the evening of February 4, Spaatz had a discussion with Maj. Philip Cochran, the commanding officer of the 58th Fighter Squadron.[33] This squadron had been so badly shot up when on ground support operations that it had to be withdrawn from combat and rebuilt. On the day in which the 33d Fighter Group (including the 58th Fighter Squadron) had been forced out of combat, the XII Air Support Command lost thirty-six aircraft while attacking enemy ground forces. A British staff history states that the Americans suffered heavy casualties because they were attempting "to maintain continuous air cover [over] the battle areas, and at the same time provide fighter escort for A–20s and P–39s." Another reason given in this staff history is that the Germans in Tunisia had been reinforced by the remnants of the Luftwaffe that had been driven out of Libya by the British.[34]

During breakfast with Spaatz the next morning, Major Cochran delineated what he thought was wrong with AAF ground support tactics. According to Cochran, the American losses "in aircraft had been brought about by sending up flights of few planes in attacks on gun positions and on patrol over troops and [no] protection of P–39s and A–20s when it was known that they would meet enemy aircraft in superior numbers."[35] He next told Spaatz that P–40 fighters should only be used when they enjoyed a three-to-one superiority over opposing enemy aircraft. In this respect, Cochran was thinking in terms of concentration of force at the point of contact with the enemy.

Part of the task of airmen like Spaatz was one of educating ground leaders. After breakfast on February 5, he went to Anderson's headquarters at Tebessa. Although the British general was not there, Spaatz discussed a number of problems with Kuter and Anderson's chief of staff, Brigadier V. C. McNabb. McNabb told Spaatz that the U.S. II Corps had recently lost "seven hundred men from attacks of dive bombers," and that Anderson "wanted the whole air effort put on ground positions immediately in front of our troops in the coming offensive." At this point, Kuter noted that Anderson had told him on the previous day that support of Allied forces was the main task of the air forces and that he, Anderson, "was not interested in the bombing of enemy airdromes such as that at Gabes." The discussion ended with McNabb saying that he "hardly thought" that Anderson "had intended to go that far."

After lunch Kuter and Spaatz went to the headquarters of the U.S. II Corps and discussed problems with Fredendall concerning air support of ground forces. Fredendall wanted aircraft flying over his forces for 48 hours from the beginning of an attack to protect his men and artillery from being dive-bombed. In addition, Fredendall "wanted his men to see some bombs dropped on the position immediately in front of them, and if possible, some dive bombers brought down in sight of his troops so that their morale would be bolstered." The American corps commander ended by saying that he had lost 300 men to dive bombers. Spaatz pointed out that he had not only already "worn out" 2 fighter groups and a light bomber squadron giving air support to ground forces but he could not continue such operations, for "the rate of replacement would not allow extravagant dissipation of available air force." He continued to say that "he wanted to give all the help that he could," but that correct employment of air power was to hit enemy "soft points" such as airfields, tank parks, motor pools, and troop convoys. Spaatz also told Fredendall "that if he maintained a constant 'umbrella' over one small section of the front with only shallow penetrations by bombers and fighters, that his available force would be dissipated without any lasting effect." Spaatz thought "that the hard core of any army should be able to take care of itself when it came to dive bombers." Fredendall then remarked that he had lost 2 batteries of artillery to dive bombers and that without direct air support he could not go on to the offensive. After repeating to Fredendall what he thought was the proper employment of aircraft, Spaatz left the U.S. II Corps headquarters.[36]

The next day Spaatz had a talk with General Porter, Fredendall's chief of staff, who flatly contradicted his commander when he informed Spaatz that very few men had been lost to enemy dive bombers, with the exception of one infantry battalion in trucks that had been caught in the open by enemy aircraft; and this occurred because of the "stupidity on the part of the Battalion Commander." According to Spaatz's account of the meeting, "Porter was emphatically of the opinion that ground troops in forward positions should be able to take care of themselves and would be as soon as they learned to open fire instead of taking cover, kept proper dispersion, and were given sufficient antiaircraft weapons." Further, Porter thought that "a defensive fear complex was being built up in the 2nd Corps. . . ."[37]

As noted above, Spaatz, Fredendall, Kuter, McNabb, and Anderson were engaged in the classic conflict between ground and air officers over the proper use of aircraft in combat. Most ground commanders in Tunisia saw aircraft as having essentially two missions: namely to protect ground forces from air attack, which was to be done by maintaining "air umbrellas" over ground positions, and to act as airborne artillery to attack targets directly in front of the ground forces. Air force officers, however, saw aircraft not as a defensive weapon or artillery piece, but rather as an offensive weapon of great flexibility, which was capable after gaining air superiority of hitting at the center of an enemy's military power. In 1943, the whole problem was made even more complex because the AAF, while being semi-independent, was still a part of the U.S. Army. Consequently, high-ranking U.S. Army ground force officers thought they should have the right to order a squadron of fighters around in much the same way as they could a tank battalion.

Before the Allies could come to any consensus on tactics and command, the Germans mounted a major attack on the U.S. II Corps on February 14. Rommel's army had withdrawn behind the Mareth Line in Tunisia by the beginning of February, and the Axis had decided to strengthen its position in Tunisia by attacking the southern flank of the Allied forces advancing from the west before the British Eighth Army in the east could renew its offensive against Rommel. Two weeks later, German armor, supported by aircraft, attacked the American 1st Armored Division between Faid and Gafsa. A large tank battle ensued in the Sidi Bou Zid region in which the Americans were defeated, losing about half their tanks. By midnight February 17/18, the enemy had advanced to the line, Pichon-Sleitla-Kasserine-Thelpte. To stop the Axis advance, the Allies threw all their reserves into the battle. By February 25 the crisis was over, and the enemy was slowly falling back eastwards with their offensive having been halted mainly by Allied artillery fire. Allied air power played a minor role in stopping the enemy in the battle at Kasserine Pass because of bad weather and the loss of airfields in the Sbeita, Gafsa, Thelept, and Tebessa regions. The

Allied Air Support Command flew what sorties it could in the face of inclement weather and the enemy's air force. But during the period February 14–22, at the height of the battle for Kasserine Pass, the Allies flew only an average of about 365 sorties a day of all kinds, excluding antishipping missions, in all of Northwest Africa.[38] The author of a RAF staff history fairly set forth the role of air power during the enemy offensive at Kasserine when he wrote that "it is apparent that air action in the Kasserine battle was not decisive."[39]

In the aftermath of the Kasserine battle, even though the Axis air forces had played a relatively small role in the engagement, there were a number of reactions to the performance of the Allied air forces. One of the more rational ones was Doolittle's, who thought that all major operations should be stopped and that the Allied strategic and tactical air forces undertake "a short, intense, planned, combined effort" to destroy the enemy air forces in Tunisia.[40] Prime Minister Churchill's bitter evaluation, however, was typical of many reactions among the Allies: "The outstanding fact at the moment is our total failure to build up air superiority in Tunisia. . . ."[41]

By this point, the airmen themselves began to see the education of land generals beginning to bear fruit. Perhaps Kasserine galvanized top commanders to take action; perhaps it was the fact that the merging of Western Desert and Northwest African operations permitted the superior British doctrinal approaches to become inculcated into American circles. Montgomery and Coningham had started the process with a "lessons learned" conference at Tripoli on February 16, a conference which received "a gospel according to Montgomery" (as Tedder phrased it), in which the British general flatly told the assembled American and British officers that "any officer who aspires to hold high command in war must understand clearly certain basic principles regarding the use of air power."[42] The words were Montgomery's; the ideas those of Coningham. Since the great value of air power is its "flexibility," said Montgomery, there is the capability of making mass attacks on one target and then conducting mass attacks on a completely different type of target. It was clear that air operations had to be carefully planned in conjunction with those on the ground (not merely directed by ground authorities), so that the full weight of mass air attack could be placed on targets of greatest importance at any particular time. If aircraft were commanded by ground force leaders, air power would lose its flexibility, and would not be able to conduct such mass attacks. To obtain the greatest possible assistance from an air force, both air and ground commanders had to not only plan the battle together, but both staffs had to work to insure implementation of these plans, and the two staffs should be colocated to facilitate ease of communications. In Montgomery's words:

> The commander of an army in the field should have an Air H.Q. with him which will have direct control and command of such squadrons as may be allotted for operations in support of his army.

Such air resources will be in support of his army and not under his command.

But through his Air H.Q., the army commander, can obtain the support of the *whole striking force* in the theatre of operations because of the flexibility of air power.

Once this flexibility is destroyed, or is negated in any way, then the successful outcome of the battle becomes endangered.[43]

Coningham amplified Montgomery's remarks, stating quite simply: "The Soldier commands the land forces, the Airman commands the air forces: both commanders work together and operate their respective forces in accordance with the combined Army-Air plan, the whole operation being directed by the Army Commander." Noting "fundamental" differences between ground and air operations, the knowledgeable RAF leader suggested that while the army fights the land battle, the air force must fight two battles. It must first destroy the enemy air force either on the ground or in the air to secure air superiority. Once achieved, then the full weight of the air force could be directed at attacking enemy ground forces. He refuted the notion that any single officer had the skills to command both an army and an air force at the same time, for it required a lifetime of study "for a sailor, a soldier, or airman to learn his profession," in what Coningham termed "this technical age." To make certain that everybody know about the doctrine and methods of the Western Desert Air Force, as reflected at the Tripoli meeting, Coningham sent copies of his own speech to every ranking officer in Tunisia.[44]

Eisenhower, after consulting Spaatz and Tedder, agreed that the

Field Marshal Erwin Rommel and his men in North Africa.

doctrine for the employment of tactical air power would be the one set forth at the Tripoli meeting. Coningham's speech at Tripoli and the New Zealander's conduct of tactical air warfare subsequently have been considered by many American airmen to be the charter for both U.S. Army Air Forces tactical air doctrine during the remainder of World War II, as well as that of its postwar successor, the United States Air Force. Indeed, after the war, Coningham restated the basic principles which he felt should be followed by a successful tactical air force commander, namely:

> Air superiority is the first requirement for any major operation.
>
> The strength of air power lies in its flexibility and capacity for rapid concentration.
>
> It follows that control must be concentrated.
>
> Air forces must be concentrated in use and not dispersed in penny packets.
>
> The Commanders and their two staffs must work together.
>
> The Plan of Operation should be mutually adjusted and combined from the start.[45]

When named commander of a combined Northwest African Tactical Air Force in February 1943, Coningham issued his first "General Operational Directive" amidst the Kasserine crisis. The directive stated that the first objective was to gain air superiority over Tunisia by conducting "a continual offensive against the enemy in the air," and by "sustained attacks on enemy airfields." Tedder predicted that "Coningham is not going to have any easy time to get rid of the fantastic ideas of soldiers controlling aircraft." But Tedder proved wrong on this point. Two days after Coningham issued his directive, Allied ground commanders were forced by Alexander to totally reverse their position on control and employment of tactical aircraft. During a meeting with Eisenhower, Coningham, Kuter, and several other Allied staff officers on February 22, Alexander, the new commander of all Allied ground forces in North Africa, authorized Kuter to quote him (mainly for American consumption) as saying: "I shall never issue any orders on air matters. The airmen must be the final authority on air matters." The next day, Kuter reported to Spaatz that Alexander had overruled both Anderson and Fredendall on the issue of air umbrellas for the ground troops, and that aircraft of the Northwest African Tactical Air Force were going to be employed offensively as called for in Coningham's directive.[46]

Casablanca and the Creation of the Northwest African Air Forces

During late January and early February 1943 at Casablanca, Churchill, Roosevelt, the Combined Chiefs of Staff and numerous advisers changed

245

the command structure of the Allied air forces in the Mediterranean and planned Allied strategy for the future conduct of the war. One of the many decisions made during the Casablanca meeting was to change the entire Allied command structure in the Mediterranean. Eisenhower was appointed Commander in Chief of all Allied forces in the Mediterranean, with three deputy commanders who were British officers. Cunningham was named commander of all Allied naval forces in the Mediterranean; Gen. Sir Harold Alexander was to be Deputy Commander in Chief and was placed in command of the 18th Army Group consisting of all Allied ground forces in the Mediterranean. Air Marshall Sir Arthur Tedder was named Commander of all Allied Air Forces in the Mediterranean. It was intended by the CCS that this new command structure would go into effect in February, after the British forces in Libya had joined the Allies in Tunisia.[47]

It was understood by all that victory in Tunisia depended on the Allies gaining air superiority in the central Mediterranean and that this could not be done until the Allied command structure in North Africa was reformed. What the CCS did was to agree to a plan put forth by the British entitled "System of Air Command In The Mediterranean." This scheme called for a single commander in chief of all Allied air forces in the Mediterranean. This new command would consist of the Northwest African Air Forces (Spaatz), the AOC-in-C, Middle East (Air Chief Marshal Sir Sholto Douglas), and AOC Malta (Air Vice Marshal Sir Keith Park). For operations in Tunisia, Spaatz's command would be subordinate to Harold Alexander.[48] The American Joint Chiefs of Staff agreed with the British proposal for a "unified command" of all Allied air forces in the Mediterranean. After the meeting had ended, Marshall informed Portal that the appointment of Tedder to be the new commander in chief of all the Allied air forces in the Mediterranean would be agreeable to the Americans. Tedder was a natural choice for the position, for in addition to serving as AOC-in-C Middle East, many of his ideas were incorporated in the directive establishing the new Mediterranean Air Command.[49]

The most important force under Tedder's command was Spaatz's Northwest African Air Forces (NWAAF), which were to operate over Tunisia and the Central Mediterranean. These forces were activated on February 18, while the Allied Air Force and the Eastern Air Command were abolished, and the Twelfth Air Force ceased to exist except on paper for legal and administrative purposes.[50]

The Northwest African Air Forces were divided into three major combat commands and several support organizations along functional rather than national lines. Coningham, a New Zealander and former commander of the Western Desert Air Force, was placed in command of the Northwest African Tactical Air Force, which supported Allied ground forces. His second in command was Kuter. The Northwest African Strategic Air Force, consisting of all American heavy bombers, some medium bombers, plus their fighter escorts and two squadrons of RAF Wellingtons, was placed under the command of Doolittle. The Northwest African Coastal Air Force, commanded by Air Vice Marshal Hugh P. Lloyd, conducted maritime missions and was responsible for the defense of North African ports. These air forces were formed out of units of the Twelfth Air Force, the Western Desert Air Force, and the Eastern Air Command.[51]

Allied Conquest of Southern Tunisia

On March 8, Coningham's headquarters issued, after lengthy consultations with Alexander and the staff of the 18th Army Group, an outline of the Northwest African Tactical Air Force strategy for the conquest of Tunisia in three major phases. Phase A was the support of an attack eastward by the U.S. II Corps to take Gafsa and to "operate towards Maknassy." The objective of Phase A was to threaten to cut off the Axis forces facing the British Eighth Army at the Mareth Line. Phase B called for the British Eighth Army and the U.S. II Corps to clear the enemy out of Tunisia south of Gabes. And Phase C was the final assault on northern Tunisia by the Allies.

During the accomplishment of Phases A and B, the clearing of the Axis forces from southern Tunisia, the Northwest African Tactical Air Force had to gain air superiority over the Axis forces in southern Tunisia. The first step would be the construction of radar early warning and fighter control systems to cover the regions over which the ground forces would fight and the construction of a number of all-weather airfields in the Thelepte region as well as others in central Tunisia. The next step was to plan for and amass the necessary supplies for units of 242 Group, enabling them to reinforce the XII Air Support Command and supply the Western Desert Air Force when it moved into central Tunisia. It was the mission of the XII Air Support Command and 242 Group to attack any enemy aircraft found in the air while conducting a continuous series of attacks on enemy airfields in Tunisia, with the objective of either destroying the Axis air force or pinning it down in northern and central Tunisia. At the same time, the British Eighth Army, supported by the Western Desert Air Force, was to break through the Mareth Line and advance northward to the Gabes region.[52]

On March 17 the U.S. II Corps, under the command of Maj. Gen. George S. Patton, who had replaced Fredendall, began Operation WOP, which called for a series of limited attacks to threaten the communications of the enemy forces in southern Tunisia. The Americans attacking south and then east met slight enemy opposition, and even though the weather was bad, by March 18, units of the U.S. II Corps had taken Gafsa and El Guettar. At the same time, other elements of the U.S. II Corps drove east

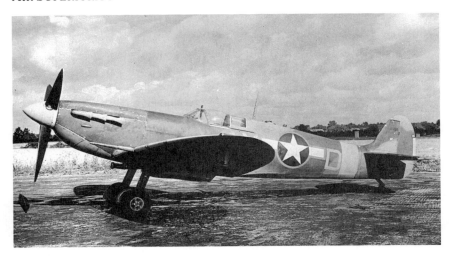

**The graceful Supermarine Spitfire, Britain's legendary fighter, was also
flown by American pilots during the war in the Western Desert.**

to take Maknassy on March 21, which was about fifty miles from Mahares
on the Golfe De Gabes.[53]

Attack aircraft of the XII Air Support Command bombed and shot up
enemy ground forces in support of the U.S. II Corps. Because of the rain
during the week of March 13–19, the Northwest African Tactical and Strategic Air Forces flew only slightly more than 700 sorties, dropping 241,680
pounds of bombs, most of which were expended on shipping targets.
Though the Allies thought on March 20 that the Axis still had some 435
combat aircraft in Tunisia, the Northwest African Air Forces' weekly intelligence summary dated March 22 proclaimed that "one fact stands out from
all reports, this being that NAAF has air superiority in North Africa at
present."[54] In other words, the author of this intelligence summary considered "air superiority" to refer to the fact that the enemy lacked the ability
to prevent the Allies from employing aircraft at the time and place of their
choice, and not that the Axis no longer had any combat aircraft.

The air plan for Phase B, breaking through the Mareth Line, was decided during a meeting on March 12. Coningham directed that the XII Air
Support Command and 242 Group would attack enemy airfields by day and
by night to "endeavor to neutralize and divert the attention of the enemy
air forces from the Eighth Army front. . . ." This would permit the Western
Desert Air Force to be devoted to support the British Eighth Army during
the attack on the Mareth Line.[55] Coningham requested that aircraft of the
Northwest African Strategic Air Force undertake attacks on enemy airfields before and during the assault on the Mareth Line in order to increase

the weight of the Allied attack on enemy airfields.[56] The heavy attacks on
enemy airfields in Tunisia, before and during the assault on the Mareth
Line, while not destroying the Axis air forces in Tunisia, were successful
to the extent that during the British assault of the Mareth Line only five
enemy aircraft appeared over the battlefield.[57]

On March 20, the British Eighth Army's attack on the Mareth Line
began. This position was a system of interconnected strong points running
from the sea in the east to the almost impassable steep-sided Matmata
Mountains in the west. Rommel knew that the Mareth Line could be outflanked by a force moving northward across the desert west of the Matmata
Mountains to the region of El Hamma, and then attacking in a northeast
direction between Chott El Fedjadj and the sea, cutting off the defenders of
the Mareth Line. This is exactly what Montgomery accomplished by
mounting a frontal assault on the fortifications on his right flank, while at
the same time the New Zealand Corps made a 150-mile march north along
the west side of the Matmata mountains arriving before El Hamma on
March 21. The British 50th Division on the night of March 20/21 attacked
the eastern end of the Mareth Line and at considerable cost made a lodge-
ment on the edge of the enemy position. But by March 23 it was clear that
the British Eighth Army could not, even with strong air support, smash its
way through the Mareth Line. Then, Montgomery ordered the British 1st
Armoured Division to join the New Zealand Corps before El Hamma and
ordered the New Zealanders to push on past El Hamma even before the
arrival of the British 1st Armored Division. Meanwhile, the enemy had
moved forces into positions around El Hamma, which were able to halt the
advance of the New Zealanders almost as soon as it began.[58]

After several days of fighting and numerous attacks by the Western
Desert Air Force on targets in the enemy's rear as well as frontline positions,[59] the British turned to air power to smash their way through the enemy positions blocking the Gabes Gap in the El Hamma region. The air
plan for the second attack against the Axis forces at El Hamma was made
by Air Vice Marshal Harry Broadhurst, the AOC of the Western Desert Air
Force. During the period between the two attacks enemy targets around
Mareth were hit in the daytime by light bombers. And during the two nights
before the ground assault, aircraft of the Western Desert Air Force were
used to attack the enemy anywhere that targets could be found. The objective was to destroy enemy vehicles and telephone lines in the El Hamma
region, and to deprive the enemy of sleep. In two nights about 330 sorties
were flown, during which over 400 tons of bombs were dropped.[60]

On March 26 in the late afternoon, fifty-four light bombers conducted
a "pattern bombing" attack on targets near El Hamma to further disrupt
the enemy. Right on the heels of the light bombers came the first group of
fighter bombers which machinegunned and bombed enemy positions from
the lowest possible height at fifteen-minute intervals. The pilots were

ordered to attack preset targets and then to shoot up enemy gun crews with the objective of putting enemy artillery and antitank guns out of action by killing the men who manned them. Twenty-six squadrons of fighter bombers strafed and bombed the enemy for two-and-one-half hours, while a squadron of Spitfires flew top cover for the fighter bombers.

At 1600, half an hour after the fighter-bomber attacks began, British and New Zealand forces attacked with the sun at their backs, which was a favorite enemy tactic. The Allies advanced behind an artillery barrage "creeping at a rate of one hundred yards every three minutes, thus automatically defending the bomb-line." Allied fighter bombers bombed and strafed in front of the artillery barrage. The combined air attacks and the artillery fire were too much for the enemy, and by the time the moon rose, British armor and New Zealand infantry broke through the Axis defenses. Within two days the New Zealanders took Gabes, and the British Eighth Army was marching north through the gap between the sea and Ghott El Fedjadj.[61]

The Allied use of aircraft during the Mareth Line battles was a classic example of the great flexibility of air power. While the XII Air Support Command and 242 Group pinned down the enemy's air force by attacking their airfields, the Western Desert Air Force blasted a path for units of the British Eighth Army to pass through the defenses at El Hamma. Air Vice Marshal Broadhurst thought that the battle fought on March 26 at El Hamma by the British Eighth Army and the Western Desert Air Force was "an example of the proper use of air power in accordance with the principle of concentration."[62] The Allied breakthrough at El Hamma resulted in the clearing of southern Tunisia. But this successful operation did not destroy the Axis air forces in Tunisia, for Allied intelligence on the eve of the battle estimated that the Axis still had some 425 combat aircraft in North Africa. Likewise, this battle did not stop the enemy from bringing in supplies and men to Tunisia.

Operation FLAX

At the end of the Tunisian campaign, Allied intelligence estimated that during the first 4 months of 1943 enemy transport aircraft carried an average of 7,675 tons of cargo per month from Italy to Tunisia. To carry the supplies to Tunisia the Germans had some 200 Ju–52s and about 15 Me–323 transport aircraft, which were escorted during daytime flights by as many as 100 fighters. Of course, the Italians similarly used cargo aircraft in resupply of their forces. When the transports arrived in Tunisia, usually at airfields near Tunis and Bizerta, they were unloaded and refueled, while fighters based in Tunisia flew overhead cover to protect them from Allied attack. In the first months of 1943, the Allies made no *systematic* attempt to stop movement of enemy transport aircraft between Europe and Tunisia as part of any overall air superiority campaign.⁶³

During March, Doolittle submitted to Spaatz a scheme, code-named FLAX, which called for the Northwest Africa Strategic Air Force to attack and destroy the entire enemy force of transport aircraft and their fighter escorts. The idea was not new; 242 Group and the Eastern Air Command had planned such an attack for months before Doolittle advanced FLAX for consideration. The plan was complex, but if it could be brought off, it would result in ending the enemy's ability to supply its forces in Tunisia by air. To carry out FLAX, Doolittle needed a great deal of information, such as the times of departure and arrival of enemy transports at various airfields plus the routes flown in and out of Tunisia. The required information was supplied by ULTRA intercepts and by the RAF's "Y" Service which handled interception, analysis, and decryption of wireless traffic in low-and medium-grade codes and ciphers. Tedder and Spaatz approved FLAX on April 2, 1943.⁶⁴

On the first day of FLAX, April 5, 1943, Northwest Africa Air Forces undertook 12 missions. At 0630, 26 P–38s of the 1st Fighter Group began a sweep of the Sicilian Straits, and at 0800 over Cape Bon they intercepted 110 enemy aircraft, 50 of which were thought to be transports, proceeding towards Tunisia. American fliers claimed 16 enemy aircraft destroyed in the ensuing battle. At the same time, 18 B–25s of the 321st Bomb Group, escorted by P–38s from the 82d Fighter Group, began an antishipping sweep between Sicily and Tunisia. The Americans attacked an enemy convoy escorted by 3 destroyers and claimed hits on 2 merchantmen and the destruction of 1 destroyer. The P–38s attacked the convoy's air cover and claimed 16 enemy aircraft downed at the cost of just 2 P–38s.

American air attacks on Sicily began at 0915 that day when 36 B–25s of the 310th Bomb Group, escorted by 18 P–38s of the 82d Fighter Group, took off for the island. The B–25s dropped 2,442 20-pound fragmentation bombs on some 80 to 90 aircraft parked on the airfield at Bo Rizzo. At the same time, heavy bombers of the 301st Heavy Bombardment Group conducted a similar attack on the Boca di Falco airfield, dropping 2,448 twenty-pound fragmentation bombs on 100 to 150 enemy aircraft parked there. Some 50 B–17s of the 99th Heavy Bombardment Group similarly struck other Axis airfields on Sicily as well as the field at El Aouina near Tunis in North Africa. That afternoon, P–38s made two more sweeps of the straits between Sicily and Tunisia but failed to encounter any enemy planes. For the day, the Northwest African Strategic Air Force claimed 40 enemy aircraft shot down and another 20 destroyed on the ground. The Axis admitted having 25 aircraft destroyed and 67 damaged.

FLAX was repeated on April 10 as twenty-eight P–38s of the 1st Fighter Group conducted another sweep over the Sicilian Strait. The Americans intercepted some sixty-five enemy aircraft and claimed to have shot down

251

AIRCRAFT INVOLVED IN THE NORTH AFRICAN CAMPAIGNS (*clockwise from upper left*): **B–25s come in over wrecked Nazi planes to land at their base in North Africa; Ju–52s in Tunisia; Me–109 wreckage in the desert; P–40.**

twenty-eight of them. That same morning, eighteen B–25s and twenty-five P–38s intercepted twenty-five Ju–52s and a number of other aircraft while conducting an antishipping sweep. The Americans claimed to have downed twenty-five enemy aircraft, twenty of which were transports. Most of the transports apparently were carrying gasoline, for they burst into flames and exploded when hit by gun fire. An additional four Ju–52s were shot down by Spitfires of the Northwest African Tactical Air Force. The following day, two additional P–38 sweeps took place over the Sicilian Straits, which resulted in thirty-two more enemy aircraft claimed shot down. FLAX represented an attritional response designed to win air superiority as well as to aid the ground fighting in Tunisia.[65]

The Western Desert Air Force assumed responsibility for FLAX operations in mid-April, since its aircraft operating from fields north of Sousse could easily operate over the north coast of Tunisia. The problem for British planners, however, was to ascertain the best time and place for interception of the enemy given the relatively short time-over-target leeway afforded the P–40s and Spitfires of the command. In order to intercept enemy transports, fighter patrols had to be maintained over the entire area. At first the British used small groups of fighters spread over "the maximum space and time because this would increase the chance of interception." This tactic was tried on April 16 when thirteen Spitfires intercepted a number of enemy transports escorted by more than 15 fighters. The out-numbered British lost two aircraft, claiming ten enemy planes in return.

The Western Desert Air Force adopted "a policy of annihilation" after April 16, which meant that sweeps were never again to be carried out by less than 3 squadrons of P–40s with a squadron of Spitfires providing top cover. According to an RAF staff history, this strategy resulted in most of the fighters of the Western Desert Air Force being devoted to FLAX, "following the basic principle of concentration in time and place which had been too often neglected in the past." On April 18, the Western Desert Air Force staged the famous "Palm Sunday Massacre" when 4 squadrons of P–40s from the AAF 57th Fighter Group, with top cover provided by RAF Spitfires of No. 92 Squadron, caught 130 enemy aircraft over Cape Bon. As the American planes attacked the enemy transports, some enemy aircraft were seen to crash land either in the sea or on land to avoid the P–40 gunfire. When the battle ended, the Western Desert Air Force estimated that 74 enemy aircraft had been destroyed with a loss of 6 Allied fighters. Early the next morning, 36 P–40s of the South African Air Force's 7th Wing intercepted 26 enemy aircraft, and when the fighting was over the South Africans claimed to have destroyed 15 enemy planes. The last major action of FLAX occurred on April 22 when South African P–40s and American aircraft from the 79th Fighter Group attacked a number of the giant Me–323 transports and their escorts. When the shooting ended, the Allies claimed 38 enemy aircraft had been shot down.[66]

Following the debacle on April 22, the Axis stopped sending large flights of transports to Tunisia during the daytime. They now tried to dispatch individual transports to Tunisia at night, making it possible for about seventy aircraft to make the flight each night. But, even under cover of darkness, the enemy transports faced the possibility of being shot down by British night fighters that operated freely over northern Tunisia.

German records indicate that by the end of April, 105 Ju–52 transports had been destroyed, an additional 22 damaged, and 19 Me–323 transports had been lost. Whether the German figures are used or the claims of Allied pilots, the overall effect of Operation FLAX, when combined with losses then taking place in Russia, was that Axis air transport units received blows that greatly increased the problems of resupplying Axis ground forces in Tunisia. FLAX enabled the Allies to use their newly won air superiority to dramatically affect the ground balance. As one German naval officer in Rome noted in the spring of 1943: "For the Luftwaffe, the Mediterranean had become a bottomless pit" into which the Germans poured aircraft without result.[67]

Victory in Tunisia

As early as March 20, the Allies anticipated Axis evacuation from Tunisia, and by early April, Spaatz's headquarters had issued a plan for interdicting such an evacuation by the Northwest African Air Forces. However, the Axis decision to fight to the end in Tunisia enabled the Allies to achieve their strategic objective—"to destroy the Axis forces in Tunisia as early as possible."[68]

During the first months of 1943, Allied air forces in the editerranean conducted a number of attacks on airfields in Sicily, Tunisia, and Sardinia, with the objective of destroying the enemy's ability to carry out air operations. Between February and mid-April, Allied aircraft (including those on FLAX missions), struck airfields in Sardinia 14 times, those in Sicily 16 times, and Tunisian airfields approximately 113 times. The Allies estimated that these attacks had destroyed 180 enemy airplanes and caused unspecified collateral damage to equipment, runways, buildings, munitions and fuel stockpiles, as well as killing and injuring personnel. All of this significantly reduced the Axis air forces' abilities to conduct offensive operations.

The defeat of the enemy air forces in Tunisia and the Central Mediterranean was a slow process, similar to grinding down a metal object with a file. Raids on Axis airfields might be dramatic, but their results were slow to appear. In November 1942, Axis air forces attacked Allied convoys and ports in the central and western Mediterranean with an average of forty sorties a day. By January 1943, enemy sorties averaged only fifteen to twenty per day, and this figure was further reduced in February and March to ten or twelve, and in April to only about six sorties per day. This decline resulted from the increasing weight of Allied air attacks wresting air superiority from the Axis.[69] Many operational Axis aircraft moved from offensive operations to defensive roles in protection of convoys, airfields, and communications.

The aircraft of the Allied Mediterranean Air Command outnumbered the Axis aircraft operating in the theater by a ratio of about 2 to 1. On April 16, the Allies had 3,241 combat aircraft, while the Germans and Italians each had an estimated 900. (See Table 5–1) The relative strength of Allied air forces in the Mediterranean, as compared with the Axis air forces, was even greater than these figures indicate, for at any given time about 80 percent of the Mediterranean Air Command's aircraft were serviceable compared to about 58 percent for the Germans and 50 percent for the Italians. In fact, the Allies probably had 1,600 more serviceable aircraft available at any one time than their Axis enemies.[70]

Air strength comparability remains difficult to judge even by 1943. In many respects, comparing differences in aircraft performance proves no more helpful than statistical comparisons. Certainly, the Axis had no long-range, heavy bombardment aircraft like the B–17 or B–24. Comparing medium bombers such as the American B–25s and B–26s with German Ju–88s is difficult and of doubtful value. In general, although Allied bombers were superior to Axis bombers, only the latest model Spitfire could equal German FW–190 or Me–109 fighter aircraft in speed, climb rate, and maneuverability. The German twin-engine Me–110 fighter was no match for the American P–38, while the only dive bomber used was the German Ju–87 Stuka. Only the British used antiques like the Fleet Air Arm Albacores, yet such aircraft were part of a powerful air team, for they marked targets for medium and heavy night bombers.[71] Added to the question of materiel, other factors affecting air strength included skill and training of aircrews and commanders; command and control; doctrine, strategy and tactics; as well as logistics and technology.

By the middle of April 1943, the Allied air forces were superior to the Axis air forces in the Mediterranean. The Allies had more, if not better, aircraft than the Axis. Allied aircrews were becoming more proficient with each passing day, while the Axis lagged badly in the use of new technology such as radar. Allied logistical support had been strengthened, while the Axis forces in Tunisia lived on a hand-to-mouth basis because of the air-naval blockade. In matters of tactics, doctrine, and command and control, the Allied air forces were becoming increasingly skillful. Strategically, the most powerful of the Axis air forces, the German Luftwaffe, was fighting a three-front war against the Anglo-Americans in the Mediterranean and Northwest Europe, and with Russia in the east. What would decide the air

TABLE 5–1

Axis Mediterranean Air Strength, April 1943

Tunisian Air Corps	Aircraft Strength
53d Single Engine Fighter *Geschwader* (Me–109)	90
77th Single Engine Fighter *Geschwader* (Me–109)	90
3d *Gruppe*/1st Close Support *Geschwader* (Me–109)	25
3d *Gruppe*/4th Close Support *Geschwader* (FW–190)	25
2d and 4th *Staffeln*/14th Reece. Gruppe (Me–109)	16
Desert Rescue *Staffel* (Fiesler Storch)	21
Mine Detector *Staffel* (Ju–52)	3
Total	270

Note: In addition, the Luftwaffe could draw from forces elsewhere in the Mediterranean totaling 767 aircraft capable of immediate deployment.

Source: Felmy, "The GAF in the Mediterranean Theater of War" Air Ministry, German translation VII/25.

war ultimately was that Germany was in a race with its enemies, which would be won by the side that could produce the most trained aircrews and modern aircraft, as well as other weapons such as radar. By the middle of April 1943, it was fast becoming apparent that Germany was losing that struggle. Nevertheless, this did not mean that the air war in Tunisia or in Europe would be a walk-over for the Allies. The Germans in Tunisia, as later in Europe, would fight to the last aircraft and rifle round, and would not surrender until there was no other alternative.

The Axis forces in Tunisia, as well as those supporting the North African effort, were now being attacked by Allied air power, which grew stronger daily. The weight of Allied air attacks in the Mediterranean in April 1943 could not be compared with those in Northwest Europe over the next two years. However, in 1943, it was nevertheless unprecedented. During the period March 29 through the night of April 21/22, bombers of the Northwest African Strategic Air Force and the Middle East Air Command flew 997 sorties against enemy airfields, communications, and tactical targets, not counting attacks on ports and ships. The estimated daily average for all Allied combat sorties was 1,171.[72] During the period 1800 hours April 4 to 1800 hours April 5, the Northwest African Tactical Air Force flew more than 800 sorties over Tunisia, while the Northwest African Strategic Air Force flew some 178 sorties. In the course of these sorties, the Northwest African Strategic and Tactical Air Forces lost 6 aircraft with another 7 missing, while they claimed to have shot down 84 enemy planes.[73] Between April 10 and 16 Allied aircraft flew 51 major missions, dropping 2,421,520 pounds of bombs on enemy targets in the central Mediterranean and Tunisia, but claimed to have destroyed in the air alone, 134 enemy aircraft. The highlight of this week was the mission carried out by 24 B–17s on April 10 against the Italian naval base at La Maddalena on Sardinia, during which the Italian cruiser *Trieste* was sunk and the cruiser *Gorizia* was damaged. During this week, with the exception of some reconnaissance flights and minor attacks on Allied shipping and ground forces, the greater part of the enemy's air forces were deployed on purely defensive missions. Allied air power had the Axis air forces distinctly on the defensive on the eve of the final Allied offensive in Tunisia.[74]

The offensive that would destroy remaining Axis forces in North Africa, code-named VULCAN, was scheduled to begin on April 22. Coningham began preparations on April 14 by issuing a directive for the employment of fighter aircraft in Tunisia. Tunisia was divided into two regions for purposes of fighter aircraft control, one under the command of the Western Desert Air Force and the other by the 242 Group, with the aircraft of the XII Air Support Command controlled by 242 Group's operations room. Allied radar was established to cover all the air space over both Allied and Axis held areas in Tunisia. Information of enemy aircraft movements obtained by this radar network was forwarded to the 242 Group operations room and the Western Desert Air Force so that the movement of both enemy and Allied aircraft could be closely monitored throughout the offensive.[75]

Operational orders for VULCAN were issued on April 16. The main land assault to capture Tunis would be made by the British First Army, which was reinforced by transferring the British X Corps from the British Eighth Army. The British First Army would attack northeast from the Medjez salient. The U.S. II Corps would take Bizerta and the region north of Mateur, between the northern flank of the British First Army and the sea. The French XIX Corps would attack along the southeastern flank of the British First Army, and the British Eighth Army, whose front was the area between the French XIX Corps and the Tunisian east coast, would have a "divisionary [sic] and containing role" in VULCAN. The British Eighth Army would attack the enemy in the Enfidaville region before the main Allied attack by the British First Army, and attempt to draw Axis forces away from the objectives of the British First Army and the U.S. II Corps.[76]

At the same time as the plan for the Allied ground forces was presented, Coningham issued a directive for the conduct of tactical air operations during VULCAN. Phase one of the air plan called for the aircraft of the Northwest African Air Forces to begin an all out assault, day and night, on April 18 against all enemy airfields in Tunisia. The Northwest African Strategic Air Force would attack the airfield at Bari where most enemy supply transport aircraft landed in Tunisia. The Northwest African Coastal Air Force would conduct night intruder operations to intercept enemy transport aircraft enroute to Tunisia. Phase two of the air plan would begin on April 22 with the main Allied ground attack. The main objective of this air effort would be "to assist the land forces." Reconnaissance operations would be undertaken to see if the enemy were attempting to withdraw from Tunisia. At first light each day, Allied fighter bombers would conduct armed reconnaissance flights with the objective of gaining information as well as attacking targets of opportunity. "Continuous light bomber and low flying fighter attacks were to be undertaken in the battle area to assist the progress of land forces." The Northwest African Strategic Air Force was to attack airfields in Sicily and enemy supply lines both at sea and in the air, while the Northwest African Coastal Air Force would continue night intruder operations. The objective of the air plan for VULCAN was to use every possible Allied aircraft to attack the enemy until the Axis forces in Tunisia were destroyed.[77]

Between April 17 and 23, Allied aircraft flew more than 5,000 sorties against enemy airfields, shipping, troops, supply dumps, and vehicles. Enemy airfields were subjected to major attacks 24 times, during which Allied aircraft dropped 727,168 pounds of bombs. The effort against airfields was a little under half of the Allied air effort during the week April 17–23.[78] The enemy, because of the great value of Allied air attacks, withdrew a majority of their aircraft from Tunisia to Sicily and Italy. Those Axis aircraft that remained in Africa were fighters deployed to defend Tunis and Bizerta.[79]

On April 22, the main Allied ground attack began when the British V Corps attacked enemy positions north of Medjez el Bab. On April 24 Allied intelligence estimated that there were 157,900 Axis troops in Tunisia,[80] supported by approximately 140 aircraft.[81] With the beginning of the last Allied offensive in Tunisia, the Northwest African Tactical Air Force flew 716 sorties over Tunisia during daylight hours. Allied aircraft attacked enemy ground positions in support of the Allied ground forces and conducted offensive fighter sweeps, but these later operations were for the most part unsuccessful for the "German Air Force was not conspicuous and was unwilling and difficult to engage."[82] The offensive that would destroy the Axis forces in North Africa began with the Allies having almost total air superiority over Tunisia and the Sicilian Strait.

The British First Army and the U.S. II Corps slowly advanced towards Bizerta and Tunis, meeting strong resistance from enemy ground forces. Allied troops had to fight for each hill and ridge. During the last week in April, the Northwest African Tactical Air Force attacked enemy airfields and maritime targets, while fighters and fighter-bombers attacked enemy frontline positions and vehicles again and again, meeting almost no resistance from the enemy air forces. During this period, 1,410,956 pounds of bombs were dropped by Allied aircraft even though there were several days of bad flying weather.[83]

In the first week of May, the enemy air forces in Tunisia flew between 70 and 200 sorties a day, most of which were defensive in nature. An Allied intelligence summary describes enemy air activity as attempting "to hold back the tide with a thimble." On May 6, the Allies flew 200 sorties against enemy shipping and Sicily, while Allied aircraft at the same time flew about 1,205 sorties attacking enemy ground forces. A large number of these sorties were directed against an area 1,000 yards deep by 4 miles long in front of the British First Army, which "literally pounded the enemy into submission."[84]

On May 7, the enemy defenses of Tunis and Bizerta cracked, and in the afternoon units of the British First Army reached the center of Tunis, while the U.S. 1st Armored Division captured Ferryville and the U.S. 9th Division seized Bizerta.[85] The next day, Cunningham ordered every available destroyer into the Sicilian Strait with orders to "Sink, burn and destroy. Let nothing pass."[86] The capture of Bizerta and Tunis split the Axis forces in half, but the fighting continued until May 13, when the last pocket of enemy ground forces surrendered. At the time, it was estimated that fewer than 1,000 enemy troops escaped from Tunisia. The last air operation in Tunisia was an attack by aircraft of the Northwest African Tactical Air Force against a group of enemy troops penned-up in a pocket north of Enfidaville.[87]

The annihilation of the Axis forces in Tunisia was the first great victory of the western Allies in the European theater during World War II. A huge but unknown number of Axis prisoners were taken at the end of the campaign in North Africa. One authority states that 238,243 members of the Axis armed forces were captured, while an 18th Army Group calculation puts the total at 244,500 Axis prisoners. Americans "estimated" that 275,000 enemy soldiers had been captured. No matter what the true number of Axis troops that were taken, it is clear that they numbered in the many thousands. Between April 22 and May 16, the Germans had 273 aircraft shot out of the skies, and over 600 German and Italian aircraft were found abandoned around Tunis, Bizerta, and on Cape Bon.[88]

Aftermath: FM 100–20

The Tunisian campaign had a profound effect on the doctrine and organization of the U.S. Army Air Forces as well as on its relations with Army ground forces. At the end of the campaign, American airmen were not going to relinquish the concept of equality between air and ground commanders nor would they let Western Desert Air Force doctrine disappear from their own tactical practices. Still, codification and institutionalization of "lessons learned" required additional work. Merely educating air and ground leaders proved to be a continuing problem.

The campaign to impose doctrine and command principles of the Northwest African Tactical Air Force upon the entire AAF as well as ground forces began during the final days of the Tunisian campaign. Air leaders like Kuter continued to battle ground staff officers planning for continued subordination of air-to-ground requirements in future operations such as the invasion of Sicily. Lt. Gen. Ben Lear, commanding the Army Ground Forces in the United States, in a memorandum to the Army's Chief of Staff, George C. Marshall on May 17, attacked Montgomery's *Some Notes on High Command in War,* which enunciated Western Desert Air Force doctrine. Lear objected to proposed changes in organization and command of tactical aircraft units because they would further separate air and ground forces; prevent air support of ground forces until air superiority had been first achieved; and place control of tactical aircraft in the hands of the air commander, which would result in "no attachment of air to ground," and "no decentralization of air support." Even some aviators like Brig. Gen. Robert Candee complained that the Air Force had "swallowed the RAF solution of a local situation in North Africa hook, line and sinker, without stopping to analyze it or report it in 'Americanese' instead of British speech."[89]

By May, however, the airmen had not only the support of in-theater leaders like Eisenhower and Alexander, but had taken their case to Washington. Marshall already understood the need for codification of the new principles of air power evidenced in Tunisia. On April 24, he had ordered that a new manual be written on "the command and employment of air power." He directed that this manual delineate the concept that "land power and air power are co-equal" and that "the gaining of air superiority is the first requirement for success of any major land operation." Therefore, air forces "must be employed primarily against the enemy's air forces until air superiority is obtained." Marshall was undoubtedly reflecting what men like Kuter had been communicating back through their own air leader, "Hap" Arnold, commanding the Army Air Forces in Washington. Perhaps the words of Marshall's directive were those of Arnold, but they captured the thoughts of Kuter, Spaatz, Coningham, and others that "control of available air power must be centralized and command must be exercised through the air force commander if this inherent flexibility and the ability to deliver a decisive blow are to be fully exploited." So, Marshall's directive stated in no uncertain terms that the manual writers should include a statement to the effect that the commanders of land and air forces are to be under a "superior command . . . who will exercise command of air forces under his command through the air force commander. The superior commander will not attach Army Air Forces units to units of ground forces under his command except when such ground units are operating independently or isolated by distance or lack of communication."[90]

In May, Maj. Gen. George E. Stratemeyer, the Chief of the Air Staff in Washington, met with General Alexander while passing through Tunisia and wrote back to Arnold how positive the British were concerning centralization of air power in the hands of air commanders. Kuter, just before he departed Tunisia for a new billet as Assistant Chief of the Air Staff for Plans, also sent Arnold a long and detailed report on May 12 concerning how the Northwest African Tactical Air Force functioned and recommended that all AAF tactical units be organized and employed in the same manner. He reiterated this in a press conference at the Pentagon on May 22, recounting the main points of the argument that emphasized equality of air and ground commanders, centralized control of tactical air power, and the need for gaining air superiority over the battlefield. Several weeks later, Kuter sent Coningham a copy of his press statement and told the New Zealander that a "radical change of heart within the War Department [is] indicated by the fact that this release was cleared at all."[91]

On June 9, under the direction of the G-3 Division of the U.S. Army General Staff, a committee consisting of Col. Marton H. McKinnon, Commandant of the Air Support Department of the School of Applied Tactics; Col. Ralph F. Stearley, Commander of the 1st Air Support Command; and Lt. Col. Orin H. Moore, Armored Forces liaison officer at the AAF Headquarters, drafted FM 100–20, *Command and Employment of Air Power*. This new manual, which was first issued on July 21, 1943, set forth the doctrine, organization, command requirements, and strategy of a tactical air force as outlined in Marshall's memorandum of April 24, and in Coningham's and Montgomery's talks on February 16 at Tripoli. FM 100–20 established the equality of air and ground force commanders. It asserted that centralized command of combat aircraft was essential to obtain "the inherent flexibility of air power" which "is its greatest asset," for it gave the commander of a tactical air force the ability to mass his aircraft to attack the decisive targets and the fully exploit the hitting power of tactical air power. According to the manual writers, overall command of air and ground forces would be conducted by a theater commander who would be responsible for all operations. Also, this manual stated that the first requirement for success of ground operations was gaining air superiority over the battlefield.[92]

In many ways, because of the manner in which the manual was written and subsequently used by the AAF, the implications of independence from ground force control somewhat overshadowed other key points brought out in this publication. The breakdown of types of tactical air missions and the separate chapters devoted to strategic air forces, tactical air forces, air defense, and air service commands were important developments resulting from wartime experience. Moreover, the discussions of tactical air operations especially incorporated many lessons derived from Tunisia. The missions, ranked by priority, highlighted securing "the necessary degree of air superiority," for example. This would be accomplished by attacks against aircraft in the air and on the ground, and against those enemy installations that "he requires for the application of air power." Priorities then followed for interdicting the movement of hostile troops and supplies into the theater of operations or within the theater, followed by participation in a combined effort of the air and ground forces, in the battle area, to gain objectives on the immediate front of the ground forces.[93]

For the first time, actual combat permitted AAF and Army officers to identify the actions necessary for acquiring air superiority. They incorporated those actions into a particularly pivotal paragraph in FM 100–20:

> The primary aim of the tactical air force is to obtain and maintain air superiority in the theater. The first prerequisite for the attainment of air supremacy is the establishment of a fighter defense and offense, including RDF (radio direction finder), GCI (ground control interception), and other types of radar equipment essential for the detection of enemy aircraft and control of our own. While our air superiority is maintained, both the ground forces and the air force can fight the battle with little interference by the enemy air. Without this air supremacy, the initiative passes to the enemy. Air superiority is best obtained by the attack on hostile airdromes, the destruction of aircraft at rest, and by fighter action in the air. This is much more effective than any attempt to furnish an umbrella of fighter aviation over our own troops. At most an air umbrella is prohibitively expensive and could be provided only over a small area for a brief period of time.[94]

Publication of FM 100–20 caused mixed reactions among the American military. Arnold ordered copies distributed to every AAF officer, while the Army ground forces generally considered the manual an AAF "Declaration of Independence" and held varying degrees of "dismay" about its contents. Some airmen thought the document too British in content, while Maj. Gen. Orvil Anderson disapproved the separation of air power into distinctively strategic and tactical catagories.[95] Whatever the opinions, the War Department publication gave the air force position a note of authority and a corpus of doctrine that would remain basic for the duration of the war and beyond. It was British doctrine à la Coningham, but it had been learned and absorbed by American air force officers working together with their Allies to destroy enemy air power. FM 100–20 provided the basic tenents from which the AAF could launch additional air campaigns in Sicily, Italy, Northwest and Southern France, as well as in the Pacific.

Notes

1. AAF Historical Division, *The Twelfth Air Force in the North African Winter Campaign: 11 November 1942 to the Reorganization of February 1943* (Washington, 1946), pp 80–81.

2. Public Record Office (Kew, UK), AIR/20/2107, "Axis Air Operations: North Africa and Mediterranean, The Last Phase in North Africa, Jan 1, 1943–May 12, 1943." Hereafter this archive will be cited as PRO.

3. AAF Historical Division, *The Twelfth Air Force*, p 30.

4. Kent R. Greenfield, *Army Ground Forces and the Air-Ground Battle Team including Organic Light Aviation* (n.p., 1948), pp 1–22; Christopher R. Gable, "The U.S. Army GHQ Maneuvers of 1941" (Unpublished Ohio State University Ph.D. Dissertation, 1981), pp 65–67, 70–71, 97–99, 310–13.

5. Air Ministry, *Air Support* (n.p., 1955), pp 7–45; W. A. Jacobs, "Air Support for the British Army, 1939–1943," *Military Affairs* (Dec 1982), XLVI, pp 174–82.

6. *Ibid*, pp 19–37; PRO, AIR/20/4133, pp 57–59; also "The Twelfth Air Force in the Invasion of Northwest Africa," History of the Twelfth Air Force, n.d., A6191/650.01–2, 1942–1944 (USAF Historical Center, Maxwell AFB, Ala.).

7. AAF Historical Division, *The Twelfth Air Force*, p 59; Welsey Frank Craven and James Lea Cate, eds, *The Army Air Forces in World War II* (Chicago, 1949; reprint, Washington, 1973), Vol II: *Europe: TORCH to POINTBLANK August 1942–September 1943*, chap 2, especially pp 78–85.

8. *Supplement to the London Gazette*, Nov 6, 1946.

9. PRO, AIR/41/33, f. 57.

10. AAF Historical Division, *The Twelfth Air Force*, pp 40, 44, 46, 51.

11. Office of Air Force History, 612.620–2. Notes on Interview with Brig Gen G. A. Davidson; Alfred M. Beck, Abe Bortz, Charles W. Lynch, Lida Mayo, and Ralph F. Weld, *The Corps of Engineers: The War Against Germany* (Washington, 1984), chap V, pp 4–14. Much of the Office of Air Force History (AFCHO) at Bolling Air Force Base collections are on microfilm. Each document is numbered and hereafter documents from this collection will be cited by their numbers and title.

12. AAF Historical Division, *The Twelfth Air Force*, pp 44, 49–50, 74.

13. Craven and Cate, *AAF in World War II*, Vol II: *TORCH to POINTBLANK*, pp 83–90.

14. *Ibid.*, pp 91-104.

15. Memo, Nov 30, 1942, Box 97, Spaatz Papers, Library of Congress (LC).

16. Air Historical Branch of the Luftwaffe, "A Tactical Appreciation of the Air War in Tunisia," Oct 31, 1944 [translated by British Air Ministry], p 10.

17. Arthur Tedder, *With Prejudice: The War Memoirs of Marshal of the Royal Air Force Lord Tedder G.C.B.* (Boston, 1966), p 370.

18. *Ibid.*, pp 362-366.

19. Memo, Nov 30, 1943; Memo, Dec 2, 1942; Memo, December 3, 1942; All Box 97, Spaatz Papers, LC; Tedder, *With Prejudice*, pp 371–72; 772.

20. Doolittle to Spaatz, Dec 25, 1942, Box 19, Doolittle Papers, LC.

21. PRO, AIR/8/1035, Welsh to Portal, Jan 12, 1943.

22. Memo, Dec 29, 1942; Memo, Dec 30, 1942, both Box 97, Spaatz Papers, LC; PRO AIR/8/1035 J. S. M., Washington to War Cabinet, Jan 1, 1943.

23. PRO, AIR/8/1035, Portal to Churchill, Jan 1, 1943; Portal to Secretary of State for Air, Jan 1, 1943; USFOR London to Freedom Algiers, Jan 4, 1943, Box 274, Arnold Papers, LC.

24. PRO, AIR/8/035, Eisenhower to Combined and British Chiefs of Staffs, Jan 4, 1943; Constitution and Activities of Allied Air Forces, Jan 5, 1943, as well as Headquarters Allied Air Force, General Order Number 1, Jan 7, 1943, both Box 10, Spaatz papers, LC; and Craven and Cate, *AAF in World War II*, Vol II: *TORCH to POINTBLANK*, pp 107–09.

25. PRO, AIR/8/1035, Minutes by ACAS(P) for CAS, Jan 5, 1943; PRO, AIR/8/1035, Air Ministry to Britman, Washington, Jan 11, 1943; Air Ministry to Eisenhower, Jan 11, 1943.

26. Tedder, *With Prejudice*, pp 396–98; PRO, AIR/23/6572, Order by Eisenhower, Criticism and Disparagement of Allies, Feb 5, 1943.

27. George F. Howe, *Northwest Africa: Seizing the Initiative in the West* (Washington, 1957), pp 369-71.

28. PRO, AIR/20/2568, Mediterranean Air Command to Air Ministry, Feb 28, 1943.

29. Lecture given by Vice Air Marshal Sir A. Coningham . . . (Tripoli, Feb 16, 1943), Box 12, Spaatz Papers, LC.

30. Memo by Spaatz, Jan 21, 1943, Box 10, Spaatz Papers, LC.

31. PRO, AIR/41/33, f. 77.

32. Some principles on air employment followed in Tunisian campaign, Feb 3, 1943, Box 10, Spaatz Papers, LC.

33. Memo by Spaatz, Feb 4, 1943, Box 10, Spaatz Papers, LC; Craven and Cate, *AAF in World War II*, Vol II: *TORCH to POINTBLANK*, p 139.

34. PRO, AIR/41/33, pp 77–78.

35. Memo by Spaatz, Feb 5, 1943, Box 10, Spaatz Papers, LC.

36. *Ibid.*

37. *Ibid.*

38. I. S. O. Playfair and C. J. C. Molony, *The Mediterranean and Middle East* (London, 1966), vol IV, p 303.

39. PRO, AIR/41/33, f. 80.

40. Doolittle to Spaatz, Feb 24, 1943, Box 12, Spaatz Papers, LC.

41. PRO, AIR/8/1085, Churchill to Portal, Feb 25, 1943.

42. Tedder, *With Prejudice*, pp 398–403.

43. *Ibid.*, pp 396–97; also B. L. Montgomery, *Some Notes on High Command in War* (Tripoli, 1943), p 2.

44. Talk by Air Vice Marshal Sir A. Coningham (Tripoli, Feb 16, 1943), Box 12; also, Coningham to Spaatz, Mar 1, 1943, Box 11, both Spaatz Papers, LC.

45. Memo by Spaatz, Feb 17, 1943, Box 10, Spaatz Papers, LC; Sir Arthur Coningham, "The Development of Tactical Air Forces," *Journal of the Royal United Service Institution* (May 1946), vol 91, p 215; Riley Sunderland, *Evolution of Command and Control Doctrine for Close Air Support* (Washington, 1973), pp 13–14; Richard H. Kohn and Joseph P. Harahan, eds, *Air Superiority in World War II and Korea* (Washington, 1983), pp 29–41.

46. Coningham Directive, Feb 20, 1943, Laurence Kuter Papers, U.S. Air Force Academy Library, Colorado Springs, Colo., hereafter cited USAFA; Tedder, *With Prejudice*, p 398; Laurence S. Kuter, "Goddamit, Georgie! North Africa, 1943: The Birth of TAC Air Doctrine," *Air Force Magazine*, Feb 1973, p 55.

47. Craven and Cate, *AAF in World War II*, Vol II: *TORCH to POINTBLANK*, pp 113–15.

48. PRO, AIR/8/1035, Combined Chiefs of Staff, Systems of Air Command in the Mediterranean, Jan 20, 1943.

49. Tedder, *With Prejudice*, p 372.

50. Howe, *Northwest Africa*, pp 354–55; Memo by Col Cook, Feb 23, 1943, Box 10, Spaatz papers, LC.

51. 612.193, General Orders by Spaatz, Feb 18, 1943, AFCHO; also General Order Number 1 by Tedder, Feb 18, 1943; Memos of conference, Feb 19, 1943, and staff meeting, Feb 21, 1943, all Box 10, Spaatz Papers, LC.

52. Memo by Spaatz, Feb 23, 1943, Box 10, Spaatz Papers, LC; 614.201-1, Outline of Operational Plan by Coningham, Mar 6, 1943, AFCHO.

53. Howe, *Northwest Africa,* pp 542–51.

54. 612.606–1, Weekly Intelligence Summary No. 18, Period from 001 Hours Mar 13 to 2400 Hours Mar 19, 1943; Weekly Intelligence Summary No. 19, Period from 001 Mar 20 to 2400 Hours Mar 26, 1943, both AFCHO.

55. PRO, AIR/41/33, f. 103; AIR/41/50, pp 489–500.

56. NATAF to NAAF, Mar 17, 1943, Box 12, Spaatz Papers, LC.

57. PRO, AIR/41/33, ff 104–05.

58. Playfair and Molonoy, *The Mediterranean and Middle East,* vol IV, pp 338–43.

59. PRO, AIR/41/50, pp 500–03.

60. PRO, AIR/41/50, p 506.

61. PRO, AIR/41/50, pp 506–09; Playfair and Molony, *Mediterranean and Middle East,* vol IV, pp 345–55; 614.4501–1, The Eighth Army Breakthrough at Hamma on Mar 26, 1943, AFCHO.

62. PRO, Air/23/1708, The Eighth Army Breakthrough at Hamma on Mar 26, 1943; Comment by A.O.C. Tactical Air Force.

63. PRO, ADM/223/49, p 8; 615-308.–2, Effect of Weather Conditions on Enemy Air Transport Activity, Mar 26, 1943, AFCHO; Fritz Morzik, *German Air Force Airlift Operations* (Maxwell AFB, Ala., 1961) p 133.

64. Doolittle to Spaatz, Mar 22, 1943, Box 19, Doolittle Papers, LC; Aileen Clayton, *The Enemy is Listening: The Story of the Y Service* (London, 1980), p 236; Memo of A Conference, Apr 2, 1943, Box 11, Spaatz Papers, LC.

65. The Battle Story of FLAX, Box 19, Doolittle Papers, LC; Operations Bulletin, Number 1, for period ending Apr 30, 1943, Box 14, Spaatz Papers, LC; and Craven and Cate, *AAF in World War II,* Vol II: *TORCH to POINTBLANK* pp 189–91.

66. *Ibid.*

67. PRO, Air/41/50, pp. 521–25. Until gun sight cameras came into use, pilots and gunners always over estimated the number of enemy aircraft shot down. The problem is made more difficult by the fact that different services have different definitions of what constitutes a destroyed aircraft as opposed to a damaged one.

68. Plan of action to meet attempted evacuation of Tunisia by Axis forces, Mar 20, Box 11; Operations order Number 4, Apr 3, 1943, Box 12, Spaatz Papers, LC; PRO, AIR/20/2567, Alexander to Churchill, Apr 2, 1943.

69. PRO, Air/20/5796, Appreciation of the Effects of Allied Air Force Attacks on Axis Airfields in Sardinia, Sicily, Tunisia, 1943.

70. Playfair and Molony, *Mediterranean and Middle East,* vol IV, p 400.

71. Cf. *Jane's All the World's Aircraft, 1943-44* (New York, 1945).

72. Playfair and Molony, *Mediterranean and Middle East,* vol IV, pp 391, 401.

73. 612.307, Operational Summary No. 44, Period end 1800 Hours Apr 5, 1943, AFCHO.

74. 616–606–1, Weekly Intelligence Summary No. 22, Period from 001 Hours Apr 10 to 2400 Hours Apr 16, 1943, AFCHO.

75. Control of Fighters in the Final Phase of the Tunisian Campaign, Apr 14, 1943, Box 12, Spaatz Papers, LC.

76. PRO, Air/23/17111, Final Phase, Army Plan, Apr 16, 1943.

77. 614.201–1, T.A.F. Operational Plan for the Final Assault on Tunis, Apr 16, 1943, AFCHO.

78. 612.606–1, Weekly Intelligence Summary No. 23, Period from 0001 Hours Apr 17 to 2400 Hours Apr 23, 1943, AFCHO.

79. PRO, AIR/41/33, f. 111.

80. 612.606–1, Weekly Intelligence Summary No. 24, Period from 0001 Hours Apr 24 to 2400 Hours Apr 30, 1943.

81. 612.606–1, Weekly Intelligence Summary No. 23, Period from 0001 Hours Apr 17 to 2400 Hours Apr 30, 1943, AFCHO.

82. 612.307, Operational and Intelligence Summary No. 61, for the period ending 1800 Hours April 22, 1943, AFCHO.

83. 612.606–1, Weekly Intelligence Summary No. 24, Period from 0001 Hours Apr 24 to 2400 Hours Apr 30, 1943.

84. 612.606–1, Weekly Intelligence Summary, No. 25, Period from 0001 Hours May 1 to 2400 Hours Apr 30, 1943.

85. Playfair and Molony, *Mediterranean and Middle East*, vol IV, pp 442–43.

86. A. B. Cunningham, *A Sailor's Odyssey: The Autobiography of Admiral of the Fleet Viscount Cunningham of Hyndhope* (New York, 1951), p 529.

87. PRO, AIR/41/33, ff. 112–13.

88. Playfair and Molony, *Mediterranean and Middle East*, vol IV, p 460.

89. Memo by Spaatz, May 3 and 4, 1943, Box 11, Spaatz Papers, LC; Beam to Kuter, Apr 28, 1943; Kuter to Beam, May 6, 1943; Training Memorandum Number 33, Air Support; Senior Air Staff Officer, Northwest African Tactical Air Force, May 6; Kuter Papers, USAFA; Candee quoted in Robert Frank Futrell, *Ideas, Concepts and Doctrine* (Maxwell AFB, Ala., 1971), p 69.

90. Stratemeyer to Arnold, May 7, 1943, Box 11, Spaatz Papers, LC.; also Memorandum for the Chief of Staff by Lt. Gen. Lear, May 17, 1943, Kuter papers, USAFA; Kuter to Commanding General, Army Air Forces, May 12, 1943, Kuter Papers, USAFA. Enclosed with Kuter letter were:

    1) 18th Army Group Operational Instructions No. 1, May 20, 1943.

    2) Coningham's General Operational Directive to the Northwest African Tactical Air Force, Feb 20, 1943.

    3) Coningham's Outline of Operational Plan for Northwest African Tactical Air Force, Mar 8, 1943.

    4) Coningham's T.A.F. Operational Plan for the Final Assault on Tunis, Apr 16, 1943.

    5) British 1st Army's Operational instructions No. 37, Apr 19, 1943.

    6) Text of talk given by Coningham at Tripoli, Feb 16, 1943.

    7) B. L. Montgomery, *Some Notes of High Command in War* (Tripoli, 1943).

    8) Alexander to Coningham, May 1943.

91. 614.505, Statement made by Brig Gen Laurence S. Kuter at a Press Conference at the Pentagon, May 22, 1943, AFCHO; PRO, AIR/23/7439, Kuter to Coningham, Jun 26, 1943.

92. Memorandum for the Assistant Chief of Staff, G–3, by the Chief of Staff, OPD 384 (4–24–43), Kuter Papers, USAFA; Futrell, *Ideas, Concepts, Doctrine*, pp 69–70; U.S. War Department, *Field Service Regulations, Command and Employment of Air Power*, FM 100–20, Jul 21, 1943, pp 1–2; Kohn and Harahan, *Air Superiority*, p 34.

93. FM 100–20, pp 3, 9–10.

93. *Ibid.*, p 11.

94. Futrell, *Ideas, Concepts, Doctrine*, p 69.

Bibliographical Essay

There is a large amount of manuscript and printed materials on the campaign in Tunisia. In the United States the logical place to begin is the National Archives and Records Administration (NARA), but when inquiries were made by this author, NARA officials advised that the records of the AAF during the Tunisian campaign were closed because they are intermixed with intelligence records concerning the Balkans. This situation is not as great a setback as it would first appear, for four major collections of manuscripts exist on the operations of the AAF during World War II in Tunisia in Washington, D.C. In the Office of Air Force History at Bolling AFB, there is a large collection of AAF records on microfilm containing orders, reports, and intelligence summaries on the AAF in Tunisia. In the Library of Congress there are the papers of Generals Arnold, Doolittle, and Spaatz. For Tunisia, the Spaatz papers are the most useful. There is also a small collection of Kuter papers in the Library of the U.S. Air Force Academy; also the U.S. Army's Military

History Institute at Carlisle Barracks, Pennsylvania, holds, a number of AAF field manuals.

In Great Britain the largest, and perhaps the only collection of manuscripts on the Tunisian campaign, is held by the Public Record Office at Kew. AIR/8/1035, 1085; AIR/20/2107, 25–67–68, 4133, 5796; and AIR/23/1708, 1711, 6572, 7439 contain numerous reports, correspondence, and other documents relating to the air war in Tunisia. AIR/41/33 and 50 are two unpublished staff studies of air operations in Tunisia. ADM/223/49 is a study based on ULTRA decrypts contained in DEFE/3/588–96 produced by the Admiralty's Operational Intelligence Center on the movement of shipping and supplying of the Axis forces in Tunisia.

There are a number of official histories of World War II that cover the air campaign in Tunisia. Most important are the first two volumes of Wesley Frank Craven and James Lea Cate, *The Army Air Forces in World War II* (Chicago: University of Chicago Press, 1948–1958; reprint, Office of Air Force History, 1973) treating the plans and early operations of the war, and Europe from Operation TORCH to POINT-BLANK. The British official history of the Tunisian campaign is volume four of I. S. O. Playfair and C. J. C. Molony, *The Mediterranean and Middle East* (London: HMSO, 1954). The operations of the U.S. Army in Tunisia are covered by George F. Howe, *Northwest Africa: Seizing the Initiative in the West* [The United States Army in World War II: The Mediterranean Theater of Operations] (Washington: Office of the Chief of Military History, Department of the Army, 1957). The engineering problems of the U.S. forces in Tunisia can be studied in Alfred M. Beck, Abe Bortz, Charles W. Lynch, Lida Mayo, and Ralph F. Weld, *The Corps of Engineers: The War Against Germany* [The United States Army in World War II: The Technical Services] (Washington: Center for Military History, Department of the Army, 1985). For a look at Allied intelligence operations during the fighting in Tunisia, volume two of F. H. Hinsley, E. E. Thomas, E. F. G. Ransom, R. C. Knight, *British Intelligence in the Second World War* (London: HMSO, 1979) should be considered. There are several official histories of forces other than the Americans and British who fought in Tunisia, such as the South Africans and New Zealanders, which give the reader a better understanding of the campaign.

Over the years, the Americans and British have produced a number of printed and mimeographed works which indirectly relate to the Tunisian campaign. For example, there is B. L. Montgomery, *Some Notes on High Command in War* (Tripoli: British Eighth Army, 1943). There are two staff studies which deal with the early operations of the AAF in North Africa; AAF Historical Division, *The Twelfth Air Force in the North African Winter Campaign: 11 November 1942 to the Reorganization of February 1943* (Washington, 1945) and the *Ninth Air Force in the Western Desert Campaign* (Washington, 1945). Also, there are several government publications dealing with problems such as tactics, command, control, and doctrine. For example, the RAF produced *Air Support* (N.P.: Air Ministry, 1955). The American armed forces have produced works such as Robert Frank Futrell, *Ideas, Concepts, Doctrine: A History of Basic Thinking in the United States Air Force, 1907–1964* (Maxwell AFB, Ala.: Air University, 1971); Kent Robert Greenfield, *Army Ground Forces and the Air-Ground Battle Team including Organic Light Aviation* (Washington: Historical Section, Army Ground Forces, 1948); Fritz Morzik, *German Air Force Airlift Operations* (Maxwell AFB, Ala.: Air War College, 1961); Riley Sunderland, *Evolution of Command and Control Doctrine for Close Air Support* (Washington: Office of Air Force History, Headquarters U.S. Air Force, 1973); and Richard H. Kohn and Joseph P. Harahan, eds., *Air Superiority in World War II and Korea* (Washington: Office of Air Force History, 1983).

The air war in Tunisia cannot be understood without consulting memoirs and printed documents such as those of Arthur Tedder, *With Prejudice: The War Memoirs of the Royal Air Force Lord Tedder G.C.B.* (Boston: Little Brown and Company, 1966); Aileen Clayton, *The Enemy is Listening: The Story of the Y Service* (London: Hutchinson & Co., 1980); A. B. Cunningham, *A Sailor's Odyssey: The Autobiography of Admiral of the Fleet Viscount Cunningham of Hyndhope* (New York: Hutchinson & Co., 1951); and L. B. Montgomery, *The Memoirs of Field Marshal the Viscount Montgomery of Alamein, K.G.* (New York: The World Publishing Company, 1958). Two sets of printed documents must also be consulted, namely Martin Blumenson, ed., *The Patton Papers, 1940–1945* (Boston: Houghton Mifflin, 1972) and volume II of *The Papers of Dwight David Eisenhower: The War Years* (Baltimore, Md.: Johns Hopkins University Press, 1970), ed., Alfred D. Chandler, Jr.

In addition, three articles help provide an understanding of the air war in Tunisia. Laurence S. Kuter, "Goddammit, Georgie! North Africa 1943: The Birth of TAC Air Doctrine," *Air Force Magazine* 55 (Feb 1973); W. A. Jacobs, "Air Support for the British Army, 1939–1943," *Military Affairs* XLVI (Dec 1982); and Sir Arthur Coningham, "The Development of Tactical Air Forces," *Journal of the Royal United Service Institution* 91 (May 1946). Technical information about various types of aircraft used in the Tunisian campaign can be found in *Jane's All the World's Aircraft, 1943–44* (New York: The Macmillan Company, 1945). Other useful information can be found in the official dispatches of the Allied commanders located in various issues of the *London Gazette.*

Martin B–26 Marauder, resplendent in invasion markings, returns from a strike over occupied France during the Normandy landing.

6

Operation OVERLORD

W. A. Jacobs

On the 6th of June 1944, British and American forces launched Operation OVERLORD, the invasion of Northwest Europe. Air superiority made a vital contribution to the success of that invasion and the operations that followed. It was a superiority that manifested itself in two quite distinct ways. First, the Luftwaffe was unable to act with any decisive effect against the landings and subsequent Allied operations. At best, it could only mount nuisance raids at night. Second, the Allied air forces gained the operational freedom to conduct reconnaissance and to attack lines of communication, equipment, supplies, and enemy troops effectively.

When the planning for OVERLORD first began in 1943, two proven strategies existed for gaining air superiority. The first, initially developed in the First World War, concentrated on gaining superiority in a specific operational area by air fighting. The second method, complementary to the first, had been employed in each major campaign since 1939. The aim was to gain superiority in a larger zone, including both the battle area and the lines of communication leading to it, by a combination of air fighting and attacks on the operational infrastructure of the enemy air force—its airfields, maintenance services, and supply system. In each case, the object was to gain the freedom to conduct one's own air operations while denying that freedom to the enemy.

There were serious problems, however, in applying these two strategies to Operation OVERLORD. Chief among them was the fact that the Luftwaffe's airfields in France were closer to the invasion beaches than were the Allied fields located in southern England. That greatly reduced the time each Allied fighter could spend over the battle area, a grave disadvantage in any traditionally conceived fight for air superiority. The Allied fighter forces, obliged to operate at maximum intensity at extreme ranges, would suffer a decline in their strength as the battle progressed. These difficulties made a third strategy, previously untried, especially important. This was the attempt to gain a general air superiority in northwest Europe by attacking the production of enemy aircraft, forcing a decline in the Luftwaffe's frontline forces and generally weakening its fighting powers.[1]

The Allied authorities never produced a single coherent plan that integrated the strategies for local and general air superiority. Senior Allied airmen disagreed about the relative importance of each of the three strategies, and there was no unified command of the Allied air forces to iron out differences and make all parties conform to a single plan.[2] The operations that achieved air superiority for OVERLORD were largely planned and directed by two separate and independent groups of airmen, one in the strategic air forces, the other in the tactical, often following different agendas, sometimes cooperating, sometimes not.

Despite the absence of unified planning and command, the Allies employed each of the three air superiority strategies against the Luftwaffe in a roughly complementary fashion. The British took the first steps very early in the war not as a preparation for OVERLORD, but as part of the defense of the United Kingdom. The air battles of 1940 and 1941, the development of British air defenses, and the dispersal of the Luftwaffe's limited offensive strength to other fronts in 1941 and 1942 established an air superiority over the United Kingdom, which ensured that the Allied base of operations remained relatively free from effective German attack throughout the critical struggles of 1943 and 1944.

The attempt to gain a general air superiority by attacking aircraft production began in mid-1943 and reached a peak in April 1944. Toward the end of this period, the emphasis in this campaign began to shift toward deliberate attrition of the frontline strength of the Luftwaffe by air combat and attacks on the airfields in the *Reich* (the deep infrastructure). The American strategic air forces made their first attacks on synthetic oil production in May 1944 as part of this strategy.

In late April and early May of 1944 the tactical air forces began systematic attacks on the Luftwaffe's close infrastructure of airfields and maintenance facilities in France, which were continued through the period of the invasion itself. On D-day this effort was complemented by a massive air cover over the fleet and the invading armies, supplemented by attacks on the enemy's warning and aircraft reporting system. The combination of air cover and attacks on Luftwaffe infrastructure continued throughout the months of June and July 1944 until something approaching air supremacy in western Europe was achieved in August.

German strategy developed along somewhat different lines. The Luftwaffe had pioneered the use of the two traditional air superiority strategies to overpower their opponents in Poland, France, and the western Soviet Union. But the Luftwaffe had failed to gain air superiority over Great Britain and to maintain it in Soviet Russia and the Mediterranean. As a consequence, by the middle of 1943 the Germans faced regional enemy air superiorities in the Mediterranean and on the Eastern Front as well as the beginning of an American campaign aimed at achieving a general air superiority by attacking the very existence of the Luftwaffe. In addition, Germany had to confront a mounting RAF Bomber Command offensive against its major cities and the prospect of a determined Allied campaign to gain a local superiority in France that would support an invasion sometime in the near future.

To deal with this grave situation, some German authorities like Field Marshal Erhard Milch, the State Secretary for Air, favored concentration on fighter production and air defense of the *Reich*. Others, like Hitler and *Reich* Marshall Hermann Goering, the Commander in Chief of the Luftwaffe, wanted bombers for reprisals against Great Britain. Still others pressed for an expansion of the ground attack force. Unlike the Allies, however, the Germans did not possess the resources to pursue so many policies simultaneously.[3] In the meantime, the wastage of the smaller bomber force in reprisal attacks in early 1944 meant that the Luftwaffe had very little offensive power to throw into the struggle against the Allied air forces or the ground and naval forces when the invasion in the west began. The best that the Luftwaffe could do was to contest the Allied campaign for general air superiority with the *Reich* air defenses and then, when the invasion started, shift fighter resources to the battle area in western France to resist the Allied attempts to gain a local air superiority.[4]

Allied and German Comparative Strength

When OVERLORD was launched, the British and Americans possessed all the advantages that came with superior numbers. At the end of May 1944, the total frontline strength of the Luftwaffe in Russia, Southeast Europe, the Mediterranean, occupied Northwest Europe, and the *Reich* stood at 6,832 aircraft of all types. By comparison, the total Allied air forces based in the United Kingdom alone amounted to 12,617.[5] When one adds in the Allied forces in the Mediterranean and the Soviet Air Force in the east, it takes little imagination to recognize that the Luftwaffe was overwhelmed by sheer weight of numbers.

Differences in long-term air policy and in total war production capacity were the principal reasons for this great disparity in strength.[6] (See Figure 6–1) Hitler's decision for war in 1939 caught the Luftwaffe in the middle of

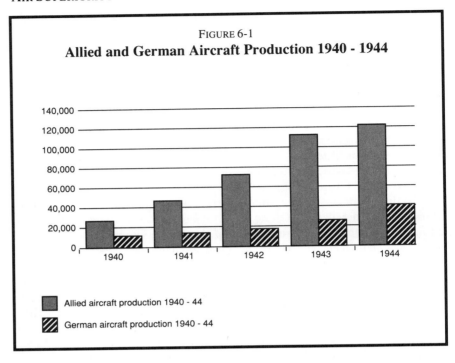

FIGURE 6-1
Allied and German Aircraft Production 1940 - 1944

Allied aircraft production 1940 - 44

German aircraft production 1940 - 44

its rearmament program.[7] The Luftwaffe went to war with a reasonably well equipped and trained frontline force, balanced between modern fighters and medium bombers. But it had insufficient reserves of men and materiel to sustain combat operations.[8] These deficiencies caused no embarassment until the Battle of Britain because the campaigns were short and decisive. When Hitler attacked the Soviet Union in June 1941 and declared war on the United States in December of that year, he enlarged the war but failed to put the Luftwaffe on an appropriate production and training footing.[9] Hitler and Goering seem to have been aware of the importance of large numbers in modern air warfare, but they were either unwilling or unable to take the measures necessary to significantly expand the Luftwaffe before 1943.[10]

The British and the Americans also entered the war long before their rearmament programs were completed. But, in contrast to Germany, they not only aimed at very high levels of aircraft production, they achieved them as early as 1942. Indeed, from 1940 to 1943 Great Britain *alone* outproduced Germany in numbers of aircraft.[11] In 1941 the United States produced two and one-half times the German output of aircraft. In 1943 this gap stretched to nearly three and one-half times German production.[12] This was a crucial advantage in a struggle for air superiority that was essentially a war of attrition.

The critical decisions about production greatly influenced the approaches of the combatants to aircrew training.[13] The German failure to increase production and to expand the size of the frontline force early in the war meant that there was no great pressure to enlarge the training organization. To the extent that they had a choice in the matter, the Luftwaffe leadership was far more interested in supporting active operations than in providing for a long-term air war.[14] The problems created by this shortsighted policy became apparent in mid-1942 when aircrew losses began to exceed the output of the training schools by a considerable margin. To meet the increased demand for aircrews, the training establishment had to have more aviation gasoline, more instructors, and more operational aircraft. It received few of these, in large measure because the Luftwaffe leadership could not be persuaded to make the necessary sacrifices in operations to build up the training program. Worse still, the operational forces diverted instructors and aircraft to the immediate needs of the front. In the face of these difficulties, the training establishment had to cut the number of hours of training received by each pilot and reduce radically the amount of time spent flying in operational aircraft before pilots were sent to operational units. This reduction resulted in a doubling of the numbers of aircrews produced in 1943 over 1942, but the quality of the performance of the average pilot began to fall off, especially in the last half of 1943. In addition, when the higher authorities finally adopted a program of radical expansion of aircraft production, the increased output could not be translated into effective frontline strength because, in large measure, the pilots did not exist to fly the new aircraft.[15]

The American and British training record was quite different. In the early stages of the war, especially during the Battle of Britain, the RAF was hard pressed to train pilots as rapidly as they were being lost. However, by 1941 the British government's commitment to a long war had produced a training establishment aimed at providing for replacements, the continuing expansion of the force, and the accumulation of reserves. After mid-1942 the total RAF training hours per pilot began to climb significantly while, as noted above, the figure for Luftwaffe pilots had begun to decline markedly. This gap continued to widen, chiefly because of the continued deterioration of the quality of the Luftwaffe training program. By mid-summer of 1944 the average RAF pilot was receiving three times as much training as his German counterpart.[16]

Much the same kind of record was achieved in the U.S. Army Air Forces, on a much larger scale.[17] In 1939 plans called for the training schools to produce 1,200 pilots a year; a year later the target was raised to 7,000. In 1941 the AAF moved the goal upward to 30,000. In 1943, the AAF training schools actually churned out no fewer than 82,700 pilots. So successful was the program that it appeared that the AAF possessed a surplus of pilots and accordingly raised its educational and physical standards at the end of 1943. Remarkably, this expansion of the force was paralleled by a steady increase in the total number of hours of training given to each pilot. Between late 1942 and mid-1943, the average AAF pilot received somewhat less training than his ally in the RAF and more than his enemy in the Luftwaffe. After July 1943 the AAF average drew level with the RAF and then pulled slightly ahead in 1944. By mid-1944 future Allied pilots were receiving between 320 and 400 flying hours of training, as compared with just over 100 for Luftwaffe cadets.[18] The Luftwaffe was caught in an increasingly vicious circle. As its less qualified pilots entered the force, they were killed or injured at increasing rates because they had to fight fresh pilots who were better trained as well as the veterans whose experience made them more lethal adversaries with each passing day.

There were also major differences in force structure between the Luftwaffe and the Allied air forces. The Luftwaffe began the war with a balanced force containing fighters, dive bombers, medium bombers, and reconnaissance and transport aircraft. By mid-1943 the medium bomber force had suffered a severe decline in numbers and adequately trained aircrew, a fact that greatly reduced the offensive weapons available to the Luftwaffe in any struggle for air superiority. The Germans did not possess a long-range heavy bomber force at the start of the war, nor did they succeed in developing a reliable machine of this type in any quantity during the conflict. Many German airmen recognized the offensive potential represented by the strategic bomber. Yet the combination of raw material and petroleum constraints, design problems, and the clear need to develop first those forces capable of directly supporting the large land operations that would begin immediately in any war in which Germany became involved prevented the development of such a force before the war.[19] Some effort was invested in a strategic bomber project during the war, but poor organization and leadership, the old resource problems, and a bad aircraft design produced only small numbers of a very unreliable machine (the He–177).[20] By mid-1943, the Luftwaffe was an air force suffering from a steady deterioration in its effective offensive power. In contrast, the large and growing force of American and British long-range bombers allowed the Allies to attempt to gain a general air superiority by attacking the production of aircraft, key supplies like aviation gasoline, and the operational infrastructure in the *Reich*. In addition, the very large Allied force of medium bombers and fighter-bombers also gave the Allies the clear offensive edge in any contest for local air superiority.

Both sides possessed modern high-performance fighter aircraft. The best evidence seems to indicate that, with the exception of the American long-range fighters, neither side enjoyed any major performance advantages in this type of aircraft. As the Military Analysis Division of the United States Strategic Bombing Survey (USSBS) noted:

276

An overall comparison of our fighters with German although each aircraft had its good and bad points, in the last analysis, the difference in performance was not great enough to give either side a decided advantage.[21]

Detailed analysis generally supports this conclusion. Of the three major American fighters, the P–38 Lightning was the first to be thrust into the long-range escort role, but it proved to be unsatisfactory. At high altitude the Lightning was faster than either of its German opponents, the Me–109 and the FW–190, but it quickly encountered buffeting in a dive. Moreover, the Lightning's engines simply did not stand up well to the extremely cold temperatures of high-altitude operation over northwest Europe. Supercharger regulators froze up; faulty oil cooling and carburetor problems led to engine failure. In addition, the cockpits were so cold that pilot efficiency suffered badly. According to the USSBS report, many P–38 pilots were confident in their ability to handle all opposition below 20,000 feet, but were more diffident about their chances at higher levels.[22] Some of the P–38's problems were heightened by the pressure of operations on maintenance. The Lightnings were the only long-range escorts available in November and most of December 1943. Many aircraft were pushed into operations when they should have been held back for various repairs.[23]

The first model of the P–47 Thunderbolt was also inadequate in aerial combat except at very high altitudes. Because its performance against the current models of FW–190 and Me–109 fell off at middle and lower altitudes, pilots tended not to follow the enemy down, even though the Thunderbolt had superior diving speed. With modifications that included a paddle-blade propeller and water injection boost, Thunderbolt pilots came to believe that they could fight effectively at any altitude.[24]

The Thunderbolt also had a well-deserved reputation for ruggedness. Its radial engine and sturdy airframe made it more resistant to battle damage. This quality contributed greatly to its effectiveness both as a fighter and as a fighter-bomber. Its greatest drawback, and the one which proved to be an important limitation on its usefulness in the struggle against the Luftwaffe, was its thirst for gasoline. Like the P–38, it did not possess the radius of action necessary for deep penetrations of German air space.[25]

The P–51 was the one American fighter for which some margin of technical superiority could be claimed. How significant or decisive this margin was is still a matter of some disagreement. Despite its belief in the rough equality of German and Allied fighters, the Strategic Bombing Survey's Military Analysis Division believed that the P–51 possessed "an all-round superiority" and that it "provided the balance which led to the domination of the German skies."[26] The Division thought that the Mustang, particularly in its B and C models, had a performance edge over the Me–109 and FW–190 at all altitudes. The Mustang's liquid-cooled engine made it less resistant to battle damage, however. The fact that the P–51 most often went into initial combat with full internal fuel tanks (having drawn from the external drop tanks during the run up to the rendezvous with bombers) had some adverse effect on its rate of climb. These difficulties were offset by its high combat performance and great endurance, a combination which the authorities in German, American, and British air forces had not believed possible earlier in the war, and one which allowed the Eighth and Ninth Air Forces to carry effective fighter air combat deep into enemy territory.[27]

Some German sources drew slightly different conclusions about relative fighter performance. Gen. Adolf Galland, the Air Officer for Fighters on the German Air Staff, believed, for example, that the improved models of the two German fighters remained superior to the P–47 up to about 22,000 feet.[28] A study prepared by the German Air Historical Branch in late 1944 concluded that recent modifications of the Me–109 made it equal to all Allied fighters at all altitudes. The FW–190 was thought to be equal in performance up to about 13,000 feet, above which it proved less capable.[29]

RAF Fighter Command Supremacy

The struggle for air superiority in western Europe began not in 1943 or 1944, but in the summer of 1940. It was a struggle between the German forces based in France and the Low Countries (mostly under *Luftflotte* 3) and RAF Fighter Command, which possessed the first modern air defense system featuring radar, high performance interceptor fighters, and ground control of combat operations. By the early winter of 1940, Fighter Command had succeeded in imposing prohibitive rates of loss on the German attackers in large daylight raids. This forced the Luftwaffe to shift its medium-bomber forces to night operations and turn to small-scale fighter-bomber and fast light-bomber raids in daylight. During the next two years, Fighter Command's night defenses were greatly improved to the point where they could impose prohibitive losses on any large-scale attacks. Consequently, after the summer of 1941, the Luftwaffe was unable to deliver large, accurate, and persistent attacks against any target system in the United Kingdom and its immediate coastal waters.[30]

Some part of the Allied air superiority achieved over the United Kingdom was the result of German policy. The attack on the Soviet Union in 1941 and the expansion of the war in the Mediterranean required the transfer of the bulk of the bomber forces to those theaters from France and the Low Countries.[31] The Luftwaffe bomber force was not large enough, nor backed by a sufficiently large flow of aircraft and crew replacements, to carry on major operations in three separate theaters. Such bombing of British targets as did take place did not concentrate on any useful target system. In fact, from September 1940 right through to the first six months of 1944, German bombing in the west was dominated by the idea of reprisal for Bomber Command's area attacks on German cities. The limited effort available to the Luftwaffe was largely wasted in attacks on British cities, chiefly London, supplemented by small scale "tip and run" raids. Such attacks could not interfere with Allied air operations, significantly damage British industry, or hinder sea communications.[32]

The air superiority over the United Kingdom created by the work of Fighter Command and augmented by the failures of German policy was clearly demonstrated between January and June of 1944. The Luftwaffe had accumulated a small bomber force of some 500 aircraft for operations in the west. Hitler and Goering determined that this force was not to be conserved and trained for operations against the forthcoming Allied invasion, but was to be employed in reprisal raids against London. These raids were carried out at night, were inaccurate, and suffered an average casualty rate of six percent of sorties. They damaged or destroyed property and caused some loss of life, but they did not interfere with preparations for OVERLORD. The few raids directed against south coast ports were entirely ineffective.[33]

Fighter Command (now known by the infelicitous title of Air Defence of Great Britain or ADGB) was also successful in preventing the Luftwaffe from carrying out one of its most important tasks—daylight aerial reconnaissance of the Allied buildup areas. British records show that, between January and June 1944, *Luftflotte* 3 made no more than thirty-two such flights (exclusive of any over coastal waters). From late April right through the invasion period, ADGB maintained standing patrols over the key assembly areas for the Allied fleets. In the same period, the Luftwaffe intensified its efforts, flying daily reconnaissance sorties. Only two of these actually made landfall in the Plymouth and Falmouth areas. During the first week of June 1944, when the Allied armada was collected at the ports, loaded with troops and equipment, and then marshalled at sea, only one German daylight reconnaissance sortie, over the Margate area, was recorded. This form of air superiority directly contributed to the tactical surprise achieved by British and American forces on D-day.[34]

POINTBLANK: Strategic Bomber Offensive

The Allies set in motion their campaign to gain a general air superiority over the Luftwaffe at the Casablanca Conference in January 1943. The overall objective of the strategic bomber forces was to aim at the "progressive destruction and dislocation of the German military, industrial and economic system and the systematic undermining of the morale of the German people" in order to "fatally" weaken their "capacity for armed resistance."

More specifically, they were to attack a group of key target systems, among which the German aircraft industry was ranked second. In June, the Allied Combined Chiefs of Staff issued a new policy to govern the strategic bomber offensive—the POINTBLANK Directive. In that document, the German aircraft industry, particularly that part of it devoted to fighter production, was elevated to the status of an "intermediate" objective second to none. The idea behind this particular language was that air superiority was not an end in itself, but the means to strategic attack on other key target systems. The air superiority and the attack on other systems were part of the preparation for OVERLORD, but many American and British airmen privately believed that the strategic bombing campaign would be decisive, reducing the invasion to a mere exercise in occupation.[35]

Three commands made up the Allied long-range heavy bomber forces—RAF Bomber Command, and the American Eighth and Fifteenth Air Forces. Air Chief Marshal Sir Arthur Harris, the Commander in Chief of RAF Bomber Command, was completely unconvinced of the merits of any attempt to attack limited and specific target systems, an approach he derided as "panacea" bombing. He thought such an approach was tactically unfeasible and he believed fervently in Bomber Command's powers to bring Germany to defeat by destroying her major cities.[36] Sir Arthur Harris's views ensured that the POINTBLANK Directive was written to permit him enough latitude to carry on with his campaign. Elements of the RAF Air Staff, chiefly the Director of Bomber Operations (Air Commodore S. O. Bufton) and the Deputy Chief of Air Staff (Air Marshal Sir Norman Bottomley), believed that the attack on the aircraft industry was so important that Bomber Command ought to join in, despite the obvious tactical difficulties. As 1943 wore on and the American Eighth Air Force ran into grave difficulties in its attempts to carry out the POINTBLANK Directive, Bufton and Bottomley pressed Sir Arthur Harris to change his views.[37] Not until February 1944, almost eight months after POINTBLANK had begun, did Bomber Command attack Schweinfurt, one of the most important targets in the POINTBLANK program. The British Official History regards this attack as the first blow of a genuine "Combined Bomber Offensive."[38] As a result, in the first stages of the campaign for a general air superiority, the main burden fell on the Eighth Air Force and its commander, Maj. Gen. Ira C. Eaker. The Fifteenth Air Force was not formed until late 1943, and it made few significant attacks on the German aircraft industry until the next year.

General Eaker's efforts to implement the POINTBLANK Directive were frustrated by several key problems. The first was a considerable improvement in the German flak and fighter defenses. The POINTBLANK plan, to which Eaker was a major contributor, had recognized that growth in the enemy's fighter force might imperil the attack on vital areas of

Air Chief Marshal Sir Arthur Harris (*center, standing*), **the Commander in Chief of RAF Bomber Command, studies bomb damage assessment photos.**

the war economy and had endeavored to meet that threat by concentrating first on the German fighter industry.[39] The problem was that the existing German air defenses stood in the way of an effective assault on that industry.

Initially, Eaker was confident that he could successfully attack any target in Germany with an unescorted force of some 300 heavy bombers and suffer no more than four percent losses.[40] He, along with many other American airmen, believed that the defensive air combat power in the heavy bomber force would be adequate to carry strategic attacks to the aircraft industry for a period long enough to force a decline in aircraft production and in frontline strength. This optimism soon proved to be unfounded. It was one thing to attack targets in France and Belgium with heavy escort from RAF Fighter Command and the VIII Fighter Command. It was another to attempt to operate in German air space without any fighter escort. Large-scale deep penetration raids against ball-bearing targets at Schweinfurt in August and October 1943 led to very heavy losses in the Eighth Air Force. The cost in heavy bombers expressed as a percentage stood at 5.5

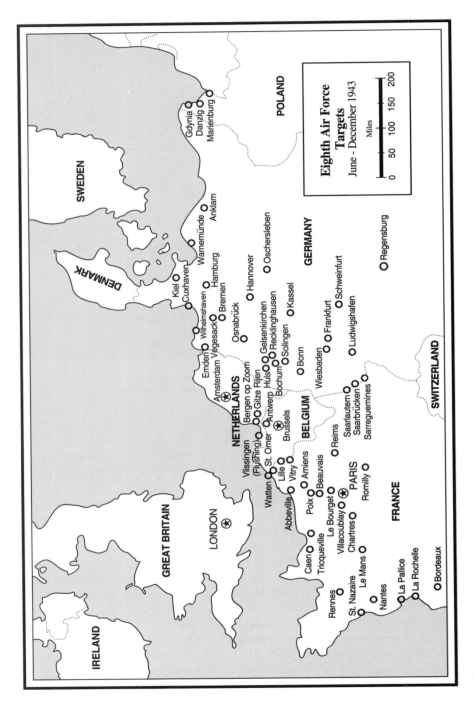

Eighth Air Force Targets
June - December 1943

Miles
0   50   100 150 200

IRELAND

GREAT BRITAIN

LONDON

SWEDEN

DENMARK

Kiel
Cuxhaven
Wilhelmshaven
Warnemünde
Anklam
Hamburg
Bremen
Osnabrück
Hannover
Oschersleben
Emden
Amsterdam
Vegesack
Bergen op Zoom
Gilze Rijen
Gelsenkirchen
Recklinghausen
Kassel
Antwerp Huis
Bochum
Solingen
Bonn
Wiesbaden
Frankfurt
Schweinfurt
Ludwigshafen
Regensburg

NETHERLANDS

BELGIUM

Vlissingen
(Flushing)
St. Omer
Brussels
Watten
Lille
Vitry
Amiens
Beauvais
Reims
Saarlautern
Saarbrücken
Sarreguemines

GERMANY

SWITZERLAND

POLAND

Gdynia
Danzig
Marienburg

Abbeville
Poix
Le Bourget
Villacoublay
Chartres
PARIS
Romilly

FRANCE

Caen
Tricqueville
Rennes
St. Nazaire
Le Mans
Nantes
La Pallice
La Rochelle
Bordeaux

282

percent of credited sorties in July, rose to 6.0 in August, fell by half in September when the Eighth largely refrained from attacking German targets, and then rose sickeningly to 9.2 percent in October.[41] Unescorted heavy bombers could not gain the necessary degree of air superiority over the Luftwaffe in being in order to attack effectively the Luftwaffe in prospect.

In the early period of the struggle for general air superiority, Eaker did not receive aircraft from the United States at the rate laid down in the POINTBLANK plan. His logistical and maintenance services were inadequate, in part because Washington had not furnished sufficient trained personnel to make up for those diverted to the war in North Africa, and in part because of organizational difficulties in the theater. To make matters worse, an adequate flow of trained aircrew to expand the force and to provide replacements did not materialize.[42]

Under the POINTBLANK plan, the heavy bomber strength of the Eighth Air Force was to increase to 944 by June 30, 1943, 1,192 by September 30, and 1,746 by December 31.[43] The actual numbers made available fell short: 800, 1,000, and 1,630 respectively (daily averages for the months of July and October 1943 and January 1944). The difficulties of the logistics system in the theater are illustrated by the figures for bomber aircraft on hand in the tactical units in the same months: 589, 763, and 1,082. The shortcomings of the aircraft maintenance system are made clear by the relatively low numbers of aircraft serviceable for action: 378, 535, and 842. The aircrew situation made things even worse. In July, Eighth Air Force possessed no more than 315 crews for 378 aircraft; in October, the situation was no better—479 crews for 535 aircraft.[44]

Eaker's problems were not viewed sympathetically in Washington. For over two years, Gen. Henry H. Arnold, the Commanding General of the Army Air Forces, and friends of the AAF in the Roosevelt administration, the press, and the Congress had defended the idea of a strategic bombing offensive against Germany from the competing demands generated by all the other theaters of war. Arnold was now under great pressure to deliver. The spectacle of the Eighth Air Force stalemated by German defenses and unable to apply what had been expected to be decisive destruction was most unwelcome. Arnold's staff came to interpret the low frequency of deep penetration raids on German targets, the casualties incurred in those raids, and the continuing effectiveness of the German air defenses as evidence of a failure of leadership.[45] Arnold himself, in fact, had pressed General Eaker for quick results as early as June 1943. He urged Eaker to dismiss those responsible for poor maintenance, ignoring the fact that Eighth Air Force's maintenance establishment had been gutted for Operation TORCH (the invasion of Northwest Africa in November 1942) and had only slowly been restored. As if Eaker were somehow guilty of avoiding responsibility, Arnold admonished, "You must play your part."[46] He ques-

Republic's hefty P–47 Thunderbolt was the finest multipurpose American fighter of the Second World War.

tioned the tactical organization and the formations employed by the Eighth.[47] Arnold's growing impatience was not limited to Eaker. In October, he wrote a rather intemperate letter to Sir Charles Portal, the RAF Chief of Air Staff, complaining that neither RAF Fighter Command nor Bomber Command had lent sufficient aid to the daylight strategic bombing offensive.[48]

At the Sextant Conference in November, Arnold gave full vent to his frustration with Eaker's leadership.

> They [Eighth Air Force] had not changed their technique. He [Arnold] had sent a series of inspectors to the UK to try and probe into the reasons for this. In other theaters sixty or seventy percent of available aircraft were used in operations. In the UK, only fifty percent were used....There were approximately 1,300 bombers supplied to the UK....In spite of this, only once in the last month had 600 aircraft taken part in operations in one day....The failure to destroy targets was due directly to the failure to employ planes in sufficient numbers. A sufficient weight of bombs was not being dropped on the targets to destroy them, nor was the proper priority of targets being followed....At present, the necessary drive and ideas were coming from Washington. He believed that more aircraft were being sent to the UK than were being effectively used and that unless better results could be achieved no more planes should be sent.[49]

Gen. George C. Marshall, U.S. Army Chief of Staff, then added that he "believed that a commander in England was required who could give full consideration to the many problems involved and impart the necessary drive."[50]

General Eaker's tenure at Eighth Air Force was soon to end. He suffered the common fate of those commanders sent into battle too soon with too little. In January 1944, Eaker moved to the Mediterranean where he assumed the direction of the Allied air forces in that theater. With Eaker's transfer, the primary responsibility for POINTBLANK now shifted to Lt. Gen. Carl Spaatz who commanded a new headquarters—United States Strategic Air Forces in Europe (USSTAF)—which directed the operations of both the Eighth Air Force and the new Fifteenth Air Force operating from bases in southern Italy. Maj. Gen. James Doolittle assumed command of Eighth Air Force.[51] (See Figure 6–2)

General Spaatz and his deputy, Maj. Gen. Frederick L. Anderson, were determined to carry out POINTBLANK as originally designed. They wanted to strike decisive blows at the German aircraft industry and then to shift the strategic bombing effort to a target system that would bring the Germans to their knees. Spaatz had long believed in the ability of the strategic air forces to bring about German defeat without an invasion. When he first came to London, he feared that there would be "no opportunity to carry out any air operations of sufficient intensity to justify the theory that Germany can be knocked out by air power alone."[52] He thought that it would be "an emasculation of heavy bomber capabilities" to restrict the role of the strategic air forces to the achievement of air superiority for the invasion.[53] He apparently thought Operation OVERLORD to be dangerous and unnecessary, a view which he expressed in a conversation with Maj. Gen. Hoyt Vandenberg, the American Deputy Commander in Chief of the Allied Expeditionary Air Forces (AEAF), held in April of 1944:

> General Spaatz stated that he feared that the allied forces might be batting their heads against a stone wall in the OVERLORD operation. If the purpose of OVERLORD is to seize and hold advanced air bases; this purpose is no longer necessary since the Strategic Air Forces can reach all vital targets in Germany with fighter cover.... It is better to win the war surely than to undertake an operation which has really great risks.[54]

Arnold reinforced the sense of urgency at USSTAF headquarters. He wrote Spaatz in January to tell him to stop "pecking away at the German aircraft industry."[55] He went so far as to send his Chief of Staff, Maj. Gen. Barney Giles, to London to convey his feelings and to urge a ruthless persistence in attacking the Luftwaffe. Among other things, Giles was to tell Spaatz that he should be prepared to risk losing no less than 600 heavy bombers per month in order to beat down the Luftwaffe.[56]

Thus encouraged, Spaatz and Anderson aimed at carrying out a plan, first developed at Eighth Air Force headquarters in the early autumn of 1943, to strike a highly concentrated series of blows which, they believed, would more or less finish the job at one go. Also, partly in response to the

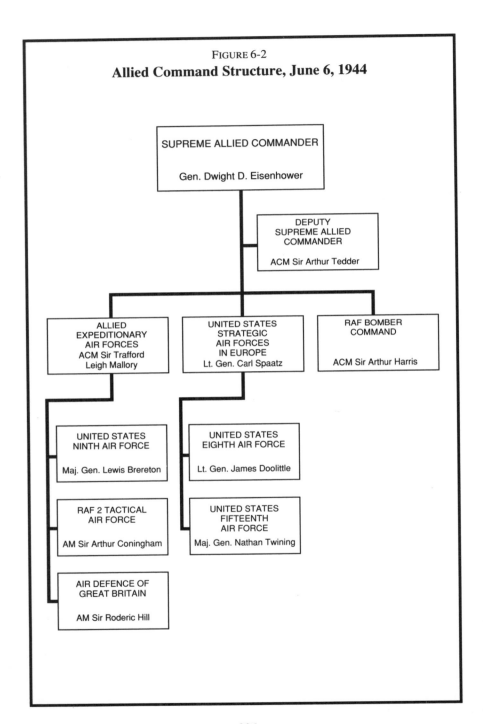

Figure 6-2

Allied Command Structure, June 6, 1944

SUPREME ALLIED COMMANDER

Gen. Dwight D. Eisenhower

DEPUTY
SUPREME ALLIED
COMMANDER

ACM Sir Arthur Tedder

ALLIED
EXPEDITIONARY
AIR FORCES
ACM Sir Trafford
Leigh Mallory

UNITED STATES
STRATEGIC
AIR FORCES
IN EUROPE
Lt. Gen. Carl Spaatz

RAF BOMBER
COMMAND

ACM Sir Arthur Harris

UNITED STATES
NINTH AIR FORCE

Maj. Gen. Lewis Brereton

UNITED STATES
EIGHTH AIR FORCE

Lt. Gen. James Doolittle

RAF 2 TACTICAL
AIR FORCE

AM Sir Arthur Coningham

UNITED STATES
FIFTEENTH
AIR FORCE
Maj. Gen. Nathan Twining

AIR DEFENCE OF
GREAT BRITAIN

AM Sir Roderic Hill

pressure from Washington, they began to emphasize the attrition of the existing Luftwaffe frontline force in the air and on the ground.[57] Weather prevented the implementation of the plan—code-named ARGUMENT—until late February. Then, between February 20th and 25th, the Eighth and Fifteenth Air Force, under USSTAF's direction, carried out a series of massive air raids against the German aircraft industry, attacking nearly ninety percent of the facilities producing single-engine fighters. These raids, which quickly came to be known as BIG WEEK, were thought by Generals Spaatz and Anderson, along with key members of their staffs, to have seriously crippled aircraft production. Far from concluding such attacks, however, BIG WEEK began a period in which American bombs literally rained on German aircraft factories. In February, the Eighth and Fifteenth Air Forces dropped 5,234 tons of bombs on those targets; in March, the total fell slightly to 4,516 tons; but in April, it rose to the highest figure of the war, just over 10,000 tons.[58]

Attacks on this greatly increased scale were possible because the Eighth was a much bigger force than the one Eaker had possessed in the summer and early autumn of 1943, and it was growing stronger every day. (See Figure 6–3) In February 1944 the Eighth possessed an average of 1,852 heavy bombers of which no fewer than 1,046 were serviceable. Still more important was the fact that an average of 1,155 aircrews were available.[59] These circumstances allowed the dispatch of no fewer than 1,000 heavy bombers on the first day of BIG WEEK, almost three times as many as had set out on the Schweinfurt raid in August the previous year. In addition, the once fledgling Fifteenth Air Force based in Italy had grown to a heavy bomber strength of 835 Liberators and Fortresses, 570 of which were serviceable.[60] Under Spaatz's direction, this force was also thrown into the attack on German aircraft production.

Apart from these significant increases in heavy bomber strength, escort fighters were now available in much greater numbers. When the offensive against aircraft production opened in 1943, VIII Fighter Command was not capable of providing escort beyond western France and the Low Countries. It had long been thought in both the RAF and the AAF that a long-range escort fighter was a contradiction in terms. It was not believed possible to produce a fighter with range equal to that of the bomber force without seriously compromising its performance. In addition, there was no urgency in finding a solution to this problem because of a longstanding confidence in the ability of American day bombers to defend themselves against enemy fighters. But, by June 1943 it had become clear that VIII Fighter Command had to provide escort if the Eighth Air Force were to carry on the strategic air offensive. Following an inspection visit, Robert Lovett, the Assistant Secretary of War for Air, wrote General Arnold to emphasize the need for increased escort.[61] This note galvanized Arnold into action. He told his Chief of Air Staff:

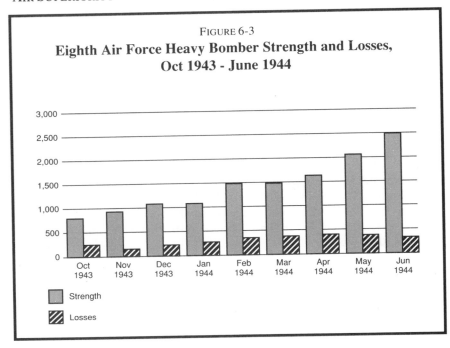

FIGURE 6-3

**Eighth Air Force Heavy Bomber Strength and Losses,
Oct 1943 - June 1944**

Within the next six months, you have got to get a fighter that can protect our bomb-
ers. Whether you use an existing type or have to start from scratch is your problem.
. . . By January 1944 I want fighter escort for all of our bombers from UK into
Germany.[62]

By January 1944 three important things had been accomplished.
Despite many difficulties, external droptanks in sufficient quantities had
been produced; tactics and flying procedures had been worked out to
extend range; and, the AAF had found a fighter that did combine great
range with high combat performance—the P–51 Mustang.[63] In its original
version, the P–51 had proved unsuitable as a fighter because its high-altitude performance left much to be desired. The British experimented by
replacing the Mustang's original Allison engine with a Rolls-Royce Merlin.
The new combination of engine and airframe not only improved the P–51's
combat performance, it also significantly increased its endurance. A long-
range high performance escort fighter was now possible. Fighters of this
type began to arrive in the United Kingdom late in 1943.

Early American escort tactics were modeled on the RAF practice of
providing short-range escort in the form of an "umbrella" over the bomber
formation. The fighters assembled separately and rendezvoused with the
bomber formation on its way to the target. Once they joined up, they
weaved over the formation, a tactic necessary because of the considerable

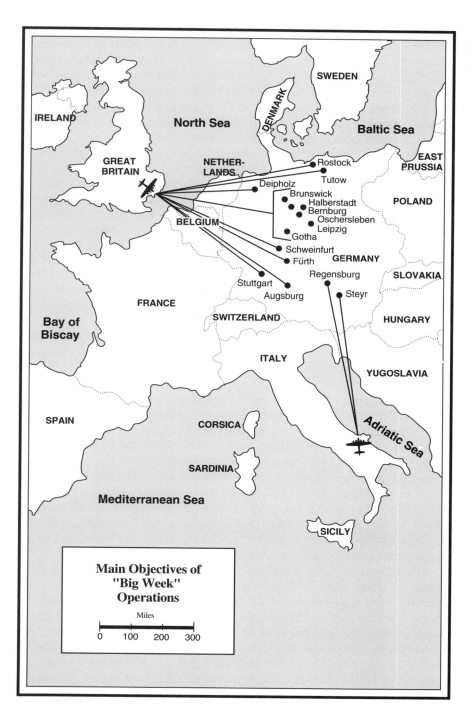

IRELAND

North Sea

SWEDEN

DENMARK

Baltic Sea

GREAT
BRITAIN

NETHER-
LANDS

EAST
PRUSSIA

Rostock

Tutow

Deipholz

POLAND

Brunswick
Halberstadt
Bernburg
Oschersleben
Leipzig

BELGIUM

Gotha

Schweinfurt

Fürth

GERMANY

Regensburg

SLOVAKIA

FRANCE

Stuttgart

Augsburg

SWITZERLAND

Steyr

HUNGARY

Bay of
Biscay

ITALY

YUGOSLAVIA

SPAIN

CORSICA

Adriatic Sea

SARDINIA

Mediterranean Sea

SICILY

**Main Objectives of
"Big Week"
Operations**

Miles

0   100   200   300

difference in speeds between bombers and fighters. If the fighters had throttled back, they would have been vulnerable to sudden attack by enemy fighters. Weaving, of course, severely cut down the effective combat radius of the fighters. The type of escort provided was described as "close," that is, the fighters were obliged to keep near to the bomber formation and to fend off enemy attacks. The escort was forbidden to pursue the enemy or to sweep ahead or to the sides of the bomber formation on the assumption that such tactics opened the bombers to enemy attack.[64]

Improved fuel capacity from increased internal tankage and the addition of drop tanks helped greatly to increase the range of fighter escort. Greater numbers helped as well. A larger fighter force, for example, allowed the development of the relay system under which individual formations of one or two groups would fly more or less direct courses to prearranged rendezvous points along the course of the bombers. A P–51 group, for example, did not escort B–17s all the way to Berlin from the coast of France. Instead, the Mustangs flew a direct course to a point a few minutes short of the target where, if the navigation was correct and the time-keeping of both forces accurate, they would meet the bomber formation (from which a previous relay of P–47s or P–38s was departing).[65]

Greater numbers also allowed a modification of escort techniques in favor of offensive tactics. Beginning in January 1944 fighters no longer stuck to the principle of "close" escort. After rendezvous, a fighter group would deploy into one eight-plane section to provide top cover for the bomber formation, two such sections to provide cover from each flank, and one formation of squadron strength to range out to the front. The flanking escort was allowed to move away from the formation to engage enemy fighters flying on parallel courses waiting for a favorable opportunity to attack. The lead squadron swept ahead, and increasingly, the escort was encouraged to pursue enemy aircraft as they retired. "Area support" was a further modification. Formations of fighters in one- or two-group strength were assigned the task of sweeping ahead of the bombers to catch enemy fighters as they were assembling their formations. By April fighters were also returning from their escort relay by descending "to the deck" and carrying out strafing attacks on airfields.[66]

The effects of these developments on the tactical situation were significant. They made it difficult for large formations of defenders to assemble. They easily overpowered the slow and cumbersome twin-engine fighters carrying rockets that had caused so much grief in 1943. The new tactics greatly enlarged the zone of danger to the Luftwaffe fighters by extending combat all the way back to airfields in the *Reich*. By early spring of 1944, even Luftwaffe training fields scrambled their aircraft during an air raid in order to avoid being caught on the ground by returning escort fighters.

Gen. Carl Spaatz talking to Wing and Group Commanding Officers during an inspection of the U.S. Army Eighth Air Force installations; to his right are Lt. Gen. James Doolittle, Commanding General of the Eighth Air Force, and Maj. Gen. William E. Kepner, Commanding General of the 2d Air Division; *below*: the P–51 Mustang provided the long-range escort needed in 1944 for the strategic air offensive.

The increased strength of the Eighth Air Force and the development of long-range fighter escort made possible BIG WEEK and the attacks against aircraft production that followed. How much did these attacks contribute to air superiority for OVERLORD? It appears that the results were mixed. Ironically, the only period in which the bombing attacks actually forced production down was in the last six months of 1943, when the Eighth Air Force was forced to operate with small forces and inadequate escort. In July 1943 German monthly production of all types, including gliders, reached a peak of 2,475. It remained very close to that figure for the next three months. It fell to 2,111 in November and again to 1,734 in December. The fall was most pronounced in single-engine fighter production at which most of the attacks were aimed. Again, the peak was reached in July when 1,263 were produced. By December, the total had fallen to 687.[67]

In January 1944 overall production was restored to 2,445. It fell to 2,015 in February. Beginning in March, the overall total rose each month to reach a peak of 4,103 in September after which it fell to between 3,000 and 3,500 per month. Fighter production followed a roughly similar track. It rose from the December low to 1,555 in January 1944. February brought a decline to 1,104, but by March the figure was restored to 1,638. Again, increases were recorded each month to reach a peak of 3,375 in September 1944.[68] (See Figure 6–4)

The strategic bombing campaign did exact, however, a considerable toll from the levels of output the Germans had planned to produce. Bombs destroyed and damaged factories, equipment, and aircraft. The dispersal of the industry, ordered after the BIG WEEK bombings, contributed further to losses of production. The USSBS estimated that the attacks delivered in the year beginning in August 1943 cost the Luftwaffe between 5,000 to 10,000 airplanes.[69] This helped to ensure that the already considerable margin of numerical superiority enjoyed by the Allied air forces continued to grow in 1944.

Why did the strategic bombing offensive not bring a halt to the expansion program and reduce production capacity as planned in POINTBLANK? First of all, the German plant capacity that existed as early as 1941, measured in factory space and tools, was probably adequate for the peak production of aircraft actually reached in 1944 (if undisturbed by attack).[70] Up until the crisis created by strategic bombing in early 1944, most German aircraft factories still worked only single shifts. From March of 1944 on, double shifts and seven-day work weeks were put into effect in undamaged and newly dispersed plants, measures which had a positive effect on production and largely compensated for the loss of capacity from bombing.[71]

The weak attacks of 1943, which were aimed primarily at assembly plants, fell on the industry at a time when it was beginning a major

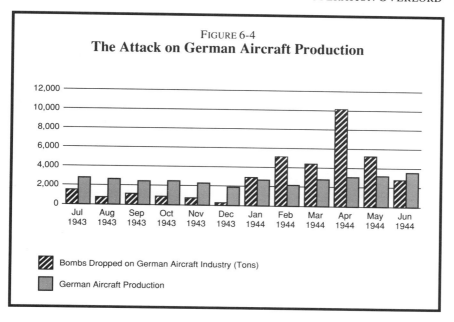

FIGURE 6-4
The Attack on German Aircraft Production

Bombs Dropped on German Aircraft Industry (Tons)

German Aircraft Production

program of expansion. This had the effect of "backing up" and "filling" the production pipeline for the surge in production that began to occur right in the middle of the heaviest attacks in the first four months of 1944.[72]

The dispersal of the industry made it a much less profitable target. Some individual manufacturers had begun dispersal on their own in 1943, but it was not until late February and early March 1944 that government-ordered dispersal was begun. Dispersal had its costs; the USSBS Aircraft Division believed that dispersal might have cost at least as much production as bombing destruction did. It greatly increased overhead labor costs; made the handling of engineering and program changes more difficult; shortened production runs, increased tool and jig requirements, and, above all, greatly increased the industry's dependence on the transportation net. When the transportation system came under increasing attack in the late summer and autumn of 1944, the Germans were forced to revert to industrial concentration, this time in underground factories. In the interim, however, the dispersal of production significantly increased both the number of targets and the difficulty in identifying them.[73]

There were some shortcomings in the type of weapons employed by the attackers. The standard bomb used by the Army Air Forces in most of these attacks was the 500-pound general purpose (GP). It was quite simply too small for the job. It tended to do a relatively good job of destroying buildings while leaving valuable machinery much less damaged. Larger

293

bombs would probably have done a more effective job. Also, a greater proportion of incendiaries might have increased the extent of useful destruction.[74]

The *timing* of the relatively weak early attacks on production was important. They were the only attacks that actually drove production levels down, particularly in single-engine fighters. And they achieved this when the German authorities were attempting, for the first time, to expand the industry and significantly improve the air defenses of the *Reich*. In combination with other factors, this meant that the Luftwaffe failed to improve its position vis-à-vis the Allied air forces in 1943 before the Allies were able to greatly increase the scale of their attacks.

The expansion of production achieved in 1944 did not at any time lead to a significant increase in Luftwaffe frontline strength. No fully satisfactory answer has yet been produced for this problem. A large number of Luftwaffe records were destroyed and many of the surviving ones have been difficult to decipher. With confidence, one can say that a significant proportion of the expanded production that did not turn up in frontline strength was destroyed at the factory, in transit, on operational airfields, or in combat. The sources agree, however, that attrition did not account for the whole of the problem. The balance might be accounted for, in part, by declining standards of record-keeping in the last year of the war. Another explanation favored by USSBS investigators was that certain officials, chiefly Karl-Otto Saur, the head of the special Fighter Staff under Albert Speer, were not above altering the books to make their production efforts look better than they really were.[75]

Attrition of the Luftwaffe-in-being clearly contributed more than the attacks on production to the cause of Allied general air superiority. Attrition received greater emphasis when General Spaatz assumed command of USSTAF, partly because of the urgency of the need to make progress against the Luftwaffe, and partly because he increasingly had the means to carry combat to the Luftwaffe in his rapidly growing escort fighter forces. Shortly after his arrival in London, Spaatz told his chief planner, Col. Richard Hughes, "... it is my belief that we do not get sufficient attrition by hitting fighter factories...." He went on to tell Hughes that in selecting targets he was to keep in mind that the mission was to destroy the German Air Force: "We will hit primary objectives [aircraft factories] when weather permits, but at other times will choose targets ... which will bring their fighters into the air."[76]

By the end of February, USSTAF had elevated attrition of the Luftwaffe frontline force to the top of its priority list. There were two reasons for this. Spaatz and Anderson, along with key members of their staffs, believed that the BIG WEEK raids had seriously crippled aircraft production. What was now required was to "police" the industry in order to keep aircraft production at a low level and to inflict combat losses on the

Luftwaffe in order to reduce its frontline strength before the launching of OVERLORD. Spaatz told the Eighth and Fifteenth Air Forces at the beginning of March that they were now to plan their operations with a view, not to avoid the German defenses, but to "invite air opposition when we have fighter escort."[77]

Spaatz and his staff also thought that the decisiveness of their attacks in February opened the door to a strategy that promised not only continued attacks on the Luftwaffe but also the defeat of the whole German war effort. They believed that the opportunity now existed to demonstrate the ability of strategic bombing to win the war. Spaatz wrote to Maj. Gen. Nathan Twining, Commander of the Fifteenth Air Force in Italy, to say that the February raids had placed USSTAF "on the threshold of our real purpose; the piece by piece demolition of the German war machine by precision bombing."[78] Early in February, General Anderson directed the USSTAF planners to produce a plan of operations to be implemented after the completion of the major attacks against aircraft production. Special urgency existed because OVERLORD was approaching and the time to make a convincing demonstration of strategic air power was shrinking. Anderson also wanted to prevent the strategic air forces from becoming too closely tied to a proposal made by the AEAF planners to use the strategic air forces to attack transportation targets in France.[79]

USSTAF's deliberations were governed by three requirements. The plan had to contribute to the existence of air superiority at the time of the invasion. A plan that did not do that had no hope of being approved. It also had to "favor a RANKIN," that is, it had to hold out the promise of bringing about a German collapse without a major invasion. Finally, in the event such a collapse did not materialize, it must make a maximum contribution to the success of OVERLORD. Synthetic oil production was the target system which best met these requirements because the Luftwaffe would fight in defense of such vital targets and suffer attrition. Success would deprive the Luftwaffe of aviation gasoline; it might precipitate a collapse of the German war effort altogether. Failing that, it would at least seriously undermine the fighting power of the German army by limiting its mobility.[80]

The month of March saw an intense debate between USSTAF and its supporters on the one hand and AEAF and the advocates of the assault on the French railway system—the Transportation Plan—on the other. These arguments culminated in a meeting of March 25 at which Gen. Dwight D. Eisenhower, the Supreme Allied Commander, adopted the Transportation Plan. He and his deputy, Air Chief Marshal Sir Arthur Tedder came to believe that the effects of the Oil Plan would occur too late to have an immediate bearing on the invasion itself.[81] This did not mean, however, that the Oil Plan was entirely set aside. Eisenhower and Tedder both believed that air superiority should continue to be the first charge on the efforts of the strategic bombers. Their directive issued to the strategic bomber forces in mid-April emphasized that point.[82] Within a few days of the decision against the Oil Plan, Spaatz approached Eisenhower and reminded him of the urgent need to continue to inflict heavy attrition on the Luftwaffe. He said that the only way this could be done was to attack targets that the Luftwaffe would defend and the best targets for this purpose were those involved in synthetic oil production.[83] In effect, Spaatz now represented the Oil Plan as a continuation of the air superiority part of POINTBLANK, not as the development of a new strategy. One source asserts that Spaatz threatened to resign if he were not allowed to open the oil offensive.[84] Whether the threat was made or not, Eisenhower did agree that Spaatz should make some "experimental" attacks on oil targets.[85]

The first of these attacks began in early May. On May 5, the Fifteenth Air Force bombed the crude oil refineries in Romania; on the 12th, Eighth Air Force struck the first blows at German synthetic petroleum production. The Eighth hit those targets again on the 28th and 29th of May. These attacks caused a formidable reaction from the German defenses and inflicted considerable attrition on the enemy. That, of course, helped to hold down frontline strength and to continue the exchange of experienced German pilots for poorly trained ones. It does not appear, however, that Luftwaffe operations were made to suffer significantly from fuel and lubricant shortages in May or June of 1944. These seem to have had their greatest impact beginning sometime in late August.

To understand this, it is necessary to look first at the relation between aviation gasoline consumption and production.[86] (See Figure 6–5) Consumption rose each month between January and May of 1944. In January, it stood at 122,000 metric tons. Rising to 156,000 tons in March, it peaked at 195,000 tons in May. In June, it fell, but only to 182,000 tons. It fell again in July, to a figure roughly equal to the level consumed in February. After July, however, the decline was steeper, to 115,000 tons in August, and then down to a mere 60,000 in September.

Aviation gasoline production shows a somewhat different picture. It expanded in the first three months of the year, from 159,000 tons in January to 181,000 in March. A slight decline occurred in April, and the May figure stood at 156,000 tons. The drop in production in June was dramatic, to 52,000 tons. From there it fell to a mere 10,000 tons in September.[87]

For the first four months of the year, production exceeded consumption, with the margin narrowing from about 37,000 tons in January to just over 10,000 in April. This allowed the accumulation of reserve stocks, which were employed to keep the level of Luftwaffe operations up while the production of aviation gasoline fell. The deficit in production amounted to nearly 30,000 tons in May and grew to 130,000 in June. From there on it narrowed because Luftwaffe operations fell off rapidly.[88]

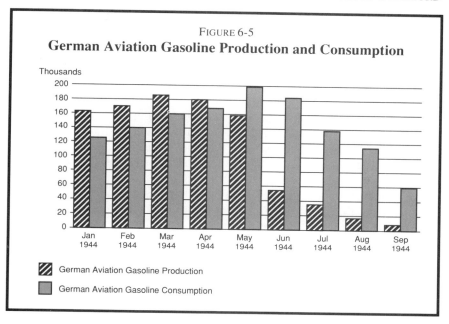

FIGURE 6-5

German Aviation Gasoline Production and Consumption

German Aviation Gasoline Production

German Aviation Gasoline Consumption

These figures make it clear that the impact of the oil attacks on the Luftwaffe, while ultimately very serious, if not crippling, was not significant in May and June. To be sure, the aviation fuel situation had been difficult for some time. Fuel shortages had led to the curtailment of training hours as early as 1942. There is ample evidence of strict conservation policies and occasional local shortages of fuel, especially after the heavy attacks on communications in France. But the supply of aviation gasoline does not appear to have exercised a decisive constraint on Luftwaffe operations in France until some time in August 1944.[89]

The oil offensive was more important for the attrition that it inflicted on the Luftwaffe, the continuation of a process that had begun much earlier in the summer of 1943 and carried on right through the development of the strategic offensive against aircraft production. The losses endured by the Luftwaffe in mid-1943 in the Mediterranean and in Russia were so severe that the High Command was forced to reduce operations on the periphery and concentrate forces for the defense of the *Reich* against the bomber offensive. In the fight between the rapidly developing day air defenses and the struggling Eighth Air Force in late 1943, both sides suffered heavily. We have already seen that the Eighth lost heavy bombers equal to 9.2 percent of credited sorties in October, easily the worst month of the campaign in that respect. But the cost to the Luftwaffe was equally great.

At the time, it was difficult to know what to make of the inflated claims submitted by the Eighth's air gunners, except to admit that they were too high. Inflated they certainly were, but in October the Luftwaffe lost no less than 41.9 percent of the fighter establishment with which it had entered the month.[90]

In short, both the attackers and the defenders suffered casualties at a very high rate in 1943. The difference between the two was to be found in the fact that the production and replacement pipeline continued to expand the Allied air forces and to maintain the level of aircrew quality, while the Luftwaffe was barely able to maintain its frontline strength with aircrew of diminishing quality.

The first six months of 1944 continued the basic pattern laid down in 1943. In January, the Eighth Air Force wrote off 211 bombers. The figure continued to rise to 409 in April, then fell off slightly to 366 in May and more significantly to 280 in June.[91] The Eighth also lost increasing numbers of fighters over this period, the toll rising from a January low of 65 to a June high of 242. Expressed as a percentage of credited sorties, however, the heavy bomber losses fell when compared to the horrors of August and October 1943. The highest percentage was 3.8 in January; by May it had fallen still further to 1.1. (See Figure 6–6) These changes were the consequence of a greatly expanded force and the provision of deep fighter escort. In July of 1943, the average number of heavy bomber aircraft available for operations was 378. By January 1944, the figure had climbed

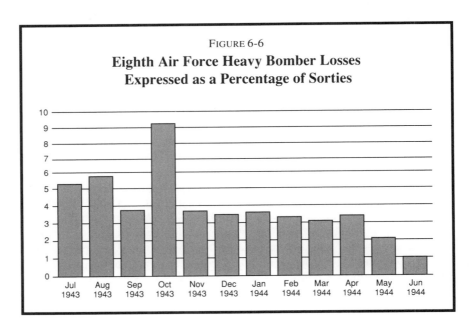

FIGURE 6-6

**Eighth Air Force Heavy Bomber Losses
Expressed as a Percentage of Sorties**

to 842, more than doubling the force. By May, the figure had doubled again to 1,655.[92]

In the first quarter of the year, the Luftwaffe lost 4,107 airplanes destroyed or missing on all fronts; in the second, 5,541.[93] *Luftflotte Reich* and *Luftflotte* 3, the organizations defending Germany and occupied western Europe, lost 733 aircraft in January. The total rose steeply in the ensuing months to 931 in February, 1,070 in March, 1,216 in April, 1,267 in May, and 1,431 in June.[94] In March, the worst month for German fighter losses in all theaters, no less than 56.4 percent of the total fighter establishment on hand at the beginning of the month was destroyed.[95]

The casualties in aircrew imposed on the Luftwaffe by strategic bombing (and operations in other theaters in 1943) prevented the rise in aircraft production from being translated into an increase in frontline strength. In fact, attrition forced a modest decrease. On June 30, 1943, frontline Luftwaffe fighter strength stood at 1,361 operational aircraft in all theaters. By April 30, that figure had fallen to 1,114.[96] More important still, the losses in aircrew were not made good by replacements of equal caliber.

The Luftwaffe, however, was not being driven from the skies in any absolute sense. Its fighters and antiaircraft guns were able to shoot down aircraft and to kill aircrews in numbers similar to those of the preceding year. They had not, however, succeeded in raising the level of destruction to keep pace with the growth in the American strategic bomber and fighter forces. Between October 1943 and May 1944, the operational strength of the Eighth Air Force heavy bombers had grown from 535 to 1,655; its operational fighter force had increased from 426 to 882.[97] In the same period, the American Fifteenth Air Force based in Italy had grown from a serviceable strength of 206 heavy bombers and 163 fighters to 933 bombers and 319 fighters.[98] What this meant was that a daylight attack by the Eighth Air Force in August of 1943 could put up a maximum of about 400 bombers escorted by 200 fighters part of the way. In May 1944, the Eighth Air Force routinely put in attacks of over three times that number of bombers fully escorted (when things went right) by three times the August number of fighters. Against this, the Luftwaffe could make a maximum effort of no more than, perhaps, 400–600 sorties. Moreover, the Eighth could make raids of this size as often as weather (and the flak damage repair services) would allow. The Luftwaffe was not capable of a similarly sustained effort. Consequently, the general air superiority achieved by the Allies before D-day amounted to the freedom to conduct daylight aerial operations over Germany. By holding back the expansion of the Luftwaffe frontline, by forcing a decline in the quality of German aircrew, and by denying the Germans the opportunity to conserve their forces in anticipation of the invasion, this achievement made a considerable contribution to the success of OVERLORD.

It was the responsibility of Air Chief Marshal Sir Trafford Leigh-Mallory, the Commander in Chief of the Allied Expeditionary Air Forces, to ensure local air superiority on the day of the invasion. He had three major forces at his disposal—the American Ninth Air Force, the RAF 2d Tactical Air Force and the Air Defense of Great Britain (ADGB, which was formerly Fighter Command).

Leigh-Mallory did not see the problem of air superiority in the same light as Generals Spaatz and Anderson, or for that matter, Sir Charles Portal, the Chief of Air Staff of the Royal Air Force. Leigh-Mallory had spent much time in the interwar period specializing in what the British called "Army Cooperation"—reconnaissance and close air support. In 1937 he assumed the command of 12 Group in the recently formed Fighter Command. In October 1940 he moved to 11 Group, the frontline force in the main fight against the Luftwaffe. From there he became head of Fighter Command in November 1942. He was a leading force in the transformation of Fighter Command from a force exclusively devoted to air defense to one capable of major offensive operations. He presided over the formation of the new Army Support squadrons in 1943 as well as the creation of 2d Tactical Air Force, the organization intended to provide support to the British Army in OVERLORD, and he directed the continued development and technical improvement in British air defenses. In short, he was one of the four or five senior Allied airmen most knowledgeable about local air superiority, but, aside from the cooperation provided by Fighter Command to the Eighth Air Force in the form of withdrawal support for its attacks, he had little experience with the inner circles of the strategic bomber offensive. He simply did not share the hopes and ambitions of the champions of POINTBLANK.[99]

Leigh-Mallory's perspective also differed because the tasks for which he was responsible were more varied and complex than those faced by the strategic bomber commanders. He had to plan the full range of air operations in support of OVERLORD. His long list of responsibilities included operations against the Luftwaffe bases in France and the Low Countries, attacks on the German lines of communication, direct support of the British and American armies on the battlefield, air cover of the invasion fleets and the sea lanes over which supplies were to flow to the invading forces, air defense of the British bases from which the invasion was to be launched, the execution of airborne operations, and, finally a large share of the tactical reconnaissance provided to the Allied armies. To these tasks he applied three basic ideas, each of which brought him into direct conflict with most of his colleagues among the senior air commanders.

First, he believed that the completion of the POINTBLANK attacks on aircraft production was not a prerequisite for the success of the invasion. The reduction of the frontline strength and the production base of the

Bursts of deadly enemy flak explode around a formation of B–17 Flying Fortresses during a mission over Germany.

Shattered remains of Schweinfurt after bombing attacks from Eighth Air Force.

Luftwaffe prior to the landings was an important objective, but Leigh-Mallory thought that the decisive moment for the achievement of air superiority would come at the time of the invasion. The Luftwaffe was certain to conserve its forces in order to strike a massive blow at the invasion forces. He was confident that the fighter forces at his disposal would be able to meet this threat and inflict a decisive defeat on the Luftwaffe.[100]

Leigh-Mallory and his planners also believed that the number and the scope of the tasks he would be called upon to perform would grow rapidly as the invasion approached.[101] Before the assault was launched, he could structure his operations in phases, first giving emphasis to one task, then shifting to another, taking account of the weather and the state of his forces. When the landings began, he would no longer be permitted that luxury. The demands of a combined arms battle would appear all at once, and he would be compelled to deal with them simultaneously, or risk the failure of the whole precariously balanced operation. He was, therefore, anxious that the strategic air forces assume responsibility for key tasks in order to allow him to use his fighter and medium bomber force more effectively.

Leigh-Mallory was also aware that the Allied landing forces, having to be reinforced and supplied by sea while the German defenders could depend on land communications, would be at a severe disadvantage, especially in the critical period immediately following the landings. Accordingly, he approved a plan drafted at his headquarters—the Transportation Plan—that called for the employment of both Eighth Air Force and RAF Bomber Command in a program of heavy attacks on the French and Belgian railway networks for a period of about sixty days preceding the invasion.[102] This plan ran head-on into General Spaatz's determination to conserve his force for decisive blows against the German war economy.

Leigh-Mallory's planners believed, as did most airmen, that relative airfield position was critical in a struggle for local air superiority. In that light, it appeared that the Luftwaffe would enjoy the advantage of having its airfields much closer to the landing area, permitting greater intensity of operations and endurance over the battle.[103]

The Allied Expeditionary Air Force (AEAF) staff looked to a number of remedies for this problem. First of all, they expected some diversions would slow down the rate of Luftwaffe reinforcement in the area, and they hoped that the strategic offensive would generally weaken the enemy's frontline force.[104] The Luftwaffe's advantages in position could be eliminated if the major airfields within a 110-mile radius of Caen were attacked, forcing the enemy to operate from fields considerably further away from the landing areas.[105] It was also vital for the armies to capture ground suitable for airfields as quickly as possible.[106]

This delicately balanced strategy broke down in January 1944 when General Montgomery arrived in London and proceeded to direct a revision to the original OVERLORD plan which, among other things, widened the frontage of the assault. To Leigh-Mallory and his planners, this reduced the likelihood that the open ground beyond Caen would be captured early. To offset the probability of a slower rate of airfield development in France, AEAF now thought that the radius within which airfields would be attacked should be enlarged from 110 miles to 130 miles.[107]

Leigh-Mallory published the final version of the overall air plan on April 15, 1944. He proposed to attack about 50 major operational bases and satellite landing grounds within the 130-mile radius. Because there were too many targets to leave the task to the last few days before the landings, the attacks were to be carried out in phases; first, against the installations that took the longest to repair, such as maintenance facilities, and second, against airfield surfaces. AEAF scheduled the first series of attacks to begin on D–21, the second on D–5.[108]

At this point, Leigh-Mallory and Spaatz clashed again. USSTAF and Bomber Command had attacked French and German airfields as secondary targets and targets of opportunity in the period between January and April. USSTAF, however, was getting restive about airfield attacks. Shortly after Leigh-Mallory issued his plan, General Anderson directed one of his staff to look into the matter remarking, "It is believed that the number of bombs striking on airdromes, near airdromes, airfields and in wooded areas, results in an entirely undue excessive waste of effort."[109] Spaatz wrote to Eisenhower on May 5:

> No allocation of effort by the Strategic Air Forces is recommended in the case of airdromes in the battle area. These targets can be attacked more profitably by lighter forces, particularly when occupied. Further, there are so many demands for heavy bombers that there is no chance of effort being available.[110]

The following day Spaatz put his case to Leigh-Mallory, saying that it was more important to attack airfields in Germany from which long-range bomber attacks might be launched against the invasion. He was seconded by Air Vice-Marshal Oxland, the representative from Bomber Command to AEAF, who claimed that the plan demanded more effort than his command could make available. Leigh-Mallory did not budge, saying that coverage of the operational fields in the 130-mile radius was more important. It was finally agreed that AEAF intelligence would, in consultation with the intelligence branches of the other concerned commands, work out a priority table for airfields. In the interim, Spaatz agreed to attack airfields as a fourth priority behind the Luftwaffe, the secret weapons sites (from which V–1 Buzz Bombs were launched beginning in June), and the Transportation Plan targets.[111]

Leigh-Mallory changed his mind the next day. He had apparently come to believe that the attack on German lines of communications and the delay of enemy reinforcements was more important than the attack on airfields, given what was known about the declining capabilities of the Luftwaffe. He maintained this view well into the period after the invasion. For example, when he introduced proposals for blocking road movement into the battle area at an Allied Air Commanders' meeting on June 3, an acrimonious discussion followed in which both Tedder and Spaatz argued that there was now a pressing need to make attacks on airfields. Leigh-Mallory emphasized the depth of his conviction about the priority of transportation targets by threatening to resign. Tedder "arbitrated" by splitting the difference, allocated one-half of USSTAF's effort to airfields (outside the battle area) and the other half to lines of communications.[112]

In keeping with the reduced priority given to airfield attacks, the Allied air forces did not complete Leigh-Mallory's original program. Only thirty-four of about fifty fields were attacked prior to the invasion. After the landings began, however, attacks on airfields again absorbed a larger proportion of the air effort.[113]

Prior to the invasion, these attacks led to the destruction of very few aircraft largely because the Luftwaffe High Command refused to transfer any large numbers of aircraft to *Luftflotte* 3 before the invasion actually occurred. Dispersal, camouflage, and frequent transfers of units also kept losses low.[114] After the invasion, the destruction of aircraft on the ground picked up a bit, simply because there were more targets.

Airfield attacks had two other very positive effects. They forced the Luftwaffe back to airfields further in the rear and eliminated the position differential that had so worried Allied planners for so long. This largely compensated for the slowness with which Allied airfields were developed following the landings. Secondly, when the Luftwaffe moved to the rear, they occupied fields that were inadequately prepared, a condition which reduced serviceability and made it difficult, if not impossible, to make up for numerical inferiority with a greater intensity of operations.[115]

To ensure local air superiority on D-day itself, AEAF worked out a plan to employ virtually the whole of the available fighter strength of the Allied air forces. To begin with, the bases and embarkation ports of southern England were covered by the ten squadrons of day fighters and seventeen squadrons of night fighters under the control of the Air Defence of Great Britain. Six groups of P–38s from the Eighth Air Force provided cover over the shipping lanes to a point about fifteen miles from the enemy coast. They were employed in patrol relays of four squadrons at a time. AEAF chose the P–38 for this work because there was little chance that its silhouette could be mistaken for that of an enemy plane, an always important consideration given the uncertain state of naval flak fire discipline. AEAF detailed fifty-one squadrons to provide cover over the French coast from a line about five miles inland to the edge of the patrol area of the P–38s. Spitfires of 2d TAF flew at the lower altitudes in patrols of six squadrons while a P–47 relay of three squadrons flew high cover. The whole of VIII Fighter Command—the long- range escort fighters—flew perimeter patrols outside the battle area. Leigh-Mallory held back a reserve of some thirty fighter squadrons, with six at the highest state of readiness for instant commitment to threatened areas. The defense of the shipping lanes and of the beaches at night was in the hands of ADGB and RAF No. 85 Group.[116]

AEAF laid on a host of offensive measures as well. As a preliminary step AEAF had begun to attack the German long- range aircraft warning and reporting stations as early as May 10. On May 17, these raids were extended to the night fighter control stations. RAF 2d TAF attacked some forty-two sites in the last week of May. RAF Bomber Command raided the four highly important jamming stations located in the west on the night of June 3/4. That night, ninety-five heavies from Bomber Command, using markers laid by Oboe-controlled Mosquitos, completely took out the Luftwaffe's wireless intercept station for northwest France. Two combined air and naval diversions employing elaborate electronic "spoofing" were laid on to attract the attention of the radar stations that remained active. In addition, a major electronic jamming barrage was employed for over five and one-half hours to cover the flight of the airborne forces and the night air attacks.[117] Exact assessment of the effects of these measures is not possible. But it is clear that the landing forces achieved tactical surprise; the airborne flights were not attacked by fighters (although they did take casualties from flak); and, in general, the aircraft warning and reporting services of the Luftwaffe worked very badly, if at all. AEAF calculated that, on the night of June 5/6, no more than eighteen percent of German radar coverage in northwest France was functioning.[118]

The Luftwaffe forces deployed to meet this onslaught were weak and badly dispersed. *Luftflotte* 3, the Luftwaffe command in the west, possessed about 325 bombers of one description or another. Approximately 180 of these were the antishipping forces of *Fliegerkorps* X and *Fliegerdivision* 2 based in southern and southwestern France. The remainder were in northwestern France, Belgium, and Holland. On paper these forces were capable of doing some damage, but they contained a very high percentage of untrained crews whose ability to find targets and hit them was suspect. Worse still, they could not expect to attack in daylight without a powerful escort of fighters. *Luftflotte* 3 possessed only about 170 single-engine fighters. The ground-attack forces were pitiful, numbering only about 75 aircraft. *Luftflotte* 3 had requested more of these, but the Luftwaffe High Command decided that the Russian threat to the Romanian oilfields was more serious and kept over 500 aircraft of the fighter-bomber force deployed in the east.[119]

The High Command had planned to meet the invasion threat by transferring the bulk of the fighters in *Luftflotte Reich* to *Luftflotte* 3. Fields and

305

stocks of fuel and munitions were prepared to receive this force. One German source indicates, however, that these preparations were miserably inadequate. The administrative authorities (*Luftgau* 3) had not constructed headquarters buildings; dispersal points were not organized; there was a complete lack of splinter screens, trenches, dug-outs, shelters, and communications installations.[120]

Perhaps the most important point to note about the Luftwaffe preparations to meet the invasion is that the decision to withhold reinforcement of *Luftflotte* 3 from Germany until the invasion had actually begun made it impossible to intervene with any effect during the first hours of the landings. The first German sorties flown against the beachheads occurred in the afternoon. The total amounted to less than 100, mostly by single-engine fighters. When night fell, the bomber and torpedo-bomber forces flew about 175 sorties against the landing forces. They were attacked not only by Allied night-fighters (ADGB and No. 85 Group) but also by their own flak. These could not be classified as anything more than harassing attacks.[121]

Reinforcement from Germany began quickly. By June 10 about 300 fighters had been flown to the west. The poor state of base preparation, the incessant attacks on airfields, and the attacks on aircraft and ground crews in transit (made possible by ULTRA information) greatly weakened the effect of these moves. Further confusion was created when the plan to employ a good portion of this force as fighter-bombers came unstuck. By June 10 about 25 percent of the fighter force was operating in the ground attack role, and on the 11th, *Luftflotte* 3 issued orders to fit all fighters with bomb racks. With the poor state of training for this work, however, losses were high and the effort entirely ineffective. Accordingly, on the 12th, Luftwaffe High Command ordered that henceforth all fighters were to concentrate exclusively on enemy aircraft.[122] No wonder that the Chief of Staff of *Jagdkorps* II (the main fighter command) was moved to complain about the lack of organization and grip in the Luftwaffe higher command.[123]

The constant Allied pounding of airfields in the days and weeks after the invasion (interrupted only by bad weather), accompanied by strong fighter patrols over the battle area, prevented the Luftwaffe from improving its effort significantly. In day action, Allied fighters intercepted attacks before they reached the frontline, forcing the Germans to expend ammunition and fuel (in the case of fighter-bombers, to jettison their loads), and to return to their fields. The interception of Allied medium and fighter bomber attacks was not effective because of poor performance by the German warning and reporting service and pilot inexperience. This meant that the fighter forces were obliged to attack in small groups and to confine the bulk of their activity to attempting to protect the army's lines of communication and to drive back the very dangerous Allied artillery spotting planes.[124]

The Luftwaffe bombing force was also ineffective. After about a week of night attacks against the bridgehead, the combination of Allied barrage balloons, searchlights, flak, and night fighters forced all bombing to be done from relatively high altitudes which further degraded the accuracy of their attacks. From June 12 on, the whole of the bomber force went over to minelaying, averaging between sixty and seventy sorties per night. These efforts caused some difficulties to the Allies, but the decisive effect hoped for was not achieved.[125]

On both sides, the losses in aircraft and crew sustained in June were considerable. The German air defenses extracted a considerable toll, much of it due to flak. The Eighth Air Force, for example, lost 534 aircraft, just over half of which were fighters. Ninth Air Force losses jumped from 174 in May to no less than 381 aircraft of all types in June. RAF Bomber Command, operating almost exclusively in the west, lost 293 aircraft in June, a figure exceeded in the first six months of the year only by the carnage of January when it was attacking Berlin. RAF 2d Tactical Air Force also took significant casualties. But, as in the case of strategic air operations over the *Reich*, the continued ability of the German air defenses to cause casualties had little or no tactical or strategic effect on Allied air operations, largely because of the huge Allied advantages in numbers and because of the production and replacement pipelines standing behind the fighting forces.

June was also the worst month of the year for the Luftwaffe. *Luftflotte Reich* and *Luftflotte* 3 lost 1,181 planes on operations and a further 250 to accidents.[126] The Luftwaffe could not accumulate enough force size and crew experience to do anything more than harass Allied ground and air operations. It did not intervene with any effect against the most vulnerable stage of OVERLORD when the first amphibious assaults were made; it could not effectively attack the troops, equipment, and supplies crammed into the congested beachhead, and it could not impose anything approaching a prohibitive loss rate on the operations of the Allied fighter-bombers. The best that could be said is that its harassment forced AEAF to continue to invest a considerable effort in air superiority operations, which was, as a result, not available for close support in the battle area. It is doubtful that this was a significant cause of the slowness with which the Allied ground forces broke out of the beachhead.

Top-ranking American officers visit airfields on French soil soon after D–day *(from left to right)*: **Lt. Gen. Omar Bradley, Gen. Henry Arnold, Adm. Ernest J. King, Gen. Dwight Eisenhower, and Gen. George Marshall.**

The Intelligence Contribution

What role did intelligence play in the battles for general and local air superiority? The material most useful to Allied air commanders was information about strategic and tactical intentions, frontline strength, production of aircraft, the location of operational units, tactics employed by those units, and the damage done by air attacks. To get that information, Allied intelligence agencies relied on many sources including after-action debriefing of aircrews, aerial reconnaissance, agent information, and signals intelligence. In two of these areas, the Allies had considerable advantages. By 1944, both the RAF and AAF had invested heavily in aerial reconnaissance and photo interpretation, which played a key role in the air superiority campaign. In signals, the Allied wireless intercept organizations ("Y" services) were excellent both in traffic and content analysis. The most spectacular Allied intelligence asset, however, was the ability to decode German wireless traffic in various high-level ENIGMA codes—the ULTRA secret. The Luftwaffe was more prone to use radio than the other services and, in general, its radio security procedures were more lax. From 1940 through to the end of the war, the British intelligence agencies charged with the task of decoding these transmissions found the Luftwaffe traffic easiest to break into.[127]

The contribution made by intelligence to the achievement of air superiority was considerable, but uneven. It is always difficult to get hard information on enemy strategic intentions. For almost all of the war, the Allies relied on the time-honored practice of inferring intentions from enemy action. The major problem with this approach was that one could derive quite different estimates of policy from the same action. A good example was the attempt to understand what the Luftwaffe strategic policy was when German resistance was so weak against the raid on aircraft factories on February 20, 1944, as well as the raid on Berlin on March 9, 1944. Were the Germans tactically exhausted on those days? Did weather conditions hinder them? Were they following a policy of deliberate conservation of force, or were they beaten in a more absolute sense? If they were conserving their forces, were they doing it to accumulate strength in order to deal a massive blow against a future raid or to intervene against the Allied invasion?[128] The only way to answer these questions was to keep on attacking.

A good illustration of the weakness of intelligence in the area of strategic intentions was the estimate of what the Luftwaffe intended to do when the invasion started. We have already seen that Leigh-Mallory and his staff expected a big air battle extending over several days. They came to this conclusion very early in the planning process and stuck to it right up to the end, although by May, Leigh-Mallory was sufficiently convinced of the power of his fighter forces and the general weakness of the Luftwaffe to want to ease up on airfield attacks in order to put more resources into the attack on lines of communications. Belief in an impending air battle should not, however, be dismissed as a misguided notion peculiar to someone not convinced of the decisive effects of strategic bombing. As important a champion of that strategy as General Arnold expected there would be a major air struggle over the invasion beaches.[129] He held that view despite the optimistic assessment of the effects of the attacks on aircraft production made by USSTAF in London and his own staff in Washington. What seems to have been the case is that, in the absence of solid intelligence, Leigh-Mallory and Arnold, as well as many others, concluded that the Luftwaffe High Command would do what they themselves would do in similar circumstances.

Intelligence on tactical intentions was better. After-action debriefing provides a fairly good picture of enemy tactics, especially as the fund of experience in deep-penetration operations grew. Very little warning was given about the adoption of new weapons (such as the air-to-air rocket) or techniques, however. One exception to this pattern was the advance notice of the Luftwaffe's formation of special assault squadrons in late 1943 for the special purpose of driving home attacks against the bomber formations at very short ranges.[130] During and after the invasion, signals intelligence, including ULTRA, often provided warning of impending enemy raids before they were launched and picked up on radar. What little effort the Luftwaffe could mount against the beachhead, principally at night, was blunted, at least partly, because of good signals intelligence.

Intelligence estimates of enemy aircraft production were poor. (See Figure 6–7) Early on in the war, Air Ministry intelligence tended to overestimate German aircraft output, sometimes by a considerable margin. By mid-1943, the situation had improved dramatically, and Air Ministry assessments of production and first line strength were remarkably accurate. In 1944, especially after the heavy attacks on production in February, the estimates went badly awry. The Air Ministry, for example, thought that the average monthly production for the first six months of 1944 amounted to 1,870 aircraft, down from 2,115 in the last half of 1943. In fact, German production actually rose to an average of 2,811 per month, almost 1,000 aircraft more than the intelligence figure. Almost all of this error was to be found in estimates on single-engine fighter production.[131]

Some wildly optimistic assessments of the effects of the BIG WEEK attacks were made at USSTAF. General Spaatz thought that fighter production had been cut in half for at least one and maybe two months.[132] As we have already seen, Colonel Hughes, USSTAF's chief planner, believed that

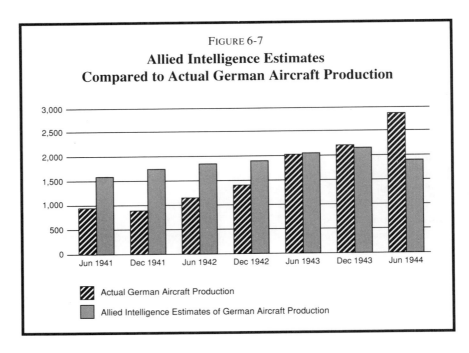

FIGURE 6-7

**Allied Intelligence Estimates
Compared to Actual German Aircraft Production**

the blows struck had been so decisive as to allow the strategic air forces to turn toward their main aim, the assault on the vital centers of war production.[133] The Enemy Objectives Unit attached to the American Embassy, and the source of much of USSTAF's intelligence analysis of German targets, prefaced its assessment of the February attacks with the caveat that it was still too early to draw definitive conclusions, and then went on to say that it appeared that single-engine fighter production had fallen from 950 to 250 per month, and twin-engine fighters from 225 to 50 per month. If further attacks were carried out, they thought single-engine production might be cut to 15 percent of pre-raid levels.[134] There was no less optimism in Washington where, as late as April 20, the Assistant Chief of the Air Staff for Intelligence estimated that strategic bombing had reduced single-engine fighter production in March to less than 500 aircraft, when the actual figure was just over 1,300.[135]

How could the estimates have gone so far wrong? The intelligence officers and their commanders seem to have fallen into an old trap—the tendency to see what one expects to see. Many had high expectations of the huge impact that would follow concentrated attack on aircraft production, and that is quite simply what they saw. The evidence from photo reconnaissance showed over seventy-five percent of the buildings associated with fighter production damaged in one respect or another. The difficulty was, as the USSBS Aircraft Industry Division pointed out, that heavy machinery and tools remained more or less intact.[136] The quality of intelligence on aircraft production fell off considerably after dispersal of the industry.

Perhaps the most important culprit was the misunderstanding of the German economy. It was widely assumed in Allied intelligence circles that the Germans had been running an efficiently organized, tightly-strung war economy ever since the promulgation of the Four-Year Plan in 1936. In fact, nothing of the sort existed until at least late 1942. The failure to spot the reserves of capacity in the German economy accounted for a good deal of the overestimation of the effects of strategic bombing in general and of the attack on the aircraft industry in particular.[137]

The direct consequences of this intelligence failure on the course of the campaign for air superiority do not appear to have been severe. A mistaken optimism about the effects of the February raids certainly did not mean that aircraft factories were thereafter left alone. In fact, as is explained above, the tonnage of bombs dropped on those factories in March, April, and May of 1944 was much greater than in February. The decision to emphasize attrition in strategic air action was greatly influenced by the mistaken certainty of success in the February attacks, but it cannot be said that this was an incorrect decision. Given the Luftwaffe's poor training position, and the obvious need to keep its frontline strength down, a policy of attrition made great sense regardless of what was happening to

311

production. USSTAF appears to have made a good decision on the basis of bad evidence.

The picture in other areas was more positive. ULTRA, for example, provided much information that indicated the strains and stresses that were being imposed on individual Luftwaffe formations during the course of the bombing offensive. ULTRA revealed the shortages in combat pilots that were brought on by intensive air operations as early as the last few months of 1943.[138] Information of this kind encouraged USSTAF to persist in the emphasis on attrition. Also, this information probably contributed to the growing confidence with which AEAF approached the impending air battle over the invasion beaches. The Luftwaffe might intervene, but it could not be expected to be effective or to persist in a large-scale effort.

ULTRA information was also helpful in operational planning. Intercepts of German weather reports, particularly the excellent ones put out by the SS at Cracow, were valuable aids. Knowledge of order of battle and disposition of the fighter and flak defenses contributed greatly to mission planning. Analysis of German fighter radio traffic took on much greater importance as time went on, providing knowledge of take-off times, assembly routes, and rendezvous points. In the first part of the daylight strategic bombing campaign, this information was used for planning evasive tactics and the relays of the escorts. Its value increased, of course, when tactics became more aggressive and a portion of the escort ranged ahead of the bomber formation to attack the defenders while they were assembling. When the assault against the Luftwaffe forced the defenders to operate from bases deeper in Germany, the quality of radio interception decreased, and the Eighth Air Force began to use a new intelligence tool that the Fifteenth had pioneered beginning in February: airborne radio-intercept stations.[139]

In addition, ULTRA provided confirmation of the wisdom of the experimental attacks on oil. The day after the first of these attacks (on May 12), an ULTRA intercept indicated that a transfer of flak from the Eastern Front to France (*Luftflotte* 3) was diverted to provide additional flak support to the hydrogenation plants. In addition, flak batteries operating in protection of certain aircraft factories were to be similarly redeployed.[140]

Signals intelligence proved to be even more valuable in the fight for local air superiority. "Y" Service and ULTRA often provided warning of enemy raids in advance of radar plots. More importantly, ULTRA helped to blunt the Luftwaffe strategy of mass reinforcement. It gave notice of movement orders, including times of departure and arrival, as well as identifying the airfields to which transfers were being made. After Allied attacks on those fields were made, ULTRA picked up German damage reports that were particularly valuable, either as a complement to or substitute for aerial reconnaissance. The latter function was very important in the bad weather of the summer of 1944.[141]

It appears that, on the whole, tactical intelligence of all kinds was better than strategic intelligence. Furthermore, it also seems that this intelligence was of greater use in the battle for local air superiority than it was in the attempt to gain a general theater superiority. Strategic intelligence seems to have been marred by faults in the sources and in the analytical habit of seeing in the data what was expected. Perhaps the best that can be said is that while intelligence made a considerable contribution to the air superiority campaigns, it did not make a decisive one.

Assessment

The air superiority achieved for Operation OVERLORD was largely the product of vastly superior Allied production and training efforts that were begun very early in the war. Some marginal advantages in technology and some greater ones in intelligence contributed to the result. Overall, the struggle for control of the air in western Europe was a war of attrition. The German failure, for one reason or another, to build a larger air force, to expand its effective offensive power, and to support it with a proper training program contributed directly to the outcome.

Three campaigns effectively translated superior numbers and training into a practical Allied domination of the air. RAF Fighter Command's successful struggle to prevent the Luftwaffe from carrying on effective offensive air action over the United Kingdom and its coastal waters established a secure base for conducting Allied air operations, for producing and accumulating materiel, and for assembling and training the invasion armada.

The strategic bombing campaign for general air superiority did not succeed by reducing the production of German aircraft. After an initial decline in 1943, production continued to climb, especially in fighters, right through the invasion up to September of 1944. The strategic offensive did gain air superiority for its own operations, however, largely by applying greater numbers and by carrying offensive air combat to German air space itself with the long-range fighter escort. The attrition caused by these operations kept the Luftwaffe from translating improved production into an enlarged frontline force. It also forced a continued decline in the average quality of German aircrew, measured by the extent of their training and their performance in combat.

The inability to expand the frontline force meant that the Luftwaffe had to enter the critical period of 1944 with numbers barely adequate to meet the demands of only one of the major theaters of operations in which the German armed forces were committed. The decision to keep special-

313

ized fighter-bomber forces in the east and to retain the bulk of the fighter forces in the *Reich* until the British and the Americans actually landed in France effectively deprived the Luftwaffe of the chance to intervene in the earliest and most vulnerable moments of the invasion. Moreover, the intensity of operations forced on the *Reich* air defenses by strategic attack in effect prevented the Luftwaffe from conserving forces in order to train them for both defensive and offensive roles when they were committed to the battle in the west.

The campaign for local air superiority in western France before the invasion did greater damage to the close operational infrastructure of *Luftflotte* 3 than it did to aircraft. When *Luftflotte* 3 received its reinforcements shortly after D-day, they had to operate with airfields, maintenance facilities, radar, and communications that had been badly damaged by Allied air attack. The combination of offensive and defensive measures taken by AEAF on D-day, and in subsequent weeks, ensured that *Luftflotte* 3, even when augmented by reinforcements from the *Reich*, could not use large forces effectively and persistently in any offensive or defensive operation. By August 1944, the Luftwaffe in France was an utterly spent force. Allied air superiority had become air supremacy.

Notes

1. JCS 442, Aug 5, 1943, "Operation OVERLORD;" RAF Air Historical Branch (hereafter cited as AHB), "The Liberation of Northwest Europe," vol I, pp 69-70.

2. The question of the muddled Allied air command has not yet received adequate treatment. For coverage of this subject in the official histories, see W. F. Craven and J. L. Cate, *The Army Air Forces in World War II,* vols II and III (Chicago, 1949; reprint, Office of Air Force History, 1983), and Sir Charles Webster and Noble Frankland, *The Strategic Air Offensive Against Germany,* vols II and III (London, 1961).

3. For a very good recent analysis of the German failure to develop a larger air force, see R. J. Overy, *Goering, The "Iron Man"* (London, 1984), chap 7.

4. On the confusion in German strategy, see *Ibid.;* and Williamson Murray, *Strategy for Defeat: The Luftwaffe, 1933–1945* (Maxwell AFB, Ala., 1983) pp 222–24, 245–55. On Luftwaffe strategy to meet the invasion in the west, see AHB, *The Rise and Fall of the German Air Force, 1933–1945* (London, 1948), pp 316–25; and Murray, pp 277–85.

5. AHB, "Luftwaffe Strength and Serviceability Tables, 1938–45," USAF Historical Research Center (AFHRC) K5002, fr 0432–5; AHB, "The Liberation of Northwest Europe," III, appendix 1, AFHRC 23357, fr 1050.

6. The best introduction to a comparative analysis of aircraft production is R. J. Overy, *The Air War, 1939–1945* (New York, 1982), PB edition, pp 149–84.

7. For a excellent discussion of this background, see Klaus Maier, "Der Aufbau der Luftwaffe und Ihre Strategisch-Operation Konzeption Insbesondere Gegenueber den Westmaechten," in *Deutschland und Frankreich, 1936–1939* (Munich, 1981), and the section on the Luftwaffe in Wilhelm Deist, *The Wehrmacht and German Rearmament* (London, 1981). A very good recent account can be found in Murray, *Strategy for Defeat,* pp 1–21. An important feature to note about this last work is its extensive use of German sources.

8. AHB, *The Rise and Fall of the German Air Force, 1933–1945,* pp 21–33.

9. United States Strategic Bombing Survey (USSBS), "Aircraft Division Industry Report" (ADIR), pp 21–3.

10. This was in part the product of a considerable underestimate of the production of potential adversaries. Overy, *The Air War,* pp 22–23. See also Overy, *Goering,* chap 7.

11. Overy, *The Air War,* table 12, p 150.

12. *Ibid.* On American aircraft production, see Craven and Cate, *The Army Air Forces in World War II,* vol VI, pp 263–361; also I. B. Holley, *Buying Aircraft: Materiel Procurement for the Army Air Forces* (Washington, 1964).

13. For a comparative overview of Allied and German training, see Overy, *The Air War,* pp 138–45.

14. Richard Suchenwirth, *Historical Turning Points in the German Air Force War Effort* [USAF Historical Study #189] (New York, 1968), pp 20–21.

15. *Ibid.,* pp 21–28; AHB, *Rise and Fall,* pp 203–05, 314–16; USSBS, Military Analysis Division (MAD), "The Defeat of the German Air Force," pp 3-6; USSBS, MAD, Interrogation of Lt. Gen. Werner Kreipe, Jun 4, 1945, National Archives and Records Administration (NARA), RG 243, Box 1.

16. USSBS, MAD, "The Defeat of the German Air Force, figures 8–9.

17. For a survey of the American aircrew training program, see Craven and Cate, *Army Air Forces in World War II,* vol VI, pp 600–29.

18. USSBS, MAD, "Defeat of the German Air Force," figure 9.

19. Murray, *Strategy for Defeat,* pp 6–13.

20. *Ibid.,* p 250. Only 35 of these machines were available for the "Baby Blitz" in Jan 1944. The development of the He–177 had been badly hampered by the requirement that it be able to dive-bomb and by its unique design featuring coupled engines. They had a demonstrated tendency to overheat and catch fire.

21. USSBS, MAD, "The Relative Performance of British and American Fighters Against German Fighters," p 13, NARA, RG 243, Box 1.

22. *Ibid.,* p 16–17; History, IX Fighter Command and IX Tactical Air Command, Mar 1 to Mar 31, 1944, Quesada Papers, Library of Congress (LC), Box 5.

23. Kepner (C.G., VIII Fighter Command) to Giles, Dec 27, 1943, Arnold Papers, LC, Box 105.

24. USSBS, MAD, "Relative Performance," pp 16–17.

25. For a comparison of the endurance of the three principal AAF fighters under a variety of combat loads, see W. A. Jacobs, "Tactical Air Doctrine and AAF Close Air Support in the European Theater, 1944–45," *Aerospace Historian,* March 1980, p 47.

26. *Ibid.,* p 21.

27. *Ibid.,* 20–21.

28. USSBS, MAD, Interrogation No. 34, NARA, RG 243, Box 1.

29. Luftwaffe General Staff, 8th Abt, "Problems of German Air Defence in 1944," Nov 5, 1944, AFHRC A5421, fr 1063.

30. The best introduction to the history of British air defense is Basil Collier, *The Defence of the United Kingdom* (London, 1957). More detailed analysis of many subjects may be found in AHB's narratives, "The Air Defence of Great Britain," vols I–IV, AFHRC, reels 23361–3.

31. AHB, *Rise and Fall,* p 165; Murray, pp 72–81.

32. Collier, *Defence of the United Kingdom,* pp 261–330.

33. *Ibid.,* appendix XLII, p 520.

34. AHB, "The Air Defence of Great Britain," vol V, p 188, AFHRC 23363.

35. The texts of the Casablanca and POINTBLANK Directives are printed in Webster and Frankland, *Strategic Air Offensive,* vol IV, pp 153–54, 158–60. See the opinions expressed by Sir Arthur Harris (C-in-C, RAF Bomber Command) in Harris to Sir Charles Portal (Chief of Air Staff), Jan 13, 1944, PRO-AIR 2/7080, and Lt Gen Carl Spaatz in Daily Journal, Jan 21, 1944, Spaatz Papers, LC, Box 14.

36. For Sir Arthur Harris's views, see Webster and Frankland, *Strategic Air Offensive,* vol II, pp 10–52.

37. *Ibid.,* pp 34–35, 62–66.

38. *Ibid.,* p 70.

39. CCS 217, May 14, 1943. German fighter strength was considered "an intermediate objective second to none in priority."

40. Bernard Boylan, "The Development of the Long-Range Escort Fighter," [USAF Historical Study #116] (Maxwell AFB, Ala., 1955), p 68.

41. "Statistical Summary of Eighth AF Operations, European Theater, Aug 17, 1942 to May 8, 1945," AFHRC A5871, fr 0855.

42. A good account of these problems from a perspective admittedly sympathetic to Gen. Eaker may be found in Webster and Frankland, *Strategic Air Offensive,* vol II, pp 32–52.

43. CCS 217, May 14, 1943.

44. "Statistical Summary of Eighth AF Operations," AFHRC A5871, fr 0840.

45. For the views of key members of the Plans Division at AAF Headquarters, see Loutzenheiser to Kuter, Nov 30, 1943; Kuter to Loutzenheiser, Dec 4, 1943, on AFHRC A1376, fr 0900; A1377, fr 0827-8.

46. Arnold to Eaker, Jun 15, 1943, Arnold Papers, LC, Box 48.

47. Arnold to Eaker, Aug 1, 1943, Arnold Papers, LC, Box 48.

48. Arnold to Portal, Oct 14, 1943, cited in Webster and Frankland, *Strategic Air Offen-*

sive, vol II, p 42. The original of Portal's reply dated Oct 24, 1943, is in Arnold Papers, LC, Box 49.

49. CCS, 134th Mtg, Dec 4, 1943.

50. *Ibid.* For an example of AAF staff thinking, see also Giles to Arnold, Nov 30, 1943, Arnold Papers, LC, Box 114.

51. Maj Gen James Doolittle assumed command of the Eighth Air Force which now became a purely operational command with virtually no policymaking responsibility.

52. Daily Journal, Jan 21, 1944, Spaatz Papers, LC, Box 14.

53. Spaatz to Eaker and Doolittle, Mar 4, 1944, Spaatz Papers, LC, Box 143.

54. "Notes of a Conference Between Generals Spaatz and Vandenberg," Apr 10, 1944, Spaatz Papers, LC, Box 14.

55. Arnold to Spaatz, Jan 14, 1944, Arnold Papers, LC, Box 105.

56. Arnold to Giles, Jan 5, 1944, AFHRC A1377, fr 1474–75.

57. Diary, Spaatz Papers, LC, MD, Box 14; Anderson to Kuter (AC/AS Plans), Feb 1, 1944, Spaatz Papers, LC, Box 143.

58. USSBS, ADIR, table V–2, p 58.

59. "Statistical Summary of Eighth Air Force Operations," AFHRC A5871, from fr 0840.

60. "Statistical Story of the Fifteenth Air Force," NARA, RG 243, Box 84.

61. Lovett to Arnold, Jun 18, 1943, Arnold Papers, LC, Box 127.

62. Arnold to Giles, Jun 22, 1943, Arnold Papers, LC, Box 127.

63 The best secondary account is Bernard Boylan, "The Development of the Long-Range Escort Fighter" [AF Historical Study #116].

64. This analysis of the development of fighter escort tactics is based on two principal sources: "Eighth Air Force Tactical Development, August 1942 to May 1945" (copy in AF/CHO Library); and AAF Evaluation Board (ETO), "Tactics and Techniques Developed by VIII Fighter Command," Oct 27, 1944, AFHRC A1174, fr 0500-82.

65. AAF Evaluation Board (ETO), "Tactics and Techniques," fr. 0523.

66. *Ibid.,* p 23–24.

67. USSBS, "Effect of Strategic Bombing on the German War Economy" (ESBGWE), appendix table 101, p 276.

68. *Ibid.*

69. *Ibid.,* p 158.

70. USSBS, ADIR, pp 21–22.

71. *Ibid.,* p 83.

72. *Ibid.,* p 84.

73. *Ibid.,* pp 23–26.

74. *Ibid.,* p 8.

75. USSBS, ESBGWE, p 159; USSBS, *Overall Report (European War),* pp 19–21.

76. Daily Journal, Jan 4, 1944, Spaatz Papers, LC, Box 14.

77. Spaatz to Doolittle and Twining, Mar 2, 1944, Twining Papers, LC, Box 118.

78. Spaatz to Twining, Mar 2, 1944, Twining Papers, LC, Box 118.

79. Anderson to Kuter, Feb 11, 1944, Spaatz Papers, LC, Box 143.

80. Intvw, Col Philip Hughes (Chief Planner, USSTAF), Mar 20, 1944, Spaatz Papers, LC, Box 135; "Plan for the Completion of the Combined Bomber Offensive," Mar 5, 1944, PRO-AIR 37/1025.

81. The minutes of this meeting are in PRO-AIR 8/1190. Tedder's views are summarized in a paper he prepared for the meeting: "Employment of Allied Air Forces in Support of OVERLORD," Mar 24, 1944, PRO-AIR 37/1028.

82. Eisenhower's directive, drafted by Tedder, placed attacks on the Luftwaffe in first priority and attacks on communications in second. A copy of the directive is printed in Webster and Frankland, *Strategic Air War,* vol IV, appendix 8, xxxviii, pp 167–70.

83. Spaatz to Eisenhower, Mar 31, 1944, PRO-AIR 37/1011.

84. W. W. Rostow, *Pre-Invasion Bombing Strategy* (Austin, Tex., 1982), p 148, n 28. This work is a very interesting account of the view from inside the USSTAF world.

85. Diary, Apr 19, 1944, Spaatz Papers, LC, Box 14. Spaatz always maintained that air superiority was his first priority throughout the period of strategic debate in March and April of 1944. Spaatz interview with B. C. Hopper (USSTAF Historian), May 1945, Spaatz Papers,

Box 135. Hughes, however, told Hopper in June 1944 that the Oil Plan had not been approved on its merits. The emphasis on its contribution to air battles and hence to air superiority was, in his words, "a pretext." Hughes interview with B. C. Hopper, Jun 13, 1944, Spaatz Papers, Box 135. On the other hand, General Anderson noted on Apr 19: "In view of the lack of fighter reaction, we are more anxious than ever to secure two days of grace in which we can attack targets of our choice in an effort to force the attrition of the German Air Force." Anderson Journal, Apr 19, 1944, Spaatz Papers, Box 316, all LC.

    86. The figures discussed in this and succeeding paragraphs are taken from USSBS, *Overall Report (European War)*, p 44, and USSBS, *ESBGWE*, table 42, p 80.

    87. USSBS, *ESBGWE*, table 42, p 80.

    88. *Ibid;* USSBS, *Overall Report (European War)*, p 44.

    89. AHB, *The Rise and Fall of the German Air Force*, pp 334–35.

    90. Murray, *Strategy for Defeat*, p 226. Prof. Murray's work has served to draw our attention to the very significant casualties absorbed by the Luftwaffe in the early and relatively weaker period of the daylight bombing offensive.

    91. "Statistical Summary of Eighth AF Operations," AFHRC A5871, fr 0855.

    92. *Ibid.*, fr 844.

    93. Webster and Frankland, *Strategic Air War*, vol IV, appendix 49, table xxvii, p 500.

    94. These figures are compiled from the tables constructed by the British Air Ministry, Air Historical Branch, from German records: "Luftwaffe Losses in the Area of Luftflotte *Reich*, January to April, 1944"; "Luftwaffe Losses in the Area of Luftflotte Reich, May 1944"; "Luftwaffe Losses in the Area of Luftflotte Reich, June 1944"; "Luftwaffe Losses on the Western Front, January through April 1944"; "Luftwaffe Losses on the Western Front, May, 1944"; and "Luftwaffe Losses on the Western Front, June 1944." These are found on AFHRC K5002 and K5003.

    95. Murray, *Strategy for Defeat*, table LII.

    96. "Luftwaffe Strength and Serviceability Tables"

    97. "Statistical Summary of Eighth AF Operations," AFHRC A5871, fr 0840–1.

    98. "Statistical Story of the Fifteenth Air Force," NARA, RG 243, Box 84.

    99. Leigh-Mallory left no memoir and no biography has been done. He was killed in an air crash on his way to assume the post of Air C-in-C, SEAC. See the entry in the *Dictionary of National Biography*.

    100. Leigh-Mallory expressed these views on several occasions, beginning as early as mid-1943 when he first assumed planning responsibility for OVERLORD operations. Spaatz openly disagreed from the time they first discussed this subject. Diary, Jan 3, 1944, Spaatz Papers, LC, Box 14; Minutes, SCAEF Meeting, Jan 21, 1944, PRO-AIR 37/1011.

    101. AHB, "The RAF in the Bombing Offensive Against Germany," vol VI, AFHRC 23355.

    102. There were several drafts of the Transportation Plan. What appears to be the third draft is in PRO-AIR 37/1028.

    103. JCS 442, Aug 5, 1943, "Operation OVERLORD."

    104. *Ibid.*

    105. AHB, "The Liberation of Northwest Europe," vol I, p 125.

    106. *Ibid.*, p 70.

    107. *Ibid.*, pp 75–76, 125–26.

    108. *Ibid.*, pp 126–28.

    109. Anderson to Director of Operations, Apr 25, 1944, AFHRC A5615, fr 0458.

    110. Spaatz to Eisenhower, May 5, 1944, AFHRC A5687A, fr 0500.

    111. "Minutes of a Meeting held in the Air C-in-C's Office Headquarters, AEAF, on Saturday, May 6, 1944, to Discuss Bombing Targets," PRO-AIR 37/1041.

    112. Minutes, Allied Air Commanders' Meeting, Jun 3, 1944, PRO-AIR 37/563.

    113. AHB, "The Liberation of Northwest Europe," vol III, pp 33–34.

    114. 8th Abteilung, Luftwaffe General Staff, "Some Aspects of the German Fighter Effort During the Initial Stages of the Invasion of Northwest Europe," Nov 18, 1944, AFHRC A5421, fr 1017. The author of this report, Oberst Hettig, had been Chief of Staff of II *Jagdkorps*, the main fighter organization in *Luftflotte* III before and during the invasion.

    115. *Ibid.*, fr 1019.

    116. AHB, "The Liberation of Northwest Europe," vol III, pp 15–17, 69–76.

117. *Ibid.*, pp 31–33.

118. *Ibid.*, p 32.

119. The details in this account are drawn chiefly from two important secondary sources: AHB, "The Rise and Fall of the German Air Force, 1939–1945," pp 323–33; and Murray, pp 279–84. Useful German contemporary sources are two reports prepared for the 8th Abteilung the Luftwaffe General Staff: "Some Aspects of the German Fighter Effort During the Initial Stages of the Invasion of Northwest Europe," Nov 18, 1944; "Air Operations Over the Western Front in June 1944," Aug 27, 1944. These are available in translations made by RAF AHB on AFHRC A5421.

120. 8th Abteilung, Hettig Report, fr 1019. Murray quotes this document on page 281.

121. AHB, "Rise and Fall," p 330.

122. AHB, "Rise and Fall," p 331.

123. 8th Abteilung, Hettig Report, fr 1021–28.

124. *Ibid.*, fr 1021.

125. AHB, "Rise and Fall," pp 330–31.

126. On sources for Luftwaffe losses, see note 94 above. For American losses, see "Statistical Summary of Eighth AF Operations, Aug 17, 1942 to May 8, 1945," AFHRC A5871, fr 0840–1; "Statistical Summary of Ninth AF Operations, Oct 16, 1943 to May 8, 1945," AFHRC B5587, fr 1621–627.

127. On the vulnerability of Luftwaffe transmissions, see Ralph Bennet, *ULTRA in the West* (New York, 1980), p 7 and F. H. Hinsley, *et al.*, *British Secret Intelligence in the Second World War*, vol I (London, 1979), appendix 1. To compare the vulnerability of Luftwaffe cyphers with those employed by other agencies, see the table in Hinsley, *et al.*, vol II (New York, 1981), appendix 4, "Enigma Keys Attacked by GC and CS up to mid-1943."

128. Anderson Journal, Mar 3, 1944, Spaatz Papers, LC, Box 316.

129. Arnold to Spaatz, Apr 24, 1944, Spaatz Papers, LC, Box 14.

130. USAAF, *ULTRA and the History of the United States Strategic Air Force in Europe vs. the German Air Force*, (hereafter cited as USAAF-ULTRA) (Frederick, Md., 1980), pp 61-62. (This report was originally written in 1945.)

131. USSBS, AIDR, table V–7, p 74.

132. Spaatz to Twining, Mar 2, 1944, Twining Papers, LC, Box 118.

133. Intvw, Col R. D. Hughes, with USSTAF Historian, Mar 20, 1944, Spaatz Papers, LC, Box 135.

134. Enemy Objectives Unit, "Use of Strategic Air Power after Mar 1, 1944," Feb 28, 1944, AFHRC A5615, fr 0681. Key figures in the EOU were W. W. Rostow, C. P. Kindleberger, and Carl Kaysen, all of whom were to become well-known academics in the postwar period.

135. AC/AS, Intelligence, "Strategic Aerial Bombardment of Europe, Jan 1 to Mar 31, 1944," Mar 20, 1944, AFHRC A1254, fr 1456.

136. USSBS, ADIR, pp 8, 73. Interestingly, an intercepted report of the Japanese Naval Attaché to his superiors in Tokyo (an item produced by MAGIC) reported that he had information from Field Marshal Milch that monthly production during February and March was 1,400 fighters. Apparently this was dismissed because of Milch's supposed interest in impressing his ally by inflating the figures. This is a useful example of the self-defeating cleverness one sometimes finds in intelligence analysis. USAAF-ULTRA, pp 91–92.

137. For an extended discussion of the Allied understanding of the German economy during the war, see Hinsley, *British Secret Intelligence,* vol I, chap 7; vol II, chap 18; vol III, chap 30 (New York, 1984).

138. *Ibid.*, vol III, pp 317–18.

139. *Ibid.*, pp 320–22.

140. USAAF-ULTRA, pp 98–99.

141. For information about the impact of intelligence on air superiority operations in France, see USAAF-ULTRA, pp 107–44; Ronald Lewin, *ULTRA Goes to War* (New York, 1978), pp 298, 329–35; and Ralph Bennet, *ULTRA in the West* (New York, 1980), pp 52–58, 85-86. The Hinsley series, volumes I–IV, has provided a good deal more about this subject.

Bibliographical Essay

The struggle to gain air superiority for OVERLORD and the strategic bombing campaign of which it formed a part have been among the most widely discussed subjects in the literature of the Second World War. A short essay of this kind cannot hope to be exhaustive, but a few of the most reliable and interesting items can be identified.

Even after a considerable passage of time, the official history—*The Army Air Forces in World War II*—edited by Wesley Frank Craven and James Lea Cate, 7 vols, (Chicago: University of Chicago Press, 1948–58; reprint, Office of Air Force History, 1983) remains a solid piece of scholarship. Its major shortcomings are to be found in those subjects that it fails to treat or passes over lightly, chiefly intelligence and the less edifying aspects of the organizational politics of high command. Of equal importance to the subject are the four volumes of the British official history, *The Strategic Air Offensive Against Germany,* 4 vols (London: HMSO, 1961), written by Sir Charles Webster and Noble Frankland. This work is especially important for its repeated emphasis on the fact that air strategy was (and, by implication, still is) dominated by operational factors. A good single-volume introduction to the strategic air war is Anthony Verrier, *The Bomber Offensive* (New York: Macmillan, 1969). Basil Collier's *The Defence of the United Kingdom* (London: HMSO, 1957) is essential to understanding the achievement and maintenance of air superiority over the Allied base of operations. All four volumes of the newest of the official histories have been published—*British Intelligence in the Second World War* by F. H. Hinsley, *et al.* (London: HMSO, 1978–84). While they do not satisfy our curiosity in every respect, they are clearly superior to anything else on this subject, official or private. The failure to produce an American counterpart is to be regretted.

The best single volume is R. J. Overy, *The Air War, 1939–1945* (New York: Stein and Day, 1980). Its coverage is comprehensive, its analysis is comparative, and its interpretation judicious. Overy's *Goering: The "Iron Man"* (London: Routledge and Kegan Paul, 1984) is of a similar quality. Among the general histories of the Luftwaffe, two are most important. The British Air Ministry study, *The Rise and Fall of the German Air Force, 1939–1945* (London: HMSO, 1948; reprint, New York: St. Martin's, 1983) is dated but contains some useful information. Williamson Murray's *Strategy for Defeat: The Luftwaffe, 1933–1945* (Maxwell AFB: Air University Press, 1983) is a recent and important addition to the literature. Murray has made extensive use of the German archival material originally held by the British Air Ministry and subsequently returned to Germany. He has emphasized how critical the production decisions made early in the war were to the defeat of the Luftwaffe. He has also made the valuable point that the attrition inflicted by the suffering Eighth Air Force in the last six months of 1943 was a very important contribution to air superiority in 1944.

Good German scholarship has begun to appear in recent years. To date it has concentrated principally on the rearmament period and the early part of the war. Especially important are: Klaus Maier, "Der Aufbau der Luftwaffe and Ihre Strategish-Operative Konzeption Insbesondere Gegenueber den Westmaechten," in *Deutschland und Frankreich, 1936–39* (Munich: Artemis Verlag, 1981), and the section on the Luftwaffe in Wilhelm Deist, The *Wehrmacht and German Rearmament* (Toronto: University of Toronto Press, 1981). The tendency of the Luftwaffe leadership to concentrate narrowly on operations to the exclusion of the problems of production, logistics, and training is brought out in Horst Boog, "Higher Command and Leadership in the German Luftwaffe, 1935–45," *Air Power and Warfare* (Washington: Office of Air Force History, 1979) pp 128–58; and "The Luftwaffe and Technology," *Aerospace Historian*, September 1983, pp 201–06. Also important are the sections on the Luftwaffe and the air war in volumes one and two of *Das Deutsche Reich und die Zweite Weltkrieg* (Stuttgart: Deutsche Verlags-Anstalt, 1979).

Eighth Air Force has not been as well served as RAF Bomber Command in its historians. Most treatments of the former have been rather shallow popular histories that have not delved into anything but the technical side with any persistence. Max Hasting's *Bomber Command* (London: Michael Joseph, 1979) is a stimulating work of the kind that could be read with profit by any serving officer. Nothing serious has been done for Fifteenth Air Force. USSTAF, AEAF, and SHAEF (Air) await their historians. Historical narratives for the latter two organizations can be found in the Public Record Office at Air 37/1057–60. Narratives exist both for SHAEF (AIR) and AEAF in the Public Record Office. No serious study has yet been done of the British or American Air Staffs.

There is also a dearth of good biographies. Thomas Coffey's *Hap: The Story of the U.S. Air Force and the Man Who Built It* (New York: Viking, 1982) is a popular and largely uncritical history. James Parton's *"Air Force Spoken Here": General Ira Eaker and the Command of the Air* (New York: Adler and Adler, 1986) and David Mets's *Master of Airpower: General Carl A. Spaatz* (Novato, Calif.: Presidio Press, 1988) are of particular interest since they are recent publications and are the first full-length biographies of their subjects. Denis Richards's *Portal of Hungerford* (London: Heinemann, 1978) is the authorized biography. No biographies have been done of Tedder or Leigh-Mallory; Harris has received ample treatment in Webster and Frankland, in Hastings, and in Charles Messenger, *"Bomber Harris" and the Strategic Bomber Offensive* (New York: St. Martin's, 1984). DeWitt S. Copp's two volumes—*A Few Great Captains* and *Forged in Fire* (New York: Doubleday, 1980, 1982)—are a useful attempt at a "collective biography" of the American air leadership.

Of the senior air commanders, only Arnold and Tedder produced memoirs, although Harris's *Bomber Offensive* (London: Macmillan, 1947) might also be included in that category. Tedder's *With Prejudice* (London: Cassell, 1966) is the best of the three. Recently, there have appeared two very interesting accounts from persons who were rendering advice at high levels—Lord Zuckerman's *From Apes to Warlords* (London: Hamish Hamilton, 1978) and W. W. Rostow's *Pre-Invasion Bombing Strategy* (Austin: University of Texas Press, 1982). These represent two opposing views of the merits in the great dispute over oil and transportation.

Among the printed sources, by far the most useful are the reports of the United States Strategic Bombing Survey. The *Aircraft Division Industry Report* and the *Effects of Strategic Bombing on the German War Economy* are indispensable to any serious student of the air war. David MacIssac has published an edited version of the Survey's most important reports in ten volumes (New York: Garland Press, 1976).

The struggle for air superiority was in large measure a *Materielschlacht*. The sections on production in Overy are essential reading. For the Luftwaffe, see E. L. Homze, *Arming the Luftwaffe* (Lincoln: University of Nebraska Press, 1976) and Overy, "The German Pre-War Aircraft Production Plans" *English Historical Review*, XC (1975). The USSBS *Aircraft Division Industry Report* is an important source for wartime production. The British record is discussed in M. M. Postan, *British War Production* (London: HMSO, 1952); the American in I. B. Holley, *Buying Aircraft: Materiel Procurement for the Army Air Forces* (Washington: GPO, 1964).

On the American and British side there is a wealth of manuscript resources. British records are, especially in cases of policy disputes, somewhat more illuminating because British administrative practice was more orderly and employed formal internal memoranda ("minutes") much more than was the case in the AAF. AEAF and SHAEF (AIR) papers are found at Air 37 in the Public Record Office; Bomber Command at Air 14; and Chief of Air Staff at Air 8. Many valuable documents from lower echelons in the Air Staff may be found by persistent searching in Air 20, Unregistered Papers. One can find, for example, papers originally written by staff of the Directorate of Bomber Operations. Sir Charles Portal's papers are in the keeping of the Library, Christ Church, Oxford. On the American side there are three large collections deposited in the Library of Congress Manuscript Division—the Arnold, Spaatz, and Eaker Papers. Each contains a marvelous set of correspondence. The Spaatz Papers also have Daily Journals and the transcripts of some interviews made by the USSTAF Historian, Dr. Bruce Hopper, in 1944 and 1945. Other valuable manuscript items are held by the USAF Archives at Maxwell AFB. Of particular interest are documents generated by Eighth Air Force, USSTAF, and of course, AAF Headquarters itself. Especially important are internal memoranda, reports, plans, and statistical material. Given the eternal mysteries of the War Department decimal filing system, however, one is condemned to the hunt-and-hope technique in utilizing these materials.

7

Air Superiority in the Southwest Pacific

Joe Gray Taylor

The Japanese achieved their initial objectives in World War II in a much shorter period than they had anticipated. They had incorporated the oil resources of the East Indies into their empire, had cut off the Burma Road, the only land route by which supplies could reach China, and had established a defensive perimeter that extended from northern Papua in eastern New Guinea to Rabaul in New Britain, the northern Solomon Islands, the Gilbert Islands, the eastern Marshall Islands, and Wake Island. In addition to Rabaul, this perimeter was backed by strong bases at Truk in the Caroline Islands, at Saipan in the Marianas, and bases soon to be developed in the Philippine Islands. The ease of their early conquests led the Japanese to launch offensives in May of 1942 that were intended to conquer Port Moresby on the southern coast of New Guinea, to occupy the southern Solomon Islands with the eventual objective of cutting off American sea lanes to Australia, to occupy Midway Island west of Hawaii, and to occupy positions in the Aleutian Islands.

This second Japanese offensive was mainly a failure because of United States naval victories in the Battles of the Coral Sea and of Midway in May and June of 1942, but these defeats made no great difference in overall Japanese strategy. That strategy was to make an Allied offensive against the newly expanded Japanese empire so expensive in blood and treasure that the United States and its Allies would have no choice but to negotiate a peace favorable to Japan.

Planning for the Pacific Campaign

The basic strategy of the United States and her Allies was to defeat Germany first and then finish off Japan. However, it was not possible to take a completely defensive posture in the Pacific, because even after the Battle of the Coral Sea, the Japanese continued to move down the Solomon Island chain toward the supply lines to Australia and subsequently mounted a land attack against Port Moresby from the north coast of New Guinea. When these drives had been checked, as they were before the end of 1942 on Guadalcanal and in the Owen Stanley Mountains of New Guinea, Allied forces were able to continue a limited offensive.

Because of the great distance in the Pacific, active American theaters were created. The Central Pacific theater under Adm. Chester Nimitz would conduct the main American offensive toward the Japanese home islands (but its campaigns will seldom appear in this account). To fight the battle of Guadalcanal and then to move northward up the Solomons, the South Pacific theater was formed, first under Vice Adm. Robert L. Ghormley and then under Adm. William Halsey. The basic objective in the South Pacific was the great fortress the Japanese had established at Rabaul, on northern New Britain. When the South Pacific command had served its purpose, it was to be absorbed into the Southwest Pacific Area (SWPA) command, which had been established in Australia under Gen. Douglas MacArthur.

The mission of the Southwest Pacific Area was to defend Australia and then to establish Allied control over Papua (eastern New Guinea) as soon as possible. SWPA was also expected to play a major role in the capture, or as later decided, the neutralization,* of Rabaul. Finally, SWPA was assigned, over the objections of the Central Pacific command, the mission of advancing westward along the New Guinea coast, and then northward to free the Philippine Islands from Japanese occupation.

Air superiority was essential to the accomplishment of these Allied objectives. Air superiority may be defined as a condition in a given geographical area in which the air arm of one side was strong enough to successfully defend air, ground, and naval bases, naval units at sea, and ground forces in action from attacks by enemy air. Likewise, the air arm possessing air superiority could carry out successful offensive operations against enemy air bases, ground units, and naval craft and installations, and could overcome the enemy air force's air defense efforts. Air superiority, if successfully exploited, could lead to air supremacy, a condition in which enemy air, with the possible exception of occasional reconnaissance missions

---

*The word neutralization, as used in this essay, means to render a base or other position still occupied by an enemy incapable of any longer making a significant contribution to the enemy's war effort.

and small scale harassing strikes at night, simply could not operate in a given area.

This essay will deal with the achievement of air superiority in both the South Pacific and the Southwest Pacific. Because the two theaters shared Rabaul as a common objective, the two efforts simply cannot be separated. First it was necessary to gain air superiority over Port Moresby. Then as Allied forces moved nearer Rabaul or along the coast of New Guinea, air superiority had to precede the amphibious operations by which this movement was accomplished.

The first task facing Allied air, however, was to achieve air superiority over the southern Solomons and over Port Moresby, which was no small task. Incredible as it may seem, the Army Air Forces entered the Second World War without any real idea as to how air superiority was to be obtained or maintained. Doctrine and tactics were developed on a trial-and-error basis after the war began.

During the First World War, pursuit aircraft (later designated fighter aircraft) had been dominant in aerial warfare, and for some years after the end of hostilities fighter aircraft continued to dominate the thinking of American air officers. For a number of reasons, however, the role of fighter aircraft came to be neglected in theory and in practice. Since fighter aircraft, in the actual course of the Second World War, would play an absolutely essential role in the achievement of air superiority and, as it turned out, in carrying out a strategic bombing campaign, this neglect had most serious consequences.

The fighter aircraft of the late 1920s and the early 1930s were little faster than the bombers of the same period, and even now it is a truism that interceptors must be much faster than bombers in order to attack them successfully. The speed factor seemed especially important after it became evident that the four-engine Boeing B–17 would be the primary U.S. bomber. Unfortunately for thousands of bomber crewmen who were shot down by German and Japanese fighters in 1942 and 1943, the speed of fighter aircraft approximately doubled between 1930 and 1940; the speed of the B–17 remained the same, or even declined as more defensive armament was added. In defense of Air Corps thinking, it should also be noted that war scenarios of the 1930s assumed an attack upon the continental United States by sea. Certainly bombers might be expected to play a much greater role than fighters in turning back such an invasion.[1]

The primary reason for the neglect of the role of fighter aircraft was adherence by the majority of Air Corps officers to the doctrine of strategic bombing. The strategic bombing advocates maintained that bombardment aircraft, striking at an enemy's heartland, could destroy an enemy's ability as well as his will to make war. In the minds of American air officers this relatively cheap victory was going to be accomplished by "daylight precision bombing." Such Air Corps leaders as Henry H. "Hap" Arnold,

325

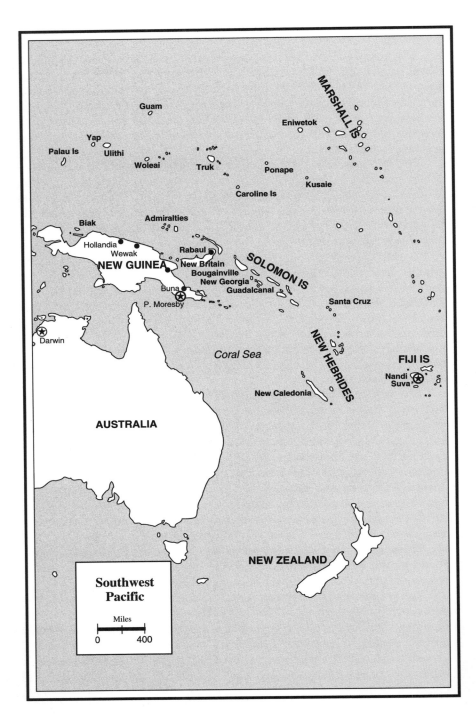

Southwest
Pacific

Miles

0   400

326

Ira C. Eaker, Harold L. George, Lawrence S. Kuter, and Haywood S. Hansell, among others, believed that bombers would not only be fast enough to get through to their targets without unacceptable losses, but after the speed of fighter aircraft had increased so rapidly, the bombers would also be able to fight their way through to their targets. In the grim laboratory of war, of course, the B–17 and the B–24 could not speed safely to their targets in daylight; they could not fight their way through without unacceptable losses; and when faced with enemy antiaircraft fire and interceptors over the target, their bombing was far from precise. Nevertheless, it was to this strategy that the Air Corps was committed, and as a result, the development of doctrine, tactics, and even the aircraft for the interception of enemy bombers and the escort of our own, was neglected.[2]

The aftermath of this neglect would have been even more serious had not a few officers been more farsighted than their peers. The most important of these was Capt. Claire Chennault, instructor in pursuit tactics at the Air Corps Tactical School. Chennault was one of the few officers in the 1930s who gave serious thought to fighter tactics. He experimented with the two-plane element as the basic combat unit for fighters. He also insisted that it was possible to establish an intelligence net to make effective interception of bombers possible. On one occasion he set up a civilian-manned telephonic net that enabled him to have fighters exactly in place for interception when war-game bombers arrived at their target. Not even Chennault, however, seems to have appreciated the importance of the fighter as an offensive weapon against enemy air. In the Southwest Pacific, this and much more had to be learned under combat conditions.[3]

When war broke out over Pearl Harbor, the fighter aircraft in service in the United States armed forces were almost all obsolete and at a definite disadvantage when pitted against Japanese fighters. The P–39 Bell Aircobra was in production for the Army Air Forces, but in combat it was to prove a great disappointment. Designed in 1936, it had a slow rate of climb, was not particularly maneuverable, and performed poorly at high altitude. Its maximum range was only 600 miles, which was also a serious impediment. The P–40 was a much better plane, even though it was designed only a year later. It was not quite as fast as the P–39 at medium altitudes, but given time it could climb to well above 20,000 feet. Compared to Japanese fighters, the P–40 was not as maneuverable, but it had two significant advantages: its rugged construction and the fact that it could dive faster than lighter Japanese aircraft. Used correctly, the P–40 was equal to or even superior to the Japanese fighters of 1942 and 1943, but it too was handicapped by a limited range.[4]

The United States Navy had several hundred F2A–2 Brewster Buffalo fighters at the beginning of the war, but these obsolete planes, though they saw combat at Midway and in Allied hands elsewhere, were far from equal to Japanese fighters. Much more reliable was the F4F Grumman Wildcat, which first saw action over Wake Island and later played a major role in the Battle of Guadalcanal. The P–40 and the F4F were the mainstays of American air defense during the first two years of the war in the Pacific, but the Army Air Forces' P–38 Lightning, P–47 Thunderbolt, and P–51 Mustang, and the Navy's F4U Corsair and F6F Hellcat, would get into action in time to play an important role in the final achievement of air superiority in the Pacific.[5]

In the first few months of World War II, the air power of the United States suffered defeat after defeat in the Pacific. Aircraft at Pearl Harbor were parked close together in the open, simplifying the task of Japanese bombers and fighters; and the Japanese effected complete surprise. In the Philippines, the Army had been alerted by the attack on Pearl Harbor, and overcast skies delayed the Japanese attack. Even so, and for reasons still not understood, the American air command was caught with its planes, including a sizable proportion of the nation's heavy bomber strength, on the ground. There they suffered destruction comparable to that in the Hawaiian Islands. In Indonesia, then the Dutch East Indies, American and some Dutch air resistance was perhaps a bit more effective than in the Philippines, but not significantly so. Certainly it was not enough to delay the Japanese occupation of those islands.[6]

Many reasons may be given for the dramatic success of the Japanese in the first months after Pearl Harbor. Surprise was a major factor. Certainly in December 1941 the Japanese were better prepared for war than was the United States, but their superiority in materiel was not so great as is often assumed. In Hawaii and the Philippines there were enough American fighters and bombers to have offered strong resistance and perhaps even to have prevented the establishment of Japanese air superiority. A significant number of the Allies' men and planes were fed into the battle for the East Indies, but they arrived in driblets and were often destroyed one way or another before they got into combat. Some vitally needed fighters were never even assembled after arrival. The Japanese quickly achieved air superiority, put an umbrella of fighter planes over their invading land and naval forces, sent their bombers against Allied forces, and went where they willed.[7]

The Japanese also had some advantage in quality of men and materiel. Japanese aircraft were more maneuverable than American aircraft, and they had significantly greater range. Range was of tremendous importance in the vast reaches of the Pacific Ocean, and maneuverability made the Japanese fighters far superior to Allied opponents until new tactics took advantage of the armor, the more powerful engines, and the greater weight of American aircraft. The Japanese pilot training program was longer and more rigorous than that of the U.S. Army Air Forces and even that of carrier pilots of the U.S. Navy. Fortunately for the Allies, the number of these

The Curtiss P–40 (*above*) and the Grumman F4F Wildcat (*below*) were the
mainstay U.S. fighters during the early years of the war in the Pacific.

highly trained Japanese pilots was not large, and as war took its toll, Japan was never able to replace them. The United States did not have nearly as many military pilots in combat units in December 1941 as did the Japanese, but an effective training program that would redress the balance was already in operation.[8]

Once the Japanese began winning, momentum was on their side, and they took full advantage of it. The small size of the ground units they deployed appeared at first glance to have constituted almost a reckless gamble, but they had air and naval superiority, and only in the Philippines did they encounter significant ground opposition. The Japanese, once ridiculed in the American press, became for a short time almost supermen, and their air arm seemed, at least to the public and the beleaguered soldier or sailor who suffered under its attacks, a superior air force. However, this was not actually the case. All the Allies had to do was to mobilize and to adapt. The Japanese advance was checked less than six months after it began, and from mid-1942 onward, though there would be many anxious moments, the tide of war flowed in favor of the Allies. The achievement of air superiority and its retention were a vital part, perhaps the most essential part, of the Allied effort to check Japan's military ambitions and then effect her complete defeat.

Battles of the Coral Sea and Midway

Victories had come so easily and with such light losses that the Japanese high command decided to speed up the timetable for establishing an expanded defensive perimeter, with the intention of making American attempts at a counterattack more difficult and prompting a decisive engagement with the U.S. Navy. The Japanese plan was first to take Tulagi in the Solomon Islands and Port Moresby on the south coast of New Guinea, bringing northern Australia under the threat of invasion; then to occupy Midway Island and eventually Samoa, Fiji, and New Caledonia so as to cut off communications between the United States and Australia.

In attempting to achieve the first part of their plan, the Japanese became embroiled in the Battle of the Coral Sea, the outcome of which provided a strategic victory for the United States. The Japanese force ordered to occupy Port Moresby eventually turned back with its mission unaccomplished. Land-based Japanese planes from Rabaul in New Britain and land-based Allied planes from northern Australia and Port Moresby had a slight role in this battle; basically it was a contest between Japanese and American carrier aircraft. Japanese bombers sank the carrier *Lexington,* and the Japanese lost a light carrier. Japanese plane losses were somewhat greater than those suffered by the Americans, and probably a greater proportion of the American airmen were rescued. The Japanese Navy had suffered some aircraft losses at Pearl Harbor, and a raid into the Indian Ocean to Ceylon subsequently brought higher losses. Three of the five carriers that participated in this raid lost so many planes and pilots that they had to return to Japan for replacements. It was also noted that the replacement pilots were not as skilled as their predecessors. These three carriers were not available for the Coral Sea and Midway battles. The loss of one carrier and serious damage to another in the Coral Sea further reduced the force available to the Japanese.[9]

Probably more important than the strategic defeat of the Japanese in the Coral Sea were the lessons learned by the U.S. Navy. The battle clearly proved that the existing Navy carrier planes were inferior to the Japanese planes and that they must be replaced as soon as possible. Further, it was demonstrated that carriers should have a greater proportion of fighters among the aircraft carried; at one time it was necessary to use SBDs (Douglas Dauntless dive bombers) as fighters to oppose Japanese torpedo bombers. It also became evident that carrier-based fighters should have greater range in order to intercept attacking enemy aircraft at a distance from the carriers they were protecting. Additional fighters were aboard the carriers less than a month later when they went into battle at Midway.[10]

The U.S. naval forces that survived the Coral Sea battle hastened back to the Central Pacific where a much more powerful Japanese fleet was known to be advancing on Midway Island. The surviving carrier, the *Yorktown*, was joined northeast of Midway by the carriers *Enterprise* and *Hornet*. They managed to remain undiscovered until their dive bombers were raining fatal destruction upon three of the four Japanese carriers in the action; the fourth survived long enough to launch a strike that mortally wounded *Yorktown*, but was then sent to the bottom. Plane losses were exceptionally high for the American carriers, but a substantial number of downed airmen were rescued. Midway was without question a decisive American victory.[11]

Although it was not fully apparent at the time, the battle was actually a turning point because it established the superiority of U.S. carrier-borne aviation over Japanese carrier-borne aviation for the remainder of the war. In other words, the U.S. Navy had established air superiority in the Pacific so long as American carriers were out of range of land-based Japanese air power. The productive capacity of American shipyards and the aviation training program in the United States would expand this superiority as the war progressed. The most important factor in this achievement was undoubtedly the losses inflicted on Japanese flying personnel. Men who were the product of several years of intensive training were lost to Japan forever, and years were not available for the training of replacements.[12]

Japan was far from admitting defeat in mid-1942. On the contrary, it was operating a seaplane base at Tulagi and building an airfield on

Guadalcanal in the southern Solomons, posing a very real threat to Allied communications. As noted previously, the plan to occupy Port Moresby had not been abandoned. Since the sea route had been denied them, the Japanese decided to move against this objective by land. On July 21, a landing was made at Buna, on the north coast of New Guinea, and troops began advancing across the Owen Stanley Mountains. Because Australia's best troops had been sent to North Africa and Singapore, the advance was opposed by poorly trained and poorly equipped militia. The Japanese quickly established an airfield at Buna and seemed well on the way to establishing air superiority over eastern New Guinea. Rabaul was the base for both the Solomon Islands and the New Guinea offensives, and from Rabaul, Japanese fighters and bombers could reach both Port Moresby and, if necessary, Guadalcanal.

Guadalcanal

On August 7, 1942, U.S. Marines went ashore at Tulagi, where they met heavy resistance, and at Guadalcanal, where the Japanese labor troops working on the airfield fled. The ease of the Guadalcanal landing was deceptive because it was the beginning of a battle that would last into February of the next year and would cost each of the contending powers thousands of lives, hundreds of aircraft, and scores of ships before it was resolved. The real objective of this struggle was the airfield on Guadalcanal, Henderson Field as it was quickly named, the possession of which was the key to the control of the southern Solomon Islands.

Douglas TBD Devastators on board the USS *Enterprise* prior to take off for the Battle of Midway; only four of these torpedo-bombers returned.

Japanese fighters burn on an island airstrip following an attack by Fifth Air Force bombers.

The Japanese had a number of advantages at the beginning of this struggle. The Imperial Navy was still stronger than the U.S. Navy, although the disparity was not nearly so great as it had been just after the attack on Pearl Harbor or just before the Battle of Midway. Japanese fighter aircraft were still far more maneuverable than American planes, and American pilots had not yet learned fully how to take advantage of their planes' strong points. Probably most important of all, Japanese fighters and bombers had the range to operate over Guadalcanal from their main base at Rabaul, though closer bases were soon built on nearby New Georgia and Bougainville. At the time of the American landings, B–17s were the only land-based American aircraft that could operate over Guadalcanal from existing bases, and they were very few. Even when Allied fighters and dive bombers were based at Henderson Field, they did not have nearly the range to strike the Japanese base at Rabaul.

The landings on August 7 were supported by carrier aircraft, which were able to turn back a hastily mounted Japanese attack on that day. Much heavier bombing attacks, delivered by torpedo bombers and dive bombers under fighter escort, came in the next day, and one American transport was lost. More important, however, the naval commander was convinced that carriers could no longer operate safely in the Guadalcanal area, and the withdrawal of the carriers meant the withdrawal of all ships. For eleven days, the Marines were defenseless against air attack except for a limited number of antiaircraft guns. Much of the materiel not landed was needed to put the airfield into operation. Fortunately, the Japanese had left some equipment behind, which was used. The field was ready for a limited number of aircraft on August 20.[13]

The real air struggle for Guadalcanal began on that date, for on August

20, escort carrier *Long Island* launched nineteen Marine Corps F4Fs and twelve Marine SBDs that landed at Henderson Field. Two days later part of the AAF 67th Fighter Squadron arrived with P–400s (export versions of the P–39). A complement of Naval SBDs from the *Enterprise* landed on August 24, and nineteen more F4Fs and twelve more SBDs came in before the end of August. This was not enough. The aircraft that arrived on the 20th were in action the next day. Combat losses were surprisingly low in view of the amount of flying done. American pilots claimed five or six Japanese planes for each American plane shot down, and operations went on steadily day after day. Furthermore, many planes were lost in takeoff or landing accidents on the primitive airfield, and some were destroyed by the Japanese bombing attacks. The P–400s proved practically useless in air combat and were relegated to supporting ground troops.[14]

The pilots defending Guadalcanal had some help. Aircraft carriers joined in the fight at crucial moments, but this could be only at times of crisis. Not until Luzon in 1945 would the United States have enough carriers and the Japanese air force be weak enough, for these precious ships to remain in combat for more than a few days at a time. As it was, two of the three carriers in the South Pacific in August of 1942 were lost before the Battle of Guadalcanal was over, and *Enterprise,* the survivor, was badly damaged. B–17s based at Espiritu Santo performed valuable reconnaissance and, eventually, by staging through Henderson Field, were able to strike at Japanese bases in the northern Solomons, even though they were weak blows. Navy PBYs (Catalinas) also performed valuable reconnaissance and now and then delivered bombs—and once torpedos—at shipping targets. Southwest Pacific bombers struck at Rabaul from Port Moresby, but these too were relatively weak attacks. Yet, in a fight so close as Guadalcanal any help was much to be desired.[15]

Also to the advantage of Henderson Field's aerial defenders was the great distance the attacking Japanese aircraft had to fly. This meant that planes coming from Rabaul had to arrive near the middle of the day or later, so there was some respite in the mornings and afternoons. Early warning radar, not so efficient in 1942 as it would be later in the war, enabled work on the airfield to continue until shortly before Japanese bombs began to fall. Almost certainly, however, the greatest blessing for the defenders of Henderson Field was the fact that the Australians, in evacuating the Solomons, had left behind coastwatchers. These brave men gave warning of Japanese attacks long before (sometimes almost an hour) the bombers arrived overhead. The advance notice gave the hard-pressed F4Fs time to get to altitude from which they could strike the Japanese bombers and fighters from above. The advantage of altitude did much to make up for the Wildcats' disadvantages.[16]

The survival of American air power on Guadalcanal, in the final analysis, depended upon the survival of the airfield. The base could not survive without a flow of supplies, especially gasoline, and the Japanese Navy made every effort to cut these essentials off. Obviously the field could not operate if it was overrun by Japanese infantry, and this too the Japanese attempted with all their might. The field could not be used if it was kept out of operation by bombs from Japanese aircraft; this too the enemy attempted. But Henderson Field was also subject to Japanese naval and artillery bombardment. The Japanese Navy soon ceased operations about Guadalcanal by day, largely because it came under attack by SBDs, but for weeks it operated at night almost with impunity. Nonetheless, the field survived because the Allies rushed in supplies and reinforcements in daylight, enemy bombing was relatively ineffective, the Marines and the Army infantry that arrived later valiantly held their lines, and the engineers and Seabees (Naval Construction Battalions) on Guadalcanal risked their lives filling bomb craters and shell holes so that the F4Fs and SBDs could continue to operate.[17]

In October and November the Japanese made their supreme effort to dislodge U.S. forces from Guadalcanal. On October 13, ninety Marine, Navy, and Army Air Forces planes were operational at Henderson Field, though their gasoline supply was low. The Japanese, determined to establish air superiority, had strongly reinforced Rabaul's airfields in late September and had begun heavy raids on Henderson Field. These attacks reached their peak on the morning of October 13 and Japanese artillery joined in the bombardment. Fifty-three bombs and shells hit the runway, and at one time the Seabees repaired thirteen craters and shell holes while planes waited to land. Then that night came the worst experience endured by the men at Henderson Field: a naval bombardment that included 14-inch shells from battleships. When sunrise came, only forty-two planes were in flying condition. These planes could not fly from the regular runway. However, parallel to the runway was a grass strip that was usable when dry, and it was prepared so that fighters and dive bombers were able to take off there. This was the low point, and from the end of October on, the Allied air strength on Guadalcanal increased steadily. The air battles of October and the Allied naval surface victories of November brought an end to Japanese attempts to reinforce Guadalcanal. Having successfully defended their base, Allied air units could now seek air superiority over the Solomons.[18]

Eastern New Guinea

By mid-1942, remnants of defeated air units from the Philippines and the East Indies, a few Royal Australian Air Force units, a Dutch medium bombardment squadron, and hastily trained replacements from the United

335

Above: **Marines storm ashore in the Solomon Islands in August 1942;**
below: **Repairs being made to the airstrip at Henderson Field after Japanese bombs fell there.**

States provided the aerial defense of Australia. Aircraft from Port Moresby, the most advanced Allied air base to the north, and from Darwin, in northwestern Australia, opposed the Japanese in the East Indies. By the middle of August 1942, Darwin had undergone twenty-seven heavy bombing attacks, and Port Moresby seventy-eight. Japanese losses were not high; strikes at Darwin were intercepted only sporadically, and at Port Moresby, where about five minutes warning was all the defenders received, interception was almost impossible. The defending fighters were P–40s and P–39s, both of which required ample warning to reach the altitude at which Japanese bombers normally operated. When the Japanese took Lae, Salamaua, and then Buna on the north coast of New Guinea and built airstrips in those places, the danger to Port Moresby became much more acute.[19]

As of June 31, 1942, total American air personnel in the Southwest Pacific, all stationed in Australia or at Port Moresby, numbered 20,000. On paper they manned 5 bombardment groups and 3 fighter groups, but 1 heavy group had no aircraft, and the men and B–17s of the 19th Group were exhausted after fighting through the Philippine and East Indies campaigns. The 38th Medium Bombardment Group did not receive its B–25 Mitchell aircraft until September, and two of its squadrons were retained in the South Pacific. The 22d Medium Group, equipped with B–26s Marauders, had been in action since April. The 3d Bombardment Group had a motley assemblage of A–24 (SBD), A–20 (Havoc), and B–25 aircraft. Based in Australia, these bombers had to stage through Port Moresby and then climb over the Owen Stanley Mountains to reach their targets. B–17s that bombed Rabaul were away from their base 48 hours and in the air 18 hours. P–400s of the 8th Fighter Group were at Port Moresby, the 49th Fighter Group was at Darwin with P–40s, and P–39s of the 35th Group were in northern Australia. In addition, the Royal Australian Air Force (RAAF) had 2 squadrons of P–40s at Moresby and about 30 reconnaissance planes (PBY Catalinas and Lockheed Hudsons) in action.[20]

Maj. Gen. George C. Kenney took command of the Allied Air Forces in Australia on August 4, 1942. He made a quick tour of the theater and informed General Douglas MacArthur that he would make achievement of air superiority his first priority. He realized, however, that it would also be necessary to aid the invasion of Guadalcanal by attacking air bases and shipping in the neighborhood of Rabaul. Thus, he sent eighteen bombers over Rabaul in daylight on August 7, the day of the Guadalcanal landing. The Japanese intercepted vigorously, with the result that one B–17 was shot down and nearly all damaged to a greater or lesser extent. Two days later, the Japanese damaged all of seven B–17s over Rabaul, and two of them were wrecked when they attempted to land. Without fighter escort, not even the redoubtable Flying Fortress could mount sustained daylight

337

attacks against a strongly defended target, and for the remainder of the year attacks on Rabaul were at night.[21]

While AAF B-17s and to a lesser extent RAAF PBYs were striking as best they could at Rabaul airfields and shipping, other aircraft were not idle. Fortunately for General Kenney, the Guadalcanal battle absorbed most of the Japanese air effort, but the Japanese land advance from Buna over the mountains toward Port Moresby brought them eventually within twenty-six miles of their goal. If he was to retain his base in New Guinea, Kenney had to render all possible aid to the ground forces opposing the Japanese advance, which he did. Attempts to interdict supplies and reinforcements coming into Buna by sea were not particularly successful. Lack of experience was partly responsible, but so was the fact that the Japanese usually provided air cover for their convoys, and the A-20s and B-26s that made the attacks were understandably inaccurate when under fighter attack. Once again, the need for fighter escort was demonstrated.[22]

Because the war in Europe took precedence over the Pacific War, and the desperate fighting in and over Guadalcanal had temporary priority over New Guinea, the Fifth Air Force, created on September 3, 1942, as a headquarters for the American components of the Allied Air Forces in SWPA, had limited resources for the air superiority battle over Papua. P-40s, P-39s, and P-400s could cross the Owen Stanley Mountains and strike Japanese targets, but they could not fight long air battles with enemy fighters. Their tactics had to be offensive, not defensive. Twenty-five P-38s had arrived in Australia in mid-August, and these twin-engine fighters would give the Fifth Air Force the range needed. Unfortunately, the fuel tanks proved to be defective and had to be rebuilt. It was December before the P-38s could engage in full-scale combat in SWPA. B-26s and B-25s had enough range to attack airfields on the north coast of New Guinea, and by adding bomb-bay tanks to A-20s, "Pappy" Gunn, an inventive genius who served American air power well in the Southwest Pacific, gave these light bombers the range they needed to cross the mountains and strike the north coast. Gunn also added four .50-caliber machineguns to the firepower of the A-20s and made them formidable strafing aircraft.[23]

By August 1942, improved airstrips at Port Moresby permitted Allied aircraft to intensify strikes against Japanese airfields on the north coast of New Guinea. In general, B-26s and B-25s bombed from medium altitude, P-40s glide-bombed, approaching their targets at an angle of about thirty degrees, and other fighters and A-20s strafed. It must be emphasized that Australians played as great or perhaps a greater role in this campaign than American pilots and crews. These attacks kept the runways at Lae, Salamaua, and Buna out of commission part of the time, and they destroyed some Japanese aircraft on the ground and some in the air, but they did not prevent reinforcement from Rabaul. On August 17 a Japanese attack on

338

Port Moresby destroyed eleven Allied aircraft on the ground. Near the end of August, however, radar was installed fifty and thirty miles northwest of Port Moresby, and thereafter Allied fighters were usually able to intercept successfully Japanese daylight attacks. In June, Australian forces had occupied Milne Bay, at the eastern tip of New Guinea, and soon two squadrons of RAAF fighters were stationed there. They played a major role in repulsing a Japanese attempt to take Milne Bay.[24]

On August 25, P–400s swept the Buna strip and claimed ten Japanese planes destroyed on the ground. his was soon followed by another notable strike on September 12, when reconnaissance reported twenty planes on Buna strip. A–20s then went in at treetop level with fragmentation bombs suspended from parachutes (a weapon General Kenney had helped develop before the war) and claimed to have destroyed seventeen of the enemy planes. Attacks on Lae, Salamaua, and Buna continued on an almost daily basis, and on November l, Kenney noted that he had not seen or heard of a Japanese plane over New Guinea in daylight for five weeks. He was confident enough of his local air superiority to move large numbers of ground troops to the Buna area by air transport and to accept the obligation of providing a large share of their supplies. Kenney was proving, despite some opposition from Washington, that persistent air attacks upon enemy air bases could sometimes persuade the enemy that the constant effort needed to keep a strip in operation was simply not worth its cost.[25]

Air superiority over eastern New Guinea was maintained throughout the remainder of 1942. The Japanese could still strike Papuan targets; Port Moresby remained within range of Rabaul, and a raid of about one hundred Japanese planes struck there as late as April 1943. Almost half these raiders were claimed shot down, however, demonstrating Allied control. By the first days of 1943, the Allied forces were much stronger. General Kenney's three fighter groups were now veteran outfits, and one was equipped with P–38s, the aircraft that became the backbone of Allied fighter strength in the Southwest Pacific for most of the remainder of the war. Perhaps more important, work on an airfield complex at Dobodura, near Buna, had begun in November 1942. When a road from Oro Bay to Dobodura was completed in early 1943, Dobodura became the main advance base for Allied Air Forces in the Southwest Pacific.[26]

Lessons From 1942

The Allies learned a number of important lessons during the 1942 aerial battles over Guadalcanal and Papua. Fighter pilots quickly discovered that the turning tactics of the First World War and the Battle of Britain were suicide when attempted against the superbly maneuverable Japanese fighters. American fighters needed more range; superior Japanese range meant that most air combat in 1942 was over Allied bases, not over Japanese bases. Also, inadequate fighter range meant that American bombers attacked Japanese bases and Japanese shipping without escort, which made them vulnerable to enemy interception. General Kenney himself wrote: "our own short-sightedness, mine included, didn't put the range in our fighters to do this job out here."[27] Nor did American bombers have enough defensive firepower. The B–17 was able to defend itself better than other bombers, but experience demonstrated that it could not operate unescorted in daylight without unacceptable losses. Even the faster B–25, which at that time had only one forward-firing machinegun, proved vulnerable to head-on attacks from Japanese fighters. Incidentally, after heavy losses in New Guinea, General Kenney decided the A–24 was too slow and too defenseless and phased this plane out of the Allied Air Forces.[28]

The Japanese advance eastward and southward in the Pacific had been accomplished by capturing an air base, sometimes with the aid of carrier aircraft, then extending air cover for the next operation from that air base. It was quickly obvious that if the Allies were to mount a counteroffensive, it must be of the same nature. Guadalcanal and Papua were the beginning of this process. The largely unopposed landing at Guadalcanal was made under the short-lived cover of carrier aircraft, but further advances could be covered by aircraft based on Guadalcanal. The move to the north coast of New Guinea was protected and supported by planes based at Port Moresby. Yet, before there could be further advances, bases had to be established on the north coast. The distances that made establishment of forward bases necessary also made advanced headquarters necessary to control operations from these bases.

Essential to the achievement of air superiority was warning of Japanese air attacks. Coastwatchers had a major part in providing warning both in the Southwest Pacific and in the South Pacific, but it was in the latter battles that they played the most critical role. At the beginning of the war, American radar was primitive and unreliable, but by the end of 1942 much improved equipment was available. It became normal for Allied bases to have at least thirty minutes warning before a Japanese air attack arrived overhead.[29]

The first year of the war saw the development of equipment and tactics enabling American aircraft to meet the Japanese on more than equal terms most of the time. American bombers were given more firepower, and more frequently they had fighter escort. American fighters used tactics that more than compensated for their lack of maneuverability. In the first place, their armor, self-sealing tanks, and heavier engines enabled them to take more punishment than the Japanese interceptors. Whenever possible, therefore, Allied fighters engaged the Japanese from higher altitude and then, if necessary, dove out of the fight. Seldom could a Japanese aircraft match the speed of an American plane in a dive. The American pilots, if they still had fuel and ammunition, could use the speed built up in the dive to climb back to altitude and reenter the battle.

American fighter planes fought in two-plane elements comprising a lead pilot and a wingman. The primary task of the wingman was to protect the lead pilot from attacks from the rear, but it must not appear that he was left completely exposed. The two-plane element "wove" in and out so that each man to some extent protected the other's tail. These tactics had been used by the American Volunteer Group in China and Burma, but Gen. Claire Chennault, who had introduced them there, gave credit to a German officer in the First World War for inventing them. Naval pilots often referred to the procedure as the "Thach weave," so named in honor of Lt. Comdr. J. S. Thach, who served aboard the *Lexington* and who presumably introduced the tactic to carrier pilots. Above all, as stated earlier, American fighter pilots learned, too often the hard way, that they must never "dog-fight" with the ZEKES, TONYS, and OSCARS with whom they disputed the Pacific skies.[30]

Neutralization of Rabaul

In the Southwest Pacific, the long battle for Buna ended in mid-January 1943. In the South Pacific, the Japanese finally evacuated Guadalcanal in February. These two victories gave the Allies the initiative, but so long as the Japanese could operate freely out of Rabaul, no advance toward Japan could be mounted. Rabaul thus became the next objective of Allied forces. Initially, the plan was to capture this New Britain position, but Adm. Ernest J. King in October 1943 persuaded the other members of the Joint Chiefs of Staff that Rabaul could be bombed into impotence. When that neutralization had been accomplished, then the advance to the west and to the north could be undertaken.

South Pacific forces were still far from Rabaul; heavy bombers could reach that target from Guadalcanal, but they could not be escorted by fighters nor aided by light or medium bombers. From Dobodura, Southwest Pacific forces could strike Rabaul, employing not only heavy bombers but also medium bombers, and they could look to P–38 fighters, now in operation in New Guinea, for protection from Japanese interceptors. Southwest Pacific forces, however, could not concentrate completely on Rabaul, because they also had to deal with a Japanese air threat from Madang and Wewak, farther west in New Guinea. Kenney's forces would strike Rabaul sporadically but it would be necessary for South Pacific forces to inch their way up the Solomons chain, establishing local air superiority as they went, before Rabaul could be permanently neutralized.[31]

During the fighting on Guadalcanal, the Japanese had very cleverly constructed an airfield at Munda, on New Georgia, the next large island up the Solomons chain from Guadalcanal. Hanging palm treetops on cables stretched over the strip, the Japanese prevented discovery until the field was ready to go into operation. This obviously had to be the next target of the South Pacific forces. As an intermediate step, the Russell Islands, sixty-five miles nearer Munda than Henderson Field, were occupied before the end of February. The Japanese were anything but passive while the occupation of the Russells and preparations for the invasion of New Georgia continued. Guadalcanal became a more lucrative target for the Japanese every day as airfields were extended and improved and supplies accumulated. They attempted, as late as June, to establish control of the air over the southern Solomons. Very heavy attacks were mounted on April 1, April 7, May 13, and especially on June 16, when well over 100 Japanese planes made an apparently all-out effort. Allied claims of enemy aircraft destroyed were certainly exaggerated—during World War II they almost always were—but they amounted to 180 fighters and bombers during these attacks. Allied losses were only a fraction of this, and many of the downed American and New Zealand pilots were rescued to fight another day. Whatever the Japanese losses were, they were great enough that it was impossible for them to keep up the steady, regular, and sustained bombing that experience proved necessary for the neutralization of a base.[32]

Allied air forces in the Solomons were a remarkable example of inter-service and international cooperation, and they were far stronger in 1943

The Grumman F6F Hellcat became the principal carrier-borne fighter for the U.S. Fleet after 1943, gradually replacing the Wildcat.

than they had been in 1942. They still had the coastwatcher network on the islands to the north to give warning of impending attack, and the radar installations on Guadalcanal had been much improved. The new airstrips in the Russell Islands made it possible to intercept the Japanese farther from their Guadalcanal targets and to engage them for a longer period of time. Perhaps more important was the fact that new and better aircraft were beginning to arrive. AAF P–38s came to the South Pacific as they did to the Southwest Pacific. The F4Fs of the Marines were replaced by F4Us, and the Navy squadrons assigned to Guadalcanal began flying the F6F Hellcats that would be the main Navy fighter for the remainder of the war. The Royal New Zealand Air Force was still equipped with P–40s. When the Japanese made their all-out effort of June 16, they flew into a defensive disposition that had P–38s at 30,000 feet, F6Fs and F4Us next, then P–40s and F4Fs, and finally P–39s at 20,000 feet. As important as new and better aircraft were, just as important were the Seabees and engineering units and improved engineering equipment that made it possible to construct new airstrips and improve existing ones with a speed that the Japanese found almost unbelievable.[33]

There was a definite limit to how much support South Pacific aircraft could give to the invasion of New Georgia. SBDs and fighters, especially after the SBDs were equipped with belly tanks, could keep Munda and other New Georgia strips neutralized, but Japanese bases on Bougainville were out of range of all but heavy bombers. The B–24 Liberators that were replacing B–17s everywhere in the Pacific made unescorted daylight attacks on Buin airstrip (Bougainville) on February 13 and 14, and 5 of the 15 participating bombers were lost. Thereafter, attacks out of fighter escort range were made at night, but night bombing was ineffective. From Port Moresby, Southwest Pacific heavy bombers had been striking Rabaul, Kavieng (New Ireland), and Kahili (Bougainville) air bases since the late summer of 1942. Gen. Ennis C. Whitehead, commanding the advanced headquarters of the Fifth Air Force, believed correctly that these night strikes did little damage. The Japanese could still operate effectively, and South Pacific forces would have to fight them in the air. Furthermore, the Japanese were bringing air reinforcements into Rabaul, and Japanese pilot performance in June and July 1943 indicated that fresh replacements had taken over from the tired survivors of the long air war over Guadalcanal. This was indeed the case. Japanese Adm. Isoroku Yamamoto stripped his carriers of 200 planes and crews and threw them into the Solomons battle.[34]

Allied forces landed on Rendova and New Georgia on June 30, 1943, beginning a land battle that would last into August. On the day of the landings a fighter director crew and equipment functioned aboard the destroyer *Jenkins,* and Air Command Solomons Islands (COMAIRSOLS), which had been designated headquarters of the multiservice and multina-

343

tional Allied air forces, provided a combat air patrol (CAP) of 32 fighters over the landings. This CAP required the total assignment of 96 fighters, and the commitment was continued for 30 days. The Japanese air reaction was initially strong, but Allied fighters inflicted such heavy losses on the attackers that after June 15, attacks came at night, or at dusk when the fighter cover had left station in order to have daylight for landing. COMAIRSOLS planes struck at Japanese airfields when possible, but basically the battle continued to be fought between planes aloft. This aerial battle was a decided Allied victory, with 358 enemy aircraft claimed destroyed for a loss of 71 Allied fighters and 22 bombers. A large number of Allied aircrews were rescued by PBYs, thus contributing mightily to morale.[35]

The next major Allied objective in the Solomons was Bougainville, but more airfields were needed before an attack could be mounted. As soon as enough fighters to provide cover could operate from New Georgia, the Allies moved against Vella Lavella. Landing at a point unoccupied by Japanese troops, the assault forces met only a slight resistance from the air. The Japanese should have done better here; their target was within close range of their major base at Kahili and an early raid knocked out the main Allied radar set so that adequate warning was impossible. Even so, by August 26 the defending fighters from Munda had downed 43 fighters, 5 dive bombers, and a float plane for the loss of a F4U. Some damage was suffered, but work on an airstrip continued steadily, and by October 15, Vella Lavella could handle one hundred aircraft.[36]

Completion of this latest airfield was well-timed since the Allies would need every plane they could send up from every possible base to permit landing at Bougainville to go forward on November 1, as scheduled. It was necessary that Bougainville be captured, for airfields on that island were an essential part of the plan to neutralize Rabaul by air action.

General Kenney's Allied Air Forces from the Southwest Pacific had a major role in protecting the Bougainville operation by strikes at Rabaul. The Fifth Air Force went strongly on the offensive in October. B–24s had replaced B–17s in all combat units, and sufficient P–38s were available to escort them. From the new bases in Northern New Guinea, AAF B–25s and RAAF Beauforts could strike Rabaul. On October 12 a massive attack, by Pacific standards, sent 70 B–24s, 107 B–25s, 12 RAAF Beauforts, and no less than 117 P–38s over the Rabaul airfields. Participants in this mission claimed to have shot 26 Japanese planes out of the air and to have destroyed 100 on the ground. For the rest of October heavy and medium SWPA bombers and fighters were over Rabaul almost every day that the weather per- mitted. The B–24s bombed from medium altitude, the B–25s bombed and strafed at treetop level, and their pilots claimed great destruction of Japanese aircraft as well as of shipping and other targets. Certainly the ability of the Japanese to operate in the Solomons was significantly reduced.[37]

Planes from the South Pacific could not strike Rabaul as easily as the Allied Air Forces from New Guinea, but they could spread destruction over Japan's airfields in the Solomons. By October, Air Command Solomons Islands (COMAIRSOLS) had something more than 200 fighters, about 175 of them at bases from which they could escort bombers to Japanese targets. Within reach of Japanese targets were 100 SBDs on Munda, 48 TBFs and 48 B–25s in the Russells, and 52 B–24s based on Guadalcanal. Navy PBYs and PB4Ys, and RNZAF Venturas were also available but were used almost entirely for reconnaissance and rescue work. Attacks were mounted on Japanese airfields every day that weather permitted, SBDs dive-bombing, fighters glide-bombing, B–24s striking from up to 20,000 feet, and the B–25s roaring in at tree-top level. It is very significant that by mid-October the ratio of fighter escort to bombers could be cut in half, and that by the end of October bomber strikes were hitting these Japanese airfields in daylight without fighter escort. The fields on and near Bougainville were definitely being beaten down, with the final blow delivered November 1 by planes from carriers *Saratoga* and *Princeton*.[38]

Despite efforts to mislead them, the Japanese were quite sure that the Allies would attack Bougainville, and early in the morning on D-day, November 1, Japanese dive bombers showed up at the Allied invasion site with a heavy fighter escort. Fine work by a CAP of 8 NZRAF P–40s and AAF P–38s so disorganized this attack that the bombers made no hits and only one near miss. One hundred of the carrier aircraft recently arrived at Rabaul came in shortly after noon, but they too failed to inflict serious damage on the landing force; they were preoccupied, in fact, with defending themselves against 34 mixed fighters that covered the unloading at the beachhead. That night the Navy won the surface battle of Empress Augusta Bay, but the Allied task force came under heavy Japanese air attack the following morning. The fighters and naval antiaircraft fire of COMAIR-SOLS exacted a heavy price, yet only two American ships were damaged. There would be little daylight offensive action by Japanese airmen during the battle for Bougainville. They would be too busy defending their own bases at Rabaul.[39]

Attacks against Rabaul to prevent Japanese interference with Allied landing on Bougainville were fine examples of cooperation between land-based and carrier-based air, and between the various services and various Allies. Bad weather over Rabaul protected it against strikes from New Guinea on November 1, but the next day seventy-five B–25s escorted by eighty P–38s reached this primary target. The B–25s struck at shipping in the harbor, but they were hotly engaged by the Japanese defenders. Allied losses were so high (twelve B–25s and as many P–38s) that General Kenney launched no more daylight attacks for two days. On November 5, however, an attack by the entire air strength of *Saratoga* and *Princeton,* twenty-three TBFs, twenty-two SBDs, and fifty-two F6Fs, hit shipping in Rabaul harbor at 1130 while COMAIRSOLS fighters protected the carriers. They claimed to have shot down at least twenty-five intercepting fighters. Less than an hour later, twenty-seven Fifth Air Force B–24s struck Rabaul, encountering weak opposition. Two days later the B–24s returned; the bombers and P–38s claimed the destruction of twenty-two Japanese fighters in the air and twelve fighters and bombers on the ground. Until November 11 attacks on Rabaul were at night, but on that day carrier aircraft returned, this time from *Bunker Hill* and *Independence* as well as *Saratoga* and *Princeton.* The Navy claimed to have destroyed twenty-four Japanese interceptors. Once more, the carriers were protected by land-based fighters while their planes struck at the enemy. During the first two weeks of November, the Allied losses over the Solomons and New Britain were far less than the Japanese losses. Perhaps just as important, carrier-trained Japanese aircrews had been greatly depleted.[40]

Attacks on Rabaul from New Guinea were delivered at night from mid-November on, and most of the remainder of the work of reducing Rabaul to impotence was carried out by South Pacific forces. Until December, COMAIRSOLS planes occupied themselves primarily with keeping Japanese bases in the Solomons inoperable. Japanese night attacks on the Bougainville beachhead were not enough to prevent Seabee and New Zealand engineer units from completing the first of the Allied airstrips planned for that island on December 9. The next day seventeen Marine F4Us landed and began operations out of the field. The Bougainville base was first used offensively on December 17 when a Marine fighter sweep led by Maj. Gregory "Pappy" Boyington roared over Rabaul, destroying seven Japanese planes but losing three. For the remainder of December, fighter sweeps and heavy bomber strikes made life uncomfortable at Rabaul, but did not appreciably lessen the Japanese ability to defend the airfield. It was apparent that B–25s, TBFs, and SBDs would have to join the B–24s, and two more Bougainville strips were built for them, one being completed on the last day of December, the other on January 9.[41]

With fighters in place on Bougainville, and the additional airstrips available for basing or staging through light and medium bombers, the fate of Rabaul was sealed. The Japanese kept pouring in reinforcements, but they could not stem the tide of the Allied air assault. The B–24s of the Thirteenth Air Force, a command created to administer the AAF components of COMAIRSOLS, were returned to night strikes, but every day that weather permitted, fighter sweeps and/or bomber attacks hit the airdromes, the harbor, and other installations at Rabaul. When it became apparent that Kavieng was partially replacing Rabaul, Fifth Air Force B–24s and

RAAF Beauforts began striking that base on New Ireland. These efforts were supplemented by low-level B–25 and A–20 strikes on January 15 which cost 4 B-25s and 2 A–20s. Already Kavieng had been savaged by bombers and fighters from *Bunker Hill* and *Monterey* on December 25, December 26, and January 5. During January COMAIRSOLS sent over Rabaul 180 B–25 sorties, 368 SBD sorties, 227 TBF sorties, and 1,850 sorties by Navy and Marine F4Us and F6Fs, Army P–38s and New Zealand P–40s. Despite reinforcements, Rabaul was rapidly weakening by the end of January.[42]

South Pacific forces made 32 strikes on Rabaul in January and were intercepted 27 times by an average of 47 Japanese aircraft. Allied fighters and bombers claimed to have shot down 471 of these interceptors, but on January 30 more than 30 planes rose to defend their bases. The Japanese continued to send in reinforcements. During the first 19 days of February, Allied bombers flew 1,336 sorties, but it is significant that the number of fighter sorties was proportionately less, only 1,579. With the harbor practically empty of shipping, the light bombers turned to antiaircraft installations while the heavy and medium bombers struck at runways and dispersal areas. On February 19, the usual strike on Rabaul was intercepted by about 50 fighters. Except for a few single-plane incidents, this was the last interception. On the date noted, February 19, American carrier forces struck

Fifth Air Force Commander, Lt. Gen. George C. Kenney (*right*) **and his Deputy Commander, Maj. Gen. Ennis C. Whitehead** (*center*), **meet with Lt. Gen. William S. Knudsen, a visitor to the base on New Guinea.**

the great Japanese base at Truk, through which planes destined for Rabaul were staged. This strike had a field day with the aerial defenders claiming more than 200 planes destroyed in the air and on the ground. The Thirteenth Air Force would soon be withdrawn from the South Pacific, but Marine, Navy, and RNZAF planes would continue the bombing and strafing of Rabaul for the rest of 1944. The great base was neutralized, but it had to be kept neutralized if Allied air superiority over New Britain was to be maintained.[43]

The long struggle for the neutralization of Rabaul taught many lessons, even though some of them could not be learned until the war was over and Japanese personnel involved could be interviewed. It was demonstrated clearly once more over Rabaul that bombers could not operate unescorted in daylight against fighter opposition without unacceptable losses. Likewise, it was shown that heavy bombers alone, even if provided with escort, could not knock out of commission an active base subject to reinforcement. It was learned only after the war that the hundreds of night sorties against Rabaul had accomplished little except to lower the morale of the defenders. The neutralization of Rabaul was a slow business, demanding constant effort. Sporadic attacks gave the defenders ample time to repair damage. The October and November strikes against Rabaul were useful in preventing Japanese attacks on the Allies in Bougainville and in New Guinea. Except for reducing the number of highly trained Japanese pilots, these assaults did not bring Rabaul any nearer impotence in November of 1943 than it had been in November 1942. It was the incessant attacks, mounting in intensity, of December 1943, and especially of January and February 1944, that brought Rabaul to the point that it was probably more of a liability than an asset to Japan. Certainly Rabaul could no longer make any significant contribution to the Japanese war effort. But even then, the bombing and strafing of light bombers and fighters had to be continued to make sure that Rabaul did not rise again.[44]

One trend that had begun in 1942 was very noticeable before the end of the Rabaul campaign. The Japanese pilots of early 1944 were poor substitutes for those who had flown over Pearl Harbor. The loss of naval pilots had been high at the Coral Sea and at Midway, and the loss of both Army and Navy pilots had been notable in New Guinea. Not only were replacements from the homeland used up in the fighting over the Solomons and Rabaul, but the combined fleet of Japan was stripped of half its carrier fighter pilots and of a far greater proportion of its dive bomber and torpedo bomber pilots. The carriers had to return to Japan to train replacements, and in the home islands a shortage of oil limited the operations of the carriers and the number of hours in the air that trainees could have. When the fleet sortied in response to the U.S. invasion of the Marianas in mid-1944, its undertrained pilots were simply incompetent to deal with American pilots in the "Marianas Turkey Shoot." Thus achievement of

348

air superiority over Rabaul facilitated the establishment of air supremacy elsewhere.[45]

Wewak

While South Pacific forces were moving up the Solomon Islands chain toward Rabaul, General Douglas MacArthur's Southwest Pacific forces were consolidating their hold upon the northern coast of New Guinea, contributing to the isolation of Rabaul, and at the same time establishing bases for an advance westward in New Guinea and then northward to the Philippines. Advances planned by Southwest Pacific Headquarters were threatened by the Japanese air forces at Rabaul, but Rabaul commanders were in general more concerned with the battles takingplace in the Solomons than with Allied advances in New Guinea. Attacks on New Guinea from the north were, therefore, rather sporadic. Of much more concern to SWPA commanders was growing Japanese air strength at Wewak, some 500 miles northwest of the still developing Allied base at Dobodura. By the end of July 1943 some 200 Japanese aircraft were in place at Wewak, where there were 3 airfields and the other installations needed for a major air base, all heavily defended by antiaircraft emplacements.[46]

Heavy bombers could reach Wewak from Port Moresby or Dobodura, but by the spring of 1943 there was no thought of sending them there in daylight without fighter escort. B–25s and P–38s also could reach Wewak from Dobodura, but operating at extreme range, they badly needed an intermediate base where damaged planes, or those low on fuel, could find refuge on the return flight. Bases closer to Wewak were definitely needed for supporting fighters, and two were established before the end of the summer of 1943. The first was at Tsili Tsili, redubbed Marilinin by General Kenney, who feared that the real name might be descriptive. Here natives cut out a runway suitable for fighter operations before the end of July. Kenney had carefully kept his planes away from Wewak, hoping to lull the Japanese into a false sense of security. Thus, the stage was set for one of the most effective airfield strikes of the Second World War.[47]

By mid-August, 2 heavy bomb groups operating from Port Moresby had 12 B–17s and 52 B–24s in commission, and Kenney's other bomb groups had 58 B–25s that had been modified to give them 6 forward-firing machineguns and an attack radius of 550 miles. His strength in P–38s, the only fighters with range for long-range escort, was well over 100.[48]

Every available bit of this strength was thrown against Wewak's 4 airfields on August 16, when intelligence reported that more than 200 Japanese fighters, light bombers, and medium bombers were there. Heavy bombers began taking off from Port Moresby at 2100 and continued until

349

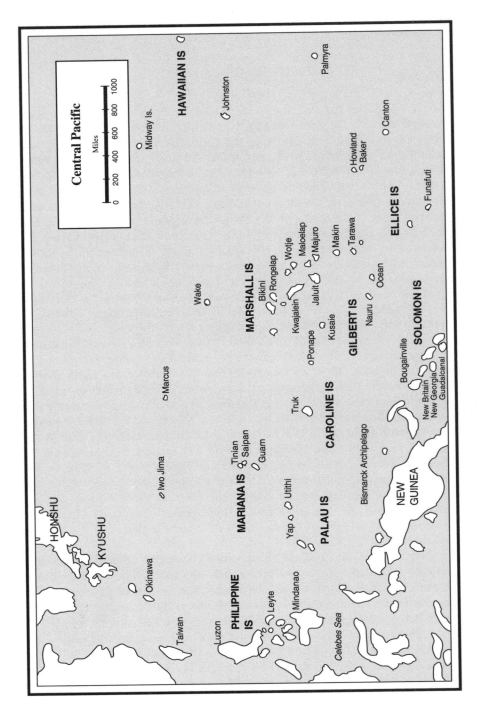

Central Pacific

Miles

0   200   400   600   800   1000

HONSHU
KYUSHU

Okinawa

Taiwan

PHILIPPINE IS

Luzon

Leyte

Mindanao

Celebes Sea

Iwo Jima

MARIANA IS
Tinian
Saipan
Guam

Yap Utithi

PALAU IS

Marcus

Truk

CAROLINE IS

Bismarck Archipelago

NEW GUINEA

New Britain
New Georgia
Guadalcanal

Bougainville

SOLOMON IS

Wake

MARSHALL IS
Bikini
Rongelap
Kwajalein
Jaluit
Kusaie
Ponape

Wotje
Maloelap
Majuro
Makin
Tarawa

GILBERT IS

Nauru
Ocean

Midway Is.

Johnston

HAWAIIAN IS

Palmyra

Canton

Howland
Baker

ELLICE IS

Funafuti

350

midnight. The lead bomber of the stream dropped its bombs soon after midnight, and the rain of explosives, incendiaries, and fragmentation bombs continued until after 0300. How much damage this night bombing inflicted upon the Japanese at Wewak will never be known. Probably it was not great, but the purpose of the attack was to delay the takeoff of Japanese planes early the next morning, and this was accomplished.

Two squadrons of B–25s that took off from Port Moresby encountered very bad weather, and only 3 of the bombers reached their target. All but a few of those leaving Dobodura reached Wewak, and 32 of them swept over the Japanese airfields, strafing and dropping parafrags, the bombs that had already proved their usefulness in Papua. It is doubtful that this strike destroyed 200 planes on the ground, certainly not 250 as some averred, but the number was almost certainly well over 100. The next day, August 18, a similar mission was mounted, but this time the attack of the B–24s did not ground the Japanese fighters, and 52 B–25s encountered fierce fighter opposition. One Mitchell was lost, but the escorting P–38s claimed 15 enemy fighters for a loss of 2. Wewak, like Rabaul, would be reinforced, and Allied forces would attack the base again and again, but the strikes of August 17 and 18 established Allied air superiority from Marilinin to Wewak. This superiority might be challenged, but it would never be overcome. The accomplishment of objectives on the Huon Peninsula of New Guinea, in southern New Britain, and in the Admiralty Islands could now proceed.[49]

The Allied surface offensive on the Huon Peninsula began on September 4 with an amphibious attack on the Japanese base at Lae. Australian infantry was firmly ashore before the day was over. This marked the beginning of a period of astonishingly successful international cooperation between the Australians and Americans, and intraservice cooperation among the Seventh Fleet of the United States Navy, American and Australian ground forces, and the AAF and RAAF ground and air units. Before the end of the war, American carriers would add another ingredient to this mix. The Japanese air force resisted the landing, but fighter cover directed by an AAF team aboard the destroyer *Reid* vectored American fighters so as to turn back most attacks. The success of the operation was never endangered. On the next day, one of the most spectacular operations of the entire war in the Southwest Pacific took place as paratroopers descended upon Nadzab, already selected as the site for a new American air base. Nadzab quickly became a major fighter base, especially after a road from Lae permitted bringing in supplies by sea. On September 22, another amphibious invasion brought the occupation of Finschhafen. In the interior, the Australians moved up the Markham Valley to Gusap, where two fair weather strips and a 5,000-foot asphalt strip were serving a fighter squadron as early as November 1, 1943.[50]

The Allied Air Forces in August and September 1943 still had a major part to play in the neutralization of Rabaul. It was believed at the time that the seizure of Arawe and Cape Gloucester, at the southern end of the island of New Britain (Rabaul lay on the northern end) was an essential part of the neutralization. Probably this was not the case, but hindsight is always better than foresight. It certainly was essential that the flank of the advance along the coast of New Guinea be protected, and the seizure of the Admiralty Islands provided this protection, as well as furnishing a magnificent anchorage. It must be understood, however, that support of these operations absorbed much of the Southwest Pacific air effort from September 1943 through March 1944. This effort was certainly not wasted; it resulted in the destruction of many Japanese aircraft and contributed significantly to the neutralization of Rabaul. But if it had been possible to devote all this effort to Wewak, the air superiority that had been achieved over eastern New Guinea could have been converted into air supremacy far more quickly.

In the meantime, the campaign against Wewak continued. From the attacks of August 17–18 until the end of the month, B–24s flew 102 sorties over Wewak and B–25s flew 21. Perhaps more important, attacks on other Japanese positions in New Guinea forced fighters from Wewak to come out and fight. Counting the first raids, during August the B–24s claimed to have shot down 35 enemy aircraft for the loss of 3 bombers; B–25s claimed 22 enemy fighters for the loss of 5 bombers; and American fighters claimed 69 Japanese planes for a loss of 6 P–38s. During this summer, General Kenney's forces were growing stronger. The number of P–38s, his preferred fighter because of range and the twin engines that saved so many lives on overwater flights, was significantly increased. Supplementing the additional P–38s, he received the P–47, the giant single-engine Republic Thunderbolt. Even though P–47s had to have droppable auxiliary fuel tanks to give them the range necessary in the Southwest Pacific, and given that there was initially some pilot prejudice against these aircraft, they proved to be a valuable addition to the fighter inventory. No additional fighter types would come to the Southwest Pacific until P–51 Mustangs arrived late in 1944.[51]

The number of Japanese fighters and bombers on the four airfields at Wewak and shipping in the harbor increased until September 27, when another major strike took off from Allied airfields; eighteen B–24s, ninety-seven B–25s, and sixty-eight P–38s struck at the airfields and at shipping. The B–25s reported they had destroyed forty Japanese planes on the ground, and fighters and bombers together took credit for nine shot out of the air. Even so, the Japanese—the Japanese Fourth Air Army in this case—continued to pour aircraft into Wewak.

During all this time bases nearer and nearer to Wewak were being developed, and P–47s, P–40s, and P–39s began to join the strikes. Whenever adequate targets developed, the bombers went out. On November 27,

Above: A North American B–25 Mitchell drops its bomb load on a Japanese freighter, which is lying at anchor in Wewak harbor. *Below:* U.S. B–25s strafe and drop fragmentation bombs on Kawasaki Ki–61 fighters in the Wewak area.

353

sixty-seven B–25s claimed fifteen planes destroyed; the next day forty-eight B–24s hit the strips. B–24s returned on December 1, but were intercepted by nearly fifty fighters; escorting P–47s claimed eleven of the Japanese planes, but three B–24s were lost. The Japanese at Wewak fought on through the rest of 1943 and early 1944.[52]

By early 1944, General MacArthur's decision to bypass the Japanese Eighteenth Army at Wewak was firm. Allied forces would instead land at Hollandia, more than 200 miles farther west along the New Guinea coast. The persistent Fourth Air Army could not be bypassed, however. It was imperative that Wewak be rendered helpless insofar as air power was concerned. Constant blows since August of 1943 had damaged the base, but it was still operational. By early 1944, however, Allied bases at Nadzab and Gusap had been developed to handle bombers, and fighters were available there as well as at Saidor and Finschhafen. Adequate aircraft were available, including 265 B–24s, 154 B–25s, 172 A–20s, and more than an adequate number of fighters. By March, the time was ripe to deal the final blow to Wewak as an air base.[53]

This final assault began on March 11, 1944, and continued every day through the 27th except for one day when the weather made sorties impossible. In the beginning, fighters gave cover while B–24s struck the runways and antiaircraft installations with 1000-pound and 2000-pound bombs. The B–25s and A–20s swept over the strips at low altitude, striking at aircraft, personnel, and any installations that seemed worth bombing and strafing. Japanese fighter-interceptors were ineffective during the first 4 days; thereafter the antiaircraft gunners, their fire growing weaker every day, gave the only resistance encountered. As Japanese antiaircraft fire at Wewak weakened, the B–24s began making single four-minute bomb runs at medium altitude—10,000 to 13,000 feet—and under these circumstances the Norden bombsight was almost as accurate as the claims made for it. All told, B–24s flew 1,543 sorties, B–25s flew 488, and A–20s flew 555 between March 11 and 27. When they were through, no air base was left; the Japanese Eighteenth Army had nothing to defend. Runways were cratered and useless. The equipment used to repair them had been destroyed. Fuel storage facilities were blasted and burned, and the few buildings the Japanese had erected were leveled. The commander of the Fourth Air Army flew his headquarters to Hollandia, more than 200 miles away, ordering the remaining personnel to make their way by land through jungle and swamp and over mountains. Most of the pilots who defended Wewak were already dead; the vast majority of those air crew and ground crew personnel who attempted the walk to Hollandia died along the way. Those who reached Hollandia walked into a death trap.[54]

The Advance to Hollandia

In the long, drawn-out campaigns against Rabaul and Wewak, the Allies had learned much about what was required to neutralize an air base. Neutralization required a sustained effort by heavy, medium, and lighter bombers adequately protected by fighters. Bombing and strafing had to be continued until aircraft based at the target airfields had been destroyed, and until the facilities and runways had been so damaged that effective reinforcement was impossible. This knowledge would be applied to Hollandia and would produce a remarkably rapid victory in comparison to those that had gone before. Hollandia was outside the range of any Allied fighter aircraft in New Guinea except for the newest model P–38, which had an additional 150 gallons of gasoline capacity. Fifty-eight of these had arrived in the theater, and the process of converting 75 older models to like performance as well was underway. There was no possibility of a combat air patrol being maintained over landings at Hollandia because of the distance, so it was obvious from the beginning that aircraft carrier support would be necessary. But it was also believed that aircraft carriers could not remain within range of a major Japanese air base until that base had been at least crippled, or preferably completely neutralized. Thus, less than a month after Wewak had been finally disposed of, the Allied Air Forces had to turn their attention to Hollandia.[55]

The Thirteenth Air Force came under SWPA command on March 25, 1944, and its units were physically transferred to the Southwest Pacific Area as rapidly as possible. Air Northern Solomons (AIRNORSOLS) was created to control the remnant of Navy, RNZAF, and Marine Corps planes devoted to keeping Rabaul neutralized. A new Headquarters, Far East Air Forces, still under General Kenney's command, came into being on June 14, 1944, to control Fifth and Thirteenth Air Forces, the RAAF, and Dutch units based at Darwin. Fifth Air Force came under the direct command of Maj. Gen. Ennis Whitehead. Thirteenth Air Force heavy bombers, though much less numerous than the B–24s of Fifth Air Force, were able from the Admiralty Islands to give necessary support to the Central Pacific Theater and to take over some other tasks that would have fallen to Fifth Air Force. This left practically all units of Fifth Air Force free to concentrate upon Hollandia.[56]

While he waited for his P–38s to be readied for the neutralization of Hollandia, General Kenney sent his B–24s over the target at night, seeking to trick the Japanese into believing that he could not provide daylight escort. P–38 pilots were ordered not to go west of Tadji, considerably east of Hollandia, and were ordered to run for home as though low on fuel after fifteen minutes combat that far east. This deception was seemingly successful. The Fourth Air Army accumulated some 350 aircraft at Hollandia, so many that they had to be lined up wingtip to wingtip, as American planes

355

had been at Pearl Harbor, and as Japanese planes had been at Wewak in August of 1943.[57]

By March 30, 1944, enough long-range P–38s were ready to escort bombers to Hollandia. On this first daylight strike, Generals Kenney and Whitehead sent only heavy bombers, operating at high altitude, along with fighter escorts, because they suspected that the Japanese might have laid an antiaircraft trap along the valley route through which the lighter, low-altitude bombers would have to fly to effectively strike the 3 airfields. This was an unnecessary precaution, but the B–24s were able to do great destruction on their own. Sixty-one of them dropped 1,286 clusters, weighing 120 pounds each, and containing small fragmentation bombs more destructive than hand grenades. They also dropped 4,612 twenty-pound fragmentation bombs that were even more destructive. Japanese fighters, some 30 of them, rose to challenge the attackers, but they were easily dispersed by the fighter escort. Photographs taken after the mission showed at least 73 fighters and bombers destroyed on the ground.[58]

The heavy bombers and fighters flew again the next day, March 31, and the B–24s once more carried mainly fragmentation bombs. One more interception was weak and ineffective. This strike raised the total of aircraft claimed destroyed on the ground to 208. The Japanese now apparently realized that Hollandia was doomed. That night they began flying planes out. The headquarters of the Fourth Air Army made another pilgrimage in search of operational safety. It had moved from Rabaul to Wewak, from Wewak to Hollandia, and now it sought a more restful area in the Celebes. Unfortunately for Japan, it left behind in New Guinea some 20,000 aircraft maintenance men.[59]

The weather over Hollandia was too bad for aerial operations on April 1 and 2, but on April 3 the Allied Air Forces returned for the kill. Sixty-six B–24s this time carried 1000-pound bombs, which they dropped from 10,000–12,000 feet on still-active antiaircraft positions. Some 30 Japanese fighters managed to take off, but they were apparently not eager for combat—or perhaps not well enough trained to know how to be aggressive. Just behind the B–24s came 96 A–20s, strafing and scattering parafrags. They were assailed by fighters, but escorting P–38s shot down 12 while losing only 1 of their own number. Less than an hour later, 76 B–25s came over the Hollandia fields at treetop level, seeking whatever the A–20s might have left behind. They saw only 3 Japanese fighters, and the escorting P–38s shot down all of them. When the Army occupied the Hollandia airfields a little more than 3 weeks later, some 350 destroyed aircraft were on and beside the runways. In this one instance, and it is a rare one, air claims of damage done to the enemy were apparently more conservative than the reality.[60]

The strike of April 3, did not completely neutralize Hollandia's airfields. The Japanese capacity to fill in crater holes on earthen runways was amazing, and planes from farther west staged into Hollandia several times before the invasion. Nonetheless, the Allied Air Forces had established air superiority over Hollandia in a few all-out missions. When the Navy's Task Force 58 arrived to cover the invasion, it found few aerial targets either on the ground or in the air, and total naval claims in New Guinea were only eighty-one aircraft from April 20 through April 24; many of these kills were made farther west than Hollandia. It should perhaps be noted that air superiority provided no protection against the weather. Allied bombers continued to strike Hollandia until D-day, April 22, and on April 16, known afterward as "Black Sunday," a weather front closed in over the Markham Valley before bombers had returned from their strikes. Nineteen bombers were lost, twenty percent of those on the mission.[61]

Back to the Philippines

Hollandia was invaded on April 22, and the airfields were quickly secured. With Japanese air no longer the threat it once had been and with aircraft based at Hollandia, Southwest Pacific forces could speed up their advance. On May 18 they landed on Wakde Island, approximately 140 miles northwest of Hollandia; and then pressed westward, landing on Biak, an island off the New Guinea coast, roughly 325 miles from Hollandia. On July 2 Allied forces stormed ashore on Noemfoor Island, 75 miles west of Biak, and on July 30, American troops, meeting practically no resistance, went ashore at Sansapor and Mar, at the western tip of New Guinea. The last landing before the Philippines was on the island of Morotai, between New Guinea and the southernmost of the major Philippine Islands, Mindanao.[62]

In the summer of 1944, the Allies had planned that General MacArthur's Southwest Pacific forces should move into Mindanao following the establishment of air bases on Morotai. This was rather a bold plan, because Mindanao was 350 miles from Morotai, and land-based air cover of the invasion would be very limited. On the other hand, with the Thirteenth and Fifth Air Forces, the number of heavy bombers available for this operation was much greater than had been the case earlier. Also, although the Japanese were known to be flying aerial reinforcements into the Philippines, they had ceased to put up much of a fight in the East Indies. It seemed quite possible that the carriers that would cover the Mindanao landings and the land-based bombers and fighters from Morotai could quickly counter Japanese aerial resistance to a Mindanao landing. Then the Allied forces could move on to Leyte, in the central Philippines, and then to Luzon in the north, the main island of the archipelago.[63]

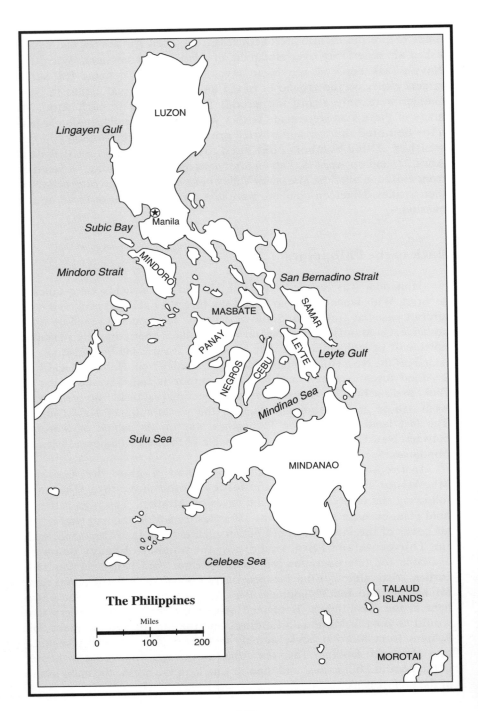

LUZON

Lingayen Gulf

Subic Bay   ⭐ Manila

MINDORO

Mindoro Strait

San Bernadino Strait

SAMAR

MASBATE

PANAY

LEYTE

Leyte Gulf

NEGROS   CEBU

Mindinao Sea

Sulu Sea

MINDANAO

Celebes Sea

TALAUD ISLANDS

MOROTAI

The Philippines

Miles

0   100   200

358

Subsequent developments made the plan to invade Mindanao seem conservative. Admiral William Halsey's Task Force 38, the main strike force of the U.S. Navy, set sail from Eniwetok for the Palaus and the Philippines. This fleet included 9 fleet carriers and 8 light carriers with a plane complement of well over 500 F6Fs, 315 dive bombers (SB2Cs, or Helldivers), and almost 250 torpedo bombers. Obviously this was a major concentration of air power in itself. After striking the Palaus, scheduled for early invasion, Halsey on September 9 and 10 struck at Mindanao. The Japanese on Mindanao did not even attempt to intercept Halsey's aircraft. On September 12, Halsey moved to the north and hit the central Philippines. Here there was more resistance than at Mindanao, but it was still feeble. One of Halsey's pilots, who was shot down over Leyte and then rescued, understood from the people of Leyte that there were no Japanese on the island. Halsey recommended to Admiral Nimitz, who passed it on to the Joint Chiefs of Staff, that the scheduled landings in Mindanao, as well as others in the Palaus and at Yap Island, be cancelled and that all the troops and naval forces thus made available be thrown into an early invasion of Leyte.[64]

The Joint Chiefs of Staff decided to bypass Mindanao and Yap but to carry out the invasion of the Palaus. The troops originally intended for Yap and already at sea were sent on to General MacArthur to participate in the invasion of Leyte, as recommended by Halsey. The landing was scheduled for October 20, and much had to be done before it could take place. The Philippines, except for Mindanao, were out of range of all FEAF aircraft. Only heavy bombers could reach Mindanao, but after Morotai was developed, long-range fighters from there could escort such bomber missions. Except for that, however, all preparatory bombing for the invasion of Leyte and protection of the landings until satisfactory airfields could be established on the island would be the task of the Navy.

In the Philippines, Japanese air was still strong, and the reinforcement route from the home islands by way of the Ryukyu Islands and Formosa was a short one. More important, a new factor would appear in the air struggle over Leyte, the Japanese suicide pilot, or *kamikaze*. In the previous air operations in the South and Southwest Pacific, when most, or even a considerable portion of the Japanese planes mounting an attack were destroyed, the attack was usually rendered ineffective. To accomplish this normally required air superiority, but not necessarily air supremacy. In the Philippines, Allied targets, and especially ships, were not safe so long as there was one Japanese pilot alive with access to one operational aircraft. Not even air supremacy was enough; every Japanese aircraft within range had to be rendered inoperable, or a *kamikaze* attack was possible. And the *kamikazes* brought about this change just at the time when SWPA forces moved out of the zone of air supremacy they had established in New Guinea.[65]

The preinvasion achievement of air superiority north of Mindanao had to be accomplished by the U.S. Navy to the extent that it was to be accomplished at all. Leaving Ulithi just after the passage of a typhoon, 17 carriers and other ships of Task Force 38 sailed northward and struck the Ryukyu Islands on October 10. In the Ryukyus the task force claimed 111 enemy aircraft destroyed and great damage to shipping. Next the bombers and fighters struck at Aparri, on the northern tip of Luzon. The strike, a relatively small one, cost the fleet 7 aircraft and destroyed perhaps twice that many on the ground. Formosa was the next target, and the Japanese commander was expecting the attack. He had well over 200 fighters available, plus a force of fighters and bombers on Kyushu that he expected to use for a counterattack. On October 12, no fewer than 1,378 Navy sorties were flown over the Japanese installations on Formosa. Considerable destruction of installations was achieved, and the destruction of Japanese fighters was so complete that when the carriers' third wave struck the island, they met no opposition. American losses had been high, however, no less than 48 aircraft.[66]

Now Halsey turned back toward the Philippines, and strikes were launched against Luzon. The main task now, however, was to protect the landings on Leyte that began on October 20. Task Force 38 had destroyed over 500 Japanese planes, but the Japanese air force in Formosa and the Philippines was far from defeated. The Leyte beachhead would be under Japanese air attack so long as it was active, and the Allies would encounter damaging air opposition until the beachhead at Luzon was secure. Carrier-based air power could not do the persistent pounding that would have been necessary to neutralize the scores of airfields on Formosa and Luzon. Even if Task Force 38 had destroyed every aircraft on Formosa and Luzon, and it certainly did not come close to that, it could not stay on station forever. As soon as it was withdrawn, more planes from the homeland could be funnelled down the Ryukyu Islands. The ground forces that landed on Leyte were back in the position of those who landed at Guadalcanal in 1942, utterly dependent upon carrier-based air support until bases for land-based planes could be constructed.[67]

The Japanese effort over the beachhead was sporadic, consisting of raids by a relatively few planes at a time. Under the circumstances that had prevailed before October 1944, they would have inflicted some damage by bomb and torpedo attacks, but nothing that could have menaced the landings. But now the *kamikaze* was on the scene. There had been instances of damaged Japanese planes deliberately seeking to crash into an American ship rather than into the water earlier in the war, even a few cases of doomed American pilots diving into Japanese ships. But there was a difference between the man, already lost, who sought to do as much damage as possible to the enemy as he died, and the man who took off with the intention of crashing his plane into an enemy target. The target was almost always a ship, because ships were so especially vulnerable to this type of attack.

The landings at Leyte went well, and the ground troops were soon firmly established ashore. This landing brought out the Japanese fleet and led to the Battle of Leyte Gulf. However, the Japanese naval air force was already reduced to such straits that the carriers in this engagement served only as bait to draw Admiral Halsey away from the beachhead so that surface forces might be able to attack American shipping. This battle was, of course, an overwhelming victory for the United States Navy, and the Imperial Japanese Navy as such was no longer a factor in the war. But Imperial Japanese Navy aviators, because of their willingness to sacrifice their lives to deliver a blow, most definitely were a factor, and they inflicted heavy losses on Allied naval forces, especially the escort carriers that were scheduled to cover and provide ground support for the troops ashore.

The *kamikaze* attacks during the Leyte campaign might not have been so devastating had the establishment of air bases on the island gone as planned. Unfortunately, the invasion had been made at the rainiest time of the year, and the soil on Leyte proved to be extremely difficult to make into runways that could stand the shock of landing aircraft. Steel planking was laid down, but it was soon driven into the mud, causing many accidents, and, of course, accidents reduced still further the few land-based planes available. General Kenney was able to bring in thirty-four P–38s on October 27, but this was not nearly enough to defend the airfield adequately, much less to carry out all the other work needed to be done. The escort carriers that had been giving what air defense and support the beachhead had received during the first week after the invasion had suffered such heavy losses and damage during the Battle of Leyte Gulf and from *kamikaze* attacks that they could no longer accept the responsibility for air defense. Yet the Japanese, *kamikaze* and otherwise, kept coming. Seldom were more than a dozen aircraft involved, and often only three or four, but there was so much shipping in the harbor, and the beach was so crowded, that bombs or bullets delivered almost anywhere did damage. The original thirty-four P–38s were reduced to twenty very shortly.[68]

The truth of the matter was that the Far East Air Forces had lost air superiority to such an extent that the Japanese were able to reinforce Leyte massively. For the first time since before the Battle of the Bismarck Sea in March 1943, entire Japanese convoys were able to get to a besieged base and land reinforcements. These reinforcement efforts were costly, and not a few Japanese soldiers landed on Leyte's shores without their equipment. Yet the transports and destroyers loaded with troops made the perilous run from Luzon to Leyte. As the airfields on Leyte gradually improved, medium bombers were staged through to bomb and strafe the ships bringing reinforcements, and fighters based on Leyte became antishipping bombers.

Night attacks on the airfields were so annoying that General Kenney brought a Marine Air Group into Leyte, primarily for air defense. One Marine squadron had radar-equipped F6Fs for night fighting and was used to replace the AAF P–61s originally assigned. The P–61 was heavy and comparatively slow. It was a satisfactory defense against bombers, which were even slower, but the Japanese night attacks on the Leyte airfields were delivered mainly by fighter-bombers that simply outran the P–61s. The Marine night-fighter squadron was able to deal with the Japanese fighter-bombers, and the other three squadrons, equipped with F4Us, had been functioning as fighter-bombers in the Solomons, so they contributed to the striking force available for use against Japanese shipping. This was another example of the interservice cooperation that characterized the war in the Southwest Pacific.[69]

It should not be thought that the Japanese were opposed only by the beleaguered forces on Leyte. B–24s of the Fifth and Thirteenth Air Forces struck airfields in the southern and central Philippines every day that weather permitted, but these attacks were limited to fields no farther north than Leyte because of the distance from New Guinea bases. Even when Thirteenth Air Force heavy bombers moved into Morotai, they could not reach the main Japanese bases on Luzon. Even so, heavy bomber strikes on Japanese airfields east, west, and south of Leyte were highly useful because they interfered with reinforcement of the Philippines from the East Indies. On the other hand, Luzon was the center of Japanese power in the Philippines, and it was out of reach of AAF bombers.

Luzon would not escape Allied attention, however. By November 3, Admiral Halsey had replenished his mighty naval force, and after coordination with General MacArthur concentrated upon the Luzon airfields. The strikes were not as heavy as they otherwise might have been because it was necessary to maintain so many fighters over the fleet as defense against *kamikazes*. Nevertheless, the Japanese suffered heavily. The naval aviators believed they had destroyed 439 aircraft, which were widely dispersed and even concealed at long distances from their runways, and they sank significant amounts of shipping.[70]

Although General Kenney never said "we have lost air superiority," he was nonetheless keenly aware of this fact in October and November. He wrote General Arnold a long letter on November 14, in which he noted that "carrier-based aircraft, even in the overwhelming numbers we are using, do not supply the answer for air cover and support. . . . They simply do not have the staying power and therefore do not have the dependability of land-based aircraft." In the same letter he said, "I believe that it would be a mistake to take this operation as a criterion for the

A B–25 roars in to attack a Japanese vessel carrying reinforcements to the Japanese base at Leyte.

future. As long as the enemy is ready to fight and has the means to do it, amphibious operations should be made only after his air forces are destroyed or pushed back so far that they cannot effectively oppose the expedition."[71]

Even after forty years, it is easy to see from the record that the Leyte operation was beginning to exasperate the commanders, the pilots, and the troops on the ground. Relations between Kenney, MacArthur, and Adm. T. C. Kinkaid, commander of MacArthur's Seventh Fleet, had been remarkably good thus far in the war. Now, when Kinkaid complained that Kenney's fighters did not give his battleships adequate protection against *kamikazes*, Kenney told him to put his story in writing, "and I would then prefer charges against him for false official statements." Even General MacArthur seems to have engaged in a shouting match with the admiral on at least one occasion.[72]

The Japanese were still pouring ground forces into Leyte and aerial reinforcements into Luzon and the Visayas throughout November. The turning point of the Leyte campaign came on December 7 when the American 77th Division landed at Ormoc, which had been the main Japanese landing point. By now, more American planes were available on the still poor Leyte airfields, and P–38s provided air cover that Admiral Kinkaid described as the finest he had seen in the Southwest Pacific. The P–38s claimed 53 Japanese planes shot down, P–47s claimed 2 more, and an F6F destroyed a bomber over Ormoc that night; but *kamikazes* sank a destroy-

363

er, a transport, and a landing ship, and they damaged a number of others. Supply convoys to Ormoc, particularly the second one on December 11–12, suffered heavy and costly Japanese air attacks, but yet the supplies were delivered. The Japanese, on the other hand, were now cut off from resupply; they would continue to fight to the death and to inflict casualties, but their fate was sealed.[73]

Insofar as time would allow, land-based air support would be made available for Allied landings on Luzon, eventually scheduled for January 9, 1945. All of Luzon would be within range of aircraft based on the neighboring island of Mindoro, and General MacArthur was determined, despite the air battle still raging over Leyte and the adjacent waters, to take that island and establish airfields there. Army Air Forces aircraft could play only a minor role in the invasion of Mindoro; the landing sites were more than 250 miles from Leyte, which meant that only long-range P–38s could give significant cover. The brunt of protecting the convoys to Mindoro would have to be borne by Admiral Kinkaid's escort carriers, and they would have all they could handle. Fortunately, Admiral Halsey's fast carriers returned to Luzon for a number of strikes. More than 200 Japanese planes were destroyed in the air and on the ground, but carrier plane losses were not light, and three carriers were damaged by *kamikazes*. Halsey felt it necessary to withdraw until better tactics for defense against suicide planes had been developed.[74]

In support of the Mindoro attack, Far East Air Forces bombers pounded the fields they could reach in the southern and central Philippines. General Kenney believed that these strikes had destroyed 121 Japanese planes in the air or on the ground on December 13, but this was considerably more than intelligence estimates attributed to his forces. Much more effective, since they had targets, were the fighters and bombers of Task Force 38, which came back to Luzon for three days, December 14–16, and claimed 270 aircraft destroyed for a loss of 27. Even if these claims were not exaggerated, there was still a substantial number of possible *kamikazes* on the island. However, Admiral Halsey, at this time, suffered no ship losses. He had reduced the number of bombers and increased the number of fighters on his carriers, had devised a method that prevented *kamikazes* from finding carriers by following their planes home, and had put a fighter patrol over every known Japanese air base within striking range of the task force. Despite all of this, the convoys to Mindoro would suffer terribly from suicide attacks.[75]

Proving that there were Japanese planes left in the Visayas and on Luzon, the main Mindoro attack force was surprised in the middle of the afternoon on December 13 by a bomb-laden dive bomber that crashed into the cruiser *Nashville* killing 133 men, including the designated air commander for Mindoro, and wounding 190 more. Two hours later, another *kamikaze* crashed into the destroyer *Haraden*, inflicting another 38 casualties. So efficient had amphibious assault become by the end of 1944, however, that despite *kamikaze* attacks, all the ships carrying men and supplies, with one exception, were unloaded and on the way back to Leyte by 1900 on December 14. The six escort carriers that supported the landing remained through December 16. Engineers on Mindoro had a fair weather strip ready for fighters on December 20, but the loss of a 1,000-barrel gasoline dump to Japanese air attack slowed down operations for a time. Air cover from December 26 on was all that could be expected, though certainly not all that sailors could have desired, for losses continued to be heavy. Relief came only when the *kamikazes* shifted their attention to convoys on their way to invade Luzon.[76]

The purpose of the Mindoro occupation, of course, was to provide land-based air for the support of landings on Luzon and of ground operations after the landing. Fighters from Mindoro could cover heavy bomber attacks on Luzon airfields, and these began on December 22. The strength and frequency of these B–24 strikes was limited, however, because the bombers had to stage through crowded Tacloban Airfield on Leyte on their way home to Anguar in the Palaus. Fighters from Leyte were making sweeps over Luzon before the end of November, and in December, B–25s began to strike northward from Leyte. Mindoro-based planes attacked Japanese shipping trying to make its way into and out of Luzon, and some targets important to the invasion were bombed. Probably more important than anything else, however, was the fact that Mindoro-based fighters could play a large role in protecting Luzon-bound convoys. Adm. Samuel Eliot Morison, the Navy's official historian of the Second World War, suggested that AAF planes on Mindoro "probably saved that bloody passage from becoming a mass slaughter."[77]

It was obvious that the AAF planes based on Leyte and Mindoro could not suppress all the Japanese air power available to contest a Luzon landing. Once more, Admiral Halsey's Task Force 38 would have a major role, and in addition, no fewer than 18 escort carriers were to support the landing by providing air cover and ground support for the troops going ashore. Admiral Halsey, when weather permitted, again kept a fighter patrol over each known Japanese airfield near enough to launch strikes against his fleet or the landing force. The Third Fleet carrier planes had in the week of January 3–9, flown over 3,000 sorties, dropped 700 tons of bombs, and saved hundreds of American lives. The Luzon-bound convoys needed all the help they could get because *kamikaze* attacks continued to inflict heavy losses. Some relief came on January 8, 1945, when 80 A–20s and 40 B–25s of the Fifth Air Force staged a massive low-level strike on Clark Field, but deadly *kamikaze* strikes continued through January 12. These attacks did not delay the landings at all, and by January 12, there were no more flyable Japanese planes on Luzon, or there were no more pilots ready to make the ultimate sacrifice. Air supremacy in the Philippines had finally been achieved, and in dealing with *kamikazes* nothing else would do. This essential achievement had required the utmost effort by the AAF and the Navy air arm, with an assist from the Marines.[78]

Lessons Learned

By the end of the battle for the control of the air over Hollandia, certain general principles applicable to the attainment of air superiority in the South and Southwest Pacific had become evident. The first essential was a force of adequate fighter aircraft with well-trained and experienced pilots. Without this, no air base could be established and maintained within range of enemy air. An adequate flow of replacement planes and replacement personnel was critical because combat losses and operational losses were inevitable. If these fighter planes were to defend their bases, they must have early warning of enemy attacks. In the early phases of war in New Guinea and in the Solomons, such warning was provided by coastwatchers. Later, radar provided this vital service.

Somewhere over the horizon were the main base or bases from which enemy air action stemmed. In 1942, this was Rabaul for Allied forces in both New Guinea and the Solomons, and Rabaul continued to be the main base of operations against South Pacific forces until it was finally neutralized. But in New Guinea, by mid-1943 Wewak had come at least to rival Rabaul in importance and by the end of the year had come to exceed it. While South Pacific forces completed the neutralization of Rabaul, aided certainly by the losses the Japanese suffered opposing Southwest Pacific operations in New Guinea and New Britain, Southwest Pacific forces could devote more attention to Wewak. When Wewak was disposed of, attention could be switched quickly to Hollandia.

In order to attack the main enemy base, Allied air power had to be able to reach it. Normally this was no problem for heavy bombers—B–17s and B–24s—but the Allies originally had no fighters with the range to escort heavy bombers on long daylight missions, and experience soon demonstrated that bombers could not operate in daylight over well-defended bases without fighter escort. Therefore, the heavy bombers either attacked the main enemy base at night, or they bombed nearer, intermediate bases to which they could be escorted in daylight. To bring the main enemy bases within daylight range it was necessary either to secure airfields closer to the enemy stronghold or to extend the range of fighters and light and medium bombers.

In practice both were done. The seizure of the Dobodura area on the north coast of Papua brought Rabaul within range of Fifth Air Force B–25s and made it possible, though barely, for P–38s to escort bombers to Rabaul.

The seizure of Munda in New Georgia made it possible for F4Us and P–38s to escort heavy bombers to Bougainville from the South Pacific, and Bougainville bases put fighters and light bombers within range of Rabaul. The seizure of bases on the New Guinea coast and the literal creation of bases in the Markham and Ramu valleys brought bombers within effective escorted range of Wewak. These same bases served for launching the aerial assault on Hollandia. However, the key factor in this achievement was the modification of P–38 fighters by adding 150 gallons of gasoline so as to extend their range.

If postwar assessments were accurate, the earlier night-bombing phase of aerial assault did little damage. Certainly Japanese night bombing, while annoying, usually did Allied bases no great harm. When the first daylight attacks came, the Japanese resisted vigorously unless they had been surprised. At Wewak, in August of 1943, they were surprised and they suffered great losses. But they recovered quickly, and it took seven months more to truly neutralize Wewak. Rabaul began coming under sustained daylight attack in October 1943, maintained vigorous air resistance until February, and still bristled with ground defenses when the war came to an end. Wewak and Rabaul were battles of attrition; powerful American forces gradually grew more powerful, and the weaker Japanese forces lost more and more of the little strength they had. The greater the difference in strength between the opposing air forces, the less the proportion of loss was for the stronger and the greater it was for the weaker. American claims of Japanese planes destroyed were undoubtedly too high, but Japanese losses were far greater than Allied losses in these campaigns.

Obviously, it was better to destroy enemy planes on the ground than to be forced to shoot them out of the air. Many planes were destroyed on the ground at Rabaul over the long battle that lasted from mid-1942 to early 1944, but most often by low-level attack. Such low-level attacks as were mounted against Rabaul were directed mainly against shipping in the harbor rather than against airfields. Incidentally, in 1943 such attacks at Rabaul were unacceptably costly in men and aircraft. At Wewak and Hollandia, on the other hand, low-level strikes by A–20s and B–25s destroyed hundreds of Japanese planes on the ground and American losses were amazingly low.

The Americans at Henderson Field and the Japanese at dozens of airstrips in the Solomons and in New Guinea proved again and again that bombardment might knock out an airfield for a short time, but that it need not stay out. A runway pock-marked with a dozen craters at nightfall was often ready to receive planes before the sun rose the next morning. The larger the bombs used against runways, the bigger the craters and the more difficult they were to fill. Yet, there was a trade off, because the same number of planes dropping smaller bombs would make more craters.

Sooner or later in the course of the neutralization of an air base, antiaircraft defenses were targeted. At Rabaul and Wewak, this came fairly late in the battle. At Hollandia, part of the first daylight attack was directed at suspected antiaircraft emplacements. As these defenses were destroyed, the bombing improved; it was only natural that a pilot or bombardier who was not being shot at could concentrate better on his work. Moreover, as the antiaircraft defenses were eliminated, the big and comparatively slow heavy bombers could come down to medium altitude. Bombing from 10,000 feet was far more than twice as accurate as bombing from 20,000 feet.

Missions not directly aimed at the base being neutralized could contribute much. The first carrier strike at Truk was almost certainly instrumental in persuading the Japanese to give up the aerial defense of Rabaul. The fact that Rabaul was faced with two separate forces operating in different directions was a major factor. Had the Japanese commander at Rabaul been able to concentrate all his air power against either New Guinea or the Solomons, the battle to neutralize Rabaul would have been longer and costlier. If South Pacific forces had not been able to take over the Rabaul campaign almost totally in early 1944, the neutralization of Wewak and Hollandia would have been much more difficult. Darwin, in northwestern Australia, was a great distance from New Guinea, but strikes from there against the East Indies almost certainly kept reinforcements away from New Guinea.

Maintenance crews were just as essential as pilots to an effective air campaign. The Allies developed a marvelously inventive and efficient depot system in Australia, but it was the ground crews at the airfields that kept the bombers and fighters flying. Probably Japanese maintenance was as good as American at the beginning of the war, but by 1944 this was certainly not true. As the Allied troops moved forward, the maintenance men at the Japanese airfields they captured were either killed or fled into the jungle. Those stationed at the bypassed airfields were not harmed, but they had been eliminated from the war just as effectively as if they had been killed. After the war, the Deputy Chief of the Japanese Army General Staff estimated that not more than ten percent of the Army aircraft sent from Japan to the Southwest Pacific ever got into combat. They were grounded by mechanical problems, and then, presumably, destroyed on the ground.[79]

Engineers were just as essential as aircraft, aircrews, and maintenance men in the neutralization of Japanese bases and the resulting achievement of air supremacy. From Guadalcanal to Bougainville, from Port Moresby to Gusap, the Seabees and engineers built the wharves, the pipelines, the roads, and the runways that were essential to air base operation. Sometimes, as at Munda, they had an abandoned Japanese base to work with. But more often, as at Bougainville and at Dobodura, they had to clear a jungle, drain swamps, move huge amounts of earth, and create from nothing a base bigger and busier than most airfields in the United States.

The air forces could not have operated without the bases provided by the engineers, but before engineers could go to work, infantry had to take and hold the ground, and the Navy had to put the infantry ashore and supply it. Certainly the hardest and dirtiest work, and quite probably the most hazardous work, in achieving air supremacy was done by the Marines and by the ground troops of the United States and Australian forces who stormed ashore on tropical beaches, took the ground, and then defended it against Japanese counterattack. In the long run, naval, ground, and air action was all directed toward the achievement of air supremacy, and the Pacific campaigns were fine examples of willing and successful cooperation by all arms.

South Pacific forces first had to fight for air superiority over Guadalcanal, then New Georgia, Bougainville, and Rabaul; but with the neutralization of Rabaul, the Allies had absolute air supremacy in the South Pacific, which became almost an inactive theater. General Kenney's Allied Air Forces had had to win air superiority over Port Moresby, then over Papua, then the Huon Peninsula, and finally over Wewak and Hollandia. But with the neutralization of these last two bases, the Allies had practical air supremacy over all of New Guinea. Basically, this air supremacy had been achieved by land-based air power. Carrier strikes against Rabaul and Truk had certainly been helpful, and carrier support was essential for the long leap to Hollandia. Yet, it was land-based aircraft—from the United States, New Zealand, and Australia—that defeated Japanese air power in the South and Southwest Pacific.

In the Philippines, Allied land-based air power would be too long unavailable or too weak, and that would make a great difference. Then the *kamikazes* appeared, and that added another great obstacle. The *kamikaze* effort in the Philippines was largely improvised, but even so it inflicted damage to a degree American naval forces had not experienced since Pearl Harbor and the early months at Guadalcanal. This improved effort inflicted shocking damage: 24 ships sunk, including 2 escort carriers, 2 destroyers, and 2 minesweepers, and 57 ships damaged, including 4 battleships, 6 cruisers (some of them several times), 5 fleet carriers, and 9 escort carriers. Shipboard casualties estimated 1,230 men killed and 1,800 wounded. Use of suicide pilots was the most effective Japanese aerial tactic of the war insofar as shipping was concerned. It was indeed fortunate that the Allies were able to meet and eventually to check this measure of desperation.[80]

How were the *kamikazes* in the Philippine checked? In part they checked themselves; successful or unsuccessful, a *kamikaze* pilot flew only one mission. Secondly, although suicide tactics improved from the beginning of the Leyte campaign until the last attacks off Luzon, there was no way for those pilots who flew successful missions to pass on their experience to others. Thirdly, the *kamikaze* pilots were not the skilled veterans of Pearl Harbor, Midway, Guadalcanal, Buna, and Rabaul. In early 1945, Japan had thousands of Army and Navy planes deployed, but the pilots who were to fly them were mainly still in basic training. It did not, however, take tremendous skill to point an airplane at a ship and hold it steady until it crashed. In the long run, the *kamikazes* in the Philippines were defeated by the same tactics that had worked against Rabaul, Wewak, and Hollandia, except that the task in the Philippines was far more difficult. There were scores of enemy-held airfields to be neutralized rather than a few. In the battle against the *kamikazes*, air supremacy had to be absolute; one operational Japanese plane pilot was as great a hazard in the autumn of 1944 and the first two weeks of 1945 as ten, twenty, or perhaps even fifty planes had been in 1942 and 1943.[81]

How, then, was such absolute supremacy established? In the first place, hundreds of Japanese aircraft, *kamikazes* and otherwise, were shot out of the air. While the Japanese were contesting Allied air superiority over Leyte and the surrounding waters, and making a real contest out of it, they suffered heavy losses. The naval strikes in support of the Leyte, Mindoro, and Luzon invasions destroyed hundreds of Japanese planes, and the AAF and naval top cover for the invasion convoys took a heavy toll. Secondly, airdromes were bombed. This could not be totally accomplished in advance of invasion, as had been the case at Hollandia, but fields in Mindanao and the central Philippines were pounded steadily during the battle of Leyte, and as Allied airfields on Leyte, and later Mindoro, were finally ready for use, the Japanese fields were bombed more heavily than ever. The Navy also bombed airfields, but in the nature of things carrier-based bombers could not carry the bomb load of heavy bombers, or even medium bombers. The most effective tactic, however, as had always been the case, was to go over airfields at low level, bombing and strafing aircraft on the ground. The Navy destroyed planes on the ground this way, and before the end of the landings at Lingayen on Luzon, AAF light and medium bombers were making sweeps comparable to those that had been so effective in New Guinea. The Navy, as has been mentioned, was at times able to keep a fighter cover over all known Japanese airfields within range of the carriers, so that the pilot of a concealed Japanese aircraft committed suicide simply by attempting to take off.

The Japanese high command had sought to make Leyte the decisive battle of the Philippines campaign, but lost. In its desperate attempt to prevent an Allied victory, the Japanese turned to suicide attacks. These were far more effective than conventional air attacks, but they were not successful enough. The Japanese were far from ready to give up; the *kamikazes* would inflict far more damage at Okinawa than in the Philippines. Even so,

370

the air war in the Philippines was over for all practical purposes on January 12, 1945. By now, the awesome power of the Far East Air Forces could be devoted primarily to the support of ground troops; American infantry on Luzon probably received more direct air support than had been given to ground troops in all the preceding Pacific campaigns. This was possible because air supremacy, established at Rabaul, Wewak, and Hollandia, and then temporarily lost at Leyte, was fully restored during the invasion of Luzon.

Notes

1. Thomas H. Greer, *The Development of Air Doctrine in the Army Air Arm, 1917–1941* [USAF Historical Study No. 89] (Maxwell AFB, Ala., 1955), pp 31, 37, 67–70, *passim.*

2. *Ibid.*, pp 116–21, 129; Richard H. Kohn and Joseph P. Harahan, eds, *Air Superiority in World War II and Korea: An Interview with Gen. James Ferguson, Gen. Robert M. Lee, Gen. William Momyer, and Gen. Elwood R. Quesada* (Washington, 1983), pp 14–30; Joe Gray Taylor, "They Taught Tactics," *Aerospace Historian,* Spring 1966, *passim.*

3. Greer, *Development of Air Doctrine,* pp 59, 62–63, 82, 129; Gen George Kenney Notebooks, vol I, entry, Aug 13, 1942, currently located at Office of Air Force History, Bolling AFB, Washington, DC; Claire Lee Chennault, *Way of a Fighter: The Memoirs of Claire Lee Chennault* (New York, 1949), pp 24–26; Martin Caidin, *The Ragged, Rugged Warriors* (New York, 1967), p 107.

4. Wesley F. Craven and James L. Cate, eds, *The Army Air Forces in World War II,* 7 vols (Chicago, 1955; reprint, Office of Air Force History, 1983), Vol VI: *Men and Planes,* pp 212–13; Elke C. Weal, comp, *Combat Aircraft of World War II* (New York, 1977), pp 187–213; Enzo Angelucci, *The Rand McNally Encyclopedia of Military Aircraft, 1914–1980* (New York, 1981), p 246; Robin Higham, *Air Power: A Concise History* (New York, 1972), p 185.

5. Weal, *Combat Aircraft of World War II,* pp 187–213; Angelucci, *Rand McNally Encyclopedia of Military Aircraft,* pp 236–37, 246.

6. Craven and Cate, *AAF in WW II,* Vol I: *Plans and Early Operations, January 1939 to August 1942,* pp 151–233, 366–402; Samuel Eliot Morison, *History of United States Naval Operations in World War II,* Vol III: *The Rising Sun in the Pacific: 1931–April 1942* (Boston, 1951), pp 80–380.

7. *Ibid.*

8. Kenney Notebooks, vol I, Aug 13, 1942; Ltr, Kenney to Burdette S. Wright, Dec 8, 1942, Kenney Notebooks, vol III, both Office of Air Force History; Craven and Cate, *AAF in WW II,* Vol VI: *Men and Planes,* p xi; Lewis H. Brereton, *The Brereton Diaries: The War in the Air in the Pacific, Middle East, and Europe, 3 October 1941–8 May 1945* (New York, 1976), p 7; Morison, Vol III: *Rising Sun in the Pacific,* pp 22, 386; Angelucci, *Rand McNally Encyclopedia of Military Aircraft,* pp 224–25; Masatake Okumiya and Jiro Horikoshi with Martin Caidin, *Zero* (New York, 1956), pp 56–59; William N. Hess, *Fighter Sweep: The 5th and 13th Fighter Commands in World War II* (Garden City, N.Y., 1974), pp 1–47; Caidin, *Ragged, Rugged Warriors,* p 200; Higham, *Air Power,* p 185.

9. Frederick C. Sherman, *Combat Command: American Aircraft Carriers in the Pacific* (New York, 1950), pp 92–117; Morison, Vol III: *Rising Sun in the Pacific,* p 386; Samuel Eliot Morison, *History of the United States Naval Operations in World War II,* Vol IV: *Coral Sea, Midway and Submarine Actions, May 1942–August 1942* (Boston, 1951); Craven and Cate, *AAF in WW II,* Vol I: *Plans and Early Operations,* pp 444-51.

10. Sherman, *Combat Command,* p 117; Morison, Vol IV: *Coral Sea, Midway and Submarine Actions,* pp 14, 22–28, 42–43, 48, 53, 64.

11. Morison, Vol IV: *Coral Sea, Midway and Submarine Actions,* pp 69–159; Gordon W. Prange, Donald M. Goldstein and Katherine V. Dillon, *Miracle at Midway* (New York, 1982),

passim; Craven and Cate, *AAF in WW II,* Vol I: *Plans and Early Operations,* pp 451–62.

12. Morison, Vol IV: *Coral Sea, Midway and Submarine Actions,* pp 104–05, 131; Prange, *Miracle at Midway,* p 311; Sherman, *Combat Command,* pp 133–34; Narrative History and Chronological Order of Events, *USS Enterprise* (CV–6), May 12, 1938–Sept 25, 1945, dated Oct 1, 1945, Operational Archives, U.S. Navy Historical Center, Washington Navy Yard, (USNHC).

13. Morison, Vol V: *The Struggle for Guadalcanal, August 1942–February 1943,* pp 16, 68; Sherman, *Combat Command,* pp 162, 170; John Miller, Jr., *Guadalcanal: The First Offensive* [United States Army in World War II: The War in the Pacific] (Washington, 1949), pp 59–99.

14. Craven and Cate, *The AAF in WW II,* Vol IV: *The Pacific: Guadalcanal to Saipan,* pp 38–44; Miller, *Guadalcanal,* pp 105–10; Morison, Vol V: *The Struggle for Guadalcanal,* pp 68–77.

15. Craven and Cate, *AAF in WW II,* Vol IV: *Guadalcanal to Saipan,* pp 38–60; Morison, Vol V: *The Struggle for Guadalcanal,* pp 73–125.

16. Morison, Vol V: *The Struggle for Guadalcanal,* p 11; Miller, *Guadalcanal,* pp 107–09; Intvw, Gen William O. Brice, USMC, 1976, USAFHRC, 57; Commendation, Sept 29, 1942, Col Harold W. Bauer, Personal Papers, Personal Papers Collection, Marine Corps Historical Center, Washington Navy Yard (MCHC); Narrative History, USS *Enterprise,* 4; Sherman, *Combat Command,* pp 162–70; Intvw, W. A. Noll, Mar 23, 1943, U.S. Air Force Historical Research Center, Maxwell AFB, Ala., (USAFHRC); Intvw, Gen Nathan F. Twining, undated, 10, USAFHRC; Obumiya and Horikoshi, *Zero,* p 207.

17. Craven and Cate, *AAF in WW II,* Vol IV: *Guadalcanal to Saipan,* pp 52–58; Miller, *Guadalcanal,* pp 107–10, 146–49, 167–69; Morison, Vol V: *The Struggle for Guadalcanal,* pp 75–78, 87–122, 138–39.

18. Miller, *Guadalcanal,* p 173; Morison, Vol V: *The Struggle for Guadalcanal,* pp 149–54, 229–63; Frank O. Hough, *The Island War: The United States Marine Corps in the Pacific* (Philadelphia, 1947), pp 65–66, 73–77.

19. Vern Haugland, *The AAF Against Japan* (New York, 1948), p 155; Douglas Gillison, *Royal Australian Air Force, 1939–1942* (Canberra, 1962), pp 544–47, 583–84, 653; Craven and Cate, *AAF in WW II,* Vol IV: *Guadalcanal to Saipan,* pp 3–10; Samuel Milner, *Victory in Papua,* [United States Army in World War II: The War in the Pacific] (Washington, 1957), pp 33–55.

20. Craven and Cate, *AAF in WW II,* Vol IV: *Guadalcanal to Saipan,* pp 7–8.

21. George C. Kenney, *General Kenney Reports: A Personal Memoir of the Pacific War* (New York, 1949), pp 35–95; Chronology, Fifth Air Force, 1942–1944, USAFHRC.

22. Kenney, *Reports,* pp 35–115.

23. *Ibid.;* Craven and Cate, *AAF in WW II,* Vol IV: *Guadalcanal to Saipan,* pp 103–06; see also Gen George C. Kenney, *The Saga of Pappy Gunn* (New York, 1959), *passim.*

24. See Kenney Notebooks, July-December 1942, vols I, II, III *inter alia,* Office of Air Force History; Kenney, *Reports,* vol III, pp 45, 61–134; Richard L. Watson, Jr., *The Fifth Air Force in the Huon Peninsula Campaign* (Washington, 1946), pp 8, 19, 200–01, *passim.*

25. Watson, *Fifth Air Force in Huon Peninsula Campaign,* pp 200–01; Kenney, *Reports,* pp 110–15, 123, 131; Kenney Notebooks, Aug-Nov 1942, vols I, II, III *inter alia,* Office of Air Force History; Milner, *Victory in Papua,* pp 125–46.

26. Craven and Cate, *AAF in WW II,* Vol IV: Guadalcanal to Saipan, pp 119–28; Watson, *Fifth Air Force in the Huon Peninsula Campaign,* pp 8, 112–13; Robert L. Eichelberger in collaboration with Milton MacKaye, *Our Jungle Road to Tokyo* (New York, 1950), pp 23–24, 37–38; Karl C. Dod, *The Corps of Engineers in the War Against Japan* [United States Army in World War II: The Technical Services[(Washington, 1966), pp 198, 218–21, 257; Haugland, *AAF Against Japan,* p 164; Milner, *Victory In Papua,* p 378.

27. Kenney Notebooks, Aug 13, 1942, vol I, Office of Air Force History.

28. Kenney Papers, 1942, *passim;* Vice Adm George Carroll Dyer, *The Amphibians Came to Conquer: The Story of Admiral Richmond Kelley Turner,* 2 vols (Washington, 1970), vol I, pp 391–92; "Pappy" (Gregory) Boyington, *Baa Baa Black Sheep* (New York, 1958), pp 59, 216, 222; Intvw, Gen George C. Kenney, Aug 10–21, 1974, 10, USAFHRC; Watson, *Fifth Air Force in the Huon Peninsula Campaign,* pp 2, 10.

29. Craven and Cate, *AAF in WW II*, Vol IV: *Guadalcanal to Saipan*, pp 139, 159, 177, 239, 241; Vol VI: *Men and Planes*, pp 83, 96–97; Dod, *The Corps of Engineers*, pp 222; Ltr, Brig Gen Ennis Whitehead to Kenney, Feb 10, 1943, Kenney Notebooks, vol IV, Office of Air Force History.

30. Kenney Notebooks, Aug 11, 1942, Aug 31, 1942, vol I, and May 2, 1943, vol V; all Office of Air Force History; also Ltr, Kenney to Burdette S. Wright, Dec 8, 1942; George Odgers, *Air War Against Japan, 1943–1945* (Canberra, 1957), pp 44–67; Boyington, *Baa Baa Black Sheep*, pp 59, 216, 222; Kohn and Harahan, eds, *Air Superiority in World War II and Korea*, pp 19–20; Chennault, *Way of a Fighter*, pp 21, 113–14; John M. Lindley, *Carrier Victory; The Air War in the Pacific* (New York, 1978), pp 90–91; Gillison, *Royal Australian Air Force, 1939–1942;* Watson, *Fifth Air Force in the Huon Peninsula Campaign*, p 40.

31. Craven and Cate, *AAF in WW II*, Vol IV: *Guadalcanal to Saipan*, pp 203–80; John Miller, Jr., *Cartwheel: The Reduction of Rabaul* [United States Army in World War II: The War in the Pacific] (Washington, 1959), *passim.*

32. The First Marine Aircraft Wing, HQ USMC, Washington, DC, Historical Division, Operations Archives, USNHC, p 3; Craven and Cate, *AAF in WW II*, Vol IV: *Guadalcanal to Saipan*, pp 211–17; Haugland, *AAF against Japan*, p 144; Intvw, Gen Dean C. Strother, Aug 21–24, 1978, USAFHRC, pp 62–63.

33. Strother Intvw, 54, 62–63; Okumiya and Horikoshi, *Zero*, pp 229–30, *passim;* Intvw, Gen William O. Brice, USMC, 1976, USAFHRC, p 57; Maj Gen John P. Condon, USMC, Oral History Transcript, Dec 1970, MCHC, pp 34–38; Intvw, Lt Col Danforth P. Miller, Jr, Jun 29, 1975, USAFHRC, p 41; Watson, *Fifth Air Force in the Huon Peninsula Campaign*, p 102; Craven and Cate, *AAF in WW II*, Vol IV: *Guadalcanal to Saipan*, pp 217–19.

34. Information on Operations in the Solomon Islands from Jul 31 to Nov 30, 1942, HQ 11th Bomb Gp, Dec 3, 1942, USAFHRC, p 6; AG 373, Whitehead to Kenney, Jul 18, 1943, vol VI, as well as Kenney Notebooks, Aug 1942-Jul 1943 vols I–VI, *inter alia*, Office of Air Force History; Craven and Cate, *AAF in World War II*, Vol IV: *Guadalcanal to Saipan*, pp 205–06, 217–19, 221; Maj John N. Rentz, *Marines in the Central Solomons* (Washington, 1952), pp 140–43; Watson, *Fifth Air Force in the Huon Peninsula Campaign*, pp 128–29, 167–68, 230.

35. First Marine Air Wing, p 4; Strother Intvw, pp 60–61, 75; Dyer, *Amphibians*, vol I, p 527; Samuel Eliot Morison, *History of United States Naval Operations in World War II*, Vol VI: *Breaking the Bismarcks Barrier, 22 July 1942–1 May 1944* (Boston, 1950), p 150; Richard G. Hubler and John A. DeChant, *Flying Leathernecks: The Complete Record of Marine Corps Aviation in Action, 1941–1944* (Garden City, NY, 1944), p 2; Craven and Cate, *AAF in World War II*, Vol IV: *Guadalcanal to Saipan*, pp 222–23, 225–34; Sherman, *Combat Command*, pp 188–89; Haugland, *AAF Against Japan*, p 147.

36. Miller, *Cartwheel*, pp 175, 179–81, 184; Craven and Cate, *AAF in WW II*, Vol IV: *Guadalcanal to Saipan*, pp 237–39.

37. Kenney Papers, Apr 11, May 3, June 10 all vol V and Oct 3, 12, 15, 18, 23–25, 29, vol VII, all 1943, Office of Air Force History; "Neutralization of Rabaul: Air Evaluation Board," SWPA, May 10, 1946, pp 14, 23–25; Kenney, *Reports*, p 241, Watson, *Fifth Air Force in the Huon Peninsula Campaign*, pp 185–86.

38. Craven and Cate, *AAF in World War II*, Vol IV: *Guadalcanal to Saipan*, pp 251–55; Hough, *Island War*, p 105; Miller, *Cartwheel*, pp 235–36. 242–43; Morison, Vol VI: *Breaking the Bismarcks Barrier*, pp 286–87; Okumiya and Horikoshi, *Zero*, p 215.

39. Morison, Vol VI: *Breaking the Bismarcks Barrier*, pp 293-320; *The Bougainville Landing and the Battle of Empress Agusta Bay, 27 October–2 November 1943, Combat Narratives: Solomon Islands Campaign*, vol XII (Washington, 1945), p 46.

40. "Neutralization of Rabaul," pp 25–26, 47; Kenney Notebooks Nov, 1–26, 1943, vol VII, Ltr, Kenney to Arnold, Dec 4, 1943; Kenney Notebooks, vol VII, Office of Air Force History; *Bougainville Operation*, p 14; Sherman, *Combat Command*, pp 204–06; E. B. Potter and Chester W. Nimitz, eds, *The Great Sea War: The Story of Naval Action in World War II* (Englewood Cliffs, N.J., 1960), pp 301–09; Harris G. Warren, *The Fifth Air Force in the Conquest of the Bismarck Archipelago, November 1943 to March 1944* [Army Air Forces Historical Studies] (No. 43, Washington, 1945), pp 22–24; Morison, Vol VI: *Breaking the*

Bismarcks Barrier, pp 324–36.

41. Kenney Notebooks, Dec 25, 1943, vol VII, Office of Air Force History; "Neutralization of Rabaul," pp 30, 47; Intvw, Maj Gen Jared B. Crabb, Apr 17 and 28, 1970, USAFHRC, p 37; Sherman, *Combat Command*, p 207; Miller, *Cartwheel*, pp 269–70; Craven and Cate, *AAF in WW II*, Vol IV: *Guadalcanal to Saipan*, pp 350–51; Boyington, *Baa Baa Black Sheep*, pp 212–13.

42. "Neutralization of Rabaul," pp 33–35; Craven and Cate, *AAF in World War II*, Vol IV: *Guadalcanal to Saipan*, pp 352–53; Robert Sherrod, *History of Marine Corps Aviation in World War II* (Washington, 1952), pp 193–98.

43. "Neutralization of Rabaul," pp 31, 33–35, *passim;* Sherman, *Combat Command*, pp 209, 229–31; Kenney Notebooks, Feb 13 and Feb 19, 1944, vol VIII, Office of Air Force History; First Marine Aircraft Wing, p 6; Ltr, Whitehead to Kenney, Mar 5, 1944, vol VIII, Kenney Notebooks, Office of Air Force History; Potter and Nimitz, *The Great Sea War*, pp 338–39; Sherrod, *History of Marine Corps Aviation*, pp 193–206; J. M. S. Ross, *The Assault on Rabaul: Operations by the Royal New Zealand Air Force, December 1943–May 1944* (Wellington, New Zealand, 1949), *passim;* Vice Adm E. P. Forrestal, *Admiral Raymond A. Spruance, U.S.N.: A Study in Command* (Washington, 1966), pp 113–14; Lindley, Carrier Victory, p 114.

44. "Neutralization of Rabaul," p 47; Intvw, Maj Gen Crabb, p 39; Okumiya and Horikoshi, *Zero*, pp 280, 303–04; Potter and Nimitz, *The Great Sea War*, p 309.

45. Potter and Nimitz, *The Great Sea War*, pp 309, 338–39; Sabura Sakai with Martin Caidin and Fred Saito, *Samurai*, pp 25–35, 265–95; Intvw, Maj Gen John C. Condon, USMC, 1973, USAFHRC, pp 37, 46; Forty-Third Bomb Group Operation in the New Guinea Area, Jan 26, 1943, USAFHRC; Okumiya and Horikoshi, *Zero*, p 215; Sherman, *Combat Command*, p 218.

46. Craven and Cate, *AAF in WW II*, Vol IV: *Guadalcanal to Saipan*, p 168; Ltr, Whitehead to Kenney, May 29, 1943, vol V, Kenney Notebooks, Office of Air Force History.

47. Kenney, *Reports*, pp 251–71; Watson, *Fifth Air Force in the Huon Peninsula Campaign*, pp 188–92; Craven and Cate, *AAF in WW II*, Vol IV: *Guadalcanal to Saipan*, pp 175–76.

48. Watson, *Fifth Air Force in the Huon Peninsula Campaign*, pp 101–96.

49. Entry, Aug 17, 1943; Ltr, Whitehead to Kenney, Aug 18, 1943 both vol VI, Kenney Notebooks, Office of Air Force History; Watson, *Fifth Air Force in the Huon Peninsula Campaign*, pp 188–99, 229; Craven and Cate, *AAF in WW II*, Vol IV: *Guadalcanal to Saipan*, pp 178–80.

50. Administrative History, Commander, United States Naval Forces Southwest Pacific, 5, Chap VII, pp 6, 24; Navy Department Library, Washington Navy Yard, Washington DC; Kenney, Reports, pp 290–96; Watson, *Fifth Air Force in the Huon Peninsula Campaign*, pp 204, 207–10, 222–23; Dod, *The Corps of Engineers*, pp 230, 244, 252, 254; Craven and Cate, *AAF in WW II*, Vol IV: *Guadalcanal to Saipan*, pp 181–93.

51. Ltrs, Whitehead to Kenney, Jun 20, 1943, vol V, Aug 2, vol VI, both 1943 and Entry, Dec 17, 1943, Kenney Notebooks, vol VII, Office of Air Force History; "Airdrome Neutralization: Air Evaluation Board," SWPA, Apr 17, 1946, p 39; "Neutralization of Wewak," Mar 11–27, 1944: Air Evaluation Board, SWPA, p 143; Warren, *Fifth Air Force in the Bismarck Archipelago*, p 10; Watson, *Fifth Air Force in the Huon Peninsula Campaign*, pp 131, 143, 145, 164, 199–200, 206.

52. "Airdrome Neutralization," p 19; Memo to CG, ADVON Fifth Air Force, Oct 6, 1943, and Ltr, Kenney to Arnold, Dec 4, 1943, vol VII, Kenney Notebooks; Aug 1943–Feb, 1944, *inter alia*, vols VI, VII, VIII, Kenney Notebooks, Office of Air Force History; Kenney, *Reports*, p 351; Chronology, Fifth Air Force, Nov 1943-Feb, 1944; "Neutralization of Wewak," p 15; Craven and Cate, *AAF in WW II*, Vol IV: *Guadalcanal to Saipan*, pp 586–88.

53. "Neutralization of Wewak," *passim;* "Airdrome Neutralization," p 19; Warren, *Fifth Air Force in the Bismarck Archipelago*, pp 124–25; Kenney, *Reports*, pp 372–73; Kenney Notebooks, entry, Mar 1944, vol VIII, Office of Air Force History; Craven and Cate, *AAF in WW II*, Vol IV: *Guadalcanal to Saipan*, pp 588–91.

54. Kenney, *Reports*, p 373; Morison, Vol VI: *Breaking the Bismarcks Barrier*, pp 4–10, 28; Robert Ross Smith, *The Approach to the Philippines* [United States Army in World War

II: The War in the Pacific] (Washington, 1953), pp 6–48.

55. Craven and Cate, *AAF in WW II*, Vol IV: *Guadalcanal to Saipan*, pp 570–74.

56. Kenney, *Reports*, pp 373–77.

57. Kenney, *Reports*, pp 374–75; Kenney Notebooks, Mar 15–30, 1944, vol VIII, Office of Air Force History; Craven and Cate, *AAF in WW II*, Vol IV: *Guadalcanal to Saipan*, pp 576–93; Hess, *Fighter Sweep*, pp 157–58.

58. Craven and Cate, *AAF in WW II*, Vol IV: *Guadalcanal to Saipan*, pp 598; Morison, *Breaking the Bismarcks Barrier*, pp 30–35; Warren, *Fifth Air Force in the Bismarck Archipelago*, pp 124–25; Potter and Nimitz, *The Great Sea War*, p 344; Odgers, *Air War*, p 212; Haugland, *AAF Against Japan*, p 216.

60. "Airdrome Neutralization," p 22; Narrative History, USS *Enterprise*, p 7; Craven and Cate, *AAF in WW II*, Vol IV: *Guadalcanal to Saipan*, pp 595–96; Morison, *Breaking the Bismarcks Barrier*, pp 28–41, 65–71.

61. Haugland, *AAF Against Japan*, pp 180–81.

62. Craven and Cate, *AAF in WW II*, Vol IV: *Guadalcanal to Saipan*, 275–96; Samuel Eliot Morison, *History of United States Naval Operations in World War II*, Vol XII: *Leyte, June 1944–January 1945* (Boston, 1958), pp 8–12.

63. Morison, Vol XII: *Leyte*, p 13; Kenney, *Reports*, p 417; Haugland, *AAF Against Japan*, p 227; Sherman, *Combat Command*, pp 272, 75; Potter and Nimitz, *The Great Sea War*, p 364; Okumiya and Horikoshi, *Zero*, p 329.

64. Kenney, *Reports*, pp 417, 471.

65. Lindley, *Carrier Victory*, pp 134–37; Morison, Vol XII: *Leyte*, pp 87–93.

66. Morison, Vol XII: *Leyte*, pp 144–56; Craven and Cate, Vol V: *The Pacific: Matterhorn to Nagasaki, June 1944–August 1945*, pp 350–55; Kenney, *Reports*, pp 447–52.

67. Capt Rikihei Inoguchi and Comdr Tadashi Nakajima, formerly Imperial Japanese Navy, with Roger Pineau, *The Divine Wind: Japanese Kamikaze Forces in World War II* (London, 1959; reprint, Westwood, Conn., 1978), pp 59–106; Air Support of Pacific Amphibious Operations: A Report for Naval Analysis Division, U.S. Strategic Bombing Survey (Pacific), prepared by Commander Air Support Control Units, Amphibious Forces, U.S. Pacific Fleet, pp 11–12, NDL; Narrative History, *Enterprise*, p 7; Administrative History, Comdr U.S. Naval Forces, SWPA, p 79; Comdr, 7th Amphibious Force to CG Fifth AF, Oct 31, 1944, vol IX, Kenney Notebooks, Office of Air Force History; Sherman, *Combat Command*, pp 292–93, 305, 316; Odgers, *Air War*, p 307; Potter and Nimitz, *The Great Sea War*, p 428; Haugland, *AAF Against Japan*, pp 236–37.

68. Craven and Cate, *AAF in WW II*, Vol IV: *Guadalcanal to Saipan*, pp 368–85; Kenney Papers, Nov 26 and 30, 1944; Charles W. Boggs, Jr., *Marine Aviation in the Philippines* (Washington, 1951), pp 29–30, 114–15.

69. Craven and Cate, *AAF in WW II*, Vol VI: *Men and Planes*, pp 368–72; Morison, Vol XII: *Leyte*, pp 346–49; Dod, *Corps of Engineers*, pp 576–86; M. Hamil Cannon, *Leyte: The Return to the Philippines* [United States Army in World War II: The War in the Pacific] (Washington, 1954), pp 92–102; Kenney, *Reports*, pp 417, 451; Haugland, *AAF Against Japan*, pp 227–28.

70. Ltr, Kenney to Arnold, Nov 14, 1944, vol IX, Kenney Notebooks, Office of Air Force History.

71. Kenney Notebooks, entries, Nov 28, 1944, Nov 30, 1944, vol IX, Office of Air Force History.

72. Command History, Seventh Amphibious Force, Jan 10 1943-Dec 23, 1945, USNHC; Craven and Cate, *AAF in WW II*, Vol V: *Matterhorn to Nagasaki*, pp 381–83; Morison, Vol XII: *Leyte*, pp 375–92; Cannon, *Leyte*, pp 280–91.

73. Morison, Vol XII: *Leyte*, pp 354–60; Bernard Millot, *Divine Thunder: The Life and Death of the Kamikazes*, trans. by Lowell Baer (New York, 1971), p 76; Sherman, *Combat Command*, pp 320–21.

74. Kenney, *Reports*, pp 493–94; Craven and Cate, *AAF in WW II*, Vol V: *Matterhorn to Nagasaki*, pp 394–97; Samuel Eliot Morison, *History of United States Naval Operations in World War II*, Vol XIII: *The Liberation of the Philippines: Luzon, Mindanao, the Visayas, 1944–1945* (Boston, 1959), pp 52–29; Kenney Papers, Dec 13, 1944; Sherman, *Combat Command*, pp 322–23.

75. Administrative History, Comdr US Naval Forces, SWPA, p 88; Potter and Nimitz,

The Great Sea War, pp 430–31; Kenney Notebooks, Dec 13, 1944-Jan 4, 1945, vols IX and X, *inter alia*, Office of Air Force History; Morison, Vol XII: *The Liberation of the Philippines*, pp 17–51; Craven and Cate; *AAF in WW II*, Vol V: *Matterhorn to Nagasaki*, pp 396–401; Dod, *Corps of Engineers*, pp 586–87; Robert Ross Smith, *Triumph in the Philippines* [United States Army in World War II: The War in the Pacific] (Washington, 1963), pp 43–52.

76. Craven and Cate, *AAF in WW II*, Vol V: *Matterhorn to Nagasaki*, pp 306–08; Kenney, *Reports*, pp 500–01; Morison, Vol XII: *Liberation of the Philippines*, pp 50–51.

77. Morison, Vol XIII: *Liberation of the Philippines*, pp 87–92.

78. *Ibid.*, pp 98–102, 104–11, 15–19, 123–52; Air Support of Pacific Amphibious Operations, pp 12–13; Potter and Nimitz, *The Great Sea War*, pp 433–34; Charles W. Boggs, Jr., *Marine Aviation in the Philippines* (Washington, 1951), pp 47–48; Sherman, *Combat Command*, pp 324–25; Millot, *Divine Thunder*, p 87; Inoguchi and Nakajima, *Divine Wind*, pp 198–99; Craven and Cate, *AAF in WW II*, Vol V: *Matterhorn to Nagasaki*, pp 409–10; Kenney Notebooks, Jan 3-10, 1945, vol X, Office of Air Force History.

79. Seventh Amphibious Force: Command File, World War II: Operational Archives, USNHC, no pp; Odgers, *Air War*, pp 224–25; Potter and Nimitz, *The Great Sea War*, pp 346–48; Lindley, *Carrier Victory*, pp 125–26; Kenney, *Reports*, pp 404; Sherman, *Combat Command*, pp 272–73; Smith, *Approach to the Philippines*, pp 103–403; Samuel Eliot Morison, *History of United States Naval Operations in World War II*, Vol VIII: *New Guinea and the Marianas, March 1944–August 1944* (Boston, 1962), pp 91–145; Craven and Cate, *AAF in WW II*, Vol IV: *Guadalcanal to Saipan*, pp 615–70; Dod, *Corps of Engineers*, pp 520–69.

80. Morison, Vol XIII: *Liberation of the Philippines*, pp 1–152; Millot, *Divine Thunder*, pp 1–95; Inoguchi and Nakajima, *Divine Wind*, p 132; Smith, *Triumph in the Philippines*, pp 65–66.

81. Inoguchi and Nakajima, *Divine Wind*, p 132; "Airdrome Neutralization," p 56.

Bibliographical Essay

The study of the achievement of air superiority in the Southwest Pacific has its frustrating aspects, because no treatise, monograph, or report exists that is devoted directly to the subject. Indeed, no such air superiority study exists for the war against Japan as a whole. There are, however, three important reports by the Southwest Pacific Air Evaluation Board, entitled "Airdrome Neutralization" (1946), "Neutralization of Rabaul" (1946), and "Neutralization of Wewak" (1944). All three of these documents are located at the U.S. Air Force Historical Research Center, Maxwell AFB, Alabama, hereafter referred to as USAFHRC. The first applies to the Philippines, and the applications of the other two are obvious.

Unit histories are less useful in studying air superiority than they are in studying other aspects of air war in the 1940s. During the early months of the war, when survival fully occupied the attention of those fighting the Japanese air forces, few unit histories were kept. Later unit histories were too often maintained by a clerk who knew nothing of strategy and little more of tactics. Even well kept histories of squadrons and groups are of limited use in a study such as this because their scope is too narrow. Histories of higher headquarters are somewhat more useful, but not much. Special attention is called to three unit histories, from Fifth Air Force and located at USAFHRC: the 308th Bombardment Wing, 1943–45; the 309th Bombardment Wing 1943–45; and the 310th Bombardment Wing, 1943–45. These units were really advanced tactical headquarters for the Fifth Air Force. Activation and History, Fifth Air Force, 1941–43; History, Fifth Air Force, 1943–44, 2 vols.; and History, Thirteenth Air Force, 1943–45 (all at USAFHRC) are all useful. Also of value are the History of First Marine Aircraft Wing located at U.S. Navy Historical Center, Washington Navy Yard, hereafter referred to as USNHC and the Command History, Seventh Amphibious Force, Jan. 10, 1943–Dec. 23, 1945 (USNHC).

A few interviews with higher officers were recorded during the Second World War, but many more were transcribed in the 1960s and 1970s after oral history became fashionable. Not a single transcribed interview read in pursuance of this project dealt directly with air superiority in the Southwest Pacific, but they do tell something about tactics, and the bits and pieces of information they contain, when put together, bring some enlightenment. Among wartime interviews, "Fifth Air Force Interviews, 1942–45," and "Interview with Major General A. A. Vandegrift, USMC, on Air Operations on Guadalcanal, February 3, 1943" (both at USAFHRC) are especially useful. Recent interviews with Maj. Gen. Jared V. Crabb (1970), Gen. George C. Kenney (undated and 1974), Gen. Dean C. Strother (1978), and Gen. Nathan F. Twining (1965) are available at USAFHRC.

Gen. George C. Kenney, as Commander of Allied Air Forces and Fifth Air Force, and eventually Far East Air Forces, dominated the air war in the Southwest Pacific, and to a remarkable degree he dominates the historical sources for that war. The Kenney Papers, currently located at the Office of Air Force History, Bolling AFB, Washington, D.C., are by far the most useful manuscript sources seen, including summaries of air action, Kenney's account of conferences, and much vital correspondence. This collection obviously served as the basic source for General Kenney's memoirs, but it includes much information not included in the memoirs, some of it almost certainly omitted for public relations reasons. In addition, the General's penciled comments often shed light on events and sometimes on policies.

Located at the Marine Corps Historical Center, Washington Navy Yard (MCHC), the personal papers of Col. Harold W. Bauer and Gen. Keith B. McCutcheon, both Marines, are worth consulting. It must be repeated, however, that although these collections provide information concerning the achievement of air superiority, little in them is devoted directly to the subject. In fact, the need for and necessity of air superiority were so taken for granted that the subject is seldom even mentioned in the papers of the men engaged in achieving it.

The Office of Air Force History has produced Richard H. Kohn and Joseph P. Harahan, eds., *Air Superiority in World War II and Korea: An Interview with Gen. James Ferguson, Gen. Robert M. Lee, Gen. William Momyer, and Lt. Gen. Elwood R. Quesada* (Washington: Office of Air Force History, United States Air Force, 1983). This is an oral history consisting of a conversation in which these distinguished Air Force officers participated. Unfortunately for this present study, these men had all their combat experience in Europe during World War II or in Korea. None had served in the Southwest Pacific. The study is important, nonetheless, because it makes it crystal clear that the United States Army Air Forces entered the Second World War without any air superiority doctrine and without any real concept of the tactics to be used.

Thomas H. Greer, in *The Development of Air Doctrine in the Army Air Arm, 1917–1954* (Maxwell AFB, Ala.: USAF Historical Division, 1955; reprint, Office of Air Force History, 1985), demonstrates that most interwar thinking on the part of air officers was devoted to strategic bombing and that very little was devoted to how air superiority was to be attained. Richard L. Watson, Jr., *The Fifth Air Force in the Huon Peninsula Campaign* (Washington: Headquarters Army Air Forces, AAF Historical Office, 1946), and Harris G. Warren, *The Fifth Air Force in the Conquest of the Bismarck Archipelago November 1943–March 1944* (Washington: Army Air Forces Historical Office, 1945), provide exhaustive accounts of Fifth Air Force operations.

The official United States Army histories of the Second World War, Kent Roberts Greenfield, general editor, *United States Army in World War II* (Washington: Office of the Chief of Military History, Department of the Army), have been of considerable value for this study. Especially valuable were M. Hamlin Cannon, *Leyte: The Return to the Philippines* (1954); John Miller, Jr., *Cartwheel: The Reduction of Rabaul* (1959) and *Guadalcanal: The First Offensive* (1949); Samuel Milner, *Victory in Papua* (1953); Robert Ross Smith, *The Approach to the Philippines* (1953) and *Triumph in the Philippines* (1963); and Karl C. Dod, *The Corps of Engineers in the War Against Japan* (1966).

These volumes are essential to an understanding of the land campaigns that provided air bases that, in turn, made air superiority possible. Hamlin's volume demonstrates, from the ground force point of view, the troubles encountered in a ground battle undertaken without air superiority.

Admiral Samuel Eliot Morison's fifteen-volume *History of United States Naval Operations in World War II* (Boston: Little, Brown and Company, 1947–1962) is an important work of literature as well as excellent history, but it must be acknowledged that Admiral Morison has an understandable tendency to see things from the Navy point of view. In this respect he differs only in degree from other official service historians. Eight of the volumes in this series were essential to this study. Most useful were Vol. V: *The Struggle for Guadalcanal, August 1942–February 1943;* Vol. VI: *Breaking the Bismarcks Barrier, 22 July 1942–1 May 1944;* Vol. XII: *Leyte, June 1944–January 1945;* and especially Vol. XIII: *The Liberation of the Philippines: Luzon, Mindanao, the Visayas, 1944–1945.* Morison reveals, better than any other source, how the great air strength of the Navy fitted into the air campaign as a whole. He puts his eloquence to especially good use in describing the ravages of the *kamikazes* in Philippine waters and the role of carrier-based air in finally bringing an end to these attacks.

As might be expected, the seven-volume *The Army Air Forces in World War II* (Chicago: University of Chicago Press, 1948–1958; reprint, Office of Air Force History, 1983), edited by Wesley Frank Craven and James Lea Cate, is the most useful of official histories for the purposes of this study if for no other reason than that it contains more detail on air operations than other publications. Vol. I: *Plans and Early Operations, January 1939 to August 1942 to July 1944;* Vol. V: *The Pacific: Matterhorn to Nagasaki, June 1944 to August 1945;* and Vol. VI: *Men and Planes* are applicable to this subject. All but the last of these volumes follow the traditional pattern of military history and are geared to the chronological and geographical movement of Allied and Japanese forces across the air to the vast reaches of the Pacific. The development of air superiority and air supremacy in the South and Southwest Pacific theaters can be traced through these pages, but this development is never stressed as a central theme. The accomplishment of air superiority is described, but it is never proclaimed. The account of the Leyte campaign makes it clear that air superiority was lost there, and even makes clear why it was lost, but never directly. Considering the fact that this history was written a generation ago, however, it is remarkable how well it has stood up to the test of additional knowledge and new interpretations.

Maj. Charles W. Boggs, Jr.'s *Marine Aviation in the Philippines* (Washington: Historical Division, Headquarters U.S. Marine Corps, 1951) is concerned mainly with the role of Marine aircraft in close support of ground troops, but it describes also the important role of Marine aircraft in the air defense of Leyte. Maj. John N. Rentz's monograph, *Marines in the Central Solomons* (Washington: Historical Branch, Headquarters U.S. Marine Corps], 1952) gives due attention to Marine air in the Bougainville campaign and in the reduction of Rabaul. Vice Adm. George

Carroll Dyer, *The Amphibians Came to Conquer: The Story of Admiral Richmond Kelley Turner* (Washington: Government Printing Office, 1970), 2 vols., is an account of the Pacific amphibious operations commanded by Admiral Turner. It demonstrates how essential air superiority was to successfull amphibious landings. Finally, Vice Adm. E. P. Forrestal's *Admiral Raymond A. Spruance, USN: A Study in Command* (Washington: Director of Naval History, 1966) contributes to understanding of the achievements of air superiority in the Pacific.

The most important nongovernment published materials used in this study were memoirs, and General George C. Kenney's *General Kenney Reports: A Personal Memoir of the Pacific War* (New York: Duell, Sloan and Pearce, 1949; reprint, Office of Air Force History, 1987) is without question the most important of these memoirs. General Kenney does not talk a great deal about air superiority in this book, nor does he theorize; but he tells his readers in straightforward prose how he went about defeating the Japanese air force. He made air superiority, in fact air supremacy, his first priority when he took command, and this basic priority did not change until the skies of the Southwest Pacific were literally swept clear of Japanese aircraft. The attentive reader of Kenney's book quickly learns that winning an air war meant far more than simply outfighting an enemy in tropical skies or blasting his jungle-circled airfields. His recipe for victory included a supply system that demanded his constant attention, a steady stream of replacement aircraft and aircrews that he spent much of his time pleading for, a maintenance system that enabled his men to make the most of what they had, the development of effective tactics, and the selection of subordinate commanders who had the ability, stamina, and courage to do the work that had to be done. General Kenney's memoir is enthusiastic, bursting with pride in the accomplishments of his "kids," so much so that one can easily forgive him for an occasional inadvertant error in fact. In addition to his personal memoir Kenney also wrote *The Saga of Pappy Gunn* (New York: Duell, Sloan and Pearce, 1959), the near-legend whose inventive genius contributed significantly to the air victory in the Southwest Pacific.

Two other significant memoirs from the pens of Army Air officers are Lt. Gen. Lewis H. Brereton's *The Brereton Diaries: The War in the Air in the Pacific, Middle East, and Europe, 3 October 1941–8 May 1945* (New York: De Capo Press, 1976) and Maj. Gen. Claire Lee Chennault's *Way of a Fighter: The Memoirs of Claire Lee Chennault* (New York: G. P. Putnam's Sons, 1949). General Brereton was in the Philippines at the beginning of the war, and his book reveals much about the lack of readiness, materially and psychologically, of American forces in December 1941. Also, his diaries are perhaps the most logical and believable account of how American air strength in the Philippines came to be largely destroyed on the ground without striking a meaningful blow at the Japanese. General Chennault, of course, served in China during the war, but the early part of his memoir tells much about the attitude of most air officers toward tactical air power in general and fighter aircraft in particular in the years immediately preceding the attack on Pearl Harbor. Chennault was an expert on fighters who experimented with early warning systems even when his efforts ran counter to the wishes of his superiors. Lastly, Chennault tells of his development of fighter tactics, and he was at least as responsible as any other man for the development of the tactics that were successful in air combat against the Japanese.

Admiral Frederick C. Sherman's *Combat Command: The American Aircraft Carriers in the Pacific War* (New York: E. P. Dutton and Company, 1950) is an attention-holding account of the author's experiences as a commander of aircraft carriers. He was a participant in the Pacific War from the Coral Sea through the Luzon campaign. At the other extreme, in a sense, is James J. Fahey's *Pacific War Diary,*

1942–1945 (Boston: Houghton Mifflin Company, 1963). Fahey was an enlisted man aboard a cruiser, and his memoir includes a vivid account of what it was like to be on the receiving end of a *kamikaze* attack. Fighter ace Maj. Gregory "Pappy" Boyington's *Baa Baa Black Sheep* (New York: G. P. Putnam's Sons, 1958) is a fascinating account of the author's experiences with the American Volunteer Group in Burma and China as a squadron leader in the campaign against Rabaul and as a Japanese prisoner of war. His book also throws some light on how fighter tactics were developed in combat. Lt. Gen. Robert L. Eichelberger's *Our Jungle Road to Tokyo* (New York: Viking Press, 1950) tells little or nothing about the air war, but it certainly reveals a ground commander's reaction to the lack of air superiority over the battlefield. Two Japanese memoirs, Masatake Okumiya and Jiro Horikoshi with Martin Caiden, *Zero* (New York: E. P. Dutton and Company, 1956) and Saburo Sakai with Martin Caiden and Fred Saito, *Samurai* (New York: E. P. Dutton and Company, 1957) are valuable for what they reveal of Japanese naval pilots' point of view, especially during the battle for Guadalcanal and the subsequent campaign against Rabaul.

Two books deal directly with the startling phenomenon of the *kamikazes,* which may have been the most effective guided missile yet used in actual warfare. Two Japanese naval officers who had some personal knowledge of the origins and use of *kamikaze* tactics in the Philippines, Capt. Rikihei Inoguchi and Comdr. Tadashi Nakajima, wrote, with Roger Pineau, *The Divine Wind: Japan's Kamikaze Force in World War II* (London: Hutchinson, 1959; reprint, Westwood, Conn.: Greenwood Press, 1978). The French historian, Bernard Millot, produced *Divine Thunder: The Life and Death of the Kamikazes,* translated by Lowell Baer (New York: The Mc-Call Publishing Company, 1971), a well researched account of a suicide pilot campaign. Morison's *Liberation of the Philippines: Luzon, Mindanao, the Visayas, 1944–1945* (Boston: Little, Brown and Company, 1960), as noted earlier, gives an excellent account of the ravages of the *kamikazes* who sacrificed themselves in striking the American convoys bound for Mindoro and Luzon.

A number of commercially published secondary works and two published noncommercially in Australia and New Zealand have been of more than a little value in this study. John A. DeChant's *Devilbirds: The Story of United States Marine Corps Aviation in World War II* (Washington: Zenger Publishing Co., Inc., 1947) is a good account of Marine Corps aviation in the struggle for air superiority, especially in the South Pacific, and so is Robert Sherrod's *History of Marine Corps Aviation in World War II* (Washington: Combat Press, 1952). Frank O. Hough's *The Island War: The United States Marine Corps in the Pacific* (New York: J. P. Lippincott Company, 1947) and Brig. Gen. Samuel B. Griffith's *The Battle of Guadalcanal* (Philadelphia and New York: J. P. Lippincott Company, 1963) are not primarily concerned with the struggle in the air, but they are nonetheless valuable. George Odger's *Air War Against Japan, 1943–1945* (Canberra, Australia: Australian War Memorial 1957), is an excellent account of the not inconsiderable yet too often neglected role of the Royal Australian Air Force in the Southwest Pacific. J. M. S. Ross has provided *The Assault on Rabaul: Operations by the Royal New Zealand Air Force, December 1943–May 1944* (Wellington, New Zealand: War History Branch, Department of Internal Affairs, 1949). Gordon W. Prange, Donald M. Goldstein and Katherine V. Dillon, *Miracle at Midway* (New York: McGraw Hill Book Company, 1982); John M. Lindley, *Carrier Victory: The Air War in the Pacific* (New York: Elsevier-Dutton, 1978); and E. B. Potter and Chester W. Nimitz, eds., *The Great Sea War: The Story of Naval Action in World War II* (Englewood Cliffs, N.J.: Prentice Hall, Inc., 1960) add some detail to Admiral Morison's story of the naval side of the war in the Pacific.

The prose of Craven and Cate's *Army Air Forces in World War II* may at times be pedestrian, and the interpretation of events found therein may now and again show some unnecessary inclination toward the Air Force point of view. Yet, as noted earlier, it is amazing how little had been added to knowledge of the AAF war in the Pacific since this work was published. This is demonstrated by the paucity of other published works dealing with the Pacific role of the Army Air Forces. Vern Haugland, *The AAF Against Japan* (New York and London: Harper and Brothers, Publishers, 1949) was published before the pertinent volumes of the official history. Martin Caiden's *The Ragged, Rugged Warriors* (New York: E. P. Dutton & Co., Inc., 1967): Walter D. Edmonds' *They Fought With What They Had: The Story of the Army Air Forces in the Southwest Pacific, 1941–1952* (Boston: Little, Brown and Co., 1951): and Thomas G. Miller, *The Cactus Air Force* (New York: Harper and Row, 1969) are entertaining, but do not add a great deal of information. Ronald H. Spector's *Eagle Against the Sun: The American War with Japan* (New York: Free Press, 1985) was published too late to be used in the preparation of this essay.

8

Air War Against Japan

Alvin D. Coox

Although Japan had been waging major, undeclared hostilities against China since 1937, it was not until December 1941 that the authorities in Tokyo launched all-out war with the American-British-Dutch (ABD) powers. This essay addresses the period between the attack on Pearl Harbor and Japan's capitulation in August 1945. The achievement of other than regional Allied air superiority, however, had to await the seizure of forward bases and the development of bomber and fighter aircraft able to reach targets in the distant Japanese homeland. Inasmuch as such capabilities were not available until 1944–45, it is that climactic period of the war that will receive the preponderance of attention. And, since the ultimate unleashing of the B–29 bomber offensive overshadowed and predated the introduction of fighters, emphasis on the attainment of Allied air superiority centers on the consequences of the thrust westward across the Central Pacific, allowing the B–29 command to be relocated from China to the Marianas and built up there, and U.S. fighters finally to be based on Iwo Jima. While other American and Allied air forces broke through the periphery of the China-Burma theater, the Seventh Air Force and U.S. Navy and U.S. Marine Corps aviation fought their way through the Phoenix, Ellice, Gilbert, and Marshall Islands to Palau and the Marianas. The Seventh Air Force went on to Okinawa and took part in the last campaign against Japan. As the Allied counteroffensive unfurled and the air war progressed toward the home islands, Japanese defense planning revealed a frenzied and largely *ad hoc* dimension that was exacerbated by fatal qualitative and quantitative weaknesses. This chapter describes and assesses the course of ultimate Japanese failure and Allied success during the quest for air superiority over the strategic zone called the Inner Defense Perimeter by the Japanese.

Background

If the Japanese threat had not been so underestimated in 1941, and if Japan had been located geographically closer to North America, perhaps American war planners before 1941 would not have agreed that the strategic emphasis in case of war involving the United States must be on the Atlantic rather than the Pacific theater. The Americans were also unenthusiastic about defending British, Dutch, or French interests in Asia, and were averse to committing themselves to war in the Far East unless or until the objectives of the Japanese became entirely clear. Sympathy for beleaguered China, however, and revulsion at Japan's behavior there, engendered some remarkably aggressive private thoughts among administration officials in Washington. When Treasury Secretary Henry Morgenthau tried to influence Secretary of State Cordell Hull in favor of the Chinese Nationalist Government a year before Pearl Harbor, Hull asserted that "what we have to do, Henry, is to get 500 American planes to start from the Aleutian Islands and fly over Japan just once. . . . That will teach them a lesson." Hull then volunteered an even more startling hope: "If we could only find some way to have them drop some bombs on Tokyo."[1]

In addition to being impolitic and premature, Hull's personal comments scarcely alluded to fundamentals that would long hamper United States air operations in the Pacific: the relatively short reach of existing Army and Navy planes, as against the enormous distances that had to be traversed. To compensate for the weaknesses in range, U.S. aircraft were being ferried in 1941 to outposts as far away as the Philippines.[2] But the transoceanic routes were truly daunting. It is 2,100 miles from San Francisco to Oahu, 4,770 miles from Pearl Harbor to the Philippines, 1,400 miles from Manila to Japan. From Panama to Japan it is 8,000 miles. The Great Circle route via Alaska therefore attracted some attention, but even the Kuril Islands' approaches to Japan involve enormous distances: Paramushir is 1,200 miles north of Tokyo, 650 miles west of Attu in the Aleutians, over 1,000 miles west of Kiska. From Seattle to Tokyo via Hawaii, the distance is 6,600 miles but, even by the Great Circle, it is still about 4,900 miles from Seattle to Tokyo via the Aleutians.

While technological and geographical limitations thus thwarted any realistic American notions about contesting the skies in the Western Pacific at an early stage, "American racism and rationalism [in the words of historian David Kahn] kept the United States from thinking that Japan would attack it."[3] Despite some notable yet largely ignored exceptions, American observers tended to regard the actual threat posed to U.S. interests by the Japanese as not impossible but improbable. Shortly before his death in February 1936, Billy Mitchell remarked privately that for years Franklin Roosevelt had been espousing the erroneous "idea that a war in the Far East would be impracticable and that an attack upon us by Japan is inconceivable."[4] Presumably experts shared the President's notion to the bitter end. Thus, as late as mid-November 1941, the highly respected military critic, Maj. George Fielding Eliot, asserted that Japan was "in no case to fight a war with a group of major opponents." The Japanese Army was "sadly out of date" and Japanese air power was "almost nonexistent."[5] *Aviation Magazine* supplied the encouraging word that, "isolated from her Axis fellow aggressors . . . her air force of low offensive strength . . . Japan, if engaged in a great air war, would crumble like a house of cards."[6]

The downplaying of the Japanese menace was reinforced by ill-founded feelings of racial superiority. Naval writer Fletcher Pratt sought to systematize the various reasons why "every observer concurs in the opinion that the Japanese are daring but incompetent aviators." One explanation was medical: the Japanese are not only myopic but suffer from defects of the inner ear, affecting their sense of balance. Another theory was religious: the Japanese undervalue individual life and extol devotion to the Emperor, inducing pilots to "die cheerfully" instead of bailing out in case of trouble. A third notion was psychological: whereas pilots must operate uniquely alone, the Japanese lack individuality and therefore make poor airmen. Lastly, according to an educational theory, Japanese children play with fewer mechanical toys and receive less mechanical inculcation than any other people.[7] Former Director of the U.S. Office of Naval Intelligence, Capt. W. D. Puleston, admitted that Japan was energetic in efforts to develop naval aviation but was "usually a phase behind." Japan was unable to match American aircraft carriers in the number of planes carried, and Japanese personnel could not "send planes aloft or take them aboard as rapidly as American personnel."[8]

For their part, Japanese Navy officers did not underrate the British or the Americans, but the Japanese Army had, or professed to have, a veritable scoring system to indicate the level of contempt it felt for all national enemies. The Army's low regard for its Western ground foes in particular was partially caused by the fact that perhaps seventy percent of the hostile colonial forces in the Philippines and Southeast Asia consisted of native troops. Western military aviation was not similarly denigrated. On November 5, 1941, at an Imperial Conference, Army Chief of Staff General Gen Sugiyama said of the fighting capability of enemy air forces that he assumed it could not be regarded lightly in comparison to ground forces, since "the quality of the aircraft is excellent and their pilots are comparatively skilled."[9]

As for the views of the Japanese government and High Command on the matter of home defense, it is untrue that no consideration was given to the danger of enemy air attack once war began. Shortly before the outbreak of hostilities in the Pacific, a final Imperial Conference was held on December 1, at which time Finance Minister Okinori Kaya spoke of emergency fiscal measures that would be adopted in case parts of Japan were raided by enemy planes. The most illuminating commentary is found in the interpellation by Privy Council President Yoshimichi Hara:

> There is one thing I don't understand and that is what will happen in the event of air raids. It's admirable that you are providing a good deal of training for emergencies, such as air-raid drills, in order to avoid damage as much as possible. But in the event of a conflagration, can we bring it under control, given the kind of buildings in Tokyo, even though we may try to prevent it from spreading? What are we going to do if a large fire should break out in Tokyo? Do you have a plan to cope with it?

Planning Board Director Tei'ichi Suzuki tried to assuage Hara's concern by insisting that sufficient food had been stored, and expressing the hope that some of the people whose homes were burned could seek refuge elsewhere; for those who had to remain, there were plans to put up simple shelters. Hara retorted that it did not suffice "merely to have given some thought to the matter." The plans were inadequate; Suzuki ought to be fully prepared, but Hara would pose no further questions at this time.[10]

From the Japanese military's standpoint, the main threat to national security stemmed from the Soviet Union, which was known to possess the capability of making air strikes against Japan proper from bases in eastern Siberia. Motivated always by a preference for offensive action, the Japanese High Command contemplated neutralizing the Russian air threat by destroying or capturing the Soviet air bases in the Maritime Province at the outset of hostilities with Russia. In planning the war against the ABD Powers, the Japanese hoped to maintain tranquility on the northern front. Yet, General Sugiyama admitted at the Imperial Conference of November 5 that the Americans might set up air bases in Soviet Siberia from which to mount raids on Japan. Prime Minister Tojo agreed as to the danger, but deemed such attacks unlikely in the early period of the Pacific War. Tojo, however, was explicit in advising the military councillors that homeland air defense must not interfere with the Japanese offensives overseas. Tojo did not believe that the ABD Powers could launch major air raids on Japan for some time after hostilities broke out. In the initial phase of the war, enemy air attacks would be infrequent and staged from carriers.[11]

Thus, in the planning for and initiation of the Pacific War, Japanese military leaders paid relatively scant attention to air defense of the home islands. The High Command was convinced that the foe could be kept to a distance that would prevent land-based air raids on Japan. The possible carrier raids mentioned by Tojo and others were regarded as a minor threat; their primary purpose would be diversion of Japanese effort and enhancement of enemy morale. Conceivably, American planes could strike northern and eastern Honshu from bases in the Aleutians and Midway, and could attack central and western Japan from aircraft carriers or bombers based in Chekiang Province in China.[12]

The Homeland Defense Area comprised four military districts, each district commander serving concurrently as the commander of the tactical army. The Northern District, based at Sapporo, was responsible for defending Hokkaido; the Eastern District (headquarters, Tokyo), responsible for northern Honshu; the Central District (headquarters, Osaka), responsible for Honshu; the Western District (headquarters, Fukuoka), responsible for western Honshu and all of Kyushu. In July 1941, the General Defense Command (GDC) was established, with nationwide responsibility for homeland defense. In practice, GDC was a coordinating link between the district commands and Imperial General Headquarters (IGHQ) in Tokyo, and it possessed minor command authority.[13]

At the time of Pearl Harbor, few planes and antiaircraft guns were retained in Japan: about 100 Army and 200 land-based Navy fighters; 310 Army and 200 Navy antiaircraft pieces at most. The purpose of these defenses was to frustrate and discourage sporadic, small-scale, and retaliatory air raids. The real priority of the air forces was to take the offensive and seek out and destroy the enemy's aircraft carriers or air bases that might be set up in China. Meanwhile, IGHQ directed the GDC to provide point defense for 4 strategic military, government, and industrial locations: 1) Tokyo-Yokohama area (about 50 percent of available planes and guns); 2) Nagoya (10 percent of available resources); 3) Osaka-Kobe (20 percent of available resources); and 4) Kokura-Yawata and Shimonoseki-Moji (20 percent of available resources). Japanese sources agree that, compared to the strength sent overseas, air defense units in the homeland in 1941 were not only few but poorly trained and equipped. Antiaircraft guns were mainly 75-mm; Army fighters, the Type 97 (NATE)*, Japan's first low-wing military monoplane, in production since 1937. The air raid warning system included some primitive radar units but was primarily dependent on visual detection by military and civilian observers and radio-equipped naval picket ships stationed 500–600 miles from the coast.[14]

---

*Allied code name; Allied code names will appear initially in parentheses and then will be used to refer to the Japanese craft.

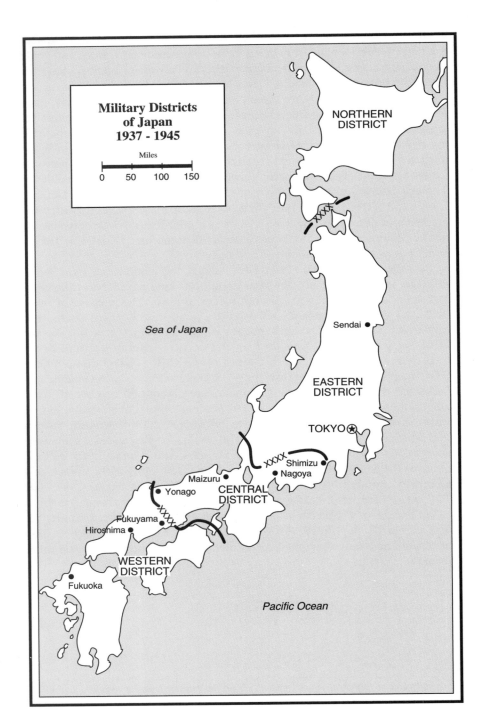

**Military Districts
of Japan
1937 - 1945**

Miles

0   50   100   150

NORTHERN
DISTRICT

Sea of Japan

Sendai ●

EASTERN
DISTRICT

TOKYO ⊛

Shimizu ●
Maizuru ●   Nagoya ●
Yonago ●

CENTRAL
DISTRICT

Fukuyama ●
Hiroshima ●

WESTERN
DISTRICT

Fukuoka ●

Pacific Ocean

388

Early Phase of the Pacific War

Diplomacy having failed to resolve the American-Japanese impasse in the autumn of 1941, Japan opted to launch "the greatest undertaking since the opening of the country," with full realization that the result would be "glory or oblivion." Most fearful of protracted hostilities, the Naval General Staff issued orders that the enemy fleet in the Hawaiian area be "reduced to impotency." Adm. Chuichi Nagumo's 1st Air Fleet carried out these instructions to the letter. The Japanese Army, whose objective was to reduce the main U.S., British, and Dutch bases in the Far East, undertook swiftly to occupy the Philippines, Guam, Hong Kong, Malaya, Burma, Java, Sumatra, the Celebes, Borneo, the Bismarck Islands, and Timor. Audacious Japanese forces unleashed powerful tridimensional assaults against this broad array of objectives throughout the Pacific and Southeast Asia. From the very outset, the Japanese naval and military air forces wrested air superiority from a motley constellation of outclassed and outnumbered American, British, Australian, and Dutch air units, whose planes were largely obsolete and universally "inferior in performance and armament to Japanese aircraft of a similar type."[15] Maj. Gen. Jonathan Wainwright, whose doomed command in the Philippines put up a longer fight than either the British or Dutch could mount in their colonies, later lamented "the futility of trying to fight a war without an Air Force."[16] It was the bleakest of times for the Allies; as Churchill put it, "We had lost the command of every ocean except the Atlantic. . . . Japan was supreme and we everywhere weak and naked."[17]

The Japanese attack on Pearl Harbor fanned elemental passions: Americans thirsted for early revenge against Japan. Senator Lister Hill called for "gutting the heart of Japan with fire."[18] Only two weeks after the disaster in Hawaii, Lt. Gen. Henry H. Arnold, Commander of the Army Air Forces, revealed what the United States was contemplating, when a senior British visitor, Air Chief Marshal Sir Charles Portal, asked about American plans for attacking Japan: "I gave him such meager information as we had on the proposed operations from eastern China, and said that preliminary negotiations indicated we would soon get permission to operate from bases near Vladivostok."[19]

On that same day, President Roosevelt had told his most senior military and naval advisors that he wanted to "[strike] back at Japan at the earliest possible moment and [he] asked everyone present to consider ways and means to attack Japan as soon as possible." The President expressed his desire, repeatedly and emphatically, for "a bombing raid on Japan proper as soon as humanly possible to bolster the morale of America and her Allies," and to carry home to the Japanese "the real meaning of war." General Arnold promptly directed the War Plans Division of the Air Staff to start planning for the retaliatory air strikes requested by Roosevelt. On

January 10, 1942, the President repeated his wish for an attack on Japan and pressed Admiral King and Generals Marshall and Arnold to "keep their respective staffs thinking of ways and means to carry the fight to the enemy and bolster public morale."[20]

It is not surprising that Roosevelt's high command had not yet devised a concrete plan. Not only had overseas air superiority been lost to the Japanese, but Anglo-American planners, as will be noted, had also accepted a Europe-first main strategy. How to reach the Japanese homeland at that early stage of the war, with the short-range surviving aircraft? The British staff, particularly Chief of the Air Staff Sir Charles Portal, advised the Americans that air strikes on Japan should be the purview of the Navy, using aircraft carriers to surprise the homeland, just as Japanese carriers had surprised Hawaii. Among the reasons for General Arnold's failure to be impressed by the British rationale was his belief that "it would be suicide for the Navy to bring their carriers within range of Japanese land-based aviation."[21] After all, the radius of action of carrier planes did not exceed 300 miles.

When the President conferred with his advisers on January 28, he reiterated the urgency of striking Japan from the air as soon as possible. General Arnold discussed the possibility of operating from North China or Russia. Roosevelt directed that the China alternative be explored, especially after being told that the distances involved in a strike from the Aleutians were too great. Unmentioned at the meeting was the fact that, of those present, Arnold and King had begun working on a daring plan spawned after the discussions on January 10. They proposed launching modified long-range U.S. Army medium bombers from an aircraft carrier deployed within striking distance of Tokyo.[22]

Already, however, by the last day of 1941, the most important decision in initial wartime grand strategic planning had been reached: to discard the widely held notion of abandoning Europe and Great Britain as lost and of launching an early counteroffensive against Japan. Instead, the Joint Chiefs of Staff (JCS) accepted, and the Combined Chiefs of Staff (CCS) formally adopted, the concept of a strategic defensive against Japan. Only after the Germans had been defeated would maximum strategic offensive operations be mounted against Japan. It was the considered opinion of the CCS that, despite Japan's entry into the war, Germany remained the primary foe, whose defeat was the key to victory; "once Germany is defeated, the collapse of Italy and the defeat of Japan must follow."[23]

The U.S. Navy understandably pressed for a more positive role in the Pacific, euphemistically termed "limited active defense," envisaging the commitment of a U.S. Army strategic air force in support of the Navy. Army Air Forces planners, in the person of Maj. Haywood S. Hansell, Jr. (supported by Lt. Col. Albert C. Wedemeyer), argued that the diversion of

American strength to the Pacific would "dilute our sparse resources beyond recognition." In this view, "failure to thwart Hirohito would lead to discomfort," whereas failure to thwart Hitler would invite disaster. The ultimate decision called for "maintaining only such positions in the [Far] Eastern theater as will safeguard vital interests and deny to Japan access to raw materials vital to her continuous war effort while we are concentrating on the defeat of Germany."[24]

The CCS spoke vaguely of the need to secure as many vantage points as possible from which the ultimate all-out offensive against Japan could be staged when additional forces became available. But the chiefs were not unaware that "the first essential is to gain general air superiority at the earliest possible moment, through the employment of concentrated air power." Piecemeal commitment of the limited available aviation must be minimized. While the main objectives of air offensive operations were delineated by Army Air Forces planners in some detail concerning Europe, "they were less definitive with regard to Japan."[25]

In this, the "lean period of the war" (as Samuel Eliot Morison phrased it), only the U.S. Navy had the reach to lunge at Japanese-held islands. A carrier strike against Wake on January 23 had to be called off, but, on February 1, American carriers and cruisers raided targets in the Marshall Islands, deep in the old Japanese Mandates. Though the objectives were peripheral and the results meager, the inflated reports boosted U.S. morale, and the strikes provided the task forces with practice in real combat. The same can be said of the well-orchestrated attacks by fast carrier forces of the U.S. Pacific Fleet against the islands of Wake, Marcus, and New Guinea on February 24, March 4, and March 10, respectively.

An American naval officer admitted that the Japanese did not mind the first U.S. carrier raids "any more than a dog minds a flea." Nevertheless, from such modest beginnings sprang the eventual major contribution by Navy air power to victory in the Pacific. Japanese naval historians find it hard to believe that the early raids by Admirals Halsey, Spruance, Fletcher, and Brown represented less than the "limited active defense" which the U.S. Navy had pleaded for in vain.[26]

The Doolittle Raid

The U.S. Army Air Forces was able to unleash one brief, indecisive, but psychologically telling blow—against mainland Japan itself—when Lt. Col. James H. Doolittle's 16 B–25 bombers, borne piggyback aboard the carrier *Hornet* within range of Honshu, struck Tokyo and 3 other cities at low level by daylight on April 18, 1942. The Japanese defenses were no better at this time than they had been prior to the opening of the Pacific

THE DOOLITTLE RAID, *Above:* One of Colonel Doolittle's sixteen B–25 bombers takes off from the USS *Hornet* on April 18, 1942, within striking distance of Honshu. *Below:* Jimmy Doolittle (*second from right*) poses with his own Tokyo bombing crew and Chinese friends after the airmen bailed out over China.

war. To cover the entire Tokyo-Yokohama-Kawasaki complex—the Kanto Sector—there were only 50 NATE fighters (244th Air Group) and 150 anti-aircraft guns. Nagoya was defended by merely 10 planes and 20 guns; Osaka, by 20 fighters and 70 guns.[27]

A War Ministry general officer asserted that the Imperial Japanese Army (IJA) and Imperial Japanese Navy (IJN) leaders' interest in air defense was "almost nil." Army officers had been arguing that no nation had ever been defeated by strategic bombing, and that bombardment of Japan was utterly impossible until a super high-altitude airplane appeared. Premier Tojo insisted that Japan was in no danger—that Japan was not Germany. By this he meant that enemy air bases were very far away and that the construction of Japanese buildings would supposedly reduce their vulnerability. They were of low height and made largely of wood. IJN publicists boasted that the "invincible Navy" would prevent even one enemy plane from penetrating Japan's air space; indeed, the conduct of air raid drills was called an insult to the Navy.[28]

In mid-January 1942, the War Ministry had proposed the first comprehensive air defense measures, including the evacuation of major urban areas, dispersion of key factories, and protection of utilities, transportation, and communication systems. Tojo rejected the plan. Evacuation, he said, was the act of a coward; and dispersal of facilities would reduce productivity. In early February, before the Doolittle raid, the War Ministry recommended at least the evacuation of women, school children, and the aged. Again Tojo refused, arguing that evacuation would wreck Japan's family-based structure. As a result of the authorities' negative attitude toward air defense precautions, according to Japanese sources, there were only two locations in all of Japan where adequate air raid shelters were in place: one at the Imperial Palace in downtown Tokyo, and another at the War Ministry headquarters in Ichigaya, also in central Tokyo.[29]

On the day of the Doolittle raid, the Japanese had ample warning but mishandled their air defenses. At 0630 on April 18, 1942, almost 6 hours prior to the dropping of the first American bombs on Tokyo, a Japanese picket vessel was able to transmit 6 messages to IJN headquarters before being sunk by a U.S. cruiser. The naval staff, however, decided to defer a counterattack because the enemy carriers were still beyond the 300-mile range within which deck planes could operate effectively. Nobody expected that long-range bombers were coming, and only a few interceptors were scrambled. For example, the Navy sent up only 4 Type 1 (BETTY) attack bombers to search for the enemy, and put 9 Zero (ZEKE) fighters on standby. Three hours after the first warning message had been received, a BETTY caught sight of aircraft of unknown type and nationality, 70 miles off shore but, though it pursued the intruders at its top speed of 270 miles per hour, it could not catch up. Nevertheless, it was able to confirm that the

393

enemy aircraft were twin-engine and large. This was the only concrete information received in Tokyo by noon, when the raid began.

A small but unspecified number of NATE fighters and DINAH command reconnaissance planes had been sent aloft on patrol in mid-morning, but they had landed to refuel when the B–25s attacked. Only after the U.S. bombers were in the Tokyo-Yokohama area did the defense command issue a tardy alert and scramble about 40 fighters and scouts. These planes began their search at an altitude of several thousand meters, and the Americans, sweeping in at 200–700 meters, had left the target area by the time the Japanese realized their error. Only 2 NATES caught up with a pair of B–25s in the Izu area and scored a nonlethal hit on an engine. One brand-new IJA Type 3 Hien (TONY) fighter tracked a B–25 near Kitaura and fired its useless training ammunition at the bomber before breaking off contact. A second TONY, armed by now, had a close call when it was attacked over Tokyo by three ZEKE pilots who had obviously never seen a TONY. By the time the mixup had been corrected, it was too late to chase B–25s.

Once the Tokyo raid was in progress, the Japanese Navy scrambled thirty BETTYS and twenty-four ZEKE fighters. Eleven ZEKES were over Yokosuka when a single B–25 struck a warship but, like the Army fighters, the ZEKES operated at too great an altitude to locate intruders. Japanese fighters were not even scrambled against the single B–25s that struck Nagoya, Yokkaichi, and Kobe, eight hours after the picket's first warning. Inexperienced antiaircraft gun crews fired many rounds and made some wild claims that embarrassed GDC but, since not one enemy bomber was found to have been downed over Japan, IGHQ made no claims when it issued its first communique. Later, parts of a B–25 that crashlanded in China were put on display in Tokyo to cover up the fact that none of the bombers was shot down over the homeland. The Japanese Navy kept on looking until April 26, without success, for the U.S. task force from which the Doolittle raid was mounted.

The casualties and damage inflicted on the Japanese by the Doolittle raid were comparatively light: about 50 persons killed and more than 400 wounded; approximately 200 houses burned. For the Americans, however, the raid thrilled the home front, coming so near the U.S. debacles of Bataan and Corregidor: "Pearl Harbor to some slight degree had been avenged, and the Japanese had been forced to swallow their proudest boast—that Tokyo could never be bombed." Admiral Halsey called the feat "one of the most courageous deeds in all military history."[30] Though none of Doolittle's bomber aircraft was brought down over Japan, none saw action again after their one-way trip to China (or, in the case of one plane, to Soviet Siberia), and this type of raid was never repeated.

Though some Japanese drew the feeble conclusion, from the evidence of the small-scale Doolittle strike, that "air raids aren't so bad, after all," a certain degree of uneasiness permeated the civilian populace. A number of military leaders did comprehend the nature of the air threat to Japan. A War Ministry general officer, for example, was astonished by the level of casualties as a factor of the minor bomb load dropped—double the ratio reported to have been caused by German air raids on England. A new civil defense plan was submitted to Tojo, with supporting documentation on England's experience and on the terrible vulnerability to strategic bombardment of the overconcentrated production base in the Kawasaki-Omori area. Tojo again stymied the proposal, though he did not reject it outright this time. Saying that Japan could not be bombed on the same scale as Germany and that needless worries were being expressed, Tojo would authorize only facilities that did not require heavy expenditures of funds and materials. Front-line combat zones, he insisted, must continue to take precedence over the demands of the home front. Although a portion of the Army General Staff was sympathetic to the War Ministry's proposition, large-scale funds were never forthcoming, and effective civil defense measures did not materialize, even after the initial shock caused by the Doolittle raid.[31]

The two services, however, did take stock of their poor performance on April 18. The Navy, which was responsible for seaward search and attack operations, had failed in both capacities, revealing insufficient patrol and intelligence collection capabilities. Charged with the main mission of air defense of the homeland, the Army had shown numerous tactical weaknesses: lack of a comprehensive warning net; delay in the transmission of information; low reliability of intelligence, caused by confusion; shortage and low capability of interceptor aircraft; insufficient training of antiaircraft gun crews, who were unacquainted with the characteristics of any aircraft and who fired blindly against low-flying planes.[32]

Japan's fighter and antiaircraft (AA) defenses obviously needed to be reinforced and upgraded. The Army set a target of tripling the number of fighters to 400 and almost quadrupling the number of guns to 1,900. By the end of April 1942, 2 AA batteries were recalled to the homeland from the Southwest Pacific and assigned to the Eastern District Army. From production, 108 more guns were allocated to that army, and another 160 guns to all the other military districts in the homeland. As for fighters, a squadron was brought back from Burma in April and assigned to the defense of Tokyo. In an effort to establish more effective tactical air units within the structure of GDC and the 1st Air Army, the 17th Air Wing was also organized under the air army and placed under the operational control of the Eastern Army command. The wing consisted of 2 fighter groups, an independent fighter squadron, and a command reconnaissance squadron. In May and June of the same year the 18th and 19th Air Wings were similarly activated and assigned to the Central and Western Army commands, respectively. These 3 wings constituted the homeland's main defense units until early 1944.

Japanese critics assert that this was no real air defense organization—only an air training setup organized into elements which could serve as a defense force in an emergency.[33]

The Japanese Army, nevertheless, took a new look at its fighter planes. The NATE, designed for dogfighting, had performed excellently on the continent, but it was obsolescent and outclassed as the mainstay air defense interceptor in terms of speed and firepower. Better suited were the Army's twin-engine Type 2 Toryu (NICK) and the new single-seater Type 2 Shoki (TOJO).[34]

The Middle Years

While the Americans' easy penetration of the airspace of the Japanese homeland and of the Imperial capital in particular had been a source of humiliation to Japanese leaders in 1942, it was certainly not the same thing as denting Japan's command of the air. The real struggle for air superiority would still have to await the appearance of long-range fighter planes and powerful land-based bombers (specifically, the B–29 Superfortress, with a range exceeding 3,000 miles, an altitude of 25,000 feet, a speed of 350 miles per hour, and a bomb load of 15,500 pounds). American strategists devised paper plans for an air offensive against Japan, similar to the one unleashed first against Germany, but the initial 2 years of the war were simply "too early to give anything more than general guidance in terms of objectives and targets."[35] After all, the B–29s did not begin to come off the assembly line until late 1943, and the new fighters needed bases within realistic range of their intended targets.

Meanwhile, Japanese strategic momentum had been checked by reversals in 1942–43, which included the Battle of the Coral Sea and the abandonment of major landings at Port Moresby in New Guinea (May 1942); the Battle of Midway (June 1942); withdrawal from Guadalcanal (February 1943); the loss of Attu (May 1943); and the evacuation of Kiska (July 1943). By the fall of 1943, the materialization of a two-prong Allied counteroffensive, mounted earlier than the Japanese expected, was already becoming apparent—the Southwest Pacific thrust under Gen. Douglas MacArthur and the Central Pacific thrust under Adm. Chester W. Nimitz.

The U.S. Army Air Forces component for the westward offensive across the Central Pacific was the Seventh Air Force which, in its own words, "was, in effect, a land-based air arm of the Navy." In February 1942, Maj. Gen. Clarence L. Tinker's Hawaiian Air Force headquartered at Hickam Field had been redesignated the Seventh Air Force. Following General Tinker's death in action in early June 1942 and the brief interim command of Brig. Gen. Howard C. Davidson, the Seventh Air Force was taken over by Maj. Gen. Willis H. Hale on June 20, 1942. Maj. Gen. Robert

W. Douglass replaced General Hale on April 15, 1944, and commanded the air force until June 23, 1945, when Maj. Gen. Thomas D. White became its last wartime commander.

The tactical core of the Seventh Air Force, on its activation, was the 18th Bombardment Wing, redesignated VII Bomber Command, and the old Hawaiian Interceptor Command, which first became VII Interceptor Command and was then redesignated VII Fighter Command in May 1942. Admiral Nimitz, in his capacity as CINCPOA (Commander in Chief, Pacific Ocean Area), was in theater command of the Seventh Air Force until mid-July 1945.[36]

The domain of the Central Pacific is enormous, dotted by 1,000 islands or atolls, singly or in clusters. From Hawaii southwest to the Gilberts, it is 2,000 miles; from the Gilberts northwest to the Marshalls, 600 miles; from the Marshalls west to the Carolines, 900 miles; from the Carolines northwest to the Marianas, 600 miles; and from Iwo Jima west to Okinawa, 1,000 miles. From the beginning of the war until November 1943, the Seventh Air Force engaged in 35 reconnaissance missions; thereafter, under a series of Navy task force commanders, it supported six amphibious landing campaigns: 1) Gilbert and Marshall Islands (Kwajalein, Eniwetok), from December 1943 to March 1944; 2) Mariana Islands (Saipan, Tinian, Guam), from March to August 1944; 3) Palau (Peleliu), from August to December 1944; 4) the Philippines (Leyte), from August to December 1944; 5) Volcano Islands (Iwo Jima), from January to March 1945; and 6) Ryukyu Islands (Okinawa), from April to June 1945. Thereafter, the Seventh Air Force took part in the final offensive against Japan itself.[37]

Admiral Nimitz's objective—to seize island air and sea bases and to secure them against enemy attacks—was achieved by "blanketing attacks on all enemy airfields within range." The Seventh Air Force operated mainly bomber aircraft—B–24s since 1942—but its fighters at various times included the P–38, P–39, P–40, P–47, P–51, and P–70. The first fighter units did not appear in the Seventh Air Force order of battle until the Marshall Islands phase, when 3 of 14 squadrons were made up of fighters (48 P–39s and 26 P–40s) based in the recently conquered Gilberts. No Japanese interceptors were encountered at Kwajalein after January 30, 1944. At Maloelap in early February, P–40s fitted with belly tanks ended Japanese air opposition, claiming 10 fighters downed and 3 probables, in a matter of minutes. Seventh Air Force fighters flew 1,058 effective sorties in the Marshalls, claimed to have destroyed or damaged 29 enemy fighters, and lost 10 of their own, including 6 to antiaircraft fire, none to interceptors, 2 to noncombat and another 2 to unknown causes.[38]

During the Marianas campaign (March–August 1944), the Seventh Air Force began operations with 12 squadrons, only 1 of which consisted of fighter aircraft, and ended with 3 squadrons of fighters and 2 flights of night

Adm. Chester W. Nimitz, Commander in Chief of the Pacific Ocean Area (CINCPOA).

Gen. Douglas MacArthur, Commander of the Southwest Pacific area (CINCSWPA).

fighters out of a total of 13 American squadrons. The Seventh Air Force had deployed its advanced headquarters to Kwajalein in the Marshalls, retained the forward tactical base at Makin in the Gilberts, and mounted strikes against Truk and Ponape from the Navy field at Eniwetok. A week after D-day on Saipan, P–47s were catapulted from escort aircraft carriers (CVE) and flew their first combat mission on the day they landed at Isley Field, now the most advanced of the Seventh Air Force bases. Two flights of P–61 night fighters, flown in from Hawaii, maintained night Combat Air Patrol (CAP) while the P–47s flew CAP from dawn to dusk. Seventh Air Force fighters conducted 1,870 sorties, claimed to have knocked out 16 enemy fighters, and lost 14 planes, 6 of which were combat-related. By helping the Navy to neutralize Truk, the Seventh Air Force also prevented Japanese air or surface attacks against U.S. bases in the Gilberts and Marshalls. Army, Navy, and Marine aircraft claimed to have destroyed 223 Japanese planes and damaged 56 at Mili, Wotje, Jaluit, and Maloelap in the Marshalls by June 1, 1944. The Seventh Air Force lost 28 planes of all types in combat during the entire Marianas campaign.[39]

U.S. carrier planes struck Iwo Jima on June 15, July 3-4, and August 3–5, 1944. The Seventh Air Force began its own raids against Iwo Jima, from Saipan, on August 16. These operations became particularly important during October and November, when very heavy bombardment bases were established in the Mariana Islands to accommodate B–29s that could strike at the heart of the Japanese homeland—something that had not been feasible or profitable from the China-Burma-India theater, despite enormous Allied logistic efforts. Well aware of the new B–29 threat, the Japanese launched a total of 80 to 100 sorties from Iwo, mostly by night, against the Marianas. The persistent U.S. air strikes against Iwo Jima, conducted by the Seventh Air Force and the Navy, contributed to the interdiction of that island and the ultimate success of the Marianas-based B–29 offensive against Japan. All large U.S. missions met interception in force—the only time Japanese air resistance was regularly encountered. Of 1,466 sorties, 661 were conducted by P–47s, which claimed to have destroyed 7 Japanese aircraft (6 of which were airborne). P–38s claimed 14 enemy planes destroyed (12 airborne) and 11 damaged (3 airborne). By December 1944, the Seventh Air Force employed 1 group and 1 squadron of fighters, out of 4 groups (and 1 photo reconnaissance flight) in action. Of its campaigns to date, the Seventh Air Force judged that "enemy bases in the western Pacific whose neutralization was entrusted to [this] AF were the source of no real disturbance to the movements of United States forces in the area, and the development of our bases in the Marianas was continued almost without any enemy interruption."[40]

The Japanese Homeland Revisited

By the time that American forces began to reconquer the Philippines (landings on Leyte in October 1944, on Mindoro in December, and on Luzon in January 1945) and to storm ashore on Iwo Jima in February 1945, the complexion of the war in general and of the air war in particular had changed dramatically. In January 1945, Admiral Nimitz established his advance headquarters on Guam. American aircraft carriers, exploiting their new numbers and their mobility, range, and punch, had proved instrumental in projecting air power westward across the Pacific, toward the innards of Japan. Shore-based air facilities were typically set up as quickly as possible, once a ground position was secured, but, as Fleet Admiral King pointed out, "there will always be a period following a successful landing when control of the air will rest solely on the strength of our carrier-based aviation."[41] In addition, for the first time, the U.S. Navy added a strategic component to its usual tactical targeting. Just before the landings on Iwo Jima, the Navy launched an intense series of carrier attacks against the Tokyo area, the first since the small raid by Doolittle from the USS *Hornet* in 1942. The new carrier strikes were designed not only to assist the Iwo Jima operation but to damage Japanese aircraft production capabilities. As Adm. Raymond A. Spruance said, "I could see no object in any longer fighting those aircraft around the perimeter, if we could by accurate bombing wreck the factories where they were being produced and so reduce the output." For the first such campaign, Admiral Mitscher's Task Force 58 of Admiral Spruance's Fifth Fleet possessed 5 task groups with a total of 17 carriers, large and small, and 1,170 embarked aircraft. Admiral Nimitz asserted that the opportunity to conduct this operation fulfilled "the deeply cherished desire of every officer and man in the Pacific Fleet."[42]

Arriving undetected 60 miles off the coast of Honshu, U.S. Navy fighters went into action on February 16 to pave the way for succeeding dive bombers and torpedo bombers. To his largely green pilots (nearly half of the air groups were on their first battle mission), Mitscher said, "[The Japanese] is probably more afraid of you than you are of him." Japanese interceptors did seem "listless" and reluctant to close. One of the task group commanders, Admiral Sherman, remarked that he was "amazed at the lack of determined air opposition. No Japanese aircraft came within 20 miles of our disposition and our planes roamed at will over the enemy's territory seeking their targets." The Americans had to contend mainly with the sometimes zero-zero weather—"the damndest, rottenest weather I could think of" (in Spruance's words). By evening, Mitscher reported that his units had destroyed 350 planes and damaged airfield installations, but had effectively hit little more than one aircraft factory. Sherman's task group alone claimed to have destroyed or damaged at least 167 aircraft. Thirty

American planes went down, several of them because of the overeagerness of green Hellcat pilots who broke formation and sought dogfights.

The weather was wretched again on February 17, but the U.S. Navy bombings and strafings continued throughout the morning. Near noon, Mitscher was obliged to end his flight operations. The Navy later judged that the strikes had been "substantial but not spectacular," although Admiral Sherman said he could see "the Rising Sun setting." The best results were achieved not against ground facilities but in air-to-air combat and in runs against parked planes, although the claims for both days were somewhat scaled down: 322–341 aircraft reportedly shot down and 177–190 wrecked on the ground. A total of 60 USN planes were lost in the course of 738 combat engagements, and a further 28 aircraft were lost to other causes. Contesting the skies with the Japanese air forces seemed to have brought about 3 days of immunity from aerial attacks for the U.S. forces on Iwo Jima.[43]

Japanese sources assert that the Naval General Staff in Tokyo did expect raids against the homeland as early as February 15, and that both the IJNAF and IJAAF went on alert promptly. But, most importantly, on February 9 the Air Defense Command had already decided to avoid engaging enemy light and medium aircraft and to try to conserve air strength for the decisive campaign in the homeland. As for the USN strikes on February 16, there was no tactical warning because the first American fighters came in at an altitude of only 1,300 feet. One IJAAF night-fighter group and all "second-class" flight personnel were ordered to take refuge at alternate airfields. Aircraft in the region that would not be committed to combat were to have their fuel drained and ammunition unloaded and be hidden far from the airstrips. Ten minutes after the initial sightings of the Americans on the early morning of February 16, the first of 4 U.S. Navy waves (estimated at 90, 90, 100, 120 planes, respectively) started attacking IJNAF and IJAAF bases in the coastal zones of Chiba and Ibaragi prefectures. In the afternoon, 3 new waves of U.S. Navy aircraft—estimated at 90 in the first, and 450 in the second and third—hit an aircraft factory and airfields deeper inland. IJAAF interceptors reported shooting down 62 U.S. planes and damaging 27, at a cost of only 37 fighters and some scout planes. Antiaircraft artillery (mainly 70-mm and 80-mm guns) and automatic cannon batteries emplaced near the airfields claimed to have shot down 19 and damaged 17 enemy planes.[44] The Japanese figures mentioned above for USN aircraft downed on February 16 are much higher than the actual losses; but U.S. claims similarly exceed Japanese losses by an even larger factor.

The Japanese Air Defense Command concluded that continuation of such combat as had been waged on February 16 would deplete IJNAF-IJAAF capabilities in short order. On the night of the 16th, the two best IJAAF air groups in the defending 10th Air Division were pulled out and ordered to disperse and seek shelter. Division Commander Maj. Gen. Kihachirō Yoshida argued that to conserve air strength contradicted the purpose of air defense. Pursuing a deliberate policy of "gradual decline" would only lead to impotence when maximum defensive strength was really needed. The core of fighter pilots' élan was the offensive; morale would be eroded, once the interceptors lost their *raison d'être*. Though impressed by Yoshida's impassioned plea, the Air Defense Command declined to lift the restriction on all-out engagement of enemy fighters, "lest strength be consumed prematurely."[45]

With their numbers reduced by losses on February 16, and by the withholding of fighter units, the Japanese put up fewer interceptors to meet the 4 waves of U.S. Navy carrier planes (estimated at 180, 90, 250, 70, respectively), which struck at airfields, factories, and maritime facilities on Honshu the next day. Nevertheless, the IJAAF claimed good results, not far off the actual mark, for February 17: 36 enemy planes shot down and 18 damaged, at a cost of 14. Antiaircraft batteries fired at the same rate as on the 16th, though 120-mm gun crews were more active. In the day and a half of air defense on February 16–17, the Japanese made the wildly exaggerated claim of having shot down 273 enemy aircraft (including 98 by IJNAF) and having damaged more than 84 (including 3 by IJNAF). As previously noted, total U.S. Navy plane losses did not actually surpass 84. But Japanese losses on the ground were far fewer than the Americans reported, because, the Japanese contend, of their good dispersion and concealment. For example, IJAAF plane losses on the ground really amounted only to 2 on February 16. Nonetheless, the Japanese admitted that many fine pilots were lost in the interceptors that crashed—more than 50 pilots in Army units alone.[46]

On February 25, in concert with a 200-bomber B–29 strike, Task Force 58 returned to the attack, since the results of the strikes on February 16–17 had obviously not been decisive and since the fast carriers were not needed at Iwo Jima. Terrible weather, however, rendered the results in the Tokyo area even less successful than during the earlier strike, and Mitscher called off further operations by mid-day; mainly secondary targets had had to be attacked. Said Admiral Sherman: "The enemy opposition was only halfhearted and Japanese planes which were not shot down seemed glad to withdraw from the scene . . . as swiftly and unceremoniously as possible. Even here, over their own capital, the enemy were notably inferior to our naval aviators in aggressiveness, tactics, and determination." Antiaircraft opposition was severe over the urban area, but "it was remarkable," added Sherman, that Japanese planes did not attack the U.S. task force at sea.[47]

The Japanese sighted about 600 U.S. Navy planes in total on the 25th. Worsening weather and heavy seas forced Mitscher to cancel a planned strike against Nagoya the next day. The Americans made an unrealistic claim to have destroyed at least 158 Japanese aircraft, but the IJA gunners'

BUILDING UP THE BOMBER FORCE IN THE MARIANAS. *Above:*
Message center and other installations of the 805th Engineer Aviation
Battalion at an air base on Saipan. *Below:* B–29s in the dispersal area
at the North Field on Guam.

more modest report of downing 9 U.S. Navy carrier planes accords with the U.S. Navy's admission. Spruance noted that "this time again the Japs made no attempt whatsoever to attack us either while we were there or on the run out. This is very different from the way they used to be, when they threw everything at you they could as long as they could reach you." In all, Task Force 58 claimed to have destroyed 393 Japanese planes in the air and more than 250 on the ground between February 16 and March 1. Though Japanese records are incomplete, their actual losses in this period amounted to perhaps 15 or 20 percent of the totals claimed by the Americans. During the same period, 84 U.S. aircraft (with 60 pilots and 21 crewmen) where lost in combat, and another 59 aircraft (with 8 pilots and 6 crewmen) were lost for other reasons.[48] These figures, too, are far lower than Japanese counterclaims.

Approaching the Climax

Once the Marianas had been seized in 1944 and the B–29 Superfortresses became available in quantity, the Army Air Forces could close down the difficult China-based bombing raids and set up shop in the Western Pacific. In personal command of Twentieth Air Force since its activation in Washington, D.C., in April 1944, General Arnold was finally able to apply his basic principle in practice against Japan; i.e., that "the main job of the Air Force is bombardment," employing large formations of bombardment planes to hit the foe. The Japanese homeland could now be struck directly and often. As U.S. analysts later remarked, "nowhere could the Japanese air forces prevent the concentration of Allied forces relatively close to their objective or force the costly disperal and other defensive measures which attend the threat of heavy and sustained air attacks." General Arnold put it simply: "In the air war with the Japanese, our strength constantly increased; theirs steadily diminished."[49]

The emphasis on bombardment aviation, to which Arnold alluded, affected the way the battle for air supremacy against Japan was fought in 1945. "One of the basic premises of Army Air Forces doctrine," air historian Robert Futrell observed, "was that its heavy bomber aircraft, flown in massed and self-defending formations, could successfully penetrate enemy defenses and perform precision-bombing attacks in daylight hours." In addition, prewar AAF doctrine evinced "little concern for the effect that hostile antiaircraft artillery fire might have on strategic bomber missions" because of the high altitudes at which the bombers operated. The most severe Japanese fighter interception against Marianas-based B–29s took place between November 24, 1944, and February 25, 1945. During that period, the Japanese concentrated fighters to defend several key areas where most of the priority industrial targets were located. Since the B–29s were still few and the Japanese interceptors were numerous, the Americans admitted that they faced "a serious but temporary problem." From a peak resistance on January 27, Japanese fighter reaction diminished steadily in intensity and in numbers.[50]

The relative lack of success of the earliest B–29 precision-bombing raids against Japan seemed to be more attributable to bad weather and strain on engines imposed by high altitudes and heavy bomb loads than to the effectiveness of Japanese air defenses. "Over Japan, we ran into problems that we hadn't foreseen," remarked Maj. Gen. Curtis E. LeMay, the Commander of XX Bomber Command in India from August 1944 and of XXI Bomber Command on Guam from January 1945. One of the unforeseen problems was a "ferocious" jet stream never before encountered by American airmen. The winds aloft over Japan interfered seriously with bomb sight computation. Japanese visual flying weather was abominable and difficult to predict. In addition, many of the U.S. flight crews were seeing combat for the first time, and the B–29s themselves had many bugs to work out. "We were feeling our way along with a new weapons system," said LeMay. Indeed, the general went so far as to suggest that most of the B–29 losses over Japan were due more to mechanical problems than to the

Maj. Gen. Curtis E. LeMay (*left*), **Commanding General of the XXI Bomber Command, and Brig. Gen. Roger Ramey, Commanding General of the XX Bomber Command, as LeMay departs for his new command in the Marianas.**

405

enemy's defense system. Another constant difficulty in deciding how to wrest air superiority from the Japanese was the lack of information on Japan and its defenses. "I could never be certain just how good my Intelligence really was," LeMay said. Before he was transferred to the Marianas, the general participated in a B–29 raid from China in September 1944 against Anshan in South Manchuria in order to observe Japanese defensive capabilities firsthand. Though his bomber was hit by flak at about 25,000 feet over the target, LeMay was unimpressed by the tactics of the Japanese fighter planes, which "turned the wrong way [and] never mounted a decent attack."[51]

General Arnold took no chances. Although, in the absence of bases for friendly fighters within reach of Japanese targets, it had been necessary to send in bombers alone, at high altitude and by day, Arnold was convinced that "all types of bombing operations must be protected by fighter aircraft. This proved essential in the Battle of Britain, and prior to that our own exercises with bombers and fighters indicated that bombers alone could not elude modern pursuit, no matter how fast the bombers traveled." As early as July 1944, Arnold had recommended that Iwo Jima—located 660 miles from Tokyo—be seized as a base for long-range fighter-escorts. Additionally, Iwo Jima would be useful as an emergency landing site, an advanced staging base and an air-sea rescue station. In July 1944, too, Arnold considered plans to send 5 very long-range (VLR) P–47 and P–51 fighter groups to support XXI Bomber Command in the Marianas.[52]

With the buildup of U.S. strategic air forces in the West Pacific, specifically the introduction of XXI Bomber Command (constituted and activated on March 1, 1944), it appeared necessary to create a theater air echelon above the Seventh Air Force, the senior air command in the region until then. In August 1944, after Army Air Forces, Pacific Ocean Areas (AAFPOA) was activated in Hawaii, the Seventh Air Force was transformed into a tactical command, controlling only its VII Fighter Command and VII Bomber Command. Component units, in turn, continued to be assigned to Navy task force commanders. Seventh Air Force fighter aircraft operational with units in 1945 were as follows:

	Seventh AF fighters operational with units	Number of night fighters included
Jan	280	28
Feb	361	54
Mar	332	43
Apr	301	45
May	540	26
Jun	481	37
Jul	526	37

The Twentieth Air Force itself was assigned the 301st Fighter Wing, and 413th, 414th, 506th, 507th, and 508th Fighter Groups, which were placed under the operational control of XXI Bomber Command.[53]

The increases in AAF aircraft inventory were significant. Whereas in August 1944 there had been 999 Army planes of all types in the Pacific Theater, by the middle of July 1945 there were 3,006 Army aircraft. AAF types and models had also changed significantly. No B–29s were in the theater in August 1944, but 985 were in place at the end of July 1945. As for Army fighters, 451 P–47Ns reached the theater between March and July 1945, and the number of P–51s rose from 8 in November 1944 to 348 in July 1945 (in addition to 74 P–61 Black Widows). Once omnipresent, the P–38s and P–39s were almost through.[54]

To exploit the impending seizure of Iwo Jima, P–51s of the 15th Group started to land on the island as early as March 6, while the fighting was still in progress. They were in action in two or three days, relieving the carrier planes by flying close-support and CAP missions at first. On March 20, a squadron of night fighters arrived. Three days later, when a second airstrip was finally ready, the 21st Group flew in. Though resistance had supposedly ended on the 16th, in late March the camp site of the 21st Group was actually penetrated by Japanese survivors, who killed forty-four Americans and wounded twice that number before being driven back. The 306th Fighter Group arrived on May 11.[55]

The Japanese Response: Conventional Approaches

Not until 1943 did Japanese Army Air Force doctrine begin to veer away from emphasis on traditional ground support tasks to the attainment of air superiority through the concentration of sizable strength for sustained air-to-air missions. Old ideas died hard, however, and attention to protracted air operations was not common. It was widely argued in IJAAF and IJNAF circles that aviation technology had not progressed sufficiently, at least so far as Japan was concerned, to develop high-speed, fast-climbing fighter planes that could operate at great altitudes, at night, or in adverse weather. Infused with the offensive spirit, IJAAF and IJNAF officers typically regarded air power as most suitable for attack, not defensive action. In the Navy, the senior staff still tended to regard aviation essentially as support for the surface fleet, geared to Jutland-type big-gun battle. Japanese military and naval successes in the first part of the Pacific War naturally fostered euphoria; Army and Navy planners gave no serious thought through 1943 to the possibility of enemy landings in Japan. It was only the deterioration of the military situation in the spring of 1944 that finally inspired Imperial General Headquarters (IGHQ) to address the question of improving the air defense of the homeland proper.[56]

First, IGHQ reduced the protective zone for which the General Defense Command was responsible. (See Figure 8–1) In February 1943, the Northern Army had already taken over the defense of Hokkaido, Karafuto (southern Sakhalin), and the Kuril Islands. Now, in March 1944, prime responsibility for the defense of Korea, Taiwan, and the Ryukyu, Bonin, and Volcano Islands was assigned to commands other than GDC; namely, the Korea Army, the Taiwan Army, the new 32d Army (stationed on Okinawa), and the Western Army. These changes left GDC with direct responsibility for defending the heart of Japan—the main islands of Honshu, Kyushu, and Shikoku. Although there were agreements between the Army and the Navy General Staffs to cooperate in defense of the homeland, in practice the conduct of Japan's air defense (other than harbors and naval facilities) lay with IJAAF and the Army's antiaircraft artillery elements.

IGHQ's second step to improve the air defense of the homeland, in March 1944, was to augment the 17th Air Wing and reorganize it as the 10th Air Division. Two months later, the division was transferred from the 1st Air Army (actually a training command) and assigned to direct control of GDC, although operational command was vested in the Eastern Army. As of October 1944, the 10th Air Division possessed about 150 fighter aircraft (organized in 5 groups) and 50 high-altitude scout planes (in an independent squadron) with which to try to defend Tokyo and the Kanto region. The division was obliged to release fighter units to assist in defense of other areas, such as the Philippines, central and western Japan, and Iwo Jima. Replacement units of uneven quality were brought in from the Kwantung Army Air Force in Manchuria.

In the spring and summer of 1944, IGHQ also upgraded the 18th Air Wing to the 11th Air Division (200 planes) under the Central Army, and the 19th Air Wing to the 12th Air Division (150 planes) under the Western Army. Apart from a small number of reconnaissance aircraft, all planes in the new air divisions consisted of fighters (6 types in all). In late December 1944, the Air Training Army was reorganized as the 6th Air Army, and several Air Training Divisions were formed. By February 1945, recognizing that the 6th Air Army was too weak to conduct such ambitious missions as attacks on the Marianas or participation in the defense of Japan, GDC limited its role to that of a strategic reserve to be committed only against enemy invasion forces. The next month, in March, the 6th Air Army had to be moved from the Kanto area to Kyushu and assigned to the Combined Fleet for the Okinawa campaign. A new IJAAF fighter wing was organized to help protect the Kanto sector against enemy carrier task forces. Training was intensified and new airfields were built.

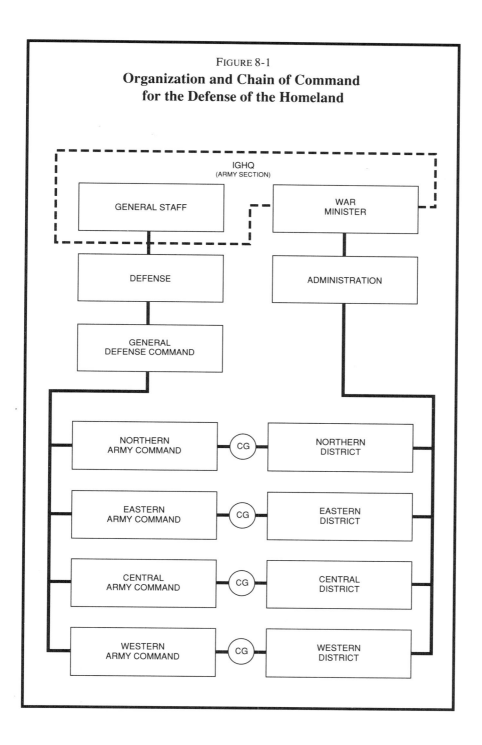

FIGURE 8-1

**Organization and Chain of Command
for the Defense of the Homeland**

IGHQ
(ARMY SECTION)

GENERAL STAFF

WAR
MINISTER

DEFENSE

ADMINISTRATION

GENERAL
DEFENSE COMMAND

NORTHERN
ARMY COMMAND — CG — NORTHERN
DISTRICT

EASTERN
ARMY COMMAND — CG — EASTERN
DISTRICT

CENTRAL
ARMY COMMAND — CG — CENTRAL
DISTRICT

WESTERN
ARMY COMMAND — CG — WESTERN
DISTRICT

With the intensification of U.S. air raids in early 1945, IGHQ decided to unify all air defense forces under one command—the new Air General Army, under General Masakazu Kawabe, effective April 15. The 1st Air Army, reorganized as an operational command, was assigned the 10th Air Division. Simultaneously with the activation of the Air General Army, IGHQ organized the 1st and 2d General Armies to take over ground defense, and the old army commands became known as area armies. Thus the 10th Air Division was now transferred from the operational command of the Eastern Army to that of the 12th Area Army.[57]

Japanese Antiaircraft Capabilities

The reach of Japanese AA guns was generally unimpressive. After undergoing the first large-scale B–29 raid in November 1944, the Antiaircraft Group reported to the Eastern Army that the enemy bombers were flying at about the maximum range of the workhorse 75-mm AA guns (30,000 to 31,000 feet), whereas the guns' effective range was a mere 17,000 to 23,000 feet. Only 120-mm guns, with a maximum range of 67,000 feet and an effective range of 47,000 feet, were deemed effective against the B–29s; but 120-mm pieces were in short supply.

An improved 75-mm AA gun was designed, calling for a maximum range of 27,000 feet, but few were manufactured by war's end. In late 1943, Japanese Army Ordnance designed a giant 150-mm piece weighing 120,000 pounds. One gun was produced in April 1945, a second in May. Both were assigned to the defense of Tokyo, where they supposedly wreaked havoc upon the B–29s.

In general, the effective vertical range of Japanese AA guns was customarily about 80 percent of the maximum listed in the manuals. Gunners groused that it was impossible to engage enemy planes flying above clouds or at night. Radar computations of the altitude of hostile aircraft were not accurate enough for AA batteries, and it was always difficult to pick up single planes. Army officers complained that the Navy's supply of AA guns, deployed to defend naval bases and naval districts, far exceeded the numbers available to the Army to protect all of the homeland. The Army repeatedly asked the Navy to release some of its AA strength for defense of Army sectors of responsibility, but few guns were ever turned over.

Against low-flying aircraft, the most commonly used Japanese Army AA automatic cannon was the 20-mm Hoki, which had a vertical range of 3,200 feet. Unable to develop a design of a more formidable piece in the 25-mm or 30-mm class, the Army in 1942 purchased various guns produced by Rheinmetall in Germany. The versatile 37-mm Flak version looked good, and the decision was taken to go into production. However, only a few test models of the Flak version had been produced early in the war, when the superior Swedish Bofors 40-mm automatic cannon (which had been employed by the British enemy) caught the fancy of the Japanese Army. Production was then converted from the Rheinmetall to the Bofors model; yet the conversion was too late, and only one 40-mm automatic cannon was ever turned out.

As the war progressed, there was a chronic shortage of antiaircraft guns and ammunition because of the decline in industrial production. For example, the Army's output of AA guns and shells in May 1945 declined to 60 percent and 53 percent, respectively, of April's production. In the spring of 1945, Japanese AA assets on Kyushu, the first objective of the expected enemy invasion of the homeland, were deployed as follows:

1) Covering Northern Kyushu (Yawata steel works, port of Waka-matsu)—120 guns (including only 12 120-mm), 96 searchlights (maximum range 26,000 feet), less than 2 machine cannon batteries (mainly 20-mm), 30 barrage balloons;

2) Covering airfields and railways—150 guns, 10 machine cannon batteries;

3) Covering Hakata, Nagasaki—60 guns, 30 searchlights, 1½ machine cannon batteries;

4) Covering Kurume, Omuta, and bridges—36 guns;

5) Covering Kumamoto, airfields, factories, and bridges—36 guns, 1½ machine cannon batteries.

When Lt. Gen. Kametoshi Kondō assumed command of the 10th Air Division in March 1945, he tried to reinforce the AA defenses of his bases in the Tokyo area, but about the best he could do was to augment fire power by modifying a number of his automatic cannon and to install some improved plotting radar apparatus. Actually, the Army and the Navy engaged in fierce competition to develop and acquire radar facilities. According to one Japanese technician, the intent of the AA defenses was more psychological than practical: "Apparently the brass felt better when antiaircraft guns could be heard firing during an air raid. The sound conveyed the impression that something effective was being done to deal with the air attacks." There were cases when unsuccessful AA unit commanders were reprimanded by superiors or transferred.[58]

Limited though the Japanese antiaircraft capability was, B–29 commanders regarded flak as a greater danger to them than enemy fighters, and they adjusted their bomber formations accordingly.[59]

Japanese Interceptor Problems

Japanese fighters participating in interceptor combat usually numbered between 20 and 50 planes per air defense region, seldom reaching 100 at a time. This inability to employ sizable numbers of fighters stemmed largely from the difficulty of concentrating forces in insular Japan, which is characterized by a lack of geographical depth and by the location of all strategically crucial installations on the long Pacific coastline. Even if there had been sufficient warning of enemy raids, and sufficient numbers of interceptors to scramble, Japanese fighter planes were deficient in ceiling and rate of climb. Designed essentially for ground support at an optimum altitude of 16,000 feet, the Army's Type 2 NICK fighter required 7 minutes to climb to that altitude; its maximum ceiling was 34,500 feet. The Navy's GEKKŌ fighter needed 9 minutes 35 seconds to reach 16,000 feet; its ceiling was about 29,500 feet.

Like most Japanese AA artillery, the fighters had difficulty grappling successfully with bombers flying at an altitude exceeding 26,000 feet. By dint of rigorous training, stripped armor, and improved materiel, it became possible by the summer of 1944 to fight at an altitude of about 29,500 feet using such planes as a converted scout and a heavy bomber armed with medium-caliber weapons. Still, the long-awaited high-altitude interceptors did not progress beyond the experimental stage and were never used in combat. For example, much was expected of the Mitsubishi SHUSUI, modeled on the Messerschmitt Me–163B, a sensational rocket-powered fighter. The SHUSUI was designed with a maximum speed of 550 miles per hour at 33,000 feet, a service ceiling of 39,500 feet, and a capability of climbing to 33,000 feet in 3½ minutes. By war's end, production was underway, but only 7 prototypes had been delivered for testing.

The best that ordinary Japanese interceptors could do at 33,000 feet was to attack bombers in level flight; when they banked, they lost altitude to a serious extent. Generally, the fighters could make only one pass at a bomber. The problems were only compounded when experimental large-caliber cannon were installed on certain IJAAF fighters and heavy bombers, to enable them to cope with the B–29. A 10th Air Division officer attributed Japanese aeronautical troubles to the country's late start in science and technology. If the Japanese had had fighters capable of climbing regularly to 40,000 feet, he said, "we would have been able to do five times as well at half the cost."[60]

Crippling losses of Japanese aircraft and flight personnel rendered replacement very difficult. The new 10th Air Division Commander, General Kondō, in the spring of 1945 sought to compensate by improving tactical doctrine and procedures governing the operations of his units on guard in the vital Kanto district. Thus he directed that instead of attempting constant interception of intruding enemy planes and protection of strategic locations, fighter units should engage only targets of opportunity. Emphasis on battle against bombers should give way to training against fighters, though decisive combat even against the latter must be avoided until thorough training had been accomplished. In devising these plans, Kondō was influenced by reports of ineffectiveness of IJAAF units in coping with the U.S. Navy carrier raids of February 1945. The general was convinced that, because of the previous Japanese stress on fighter versus bomber tactics, interceptor pilots must have been unschooled in methods of identifying and engaging enemy fighters. In the case of large-scale enemy bombing raids, Kondō wanted defending fighters to conducted concentrated counterattacks, without being distracted by enemy scout planes. Kondō also wished to tighten the protection of parked aircraft, to employ decoy planes that would lure enemy aircraft within range of ground artillery, to modernize the defensive system with new radar, and to improve the maintenance and supply of aircraft and equipment.

Among the practical effects of General Kondō's directives in the spring of 1945 were a pronounced intensification of fighter versus fighter training and the delegation of responsibility to IJAAF group commanders to engage raiders, on a case-by-case basis, designed to exploit any local advantages. Surviving officers of the 10th Air Division assert that by terminating the old system of unit-wide alerts, of aimless patrolling, and of blanket area coverage, Kondō introduced flexibility of command and operation and reduced wasted effort on the part of the defenders.[61]

Of course, the various measures instituted by the Japanese were intended to enhance the air defense posture, but they came very late in the war and they did not provide appreciably more punch, quantitatively or qualitatively. Some GDC officers later admitted that unification of the Army and Navy air forces would have been the best improvement to make, by far. But even if there had been a consensus (which did not exist at the time), it was much too late to have introduced unification. Establishing new tiers of command and revamping conventional tactics of engagement could accomplish little unless the interceptor units themselves were reinforced. Since this was becoming unfeasible, an unrealistic increase in assigned defensive tasks became the rule.[62]

Evidence of the relative impotence of the Japanese air defenses occurred when General LeMay sent 334 B–29s from Guam, Saipan, and Tinian to bomb Tokyo by night and at low altitude on March 9, 1945. Taken by surprise by these new tactics, Japanese radar installations failed to detect aircraft not appearing at the usual high altitudes. As soon as it learned of the raid in progress, the 10th Air Division sent up 90 fighters, which were to work with the antiaircraft and searchlight units. By the light of the enormous fires that illuminated the skies over Tokyo, the interceptors climbed to engage the B–29s from below, but soon afterward the rising clouds of smoke obscured the visibility, and further attacks became impossible. The first U.S. bombers reported encountering "nil" fighter opposition; later B–29s called it "weak." Throughout the 3-hour raid, B–29 crewmen noted only 76 sightings and 40 passes by Japanese fighters, usually conducted when a bomber was caught in searchlight rays. While the 10th Air Division believed that their interceptors brought down a total of 15 B–29s, no bombers were actually lost to fighters. Several returning Japanese pilots were killed in crashes while trying to find their air bases that night.

In theory, the Japanese interceptors should have done better against the low-level bombers. Instead, according to Japanese air veterans, the decrease in altitude of engagement did little to improve the fighters' record. Flying at a night-time height of less than 10,000 feet, the B–29s could increase their operational radius, strike in larger numbers, and select targets more easily. This, in turn, forced the Japanese pilots into piecemeal and even more dispersed action. Hampered by insufficient early warning, at night the fighters were obliged to link up with the narrow-beam searchlight units, a fact which constricted the pilots' ability to locate and engage the bombers.[63]

The B–29s reported that Japanese flak was moderate in general and varied in accuracy and severity. Automatic-cannon batteries tended to fire too low, while heavy AA guns fired too high. The intensity of fire diminished greatly as the raid progressed. In all, flak hit forty-two B–29s, bringing down fourteen, five of whose crews were saved at sea. The loss ratio in terms of sorties was computed as 4.2 percent, which the Americans regarded as a moderate price in terms of the catastrophe visited on Tokyo by the bombers.[64] Though it lost its administration building and quarters, the 10th Air Division still retained its operational headquarters; but the staff realized that another such raid would raze the capital, paralyze the core of the government and the military, and unhinge the people's resolve to go on with the war.[65]

The Japanese Forfeit Air Superiority Contest over the Homeland

The ineffectiveness of the Japanese air defense system in coping with the disastrous B–29 offensive caused very real concern at the highest levels of government. There was fear, in particular, that portions of the country might be isolated from the remainder as the result of air bombardment of the vulnerable transportation network. Nevertheless, in spite of the trauma caused by the raid of March 9, the Japanese High Command adopted only minimal air defense countermeasures. For example, from the other air divisions in Japan a mere twenty fighters were transferred to the defense of Tokyo, and even those planes were released in about two weeks when no second B–29 offensive had materialized by then.[66]

It is apparent that defense of the endangered Pacific approaches to Japan took precedence, even at this late stage of the war in the spring of

1945, over the requirements of the homeland itself. Assigned to the defense of Japan between January and March 1945 were only about 375 interceptors—slightly less than 20 percent of the entire IJAAF and IJNAF combined inventory. The 450 fighters allocated in April constituted the largest percentage of fighters used to defend Japan during the entire war, but still amounted to merely 26.5 percent of the operational total available. Indeed, by the time the absolute number of assigned fighters finally exceeded 500 in July and August, the percentage of the fighter inventory they represented had declined to about 16.5 percent.[67] It was largely a matter of priorities, and Imperial General Headquarters had essentially opted to allow the cities to be reduced to ashes and the civilian populace to be terrorized, in favor of the employment of precious fighter assets on the fronts east and south of Japan.

Provided with a small number of fighters, replete with qualitative shortcomings and frugally committed to battle, Japanese air defense units could only mount a low-scale effort against the B–29 raids. According to XXI Bomber Command data, in the authoritative U.S. Strategic Bombing Survey (Pacific), the average number of Japanese fighter attacks per bombing mission fell off from a high of 7.9 in January 1945 to 2.2 in February, and to considerably less than 1 thereafter: March—0.2, April—0.8, May—0.3, June—0.3, July—0.02, August—0.04.[68]

The Japanese interceptors' combat performance against the B–29 was consequently unimpressive. The loss rate of the Twentieth Air Force in the Pacific theater was approximately one-third of the rate incurred by the U.S. Eighth Air Force against German interceptors. Again, according to the U.S. Strategic Bombing Survey (Pacific), the worst rate of loss of Eighth Air Force heavy bombers, in April 1943, was more than 3.5 times that of the Twentieth Air Force.[69] The highest number of B–29s lost to fighters occurred in January and April 1945, when 13 bombers were brought down per month. But the percentage as a factor of sorties flown was only 1.29 percent of 1,009 sorties and 0.37 percent of 3,487 sorties respectively. The 8 B–29s lost to fighters in May and June were 0.18 percent and 0.14 percent of 4,562 and 5,581 bomber sorties, respectively. In the first half of August, when hostilities in the Pacific War were finally terminating, only 1 B–29 was lost to interceptors—0.03 percent of 3,331 sorties. In all, the Twentieth Air Force attributed 74 of its B–29 losses to enemy fighter action between June 1944 and August 1945, a loss of 0.24 percent out of 31,387 sorties.[70] The fact that B–29 losses to fighters remained well under 1 percent from February 1945 until war's end caused American analysts to judge that "the final measure of the effectiveness of the Japanese fighter defense system was no more than fair on paper and distinctly poor in practice."[71]

Once the Japanese abandoned the contest for air superiority over the homeland and husbanded their remaining planes for use against a land invasion, they relied more on antiaircraft artillery. But the batteries could only cover the main industrial concentrations, and resistance to the air offensive was meager elsewhere. In view of the greatly enhanced number of B–29s in action, the damage rate attributable to flak did not increase. In fact, combat damage stemming from flak was trifling when bombers attacked through overcast or were unilluminated by searchlights at night. The U.S. Strategic Bombing Survey concluded that in "both fighters and antiaircraft artillery, the Japanese proved weak. Not only were these defenses inadequate, but certain technological advances used by the Germans and ourselves were not evident. In the most vital defensive effort, that against air attack on his homeland, [the Japanese] failed."[72]

Unconventional Response: The *Kamikazes*

The Japanese manufactured 65,000 military and naval aircraft during the Pacific war, but their wastage was staggering: 54,000 planes from both services. Of the losses, 20,000 occurred in combat, 10,000 in training, 20,000 for other noncombat reasons, and 4,000 in ferrying flights. During frontline operations, the 2 services lost 40,000 aircraft to all causes. (See Table 8–1) Production could not keep up with destruction.[73]

The Japanese lavishly expended the veteran, highly trained pilots with whom they started the Pacific war. IJNAF data show a loss of 17,360 flight personnel between the Pearl Harbor period and May 1945: in 1941 there were 171 losses; in 1942 there were 2,468 losses; in 1943 there were 3,638 losses; in 1944, 7,197 losses; and Jan-May 1945, 3,886 losses. The 3 highest monthly rates of IJNAF losses occurred in October 1944 (1,802), June 1944 (1,528), and April 1945 (1,510).[74]

When the replacement training program had to be escalated, the Japanese underestimated the difficulties and emphasized numbers over quality. With respect to quantity, the Japanese were outclassed as early as 1943, when the Americans turned out 82,714 pilots compared to 5,400 Japanese pilots. In that same year of 1943, the Americans manufactured 85,433 planes; the Japanese, 16,693. Qualitatively, the new Japanese aviators were a poor match for the improved Allied air forces, and indeed for their own seniors. The most advanced Japanese wartime planes proved too "hot" for the novices to handle. One of the last IJNAF veterans, Lt. Toshio Shiozuru, who had survived air battles in the East Indies, the Philippines, and off Taiwan, in March 1945 advised against using his undertrained ZEKE fighter unit at Kokubu in the homeland for combat operations, but he was overruled by his superiors.[75]

It was largely the weakness of the Japanese in orthodox air actions which caused them to go over to "special attack" forces—the suicidal sacred warriors known as *kamikazes* (Divine Wind). Including some one-

TABLE 8–1

Japanese Aircraft Losses during Frontline Operations

Dec 1941–Apr 1942	1,100	Central Pacific	3,000
Dutch East Indies	1,200	Southeast Asia	
Midway / Aleutians	300	(after May 1942)	2,200
China / Manchuria	2,000	2d Philippines	
Solomons / Bismarcks /		Campaign	9,000
New Guinea	10,000	homeland defense	4,200
Total			40,000

man *baka* guided missiles, *kamikazes* attacked ships, rammed B–29s in midair individually, and crash-landed on enemy airfields. American analysts have called the *kamikazes* "the single most effective air weapon developed by the Japanese," and have assessed the decision to ascribe so much emphasis to special-attack tactics as "a coldly logical military choice."[76]

For suicide missions, the Japanese Army deemed that at least 70 flying hours were necessary for pilots. Yet, in practice, some of the Army's *kamikaze* pilots had less than 10 hours of experience aloft. The Japanese Navy felt that 30 to 50 hours were sufficient if training planes were used for the attacks. Dive bombing was the tactic nearest to orthodox instruction. During the winter of 1944–45 and the spring of 1945, all regular training was halted in favor of suicide-pilot preparation. Expendable, low-powered trainers proved maneuverable, cheap to build, and fairly easy to fly. Because the training planes carried bomb loads of merely 50 to 250 kilograms, however, they were often loaded with extra gasoline to enhance flammability, and hand grenades were sometimes heaped around the pilot in the cockpit. The Japanese failed to heed the advice of technicians who recommended that a more powerful explosive weapon was needed to sink large warships.[77]

In the second Philippines campaign in 1944–45, the Japanese launched 650 suicide missions against ships, with a 26.8 percent effective rate of hits or damaging near misses (2.9 percent sinkings). As the fighting progressed, the scale of the suicide effort increased steadily. But the *kamikaze* campaign was still experimental, and the Divine Wind losses amounted only to approximately 16 percent of the total of IJAAF and IJNAF aircraft losses in combat.[78]

After American forces invaded Okinawa on April 1, 1945, it became apparent that the Japanese would counter by trying to saturate the skies over the Ryukyus with as many airworthy *kamikaze* planes as could be drawn directly from training units. U.S. Army intelligence officers observed that, since the assault on Okinawa, the enemy "has committed himself to a bitter, all-out, sustained air counter-offensive; he is expending air strength recklessly in recurrent massed air attacks regardless of cost."[79] Between March 26 and April 30, 1945, *kamikaze* planes sank 15 Allied ships and seriously damaged 59. Before the Okinawa campaign was over, IJNAF had flown 1,050 suicide sorties; the IJAAF, 850. The grand total was thus 1,900 sorties, a wastage rate of 63 percent of the 3,000 Japanese planes lost in combat. Twenty-six Allied ships were sunk. Allied vessels were hit 182 times, suffering damaging near misses 97 times. Calculating the number of sinkings, hits, and near misses, against the total loss of *kamikazes*, yields an effectiveness rate of 14.7 percent. Despite the 3-fold increase in *kamikaze* sorties at Okinawa vis-à-vis the Philippines campaign, the effectiveness rate had decreased by almost 50 percent. In the category of sinkings alone, the effectiveness rate at Okinawa (1.3 percent) had also diminished to nearly half of the *kamikazes'* success rate in the Philippines.[80]

From October 1944 until the close of the struggle for Okinawa, the Japanese sacrificed 2,550 *kamikaze* pilots in order to achieve 474 hits (an 18.6 percent effectiveness factor). Against Allied naval forces, the *kamikazes* hit or scored damaging near misses on 12 fleet carriers, 16 light or escort carriers, 15 battleships, and hundreds of lighter vessels. In all, between 45 and 57 ships of all categories were sunk, none larger than an escort carrier. Destroyers took the worst pummeling, by far. In 10 months, *kamikazes* accounted for 48.1 percent of all U.S. warships damaged, and 21.3 percent of all warships sunk.[81]

Coping with the *Kamikazes*

The spectacular activities of the suicide attackers posed a real threat to the success of the Allied campaign for Okinawa. Within easy range, the Japanese possessed dozens of air bases in the homeland, Formosa, the Sakishima archipelago, and China. Since no other important military operation was distracting them at the time, the Japanese could concentrate their aerial strength in the Okinawa area. Even before the first American landings at Okinawa, the U.S. Navy wanted Japanese aircraft to be smashed in their lairs, or at least as far from Okinawa as possible. Admiral Spruance recommended to Admiral Nimitz "all available attacks with all available planes, including Twentieth Air Force, on Kyushu and Formosa fields." The U.S. Navy launched its own preinvasion offensive operations with fast carrier strikes against the Inland Sea and Kyushu region on March 18 and 19, in good weather for a change. Although Japanese snooper aircraft had picked up Task Force 58 late on the 17th, 1,400 USN and USMC planes struck from early morning on March 18, ranging as far as Shikoku and Wakayama. About 45 Japanese air bases came under attack, with much better results farther inland in later strikes. The first day's results were tallied as 102–125 Japanese aircraft shot down and 200 destroyed, plus at least 100 damaged on the ground. But, having been alerted well in advance of the offensive, 50 IJNAF *kamikaze* and conventional bombers struck Task Force 58, hitting three carriers.

With respect to the USN claims, Morison understood that Japanese authorities admitted "staggering" losses of 161 out of 193 planes committed, apart from those destroyed on the ground—losses which prevented the Japanese air forces from intervening effectively in defense of Okinawa till April 6. Recent Japanese military historians doubt that many IJAAF planes were downed in combat.[82] One element of Army fighters had been sent to reinforce Tokyo's defenses, 2 squadrons of scout planes had been evacuated to Seoul, and various fighter aircraft had been ordered to take cover at their bases. The Japanese also say that their losses on the ground were relatively negligible because dispersion and concealment were handled well. They admit that antiaircraft fire accomplished little since only automatic cannon batteries provided direct defense of the airfields under attack.

Inasmuch as the Americans adjudged so many of the Japanese airfields to have been knocked out on March 18, the next day the anchorages at Kure and Kobe, well defended by antiaircraft units, became the primary targets for 1,100 U.S. carrier planes. Airfields in the Osaka-Kobe area and on Kyushu were secondary targets. In actions waged all day on the 19th, 75–97 Japanese aircraft were reportedly shot down, and another 75–225 destroyed on the ground, at a cost of 22 American planes. But *kamikaze* aircraft remained extremely active against the U.S. task force, causing serious damage to two more carriers. When the Americans were retiring on the 21st, they scrambled 150 Hellcat fighters, 24 of which intercepted 18 twin-engine BETTY bombers and 30 single-engine fighters that were pursuing the task force. The U.S. fighters reported shooting down all the Japanese planes, losing 2 or 3 Hellcats in the process. It was discovered that the downed BETTYS were carrying rocket-powered *baka* flying bombs, each manned by a *kamikaze* pilot.

From March 18–21 during U.S. naval operations, 273 enemy aircraft were estimated to have been shot down over the targets in Japan or by combat air patrols (CAP) and naval antiaircraft artillery; 255–275 planes destroyed on the ground; and 175 aircraft probably destroyed or damaged. Heavy damage was inflicted on airfields, hangars, installations, ships, power plants, oil storage facilities, warships and civilian shipping. USN and USMC aircraft losses totalled 53, not including those ruined by enemy attacks on the carriers.[83]

419

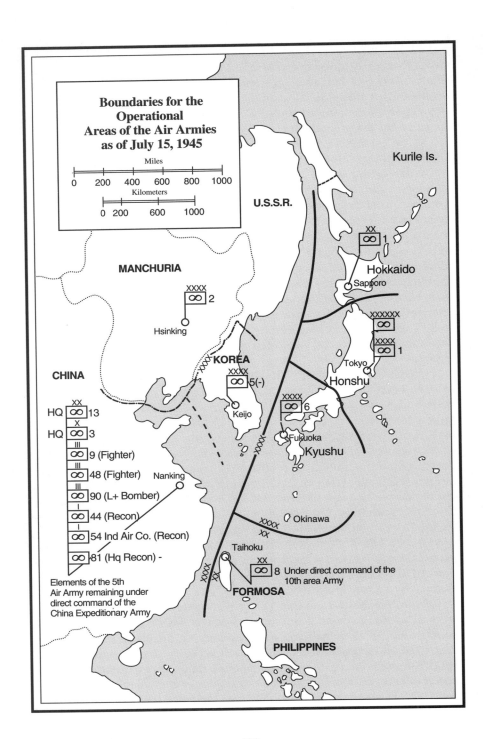

Boundaries for the
Operational
Areas of the Air Armies
as of July 15, 1945

Miles

0   200   400   600   800   1000

Kilometers

0   200   600   1000

Kurile Is.

U.S.S.R.

MANCHURIA

XX
∞ 1

Hokkaido

XXXX
∞ 2

Hsinking

Sapporo

XXXXX
∞

KOREA

CHINA

XXXX
∞ 5(-)

Tokyo

XXXX
∞ 1

Honshu

HQ XX
∞ 13

HQ X
∞ 3

Keijo

III
∞ 9 (Fighter)

III
∞ 48 (Fighter)

III
∞ 90 (L+ Bomber)

I
∞ 44 (Recon)

I
∞ 54 Ind Air Co. (Recon)

∞ 81 (Hq Recon) -

Elements of the 5th
Air Army remaining under
direct command of the
China Expeditionary Army

XXXX
∞ 6

Fukuoka

Kyushu

Nanking

Okinawa

XXXX
XX

Taihoku

XX
∞ 8 Under direct command of the
10th area Army

XXXX
XX

FORMOSA

PHILIPPINES

420

Two U.S. Navy task groups returned to Kyushu on March 28-29. Secondary targets—airfields—were hit, "a familiar story" now, in Admiral Sherman's words. About 130 carrier planes hit air facilities at Kanoya and eastern Kyushu and shipping at Kagoshima on the afternoon of the 28th. Next day, from early morning, some 600 carrier aircraft struck targets from Miyazaki and Kagoshima to Sasebo, Matsuyama, and Kochi. The rising power of the American forces was demonstrated by the fact that 2 U.S. Navy seaplanes, escorted by fighters which beat off enemy interceptors, were able to scoop up and haul to safety 2 U.S. pilots whose aircraft had crashed inside Kagoshima Bay. On April 16 the U.S. Navy task groups launched new fighter sweeps north to Kanoya, where 30 Japanese planes were downed; another 6 were splashed near the carriers.[84]

Having encountered *kamikazes* in the autumn of 1944 in the Philippines and in early 1945 at Iwo Jima, the Americans had anticipated suicide attacks to be a standard Japanese tactic. Nevertheless, as Seventh Air Force historians wrote: "For many men who had survived every other kind of fantastic battle experience, [*kamikaze*] was the most bewildering and terrifying experience of the war. It was...like being surrounded every minute of the day and night by a forest fire." Particularly unnerving was the fact that "there was no defense against [*kamikaze*] pilot short of blowing him up in the air. 'The son of a bitch dives straight at you, and what are you going to do about it?' "[85]

The sheer magnitude of the *kamikaze* effort also vastly exceeded expectations. Admiral Spruance later admitted that "none of us...foresaw the scope of the suicide plane threat while we were making our plans for Okinawa." American postwar analysts asserted that the *kamikaze* assaults caused serious losses and were regarded with great concern by the United States; "had the Japanese been able to sustain an attack of greater power and concentration, they might have been able to cause us to withdraw or to revise our strategic plans."[86]

Spruance, in fact, had had to ask Nimitz for all the air power he could proffer. Such help was forthcoming in support of Admiral Nimitz's command, including 2,000 B–29 sorties (75 percent of XXI Bomber Command's total effort during the period) diverted from bombing attacks against strategic targets in Japan to tactical strikes until May 11 against *kamikaze* fields in Kyushu, where AAF judged the greatest threat existed.[87]

VII Fighter Command also launched counteroffensive fighter sweeps from Iwo Jima and, beginning on May 14, from Okinawa. Between April 1 and June 30, the AAF fighters flew a total of 436 sweeps, those in the latter phase being strafing, bombing, and rocketing strikes against 50 airfields in southern Kyushu and the Amami and Sakishima Gunto archipelagoes. AAF analysts regarded the total P–51 effort as "not very fruitful." Although VII Fighter Command claimed to have destroyed 64 and damaged 180 Japanese planes on the ground and to have shot down

10, at a cost of only 18 (of which 11 were lost in combat), the desired objective of "widespread destruction" was not achieved. The weather was poor, and the enemy planes were hard to find, either on the ground or in the air.[88]

U.S. Bomber-Escort Missions Materialize

In early 1945, the American fighter planes in the western Pacific acquired a new and important mission: to escort B–29 bombers in raids against the enemy's homeland. On April 7, each of the 6 P–51 Mustang squadrons on Iwo Jima first sent four 4-plane sections to protect B–29s heading for targets on Honshu. By the end of June, the Seventh Air Force had flown 426 escort sorties.[89]

Although the Japanese may have expected eventually to encounter AAF fighters in such a role, they were taken by surprise when the P–51s showed up. From Japanese sources we learn of the initial IJAAF and IJNAF experiences. At about 10 in the morning on April 7, an estimated 90 (actually 101) B–29s were reported approaching the industrial zone of Musashino in western Tokyo at an altitude of 4,000 meters, usually ideal for IJAAF fighters. From Sagamihara, 24 *Hayate* (FRANK) Army fighters scrambled. Corporal N. Naitō, operating one interceptor at 7,000 meters over Oshima, detected about 30 small planes, sharp-pointed with liquid-cooled engines, flying above the B–29s. Since there had been no reports of enemy fighter-escorts, Naitō guessed that the strange planes were of the Japanese Type 3 *Hien* (TONY) family, the only operational IJAAF liquid-cooled fighter, though the rounded belly differed from that of the *Hien*. Naitō's supposition was soon disabused after he saw tracers spew from the fighters, and bullets began to hit his plane. When he went into a spin and got away, he saw the star insignia on the planes' right underwing. So these were the P–51 Mustangs, which he had heard of but never seen! When Naitō was about to enter the attack mode, P–51s came at him. Since he was low on fuel, he disengaged promptly. Eleven IJAAF planes were lost, 3 allegedly by ramming. Ground batteries fired 1,325 rounds (70-mm, 80-mm, and 120-mm).[90]

Similarly unaware of the presence of enemy fighter escorts, approximately one hundred IJNAF fighters also scrambled against the raiders. Once again, the Japanese mistook the P–51s for the *Hien*. An IJNAF squadron commander flying a two-seater *Suisei* (JUDY) fighter was shot down, as were three *Gekkō* (IRVING) night fighters and five other Japanese interceptors. The officer pilot of a *Saiun* (MYRT) scout plane was patrolling over Sagami Bay when his observer discerned what he thought were IJAAF planes to his rear. Shortly afterward, the MYRT was hit by seventeen rounds, which ruptured a fuel tank, wounded the pilot, and killed the observer. The pilot managed to bring his plane down safely at Atsugi.[91]

On the afternoon of April 7th, 153 B–29s, escorted by about 100 Mustangs, went after Mitsubishi's Nagoya factory, striking with precision from an altitude of 4,500 to 6,000 meters. Three B–29s and 2 P–51s were lost in the raid. Japanese records confirm the loss of 2 of their interceptors, the pilots ejecting safely, in battles between the IJAAF 246th Air Group and about 30 P–51s. Japanese ground batteries at Nagoya fired 1,914 rounds.[92]

According to Japanese records, the IJAAF 246th Group commander at Nagoya, Maj. T. Ishikawa, expected fighter planes to accompany the B–29s, which was why he deployed his 8 Type–4 interceptors in 2 layers at 6,000 and 8,000 meters over Ise. It became apparent that the P–51s were preceding the bombers in order to weed out interceptor defense beforehand. Ishikawa detected and attacked about 30 Mustangs approximately 1,000 meters below him, but the P–51s were superior in climb and zoomed about the IJAAF flight. One Japanese fighter was set afire, and the pilot bailed out. Ishikawa's plane was shot up. Since he could neither adjust his propeller's pitch nor fire his guns, he dived from 6,000 to 700 meters and escaped to his base. Another of his fighters had had to crash-land and was badly damaged.[93]

That B–29s could dare to conduct medium-altitude raids in the daytime was entirely due to the P–51 escorts, say the Japanese. Flying at altitudes where Japanese fighters were ordinarily at their best, the bomber formations sustained a loss of only five aircraft in the strikes on April 7 against both Tokyo and Nagoya; as a percentage of the total number of B–29s committed, this amounted to less than two percent.[94]

American analysts point out the effectiveness of the fighter escorts on April 7, noting that over the Tokyo target the last 2 bomber formations, which were unescorted, sustained 62 percent of all the Japanese interceptor attacks. U.S. sources state that the 15th and 21st Fighter Groups destroyed 21 Japanese planes that were encountered, as well as damaging 8 out of 135–160 airborne interceptors. "The Mustangs were knocking Japs down all over the sky," a B–29 gunner remembered. "For awhile . . . during the fight there were Japs parachuting down all around us. I'll never forget it."[95]

Since the Americans' round trip always entailed some 1,400 miles from Iwo Jima, about 500 miles short of the maximum range for a Mustang carrying two 108-gallon drop tanks per plane, the escorts could linger over Japan for no more than an hour, including the critical period of the B–29 bomb run. The flights were not easy for the airmen: "Pilots spent 8 hours and more in the air, and the monotony of the long over-water flights and confined conditions of the cockpits brought many fatigue problems."[96]

On the morning of April 12, five days after the initial fighter-escorted bomber raids, 119 B–29s accompanied by 102 Mustangs struck Tokyo in 3 waves from medium altitude while another 50 bombers hit the chemical factory at Koriyama and the Nakajima factory at Musashino again. This time the main target, the Nakajima plant, was damaged critically. The Japanese sent up a total of 185 Army and Navy fighters, hit 36 enemy bombers, but did not bring down even one. Seventeen interceptors were lost. The Koriyama raid failed as a diversion; Japanese fighters would not leave Tokyo, 120 miles to the south, and only 10 passes were made against the Koriyama bombers.[97]

Japanese sources explain that the advent of the P–51s fatally set back the defensive capability of the interceptors. Previously, the U.S. Navy's agile F6F aircraft, a superb bomber escort, had nullified the use of Japanese night fighters, which could "do little more than run away" when they met the Grumman Hellcat (whose record was 5,000 Japanese kills in 2 years of air combat).[98] But the night fighters could be employed well, even in daylight hours, against the B–29s, which were not as maneuverable. Now, only if there were no P–51 escorts could the night fighters, which had oblique-firing guns and were slower than single-engine interceptors, be sent against the Superfortresses. The same was true of Japanese bombers and armed scout planes that had been converted quickly into ultra high-altitude interceptors. If they were not sent up against unescorted bombers, they were useless to the Japanese defenses; and if they were committed against escorted bombers, they were doomed. But how to foretell whether the Americans were dispatching escorted or unescorted formations? Radar could not make the distinction, especially where the fighters were concerned; and it was too late when visual contact was established. Therefore, the Japanese had to regard every raid as fighter-escorted, and they would not employ night-fighter formations by day. The situation was complicated further when P–51s, guided by B–29s as far as offshore points, launched raids of their own, starting on April 19, in the Tokyo area.

If the unusable Japanese aircraft were left in the open because they could not be allowed to scramble, they would invite enemy attack, and their worth would be reduced even more. Hence it was decided to conceal them in nearby woods or to evacuate them to safer refuges, since there were few concrete hangars. For example, in mid-May 1945, Lt. Comdr. T. Minobe moved the three IJNAF fighter squadrons of his 131st Air Group from the battered Kanoya airfield to Iwakawa, also located on Kyushu but in a mountainous district. Minobe dispersed his planes and had his men plant trees, bring in cattle, erect movable dummy houses all over the area, and strew the runways with vegetation. U.S. aircraft caused few problems for the 131st Air Group at Iwakawa. Whenever enemy daytime intruders had left the region, the Japanese would quickly bring back their dispersed planes and get them ready for night action. At the forward base at Kojinya on Amami Oshima Island, Japanese engineers scooped a concealed facility, designed to support night operations, from the side of a mountain.[99] Japanese airfield battalions also boasted about the speed with which they were able to repair cratered runways.

Despite the pride that Japanese airmen retain regarding the effectiveness of their efforts at camouflage and concealment, they still feel that the Americans did not sufficiently comprehend the hardship inflicted on the defenders. The Japanese had to deal with a reduction in the number of interceptors that could scramble, the wastage of manpower and fuel, and the psychological exhaustion generated by the need for strenuous countermeasures. As for coping with fighter-escorted bombers, single-engine interceptors had a very difficult time. Few pilots could manage to combat the U.S. fighters, and those that could found it nearly impossible to shake the P–51s and close with the B–29s. The Mustangs, fast and agile, were regarded as the most powerful reciprocal-engine fighters in the enemy's arsenal; they were detested by interceptor pilots flying the outclassed Japanese night fighters. It was the feeling of IJNAF pilots that the ZEKE fighter was about equal to the Curtiss P–40 and Grumman F4F Wildcat, but no match for the powerful Vought F4U Corsair and the Grumman F6F, which was particularly disliked. One veteran Japanese flyer admitted after the war that IJNAF pilots became convinced that they were flying very inferior planes, and they "had a horror of American fighters."[100]

Not surprisingly, AAF sources are in complete agreement with the potency of fighter escorts during B–29 daylight bombing operations. It was estimated that the use of escorts reduced enemy interception by as much as 70 percent. The Japanese, it was concluded, would not press attacks against bombers in the face of the threat of P–51s and P–47s. It has also been pointed out that, "in addition to saving many B–29s from attack by enemy aircraft, the protection provided by [U.S.] fighters served to increase the confidence and morale of B–29 combat crews, thereby resulting in increased bombing efficiency." The risk that could be faced when fighter escorts were not provided for daytime bombing operations is illustrated by the events of April 24. Coming in at the unusually low altitude of 4,000 meters, 101 B–29s wrecked the radial-engine plant at Yamato outside of Tokyo, but encountered heavy resistance by fighters and flak. Though B–29 gunners claimed 14 fighters destroyed and 24 probably downed, 4 American bombers were lost and 68 were damaged.[101]

With LeMay's emphasis on low-level night raids against cities, however, the U.S. fighters were called on less frequently for escort duty than had been originally anticipated. When VII Fighter Command did provide escorts, the numbers of committed aircraft remained impressive. Thus, during the B–29 raid of May 29 against Yokohama, 101 P–51s accompanied 517 bombers by day and at high altitude. The U.S. fighters claimed to have shot down 26 and damaged 31 of some 150 Japanese interceptors they met that day; 3 Mustangs were lost. On June 10th, 107 P–51s escorted about 500 B–29s that attacked the Tokyo Bay area; and on June 26, a total of 148 P–51s covered 510 bombers that struck targets in southern Honshu and Shikoku. Against nighttime bombing operations, interceptions by Japanese fighters were never effective. Most passes occurred when bombers were illuminated by ground conflagrations or by searchlights.[102]

In scarcely more than 4 months, VII Fighter Command flew over 1,700 sorties in support of B–29s, destroyed or probably destroyed 497 Japanese planes (276 airborne), and damaged 567. The previously mentioned effectiveness of Japanese camouflage and concealment of aircraft on the ground became so pronounced, however, that "strafing of airfields yielded little return." It was evident that "the enemy's constant shifting of planes from field to field and his increased use of dispersion, dummies, and camouflage left few fat targets." Grounded Japanese aircraft did not ignite when hit by P–51s, indicating that fuel tanks had been emptied.[103]

By war's end, the B–29 bomber formations were daring to fly consistently without fighter escort. According to Gen. Henry H. Arnold, during the summer of 1945:

> . . . we bombed Japan actually at will, at altitudes of our own choosing (as low as 8,000 or even 5,000 feet) with practically no losses. In the last phase, before Hiroshima, we used B–29s without armor, and with almost no guns. When it came time to drop the atomic bomb, we were so sure that any B–29 would reach its objective without opposition that we sent the second of these preciously laden planes without escort.

General LeMay later said "the record will show that in the last 2 months of the war it was safer to fly a combat mission over Japan than it was to fly a B–29 training mission back in the United States."[104]

The Torment of the Japanese Air Forces

It should not be thought that Japanese pilots were reconciled to the High Command's decision in the spring of 1945 to preserve fighter strength for the all-out campaign that was to be waged against the expected enemy landings in the homeland. One IJAAF air defense officer remarked that "our pilots' spirit was squelched and the brilliant feats of our fighters almost vanished. We became eagles without wings." Another IJAAF officer lamented: "The enemy planes in silvery formations flew virtually unimpeded over the homeland, and the Japanese people began to wonder if their air force still existed. This eventually led to the populace's distrust of the military." War Minister Korechika Anami apologized formally to local

426

military commanders in Tokyo on July 16, 1945, for allowing enemy task forces to dominate the area around the homeland.[105]

At some point, the Japanese High Command had to face up to the consequences of having abdicated the battle for air superiority over the homeland. In June 1945, Japan was struck 36 times by an aggregate of about 4,600 USAAF, USN, and USMC planes of all types operating from the Marianas, Iwo Jima, Okinawa, and aircraft carriers. Arguments raged between Japanese staff officers, who insisted that all of the country's cities should not be allowed to die, and those who responded that it was impossible to defend the whole nation, lest the remaining fighter assets be expended even before the enemy's ground invasion began. In late June, IGHQ finally decided to adopt an air defense policy of engaging enemy planes. Even so, Japanese interceptors were only to go after bombers, because they were deemed to be most dangerous to the country as a whole, and because Japanese fighters could be expected to suffer far fewer losses in combat against bombers than against fighters. Enemy fighters should be engaged only when circumstances were "especially advantageous or absolutely necessary." It was not thought that this selective type of air defense would prevent the weakening of the people's will to resist, but it was hoped that even local successes by the Japanese air forces would exert favorable psychological effects on the populace and concomitantly adverse effects on the resolve of the enemy.[106]

On July 9, 1945, the three air divisions defending Japan were transferred from the jurisdiction of the ground armies and placed under the direct control of the Air General Army. Although that force was directed to cooperate closely with the Navy, the Army was explicitly given responsibility for the overall air defense of the country. IJAAF staff officers admit that the latest steps merely amounted to another paper plan, and that the air divisions were unable to concern themselves with the interception of raiding aircraft, but had to conserve what was left of their strength for the decisive last battle against land invasion. Given the Japanese emphasis on *kamikazes* in 1945, few fighters were left to handle the conventional air defense role. The 10th Air Division at Tokyo, for example, had only ninety-five serviceable IJAAF interceptors in five air groups as of late July.[107]

To cover the Osaka-Kobe and Nagoya districts, the 11th Air Division assembled several dozen Type 3 *Hien* (TONY) and Type 4 *Hayate* (FRANK) fighters at Kameoka, west of Kyoto. Learning on July 19 that a B–29 raid impended, 11th Air Division Headquarters at Osaka ordered interception at full strength. Too late, the division heard that the enemy raiders had been identified as fighter aircraft, and the Japanese interceptors were ordered to avoid contact. The radioed messages never got through to the IJAAF fighter units. The 16 TONYS of the 56th Air Group, patrolling at 14,000 feet, were surprised by a like number of P–51s operating 5,000 feet above them and lost 2 TONYS before they could get away. The commander of the 246th Air Group, with 16 FRANK fighters, observed the melee from a distance of 6 miles, but by the time the FRANKS could climb from 4 miles, the P–51s were gone.[108] It is noteworthy that 2 IJAAF air groups had been able to scramble a total of only 32 operational fighters at full strength, and that the air division would not authorize them to engage U.S. fighter inroads.

The cheerlessness and despair of their situation drove Japanese military and naval pilots to distraction and even to occasional rebelliousness. A case in point was the IJAAF's 244th Air Group, which had been pulled back from Kyushu to the Osaka area in mid-July 1945 to prepare for the decisive operations expected in that region. Equipped with the Army's newest single-seat fighter—the Kawasaki Ki–100 Type 5, a smooth-handling, reliable plane—Maj. Teruhiko Kobayashi and his flyers craved action against the U.S. fighters that swarmed daily over central Honshu Island. On July 16, Major Kobayashi took off from Yokkaichi with a dozen of his Type 5 interceptors, ostensibly to conduct training aloft. Inevitably, the Japanese pilots encountered the fighting that they wanted when they ran into Mustang formations. The Americans found the Type 5 to be "a complete and unpleasant surprise."[109] But though the initial combat was inconclusive, Kobayashi's immediate superiors at the 11th Air Division promptly ordered the 224th Air Group to be grounded.

Major Kobayashi's men were understandably frustrated. One IJAAF flying sergeant complained: "Why can't we use our 'hot' new planes? We fighter pilots aren't afraid to die in battle." Kobayashi bided his time. When he received information in the early morning of July 25 that hundreds of USN carrier planes were on the way to attack the Kansai region, Kobayashi assembled his unit. "We have been told not to attack enemy fighters," he said. "So why don't we just conduct battle training today?" Ordering all available planes to take off, Kobayashi led the way into the air. His 30-plus pilots followed separately, there being no time for the usual orderly takeoff sequence. F6F Grummans were already over Wakayama, heading for Osaka, but they were preoccupied with ground-strafing missions, and Kobayashi's fighters got above them. The 3d Squadron commander, Capt. Kozo Fujisawa, recalls what happened next:

> From an altitude of 4,000 meters [14,000 feet] we swooped down on one cluster of 24 enemy aircraft. Yet though we engaged them in swirling individual dogfights, the Grummans never broke formation. I set one USN plane on fire but had no time to confirm the kill. Our Type 5 fighters had the edge over the F6F in climbing and circling, but the Grummans were far better in diving and acceleration, so they could pull away from us easily. On balance, however, I think the Type 5 fighter was more than equal to the Grumman.

In this air-to-air battle of July 25, another IJAAF captain rammed a Grumman head-on. Ejecting on impact, the captain was already dead when his parachute opened. The 244th Air Group lost one more pilot in combat that day but claimed to have shot down twelve USN carrier planes. According to Japanese sources, the 343d Air Group had also sortied over the Bungo Strait the day before and had brought down twelve enemy carrier aircraft at a cost of six IJAAF interceptors. These air battles, say the Japanese, represented the last successes by their fighter planes in the defense of the homeland.[110]

U.S. records indicate that Task Force 38 launched 1,747 sorties on July 24 and 25, but that bad weather halted the round-the-clock strikes at midday on the 25th. The clash of Major Kobayashi's unit with USN fighters must have involved VF-31, which noted the rare experience of being jumped by a superior number of Japanese interceptors while its Hellcats were strafing an airfield near Nagoya on July 25. A twenty-four-year-old American officer, Lt. Comdr. Cornelius Nooy, saved an F6F from an enemy fighter. Thereupon Nooy climbed to draw off other Japanese aircraft, rejoined his flight, shot down two more enemy planes, and claimed one probable kill.[111]

As for Major Kobayashi, that IJAAF group commander had been promptly ordered to report to 11th Air Division Headquarters in Osaka, where he was reprimanded for disobeying his instructions forbidding fighter sorties and was warned that his action ran counter to the command's intention to conserve the remaining Japanese air strength. It was intimated to Kobayashi by his superiors that not only might he be demoted for his breach of military discipline but that he also faced court-martial proceedings. The major returned to Yokkaichi in a rage, drank a defiant toast to "victory," and was heard to say, "It's all O.K. with me." That very night, an official telegram of commendation arrived from Imperial General Headquarters, dissipating any thought of punishing Kobayashi. Nevertheless, the 11th Air Division sent a staff officer to the 244th Air Group with instructions to keep a watchful eye on the unit. The staff officer "stuck to Major Kobayashi like a leech," allowing him no chance for further arbitrariness.[112]

Allied Victory in the Pacific

By June 1945, the Seventh Air Force possessed a total of 1,492 planes, of which 1,006 were fighters. Most of its tactical units had reached Okinawa by July. VII Bomber Command was based at Yontan, Kadena, and Machinato. VII Fighter Command had the 4 groups of its principal force, the 301st Fighter Wing, based on Ie Shima, offshore from Okinawa itself. On July 14, the Seventh Air Force, under its new commander, Maj. Gen. Thomas D. White, was officially transferred from the Navy Tactical Air Force, Ryukyus, to the Far East Air Forces (FEAF). Having worked for years under the control of USN and USMC commanders, the Seventh Air

Force was finally able to operate as an "integrated air force" under strictly Army Air Forces command. But since the last component of the Seventh Air Force's headquarters only arrived at Okinawa on July 28, and since the staff had never before been able to direct their own elements in combat, by their own admission they were "slow to get under way." Nevertheless, they now had the novel experience of operating tactical units belonging to another service, in this case the 2d Marine Air Wing, which was responsible for the air defense of the Ryukyu Islands.[113]

FEAF assigned top priority to the neutralization and destruction of Japanese air power by attacking planes and installations, particularly the dispersal zones of the main airfields on Kyushu. In July and August 1945, Seventh Air Force fighters and bombers flew 4,442 sorties, losing only 2 planes to interceptors and 10 to antiaircraft fire. In the last 4 months of action, VII Fighter Command claimed to have destroyed or probably destroyed 497 enemy aircraft (including 276 in the air) and to have damaged 567. On July 3, V Fighter Command joined the air offensive against Kyushu, eventually building up its strength to 4 fighter groups and 2 night fighter squadrons. By war's end, V Fighter Command had lost only 1 plane to enemy interceptors and 4 to antiaircraft fire. In the absence of significant resistance by the Japanese air forces, Seventh Air Force and Fifth Air Force fighter pilots indulged in what they termed "general hell raising," attacking bridges, railroads, rolling stock, fuel storage tanks, shipping, and other targets of opportunity. Additionally, AAF fighters supported heavy bomber raids against what little was left from B–29 attacks on Japanese industry and urban centers. For example, 97 P–47s and 49 P–51s participated in an attack by 179 B–25s, B–24s, and A–26s from the Seventh Air Force and the Fifth Air Force against Tarumizu on August 5. Two days later, 18 P–47s accompanied a B–24 raid against Omuta. Kumamoto and Kurume were similarly hit by the Seventh Air Force on August 10–11. U.S. fighters still escorted the B–29s when needed. On August 10th, 102 P–51s covered strikes by 165 Superfortresses against targets from Amagasaki to Tokyo.[114]

Japanese fighters returned to the fray after the war was actually over. Four U.S. B–32s on a reconnaissance mission were attacked over the Tokyo area by fifteen interceptors on August 17, and again on the 18th; three of the Japanese fighters were shot down in the two days of clashes.[115] Japanese official combat records end with the capitulation on August 15, but it is known from oral testimony and secondary sources that for several days a number of IJAAF and IJNAF pilots, from flag rank down in the case of the Navy, deliberately sortied singly or in small formations on arbitrary, one-way suicide missions against the erstwhile enemy. The flyers' motives were frustration, grief, and humiliation. It is highly probable that the unauthorized Japanese fighter actions of August 17–18 fall into this category, originating among airmen similar to those of Major Kobayashi's defiant 244th Air Group.

Indeed, the Japanese admit that many of their own airmen had lost heart even before hostilities ended. On August 9, the chief of staff of the Air General Army had telephoned 10th Air Division Headquarters in Tokyo to stress that, although there was talk of ending the war, vigorous efforts should still be made to go on fighting and to intercept enemy raiders. Nevertheless, on August 13, when the Tokyo district was hit by USN carrier planes and Japanese fighters were scrambled effectively, the 10th Air Division commander "failed to urge his men to press the attack to the utmost [because] it seemed absurd to incur additional losses with the war obviously lost and its termination due in a matter of days."[116]

Meanwhile, the U.S. Navy had been continuing its own devastating strikes against the Japanese mainland. American warships, unchallenged from the air, had boldly shelled targets ashore since mid-July. USN and USMC carrier planes launched especially powerful attacks against camouflaged airfields in northern Honshu and Hokkaido once typhoon conditions eased up after the first week of August. Aircraft from Task Force 38 struck in force on August 9, 10, 13, and 14. The carriers' CAP fighters shot down 22 enemy aircraft, including numerous Japanese Navy B6N *Tenzans* (JILLS) and D4Y *Suisa* (JUDYS) flying singly, during the raids of August 13. Two final USN carrier strikes sortied on the morning of the 15th, the last day of the war—103 planes in the first wave, which proceeded with its attack, and 73 in the second wave, which was recalled. A flight of four F6Fs from the first wave, over Sagami Bay on their way back to the USS *Hancock*, was attacked by 7 Japanese fighters, 4 of which were shot down without loss to the Americans. Another USN flight consisting of 6 Hellcats from the USS *Yorktown*, separated from the rest of the first wave by cloud cover, was attacked near Tokyo, from behind and above at 8,000 feet, by 17 enemy fighter pilots who either did not yet know the war was over or else were mounting a last defiant challenge. In a hard-fought battle, 9 of the Japanese planes were shot down, but the Americans lost 4 of the 6 Hellcats and all 4 pilots. It was apparently the final dogfight of the Pacific War, though USN fighters downed 8 more Japanese intruders near the task force on August 15, in response to Admiral Halsey's famous order to "investigate and shoot down all snoopers . . . in a friendly sort of way."[117]

Mention should also be made of the combat contribution made by the Royal Navy (RN) to the final air and sea offensive against homeland Japan. In November 1944, a new British Pacific Fleet had been constituted under Adm. Bruce Fraser. By the spring of 1945, the British had formed a task force under the tactical command of Vice Adm. H. B. Rawlings. Rear Adm. P. L. Vian, in turn, commanded the 1st Carrier Squadron, made up of 4 aircraft carriers (later reinforced to 5). The peak British air strength available aboard 5 carriers totaled 259 fighters, including USN-type

Hellcats, Corsairs, and Avengers, as well as RN-type Seafires (a counterpart of the RAF Spitfire) and Fireflies (a heavy fighter). These fighters were employed in constant strikes against Japanese airfields and other targets on Formosa and then Sakishima Gunto in particular. British-flown Hellcats scored 47.5 air-to-air kills during their participation in the Pacific War.[118]

The crescendo of the Allied air offensive against Japan had quickened in July and early August 1945. On the 1st and 2d of August, 766 B–29s—the biggest number to date—hit Nagaoka and other targets. The largest and last series of bombing raids occurred on August 14 when 833 B–29s struck industrial and urban targets all over Japan. In the meantime, a "special unit" (to use an AAF euphemism of the time) had obliterated Hiroshima with the first atomic weapon on August 6 and Nagasaki with the second A-bomb on August 9. The fact that in each case a single B–29 could get through so easily to deliver the awesome atomic bomb unnerved the Japanese air commands. What, they were compelled to wonder, was the point of having conceded air superiority over the homeland to the enemy and of having "conserved" the remnants of the Army and Navy air forces to cope with an envisaged invasion that had become academic?

The Japanese air staffs realized, at this late hour in the war, that they would have to give up the passive practice of engaging only large formations of enemy bombers. An 11th Air Division officer remarked that "regardless of the consequences, it was clear that not even a single B–29 could [now] be ignored." The division therefore assigned its best surviving pilots and planes to patrol the skies over northern Kyushu whenever one hostile bomber was reported to be approaching. But this meant that, in practice, each lone enemy plane would have to be engaged. This was patently impossible, said a 10th Air Division staff officer. After all, by the end of the war, 2 of the 3 air divisions in the homeland had been assigned only about 50 frontline fighters each, and the third division about 100; no organic air group possessed over 34 operational aircraft. In fact, the 3 air divisions disposed of a combined total of little more than 200 operational, front-line interceptors, with another 150 in mobile reserve.[119]

Operation DOWNFALL

By July 1945, the U.S. air offensive against the Japanese home islands had devastated about forty percent of the built-up regions in sixty-six major cities, causing some thirty percent of the urban populace of the whole country to lose their dwelling places. That American bombers and fighters were freely crisscrossing Japanese skies in the absence of significant opposition from the ground or air, for whatever reason, portended the last crisis for Japan. Indeed, a number of U.S. planners and commanders became convinced that the combined impact of direct air attack and blockade could compel the final decision without an invasion. Japan had been brought to such dire straits despite the fact that the weight of the American air offensive in general "had as yet reached only a fraction of its planned proportion," as U.S. Strategic Bombing Survey analysts later observed. For example, air assaults against Japan's rail and transportation network were merely getting underway at the outset of August.[120]

Allied decisionmakers, however, were still uncertain about the decisiveness of the air and naval offensive in convincing the Japanese government and high command to negotiate an early termination of hostilities. Strategic planning therefore proceeded on the basic assumption contained in directives issued by the Joint Chiefs of Staff on April 3, 1945, that ground armies would have to be used to invade Kyushu and Honshu in order to compel Japan to capitulate unconditionally. On May 28, 1945, General MacArthur's headquarters in Manila drafted the first edition of a comprehensive "strategic plan for operations in the Japanese archipelago." The Kyushu invasion (Operation OLYMPIC, scheduled for November 1945) and the Honshu invasion (Operation CORONET, set for March 1946) were grouped under the collective code name of DOWNFALL.[121]

The OLYMPIC operation was particularly designed to project U.S. land-based air forces into southern Kyushu, with a view to supporting the second, "knock-out blow to the enemy's heart" in the Tokyo-Yokohama region. American planners had no illusions regarding the intensity or tenacity of the Japanese response. The landings were expected to be opposed by all of the enemy's available military forces using every means, and by a "fanatically hostile population" resisting to "the utmost extent of their capabilities." Once the Allies had secured control of Kyushu, the invasion forces committed to Operation CORONET would be able to draw upon a minimum equivalent of 40 land-based Army and USMC air groups and upon naval elements for direct support and blockade. The land-based "air garrison" of about 2,800 planes would specifically include 16 fighter and fighter-bomber groups and 4 night-fighter squadrons.[122]

The OLYMPIC landings would require intensive air preparation, the heaviest practicable neutralization of enemy air, ground, and naval forces capable of interfering with or limiting the success of the invasion. Attacks by carrier task groups would be coordinated with prolonged action by land-based units of the Twentieth Air Force and other air forces striking massively from the Marianas and the Ryukyus. All-out effort would peak during the ten days preceding the invasion, bringing about offensive air superiority from the outset. It was intended therefore to destroy hostile air power in Kyushu and nearby, to isolate the objective areas of Miyazaki,

433

Ariake Bay, and Kushikino, to overcome the ground defenses, and to cover the preliminary amphibious operations.[123]

Why the Japanese, after losing Okinawa, had been keeping their air forces on a tight leash, withholding commitment or strictly avoiding losses, could easily be surmised by the Americans: the enemy seemed unwilling to accept a reduction in reserves below the level deemed necessary for the final defense of the country. It was believed by MacArthur's headquarters that, through rigid economy, the Japanese would strive to replace their severe losses to date and to rebuild their inventory, not only by careful control of attempted interception of U.S. air strikes but also by concentrating in Japan all planes that could be spared from other areas. Indeed, there was evidence that the Japanese were already heavily tapping into their field forces in Manchuria to reinforce the homeland, despite the risk of weakening the Manchurian front in the face of Russia's potential entry into the war against Japan. By the time Operation OLYMPIC was to be launched, the Japanese could be expected to have had time to increase the number of planes immediately available in the homeland area to 2,000–2,500, of which 1,500–2,000 would be first-line aircraft and the rest training planes and obsolete or obsolescent models. The number, distribution, and types of Japanese airfields and landing grounds, estimated at 200 and supplemented by facilities in Korea and China, were deemed to be entirely adequate for the number of aircraft at hand or likely to come on line in the foreseeable future. According to U.S. intelligence, there was a possibility that the Japanese would withdraw their land-based aviation to the Asian mainland for protection from the neutralizing attacks. The relocated force would then operate against the enemy armies invading Kyushu by staging through fields in Japan.[124]

Initial air opposition to OLYMPIC was expected to be "as intense and violent as [the Japanese] can make it," according to U.S. intelligence, even before the actual landings. The counterattacks would emanate from northern Kyushu, southwest Honshu, Shikoku, and South Korea. American strategists, however, believed that the enemy would be quickly compelled to curtail the air defense of Kyushu, lest the all-important Tokyo area be left entirely or inadequately protected. Hence, quite early in the fighting, just as soon as it became apparent to the defenders that success on Kyushu was unlikely, the Japanese would abandon mass air attacks, after having expended no more than 500 to 800 planes in efforts to prevent U.S. landing and consolidation operations. Thereafter the Japanese would go over to the strictly defensive mode, and the scale of air effort would be reduced to intermittent sorties, involving a small number of aircraft, emphasizing suicide crashes of "uncertain proportions," mainly during hours of darkness.[125]

Though the Japanese Navy would employ its last large and midget submarines and small assault demolition or suicide craft to contest the landings during the approach and afterward, the only important naval counterthrust in defense of Kyushu might be mounted by a suicide force built around a carrier task force, if the nine aircraft carriers and two converted battleships still afloat in mid-1945 had not been destroyed in the interim. Nevertheless, in view of the reduction in the strength of the Japanese fleet, American planners judged that whatever course the Japanese Navy might choose would have had little effect on Allied operations. As for ground-launched V-type weapons, similar to the German jet-propelled V-1S, it was known that the Japanese had been trying to obtain German help in their development. Though none had appeared in the Far East to date, they might be introduced prior to the implementation of Operation OLYMPIC. Suicide-pilot "*Baka* bombs" had seen action at Okinawa, and they would undoubtedly be used in even greater numbers during the defense of the homeland.[126]

Though U.S. prognostications of Japanese response to the projected invasion of the homeland were generally accurate with respect to the intensity of reaction, they were considerably below the mark regarding the quantity of Japanese Army and Navy aircraft that had been hoarded and the proportion that would be allocated to *kamikaze* action in the last campaigns. By focusing attention on the number and length of runways and landing grounds operated by the enemy, U.S. intelligence tended to lose sight of the ubiquitous capabilities of Japanese suicide-crash aircraft. General Masakazu Kawabe, the Air General Army Commander, later said:[127]

> We believed that, despite your destruction of our major fields, we could very easily construct fields from which *kamikaze* planes could take off. Everywhere we had built little fields capable of launching *kamikaze* planes. As long as there was only a question of launching them and not getting them back, there was no question . . . We knew you would do everything in your power to destroy all our airfields, but we believed the airfields necessary for [*kamikazes*]were such simple affairs that they could be mended very quickly. We believed that by taking advantage of weather, heavy overcast, and intervals between your. . . raids, we could repair the airfields enough to keep them serviceable. Also we could use stretches of beach. . . .

Lt. Gen. Michio Sugawara, the 6th Air Army Commander, added that the battlefield in the homeland would not be 600 or 700 kilometers away from Japanese home bases, as in the Ryukyus, and that defending pilots would be "at the point of combat anywhere along the coast."[128]

While American intelligence's estimate of the Japanese stock of first-line planes was good, the analysts did not take into account the ability and willingness of the Japanese to launch *every* plane that could fly on one-way *kamikaze* missions. Yet, as the Operation DOWNFALL planners noted, the experience at Okinawa had already shown how Japanese air power would be used in all-out combat. It would feature "liberal employment of all available classes of aircraft including obsolescent types, trainers, and carrier-based planes operating shore-based . . . [supplemented by] withdrawal of aircraft from all other sectors...in order to participate in the action."[129] Japanese Air General Army staff officers asserted subsequently that the Army intended to commit "the full air force led by the commanding general. We expected annihilation of our entire air force but we felt that it was our duty."[130] Once the last designated *kamikazes* were expended, the remaining first-line conventional fighter pilots, who until then had been used to escort and shepherd the Special Attack planes, would be assigned suicide missions themselves. It is probable that at least two-thirds of the Japanese air forces' planes and pilots would have been consumed as *kamikazes*.[131] It should be noted, however, that the Japanese did not hope to win the war at this late date; they intended to inflict such fearful casualties on the foe that better than unconditional terms could be secured.

By August 1945, Japanese air units were amassing "every type of plane [they] could find, no matter how obsolete or how long in storage." The final air potential of both services in Japan and in areas of practicable reinforcement (Korea, Manchuria, north and central China, and Taiwan) was much higher than Allied intelligence's tally. The IJAAF alone possessed a maximum number of 7,800 aircraft: 2,650 ready for the *kamikaze* role (900 combat types, 1,750 advanced trainers), 2,150 suitable for conventional use, and 3,000 available but not currently effective—that is, undergoing repair or modification, still assigned to training units or in storage, etc. The last inventory of IJNAF (which was regarded as ahead of the Army in preparations, dispersal, and level of maintenance) included a maximum number of 10,100 planes; 2,700 primary trainers ready for *kamikaze* use, 3,200 orthodox aircraft, and 4,200 available but not fully effective. The two services thus had a combined total of 10,700 operational planes, of which 5,350 had been prepared as *kamikazes* and an equal number as conventional combat aircraft. If the 7,200 additional IJAAF and IJNAF planes available but not deemed currently effective were counted, the maximum number of aircraft carried in the inventories of both services' air forces would reach a grand total of 17,900.[132]

It goes without saying that the statistics for effective air potential were seriously vitiated by Japan's fundamental weaknesses, rendered irreversible by war's end. For example, with the isolation of the Japanese homeland from the Asian continent and Southeast Asia, the importation of fuel as well as natural resources dwindled seriously. Substitute aviation fuels, some bordering on desperation, were introduced (alcohol) or tested (pineroot oil, isopropyl ether, camphor oil). Since mid-1944, the Japanese had had to reduce military aviation fuel consumption at the very time that air combat was becoming crucial; the effects were felt greatly in the area of training. Even the program of orthodox air training in the Navy had to be cut to fifteen hours per pilot per month by the end of the war.[133]

TABLE 8–2

IJAAF Order of Battle, Homeland, August 1945

Unit	Commander	Location of Hq
Air General Army	Gen. Masakazu Kawabe	Tokyo
1st Air Army	Lt. Gen. Takeo Yasuda	Tokyo
10th Air Division	Lt. Gen. Kametoshi Kondō	Tokyo
11th Air Division	Lt. Gen. Kumao Kitajima	Osaka
6th Air Army	Lt. Gen. Michio Sugawara	Fukuoka
1st Air Division	Lt. Gen. Sho'ichi Sato	Sapporo
12th Air Division	Maj. Gen. Hideharu Habu	Ozuki
51st Air Division	Lt. Gen. Ai Ishikawa	Gifu
52d Air Division	Lt. Gen. Shigeru Yamanaka	Kumagaya
53d Air Division	Lt. Gen. Yutaka Hirota	Ota
20th Fighter Group	Maj. Gen. Takezo Aoki	Komaki
30th Fighter Group	Maj. Gen. Yasuyuki Miyoshi	Kumamoto

Source: Homeland Operations Record, Japanese Monograph 17, Japanese Research Division, HQ USAFE/Eighth U.S. Army (Rear); corrections by the author.

Qualitatively, Japanese military planes had deteriorated by 1944–45. They already had a history of poor performance at high altitude, unsatisfactory air-to-ground communication, short range, lack of powerful armament, chronically weak landing gear, and poor brakes. Now Japanese plane output suffered from material deficiencies and substitute components, inferior workmanship, reduced precision, and insufficient testing (many trainers received no flight testing). Other problems stemmed from clumsy flying and ferrying, rendered costly by navigational mistakes, mechanical failures, defective materials, poor upkeep, and pilot error. The ferry flight often became the test flight. IJNAF found itself rejecting thirty to fifty percent of the planes produced since summer 1944; repair of the rejected aircraft might take a precious month. In addition, the logistical and maintenance system was inadequate. Facilities for repair and engine change were few and scattered. Refueling was primitive, and spare parts were in constant short supply. There was poor technical coordination between the services and industry; duplication and secretiveness were rife.[134] The practical effects of these limitations and deficiencies had an inevitably adverse bearing on Japan's handling of the last stages of the air war and her prospects for coping with the OLYMPIC and CORONET onslaughts.

Conclusions

This chapter has emphasized the quest for air superiority in the war against Japan. But, as the official U.S. Air Force historians Wesley Frank Craven and James Lea Cate pointed out in 1953, "to win a victory over the enemy air forces was but part of the mission" of aviation in the Pacific. "It was the versatility of the AAF," added Craven and Cate, "rather than its accomplishments in any one department, which deserves principal emphasis. . . . "[135] The Seventh Air Force, for example, was tasked with a threefold mission in the final offensive against Japan. Its highest priority until the end of the war was to neutralize and destroy Japanese air power by bomber as well as fighter attacks on enemy air installations and aircraft. The second mission was to destroy Japanese shipping; and the third, to disrupt transportation and communications on Kyushu, preparatory to Operation OLYMPIC.[136]

The war against Japan was not a sea war or a ground war or an air war, but, as the Strategic Bombing Survey stressed, "a combined sea-ground-air war in three dimensions." Admiral King spoke of a "partnership of accomplishment" with the U.S. Army's ground, air, and service forces. USN and USMC carrier planes played a large part in the reduction of island objectives, particularly in the preinvasion stages. In the Marianas and Ryukyus operations, the initial strikes were carrier-borne. The Seventh Air Force joined naval aviation in the first land-based reconnaissance of the Marianas. AAF bombers and fighters, from the various commands, operated in concert to bring the air war to Japan.[137]

In addition, it should be remembered that the air war was fought by Allies in several theaters of Asia and the Pacific. Though this chapter has stressed the role of the Americans, important contributions to the victory over Japan were also made, prior to the Hiroshima and Nagasaki atomic bombings, by air elements of Great Britain (RAF), Australia (RAAF), New Zealand (RNZAF), the Netherlands (RNEI Air Force), and the Republic of China (CAF and Chinese-American Composite Wing).[138]

The achievement of Allied air superiority in Japanese skies owed much to the synchronization of U.S. offensive planning with the buildup of strength. Thus the Seventh Air Force attained its peak in terms of size and activity during the last stage of operations against the Japanese home islands. Indeed, the Seventh Air Force's maximum effort took place during the final month of the war. Whereas, until the campaign against Okinawa, U.S. air strikes had been largely focused on the neutralization of specific enemy bases such as Truk and Iwo Jima, the last offensive embraced a far-ranging effort to interdict hundreds of well-developed airfields or minor strips then within range in the homeland and environs, from Kanoya, Omura, and Oita, to Nagasaki, Kumamoto, and Kagoshima, and even Shanghai. Second- and third-priority shipping and transportation targets were already coming under U.S. air attack by war's end.[139]

438

In the process of winning air superiority, AAF units had to cope with a large number of limiting factors: enormous distances between islands in the central Pacific, posing difficulties in communication, liaison, and reconnaissance; lack of bases within reach of the enemy; limited range of aircraft; and problems of navigation and navigational aids. The small size of the islands in the central Pacific constituted a chronic challenge. Even when atolls or small reef islands proved suitable as forward bases, their limited capacity usually rendered them useful only for staging operations. As Seventh Air Force officers recalled, not until the Marianas were reached "[did we have] a base which was much larger in effect than an anchored aircraft carrier. Saipan, with an area of 46 square miles, seemed tremendous in comparison with our previous bases."[140]

The AAF in the Pacific faced still other limiting factors: a lack of supplies and a lack of shipping to haul them forward; the need to move into advanced bases before adequate facilities became available; a dearth of radar-equipped aircraft; shortages of planes, parts, and equipment; and the need to create an air-sea rescue capability. There was a lack of maintenance facilities, especially in the early phases of the war, when U.S. flying personnel often had to service their own planes. Aircraft crews were in short supply until 1944; in some months, replacement crews were not received. The Seventh Air Force, detecting inadequate training in crews that did arrive from the United States, established its own schools to teach navigation and gunnery.[141] Despite the many and vexing difficulties encountered by the AAF in the course of the air war in the Pacific, "one by one these problems were overcome," USSBS analysts concluded. The program for the final air offensive against Japan itself, they added, was "soundly conceived and executed."[142]

The Japanese, of course, contributed significantly to their own inability to control the air over their homeland. Apart from the severe technological weaknesses of their antiaircraft ordnance and interceptor planes (even when committed), the basic capabilities of Japanese air opposition and countermeasures did not impress the Americans by 1945. In the words of U.S. postwar analysts:[143]

> ... the over-all effectiveness of Japanese defenses never constituted a serious threat to the accomplishment of the mission of strategic air warfare. It is apparent after survey that even had more substantial numbers of fighters been disposed in defense of the home islands, the Japanese air strategy and concept was distinctly limited, and little appreciable effect would have been felt [by the U.S. air offensive effort]. ... Throughout hostilities the tactics of the [Japanese pilot] displayed little variation, and his techniques and skill did not improve appreciably.

The larger reasons for Japanese defeat in the air encompassed geostrategic, economic, technological, demographic, and psychological factors that lie beyond the purview of this chapter. However, several specific explanations can be adduced to account for the loss of air superiority by the IJAAF and the IJNAF to the Seventh Air Force and other components of

Allied air power. Their early successes lulled the Japanese into a false sense of security. For much too long they tended to think in terms of the feeble, outclassed Allied aviation originally encountered in Southeast Asia and China. The Japanese doctrinal approach to air power was narrow and uncoordinated. The IJAAF was typically subordinated to ground forces. Neither the IJAAF nor the IJNAF (which had a somewhat broader conception) could ever mount sustained and heavy strategic attacks at long range against economic targets or rear zones. Both services underestimated the Allies' ability to conduct such operations against Japanese industry and urban centers.[144]

The Japanese did not exploit the advantages of interior lines of communication. When time was already working against them, they frittered away their best air units in piecemeal fashion around their far-flung perimeter of strategic defense—the consequence of envisaging a relatively short and victorious war. Japanese tactical aviation was committed in driblets; operations entailing more than a hundred aircraft were few. Toward the end of the war, certainly, the low quality of Japanese planes and pilots would have prevented the massing of disciplined formations, but it was also the belief of the IJNAF that the Army Air Forces would only cooperate with it if operations were conducted over land. Navy officer Minoru Genda, the man who helped to plan the Pearl Harbor operation, later remarked that each service sought to conduct operations on its own and lacked understanding of the other branch. Not only did the IJAAF and the IJNAF fail to cooperate effectively, but the Army and the Navy competed frantically for allocations of Japan's limited supplies of raw materials and production facilities. Realistically speaking, unification of the separate military and naval air forces was an impossibility.[145]

In sheer quantities of aircraft, the Japanese manufactured a formidable number for both services during the Pacific war—65,000 of all types. But they lost a similarly formidable number of planes, over 50,000 to all causes—a catastrophic price to pay for negligible results. By war's end, it is no exaggeration to state, only hundreds of Japanese aircraft could be maintained and only scores could be operated effectively by conventional measures of military serviceability.[146] By 1944–45, it was largely the weakness of the Japanese in orthodox air operations against the newest AAF bombers and fighters, as well as against USN and USMC aircraft, that spawned two deliberate decisions on the part of the Japanese: to abandon the contest for air superiority over the homeland, and to stake everything on *kamikaze* defense of the main islands against Allied invasion. Though the former decision may be arguable politically and militarily, there can be no doubt that the *kamikaze* option was fearsome. Wrote the U.S. naval historian, Samuel E. Morison:

> Although the Navy had met the *kamikaze* by radar warning, CAP, and the proximity fuze for antiaircraft shells, and although average effectiveness of the suicide planes diminished, the prospect of thousands of them being used against our invasion forces...was disquieting.[147]

From first-hand experience, Morison described "the hideous forms of death and torture" inflicted by the *kamikazes*. Suicide attacks remained 3 to 4 times more effective against surface vessels than conventional torpedo and bomb attacks.[148]

The basic problem, as many a survivor of the *kamikazes'* attacks recalled, was that mere crippling of a suicide plane was not enough. As a task unit commander, Rear Adm. W. D. Sample, recounted events at Ormoc and Mindoro, where U.S. warships and AAF fighters repeatedly hit *kamikazes* without stopping them: "For this reason, all gunners . . . should be schooled to shoot for the plane's motor. Hit the fuselage and it keeps on coming."[149] No radical solution to the menace of the *kamikazes* was ever found, however, although the U.S. Navy detached one of its best flag officers, Vice Admiral Willis A. Lee, to establish a research and experiment unit in Maine, and specifically directed him to "devise a remedy for the *kamikaze* disease."[150] The legacy of the *kamikazes* was an expendable weapon and awesome tactics that remain relevant to air warfare in today's equivalent environment of the guided missile, and to terrorist suicide bombings.

For the Japanese of 1945, however, the *kamikazes* could not and did not affect the fundamental struggle for air superiority. Simply put, the Japanese high command had not envisaged

> the ability to achieve general and continuing control of the air . . . as a requirement in their basic war strategy, as was the planned destruction of the United States Fleet. Had this basic requirement been well understood, it is difficult to conceive that they would have undertaken a war of limited objectives in the first place. Once started on a strategic plan which did not provide the means to assure continuing air control, there was no way in which they could revise their strategy to reverse the growing predominance in the air of a basically stronger opponent who came to understand this requirement and whose war was being fought accordingly.[151]

It is true that Allied aviation could not and did not *destroy* the Japanese air forces which, for all of their qualitative debilities and numerical attrition, at war's end still possessed an intact, partly masked inventory of 17,900 to 18,500 planes of all types and all conditions. Even the seasoned carrier admiral, Frederick C. Sherman, reflected a degree of disbelief when he observed that, as late as mid-1945, "despite the many devastating attacks on their bases, the Japanese somehow were able to continue sending planes on their desperate missions."[152] But the combined and mighty efforts of the U.S. Army Air Forces, of the U.S. Navy and Marine Corps, and of their allies kept the skies open over Japan and wreaked havoc on targets below. They also contributed to the elimination of the need for a frightfully expensive ground invasion.

In achieving *de facto* air superiority, through a combination of Allied power and Japanese default, the ultimate victors were able, as General Arnold asserted, to dispatch a lone aircraft carrying an atomic bomb into enemy airspace, during broad daylight and without fighter escort, on its fateful mission to Nagasaki. Japanese commanders, holding back 10,700 operational planes, half of them *kamikazes*, from a total stock of nearly 18,000 aircraft, had had another ending in mind. The impressive statistics of Japanese military and naval assets at such a late date, however, do not detract from the achievements of the Allies in having knocked out 20,000 enemy aircraft in combat, but they shed decisive light on the indispensability of having finally projected air power deep into the innards of Japan's last perimeter of strategic defense.

Notes

1. John Morton Blum, *From the Morgenthau Diaries,* Vol 2: *Years of Urgency, 1938–1941* (Boston, 1965), pp 366–67. Morgenthau and Hull met on Dec 10, 1940. The China Lobby advocates followed a route in Washington that proceeded from Chennault and Joseph Alsop through Soong to Morgenthau to Hull. See Michael Schaller, *The U.S. Crusade in China, 1938–1945* (New York, 1979), p 73.

2. Wesley Frank Craven and James Lea Cate, eds, *The Army Air Forces in World War II,* Vol 1: *Plans and Early Operations, January 1939 to August 1942* (Chicago, 1948; reprint, Office of Air Force History, 1983), pp 174–92.

3. David Kahn, "The United States Views Germany and Japan in 1941," in Ernest R. May, ed, *Knowing One's Enemies: Intelligence Assessment Before the Two World Wars* (Princeton, 1984), p 476.

4. "That's Navy thinking," added Mitchell. Emile Gauvreau, *The Wild Blue Yonder: Sons of the Prophet Carry On* (New York, 1944), p 171, citing Gauvreau's notes of a conversation.

5. *Ibid.,* p 221.

6. Issue of Sept 1941, cited by Clive Howard and Joe Whitley, *One Damned Island After Another* (Chapel Hill, NC, 1946), pp 22–23.

7. Fletcher Pratt, *Sea Power and Today's War* (New York, 1939), pp 178–79, cited by Kahn, "The United States Views," pp 476–77.

8. *Ibid.,* p 477.

9. Nobutaka Ike, trans and ed, *Japan's Decision for War: Records of the 1941 Policy Conferences* (Stanford, 1967), p 225 (Nov 5, 1941).

10. *Ibid.,* pp 275, 281 (Dec 1, 1941).

11. Tojo's statement of Nov 4, 1941, *Homeland Air Defense Operations Record,* Japanese Monograph No. 157 (JM 157), HQ USAFFE/Eighth U.S. Army (Rear) (Tokyo, 1952), pp 2–3; Sugiyama's statement of Nov 5, Ike, *Japan's Decision,* p 227.

12. *Homeland Operations Record,* Japanese Monograph No. 17 (JM 17), HQ USAFFE/Eighth U.S. Army (Rear) (n.d.), pp 2, 6–7.

13. *Ibid.,* pp 2–5.

14. JM 157, p 2; JM 17, pp 4, 6–8.

15. United States Strategic Bombing Survey (USSBS), *Air Forces Allied with the United States in the War Against Japan* (Washington, 1947), p 3; USSBS, *Japanese Air Power* (Washington, 1946), pp 1, 4–9; USSBS, *The Campaigns of the Pacific War* (Washington, 1946), pp 49–51.

16. Lt Col Carroll V. Glines, Jr., USAF, *The Compact History of the United States Air Force* (New York, 1963), p 165.

17. Winston S. Churchill, *The Second World War,* Vol 3: *The Grand Alliance* (New York, 1950), pp 518, 522.

18. Roger Dingman, "American Policy and Strategy in East Asia, 1898–1950: The Creation of a Commitment," in *The American Military and the Far East, Proceedings of the Ninth Military History Symposium, U.S. Air Force Academy, October 1980,* Joe C. Dixon, ed (Washington, 1981), p 33.

19. Gen of the Air Force H. H. Arnold, *Global Mission* (New York, 1949), p 276. The

strategic alternatives are discussed by Alaskan Delegate Anthony J. Dimond in Gauvreau, *Yonder*, pp 207–9.

20. Lt Col Carroll V. Glines, USAF, *Doolittle's Tokyo Raiders* (Princeton, 1964), pp 5–7, 13; Arnold, *Global Mission*, p 298.

21. Arnold, *Global Mission*, pp 276–77.

22. For the genesis of the Doolittle operation and details of the White House conference of Jan 18, 1942, see Glines, *Raiders*, pp 14–19, 24–31. Also see Arnold, *Global Mission*, p 298.

23. Grace Person Hayes, *The History of the Joint Chiefs of Staff in World War II: The War Against Japan* (Annapolis, Md, 1982), pp 40–42. For earlier planning, see *ibid.*, chaps 1–2; James C. Gaston, *Planning the Air War: Four Men and Nine Days in 1941: An Inside Narrative* (Washington, 1982), *passim*.

24. Maj Gen Haywood S. Hansell, *Strategic Air War Against Japan* (Maxwell AFB, Ala., 1980), pp 10–14; Hayes, *JCS*, p 42.

25. Hayes, *JCS*, pp 51–52; Hansell, *Strategic Air War*, p 12.

26. Samuel Eliot Morison, *History of United States Naval Operations in World War II*, Vol 3: *The Rising Sun in the Pacific, 1931–April 1942* (Boston, 1948), pp 257, 260–65, 268, 387–89; present author's interviews with IJN and JMSDF officers, Tokyo, 1983–84, 1985; and BBKS, *Kaigun kōkū gaishi* (Tokyo, 1976), vol 95, pp 237–38. Also see John B. Lundstrom, *The First Team* (Annapolis, Md, 1984), *passim*.

27. JM 17, p 7.

28. Tanaka Ryūkichi, *Taiheiyō sensō no haiin o tsuku* (Tokyo, 1984), pp 72–73.

29. *Ibid.*, pp 73–74.

30. Arnold, *Global Mission*, pp 298–300; Vern Haugland, *The AAF Against Japan* (New York, 1948), p 78; Craven and Cate, *AAF in WW II*, Vol 1: *Plans and Early Operations*, pp 440–44; Cdr Walter Karig and Lt Welbourn Kelley, *Battle Report: Pearl Harbor to Coral Sea* (New York, 1944), pp 297–98; Glines, *Doolittle's*, chap 6; Morison, Vol III: *Rising Sun in the Pacific*, pp 387–98. Also see BBKS, *Kaigun*, vol 95, pp 241–42; Watanabe Yōji, *Nihon hondo bōkūsen* (Tokyo, 1982), pp 38–49; BBKS, *Hondo bōkū sakusen* (Tokyo, 1968), vol 19, pp 121–24.

31. Tanaka, *Taiheiyō*, pp 74–76; Watanabe, *Nihon*, p 49.

32. Watanabe, *Nihon*, p 49.

33. JM 157, p 33.

34. Watanabe, *Nihon*, p 50; JM 157, pp 6–9, 33–34.

35. Hansell, *Strategic Air War*, p 15.

36. USSBS, *The Seventh and Eleventh Air Forces in the War Against Japan* (Washington, 1947), p 16; Robert Frank Futrell, *Ideas, Concepts, Doctrine* (Maxwell AFB, Ala., 1974), p 81. The wartime commanders of VII Bomber Command were Maj Gen Hale, Feb 1942; Col Albert F. Hegenberger, June 20, 1942; Brig Gen William E. Lynd, June 25, 1942; Brig Gen Truman H. Landon, Jan 20, 1943; and Brig Gen Lawrence J. Carr, Dec 11, 1944. The heads of VII Fighter Command were Brig Gen Davidson, Feb 1942; Brig Gen Robert W. Douglass, Jr., Oct 1942; and Brig Gen Ernest Moore, May 1944. Maurer Maurer, ed, *Air Force Combat Units of World War II* (Washington, 1961), pp 444–45, 462–63; Howard and Whitley, *Damned Island*, pp 40–41.

37. USSBS, *Seventh AF*, pp 16, 22.

38. USSBS, *Seventh AF*, pp 4–6, 17–18, 22; Glines, *Compact History*, pp 189–92; BBKS, *Kaigun*, vol 95, pp 323–24.

39. USSBS, *Seventh AF*, pp 6–8, 17, 22; BBKS, *Kaigun*, vol 95, pp 325–26; BBKS, *Okinawa Taiwan Iwō Jima hōmen rikugun kōkū sakusen* (Tokyo, 1970), vol 36, pp 27–28.

40. USSBS, *Seventh AF*, pp 8–9, 11–12, 22; BBKS, *Kaigun*, vol 95, pp 403–04; BBKS, *Okinawa*, vol 36, pp 56, 280–86.

41. Fleet Adm Ernest J. King, *U.S. Navy at War, 1941–1945: Official Reports to the Secretary of the Navy* (Washington, 1946), p 104.

42. Vice Admiral E. P. Forrestel, *Admiral Raymond A. Spruance, USN: A Study in Command* (Washington, 1966), p 171; King, *Reports*, p 130.

43. Samuel Eliot Morison, *History of United States Naval Operations in World War II*, Vol XIV: *Victory in the Pacific* (Boston, 1960), pp 20–25; King, *Reports*, pp 130–32; Thomas B. Buell, *The Quiet Warrior: A Biography of Admiral Raymond A. Spruance* (Boston, 1974),

pp 327–31; Forrestel, *Spruance*, pp 171, 173; Admiral Fred C. Sherman, *Combat Command: The American Aircraft Carriers in the Pacific War* (New York, 1950), pp 336–37; Col Raymond F. Toliver and Trevor Constable, *Fighter Aces* (New York, 1965), pp 164–65; Robert Sherrod, *History of Marine Corps in World War II* (Washington, 1952), pp 344–46; Clark G. Reynolds, *The Fast Carriers: The Forging of an Air Navy* (New York, 1968), pp 332–34.

44. BBKS, *Hondo*, vol 19, pp 476–78.

45. *Ibid.*, pp 478, 480–81.

46. Dai-ichi Fukuinkyoku, *Hondō bōku sakusen kiroku: Kantō chiku* (Tokyo, 1950), pp 665–67; Kimata Jiro, *Rikugun kōkū senshi: Marē sakusen kara Okinawa tokkō made* (Tokyo, 1982), pp. 245–46; BBKS, *Hondo*, vol 19, p 480.

47. Sherman, *Combat*, pp 341–42.

48. Morison, Vol XIV: *Victory in the Pacific*, pp 57–59; Sherman, *Combat*, p 342; King, *Reports*, p 132; Forrestel, *Spruance*, p 183; Buell, *Warrior*, p 38; Sherrod, *MC*, pp 357–58; BBKS, *Hondo*, vol 19, p 484; Dai-ichi Fukuinkyoku, *Hondo*, pp 667–68.

49. Arnold, *Global Mission*, pp 290, 371; USSBS, *Japanese Air Power*, pp 1–2. The Joint Intelligence Committee had considered targeting Japan from the Aleutians, Chengtu, Calcutta, Broome, Darwin, and Port Moresby, as well as the Marianas. JIC, "Optimum Use, Timing, and Deployment of V.L.R. Bombers in the War Against Japan," Jan 18, 1944 (Office of Air Force History).

50. Futrell, *Ideas*, pp 77, 79, 84; USSBS, *The Strategic Air Operation of Very Heavy Bombardment in the War Against Japan (Twentieth Air Force): Final Report* (Washington, 1946), pp 19–20.

51. Gen Curtis E. LeMay, *Mission with LeMay: My Story,* with MacKinlay Kantor (Garden City, NY, 1965), pp 325, 329–31, 342–43, 345–47, 350; Futrell, *Ideas*, p 84; USSBS, *Strategic Air*, pp 11, 26–28. Also see Kimata, *Rikugun*, pp 243–45; Shimoshizu Kōsha Gakkō Shūshinkai, *Kōsha senshi* (Tokyo, 1978), chap 8, sec 1, and chap 11, sec 1; BBKS, *Manshū hōmen rikugun kōkū sakusen* (Tokyo, 1972), vol 53, pp 543–48.

52. Arnold, *Global Mission* p 291.

53. Craven and Cate, *AAF in World War II*, Vol V: *The Pacific: Matterhorn to Nagasaki, June 1944 to August 1945*, pp 521–36; Maurer, *AF*, pp 444–45, 453, 470–71; USSBS, *Seventh AF*, pp 16, 23.

54. Craven and Cate, *AAF in WW II*, Vol V: *Matterhorn to Nagasaki*, p 539.

55. Roger A. Freeman, *Mustang at War* (Garden City, NY, 1974), pp 145, 148; Craven and Cate, *AAF in WW II*, Vol V: *Matterhorn to Nagasaki*, 593–94.

56. BBKS, *Rikugun kōkū no gunbi to unyō (3): Daitōa sensō shūsen made* (Tokyo, 1976), vol 94, pp 35–36; BBKS, *Kaigun*, vol 95, p 46; JM 17, pp 12–13, 16.

57. *Air Defense of Japan*, Japanese Monograph No. 23 (JM 23), HQ USAFFE/Eighth US Army (Rear) (Tokyo, 1956), pp 11–16, JM 17, pp 12, 16–21, 40–53; JM 157, pp 6, 9–11, 28, 159–60, 162; Watanabe, *Nihon*, p 235.

58. JM 157, pp 11, 60–61, 132–33; JM 17, pp 88, 115–17, 206; Watanabe, *Nihon*, pp 110, 154, 251, 253; BBKS, *Hondo*, vol 19, pp 547–48, 615, 621–24. Also see Alvin D. Coox, "The Rise and Fall of the Imperial Japanese Air Forces," *Aerospace Historian*, June 1980, 27, p 83; and Alvin D. Coox, "The B–29 Bombing Campaign Against Japan: The Japanese Dimension," Research Memorandum (May 1982), pp 7–10, 26–28, adapted by Keith Wheeler, *et al.*, *Bombers Over Japan* (Alexandria, Va., 1982), pp 135–36.

59. USSBS, *Strategic Air*, pp 20–21.

60. Author's interviews with Ikuta, Toga, M. Hattori; Watanabe, *Nihon*, pp 155–57, 248–51; JM 157, pp 11–12, 40–42, 63, 65, 109–12; JM 17, pp 36–38; Coox, "B–29 Bombing," pp 20–22; Coox, "Rise and Fall," p 82; USSBS, *Japanese Air Power*, pp 2–3, 47–48.

61. Author's interviews with Toga, Ikuta; JM 157, pp 61, 63–68, 75–78.

62. Author's interviews with Imaoka, Ikuta, Kono; Watanabe, *Nihon*, pp 204–5, 259, 268; USSBS, *Japanese Air Power*, pp 2, 26; Coox, "Rise and Fall," p 84, citing Minoru Genda.

63. USSBS, *Strategic Air*, pp 12–15; Craven and Cate, *AAF in WW II*, Vol V: *Matterhorn to Nagasaki*, pp 614–15; JM 157, pp 72–74; Wheeler, *Bombers*, pp 168–69; JM 17, p 40.

64. Craven and Cate, *AAF in WW II*, Vol V: *Matterhorn to Nagasaki*, pp 615–17.

65. JM 157, p 74.

66. *Ibid.*

67. USSBS, *Japanese Air Power*, pp 26, 47–48, 55. Also see JM 157, pp 10–11, 81, 124, 128; Watanabe, *Nihon*, p 110.
68. USSBS, *Japanese Air Power*, pp 48–49; USSBS, *Strategic Air*, pp 19–20, 27.
69. USSBS, *Japanese Air Power*, pp 27, 48.
70. USSBS, *Japanese Air Power*, pp 48, 55; USSBS, *Strategic Air*, pp 19–20.
71. USSBS, *Japanese Air Power*, p 51.
72. USSBS, *Strategic Air*, p 21.
73. USSBS, *Japanese Air Power*, pp 30, 32–34, 74; USSBS, *Summary Report (Pacific War)* (Washington, 1946), p 9; Coox, "Rise and Fall," p 81.
74. BBKS, *Rikugun*, vol 94, pp 225, 277; Coox, "Rise and Fall," p 83.
75. Author's interviews with Kono, Ikuta; Watanabe, *Nihon*, pp 236–37; USSBS, *Japanese Air Power*, p 2.
76. USSBS, *Japanese Air Power*, pp 60, 73.
77. Author's interviews with Kono, Ikuta; JM 157, pp 14–16; USSBS, *Summary*, pp 9–10; USSBS, *Japanese Air Power*, p 71; Coox, "Rise and Fall," p 82; Watanabe, *Nihon*, pp 236–37.
78. JM 157, p 39; USSBS, *Japanese Air Power*, pp 60–65, 76; Coox, "Rise and Fall," p 82.
79. "G–2 Estimate of the Enemy Situation with Respect to an Operation Against Southern Kyushu in November 1945," GHQ, U.S. Army Forces in the Pacific, MIS/GS, Apr 25, 1945, p 5 (NARS).
80. USSBS, *Japanese Air Power*, pp 65–69, 75–76; Coox, "Rise and Fall," p 82; Watanabe, *Nihon*, pp 236–39.
81. USSBS, Summary, p 10; USSBS, *Japanese Air Power*, pp 74–79; Coox, "Rise and Fall," p 82; Dennis and Peggy Warner, with Sadao Seno, *The Sacred Warriors: Japan's Suicide Legions* (New York, 1982), pp 234, 323ff.; LeMay, *Mission*, pp 370–72. For the USN dimension, see HQ CINC, US Fleet, *Antiaircraft Action Summary, World War II* (Navy Department, Oct 1945); and Air Intelligence Group, DNI/CNO, "Defense Against Japanese Aerial Suicide Attacks on U.S. Naval Vessels, Oct–Dec 1944," 1st Suppl, Jan 1945. Also see Inoguchi Rikihei and Nakajima Tadashi, *Kamikaze tokubetsu kōgekitai no kiroku* (Tokyo, 1963), pp 40–174; BBKS, *Okinawa*, vol 36, pp 305–25; Okumiya Masatake, *Kaigun tokubetsu kōgekitai: tokkō to Nihonjin* (Tokyo, 1980), pp 1–122; *Shōwa shi no tennō* (Tokyo, 1970), vol 12, pp 4–32; BBKS, *Kaigun*, vol 95, pp 422, 445–48; Ikuta Makoto, *Rikugun tokubetsu kōkūtai shi* (Tokyo, 1983), *passim*.
82. BBKS, *Hondo*, vol 19, pp 537–39; Kimata, *Rikugun*, pp 273–74.
83. Morison, *Victory*, vol 14, pp 94–101; Sherman, *Combat*, pp 353–55; Forrestel, *Spruance*, pp 189–97; Buell, *Spruance*, pp 344–47; Toliver and Constable, *Aces*, p 170; Sherrod, *MC*, pp 359–63; Reynolds, *Carriers*, pp 337–39. Also see BBKS, *Hondo*, vol 19, pp 537, 539; Kimata, *Rikugun*, pp 273–74.
84. Sherman, *Combat*, pp 355–56, 360–61; Morison, Vol XIV: *Victory in the Pacific*, pp 112–13; Kyushu Kaigun Kokūtai, *Senkun sokuhō*, May 13–14, 1945 (BBKS Archives).
85. Howard and Whitley, *Damned Island*, pp 350, 355.
86. USSBS, Summary, p 10; Forrestel, *Spruance*, p 204.
87. LeMay, *Mission*, pp 370–72, 374; USSBS, *Strategic Air*, p 6; USSBS, *Summary*, p 10; Craven and Cate, *AAF in WW II*, Vol V: *Matterhorn to Nagasaki*, pp 627–35.
88. USSBS, *Seventh AF*, pp 12–13; Craven and Cate, *AAF in WW II*, Vol V: *Matterhorn to Nagasaki*, pp 634–35; Howard and Whitley, *Damned Island*, pp 372–80. Also see Kimata, *Rikugun*, p 303.
89. USSBS, *Seventh AF*, p 23; Freeman, *Mustang*, p 148; Craven and Cate, *AAF in WW II*, Vol V: *Matterhorn to Nagasaki*, pp 647–48.
90. Watanabe, *Nihon*, p 231; BBKS, *Hondo*, vol 19, p 542.
91. Watanabe, *Nihon*, pp 231–32.
92. BBKS, *Hondo*, vol 19, p 542.
93. *Ibid.*, pp 542–44.
94. Watanabe, *Nihon*, pp 232–33; Dai-ichi Fukuinkyoku, *Hondo*, p 672.
95. Howard and Whitley, *Damned Island*, pp 341–47; Freeman, *Mustang*, pp 148–49; USSBS, *Strategic Air*, p 20.
96. Freeman, *Mustang*, p 149. Writes Kevin Herbert: "Upon return to base after over six hours in the cramped confines of the fighter, some of the men had to be lifted out of the

plane, so stiff and exhausted were they from their immobility for that length of time." *Maximum Effort: The B–29's Against Japan* (Manhattan, Kans., 1983), p 54. Also Watanabe, *Nihon,* pp 244–45; and author's interviews with Kono and Ikuta.

97. Watanabe, *Nihon,* p 234; BBKS, *Hondo,* vol 19, p 544; Craven and Cate, *AAF in WW II,* Vol V: *Matterhorn to Nagasaki,* p 648–49, Fukuinkyoku, *Hondo,* p 672.

98. See Barrett Tillman, *Hellcat: The F6F in World War II* (Annapolis, Md, 1979), pp xi, 228–29. Also see Watanabe, *Nihon,* p 233.

99. Watanabe, *Nihon,* pp 233–34, 239–40, 242–43; BBKS, *Hondo,* vol 19, pp 545–46; Kimata, *Rikugun,* pp 256–57; author's interviews with Toga, Ikuta, and Kono.

100. Author's interviews with Nomura, Ikuta, and Kono; Watanabe, *Nihon,* p 234; Kimata, *Rikugun,* p 245.

101. Craven and Cate, *AAF in WW II,* Vol V: *Matterhorn to Nagasaki,* p 649; USSBS, *Strategic Air,* pp 20, 23. The B–29 crews appreciated their P–51 "little brothers." One bomber commander praised the Mustangs' performance on the first escort mission of April 7, 1945: "Thirty Mustangs swept the area ahead of us, and only two Jap fighters got in to us. Both of them went down smoking." Wheeler *et al., Bombers,* p 174. The "P–Five–Ones" are touchingly lauded by a grateful B–29 crewman, Kevin Herbert, in *Maximum Effort,* pp 53–54.

102. USSBS, *Strategic Air,* pp 20, 23; Craven and Cate, *AAF in WW II,* Vol V: *Matterhorn to Nagasaki,* pp xix, 651, 652.

103. USSBS, *Strategic Air,* pp 20, 23; USSBS, *Seventh AF,* p 23; Craven and Cate, *AAF in WW II,* Vol V: *Matterhorn to Nagasaki,* pp 635, 696; USSBS, *Evaluation of Photographic Intelligence in the Japanese Homeland,* Part 9, *Coast and Anti-Aircraft Artillery* (Washington, 1946), pp 1–4. Also see Morison, *Victory,* vol 14, p 311.

104. Arnold, *Global Mission,* p 371; Futrell, *Ideas,* p 85.

105. BBKS, *Hondo,* pp 554, 584; Coox, "B–29 Bombing," pp. 21–22; Watanabe, *Nihon,* p 157.

106. BBKS, *Hondo,* pp 576, 584–87; JM 157, pp 77–78; JM 23, pp 25–26.

107. Watanabe, *Nihon,* p 253; JM 157, p 81; JM 23, pp 25–27; JM 17, pp 245–46.

108. BBKS, *Hondo,* pp 609–10.

109. R. J. Francillon, *Japanese Aircraft of the Pacific War* (New York, 1970), pp 130–31.

110. Watanabe, *Nihon,* pp 260–61.

111. Tillman, *Hellcat,* p 224; Morison, *Victory,* vol 14, pp 330–31.

112. Watanabe, *Nihon,* pp 261–62.

113. USSBS, *Seventh AF,* pp 13–14, 16, 23; Craven and Cate, *AAF in WW II,* Vol V: *Matterhorn to Nagasaki,* pp 692–95, 701.

114. USSBS, *Seventh AF,* p 13; USSBS, *Strategic Air,* p 20; Craven and Cate, *AAF in WW II,* Vol V: *Matterhorn to Nagasaki,* pp 655–56, 696–99; Coox, "Rise and Fall," p 83.

115. Craven and Cate, *AAF in WW II,* Vol V: *Matterhorn to Nagasaki,* p 699.

116. JM 157, p 82; and author's interview with Toga.

117. Morison, Vol 14: *Victory in the Pacific,* pp 310–16, 330–35; King, *Reports,* pp 188–90; Sherman, *Combat,* pp 366–68, 372–74.

118. Morison, Vol 14: *Victory in the Pacific,* pp 102–7, 211–14, 249–50, 264–65, 314–16, 388; Tillman, *Hellcat,* pp 222–23; Reynolds, *Carriers,* pp 310–17, 339–40, 344–46, 366, 369–70, 372–75; King, *Reports,* pp 176, 183, 188–89; Sherman, *Combat,* pp 346, 369.

119. JM 157, pp 81–82, 125–27, 164–65; JM 23, pp 69–72; and author's interview with Toga.

120. USSBS, *Summary,* pp 16–17, 29; USSBS, *Strategic Air,* pp 1, 13–15, 30–31; Craven and Cate, *AAF in WW II,* Vol V: *Matterhorn to Nagasaki,* pp 643, 674–75, 703, 748–49, 754; Hansell, *Strategic Air War,* pp 68–69, 90–91; Hayes, *JCS,* pp 701–10; LeMay, *Mission,* p 381.

121. "DOWNFALL: Strategic Plan for Operations in the Japanese Archipelago," GHQ, U.S. Army Forces in the Pacific, May 28, 1945, NARS.

122. *Ibid.,* pp 2, 9; and Annex 3d (1) (c). Also "Brief of Staff Study OLYMPIC," Strategy Section, Strategy and Plans Group, Operations Division, War Department General Staff, Jun 23, 1945, pp 1–2, NARS.

123. "Staff Study OLYMPIC: Operations in Southern Kyushu," GHQ, U.S. Army Forces in the Pacific, May 28, 1945, pp 3–7, NARS.

124. *Ibid.,* p 4. Also see "G–2 Estimate," Apr 25, 1945, pp 1, 3–7, 13–14.

125. "G–2 Estimate," pp 28–29, 32.

126. *Ibid.*, pp 5, 7–8.

127. General Masakazu Kawabe in USSBS, *Japanese Air Power,* pp 69–70. Also see "G–2 Estimate," Encl. 10.

128. Lt Gen Michio Sugawara in USSBS, *Japanese Air Power,* p 71.

129. "G–2 Estimate," p 5. Also see "Staff Study CORONET: Operations in the Kanto Plain of Honshu," GHQ, U.S. Army Forces, Pacific, Aug 15, 1945, Annex 2a, pp 24–27, NARS; and USSBS, *Japanese Air Power,* p 68.

130. Lt Gen Noboru Tazoe and Col Minoru Miyashi in USSBS, *Japanese Air Power,* p 69.

131. *Ibid.;* author's interviews with Kono and Ikuta; BBKS, *Hondo,* vol 19, p 582; BBKS, *Kaigun,* vol 95, p 444. Also see USSBS, *Japanese Air Weapons and Tactics* (Washington, 1947), p 30.

132. USSBS, *Japanese Air Power,* pp 24, 36, 70–72, 74, 80; USSBS, *Summary,* pp 9–10, 26; Hoyt, *Kamikazes,* p 291; Warner and Warner, *Warriors,* pp 292–94. Also see Saburo Hayashi in collaboration with Alvin D. Coox, *Kogun: The Japanese Army in the Pacific War* (Quantico, Va., 1959), pp 160–61; Kamata, *Rikugun,* pp 317–22; JM 17, p 139; Watanabe, *Nihon,* p 267; BBKS, *Kaigun,* vol 95, p 422.

133. USSBS, *Japanese Air Power,* pp 23–25, 34–45, 68–69; USSBS, *Summary,* p 9; Coox, "Rise and Fall," p 84. Also see JM 157, pp 40–46, 90–91; BBKS, *Hondo,* vol 19, pp 576–77, 582; BBKS, *Rikugun,* vol 94, p 400; Watanabe, *Nihon,* p 247.

134. USSBS, *Japanese Air Power,* pp 3, 30–31, 33–34, 36; USSBS, *Summary,* pp 9–10, 18; Coox, "Rise and Fall," pp 84–85; Kimata, *Rikugun,* pp 296–302; Watanabe, *Nihon,* pp 247–48.

135. Craven and Cate, *AAF in WW II,* Vol V: *Matterhorn to the Pacific,* pp xxv–xxvi, 747–48.

136. USSBS, *Seventh AF,* p 13. Also see USSBS, *The War Against Japanese Transportation, 1941–1945* (Washington, 1947), p 120.

137. USSBS, *Japanese Air Power,* p 1; Craven and Cate, *AAF in the Pacific,* Vol V: *Matterhorn to Nagasaki,* pp 746–47; King, *Reports,* pp 103, 167, 232; USSBS, *Seventh AF,* pp 18–19.

138. See USSBS, *Air Force Allied, passim.*

139. USSBS, *Seventh AF,* pp 13–15; Craven and Cate, *AAF in WW II,* Vol V: *Matterhorn to Nagasaki,* p 743. Also see USSBS, *Japanese Transportation,* pp 95–96, 98, 119–30.

140. USSBS, *Seventh AF,* p 19.

141. *Ibid.*

142. USSBS, *Strategic Air,* p 32.

143. *Ibid.,* pp 11, 19.

144. USSBS, *Japanese Air Power,* pp 1–3, 26–27; Coox, "Rise and Fall," pp 83–84; author's interviews with Imaoka, Ohmae, M. Hattori, Toga, Kono, Ikuta.

145. USSBS, *Japanese Air Power,* pp 2–3, 26, 50; Coox, "Rise and Fall," p 84. Also Watanabe, *Nihon,* pp 128, 268; and author's interviews with Kono, Ikuta, Imaoka, Ohmae.

146. USSBS, *Japanese Air Power,* pp 28–34, 36; USSBS, *Summary,* p 9.

147. Morison, Vol V: *Victory in the Pacific,* pp 280–82.

148. CINC/USF, *Antiaircraft,* p 11.

149. DNI/CNO, "Defense," Task Unit 77.12.7 (Dec 7–17, 1944), pp 38–39.

150. Morison, Vol V: *Victory in the Pacific,* pp 280–81; Hoyt, *Kamikazes,* pp 283–302.

151. USSBS, *Summary,* p 10.

152. Sherman, *Combat,* p 361. Also see USSBS, *Summary,* pp 27–28; USSBS, *Japanese Air Power,* p 27.

Bibliographical Essay

The student of the air war against Japan finds that the subject has drawn the attention of relatively few historians, and that, where it has, the attention is ancillary to other themes. One feature pervades the literature: the Allied quest for air superiority is generally subsumed in accounts of the strategic bombardment campaign, instead of the other way around. Several reasons account for this phenomenon: Japanese homeland targets possessed a special vulnerability to aerial bombing; air and ground defenses encountered in Japan were relatively weak; and Allied ground strategy in World War II accorded priority to the European theater of operations. There was another uniqueness to the war against Japan: the spatial and geographical dimensions of the Pacific meant that carrier-based naval and Marine aviation played a major share in offensive operations, especially in the phases before land-based VLR bombers and long-reach fighters could get within effective range of Japan via the central Pacific Ocean.

The starting point for serious study of the struggle to achieve air superiority against Japan remains the durable series edited by Wesley Frank Craven and James Lea Cate in the seven–volume official history, *The Army Air Forces in World War II* (Chicago: University of Chicago Press, 1948–58; reprint: Office of Air Force History, 1983). Of particular relevance are Volume I, *Plans and Early Operations, January 1939 to August 1942* (1948); Volume IV, *The Pacific: Guadalcanal to Saipan, August 1942 to July 1944* (1950); and Volume V, *The Pacific: Matterhorn to Nagasaki, June 1944 to August 1945* (1953). Robert Frank Futrell examines doctrinal underpinnings in *Ideas, Concepts, Doctrine: A History of Basic Thinking in the United States Air Force, 1907–1964* (Maxwell AFB, Ala.: Air University, 1974).

Strategic planning is authoritatively detailed in Grace Person Hayes' recently declassified *The History of the Joint Chiefs of Staff in World War II: The War Against Japan* (Annapolis, Md: Naval Institute Press, 1982). Maj. Gen. Haywood S. Hansell provides an insider's memoirs in *Strategic Air War Against Japan* (Maxwell AFB, Ala.: Air University, 1980), and in *Offensive Air Operations Against Japan* (Air University, Jan 27, 1953). Promising more than it delivers is James C. Gaston's breezy pamphlet, *Planning the Air War: Four Men and Nine Days in 1941: An Inside Narrative* (Washington, DC: Government Printing Office, 1982).

Useful though limited sections of relevance to air superiority will be found in general histories of military aviation, such as Basil Collier, *A History of Air Power* (New York: Macmillan, 1974), and Lee Kennett, *A History of Strategic Bombing* (New York: Charles Scribner's Sons, 1982). The AAF dimension *per se* is treated briefly by Carroll V. Glines, Jr., in *The Compact History of the United States Air Force* (New York: Hawthorn Books, 1963); Alfred Goldberg, ed., in *A History of the United States Air Force, 1907–1957* (New York: Van Nostrand, 1957); and James F. Sunderman, ed., *World War II in the Air—the Pacific* (New York: Franklin Watts, 1962). *The AAF Against Japan*, by Vern Haugland (New York: Harper, 1948), is an early, still very helpful account. The U.S. Strategic Bombing Survey (USSBS) brought out many detailed monographs bearing on the Pacific theater in general and the air war in particular (Washington: Government Printing Office). Especially useful are *The Campaigns of the Pacific War* (1946); *Summary Report (Pacific War)* (1946); *Air Forces Allied with the United States in the War Against Japan* (1947); and *Strategic Air Operation of Very Heavy Bombardment in the War Against Japan (Twentieth Air Force): Final Report* (1946).

Important information on the air superiority mission is embedded in the memoirs of senior AAF officers: H. H. Arnold, *Global Mission* (New York: Harper, 1949); and Curtis E. LeMay, *Mission with LeMay: My Story*, with MacKinlay Kantor (Garden City, NY: Doubleday, 1965). Supplementing the published reminiscences are Office of Air Force History transcripts of interviews with Generals Curtis LeMay, Carl A. Spaatz, and James H. Doolittle. The Army's view from the top is briefly detailed in *Biennial Report of General George C. Marshall, the Chief of Staff of the United States Army, July 1, 1943 to June 30, 1945 to the Secretary of War*

(Washington, DC, 1946). Declassified American strategic plans for the invasion of Japan reveal data as of 1945 concerning Allied air strength, actual and projected, and evaluations of Japanese air capabilities. Thus, GHQ U.S. Army Forces in the Pacific (USAFP) produced "G–2 Estimate of the Enemy Situation with Respect to an Operation Against Southern Kyushu in November 1945" (Apr 25, 1945); "DOWNFALL: Strategic Plan for Operations in the Japanese Archipelago" (May 28, 1945); and various Staff Studies for Operations OLYMPIC and CORONET respectively, directed against Kyushu and the Kanto Plain of Honshu.

Resources pertaining to the AAF campaign to win control of the skies over Japan are disappointingly slim. In a brief monograph published in 1947, the Military Analysis Division of USSBS described *The Seventh and Eleventh Air Forces in the War Against Japan*. Clive Howard and Joe Whitley prepared an officially sanctioned but highly journalistic history of the Seventh Air Force in *One Damned Island After Another* (Chapel Hill: University of North Carolina Press, 1946). *Mustang at War* (Garden City, NY: Doubleday, 1974), by Roger A. Freeman, is short on the exploits of the P–51 fighter in the Pacific. Insightful information on the value of AAF fighter escorts appears occasionally in a bomber history such as Kevin Herbert, *Maximum Effort: The B–29's Against Japan* (Manhattan, Kans.: Sunflower University Press, 1983). Editor Maurer Maurer includes data on all AAF groups, wings, divisions, commands and air forces that fought in the Asiatic–Pacific Theater in his comprehensive compendium on lineage, *Air Force Combat Units of World War II* (Washington: Government Printing Office, 1961).

The role of the U.S. Navy in the Pacific war has received extensive coverage. Admiral Ernest J. King did not provide depth in his *U.S. Navy at War, 1941–1945: Official Reports to the Secretary of the Navy* (Washington: U.S. Navy Department, 1946); but Samuel Eliot Morison's multi-volume *History of United States Naval Operations in World War II* (Boston: Little, Brown and Co.) has become a classic. Particularly relevant to the story of USN carrier aviation are Morison's Volume 3, *The Rising Sun in the Pacific, 1931–April 1942* (1948), and Volume 14, *Victory in the Pacific* (1960). Clark G. Reynolds supplies finer detail in *The Fast Carriers: The Forging of an Air Navy* (New York: McGraw–Hill, 1968).

Autobiographies and biographies of carrier admirals abound: Frederick C. Sherman, *Combat Command: The American Aircraft Carriers in the Pacific War* (New York: E. P. Dutton, 1950); E. P. Forrestel, *Admiral Raymond A. Spruance, USN: A Study in Command* (Washington: Government Printing Office, 1966); Thomas B. Buell, *The Quiet Warrior: A Biography of Admiral Raymond A. Spruance* (Boston: Little, Brown and Co., 1974); and J. J. Clark with Clark G. Reynolds, *Carrier Admiral* (New York: McKay, 1967). E. B. Potter has written *Nimitz* (Annapolis, Md.: Naval Institute Press, 1976).

Barrett Tillman treats USN aircraft in *Hellcat: The F6F in World War II* (Annapolis, Md.: Naval Institute Press, 1979), while Raymond F. Toliver and Trevor Constable recount the deeds of the airmen in *Fighter Aces* (New York: Macmillan, 1965). USN aviation is extolled by John B. Lundstrom in *The First Team: Pacific Naval Combat from Pearl Harbor to Midway* (Annapolis, Md.: Naval Institute Press, 1984); and by Wilbur H. Morrison in *Above and Beyond* (New York: St. Martin's Press, 1983). John A. DeChant recorded the USMC air war in *Devilbirds: The Story of United States Marine Corps Aviation in World War II* (Washington: Combat Forces Press, 1952). A more recent account is Peter B. Mersky, *U.S. Marine Corps Aviation: 1912 to the Present* (Annapolis, Md.: Nautical & Aviation Publishing, 1983).

In most English–language works on the Pacific war, the Japanese foe is depicted indistinctly, if at all. Useful background will be found in such USSBS monographs as *Japanese Air Power* (1946), *Japanese Air Weapons and Tactics* (1947), *The Japanese Aircraft Industry* (1947), *The War Against Japanese Transportation, 1941–1945* (1947), *Oil in Japan's War* (1946), and *Evaluation of Photographic Intelligence in the Japanese Homeland, Part 9, Coast and Anti-Aircraft Artillery* (1946). The present author investigated "The Rise and Fall of the Imperial Japanese Air Forces" in *Aerospace Historian*, Volume 27, No. 2 (June 1980), pp. 74–86; and developed a monograph on Japanese fighter and antiaircraft actions in the Pacific War, "The B–29 Bombing Campaign Against Japan: The Japanese Dimension—A Research Memorandum Prepared Exclusively from Japanese Materials" (1982), for use by Keith Wheeler *et al.*, in *Bombers Over Japan* (Alexandria, Va.: Time–Life Books, 1982).

In the past few years, there has been new interest in the *kamikaze* pilots. An ambitious but rambling study was prepared by Dennis and Peggy Warner, with Sadao Seno, *The Sacred Warriors: Japan's Suicide Legions* (New York: Van Nostrand Reinhold, 1982). *The Kamikazes* (New York: Arbor Books, 1983), by Edwin P. Hoyt, is a journalistic account. Authentic documentation on the *kamikaze* threat can be obtained from declassified U.S. Navy sources, such as Air Intelligence Group, DNI/CNO, "Defense Against Japanese Aerial Suicide Attacks on U.S. Naval Vessels, Oct–Dec 1944" (Jan 1945); and Hq U.S. Fleet, *Antiaircraft Action Summary, World War II* (Navy Department, Oct 1945).

A few postwar recollections by surviving Japanese military and naval officers are available in English translation. Col. Saburō Hayashi wrote a succinct but carefully researched military history, *Kōgun: The Japanese Army in the Pacific War,* in collaboration with the present author (Quantico, Va.: Marine Corps Association Press, 1959). Japanese aviators' accounts will be found in Saburo Sakai, with Martin Caidin and Fred Saito, *Samurai!* (New York: E. P. Dutton, 1958); and Masatake Okumiya and Jiro Horikoshi, with Martin Caidin, *Zero!* (New York: E. P. Dutton, 1956). In the 1950s, Japanese Army and Navy consultants prepared many original monographs for use by the American military, under the aegis of the Japanese Research Division of Hq. USAFFE/Eighth U.S. Army (Rear). Particularly valuable are *Air Defense of the Homeland*, Japanese Monograph 23 (1956); *Homeland Air Defense Operations Record*, JM 157 (1952); *Homeland Operations Record*, JM 17 (n.d.); *Outline of Preparations Prior to Termination of War and Activities Connected with the Cessation of Hostilities*, JM 119 (1952); *Central Pacific Air Operations Record*, JM 50 (1953).

The most important newly available Japanese–language sources include the definitive 102-volume official military history series (*Senshi Sōsho*) written by the historians of the Japan Defense Agency (Bōeichō Bōei Kenshūsho: BBKS), as well as unsponsored works. Items in neither category have been translated from the Japanese language yet. The most pertinent official JDA volumes, published between 1968 and 1979, treat such topics as the air battles for the central Pacific, Iwo Jima, Taiwan, and Okinawa (volumes 13, 36, 62); homeland air defense measures (volumes 19, 37, 51, 57); Japanese naval aviation operations (volumes 37, 95); the air defense of Manchuria and Korea (volume 53); air base construction and operation (volume 97); and the development, production, use, and supply of aerial ordnance (volumes 87, 94). The JDA's National Institute for Defense Studies has also prepared authoritative research monographs (*Kenkyū Shiryō*), appearing between 1977 and 1983, on specific topics dealing with homeland air defense preparations. Secondary Japanese–language sources that have been of greatest application to the study of air superiority include works by Makoto Ikuta, Rikihei Inoguchi, Tadashi Nakajima, Jirō Akiyama, Kei Mitamura, Jō Toyoda, Takeo Tagata, and the Kōkuhi Hōsankai, eds.

While carrying out research in Japan in 1983–84 and 1985, the author conducted extensive personal interviews on the topic of air superiority in the Pacific war with former officers of the Imperial Army and Navy, with serving officers of the present-day Japanese Self-Defense Forces, and with Japanese historians and writers. Special acknowledgement is made of assistance rendered by Yutaka Imaoka, Masanori Hattori, Shin Itonaga, Hideyuki Tazaki, Shirō Konō, Hiroshi Toga, Ikuhiko Hata, Makoto Ikuta, Teiji Nakamura, Fumio Maruta, Katsuo Satō, and Hiroyuki Agawa. The author's earlier respondents included Ryōsuke Nomura, Toshikazu Ohmae, Sadatoshi Tomioka, Muraji Yano, Takushirō Hattori, and Saburō Hayashi. Unpublished Japanese primary documentation was also located concerning IJA and IJN air defense measures in the homeland, specifically once-classified wartime reports prepared by the Kyushu Navy Air Unit and by the 10th Air Division. A privately printed postwar military history of antiaircraft operations (*Kōsha Senshi*), dated 1978, was made available by the Shimoshizu Antiaircraft Artillery School Comrades' Society (Shimoshizu Kōsha Gakkō Shūshinkai).

Predictably, the Japanese and the Western materials teem with irreconcilable features. Still, there are sufficient points of resemblance to prove that we are studying the same struggle for air superiority, though viewed from the two sides of the hill.

9

Korea

Thomas C. Hone

Before the Korean War, "air superiority" meant to the United States Air Force (USAF) the ability to conduct air operations without "prohibitive interference" by enemy air units.[1] Gaining such control of the air was necessary to conduct effectively other operations such as air interdiction, close air support, land offensives, and amphibious landings. The assumption behind this concept of air superiority was that temporary and local superiority was sufficient to achieve the more basic goals of combat, such as the destruction of enemy forces or the conquest of territory. Air superiority was not to be won solely through aerial combat between opposing air units; it was best achieved by first destroying enemy aircraft on the ground and then occupying or bombing enemy bases, training areas, and aircraft manufacturing plants.

Yet this was not the campaign waged by the Far East Air Force (FEAF) in Korea. There, the fighter pilots of the Fifth Air Force waged a campaign of attrition warfare for over thirty months against a numerically superior enemy based in an untouchable sanctuary while FEAF bombers and U.S. Navy attack planes kept enemy airfields outside the sanctuary closed. The conditions of war in Korea did not fit basic Air Force "air superiority" doctrine, but FEAF's fighter and bomber wings (with assistance from the Navy) nevertheless won an impressive "air superiority" victory. The USAF fought the air superiority war in Korea according to doctrine developed during World War II. That doctrine, unfortunately, made no provision for the new rules of "limited war," nor was it meant for an understrength air force with global responsibilities but a peacetime budget. Nevertheless, FEAF prevailed—first against the air squadrons of

North Korea and then against the larger and more sophisticated air force of the People's Republic of China.

Background

In the summer of 1950, the Air Force was not prepared for an extended conventional air campaign in Korea. FEAF, composed of the Fifth, Thirteenth, and Twentieth Air Forces, was responsible primarily for the air defense of Japan and for strategic bombardment of Russian and Chinese targets in the event of a worldwide military conflict. FEAF began and ended its actions during the Korean War outnumbered by Soviet air forces stationed in Eastern Siberia. With the numbers and types of planes at its disposal, FEAF had no difficulty destroying the small North Korean Air Force, but, with the entry of the People's Republic of China into the war, FEAF was compelled to face the possibility that the fighting could widen— and quickly. The backdrop to the Korean War was possible Russian intervention: air strikes against U.S. installations in Japan, attacks by aircraft and submarines on U.S. Navy and allied naval units operating in the Sea of Japan and the Yellow Sea, or Russian "volunteers" flying waves of supposedly Chinese or North Korean aircraft against United Nations (U.N.) air units. To guard against possible Russian attacks, FEAF always husbanded its resources, releasing the minimum number of aircraft to combat in Korea consistent with theater requirements and United Nations command policy. FEAF really had no other choice. Until 1953, USAF Headquarters did not have the air units available to sustain its commands in both Europe and Korea should the fighting in Korea spread. By the spring of 1953, however, USAF Headquarters regarded Korea as a testing ground for new air warfare concepts and as a source of experience upon which to build a revised doctrine of air superiority.[2] On the road to that stage in its thinking, the Air Force committed the Far East Air Forces to the most frustrating weeks of fighting since the Army Air Forces had fought both the Germans and Japanese in 1942.

Korea as an Operating Theater

FEAF planning and operations were shaped by Korea's geography. North Korea borders on China and Russia—mostly the former's province of Manchuria. Manchuria was vital to the North Korean armed forces; it was both supply base and sanctuary. Manchuria was immune to both attack and blockade. North Korea could not be isolated as was Japan in World War II. Moreover, North Korea always had friendly forces at her back. On the other hand, the U.S. Navy (USN) had no equal in Japanese waters. The

Yellow Sea and the Sea of Japan were dominated by the USN, which gave United Nations forces in Korea several major advantages: tactical mobility (as at Inchon in September 1950) and a secure line of communications. Just as important, the FEAF, based in Japan, was not very far from Korea. The over-water distance from Kyushu to Korea is approximately 100 miles. Because it was so close, Japan served as the U.N.'s main rear base, with supply and repair centers for the Navy and USAF, and base camps and hospitals serving the U.N. armies. The geography of the area gave both sides potential sanctuaries and gave each side in the war special advantages and disadvantages.

Because of the limited combat radius of early jet fighters, Korean distances mattered a great deal to Air Force planners and pilots. Early models of the F–80C Shooting Star had a combat radius of only 100 nautical miles (nm). With wingtip fuel tanks (which were jettisoned when air-to-air combat threatened), the F–80C's combat radius extended beyond 225 nm. Later enlargement of the wing tanks raised the plane's radius to 350 nm, but by then it was no longer active as a fighter. The swept-wing F–86 Sabre did not do much better: the F–86F model, for example, had an initial combat radius of 250 nm. Later versions of the same model could reach 400 nm. F–86A and E models, which were the first Sabres used in Korea, had combat radii of 275 nm.[3] These ranges were not impressive, given the distances involved. From 1951 until the end of the war, for example, one of the largest Chinese MiG–15 bases was at Antung, just across the Yalu River from the major North Korean base of Sinuiju and about 120 miles northwest of Pyongyang, the North Korean capital. The U.N. airfield closest to Pyongyang was Kimpo, across the Han River from Seoul, and approximately 140 miles south of North Korea's capital. Had the battle for air superiority been fought only over Pyongyang, Chinese MiGs and USAF F–86s would have had about the same distance to travel to reach the combat zone. Unfortunately, the real battle was in "MiG Alley," which covered an area bounded by Sinuiju, Chosan, and Chongju. In the "Alley," the initiative lay with the enemy; his aircraft could time his attacks to take advantage of the limited endurance of the F–86, and MiGs—damaged or pursued by U.S. fighters—could streak for the Yalu with a good chance of landing in one piece. On the other hand, B–29s based at Kadena, in Okinawa, had no trouble reaching all of North Korea with heavy bomb loads, and there was no chance whatever that Chinese MiGs could attack B–29 bases. In short, USAF long-range strike aircraft were secure on the ground and during most of the distance to and from their targets. However, USAF fighter pilots were always restrained by the combat ranges of their aircraft.

Korea's weather was usually clear during the winter months and cloudy during much of the summer. Weather conditions were not major factors during the air superiority campaign because jet fighters commonly

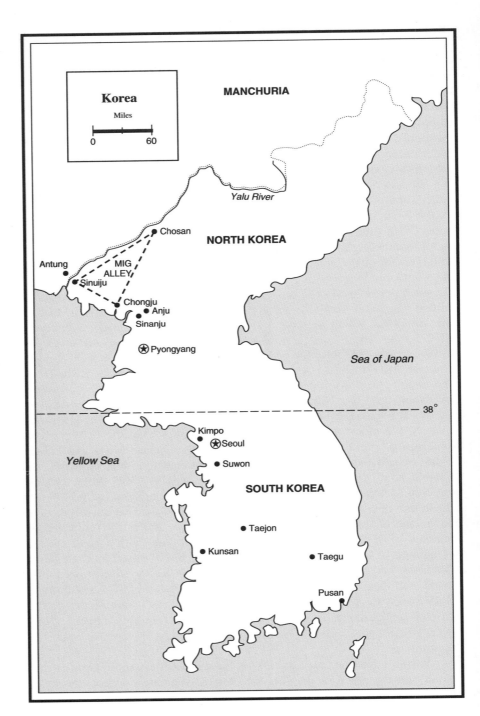

MANCHURIA

Korea

Miles

0   60

Yalu River

Antung

Chosan

NORTH KOREA

MIG
ALLEY

Sinuiju

Chongju
● Anju
Sinanju

⊛ Pyongyang

Sea of Japan

38°

Kimpo
⊛ Seoul
● Suwon

Yellow Sea

SOUTH KOREA

● Taejon

● Kunsan
● Taegu

Pusan

456

patrolled and fought above the clouds, at altitudes from 25,000 to 35,000 feet, and the B–29s could bomb without seeing their targets if necessary. More important than climate was physical setting. There were few major airfields in South Korea, and the Air Force discovered in 1950 that its civil engineering units were so understrength and so poorly equipped that it could not quickly expand South Korean fields and construct aircraft shelters and build needed maintenance hangars and housing for personnel. In the summer of 1951, for example, a year after the beginning of the war, the two squadrons of F–86 interceptors of the 51st Fighter Interceptor Wing (part of the Fifth Air Force) were based at Suwon. The runway at Suwon was only 5,000 feet long and 200 feet wide, with no taxiways or protective revetments. The aircraft parking area was small, and planes were lined up wing tip to wing tip before and after major missions. There was no arresting barrier to keep aircraft with brake problems from running off the end of the field and collapsing their landing gear. There were no large maintenance facilities; mechanics serviced planes in the parking area. There was no way for planes returning from a mission to move quickly from the runway to the confined parking area, so that jet aircraft tended to bunch up along the runway as more landed, creating the potential for a major accident were the last aircraft to touch down, blow a tire, and veer across the runway out of control.[4] The situation was a wing commander's nightmare. Yet there was nothing to be done except to shoulder the risks and upgrade the field. Suwon was 270 miles south of Sinuiju, or about as far south as the F–86s dared base. The runway at Kunsan was longer, but it was also a good 100 miles farther south, beyond the effective range of the F–86. The 51st had no choice but to improve Suwon.

Finally, Air Force personnel did not find the living easy in Korea, particularly during the first six months of the war. An official study of air operations within Korea from June through December 1950 revealed the following: 1) housing was often ramshackle; 2) USAF personnel lacked sufficient training in field hygiene, with the result that skin infections and diarrhea were "common"; 3) potable water was scarce; 4) laundry equipment was scarce, and 5) spoiled or contaminated food was far too common. Finally, cholera, typhus, typhoid fever, and malaria were widespread among Korean civilians as war action wrecked safe water supplies and created a refugee population.[5] In time, housing and sanitation problems were solved, but it took months or years to bring Korean base facilities up to the standards suited to the types and number of aircraft which were based there. As a result, it was difficult to keep adequate numbers of aircraft (both jets and piston-engined planes) operational, especially during the fall and winter of 1950–51.

Above: **A Lockheed F–80 Shooting Star fighter-bomber, using JATO take-off assistance rockets;** *below*: **When it first appeared, the MiG–15 posed a serious threat to U.N. air superiority.**

The elegant North American F–86 Sabre handily mastered the MiG–15 in fierce fighting over the Yalu.

Phase I of the Air War: June 25–November 25, 1950

When North Korean forces invaded South Korea on June 25, 1950, the FEAF did not have official permission to shoot down North Korean aircraft that attacked South Korean airfields. On June 27, FEAF was ordered to gain control of South Korean airspace in order to protect the evacuation of U.S. nationals from that country.[6] On June 29, during an inspection trip to Suwon airfield, Gen. Douglas MacArthur, commanding first U.S. and then U.N. forces in Korea, granted the request of Lt. Gen. George E. Stratemeyer, FEAF Commander, for permission to strike North Korean air bases.[7] With that, the first phase of the air superiority campaign was on. It would end approximately two months later with the destruction of the North Korean Air Force.

The strength of the North Korean Air Force when the war began was as follows: 62 Il–10 ground attack aircraft, 70 Yak–3 and Yak–7B fighters, and 22 Yak–16 transports.[8] Its opponents were the units of the Fifth Air Force, assigned the duty of defending Japan, and aircraft from 1 British and 1 USN aircraft carrier. The organization of the Far East Air Forces is portrayed in Table 9–1. The Thirteenth Air Force was based in the Philippines; the Twentieth was quartered in Okinawa and was also responsible for covering the Marianas. For immediate duty in Korea, General Stratemeyer

TABLE 9–1

FEAF Organization, 1950 and 1953

June 1950

13th Air Force (Philippines)	5th Air Force (Japan)	20th Air Force (Okinawa)
1 Fighter-Bomber Wing (FBW)	2 FBWs 1 Bomber Wing 5 Fighter-Interceptor Squadrons (FIS)	1 Bomber Wing 1 Strategic Reconnaissance Squadron 4 FIS

July 1953

13th Air Force	5th Air Force	20th Air Force	Japan Air Defense Force	Bomber Command
1 Fighter-Bomber Squadron	2 FI Wings 5 FBWs 2 Bomber Wings 2 Night FIS	1 Bomber Wing	4 FI Wings	3 Bomber wings

Note: Transport, troop carrier, and odd combat groups not listed.

Source: Korean Air War Summary, HQ, FEAF, Air Force Research Center, Air University, Maxwell AFB, Alabama.

called on the Fifth Air Force. Its fighter strength in June 1950 was as follows: approximately 216 F–80 jet fighters (9 squadrons, organized in 3 wings) and 24 F–82 "Twin Mustang" night fighters (2 squadrons). However, not all these aircraft were available for flights over South Korea because of the need to defend Japan against possible attack by Russian air units. General Stratemeyer also had available 3 squadrons of F–80s and a squadron of F–82s on Okinawa, for a total of 288 F–80s and 36 F–82s—*maximum*—available to defend Japan and attack the North Korean Air Force. Initially, coverage for FEAF air evacuation flights was provided by 3 squadrons of F–80s and a squadron of F–82s based at Itazuki, Japan. Reinforced by an additional squadron of F–80s and 2 squadrons of F–82s, the fighters (96 F–80s, 32 effective F–82s) based at Itazuki soon cleared North Korean propeller-driven aircraft from the air around South Korean airfields.[9] The 2 aircraft carriers joined the fight by launching attacks against the airfield at Pyongyang, the North Korean capital, on July 3 and 4.

As Air Force and U.N. naval air units took the offensive against the small North Korean Air Force, General Stratemeyer attempted to place all theater air assets under one commander and make that officer a key member of MacArthur's staff. During World War II, Stratemeyer had commanded Army air forces in Asia, first in India and Burma, and then, after the spring of 1945, in China.[10] He drew on his wartime experience in recommending to General MacArthur on July 8, 1950, that FEAF be given operational control over all Air Force and naval air units operating from Japan or over Korea.[11] The previous day, Stratemeyer had appointed FEAF's Vice Commander, Maj. Gen. Earle E. Partridge, Commander of Fifth Air Force and given Partridge the mission of gaining and holding air superiority over Korea.[12] On July 11, Stratemeyer met with his Navy counterpart, Vice Adm. C. Turner Joy, in an effort to form the unified command that he had recommended to MacArthur. The product of that meeting was a directive which pledged the staffs of the Navy and FEAF commanders to "coordination control," a phrase which held different meaning for FEAF and Navy commanders.[13] Stratemeyer in fact did not gain the theater-wide control of U.N. air assets which he had requested; indeed, such powers were never given FEAF during the war, and Stratemeyer and his successor, Lt. Gen. Otto P. Weyland, were compelled to rely primarily upon their personal relationships with Navy Far East Force commanders to insure interservice coordination of air efforts.[14]

Stratemeyer also had problems with General MacArthur's staff. On July 16, 1950, MacArthur's headquarters formed a target committee to allocate air strikes against North Korean military, industrial, and transportation targets.[15] General Weyland, who replaced General Partridge as FEAF's Vice Commander, had commanded tactical air units in World War II and recognized immediately that MacArthur's headquarters lacked adequate Air Force and Navy representation.[16] He and Stratemeyer were able to convince MacArthur to expand the headquarters target committee to include senior FEAF personnel. After six weeks, the headquarters committee was replaced by one staffed and organized by FEAF.[17] Though invited to participate, the Navy declined. Even without Navy membership, however, the Formal Target Committee of the Far East Air Forces served as an effective means of coordinating the U.N. air effort against North Korea and then against North Korean and Chinese air forces.[18] In the case of joint operations, such as the amphibious assault on Inchon in September 1950 that led to the liberation of Seoul, joint Air Force, Navy, and Marine committees met beforehand to divide combat air patrol, reconnaissance, and air interdiction responsibilities. It was not the system that Generals Stratemeyer and Weyland had pressed for, but it was one which, with Navy cooperation, they could—and did—learn to live with.

With the immediate threat posed by North Korean air units suppressed, the Fifth Air Force, augmented by the newly formed FEAF Bomber Command (three bomb groups), turned to assisting the U.S. and South Korean forces then under heavy pressure from mechanized North Korean ground units. Seoul had fallen to North Korean troops on June 28;

on July 20, North Korean soldiers captured Taejon; by July 31, enemy forces were past Kunsan. U.N. forces were soon bottled up in the Pusan perimeter, and most Fifth Air Force combat units were flying close support and interdiction missions. On August 25, when planning for the Inchon invasion was well underway and the Pusan perimeter was safely held, Fifth Air Force fighters were ordered to give "first priority" to attacks on North Korean aircraft. The three bomb groups of FEAF's Bomber Command (Provisional) formed on July 8, soon joined the effort against the North Korean Air Force, and, by the time the U.S. Army's First Cavalry Division crossed the 38th parallel on October 7, North Korean air units had largely ceased to operate. Major North Korean airfields were located at Pyongyang and near Hungnam. By the first week of October, with most of South Korea in the hands of U.N. troops, these bases were easily within range of a variety of Fifth Air Force and Navy aircraft, and all were bombed effectively. The bombing, along with air-to-air operations, virtually eliminated the North Korean Air Force.

The struggle for air superiority over North and South Korea in 1950 was conducted with jet and propeller-driven aircraft against a small but aggressive air force with obsolete equipment. The concept of air superiority, which the Air Force carried from World War II, served it well for this first phase of Korean operations: jet fighters (F–80s) first escorted U.N. ground attack planes and maintained barrier patrols against North Korean fighters. Once the area proximate to the battle area was secure, Fifth Air Force fighters, Bomber Command B–29s, and Navy fighters struck directly at North Korean air bases. World War II experience showed it was more efficient to destroy enemy aircraft on the ground than to wait for them in the air. Korea confirmed this element of USAF doctrine. The F–80s of the Fifth Air Force were superior to North Korea's Yak fighters, and FEAF's B–29s could place heavy ordnance loads on North Korean airfields with near impunity. The North Korean Air Force was inferior across the board. The result of the struggle was a foregone conclusion—so long as the Soviet Union and China stayed out of the conflict.

It was not certain the Russians would. Air Force historian Robert F. Futrell, for example, cited several border violations committed by U.N. aircraft during the push north by U.N. forces during the fall of 1950. An attack by two F–80s on a Soviet airfield north of the Siberian border on October 8 produced a strong Soviet protest and prompted Lt. Gen. Partridge, Fifth Air Force Commander, to set a full-scale alert in case the Russian response was more than diplomatic. Contrary to FEAF perceptions at the time, the attack may well have had a deterrent effect by demonstrating that Russian airfields were vulnerable to Fifth Air Force attack.[19] The Navy had a similar brush with Russian air units. On September 4, one of several piston-engine bombers approaching a carrier task force, which was operating in the Bay of Korea at the head of the Yellow Sea, was shot down by

Key U.S. leaders in the Korean conflict (*clockwise from top left*):
Vice Adm. C. Turner Joy; Gen.
George Stratemeyer; Gen. Otto
"Opie" Weyland; Lt. Gen. Earle
E. Partridge; and Gen. Douglas
MacArthur.

the carriers' Combat Air Patrol. The bomber, clearly Russian, had flown from the Soviet base at Port Arthur. Whether the attack was deliberate or simply a feint that went too far is not clear.[20] At the time, however, it was taken as evidence that the Soviet Union was prepared to intervene in the conflict.

The first phase of the air superiority campaign ended with U.N. air power supreme over the entire peninsula and U.N. aircraft flying out of bases in South Korea. U.N. ground forces had decimated the North Korean army by the end of the third week of October 1950, and it appeared the war would soon end without Chinese intervention and with the U.N. command in control of both North and South Korean territory. General Stratemeyer had made heavy demands on total USAF assets soon after the war began in June, and the Air Force Chief of Staff, Gen. Hoyt S. Vandenberg, had subsequently sent FEAF what reinforcements he could spare, which was not all that much: 2 B–29 groups from the Strategic Air Command, some F–80 reconnaissance aircraft, several troop carrier groups, a light bomber wing, a number of F–51 Mustang fighter-bombers, and a variety of special support units (a radio beacon unit, tactical control group, radio relay squadron, signal battalion, 3 bombing director detachments, and a night reconnaissance squadron).[21] These limited reinforcements, augmented by over 12,000 Reserve and Regular personnel dispatched to the Far East,[22] enabled FEAF to gain virtual air supremacy over North Korea. But there were still some crucial shortages. Engineers and construction equipment were scarce; there was a serious shortage of qualified photo interpreters; and a number of key personnel (bombardiers and navigators in B–29s, and aviation ordnancemen, for example) found themselves working continuous overtime through the summer and fall of 1950. Matters would get worse, however, with the entry of Chinese ground and air forces into the war in great numbers at the end of November.

Phase II of the Air War: November 26, 1950–July 9, 1951

The Joint Chiefs of Staff had feared that Korea might only be the opening round of a global war ever since North Korean forces had attacked South Korea at the end of June 1950. The Joint Chiefs had imposed restraints on the use of USAF units in the fighting in order to try to avoid widening the war in a theater where Soviet and Chinese forces held the advantages of manpower, number of aircraft, and interior lines of communication. The Joint Chiefs also decided to reinforce the North Atlantic Treaty Organization (NATO), whose military command in Central Europe was not yet a year old when the Korean War began. Accordingly, in August 1950 USAF Headquarters and the Strategic Air Command deployed a number of jet fighters and B–29s to Europe. For example, two wings of B–29s were sent to England, and one wing was placed in Labrador; supporting them were two air tanker squadrons transferred to Newfoundland.[23] This move to reinforce NATO is what constrained General Vandenberg when he refused to grant the FEAF all the reinforcements that its commander, General Stratemeyer, had requested. The evidence suggests that the SAC B–29s sent to England and Labrador were nuclear-armed.[24] This was not necessarily good news for FEAF's Bomber Command because B–29s modified for the dropping of nuclear weapons were not available for conventional bombing missions. What FEAF wanted were more conventionally armed fighters and bombers, but there were just not enough aircraft available to cover all the real or possible combat theaters simultaneously.

Through the summer and fall of 1950, the Joint Chiefs remained uncertain about Russian and Chinese intentions. In July, FEAF feared that the attack on South Korea would be followed by air attacks on U.S. bases in Japan. After the successful amphibious assault on Inchon, that fear vanished. However, the Joint Chiefs continued to be uneasy, despite the confidence of the U.N. commander, General MacArthur. In the last week of October, Chinese forces intervened in the fighting, which by that time had moved across the 38th parallel and into the heart of North Korea. Then, the Chinese seemed to withdraw, and General MacArthur claimed on November 24 that Chinese forces were not in the war except as small units of "volunteers." The next day, Chinese armies, which had crossed the Yalu River unobserved, opened a strong offensive on the ground. MiG–15 jet fighters had appeared two weeks before to harass and destroy U.N. aircraft—none of which could fight the MiGs on nearly equal terms. The massive Chinese infantry assault and MiG threat to U.S. aircraft operating near the Yalu drastically altered the course of the war. MacArthur called for reinforcements. Stratemeyer had already warned General Vandenberg that the situation was grave. He did so directly on November 7 because he believed MacArthur did not sufficiently appreciate the seriousness of the appearance of jet aircraft flying out of Manchurian bases. As Stratemeyer warned:

> The enemy, equipped with modern jet fighters, has a sanctuary in Manchuria into which I am not permitted to penetrate. His numbers are increasing and if this trend continues unchecked, his air operations will soon constitute, in my opinion, a most serious threat to overall operations of the United Nations forces.[25]

Chinese MiG pilots were not the best, and most of the U.N. aircraft they attacked escaped. But the crisis was at hand. The fast, high-flying MiGs were a threat to every U.N. aircraft they could reach. Flying from Manchuria, their range would take them only as far south as Pyongyang, but they were capable of wresting control of the air from U.N. air units along a line

465

from Sinuiju to Chosan, and they posed a real threat to reconnaissance aircraft, most of which were F–80s.[26]

At the beginning of December, MacArthur informed the Joint Chiefs that holding Korea might be impossible. Vandenberg had already agreed (on November 8) to send an F–84E and an F–86A wing to FEAF, and they arrived in the Far East during the week of December 4. The F–84s were based in Japan, and the F–86s were divided between Japan and Korea. The first mission of the Korean-based F–86s took place on December 15, the day U.N. ground forces withdrew below the 38th parallel.[27] The F–86As did well against the MiGs in December, but U.N. ground forces could not hold Kimpo and Suwon airfields near Seoul, and General Partridge, Fifth Air Force Commander, pulled the F–86s out of Korea and back to Japan in the first week of January 1951. With the F–86s in Japan, the B–29s flying from Okinawa were vulnerable to Chinese MiGs, and FEAF suspended B–29 attacks over northwestern Korea—the area known for the rest of the war as "MiG Alley."

The withdrawal of the Sabre squadrons from Korea could have proved disastrous for the U.N. command. However, the Chinese MiGs based in Manchuria (estimated at 300 in December) were not deployed aggressively to gain control of the skies above the battleground below the 38th parallel. Futrell has suggested several reasons for this. First, the Chinese and sur-

Gen. Hoyt S. Vandenberg (*left*)**, Air Force Chief of Staff, and Lt. Gen. George E. Stratemeyer, FEAF Commander, leaving FEAF Headquarters after concluding discussion of the Korean situation.**

466

viving North Korean air units had no long-range bombers of any sort and no jet bombers with which to attack U.N. ground forces. Second, though committed to supporting their ground armies, Chinese aircraft could not gain air superiority without employing MiGs, but the range of the MiGs was limited because they were not equipped with expendable, externally carried fuel tanks. Finally, the Chinese apparently feared that staging air attacks on U.N. ground units from their Manchurian sanctuary would provoke the U.S. to retaliate against Manchuria. Their concern was not without substance. The Manchurian sanctuary did not come free of charge. In effect, the Chinese lacked the kind of air force necessary to best exploit the withdrawal of the F–86s from Korea. To extend the range of their jet fighters, Chinese engineers would have to improve airfields in northwest Korea under the cover of the Manchurian-based MiGs and gradually move the MiG bases south.

Partridge, Fifth Air Force Commander, was well aware of what the Chinese might do. What he wanted and needed were the fields at Kimpo and Suwon. The 8th Army, under its new commander, Lt. Gen. Matthew B. Ridgway, got them back. On February 10, Kimpo was taken by U.N. forces; Seoul was recaptured by the middle of March. As soon as possible, F–86 squadrons returned to Korea: to Taegu on February 22, to Suwon on March 10, and to Kimpo on August 16 (F–80s had begun using Kimpo at the end of June). B–29s, shielded by Sabre patrols, cratered North Korean airfields near and north of Pyongyang in April. In May, the Superfortresses extended their daylight raids right into MiG Alley itself, with attacks on Sinuiju airfield, which the Chinese were supplying and covering from Antung, just across the Yalu. The bombers were vulnerable to the MiGs because of the latter's heavy armament (one 37-mm and two 23-mm guns) and because it was hard for the Sabres—flying from Suwon, about 300 miles from Sinuiju—to maintain adequate cover over the B–29s. Nevertheless, FEAF's air superiority campaign was successful. During their offensives against the Eighth Army in April and May, Chinese and North Korean ground forces "received no support from the Red air forces."[28] The failure of those offensives, and subsequent tactical advances by U.N. armies, were instrumental in prompting the Chinese to accept the offer of negotiations.

Tactics in Phase II of the air superiority war were drawn from World War II experience and were strongly affected by the flow of the land battle and—for the F–86 fighter squadrons—by the availability of South Korean airfields and sufficient fuel. The B–29s were controlled by FEAF's Bomber Command in Tokyo. The F–86s were under the command of the Fifth Air Force. Though there were problems employing the B–29s and the F–86s together, the problems were more the consequence of the differences between the flying characteristics of the two aircraft than of any lack of coordination between FEAF and Fifth Air Force. The F–86s and B–29s cruised at very different speeds, and the F–86s could not loiter around the fringes of the B–29 formations and still maintain enough speed to cut off MiGs making high speed passes against the piston-engine bomber.[29] Moreover, the MiGs, with their heavy armament, could do a lot of damage in one pass if they could get a good shot at one B–29. Finally, there was no ground radar coordination of fighters and bombers. The F–86s flew as a screen above the B–29s in order to keep the faster MiGs from diving down through the bombers from out of the sun. Surveillance was visual; communications were by voice radio; closure rates were significantly higher than those of World War II, and B–29 gunners tended to fire at every swept-wing fighter they saw.[30] The difficulty of operating jet fighters with piston-engine bombers was a serious obstacle to revising the bombing tactics used by the Army Air Forces in World War II. Fortunately for the FEAF and the Fifth Air Force, the Chinese MiG force was not as aggressive in the spring of 1951 as it would be a year later.[31]

Operating alone, the F–86 squadrons found they could rely on the experience of their pilots and the lack of flying skills of most of their opponents. The basic differences between the aircraft can be expressed concisely: the MiG–15 was a fast, light, highly maneuverable fighter with a slow rate of fire; the F–86 was a heavy, durable, stable, and easily flown fighter with a much higher rate of fire. Because of its light weight and powerful engine, the MiG–15 could operate effectively above 35,000 feet.[32] This gave Chinese fighter pilots a major advantage. They could respond to an F–86 attack by breaking down or up to escape. They could also cruise at high altitude and wait for an opportune moment to dash down upon formations of F–86s, or send decoys to lure flights of Sabres away from the other aircraft to a point where a group of MiGs could drop down on the USAF fighters from a position in the sun. (See Table 9–2)

On the other hand, the rate of fire of the MiG's armament (one 37-mm, two 23-mm guns) was slow, a distinct disadvantage in high speed engagements during which pilots usually had opponents in their sights for only a few seconds at most. The greater the rate of fire, the higher the chance of a kill. The 37-mm gun was a smasher; it could knock out a fighter with one shot. However, the trick for the MiG pilot was to fix an opponent in his sights long enough to score. A quick, diving pass was not enough against a fighter; against a slow moving steady flier like the B–29, the 37-mm and 23-mm guns could be devastating, however, and F–86 pilots never developed an effective daylight defense of B–29 formations.[33] The Army Air Forces had tried combining a 37-mm gun with smaller caliber armament in the P–39 of 1940–41 and had found that it was not technically possible to harmonize the very different guns to make the aircraft an effective air superiority fighter.[34] They had settled on six 50-caliber machineguns as a standard compromise of the inevitable trade-off between the mass of

TABLE 9–2

MiG–15 versus F–86: Positive and Negative Features

MiG–15

Positive Features	*Negative Features*
1) Ability to operate above 40,000 ft (50,000 for later models)	1) Loss of aircraft control at high Mach air speeds
2) High rate of climb	2) Slow defrosting of its windshield and canopy and hence reduced pilot vision
3) Quick horizontal acceleration from relatively slow speeds	3) Poor lateral-directional stability at high altitudes
4) Short turning radius	4) Low roll rate
5) Shot take-off and landing	5) Low rate of fire
	6) Short range

F–86

Positive Features	*Negative Features*
1) Superior controls— power-assisted in the F–86E and F–86F model	1) Slow rate of climb
2) High rate of fire, but poor weapon range	2) Relatively slow rate of acceleration when flying horizontal
3) High dive speed	3) Low ability to turn speed into altitude
4) Better stability in high speed turns	4) Short range, even with drop tanks
	5) Inadequate gunsight

the bullets fired and the chance that bullets would find a target. The USAF had accepted the same armament in the F–86, and the wisdom of that decision seemed proven by initial MiG-Sabre engagements. However, the decision to equip the F–86 with 50-caliber machineguns put a premium on skilled pilots, which was no problem until the USAF began to run through the supply of World War II combat veterans.

The Sabre was a responsive aircraft and could outmaneuver the MiG at altitudes below 25,000 feet. Even the F–86A, which did not have power-assisted controls, was a relatively easy aircraft to fly. Though faster than its World War II predecessors, the F–86 was actually more nimble in the hands of a skilled flier. The controls transmitted less vibration to the pilot, so that the physical strain of flying was significantly reduced.[35] Compared with piston-engine fighters, the F–86 could rapidly reach a fighting altitude, and its ability to use its weight as a source of momentum in dives partially compensated for its inability to outclimb MiGs. Nonetheless, its range was limited. There was no provision for inflight refueling, so Sabres could only extend their range by carrying drop tanks mounted below the wings. In a dogfight, however, the drop tanks were a definite hazard, so pilots would jettison them if action appeared imminent. The 4th Fighter-Interceptor Group (4th FI Group) found in its early encounters with MiGs that many of its drop tanks would not release, "and the failure of the tanks to release with complete effectiveness adversely affected pilot psychology."[36] It took about three months for 4th Fighter-Interceptor Wing maintenance personnel to learn that the problem was caused by moisture freezing in the tank's shackle assemblies at high altitudes. The tank releases were simply freezing shut under certain combinations of moisture and temperature. The 4th Wing personnel tried attaching the heaters used in the 50-caliber machineguns to the planes' tank mountings, but the gun heaters "were short in USAF supply and critically short in the Far East."[37] Air Materiel Command specialists finally hit on the solution: packing the mounting shackles with a waterproof insulating compound. The problem of wing tanks that would not drop was largely eliminated by July 1951, but it would have been a very serious problem indeed if Chinese air forces had been able to mount major MiG attacks in April and May.

Air-to-air fighter tactics were similar to those used in World War II. The major differences were closure speed (often over 1,000 miles per hour as opposing aircraft flew at each other at near mach airspeeds) and the high speed at which engagements began. The initial high speeds were often translated into rapid, high-G-force maneuvers, as MiGs and Sabres rolled, turned, and twisted to get into a shooting position. Yet the basic maneuvers were what they had been in World War II because the goal was still the same: to hold a commanding position on an opponent long enough to shoot him down. That usually meant getting on his tail and closing the range to a thousand feet or less. And, as in World War II, the task of each individual pilot was the same: to stay with his wingman or leader so as not to get caught by surprise. The difference between 1951 and 1944 was the speed with which all this was done.

Jet fighter tactics passed through three stages in every engagement: approach to the battle zone, combat, and return to base. In the approach, pilots attempted to keep their aircraft together but so arranged as to provide maximum visibility and the best initial position in a dogfight. In April and May 1951, for example, the 4th FI Group flew a series of sweeps from Suwon through MiG Alley. Each F–86 *squadron* of sixteen planes was organized into two *sections* of eight aircraft; a *section* had two *flights* of four aircraft, and each *flight* contained two *elements*. The element (leader and wingman) was the basic tactical organization.[38] The leader watched for enemy planes and attacked. The wingman, flying fifty to one hundred yards to the right of the leader and behind him, was responsible for making sure the leader was never surprised or jumped by enemy jets. The approach tactic was to spread out the four (sometimes three) flights of each squadron so that they could cover as much volume as possible without being so far apart that they could not support each other once battle began. The 4th FI Wing would assign each squadron an area of the likely battle zone, and the flights would cover that area by stacking themselves *in echelon* and by reaching it at different intervals. The first flight to sight MiGs would alert the others, and the last flight to arrive in a "covered" zone would shield those Sabres returning to base.

Engagement tactics had one object: to destroy the enemy's organization while preserving your own. That meant aggressively breaking up his larger formations. As a report by the 4th FI Group put it, "The immediate object in an attack was to break the enemy formation into two (2) plane elements or separate aircraft."[39] There was a precise logic to this tactic. In 1916, the mathematician and engineer F. W. Lanchester had shown that the real fighting differential between two military forces is the ratio of the *squares* of their strengths.[40] Given pilots and planes of comparable quality, ten aircraft are not twice as strong as five but four times as powerful— assuming that they can bring their firepower to bear. The Sabre tactic of dividing the MiG formations was thus an effort to isolate parts of the MiG force and so deal with the whole force piecemeal. The problem for the MiGs was to take advantage of their superior numbers by preventing the F–86s from breaking up their larger formations. The fact was, however, that technology and experience gave the Sabre flights an advantage: the best basic formation was the element of leader and wingman, and the USAF pilots—most of whom had combat experience in World War II—were simply better at flying it.[41]

This does not mean that MiG pilots were easy game for the USAF veterans. One official report noted that "from the beginning of the air war between the F–86A and the MiG–15, and (*sic*) aggressive spirit has pre-

471

vailed among the leaders of the MiG formations." Forty-one MiG "formations numbering up to six (6) aircraft have made attacks without losing the integrity of the formation and have demonstrated high skill in their ability to maneuver with this force."[42] MiG–15 pilots flew tight approach formations, "approximately half" of those engaged maneuvered well defensively, and MiG elements were very cohesive.[43] In addition, MiG pilots tried tactics suited to their aircraft:

1) Scissors or Butterfly. One of two aircraft "above and slightly behind a single target" would dive on the target, "go below it and pull up."[44] The second high MiG would start diving when the first was making his pass. As a result, their "target cannot pull up, dive, or turn without being subjected to fire."[45]

2) Yo-Yo. MiGs would orbit high above the F–86s and swoop down in pairs for a fast firing pass. "This tactic is frequently used by the MiGs with the aircraft in train so that the target, or targets, are under continuous attacks."[46]

3) Decoying. Sixteen MiGs chased by eight Sabres would divide into two groups of eight. The Sabres would split into two groups of four. The MiGs would split again, so that it was two F–86s on four MiGs. The MiGs would divide one last time, and the Sabres would have to choose which element to pursue. The MiG element not pursued would try to get behind the F–86 element.[47]

MiG pilots employed other tactics, as well as variations of these three, in an effort to isolate individual Sabres or to subject small groups of F–86s to a steady stream of cannon fire. When they lost the initiative, the MiGs broke or dove away *in formation* and headed across the Yalu.

F–86 pilots noticed two variations in this pattern of formation and two-plane element flying. The more dangerous case was eventually referred to as the "Honcho" pilot—a lone MiG with "skill and tenacity in his attack," able to "engage the friendly fighters who turn into his attack with ferocity and daring."[48] There is evidence these pilots were Russian; 4th Fighter-Interceptor Wing pilots certainly took that view in 1952.[49] At the same time, there were numbers of Chinese pilots in 1951 who possessed more bravery than skill. Several attacked whole flights of F–86s without—as the 4th Fighter-Interceptor Group ironically put it—"planning the future."[50] These attackers were usually shot up badly. All the MiGs employed one basic evasive tactic: running to the Yalu. This often worked in 1951 because the F–86A could not overtake a MiG–15 in a flat-out, level race. Later, when the USAF equipped its Sabre squadrons with the F–86F, it became a far tighter contest.

Withdrawal tactics were very different for the two sides. MiGs had only to reach the Yalu. The F–86s, and the bombers, reconnaissance planes, and fighter bombers that the Sabres protected, had to get below Seoul. In the early months of 1951, after FEAF's B–29s had resumed bomb-

472

ing North Korean targets near or along the Yalu, MiG pilots would try to follow U.S. aircraft as far south as Pyongyang to harass and pick off stragglers. The MiGs were aided in this work by ground-controlled intercept (GCI) radars in Manchuria, which could coordinate the various MiG formations in response to the movements of Fifth Air Force and other FEAF aircraft.[51] To foil the Chinese pilots and ground controllers, the squadrons of the 4th Fighter-Interceptor Wing constantly modified the distribution of their patrol stations and station arrival times, and guarded their radio communications. Sabre pilots also *always* turned into an attack, "regardless of the state of fuel or the number of attacking aircraft."[52]

Fourth FI Wing pilots had to learn how best to fight with and against jet aircraft—despite the fact that approximately two-thirds of them had World War II combat experience. Table 9–3 illustrates the amount of time the F–86 pilots spent training for combat. In the period January–March 1951, the F–86s were largely out of the fight in Korea, but they continued to fly from bases in Japan. Once back in Korea, they continued noncombat flying as a means of supplementing their combat experience. Fourth FI Wing estimated that F–86 pilots needed at least fifteen combat missions a month (or a minimum of twenty noncombat practice sessions) to stay in training. Yet, one obstacle to training more pilots in the U.S. for F–86 service in Korea was a shortage of Sabres for practice dogfighting.[53] In addition, after both combat and training missions, F–86 squadrons reviewed gun camera films, and squadron intelligence officers, after debriefing returning pilots on enemy tactics, prepared typed summaries of enemy moves which were quickly copied and distributed to other squadrons. North American Aviation also supplied the 4th FI Wing with material describing the F–86's flight characteristics.[54]

TABLE 9–3
F–86 Combat and Noncombat Flying Hours

	1950	1951	
	Oct-Dec	Jan-Mar	Apr-Jun
F–86 Combat Flying Hours	419	87	3876
F–86 Noncombat Flying Hours	175	5241	4772
Ratio: Noncombat to Combat	.42	60.2	1.2

Source: FEAF Korean Air War Summary, June 25, 1950–July 27, 1953.

The Fourth FI Wing was convinced that MiG pilots were learning by experience. In a sense, each side developed tactics based on combat with the other, and both sides improved from December 1950 to July 1951. In December, for example, MiG pilots lacked flight discipline; they would break formation when attacked. By July, MiG formation integrity had improved drastically. In December, the F–86 flights did not have an adequate approach tactic. They tended to arrive and depart a patrol zone together, which meant MiGs could wait on the ground and then take off at the end of the Sabres' patrol in order to catch them returning home. Staggering the arrival and departure time of F–86 flights solved that problem. In the race for tactical supremacy, however, the USAF held the advantage. MiG pilots continued to overshoot and underestimate slower jets like the F–80,[55] and there were periods when MiG activity was light—despite the need of the Chinese ground forces for relief from U.N. strike aircraft attack. Fighter combat was still a matter of element against element, and the Chinese Air Force did not have the experience necessary to challenge the 4th FI Wing squadrons on equal terms.

Compared with their counterparts in the 4th FI Wing, Navy carrier fighter pilots were at a distinct disadvantage. Beginning in July 1950, U.S. carriers on station in the Yellow Sea and the Sea of Japan employed their F9F–2 Panther jets in air superiority missions against North Korean airfields. Aircraft from the carrier *Valley Forge*, for example, reported destroying thirty-eight aircraft on the ground at North Korean bases during July.[56] In early November, however, F9Fs first encountered MiGs while attacking Sinuiju, and the Navy fighter pilots discovered their aircraft could not come close to the MiG in terms of speed, rate of climb, and service ceiling.[57] From that time on, Fifth Air Force's 4th FI Wing carried the bulk of the anti-MiG effort. Indeed, the Navy had very real doubts about the ability of its F9F combat air patrols to shield their carriers from MiG attack. The problem was not simply a function of the F9F's limited performance, however. With sufficient warning, patrolling F9Fs could be vectored to intercept attacking MiGs. Once in combat, the superior skills of the Navy pilots would tend to offset the performance limitations of their aircraft. Unfortunately, Navy Airborne Early Warning (AEW) and surface ship radars lacked the reach to give the slower F9F the time necessary to cut off approaching MiGs. The radar-F9F combination simply could not react fast enough to intercept the high-flying, speedy MiG.[58] The Navy's concern was that MiGs would decimate the combat air patrol of a carrier task force and strafe armed and fueled fighters waiting to launch on deck. The initial MiG assault would then be followed up by bombing attacks staged by conventional aircraft. This fear was never realized, but the inferior performance of Navy day fighters kept them on the sidelines of the air superiority campaign for the rest of the war.

With what limited support the Navy could offer, Fifth Air Force fighters and FEAF bombers gained air superiority in Phase II of the air war, but their victory was due as much to the weakness of their opponent as to their own skills and energy. Chinese ground forces were better at fighting U.N. and South Korean units than Chinese air units were at taking on U.N. air squadrons. Indeed, the Chinese jet air effort must be regarded as impressive simply because the Chinese Air Force was so new and because it went into action with the nimble but hard to control MiG–15. The Chinese had much assistance from the USSR, but they and the North Koreans carried the bulk of the training and combat flying burden in Korea. Fortunately for Fifth Air Force fighter bombers and FEAF B–29s, Chinese pilots were too inexperienced to keep the F–86 squadrons of the 4th FI Wing from successfully operating in "MiG Alley." With only intermittent sniping from the MiGs, U.N. air forces were able to provide U.N. ground forces in the spring of 1951 with the sort of air support the latter had received earlier in the war. (See Table 9–4)

The distribution of the Fifth Air Force's air effort was not changed by the onset of Phase II of the air war. The number of counterair, interdiction, and close support sorties increased, but at about the same rate, so that the level of the air effort changed but its distribution did not. In effect, Phase II of the air war in Korea was a stepped-up version of Phase I. That does not mean there were no variations in the specific ways in which the air superiority war was fought during the period from November 1950 to July 1951. There were some serious "ups and downs" in the campaign, and though the U.N. air forces retained control of the skies over the battle area and the approaches to it, Fifth Air Force aircraft and support personnel often worked under marginal basing and supply conditions. But the Chinese and North Koreans had problems, too. Though they operated from sanctuaries adjacent to the battlefield, their pilots were not, as a group, as

TABLE 9–4

Comparative USAF Air Efforts, July 1950–June 1951

	1950		1951	
	July-Sept	Oct-Dec	Jan-Mar	Apr-Jun
Close Support Sorties (CS)	1,996	2,646	3,140	3,347
Interdiction Sorties (I)	11,176	14,819	17,584	18,742
Counterair Sorties (A)	1,597	2,117	2,513	2,677

Source: FEAF Korean Air War Summary, June 25, 1950–July 27, 1953.

F9F–2 Panther jets over the port area of Wonsan, North Korea.

qualified as those flying for the U.N. command, and the only modern air-craft they possessed were jet fighters of limited range which were ill-suited for ground attack operations. Moreover, all their aircraft and parts were supplied by the Soviet Union, which meant that basic decisions about the Chinese air order of battle were made in Moscow. The Chinese air leaders apparently believed they could deny air superiority to the U.N. command even with these limitations. When events proved otherwise, the air superi-ority battle took a new turn.

Phase III of the Air War: July 10, 1951–July 27, 1953

In late May 1951, General Stratemeyer, FEAF Commander, was stricken with a heart attack. His formal replacement (General Partridge had taken temporary command of FEAF before returning to the U.S. to head the Air Research and Development Command) was Lt. Gen. Otto P. Wey-land, who had been FEAF's Vice Commander in 1950 (succeeding General Partridge) until he was appointed head of Tactical Air Command in April 1951. Weyland wanted to increase FEAF's interdiction campaign, and he requested FEAF Headquarters staff to examine possible Chinese and

Russian threats to a sustained bombing campaign against enemy lines of communication in North Korea. Two weeks after Weyland had requested it, FEAF Headquarters' Plans Directorate prepared a concise report on the possible character of the next stage of the Korean air battle. It was a sobering three pages.

The Communist ground offensive had been contained, and U.N. armies in Korea had successfully adopted the tactic of using their superior firepower to push Chinese ground units back to or just beyond the 38th parallel. Chinese air units had failed to support the May offensive of the Communist ground divisions and were not particularly active. The Plans Directorate, however, was watching the numbers. It estimated that the Chinese Air Force consisted of approximately 1,000 aircraft, including over 300 MiG–15s. The Chinese had deployed nearly 700 aircraft for use in Korea, including all their MiGs, plus over 150 propeller-driven fighters, and "95 bombers and 130 ground attack" planes.[59] To counter these forces, FEAF controlled, for direct use in Korea, 600 aircraft: 50 F–86s, about 285 F–80s and F–84s, 65 piston-engine Mustangs, and nearly 200 B–26s and B–29s. In terms of jet aircraft, the 2 sides were about even, but FEAF intelligence estimated that the Chinese would "equal FEAF in overall air strength in December 1951."[60] Were the Chinese allowed to continue increasing their air forces beyond that date, without hindrance, they "could force FEAF into a primarily defensive role over [FEAF] base areas in Korea, and the air control over the battle area would be in doubt."[61] The Russians had 5,300 planes in the Far East. Were they to throw their weight in with the Chinese—by covering Manchuria, say, while the Chinese devoted all their air resources to Korea—then FEAF could face military disaster.

The Plans Directorate informed Weyland that "a struggle between the CCAF [Chinese Communist Air Force] and FEAF for control of the air over Korea will determine the success of the U.N. campaign in Korea."[62] The Directorate also reported that wargames had suggested the Chinese could knock out 150 U.N. fighter aircraft in Korea in 2 days with the forces at their disposal after December 1951. In short, with more planes (especially MiG–15s) and with the benefit of recent combat experience against the 4th FI Wing, the Chinese air groups were gaining strength faster than the FEAF. Even if the Soviet Union were to stay out of the war, the Chinese could threaten U.N. air supremacy in Korea in early 1952. The Fifth Air Force had to find some way of depleting Chinese air strength while still respecting the enemy's Manchurian sanctuary. Or, the USAF had to reinforce the FEAF. Weyland responded to this assessment by pressing his superior—Vandenberg—for more F–86 squadrons. He also decided to employ B–29s aggressively against North Korean airfields.

The ground war gave Fifth Air Force reason to patrol aggressively across North Korea after August 22, when the armistice negotiations between Communist forces and the U.N. that had opened on July 10 were suspended. In September and October U.S. Army and Marine divisions battled their way into rugged territory that commanded the ground north of the Hwachon Reservoir, and Fifth air Force units supported the advance. Lt. Gen. Matthew B. Ridgway, U.N. Commander in Korea, was determined to gain a terrain advantage before winter and also convince the Chinese and North Koreans that U.S. forces would not wait passively while the Communist armies built up for a new offensive. Weyland feared that the Chinese would restore North Korean air bases in MiG Alley and then use the aircraft stationed at those fields to protect the troops restoring bombed-out runways farther south. The Chinese could, if successful, gradually extend their air units deeper into North Korea under a MiG umbrella. Eventually, they would have the capacity to support their own troops at the front with aircraft based in North Korea and to challenge the U.N.'s hold on the air. As Weyland warned Vandenberg on September 15, "If the present trend continues, there is a definite possibility that the enemy will be able to establish bases in Korea and threaten our supremacy over the front lines."[63] Vandenberg could only respond by saying that giving FEAF more F–86s would strip the air defenses of North America and NATO, which of course was something he would not do. There was always the chance that the war would spread to Europe. [The Joint Chiefs had already decided that they would sacrifice Korea if in doing so they could save Europe.]

Despite the obvious vulnerability of FEAF's B–29s to MiGs, Weyland ordered the bombers to close any North Korean airfields that the Chinese opened. The first major target was a set of new or restored North Korean airfields that could handle MiGs, including three across the Yalu from Antung and three others between Sinuiju and the Chongchon River. FEAF's Bomber Command tried using B–29s fitted with SHORAN (Short Range Radio Navigation) night bombing equipment against these airfields. However, the accuracy of the SHORAN-equipped bombers was not sufficient to halt the Chinese and North Korean engineer units, so the B–29s were sent on daylight raids with F–84s and F–86s as close and distant escorts. The daylight raids were not a success: between October 22 and 29, FEAF lost almost as many B–29s as it had through the entire war until that time.[64] Part of the problem was the proximity of MiG bases in Manchuria. There was also the problem of tactics. The Army Air Forces had learned in 1944–45 that close escort was not the best means of protecting bombers. Fighter sweeps were better because they had allowed Allied escort fighters to meet German interceptors above the latter's bases.[65] But fighter sweeps of that sort were not possible in Korea when the MiGs were based in Manchuria and the B–29s went after North Korean airfields near the Yalu. Moreover, there were so many MiGs that some were likely to seep through or circumvent even the most vigilan fighter sweep. The numbers problem had just not been severe in 1944–45 in Europe once the Allies gained bases in France. Korea was a different situation, and different tactics were required.

The different tactics called for were not really new, but it was difficult to apply them to the B–29. Fifth Air Force had first used SHORAN techniques successfully in February 1951, with its B–26 night-attack light bombers. FEAF B–29s began using SHORAN equipment in April, against built-up areas and railroad yards. SHORAN used ground-based radio transmitters (or beacons), accurate maps, and radio receivers in the B–29s to place the bombers over a target. Specially placed radio stations would transmit signals the intensity of which was a function of range. The signals of the stations overlapped, and the B–29s carried a receiver that would respond when an aircraft, navigating along the arc of one beacon, flew across the point where that beacon's signal intersected a second beacon's signal with a particular intensity. Given a sufficient number of beacons, there would be such a point of intersection above every main target.

SHORAN bombing accuracy depended upon several factors. For example, SHORAN transmitting signals dropped off in power with range, and the B–29s often flew at the limit of the SHORAN signal arcs. This meant that the bombers might be off their planned course by several hundred feet. Errors were also introduced because of mistakes in maps. In theory, the SHORAN computation personnel knew the distance of the target from the beacons and could calculate the proper level of signal that would carry the bomber over the target. They would then give that information to the B–29 navigators. Sometimes, however, the data on distances were not accurate enough. Even small errors could throw the bombs dropped by high-level bombers off target by several hundred feet. As a result, it was estimated that no more than half of the bombs dropped during SHORAN missions in September 1951 were within 500 feet of their intended targets.[66] There was another problem: bombing aircraft using SHORAN had to approach the target along one of several arcs; the defenders of airfields, which were repeatedly attacked, would soon calculate the SHORAN arcs and position searchlights, antiaircraft (AA) guns, and MiG interceptors accordingly.[67] SHORAN signals could also be jammed. The British had successfully jammed a SHORAN-like system used by the Luftwaffe in 1940, and the Chinese did attempt to jam or confuse the short-range bombing radars carried by B–29s, but FEAF SHORAN operations continued without serious electronic interference until the end of the war.[68]

The switch to night bombing actually began in April 1951, but the real jump in the frequency of such attacks took place in November and December 1951 and in the early months of 1952. (See Table 9–5) After October 1951, there were really two air superiority campaigns—one fought above the clouds by day and the other, often in the clouds, by night. The second battle pitted B–29s and their onboard electronic countermeasures (ECM) against increasingly numerous and efficient Chinese and North Korean defenses, particularly searchlight and AA gun radars. The night battle, fought over North Korean airfields, was an invisible duel, with ground radars seeking the B–29s while the bombers defended themselves with techniques first developed in World War II.

If the Chinese and North Koreans were to expand their air power south from MiG Alley, they would have to blunt the B–29 SHORAN attacks. In their efforts to do so they steadily escalated the electronic war, as the following chronology shows:

1) September 1951: Chinese/North Korean first use of radar for directing searchlights.
2) October 1951: First use of S-band AA gun fire-control radar.
3) December 1951: Over 60 S-band fire-control radars placed around four North Korean airfields and Pyongyang.
4) June 1951: Searchlight control radars used with Ground-Control Intercept (GCI) radars to guide MiGs to B–29s.
5) September 1951: B–29s drop chaff for the first time and jam Chinese/North Korean high frequency (HF) radio links.
6) October 1952: Chinese/North Korean GCI communicators switch from high frequency to VHF settings.[69]

The defenders of the North Korean airfields employed three types of radars: air early warning, fire control, and GCI. The first alerted the defenses; the second allowed aimed antiaircraft fire to be directed against the B–29s; and the third permitted ground controllers to direct MiGs (which carried no radar) to within sight of the B–29s at night. All three radars could be thwarted by overpowering them or by confusing them. Overpowering them meant jamming them with a strong signal broadcast by the bomber at the same frequency. This tactic clouded ground radar-scopes and made precise

TABLE 9–5
B–29 Night Sorties

1950	1951				1952
Oct-Dec	Jan-Mar	Apr-Jun	Jul-Sep	Oct-Dec	Jan-Mar
42	178	496	430	1032	1472

Source: FEAF Korean Air War Summary, June 25, 1950–July 27, 1953.

targeting impossible. The ground radar operators responded to this tactic by switching their radar frequencies.

The duty of the B–29 electronic countermeasures (ECM) operators was to switch their jammer frequencies as quickly as possible after any changes in ground-based radar frequencies were detected. Deceiving enemy radars was the second basic tactic; this was accomplished with chaff—thin foil strips cut at lengths that would reflect ground radar pulses. By dispensing chaff, bombers could create false targets—so many, in fact, that ground antiaircraft controllers could not tell the real bombers from the fake until the raid was over.

The use of ECM greatly reduced bomber losses, but night bombardment remained hazardous duty. The reduced accuracy of night bombing strikes forced bombers to return periodically to North Korean airfields to keep them closed. In November 1951, Weyland defined the primary mission of FEAF's Bomber Command as the systematic destruction of North Korean airfields; in December, Weyland ordered the B–29s to strike at least one important airfield every night.[70] So the Chinese and North Koreans knew the B–29s would be coming regularly. Their tactic was to pick up the approaching bombers on early warning radars, then use GCI radars to vector MiGs in toward the bomber stream. Searchlight radars would target the bombers, and a cone of lights would illuminate one B–29. MiGs would only attack when they saw a bomber illuminated by searchlight or by the moon. Directly over the target, the B–29s ran a gauntlet of flak. This was, in most respects, a replay of World War II; both sides used established tactics and proven (nearly obsolescent) equipment.

The B–29s responded to the enemy tactics with countermeasures of their own: flying at altitudes which would not produce contrails, feinting toward one target and then striking at some other field, tightening formations to place the greatest number of bombers over the target in the shortest possible time, and painting bombers nonreflective black underneath to reduce their visibility. B–29s were not allowed to drop chaff until 1951, nor were their ECM operators permitted to jam enemy GCI ground-to-plane VHF communications. The latter were listened to by Air Force and Navy radio intercept units for intelligence purposes. However, all of the intelligence material so gathered was classified Top Secret, and Bomber Command and Fifth Air Force were not convinced that the benefits gained from such intelligence were worth the added risk to B–29 groups.[71] B–29 ECM operators were also not permitted to jam enemy early warning radars. This prohibition was intended to conceal overall U.S. ECM capability so that no tactics then practiced by the Strategic Air Command would be compromised. The enemy also developed electronic counter countermeasures (ECCM). When B–29s jammed enemy fire control radars, the operators on the ground would DF (use direction-finding gear) the B–29 broadcasts to obtain a bearing on the bomber. Then the Chinese operators would use a separate height-finding radar, which had not been turned on previously, to find the bombers' altitude.[72] Defeating this system called for constant reconnaissance of enemy radars. FEAF's Bomber Command had to augment its reconnaissance force to deal with the growing quantity and sophistication of Chinese/North Korean defenses. The original RB–29 squadrons were replaced by small numbers of special "ferret" RB–50s, whose primary function was electronic intelligence. But the B–29s had to struggle through a whole year of night SHORAN bombing before receiving help from the sophisticated RB–50s.[73]

Fifth Air Force had a squadron of F–94B Starfire aircraft which were capable of escorting the B–29s on the bombers' night raids, but the "USAF had directed that the F–94s should be used only for local air-defense scrambles" because Air Force Headquarters did not want to risk losing any F–94s—with the plane's sensitive air intercept radar—over North Korea.[74] As an alternative, Fifth Air Force began employing piston-engine Marine night fighters (F7Fs) of Squadron VMF–513 ahead of the B–29s in July 1952. The F7Fs had not been designed for air intercept missions, and when they proved unable to deal with MiGs, they were replaced (November 1952) by F3D–2 Skyknight aircraft. From that point, the Marine aircraft (augmented by a Navy detachment from the carrier USS *Lake Champlain*), flying barrier patrols and top cover on the B–29s, began shooting down MiGs.[75] The early success of the Marine night interceptors, plus the entreaties made by FEAF's Bomber Command, prompted USAF Headquarters to authorize soon thereafter the use of F–94s over North Korea, where they flew barrier patrols and escorted B–29s against GCI-directed MiGs. An official USAF source credited the F–94Bs with reliable performance against MiG–15s, but that was in spite of a number of deficiencies. F–94Bs had been designed to work against piston engine bombers, and they were rushed into production with only four 50-caliber machineguns as armament. The F–94B was also relatively slow and unstable at high altitudes.[76] It had not proved effective against low-flying night intruders, but its air intercept radar was more effective at higher altitudes, away from ground clutter. In January 1953, B–29s began carrying Identification: Friend or Foe (IFF) transponders which allowed the F–94Bs to clearly distinguish bomber from MiG, and an F–94B bagged the first of several MiGs shot down by the night interceptors at the end of that month. The IFF equipment also kept the B–29s from firing on their own escorts. Fifth Air Force and FEAF both feared that the enemy air forces would field an air intercept radar-equipped fighter, but the Chinese and North Koreans never did. As the official USAF history noted, it was just as well. Night fighter tactics were far more cautious than daytime tactics, and at night, more than in daylight, the advantage lay with the attacking fighters. Fifth Air Force had trouble enough escort-

Above: **The lead B–29 during a combat mission over Korea.** *Below*: **Photo interpreters of the 548th Reconnaissance Technical Squadron check the thousands of prints produced by an RB–29 over Korea.**

ing the B–29s during the day; bomber losses to MiGs equipped with air intercept radars might have been prohibitive.[77]

FEAF's B–29s rarely attacked the increasingly heavy flak batteries that guarded select North Korean airfields and Pyongyang. There were several reasons why they did not. First, the batteries of medium-caliber guns did not throw up so great a high-level barrage that the B–29s could not weather it with their ECM techniques and tight formations that kept them over the target for the minimum amount of time. Second, the flak batteries were difficult to locate and even harder to hit. SHORAN was accurate enough to hole runways, but the accuracy against antiaircraft guns and radars was significantly less: approximately one bomb in four found the target.[78] A limited number of bombers, coupled with the need to avoid keeping them over the target beyond the minimum time necessary to hole the runway, did not make an antiflak effort worthwhile. Fifth Air Force employed both light bombers and F–84 fighter bombers in flak suppression raids, but the results were difficult to assess, particularly if the B–29s did not attack the target immediately after the flak suppression raid.[79] Navy carrier aircraft attempted to knock out radars near a number of airfields in eastern North Korea in the fall of 1952 and were also not very successful. Chinese and North Korean radar operators soon learned that switching on their equipment to track lone Navy planes brought on attacks, so they did not broadcast until there was more evidence of a major attack. By not broadcasting, or by broadcasting intermittently, they foiled the Navy's radar destruction plans.[80] The use of chaff clouds and ECM appears to have been a more economical defense against radar-directed antiaircraft guns.

Overall, the B–29 raids against North Korean airfields must be judged a success. Using World War II aircraft and tactics, FEAF's Bomber Command kept North Korean airfields closed from the fall of 1951 through July 1953. Bomber Command was not the only force that attacked the North Korean airfields. Fifth Air Force light bombers and fighter bombers also participated in the effort, as did the carrier aircraft of Naval Forces Far East—particularly after April 1953, when the Chinese and North Koreans, realizing that an armistice was likely, tried desperately to bring several runways into condition to operate MiGs. Only the B–29s, however, kept up a constant night effort under all-weather conditions. (See Table 9–6)

In 1950, B–29s flew an average of 14 night bombardment strikes a month. In 1951, the number jumped to 178; in 1952, it was 449; in 1953 until the signing of the armistice at the end of July, it was 478. Over the same period, the average number of B–29 combat flying hours generally declined. In 1950, it was 7,616 hours per month; the 1951 figure was 4,368 hours; in 1952, it was 3,834, and in 1953, 4,087. The last figure reflected the surge in bombing North Korean airfields in the 3 months before the armistice. The overall trend, however, was fewer combat hours and a greater percentage of that combat time at night.

The night raids were employed to reduce losses. (See Table 9–7) Moreover, the B–29 loss rates, even in daylight raids, were lower than comparable rates for the European theater in World War II. (See Table 9–8) Unfortunately, FEAF had no large B–29 reserve to call on, and USAF headquarters was not about to deploy B–36s or, later, B–47 jet bombers to Japan or Okinawa for use in Korea. It was a difficult situation for FEAF's Bomber Command: given obsolete or obsolescent equipment that was often in short supply, it nevertheless had a crucial assignment, and the enemy understood the importance of that assignment as clearly as did Bomber Command.

While the B–29s halted Chinese/North Korean attempts to rebuild airfields below the Yalu, the F–86 squadrons—always outnumbered—continued their daylight campaign against MiGs based in Manchuria. From the summer of 1951 on, the level of air-to-air combat increased dramatically.

TABLE 9–6
B–29 Night Sorties

		1952		1953	
Jan-Mar	Apr-Jun	Jul-Sept	Oct-Dec	Jan-Mar	Apr-Jun
1472	1237	1247	1435	1343	1568

Source: FEAF Korean Air War Summary, June 25, 1950–July 27, 1953.

TABLE 9–7
B–29 Operational Losses

1950	1951		1952		1953	
Jul-Dec	Jan-Jun	Jul-Dec	Jan-Jun	Jul-Dec	Jan-Jun	Jul
9	11	14	10	8	4	1

Source: FEAF Korean Air War Summary, June 25, 1950–July 27, 1953.

(See Table 9–9) The counterair effort rose from under five percent of all FEAF sorties to fifteen percent; it never fell below eleven percent for the rest of the war. Related figures tell a similar story. (See Table 9–10) Increases in the tempo of F–86 operations occurred as first the Chinese pressed U.N. air units in the fall of 1951 and then, in 1953, the Fifth Air Force, with four F–86 wings, sought to destroy MiGs faster than the Chinese could train pilots to fly them. Tables 9–9 and 9–10 show the increase in the counterair effort generally and in the pace of F–86 operations. Beginning in October 1951, combat between MiGs and F–86s became steady and intense, paralleling the war of attrition which Chinese armies waged on the ground. The Chinese strategy was—apparently—to wear down U.N. air and ground forces and thereby compel the U.N. command to accept a settlement favorable to the Communist belligerents. To this end, Chinese and North Korean air units mounted several major fighter offensives against the F–86 force.

The first was in the fall of 1951, when Chinese MiG units pressed their numerical advantage against the F–86s. Large numbers of MiGs were used to occupy the F–86 patrols, and additional groups of MiGs stationed themselves south of MiG Alley in order to deny Sabres withdrawing from the battle area safe passage home.[81] To offset the increased numbers of MiGs, General Vandenberg, Chief of Staff, USAF, authorized the transfer, by sea, of another wing (the 51st) of F–86s from the United States. In addition,

TABLE 9–8

Bomber Loss Rates, Korea vs Eighth Air Force in WWII

	B–29s Destroyed per 100 MiGs Encountered
Nov 1950-June 1951	4.0
Apr 12, 1951	12.5
Sep 1951-Dec 1951	1.3

	B–17/24s Destroyed per 100 German Conventional Fighters Encountered
Apr 1944-Aug 1944	18

	B–17/24s Destroyed per 100 Me–262s Encountered
Mar-Apr 1945	16 (with U.S. escort)
Mar-Apr 1945	32 (no fighter escort)

Source: "Aircraft Attrition in Korea," Operations Analysis Technical Memorandum No. 31, M.A. Olson and R.T. Sandborn, HQ USAF (Deputy Chief of Staff, Operations), Feb 11, 1952, Natonal Archives, RG 341, Entry 208, Box 13.

TABLE 9–9

FEAF Air Effort (July 1951–July 1953)

	No. of Counterair Sorties (CA)	CA as % of Interdiction Sorties	CA as a % of Total Sorties
Jul-Sep 51	2,296	15.7	4.4
Oct-Dec 51	4,435	17.4	7.4
Jan-Mar 52	7,750	40.6	14.0
Apr-Jun 52	9,945	50.5	15.3
Jul-Sep 52	7,142	53.1	12.6
Oct-Dec 52	7,851	51.9	12.4
Jan-Mar 53	6,407	57.5	11.6
Apr-Jun 53	9,945	105.9	14.2
Jul 53	2,322	99.7	11.8

Source: FEAF Korea Air War Summary, June 25, 1950–July 27, 1953.

TABLE 9–10

F–86 Operations (July 1951–July 1953)

	No. of Active F–86s on Hand	Airborne Sorties	Monthly Sortie Rate Per Aircraft	Combat Attrition Per 100
Jul-Sep 51	97	2,973	24.6	.32
Oct-Dec 51	135	4,691	25.5	.38
Jan-Mar 52	155	8,199	20.5	.24
Apr-Jun 52	163	11,749	29.3	.18
Jul-Sep 52	196	9,019	20.1	.28
Oct-Dec 52	240	10,373	20.8	.15
Jan-Mar 53	308	9,713	17.7	.14
Apr-Jun 53	331	19,763	24.0	.15
July 53	352	5,841	19.0	.15

Source: FEAF Korea Air War Summary, June 25, 1950–July 27, 1953.

General Weyland, FEAF Commander, ordered F–86s that had been rotated to Japan for training and air defense duties back to Korea. Gradually, F–86 strength did increase. Both sides introduced modified fighter models during this period: enemy pilots began flying a more powerful MiG–15, and the 51st Fighter-Interceptor Wing deployed the E model F–86. The F–86E was identical to the F–86A except that its controls were all power-operated. The powered control surfaces of the F–86E gave the plane improved stability, particularly in dives, and were therefore "of great value."[82] On the other hand, the F–86E, like the A model, lacked the power to catch a climbing MiG, so that Chinese pilots continued to avoid combat by zooming away from U.S. aircraft. Despite this advantage, the MiG pilots were unable to overcome the Sabres. F–86 pilots continued to employ very aggressive tactics which, coupled with skilled element and flight formation flying, defeated the efforts of MiGs to overwhelm the USAF fighters. Consequently, the Chinese air units could not hold control of the air above MiG Alley long enough for Communist engineers to open sufficient North Korean airfields to actually begin pushing U.N. air strength south. So long as U.N. reconnaissance planes and fighter bombers could operate behind the Sabre's screens, the Chinese and North Korean air units could not work from North Korean airfields and assist the Chinese ground armies in their campaign of attrition. At the end of December 1951, the Chinese and North Koreans suspended their efforts to restore airfields near MiG Alley.[83]

It was just as well that they did. As the official USAF history noted,

> To the men of the 4th and 51st Fighter Interceptor Wings, the early months of 1952 were times of bitter frustration...the aircraft-out-of-commission rate spiraled rapidly upward. An average of 45 percent of the Sabres had to be carried as out of commission in January 1952....[84]

Spare parts and external fuel tanks were in extremely short supply. The F–86Es, for example, had been rushed to Korea before the completion of operational suitability tests. In effect, they outran their supply chain and maintenance specialists. Fifth Air Force was also short of well-trained F–86 pilots. The original group of World War II combat veterans had been cycled home, and newer pilots had yet to be turned out in large numbers by flight schools in the United States. As an interim solution, volunteers from light bomber and transport squadrons were trained as fighter pilots. The effort was not very successful. Korea was growing rapidly into a serious, prolonged air war, but the pace of the war had nearly run beyond the ability of the Air Force to supply it.

The logistics and pilot-training problems were eventually solved, and, just when the fortunes of the F–86 squadrons seemed at their nadir, the USAF organized an effort that would produce a modified Sabre far superior to earlier models. As early as January 1951, the F–86's armament (six 50-caliber machineguns) had been criticized as too weak to knock down a MiG in the brief interval that F–86 pilots usually had to make a shot.[85] In June of that year, 4th Fighter-Interceptor Group renewed its request for a more powerful armament and also asked for a lighter aircraft.[86] Lightening the F–86 to make it more maneuverable was an option that had already been considered and rejected.[87] Like all military aircraft designs, that of the F–86 was a strict compromise. To increase the F–86's rate of climb and maximum speed, engineers could give the plane a more powerful engine, or cut its weight, or both. But they could not reduce the plane's weight without also reducing some other important military characteristics, such as endurance or armament load. The F–86 was not designed to be a daylight air superiority fighter. It was developed as an all-purpose fighter-bomber. Any serious redesign would in fact become an entirely new aircraft.

Fifth Air Force had recovered parts of a MiG–15 as early as April 1951.[88] It was soon clear that the F–86 could not be modified to the same design standards. However, fighter pilots continued to demand F–86 flight improvements and new guns and gunsights. General Partridge, who had left Fifth Air Force in June 1951 to head the Air Research and Development Command (ARDC). was well aware of the pilots' concerns. He routinely read Fifth Air Force operations reports and intelligence summaries, and he also reviewed reports filed by North American Aviation on F–86 improvements.[89] In January 1952, USAF Headquarters directed ARDC to begin a *comprehensive* program to better the combat performance of the F–86. Partridge assigned the management of the task to the Wright Air Development Center, and intensive work began on improving the F–86's rate of climb at the beginning of February. By the end of May, some solutions were ready for trial.[90] The most significant was one suggested first by North American engineers: sealing the leading edge slats on the Sabre's wings. Kits to convert the F–86's wings to the new configuration were combat tested in Korea by the 4th Fighter-Interceptor Wing in July 1952 with impressive results, and gradually all the earlier Sabre models were converted to the new wing configuration. At the end of June 1952, 4th Wing squadrons received the first production models of the new variant, the F–86F.

> That the solid leading-edge F–86F's were in combat was one of the best-kept USAF secrets, and the modification was mysteriously mentioned in American newspapers as the "new secret device" and the "new combat device" which was giving increased MiG kills.[91]

What it also produced were higher landing speeds. The original F–86s were designed with slats at their wings' leading edges that changed the wings' configuration with the speed of the airplane to give the swept-back fighter sufficient lift for lower speed landings. The swept-back wings reduced drag at high speeds but cost the aircraft lift at slower speeds, and the variable leading edges had been developed by German designers at the end of World War II to reduce the stall speeds of swept-back designs. It was a matter of compromise; to improve low-speed stall characteristics, high-speed performance was reduced. The pilots wanted to dispense with compromise. As one put it, "the air war is not won in the traffic pattern."[92]

Gun and gunsight problems were not so easily resolved. The basic problem was getting sufficient ordnance into a MiG fast enough to knock it down and at a great enough range. The longer this took, the greater was the chance that the MiG would escape or that a second MiG would get a shot in at the F–86 who was trailing the first enemy jet fighter. F–86 pilots were dissatisfied with both their guns and their sights. The 50-caliber machine-guns lacked hitting power in the very short bursts that Sabre pilots usually got off, and the gunsights of the F–86A and E models did not allow Sabre pilots to make accurate deflection shots against rapidly maneuvering MiGs. FEAF requested help from the Air Materiel Command (AMC) in the early months of 1952, and AMC engineers, with the assistance of the Air Proving Ground Command (APGC) and a panel of F–86 combat veterans, evaluated both the gyroscopic sight of the F–86A and the radar fire control system of the F–86E. Both the APGC studies and the panel agreed: the automatic radar gunsight was superior but also difficult to maintain under the operating conditions that prevailed in Korea; radar ranging could double kill probabilities and would be even more effective when the Sabres were equipped with a longer range weapon.[93] But the Sabre squadrons were not out of the woods yet. The fire control system in the F–86Fs that were shipped to Korea in the fall of 1952 was also defective. Like the system used on the F–86Es, the new radar-based calculating sight was prone to malfunction unless carefully maintained; moreover, it had not passed through a period of thorough operational test and modification. To make matters worse, the new planes were given to the squadrons "'without prior notification that the sighting system had been changed, and they were unaccompanied by necessary test equipment."[94] Even with the high-level attention that had already been given to Sabre gunsights, it still took four months "before adequate spare components and specialized test equipment were made available in the theater."[95] AMC was clearly not up to the problem of maintaining sophisticated fire control equipment under Korean operating conditions.

Improving the F–86's armament proved to be an intractable problem. What Sabre pilots wanted—and needed—were four or six reliable 20-mm guns like those carried by Navy and Marine F9Fs and F3Ds. By November 1952, the Air Force had acquired a new 20-mm gun suitable for the F–86. The Air Proving Ground Command equipped eight new F–86Fs in the 4th Fighter-Interceptor Wing with the new guns and began testing them in January 1953. The new weapons were not a success. Unfortunately, the sudden increase in air pressure around the gun muzzles when the guns were fired above 35,000 feet stalled the compressor on the F–86's engine, causing the engine to flame out. The F–86Fs could carry two 20-mm guns instead of the four tested without flaming out, but the volume and weight of fire from only two guns was no improvement over the 50-caliber machineguns. This problem had not been solved by the end of the war, so that Sabres never did have a weapon suited to their (ultimately) improved radar fire control systems.[96] What they might have done had the Air Materiel Command been able to move away from guns altogether was demonstrated by Nationalist Chinese pilots flying Sabres against Communist MiG–15s during the Taiwan Crisis of 1958 and shooting early model Sidewinder heat-seeking air-to-air missiles.

The 4th Fighter-Interceptor Wing took possession of its F–86F models none too soon. By June 1952, enemy air strength had increased to 1,830 aircraft; about 1,000 of these were MiG–15s. The Soviet Union had nearly 5,000 aircraft of all types in the Far East. Fifth Air Force had only 2 F–86 wings (163 active fighters in June) and FEAF had 3 B–29 wings (99 aircraft) to employ directly against Chinese and Russian air units. However, Fifth Air Force would have a number of the new F–86Fs in action in August, and, as noted earlier, the B–29s were prepared to employ additional ECM to overcome strengthened defenses around key North Korean targets. The odds were also far more even if the Russians stayed out of the war. The Communist Chinese Air Force again challenged the Sabres in August 1952, and through November the MiGs attempted both to overwhelm the F–86 screens and to fly around them to catch U.N. bombers and fighter-bombers that were conducting a systematic campaign of wrecking any structure of strategic importance in North Korea. This fall campaign was not a repeat of the 1951 fighting, however. In 1951, the Chinese Communist Air Force had attempted to overwhelm the Sabres with numbers of MiGs the formations of which were built from two-plane elements. In 1952, the MiGs flew in smaller overall numbers but in larger basic formations. They were also more aggressive.[97] The U.N. command believed it had to convince the Chinese and North Koreans that they could not win a war of attrition. To do so, the command ordered its air units to initiate an air pressure campaign on communist forces and their supply lines. The MiGs based in Manchuria attempted to halt this campaign but failed. The 2 F–86 wings actually increased the level of their victories over their MiG opponents even though fewer MiGs were encountered per month (September through November) than in 1951.[98]

There were several reasons for the success of the F–86 wings. First, the armament of the MiG–15s had not improved, even though MiG pilots, as a group, appeared better trained. One study of Fifth Air Force Intelligence Summaries concluded that "descriptions of actions indicate that if the MiG had fire power and gun pointing equipment comparable to the F–86, our losses would be greater."[99] Sabre pilots had also observed that MiG-15s were apparently difficult to control during high speed maneuvers. Third, Fifth Air Force's equipment and maintenance facilities had drastically improved. The new F–86Fs, for example, were the first Sabre models able to fight MiGs above 40,000 feet and F–86F pilots immediately began piling up kills. In October 1952, the Sabre patrols received the support of a new air warning and fighter director radar station located on Cho-do Island off the west coast of North Korea. The new station gave them much of the GCI capability already possessed by the Chinese Communist Air Force.

Fighter maintenance was also improved by the creation of a Rear-Echelon Maintenance Combined Operations (REMCO) maintenance and supply group for the 4th and 51st Fighter-Interceptor Wings. The REMCO concept had been applied first to light bomber and fighter-bomber wings. A REMCO was created by pooling equipment and technicians drawn from several wings stationed in Korea. The REMCO itself was in Japan, with Japanese labor and shops at hand and in use. REMCO personnel performed 100-hour checks on 4th and 51st Fighter-Interceptor Wing aircraft, as well as any major modifications and heavy repairs.[100] The REMCO organization was not without faults, but it was a means of overcoming the lack of adequate maintenance facilities at fields such as Kimpo and Suwon. The fourth reason for the high scores of the F–86 wings was the unwillingness of Chinese air forces to attack U.N. airfields in Korea for fear of U.N. retaliation in kind. FEAF had sent F–94B Starfires (all-weather, two-seat versions of the F–80) to Korea in December 1951 to combat night attacks, but concern that the characteristics of their highly classified radar fire control system might be compromised restricted F–94B deployment to reactive air defense flights until November 1952. Defense of U.N. airfields in South Korea was certainly weak in 1951 and not much improved in 1952 because of a lack of GCI radars and enough ground-based antiaircraft guns. Fortunately for Fifth Air Force, enemy air units could not or would not exploit this weakness.

There was one other reason why 4th and 51st Wing F–86s more than held their own against MiGs in the fall of 1952: superior tactics. USAF tactical doctrine was sound, and the F–86 wings constantly reviewed it. In the fall of 1952, the enemy MiGs challenged the Sabres with larger tactical formations, still hoping to wear down the F–86 wings. The tactic failed. The USAF pilots soon discovered that, if they could just get enough aircraft into the battle area, then the old rules about two-aircraft elements still applied. As one veteran pilot recalled, "In air-to-air combat, it's over like that. Snap! . . . Somebody comes in and makes a pass and gets shot down. It's a rarity for the big dogfight. Very, very rare."[101] Or, as F–86 "ace" Maj. Frederick "Boots" Blesse put it in his 1953 manual of air-to-air tactics, "If you can split the tactical formation of the enemy, more often than not his mutual support efforts against you will be ineffective."[102] As in 1950 and especially 1951, the larger MiG forces could not translate their greater numbers into tactical superiority. As groups of opposing jets met, the approaching formations broke up into two and four-plane groups. Chinese aircraft that could not maneuver for a shot or support another formation simply queued up and waited for a chance to engage. When the Sabre wings received the F–86F, they could for the first time climb and attack the MiGs "waiting in line." It must have been an extremely frustrating experience for the enemy pilots. Yet it was not unusual or unpredictable. RAF Spitfire pilots had suffered through the same sort of situation over France in 1941, when having more fighters than the Luftwaffe had not given them control of the air.[103] The Sabres were demonstrating that sheer numerical superiority was not the key factor to winning air superiority.

What really mattered was the ability of a pilot to maneuver into his enemy's "cone of vulnerability," a three-dimensional space which gradually expanded from the tail of the fighter under attack to the limit of the attacking plane's effective gun range. A Sabre's cone of vulnerability was too small to allow more than one MiG at a time to set up for a shot. A second MiG attempting to enter the same space at the same time endangered his own compatriot without significantly increasing the chance of a "kill." A MiG trying to get at a Sabre already under attack by another MiG also ran the risk of quickly becoming a target for the aggressively maneuvering Sabre. Dogfights tended to break down into one-on-one contests because of the nature of fighter tactics. In addition, Sabre pilots understood that gaining the maneuvering initiative was crucial to survival and success. Therefore, they practiced and refined techniques and maintained an aggressive spirit that gave them that initiative.

The Chinese Communist Air Force responded to their losses in air-to-air combat by fielding a force of 100 Soviet-made Il–28 jet bombers. With a loaded range of nearly 700 miles, the Il–28 "had a formidable night-attack potential."[104] The Chinese did not throw these aircraft into battle, but the threat they posed to U.N. airfields and to USN carrier task forces was clear. Indeed, from the perspective of Fifth Air Force and FEAF, the air war was steadily heating up. In the air, Korea was not a stalemate; it was escalating, and USAF Headquarters was committed to responding to every aggressive action by the Chinese and North Koreans. Fifth Air Force was ordered to equip 2 fighter-bomber wings (the 8th and 18th) with F–86Fs configured for ground attack. The plan was to train both wings in interceptor *and* ground attack tactics, so that F–86s could form tactically cohesive units that could then handle any type (ground or air) of North Korean targets. The conversion took some months; the last of the 18th Wing's squadrons to become operational in the ground-attack Sabres was ready the first week of April 1953; the corresponding date for the 8th Wing was the first week of June.[105] These and other reinforcements gave U.N. air forces the chance to show the Chinese that the U.N. could dominate any game of escalation. In fact, the USAF was now given the duty of forcing the

Chinese and North Koreans to accept the inevitability of an armistice. In 1952–53, Fifth Air Force and FEAF forces had attacked targets in North Korea of significant strategic value. In 1953, FEAF and Fifth Air Force also struck at enemy front-line armies (and their support bases, including the dam and dike system which sustained North Korean rice production) and enemy airfields. Navy carrier air wings were employed against 9 North Korean air bases, and Navy carriers continued to operate within range of Manchurian-based MiGs.[106] The goal was to show the Chinese and North Koreans that further combat would not give them better armistice terms.

At the same time, FEAF requested—and was granted—nuclear strike capability to counter a possible expansion of the air war by Chinese and Soviet forces.[107] FEAF's Director of Targets drew up lists of key Chinese and Russian airfields in case the Peoples' Republic and the USSR decided to attempt a *coup de main* in the Far East.[108] General Weyland "had long held the view that an initial atomic strike was of critical importance," and he requested, in March 1953, "expansion of FEAF's fighter-bomber attack capability."[109] He already had one squadron of F–84 fighter-bombers in training for atomic weapons delivery; he wanted two more. Then he would have a whole wing especially trained to drop recently developed tactical nuclear weapons—in addition to a still-classified number of B–29s (presumably the whole FEAF force of about one hundred) with that capability.[110] It was clear to the U.N. command that enemy ground forces were massing for another spring offensive. It was possible that the Chinese and Russians would escalate the air war to sustain that offensive.

The severity of the spring 1953 air war is reflected in Table 9–11, which compares the months just before with the months of the U.N. air assault on enemy air and field armies. Comparing the total number of F–86 sorties with those from the same period in 1952 (11,749) and 1951 (3,683) gives some idea of the magnitude of the fighting. The increased tempo of operations was possible only because there were more F–86 aircraft (see Table 9–10) and because a greater number were kept flying than in earlier campaigns. The U.N. air effort was staged to demonstrate to the Chinese that steady escalation would not be an effective strategy and might even backfire. In May, for example, General Vandenberg advocated privately that the U.S. put pressure on the Chinese through a naval blockade and by mining Chinese seaports and bombing Chinese industry.[111] In Korea, Fifth Air Force wanted to show the Chinese that the Sabre wings could shoot down newly trained Chinese pilots as fast as they could be taught to fly. In Japan, FEAF prepared for possible nuclear strikes on Chinese and Soviet targets. In Washington, the JCS felt prepared at last for a showdown worldwide, if necessary. The direct and indirect messages concerning U.S. resolve and strength apparently had their effect. When the

Chinese began their summer offensive under the cover of the clouds common during the monsoon season, their goal was to secure the best possible *post-armistice* positions. And after the armistice was signed on July 27, the primary concern of FEAF was that Washington not so deplete USAF strength in the region that the Chinese would be tempted to renew the fighting. To deter any such effort, FEAF moved to build up an effective nuclear strike capability independent of that of the Strategic Air Command.[112]

In sum, during Phase III (July 1951–July 1953) of the air war in Korea, the level of conflict gradually increased. Both USAF and enemy fighter units increased in number and strength. The air superiority campaign was fought mainly over a small number of airfields in or near MiG Alley. By keeping those fields closed, the bombers of FEAF and the fighter-bombers of Fifth Air Force compelled the Chinese MiGs to fight the F–86s. If the latter could be overwhelmed, then the air support and interdiction efforts of U.N. air forces could be assaulted directly. It was a very different situation than that faced by the Eighth Air Force in Europe in World War II. Then, U.S. aircraft had gained air superiority over Germany by forcing German fighters to attack heavily defended U.S. bomber streams and also by taking control of the air above German airfields so that German aircraft had no sanctuary. In Korea, both sides had sanctuaries, but the Chinese never had the long-range strike capability of FEAF. Korea more resembled World War I than World War II, and the F–86s and B–29s kept it that way. After October 1951, the ground war was largely static, and, in the air, both sides gradually improved their equipment and their skills and also aug-

TABLE 9–11
FEAF Air Activity, 1953

	Jan-Mar	Apr-Jun	Jul	Jul x 3*
Counterair Sorties	6,407	9,945	2,322	6,996
Total F–86 Sorties	9,713	19,763	5,841	17,523
F–86 Combat Flying Hours	14,690	26,651	7,555	22,665

Note: "July x 3" is simply the July figure multiplied by three to give a figure comparable to the other three-month periods.

Source: FEAF Korean Air War Summary, June 25, 1950–July 27, 1953.

mented their strengths. Only after U.S. war production and pilot training produced increased numbers of aircraft and pilots in 1952 was FEAF given sufficient resources to demonstrate to the Chinese that further fighting would cost more than it was worth. It may be true that a U.S. threat to use nuclear weapons was instrumental in forcing an armistice. However, the real key to maintaining air superiority over North Korea and containing the Chinese Air Force in Manchuria was the tactical prowess and aggressiveness of the Sabre pilots.

Assessment

Air-to-air combat in Korea was different than in World War II. Jet fighters approached, engaged, and disengaged at much higher speeds. Firing opportunities were brief and fleeting. Neither the MiG nor the Sabre (but especially the MiG) had armament or gunsight suited to this cascading, turbulent form of combat. As a result, losses on both sides were lower, given the number of aircraft which sortied, than during comparable battles in World War II.[113] Veteran Sabre pilots described brief engagements, and gave a lot of the credit for "kills" to a pilot's position in an attack formation (which depended on seniority) or to a pilot's ability to sneak shots at MiGs which had already reached the official exclusion zone near the Yalu.[114] On the other hand, Korea did demonstrate the superiority of high-performance jets over the best of the propeller-driven aircraft from World War II, including bombers such as the B–29. However, Korea also showed that—as in World Wars I and II—tactical training, especially at the front, was essential to tactical success. Sabre squadrons in Korea used gun camera films, analysis by intelligence officers of MiG tactics, and plenty of training flights to prepare for combat. The greatest enemy of Sabre effectiveness was the poor quality of Korean airfields, which were too short, too dirty, inadequately defended, and lacking in proper maintenance and storage facilities. These were problems the USAF never completely solved.[115]

The USAF's air superiority campaign in Korea was a success. The brunt of the campaign was carried by FEAF bombers and Fifth Air Force fighters, but other aircraft—from Navy fighters to Fifth Air Force light bombers—assisted the B–29s in closing North Korean airfields. Moreover, there was a close and positive relationship between reconnaissance and fighter-interceptor squadrons. Without reconnaissance, FEAF could not allocate its B–29s among the most significant targets or know how much the B–29s accomplished. Without the Sabre screens, however, the reconnaissance aircraft could not survive their patrols. Finally, without coordination between Fifth Air Force and FEAF, the air superiority campaign would have fallen apart. The regularity of that coordination was no accident. It was built on World War II experience and maintained through close contact between Fifth Air Force and FEAF commanders and through the many visits of General Vandenberg, USAF Chief of Staff. The USAF's combat experience, gained in a number of theaters in World War II by officers and enlisted men at all levels of command, was an asset that the fledgling Chinese Communist Air Force could not overcome—even with extensive Russian aid and some direct Russian support.

Korea showed that war experience was as important as war materiel. The U.S. Army, Air Force, and Navy were short of the latter in 1950, but the three services made up for materiel deficiencies with officers and enlisted personnel skilled in wartime operations. Fortunately for U.N. air units, the large MiG fleet of the People's Republic of China chose to wage an air war in which the experience of U.N. air personnel made the difference between defeat and victory. That experience, coupled with a gradually mobilized U.S. war economy (which eventually produced improved aircraft and tactical nuclear weapons), was decisive. FEAF and Fifth Air Force commanders, for example, relied on lessons drawn from World War II experience as they dealt with each other and with their Army and Navy counterparts. As the official Air Force history of the war noted, the close cooperation between FEAF and Naval Forces, Far East, which had developed by the end of the war stemmed "from the fortunate personalities of the commanders concerned rather than from more stable dictates of command authority and organization."[116]

Indeed, the lesson of the air superiority campaign waged in Korea was that, in a "limited" war, USAF units would be engaged in a war of attrition—a war which they could contain and even win so long as their enemy fought on terms favorable to the USAF. Were the terms of combat to change (as they did in Southeast Asia), or were the political restraints on USAF action to grow more severe (again, as happened over North Vietnam in the 1960s), then the battle might turn in favor of the enemy. But Korea did not trigger a major reevaluation of USAF air superiority doctrine, primarily for two reasons. First, the war was perceived as unusual, as the consequence of diplomatic and political miscalculation. The USAF came out of the Korean conflict determined to avoid such a struggle in the future. Second, the combined campaigns of air superiority and air interdiction appeared to have succeeded, so the notion of restructuring the light attack and fighter elements of the USAF to meet new strategic and tactical requirements on the basis of war experience was not considered. There were significant postwar changes in USAF tactical air weapons and doctrine, but they were driven mainly by the introduction of tactical nuclear weapons, not by an assessment of combat in Korea. In a sense, the success of USAF F–86s and B–29s against the air and antiair forces of the People's Republic of China obscured the vulnerability of U.S. forces to well armed opponents operating from sanctuaries. It was a lesson the USAF and USN would relearn in Southeast Asia.

Notes

1. R. F. Futrell, *Ideas, Concepts, Doctrine: A History of Basic Thinking in the United States Air Force, 1907–1964* (Maxwell AFB, Ala., 1971), p 198.

2. *Ibid.*, p 178.

3. M. S. Knaack, *Encyclopedia of U.S. Air Force Aircraft and Missile Systems,* Vol I: Post-World War II Fighters (Washington, 1978), pp 61–62, 80.

4. J. R. Lind, Analysis of F–86 Fighter Encounters with MiG–15s in Korea–March through June 1951, *Memorandum No. 47* (Aug 1, 1951), Operations Analysis Office, Fifth Air Force, pp 5–6, in the U.S. Air Force Historical Research Center at Maxwell AFB (hereafter AFHRC).

5. Korean Evaluation Project, Report on Air Operations, Jan 16, 1951, Dept of the Air Force, pp 98–99, AFHRC.

6. *Far East Air Forces Report on the Korean War, 25 June 1950–27* July 1953, vol I, p 32, AFHRC.

7. Gen G. E. Stratemeyer, *Personal Diary,* entry for Jun 29, 1950, AFHRC.

8. R. F. Futrell, *The United States Air Force in Korea, 1950–1953,* rev ed (Washington, 1983), p 19.

9. *Ibid.*, pp 3–4, 35, 58–59; *Korean Air War Summary, June 25, 1950–July 27,1953,* Headquarters, Far East Air Forces, p 2, AFHRC.

10. Futrell, *The USAF in Korea, 1950–1953,* p 2.

11. *Ibid.*, pp 47–49.

12. *Ibid.*, p 46.

13. *Ibid.*, p 50, pp 151–52.

14. *Ibid.*, p 493. For line diagrams of Far East Command organization, see J. A. Field, Jr., *History of United States Naval Operations, Korea* (Washington, 1962), p 43, p 174.

15. Futrell, *The USAF in Korea,* p 51.

16. *Ibid.*, p 52.

17. *Ibid.*, p 55.

18. *Ibid.*

19. Intvw, Col F. E. Merritt, USAF Oral History Program, pp 27–28, AFHRC. Futrell, *The USAF in Korea, 1950–1953,* p 149.

20. J. A. Field, Jr, *History of United States Naval Operations, Korea* (Washington, 1962), p 169.

21. Futrell, *The USAF in Korea, 1950–1953,* pp 68–71.

22. *Ibid.*, pp 71–72.

23. W. Burch, *et al., History of Headquarters USAF, July 1, 1950 to June 30, 1951* (Washington, 1955), in the Office of Air Force History, Bolling AFB, Washington DC.

24. D. A. Rosenberg, "American Atomic Strategy and the Hydrogen Bomb Decision," *The Journal of American History,* 66 (June 1979), p 71. See also D. A. Rosenberg, "U.S. Nuclear Stockpile, 1945 to 1950," *The Bulletin of the Atomic Scientists,* May 1982, p 30; T. B. Cochran, W. M. Arkin, and M. M. Hoenig, *Nuclear Weapons Databook,* Vol I: *U.S. Nuclear Forces and Capabilities* (Cambridge, Mass, 1984), p 11.

25. Gen G. E. Stratemeyer, *Korean Diary*, vol II, entry for Nov 7, 1950, in AFHRC.

26. Gen O. P. Weyland, *The First Jet Air War*, FEAF, 1953, AFHRC.

27. Futrell, *The USAF in Korea, 1950–1953*, p 248.

28. *Ibid.*, p 302.

29. Lind, *Memorandum No. 47*, p 18.

30. Lt Col B. H. Hinton, "MiG–15 Versus F–86A in Korea," July 25, 1951, 35th Fighter Interceptor Group, pp 19–21, AFHRC.

31. Futrell, *The USAF in Korea, 1950–1953*, p 697.

32. R. F. Futrell, *United States Air Force Operations in the Korean Conflict, 1 November 1950–30 June 1952* (USAF Historical Study No. 72) (Maxwell AFB, Ala., 1953), p 118.

33. Hinton, "MiG–15 Versus F–86A in Korea," p 18.

34. Lind, *Memorandum No. 47*, p 23.

35. Futrell, *USAF Operations in the Korean Conflict, 1950–1952*, p 126.

36. *Ibid.*, p 123.

37. *Ibid.*

38. Hinton, "MiG–15 Versus F–86A in Korea," p 16.

39. *Ibid.*

40. F. W. Lanchester, *Aircraft in Warfare* (London, 1916).

41. Hinton, "MiG–15 Versus F–86A in Korea," p 7.

42. *Ibid.*

43. *Ibid.*, p 12.

44. Lind, *Memorandum No. 47*, p 11.

45. *Ibid.*, p 12.

46. *Ibid.*

47. Hinton, "MiG–15 Versus F–86A in Korea," p 9.

48. *Ibid.*, p 10.

49. P. J. Murphy, "Political Missions," in *The Soviet Air Forces*, P. J. Murphy, ed (Jefferson, N.C., 1984), p 295.

50. Hinton, "MiG–15 Versus F–86A in Korea," p 10.

51. *Ibid.*, p 8.

52. *Ibid.*, p 17.

53. Futrell, *USAF Operations in the Korean Conflict, July 1,1952–July 27,1953* (Historical Study No. 127) (Maxwell AFB, Ala., 1953), p 60.

54. Headquarters, 4th Fighter Interceptor Group, F–86 Activities Report, May 28, 1951, to Commanding General, Air Defense Command, AFHRC.

55. Hinton, "MiG–15 Versus F–86A in Korea," p 11.

56. Pacific Fleet Evaluation Group, CINC Pacific Fleet, *Korean War, U.S. Pacific Fleet Operations*, Interim Evaluation Report No. 1, Naval Air Operations (Attack), p 312, in Navy Dept Classified Operational Archives.

57. Interim Evaluation Report No. 2, Naval Air Operations–Air Defense, p 775.

58. Interim Evaluation Report No. 5, Chapter 3: Carrier Operations, p 3–46. See also Interim Evaluation Report No. 6, pp 3–83 through 3–90.

59. HQ, FEAF Deputy for Operations, Plans Directorate, FEAF Minimum Operational Requirements for the Korean Conflict, June 24, 1951, p 2, AFHRC.

60. *Ibid.*

61. *Ibid.*

62. *Ibid.*, p 3.

63. Futrell, *The USAF in Korea, 1950–1953*, p 404.

64. *Ibid.*, pp 410–12.

65. J. E. Johnson, *Full Circle, The Story of Air Fighting* (London, 1964), p 234.

66. Futrell, *The USAF in Korea, 1950–1953*, p 409.

67. HQ, Fifth Air Force, *Communications and Electronics in Korea*, Jan 1, 1952, p 7; HQ, FEAF, *ECM History During the Korean Conflict, June 1950 to July 1953*, p 13, both USAFHRC.

68. HQ Fifth Air Force, *Communications and Electronics in Korea*, p 6.

69. HQ, FEAF, *FEAF ECM History During the Korean Conflict, 1950–1953*, pp 5–6.

70. *FEAF Report on the Korean War, 1950–1953*, vol I, p 88.

71. *Communications and Electronics in Korea*, p 12.

72. HQ, FEAF Bombardment Command, Special Narrative Report, Bombardment Operations of 98th Bomb Wing, Sept 24, 1952, p 7, AFHRC.

73. *FEAF ECM History During the Korean Conflict, 1950–1953*, p 19.

74. Futrell, *The USAF in Korea, 1950–1953*, p 614.

75. *Korean War, U.S. Pacific Fleet Operations*, Interim Evaluation Report No. 6, Chapter 3: Carrier Operations, p 3–38.

76. Knaack, *Encyclopedia of U.S. Air Force Aircraft and Missile Systems*, Vol I: *Post-World War II Fighters*, pp 101–05.

77. Futrell, *The USAF in Korea, 1950–1953*, pp 616–17.

78. *FEAF ECM History During the Korean Conflict, 1950–1953*, pp 21–22.

79. *Ibid.*

80. *Korean War, U.S. Pacific Fleet Operations*, Interim Evaluation Report No. 5, Chapter 3: Carrier Operations, pp 3–70, 3–71.

81. Futrell, *The USAF in Korea, 1950–1953*, p 414.

82. HQ, 4th FI Group, History of the 336th FI Squadron for the Month of October 1951, in *History of the 4th FI Wing for the Month of October 1951*, Nov 1, 1951, p 6, AFHRC.

83. Futrell, *The USAF in Korea, 1950–1953*, p 418.

84. *Ibid.*, p 419.

85. HQ, 4th FI Group, FA 470, Jan 7, 1951, F86–A5 Armament: Report of Conference with Active Pilots, AFHRC.

86. HQ, 4th FI Group, FA 470, June 28, 1951, Recommendation Concerning Armament Equipment for Present and Future Fighter Type Aircraft, to CG, 4th FI Wing, AFHRC.

87. D. E. DeBeau, Study of Relationships Between Military Requirements and Design Characteristics of Turbojet Fighter Aircraft, Report No. 7, Ops Analysis, D/T&R, HQ, USAF, Apr 27, 1949, Box 12, Entry 208, Air Force Operations, Technical Operations Analysis Reports, 1945–1957, Modern Military Records Branch, National Archives and Records Administration, (MMB, NARA).

88. Ltr, to Gen E. E. Partridge, CG, Air Research and Development Command (ARDC), from Brig Gen C.Y. Banfill, Dep for Intelligence, subj: MiG–15 performance, Feb 19, 1952, Partridge Correspondence File, AFHRC.

89. Ltr, Gen. E. E. Partridge, CG, ARDC, to Maj Gen G. O. Barcus, CG, Fifth Air Force, subj: Fifth Air Force Problems, Jun 10, 1952, Partridge Correspondence File, AFHRC.

90. Ltr, Gen E. E. Partridge, CG ARDC, to Col J. C. Meyer, Air Defense Comm, subj: Modification of F–86Es in Korea, May 23, 1952, Partridge Correspondence File, AFHRC.

91. Futrell, *The USAF in Korea, 1950–1953*, p 651.

92. Futrell, *USAF Operations in the Korean Conflict, 1950–1952* (USAF Study No. 72), p 122.

93. Futrell, *USAF Operations in the Korean Conflict, 1952–1953* (USAF Study No. 127), p 66.

94. *Ibid.*, p 65.

95. *Ibid.*

96. *Ibid.*, p 64.

97. D. R. Stuart, Maj. E. E. Novotny, An Analysis of F–86, MiG–15, Engagements, Sept 1952 through April 1953, *Ops Analysis Memorandum No. 63*, June 5, 1953, HQ, Fifth Air Force, pp 4–7, AFHRC.

98. *Ibid.*

99. *Ibid.*, p 8.

100. I. J. Kessler, Aircraft Service Performance Evaluation: Maintenance Workloads Generated in Korean Conflict, Vol II, *Ops Analysis Report No. 10*, Jul 8, 1952, HQ, USAF, Dep Chief of Staff, Operations, AF Operations, Tech Ops Analysis Reports, 1945–57, Box 12, Entry 208, MMB, NARA. Also, I. J. Kessler, E. C. Helfrich, and E. A. Niccolini, An Evaluation of the Fifth Air Force REMCO System of Aircraft Maintenance as Applied to F84 and F86 Aircraft in Korea, *Ops Analysis Report No. 14*, Oct 20, 1953, same office and source as Report No. 10.

101. Intvw, Gen. J. A. Roberts, CORONA ACE series, Office of Air Force History, Feb 10, 1977, p 27.

102. Maj F. C. Blesse, "No Guts–No Glory," Nellis AFB, Nev., 1953, reprinted in *USAF*

Fighter Weapons Review, Spring 1973, p 15.

103. Johnson, *Full Circle*, p 279.

104. Futrell, *The USAF In Korea, 1950–1953*, p 607.

105. *Ibid.*, pp 637–39.

106. *Korean War, U.S. Pacific Fleet Operations*, Interim Evaluation Report No. 6, Chapter 3: Carrier Operations, pp 3–83. MiGs clashed with F9F Combat Air Patrol aircraft on Nov 18, 1952, during attacks by carrier aircraft on North Korean targets near the Russian border. Though outnumbered by the attacking MiGs, the F9Fs shot down two opponents and lost none. See Field, *History of U.S. Naval Operations, Korea*, pp 440–41.

107. J. T. Kenney, History of FEAF Participation in the Atomic Energy Program, Jul 1, 1953–Jun 30, 1954, HQ, FEAF, Office of Information Services, AFHRC.

108. HQ, FEAF, *FEAF Command Historical Report*, vol I, Jan 1953, p 28, AFHRC.

109. Kenney, History of FEAF Participation in the Atomic Energy Program, Jul 1, 1953–Jun 30, 1954, p 1.

110. *Ibid.*

111. Lecture, by Gen H. Vandenberg, Chief of Staff, USAF, to Air War College, May 6, 1953, AFHRC.

112. Kenney, History of FEAF Participation in the Atomic Energy Program, Jul 1, 1953–Jun 30, 1954, pp 4–5.

113. M. A. Olson and R. T. Sandborn, Aircraft Attrition in Korea, *Ops Analysis Technical Memo No. 31*, Ops Analysis Div, DC of Staff, Operations, HQ, USAF, Feb 11, 1952, p 10, Box 13, Entry 208, AF Ops, Technical Ops Analysis Reports, 1945–1957, MMB, NARA.

114. Intvw, Gen J. A. Roberts, CORONA ACE, p 28.

115. Futrell, *The USAF in Korea, 1950–1953*, p 498.

116. *Ibid.*, p 493.

Bibliographical Essay

Government Sources

Official records of the Far East Air Forces and the Fifth Air Force are held by the U.S. Air Force Historical Research Center at Maxwell Air Force Base, Alabama. Records of the Headquarters, U.S. Air Force, are stored in the National Archives in Washington, D.C. A number of Headquarters files are still classified, although the staff of the National Archives is in the process of gradually opening them for public examination. Relevant Navy records are controlled by the Navy Department's Classified Operational Archives in the Navy Yard in Washington, D.C. However, the Navy has not declassified as many of its records as has the Air Force. Because the air superiority campaign in Korea was largely an Air Force effort, the classified nature of the many Navy records does not pose a major problem to researchers.

The main official source for this chapter was the three–volume study of Air Force operations prepared by Robert F. Futrell, *United States Air Force Operations in the Korean Conflict*, Volume I: *June 25–November 1, 1950* (USAF Historical Study No. 71); Volume II: *November 1, 1950–June 30, 1952* (USAF Historical Study No. 72); Volume III: *July 1, 1952–July 27, 1953* (USAF Historical Study No. 127). The three volumes were printed, respectively in 1952, 1955, and 1956, and all were originally classified. In 1961, Futurell, with the assistance of L. S. Moseley and A. F. Simpson, published an unclassified account of Air Force missions and achievements in Korea that was based closely on the three–volume classified study. The title of their joint effort was *The United States Air Force in Korea, 1950–1953* (New York: Duel, 1961). Slightly revised, the same work was republished in 1983 by the Office of Air Force History. Thorough, readable, and accurate, *The United States*

Air Force in Korea has not been matched by anything written since.

In his original preface to *The United States Air Force in Korea,* Futrell suggested that "time and the completion of definitive Army and Navy service histories of the Korean War will undoubtedly provide additional historical perspective which was not available to the author ... but one may doubt that the Communists will ever provide any accurate and unbiased narrative of their campaigns in Korea. ..." Futrell was right on the second point, but—as far as the air superiority war in Korea is concerned—his first prediction has not come to pass. There are two areas where his work might well be supplemented, however. The first is the field of signals intelligence; the second concerns plans to use nuclear weapons against Chinese and Russian targets had the war widened or had Chinese and North Korean forces not honored the 1953 armistice. Fifth Air Force intelligence staff documents stored at the Historical Research Center do not rely on signals intelligence—at least not directly. Message intercepts and their analysis were classified at too high a level for day-to-day staff use. The same was true for planning documents describing alternative uses for nuclear weapons. It is possible, but not likely, that the eventual declassification of records in both subject areas will significantly add to the story so ably told by Futrell.

Finally, Futrell has also prepared a lengthy study of USAF doctrine which describes how the Air Force interpreted the war in Korea: *Ideas, Concepts, Doctrine: A History of Basic Thinking in the U.S. Air Force 1907–1964* (Maxwell AFB, Ala., 1974). This study ties together Air Force tactical, strategic, and organizational development and relates changes in Air Force concepts and organization to wartime operations.

Non–government Sources

There are a surprising number of interesting and accurate articles on the air war in Korea. They fall into three general categories: 1) general discussions of air operations or studies of the logistics required to support USAF units in Korea; 2) articles describing Sabre/MiG dogfighting; and 3) short studies of the bomber operations against strategic targets and airfields. In the first category, several merit mention here. One is "The Expanding Air Force: 1 January to 1 August 1951," in *Air University Quarterly Review* (hereafter cited as *AUQR*), Vol. 4, No. 4 (1951). The U.S. Air Force grew dramatically after the beginning of the war in Korea, and this essay describes its expansion and reorganization. In *AUQR,* Vol. 6, No. 3 (1953), Gen. Otto P. Weyland reviewed the Korean conflict's air operations ("The Air Campaign in Korea"), and Vol. 48, No. 4 (1953) of *Fortune,* the high costs of air operations in Korea are detailed. Logistics are covered by two *AUQR* papers: "Air Force Logistics in the Theater of Operations," by P. E. Ruestow, Vol. 6, No. 2 (1953), and "REMCO, A Korean War development," by C. G. Nelson, also Vol. 6, No. 2 (1953).

AUQR carried a number of short pieces on air–to–air combat, including "Two Years of MiG Activity," by J. G. Albright, Vol. 6, No. 1 (1953); "Eyes, Speed, and Altitude," by G. T. Eagleston and B. H. Hinton, Vol. 4, No. 4 (1951); "Flying Training in the Fifth Air Force," by L. G. Taylor, Vol. 6, No. 4 (1953–54); "Air-to-Air Combat in Korea," by Col. H. R. Thyng, Vol. 6, No. 2 (1953); and "MiG Maneuvers," Vol. 6, No. 4 (1953). These articles include descriptions of combat by pilots, discussions of training for jet fighter dogfighting, and comments on the differences between air-to-air combat in Korea and in World War II. There are also three important *AUQR* articles on B–29 operations: in 1953: "The Attack on Electric Power in Korea" (Vol. 6, No. 2), and "The Attack on the Irrigation Dams in North Korea" (Vol. 6, No. 4), both prepared by the *AUQR*'s staff, and in 1954, "Heavyweights Over Korea: B–29 Employment in the Korean War," by the staff of Bomber Command, Far East Air Forces (Vol. 7, No. 1).

Finally, there are two excellent unclassified and unofficial studies of fighter tactics that deserve mention. Without recourse to one or both, non–pilots will find it difficult to visualize what happened in the air over North Korea during the conflict. The first is "No Guts—No Glory," by Maj. F. C. Blesse (USAF). First prepared as a mimeographed pamphlet in 1953, Blesse's guide to shooting down a MiG was reprinted in *USAF Fighter Weapons Review*, Spring 1973. A much more detailed and technical discussion is R. L. Shaw, *Fighter Combat, Tactics and Maneuvering*, (Annapolis: U.S. Naval Institute, 1985), especially Chapter One.

10

Southeast Asia

Thomas C. Hone

Aircraft of the U.S. Air Force (USAF) and U.S. Navy (USN) dominated the skies over Southeast Asia from 1964 to 1973. In those nine years, Air Force and Navy aviation units carried out approximately twenty major operations in Southeast Asia. This chapter will focus only on those operations that required U.S. aircraft to conduct campaigns to gain and then hold air superiority against the opposition of the North Vietnamese Air Force (NVAF) and North Vietnamese ground-based air defenses. The code names and dates of those particular operations are as follows: ROLLING THUNDER (March 1965–October 1968), LINEBACKER I (April–October 1972), and LINEBACKER II (December 1972). Through the course of these three operations, U.S. aircraft regularly challenged the air units and air defenses of North Vietnam (the Democratic Republic of Vietnam). The government of North Vietnam, with extensive materiel support and advice from the Soviet Union, responded by constructing the most dense antiaircraft defense system in the world. Special and detailed rules of engagement, imposed by the Secretary of Defense through the Joint Chiefs of Staff (JCS) upon Air Force and Navy air units, made the struggle between air attackers and ground defenders unique in the history of U.S. military aviation. Indeed, the Joint Chiefs argued many times during the course of ROLLING THUNDER that the special rules of engagement and the targeting restrictions imposed by the Office of the Secretary of Defense and the President on U.S. air units attacking targets in North Vietnam made the air war there not just unique but bizarre.

This chapter is concerned primarily with USAF operations over North Vietnam. The U.S. Navy's air effort during ROLLING THUNDER, LINEBACKER I, and LINEBACKER II was substantial; given the concepts which then governed aircraft carrier operations, it was also unique. However, Navy air operations will be considered only tangentially in the sections that follow. That is less an omission than it might seem because Air Force and Navy air superiority tactics were very similar, and both services had as their general purpose fighter and attack plane the F–4 Phantom. The strategy imposed upon Navy and Air Force units assigned to attack North Vietnam during ROLLING THUNDER was also the same—a "graduated response" to convince the leaders of North Vietnam that their efforts to overthrow the government of South Vietnam would prompt steadily increasing U.S. military pressure. A special focus of the bombing was the transportation of war materiel from North to South Vietnam. During LINEBACKER I, U.S. aircraft also directly assaulted massed North Vietnamese army forces which rolled over South Vietnam's borders. In LINE-BACKER II, on the other hand, the Air Force was the premier force. For eleven days, B–52 bombers, supported by a variety of tactical aircraft, carried out a deliberate and highly accurate campaign of conventional bombardment against North Vietnam's capital and major port. Bombing raids of that intensity and type had not been conducted by U.S. air units since World War II.

Through each of these operations, USAF units gained and maintained control of enemy airspace despite attacks by MiGs, antiaircraft guns, and radar-guided surface-to-air missiles (SAMs). The means by which this control was achieved are the subject of the discussion that follows.

Background

On October 21, 1964, the Joint Chiefs of Staff, in a memorandum to the Secretary of Defense, noted:

> Application of the principle of isolating the guerrilla force from its reinforcement and support and then to fragment and defeat the forces has not been successful in Vietnam. The principle must be applied by control of the national boundaries or by eliminating or cutting off the source of supply and direction.[1]

The Joint Chiefs also argued that air strikes against North Vietnam would demonstrate the seriousness of the U.S. commitment to South Vietnam and so pressure the North to end its support of the Viet Cong.[2] The Joint Chiefs did not support the view that air strikes against North Vietnam should be used as a form of retaliation for Viet Cong attacks against U.S. personnel and bases in South Vietnam.[3] Rather, the Chiefs favored "a controlled program of systematically increased military pressures against the Democratic Republic of Vietnam applied in coordination with appropriate political pressures."[4] The President and his advisers, seeking to maintain the independence of South Vietnam without involving the United States in a major war, accepted the position that a "graduated response" to a deteriorating military and political situation in South Vietnam would allow them the chance to gain their objectives (independence of the South and deterrence of the People's Republic of China) without severely straining the military resources of the United States. They were supported in this position by the senior theater military commander, Adm. U. S. G. Sharp, Commander in Chief, Pacific. Sharp's position, communicated in February 1965 to the Secretary of Defense, was that "I would hope that we . . . will act . . . in terms of a 'graduated pressures' philosophy which has more of a connotation of steady, relentless movement. . . ."[5] Sharp emphasized that "any political program...for reaching agreement on cessation of a graduated military pressures program, will be successful in proportion to the effectiveness of the military pressures program itself."[6] In short, a display of force was not sufficient to achieve the goals of the administration of President Lyndon Johnson. The bombing of North Vietnam's roads, railroads, and bridges, however, would be both a signal to the North Vietnamese and a threat to their ability to support insurgent forces in the South. A bombing campaign carried on by the United States would show intent and commitment and achieve the goal of isolating the Viet Cong. Bombing could also be started and stopped with a word from Washington, depending upon the course of negotiations between the U.S. and North Vietnam.

The *Pentagon Papers* show that the bombing of North Vietnam was advocated early and promoted frequently by the Joint Chiefs during the crucial year of 1964, when, at President Johnson's request, the Department of Defense, the Joint Chiefs, the National Security Council, and the leaders of the U.S. effort in South Vietnam tried to develop a policy that would save South Vietnam at a cost acceptable to the United States. However, the *Pentagon Papers* also reveal that the Joint Chiefs and the Secretary of Defense eventually came to disagree strongly over the proper level of the bombing campaign necessary to achieve U.S. objectives. As Admiral Sharp had argued, the "graduated pressures" program had to be effective in order to push the North Vietnamese to an agreement that the United States favored. But "effective" meant one thing to Sharp and something very different to the President and his advisers in Washington. On July 1, 1965, for example, the Secretary of Defense prepared a draft memorandum for the President in which he advocated mining Haiphong harbor, attacking North Vietnam's road and rail bridges to China, and destroying North Vietnam's MiG airfields and surface-to-air missile (SAM) sites.[7] The Joint Chiefs supported this position.

By the end of the month, however, the Secretary of Defense had changed his views, and, by September 1965, the Joint Chiefs and the Secretary were locked in conflict, with the Chiefs steadily pressing for an enlarged air war and the Secretary—with the support of the President— only slowly and reluctantly allowing USAF and USN aircraft to strike more kinds of targets in North Vietnam.[8] The *Pentagon Papers* revealed how serious and sustained the policy conflict was within the U.S. government: Admiral Sharp and the Joint Chiefs arguing against Secretary McNamara, the Central Intelligence Agency, and specialists in agencies such as the Institute for Defense Analysis. There was even strong disagreement within the Department of Defense, such as when Secretary McNamara was opposed by the administration appointee who headed the Defense Department's Office of International Security Affairs. This ongoing and serious disagreement over the precise meaning of the policy of "graduated pressures" never allowed Admiral Sharp and others in charge of U.S. air units in Southeast Asia the kind of freedom to choose targets and schedule air attacks which they desired. Instead, the agreement on only the direction of policy but not its substance involved the President and his closest advisers in day-to-day air operations, which consequently generated great tension between theater commanders in Asia and their civilian superiors in Washington. Furthermore, U.S. air units operating against North Vietnam were compelled to accept limits on their operations that were tighter and less rational than those ever imposed on U.S. aircraft flying over North Korea during the Korean War of 1950–53.

The air superiority war fought by the U.S. Air Force in Southeast Asia cannot be understood without reference to the ongoing debate over just how to apply "graduated pressure" to North Vietnam. Beginning in 1964, the Joint Chiefs, on the recommendation of the Chief of Staff, USAF, pressed for a major effort early in the campaign. By the summer of 1965, the JCS thought they had won the support of the Secretary of Defense and the President. When Secretary McNamara recommended *against* mining Haiphong and destroying North Vietnam's air defenses, however, the battle in Washington was joined. The Joint Chiefs accepted bombing restrictions, which they in fact did not favor, but hoped they would be able to get the policy changed later. The effect of this "fight and talk" position of the Joint Chiefs on U.S. air units flying over North Vietnam was profound. The latter had to wage a limited "limited war" against forces which, until and unless the general policy changed, could not be defeated. While the Joint Chiefs and Admiral Sharp kept arguing for a wider, more intensive air war, USAF and USN aircraft had to gain and regain sufficient control of the skies over North Vietnam to achieve "limited" objectives, and, until 1972, they had to do it in the face of mounting North Vietnamese defenses which they could not readily counter.

In 1964–65, the USAF was not adequately prepared for such a "limited" unlimited campaign. The problem was not doctrinal but financial. One consequence of the decision by the Joint Chiefs and the President to accept restrictions on the bombing of North Vietnam was a war of attrition in which numbers of U.S. aircraft and pilots mattered a great deal. Yet, in 1965, the Secretary of Defense refused to allow the USAF to expand its aircraft production and pilot training facilities.[9] USAF Headquarters criticized this decision as short-sighted. When, in 1967, the Secretary of Defense ordered the Air Force to increase the output of pilots and planes on the assumption that the air war in Southeast Asia would last indefinitely, it was too late to overcome quickly the already reduced capability of USAF tactical fighter squadrons in Europe and the United States.[10] There were other problems as well. The F–105 Thunderchief, which had been designed after the Korean War as a means of delivering tactical nuclear weapons against large targets such as enemy airfields, was the mainstay of first-line USAF tactical air units in the early 1960s. But the F–105 was not designed for a continuing conventional bombing campaign; it lacked all-weather and night-bombing capability, for example, as well as the endurance for long-range missions. The F–105 was designed for a tactical nuclear war against the Warsaw Pact; the same was true for the tactics taught its pilots. Both plane and tactics were at a disadvantage when flying regularly against serious air defenses in North Vietnam.

As early as 1955, the United States had officially recognized that tactical conventional air forces could conduct "military operations in which destruction and physical domination of an opponent through capture and occupation of territory" were "expressly excluded."[11] However, there was not money enough to prepare USAF tactical aviation for both this role and that of supporting the "flexible response" strategy, which stressed the importance of tactical nuclear weapons use in a major confrontation with the U.S.S.R. in Europe.[12] In any lengthy limited war, for example, tactical electronic warfare would count heavily, as it had in Korea. Yet *tactical electronic warfare* was neglected. Again, as in Korea, ground radar control of friendly aircraft and ground integration of aerial intelligence would be crucial; but the USAF was not prepared to provide either when the air war over North Vietnam heated up in the spring of 1965.[13] The administration of President John F. Kennedy, which had come into office in 1961 pledging to maximize the flexibility and combat efficiency of U.S. forces, did not remove the funding problem but instead added to it by pressuring the Air Force to develop counterinsurgency plans and forces.[14] Despite such known limitations, the Air Force and the Navy were prepared to launch an air offensive of major proportions (including strikes by B–52 bombers) against North Vietnam in late 1964. Theater air commanders knew then and in early 1965 that North Vietnam's air defenses were weak, and they wanted to attack in force before those defenses could be strengthened.

509

The F–105 Thunderchief, which lacked all-weather and night-bombing capability, was at a disadvantage against air defenses in North Vietnam.

Chronology

In the Korean War, the U.S. Air Force gained air superiority early by destroying the North Korean Air Force and its airfields. The USAF maintained air superiority in Korea by preventing the air units of the People's Republic of China from using even those North Korean air bases that were located behind the positions held by Chinese armies in North Korea. In Korea, the USAF's air interdiction campaign went on behind a shield created and maintained by forces that shot down Chinese MiGs and cratered North Korean airfields. Chinese air units had a sanctuary, but they had to leave it to assault the USAF's protective fighter screen. In Southeast Asia, however, the USAF's protective fighter screen covered only Thailand and South Vietnam. The North Vietnamese Air Force (NVAF) operated from bases that were immune to attack until the air interdiction campaign was in its third year. In addition, the North Vietnamese gradually built up a large supply of surface-to-air missiles after July 1965, and the major entry port of that supply (Haiphong) was not mined until April 1972, seven years after U.S. aircraft began attacking North Vietnam's transportation network into the South. The special advantage granted the NVAF, added to the SAM threat, made Vietnam's air war different from Korea's. Over North Vietnam, the USAF and the USN had to gain air superiority as they carried out their air interdiction missions. The air superiority war paralleled the air interdiction campaigns; hence the chronology of the latter also applied to the air superiority effort.

Rolling Thunder, the first of the three air interdiction and pressure campaigns, lasted almost exactly three years. Its air superiority side can be divided into several stages, described briefly as follows:

1. *March 2, 1965–July 23, 1965:* USAF and USN aircraft began attacking North Vietnamese supply routes south of the 20th parallel and gradually shifted their assault north. For the first month of these attacks, U.S. planes faced no fighter opposition, but North Vietnam had been training a small air force, and its MiG–17 fighters first downed USAF aircraft on April 4. By mid-May, U.S. fighters flying cover for strike formations (mainly F–105s) had countered the MiG threat. After July 10, NVAF MiGs avoided combat with U.S. planes for nearly eight months.

2. *July 24, 1965–March 1966:* North Vietnam fired the first of thousands of SAMs against U.S. aircraft on July 24. To counter the new and serious threat, U.S. air units developed electronic warfare SAM suppression aircraft and tactics. North Vietnam also began to increase its antiaircraft artillery strength to the point where, in selected areas, it surpassed in density similar artillery concentrations during World War II and Korea.[15]

3. *April 1966–February 13, 1967:* North Vietnam's air force again attacked USAF and USN aircraft, particularly the former's electronic jammers. The NVAF began employing the MiG–21 high-altitude interceptor at the beginning of this period, and by early 1967, the North Vietnamese had an integrated, layered air defense system, which required U.S. planes to employ special electronic warfare equipment and tactics. In response to the increased intensity of the war in South Vietnam, U.S. air units attacked some of North Vietnam's oil refineries, industry, and power plants, and USAF fighters mounted a major effort (Operation Bolo) to shoot down NVAF MiGs (January 1967).

4. *February 14, 1967–December 24, 1967:* U.S. planes gradually wrecked North Vietnam's power plants and industries, even targeting facilities that had been in sanctuaries. North Vietnam's military airfields were also attacked, with the exception of the main airport (Gia Lam) near Hanoi. The NVAF, at first unable to overcome U.S. aircraft formations in combat, developed new tactics in September that exploited the rules of engagement governing U.S. aircraft and temporarily threatened U.S. air superiority. By the Christmas holiday bombing halt, however, U.S. air units had driven the NVAF into its sanctuary in China.

5. *January 1968–March 1968:* U.S. planes ranged over North Vietnam, bombing in response to the Tet Offensive in South Vietnam. The major threat to U.S. aircraft at this time was antiaircraft artillery.

On March 31, 1968, President Lyndon Johnson limited the interdiction effort to the portion of North Vietnam below the 20th parallel. U.S. aircraft patrolling that area also were authorized to attack confirmed SAM sites; U.S. air commanders wanted to keep the North Vietnamese from constructing the same kind of air defense in the area of the Demilitarized Zone that already existed around Hanoi and Haiphong. After November 1, U.S. interdiction in North Vietnam ceased. However, USAF and USN air units continued to conduct numerous armed reconnaissance flights over North Vietnam for over three more years, and U.S. aviation carried on air operations in Laos that had been initiated to support the Royal Laotian Government or to sever the Ho Chi Minh trail in central and southern Laos. These actions of reconnaissance and interdiction did not have an air superiority side, however, so they fall beyond the scope of this paper.

At the beginning of April 1972, the North Vietnamese Army invaded South Vietnam across the Demilitarized Zone that separated the two countries, through South Vietnam's Central Highlands, and toward Saigon, from

A Soviet-supplied North Vietnamese SA–2 Guideline surface-to-air missile (SAM).

Cambodia. U.S. air units—both Air Force and Navy—responded with a rapid buildup that focused on the attacking enemy forces. U.S. aircraft quickly gained and then maintained control of the air over the areas of South and North Vietnam adjacent to the Demilitarized Zone. U.S. airpower also sealed the port of Haiphong and brought the new technology of "smart" bombs to bear on North Vietnam's transportation network. Previously frustrating limits on U.S. bombing were largely lifted, and LINEBACKER I (as the 1972 interdiction campaign was called) closely resembled the campaign advocated by the Joint Chiefs of Staff in November 1964. LINEBACKER I ceased on October 22, 1972, when the U.S. appeared to have reached an agreement with North Vietnam to end the fighting and to negotiate a political settlement with South Vietnam. On December 18, U.S. B–52s bombed Hanoi for the first time in the war. The negotiations had collapsed, and the B–52s and associated Air Force tactical aircraft kept up the bombing day and night as the administration of President Richard Nixon attempted to force the North Vietnamese to agree to a settlement. The B–52s halted their high-altitude conventional attacks after eleven days, and the air superiority war finally ended. In three major campaigns stretching over four years, USAF and USN fighters, bombers, and reconnaissance aircraft had never lost the ability to operate at will over North Vietnam. Their overall record of success, however, was not easily achieved, and U.S. air units found it necessary to modify and develop continuously their tactics and equipment in order to adapt to the growing sophistication of North Vietnamese air defenses.

ROLLING THUNDER Background

The first ROLLING THUNDER bombing conducted by Air Force and Navy aircraft were continuations of Operation FLAMING DART, a series of raids in February 1965 against targets in North Vietnam's southern panhandle. Both operations were planned as reprisals for Viet Cong attacks on U.S. air bases in South Vietnam. ROLLING THUNDER, however, became the generic name for the air interdiction campaign, which gradually developed from the reprisal attacks. By the end of March 1968, U.S. planes had flown over 300,000 tactical air sorties against North Vietnam,[16] yet through most of the 37 months of ROLLING THUNDER, U.S. pilots were constrained by strict rules governing what ground targets could be attacked and when air targets could be engaged.

These Rules of Engagement (ROE) could be prepared at one of three levels: the Joint Chiefs of Staff (JCS) in Washington (responding to direction from the President or the Secretary of Defense), Commander in Chief, Pacific (CINCPAC), or Navy and Air Force component commands that

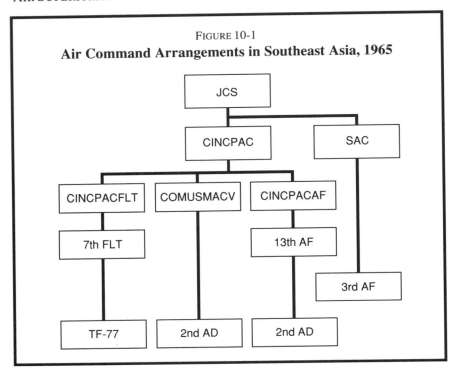

FIGURE 10-1

Air Command Arrangements in Southeast Asia, 1965

generated the specific sortie orders. (See Figure 10–1) Rules authored by the JCS covered actions in and over international waters, definitions of "friendly" and "hostile" forces, and responses of U.S. forces should attacks or threats by forces of the People's Republic of China occur. With guidance from the Joint Chiefs, Commander in Chief, Pacific (Admiral Sharp, in Hawaii) issued a number of operating restrictions. These rules defined specific geographical sanctuaries in North Vietnam, prohibited certain kinds of attacks, and set the requirements that had to be met before a suspected target could be engaged (visual identification of enemy aircraft, for example). Finally, Air Force and Navy commanders (usually in consultation with U.S. ambassadors to Laos, South Vietnam, and Thailand) in the theater issued operating rules, most of which governed the tactics of ground-attack missions, such as when certain weapons could be used to respond to ground fire against U.S. aircraft.[17] Together, these restrictions and guidelines were referred to as the Rules of Engagement, and U.S. aircrews were required to memorize them.

The Rules of Engagement that applied to ROLLING THUNDER in 1965 affected the air superiority campaign in the following ways:

1. The rules gave the North Vietnamese important geographical sanctuaries in their own country. The circular areas defined by a radius of 30 nautical miles (nm) drawn from the center of Hanoi was off-limits to U.S. aircraft. A similar but smaller exclusion zone (10 nm radius) was drawn around Haiphong. Attack were also forbitten in a zone along the Chinese border; near Loas, the zone was 30 nm wide, but it narrowed to 25 nm near the Gulf of Tonkin.[18] Within these sanctuaries, North Vietnam stationed its air force, stockpiled ammunition, and built an extensive radar network.

2. The rules freed the North Vietnamese from several major concerns. The Johnson administration, fearing possible intervention in the war by the People's Republic of China, did not close the port of Haiphong, or attack North Vietnam's irrigation and flood control system in the Red River delta, or seriously threaten North Vietnam with a seaborne invasion. As a result, North Vietnamese defense forces could concentrate their efforts and also be certain of a continuing flow of war materiel from the U.S.S.R.

3. Finally, the rules compelled U.S. aircraft to attack on clear days and only during the day unless and until very high bombing accuracies could be achieved through the use of sophisticated electronic equipment. In 1965, neither the USAF nor the USN had any choice but to bomb in clear weather during the day. Moreover, bombing attacks had to be followed by photoreconnaissance sorties, and further attacks were authorized only after a damage assessment had been made.[19] As a result, North Vietnamese air defense forces could predict the likely locations and times of U.S. air attacks—sometimes even down to the hour.

North Vietnam is not a large country. The distance from Hanoi to Haiphong is approximately 60 nm; from Haiphong north to China, the distance is 65 nm. The exclusion zones set by the 1965 Rules of Engagement covered two-thirds of the distance from Hanoi to Haiphong, and over half the distance from Haiphong to the Chinese border.

Moreover, U.S. aircraft could not pursue NVAF planes back to any airfields located in the Hanoi or Haiphong sanctuaries, even if the North Vietnamese aircraft attacked first. Relatively large areas were off limits to U.S. planes in North Vietnam. With Chinese territory as an additional sanctuary, much of the aerial battlefield was in fact a refuge for the North Vietnamese. Within one or another sector of that refuge, they based their fighter aircraft and later their SAM launching sites. As the *Pentagon Papers* later revealed, Admiral Sharp (CINCPAC) and the Joint Chiefs vigorously and regularly opposed the constraints placed on air operations by President Johnson on the advice of Secretary of Defense McNamara. As ROLLING THUNDER progressed, the pressure from CINCPAC and the Joint Chiefs, added to that of domestic political critics of the Johnson administration's war policy, gradually reduced the size of North Vietnamese sanctuaries

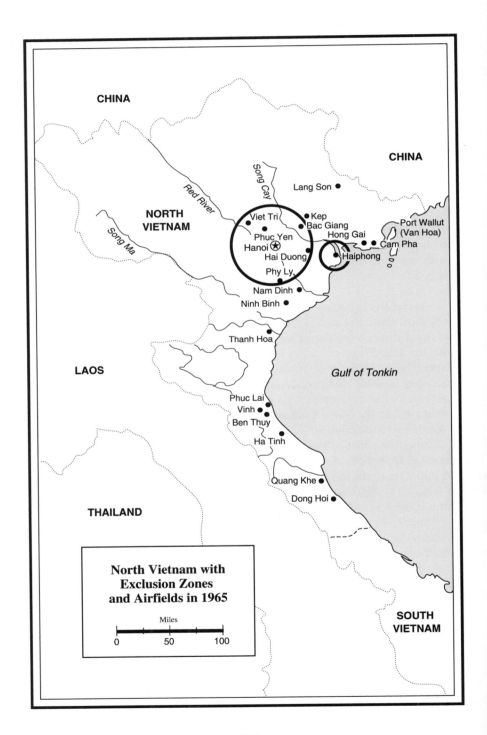

CHINA

CHINA

Song Cay

Red River

Lang Son ●

NORTH
VIETNAM

Song Ma

Viet Tri ●

● Kep
● Bac Giang
Hong Gai ●

Port Wallut
(Van Hoa)

● Cam Pha

Phuc Yen ●
Hanoi ✪

● Haiphong

Hai Duong ●

Phy Ly ●

Nam Dinh ●

Ninh Binh ●

Thanh Hoa ●

LAOS

Gulf of Tonkin

Phuc Lai ●
Vinh ●
Ben Thuy ●

● Ha Tinh

Quang Khe ●

Dong Hoi ●

THAILAND

SOUTH
VIETNAM

**North Vietnam with
Exclusion Zones
and Airfields in 1965**

Miles

0   50   100

516

and loosened the bonds that had restrained U.S. aircraft from striking many targets. By March 1968, the President had authorized the Joint Chiefs to reduce the size of the Hanoi and Haiphong sanctuaries; he had earlier authorized attacks on all NVAF airfields except Gia Lam.[20] During LINE-BACKER, in 1972, many of the restrictions that had affected ROLLING THUNDER operations were removed.[21]

To some degree, the obstacles created by ROLLING THUNDER's Rules of Engagement were offset by the proximity of U.S. bases to North Vietnam. With USN task forces steaming on "Yankee Station" as close as 60 miles to North Vietnam, U.S. air power had the southern panhandle of North Vietnam bracketed. Thailand had granted the U.S. permission in 1964 to use bases on its soil, and the bulk of USAF air strikes against North Vietnamese targets during ROLLING THUNDER originated at bases such as Ubon, Udorn, and Korat.[22] The approximate distances from those bases and from Da Nang to selected important targets are given in Table 10–1.

In effect, U.S. forces facing the North Vietnamese had sanctuaries of their own—Thailand, most of South Vietnam, and the Gulf of Tonkin. Air Force search-and-rescue teams also regularly ventured into Laos to retrieve downed U.S. aircrews. Though Navy units stationed in the Gulf of Tonkin were vulnerable to attack from the Chinese island of Hainan and the Chinese mainland, the People's Republic of China never used its own forces to combat the U.S. aircraft carriers and surface ships deployed off North Vietnam. In effect, the Gulf of Tonkin was an American lake.

The weather, on the other hand, favored the North Vietnamese. The USN, in particular, suffered because of it. When the prevailing monsoon

TABLE 10–1

Round-trip, Direct Path Distances from Selected U.S. Airfields to North Vietman

Destination	U.S. Airfields			
	Ubon (Thai)	Udorn (Thai)	Korat (Thai)	Da Nang (SVN)
Vinh	480	400	720	480
Thanh Hoa	640	480	800	600
Hanoi	800	600	960	720
Sepone (Laos) (Ho Chi Minh Trail)	140	220	300	140

Source: Aces and Aerial Victories (Washington: Office of Air Force History, 1976), p. 23.

winds were from the southwest—during June, July, and August—weather in the Tonkin Gulf was usually clear. In March and April, and September and October, the weather was uncertain. After November, the weather in the Gulf of Tonkin and over most North Vietnamese target areas was rainy and overcast. The Navy also had to ride out periodic typhoons: "In 1967, for example, it was Typhoon Billie in July. . . and typhoons Emma and Gilda in November."[23] The USAF strike forces attacking North Vietnam from Thailand did not have to worry about typhoons the way the Navy did, but the heavy clouds over target areas in winter months often made it difficult to positively identify MiG interceptors that North Vietnamese ground-control-intercept radars vectored toward USAF strike formations. Together, the rules of engagement—which required visual sightings before attacking an enemy fighter—and the weather hampered efforts by U.S. fighters to find and shoot down NVAF MiGs.[24]

From the beginning of ROLLING THUNDER in 1965 through LINE-BACKER I and LINEBACKER II in 1972, there was no single commander of *all* U.S. air assets employed against North Vietnam. In 1965, USAF air units in Southeast Asia were part of the Thirteenth Air Force, whose commander was headquartered in the Philippines. Thirteenth Air Force was subordinate to the Commander, Pacific Air Forces (PACAF), in Hawaii. In South Vietnam, air operations were controlled by the 2d Air Division, at Tan Son Nhut Airfield near Saigon. Second Air Division's chief was also the Air Component Commander subordinate to the Commander, U.S. Military Assistance Command, Vietnam (COMUSMACV). Navy carrier air units in the Gulf of Tonkin were organized as Task Force 77, which received its orders from the 7th Fleet and from the Commander in Chief, Pacific Fleet (CINCPACFLT) in Hawaii. Overall command in the Pacific was in the hands of the Commander in Chief, Pacific (CINCPAC), who reported in turn to the Joint Chiefs (JCS) and Secretary of Defense in Washington. The lines of command are illustrated in Figure 10–1. As the size of the USAF contingent in Southeast Asia grew during 1965, 2d Air Division's deputy commander was moved to Thailand and given operational control of Thai-based tactical strike and reconnaissance units. The purpose was to provide more coordination between aircraft flying into North Vietnam from South Vietnam and Thailand.[25]

As ROLLING THUNDER developed, it became clear that the command arrangements needed to be altered. The increase in USAF forces in South Vietnam and Thailand required a larger staff and more senior commanders and prompted the creation in April 1966 of the Seventh Air Force as a replacement for the 2d Air Division. The greater number of raids on North Vietnamese targets by Navy and Air Force planes also required a change. When Seventh Air Force was organized, its commander was made chairman of the Air Coordinating Committee. The function of the committee was to allocate targets and communications frequencies among U.S. strike

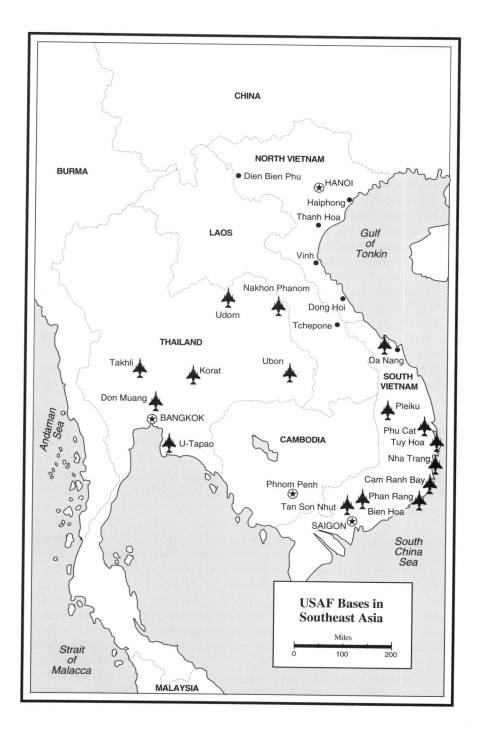

**USAF Bases in
Southeast Asia**

Miles

0   100   200

519

forces. To facilitate the committee's effort, CINCPAC, Admiral U.S.G. Sharp, divided North Vietnam into six geographic areas (called "Route Packages"). Route Package I was under control of COMUSMACV, with the Seventh Air Force planning and flying the missions. CINCPACAF, using Thirteenth and Seventh Air Force assets, was responsible for Route Packages V and VI A. The Navy was responsible for the remaining areas. The altered command structure is illustrated in Figure 10–2. Command integration existed at two levels: on the Air Coordinating Committee and at CINCPAC Headquarters, where orders were prepared for the Pacific Air Forces and the Pacific Fleet.[26]

This command structure was never satisfactory from the perspective of senior Air Force commanders. There was no overall theater commander of air assets, nor was there any Air Force/Navy joint staff. Even in South Vietnam, where the Commander, Seventh Air Force, was a component commander under COMUSMACV, interservice cooperation was limited to a formal liaison. Only in the fall of 1972 did the Army and Air Force staffs in Saigon really integrate, and only then because manpower cuts mandated by the President left senior officers little choice but to "put everybody together." On the other hand, Navy and Air Force cooperation improved as aerial surveillance and coded communications equipment became more sophisticated. In 1972, during the LINEBACKER operations, Navy and Air Force units found that the problems that had hindered their effective cooperation in the early years of ROLLING THUNDER had largely disappeared.[27]

The number of strike, reconnaissance, and fighter aircraft available to the 2d Air Division, and later to the Seventh Air Force, are given in Table 10–2. Table 10–3, which lists the percentages of aircraft types that were assigned to Southeast Asia for the years 1967–72, indicates how much of total USAF strength was assigned Seventh Air Force. Table 10–2 reveals the dramatic increase in USAF air strength during the course of ROLLING THUNDER, from 231 strike and strike support (reconnaissance, early warning, and electronic countermeasures) aircraft in June 1965, to 753 such planes 3 years later. Table 10–2 does not consider other forms of support, such as air-to-air refueling planes or search-and-rescue helicopters, even though the numbers of aircraft involved in such support operations also increased. In March 1965, for example, SAC had 4 KC–135 refueling aircraft based in Thailand; in 1972, during LINEBACKER I, the number was 110,[28] not counting additional tankers supporting B–52s and based on Okinawa. ROLLING THUNDER was a major campaign, involving large numbers of fighter and attack aircraft, and a significant percentage of overall USAF tactical aircraft strength.

Tables 10–2 and 10–3 also indicate that the USAF relied heavily on aircraft that were near the end of their useful operational lives. Primary examples were the F–100, the F–104, the RF–101, and the F–102. In 1964

TABLE 10–2

Tactical Aircraft in Southeast Asia Theater by Aircraft Type
1965–72

Aircraft Type	1965	1966	1967	1968	1969	1970	1971	1972
F–4C	18	190	160	47	48	0	0	41
F–4D	0	0	19	171	161	146	145	229
F–4E	0	0	0	0	79	66	71	126
F–100 D/F	69	87	198	273	203	170	59	0
F–104 C/D	13	8	16	0	0	0	0	0
F–105 D/F	79	126	132	108	70	65	12	30
RF–4C	0	19	60	75	81	56	37	38
B–55 B/C	10	18	19	35	30	6	15	19
RF–101C	25	28	25	16	18	NA	0	0
F–102A	17	22	23	22	16	4	0	0
EC–121D	NA	NA	6	6	6	6	3	4
Total	231	498	658	753	712	519	342	487

Note: These numbers reflect aircraft "on hand," which is a slightly larger figure than that for aircraft "ready." The "ready" figures, however, did not extend across all years. NA means "not available." The F–105s from 1972 were G model aircraft.

Source: USAF Statistical Digest, Fiscal Years 1965–1972, HQ, USAF Washington, D.C., Tables Eight and Nine.

and the early part of 1965, the major threat to U.S. planes attacking North Vietnam was antiaircraft fire, so older U.S. planes were suitable for missions over both North and South Vietnam. Table 10–4 gives the types and ranges of North Vietnamese antiaircraft guns. In September 1964, North Vietnam possessed only about 1,400 antiaircraft guns of all types, and they were supported by only 22 early warning and 4 fire control radars.[29] By March 1965, the North Vietnamese had increased the number of early warning radars to 31 and the number of fire control radars to 9, making it harder for U.S. strike forces to avoid damage. The 57-, 85-, and 100-mm guns could be radar-controlled; all fired proximity shells. The effectiveness of such weapons could be (and was) drastically increased by the use of early warning radars to track U.S. strike forces approaching and leaving target areas. Despite the growing number of antiaircraft gun batteries and supporting radars, however, what pushed the F–100 aside as an attack/ fighter plane for use over North Vietnam was the development of the NVAF and a system of surface-to-air missile (SAM) batteries. The F–100 still remained in the Seventh Air Force inventory through its effective life because it was useful in areas where the ground fire was less intense and

TABLE 10–3

Aircraft Assigned to Southeast Asia as a Percentage of USAF Aircraft of that Type, 1967–1972

Aircraft Type	1967	1968	1969	1970	1971	1972
F–4C	58	19	23	0	0	41
F–4D	4	28	32	31	35	59
F–4E	0	0	28	18	16	31
F–100 D/F	38	44	50	66	32	0
F–104C	94	0	0	0	0	0
F–105 D/F	50	41	46	48	12	45
RF–4C	27	30	30	20	14	15
EB–66 B/C	100	90	77	22	47	100
RF–101C	36	15	32	NA	0	0
F–102A	14	13	9	6	0	0
EC–121D	10	11	8	15	27	17

Note: These numbers represent the percentage of an aircraft type in Southeast Asia at the end of June of a given year.

Source: USAF Statistical Digest, Fiscal Years 1967–72, Tables Five and Eight or (in 1972) Tables Five and Nine, prepared by Headquarters, USAF, Washington, D.C.

TABLE 10–4

NVN AA Guns

Type	Most Lethal Range (ft)	Maximum Altitude (ft)
Quad 12.7-mm	1,000	5,000
Twin 14.5-mm	1,000	6,500
37-mm	1,000	10,000
57-mm	1,500-5,000	18,000
85-mm	5,000-10,000	25,000
85-mm	5,000-10,000	25,000
100-mm	3,000-20,000	30,000

Source: The Battle for the Skies Over North Vietnam, p. 122.

the air-to-air threat from enemy fighters non-existent.

Tables 10–2 and 10–3 also reveal a side to USAF activities in Southeast Asia that is frequently overlooked—the responsibility to deter any effort by the NVAF to attack U.S. air bases in Thailand or South Vietnam. The quickest way to gain air superiority was to attack an enemy's air force on the ground; the F–104s and F–102s were stationed in Thailand and South Vietnam to keep the NVAF from scoring any successes in raids by its small force of Il–28 jet bombers. Through 1967 and 1968, for example, Seventh Air Force kept a minimum of fourteen F–102s on five-minute alert at Da Nang and Udorn, with others on one-hour alert at Bien Hoa.[30] A squadron of F–104s was based in Da Nang in 1965 and then at Udorn in 1966 until replaced in July 1967 by F–4Ds.[31] These supersonic interceptors were part of Seventh Air Force's Southeast Asia area air defense. Their duties included stopping both NVAF bombers and efforts by NVAF MiGs to attack unarmed U.S. aerial tankers, airborne early warning planes, and electronic warfare platforms.

The tables on aircraft strength also demonstrate that strike support forces (reconnaissance, electronic warfare, aerial surveillance) were a major component of the USAF air contingent. In 1965, for example, RF–101s and EB–66s represented 15 percent of all tactical combat aircraft in Southeast Asia (see Table 10–2); in 1967, that figure was 17 percent (including EC–121s). As Table 10–3 shows, through much of the war, most Air Force EB–66 strength was assigned to the bombing campaign against North Vietnam. The function of the EB–66 was electronic warfare; its heavy use in Southeast Asia was just one indicator of the importance of electronic techniques to the U.S. air interdiction and air superiority campaigns. Table 10–5 supplements Tables 10–2 and 10–3 by listing the major U.S. airbases in Thailand and South Vietnam, along with the primary aircraft types and major combat units stationed at each base. Finally, Table 10–6, which presents total U.S. Navy and Air Force fixed-wing aircraft losses over North Vietnam as a percentage of all aircraft losses in Southeast Asia from all causes, tracks the ability of U.S. planes to continue air interdiction and survive in the face of improved enemy defenses.

The data upon which Table 10–6 is based also reveals that Air Force operations in Southeast Asia presented a formidable problem of base security. Many planes were damaged or lost through guerrilla attacks, or because of enemy small-arms fire from concealed positions located along landing and take-off approaches. As early as 1965, the Commander-in-Chief, Pacific Air Forces, requested aid from Chief-of-Staff, USAF, in implementing a comprehensive program of base security.[32] The Military Assistance Command, Vietnam, had taken the view that U.S. bases would be defended by South Vietnamese forces, but Gen. John P. McConnell, USAF Chief of Staff, thought U.S. ground troops should have that responsibility, and he asked the Joint Chiefs to pressure Admiral Sharp to imple-

TABLE 10–5

Major USAF Bases in Southeast Asia for Strikes Against North Vietnam During ROLLING THUNDER

Bases	Aircraft	Major Combat Units
Thailand		
Ubon	F–4C, F–4D	8th Tactical Fighter Wing (TFW) (from Dec 1965)
Takhli	F–105D, EB–66	355th TFW (from Nov 1965)
Korat	F–105D, EC–121	388th TFW (from Apr 1966)
Udorn	RF–101, RF–4C	432d Tactical Reconnaissance Wing (TRW) (from Sep 1965)
South Vietnam		
Tan Son Nhut	F–100 D/F, RF–101, RF–4C RB–66B, EC–121	460th TRW (from Feb 1966)
Bien Hoa	F–100 D/F	3d TFW (from Nov 1965)
Pahn Rang	F–100 D/F	35th TFW (from Apr 1966)
Cam Ranh	F–4C	12th TFW (from Nov 1965)
Tuy Hoa	F–100 D/F	31st TFW (from Dec 1966)
Da Nang	F–4C, F–4D	366 TFW (from Mar 1966)

Note: Unit identification for South Vietnamese bases applies only to ROLLING THUNDER.

Source: A Study of Strategic Lessons Learned in Vietnam, Vol VI, Book I, BDM Corporation (McLean, Virginia, 1980), p 6–10, 6–31.

TABLE 10–6

Fixed-Wing U.S. Aircraft Losses over North Vietnam as a Percentage of all Fixed-Wing Losses, 1966–1971

1966	1967	1968	1969	1970	1971
44%	45%	21%	.05%	2%	4%

Source: *A Study of Strategic Lessons Learned in Vietnam*, Book I, p. 6–58.

ment such a policy.[33] The other service chiefs declined, and, for the rest of the war, "the Air Force local ground defense mission did not extend beyond the legal perimeter of its installations."[34] As an official Air Force account of security problems noted, "apathy and indifference were only intermittently dispelled by a near-disaster such as the 1968 Tet Offensive," and "recreation facilities received top priority while defense works at obscure or remote locations were ignored."[35] Base construction was also a problem. Most airfields constructed or substantially modified for USAF use had to be built or altered by civilian contractors under Navy management. During 1965 alone, "16 new base supply and equipment management accounts were opened in South Vietnam and Thailand. Prior to 1965, Tan Son Nhut air base at Saigon had been the only major account in either country."[36] As an Air Force historian aptly put it, "Vietnam . . . was a small war when compared militarily with previous world wars, but logistically it was very much a large war."[37] It was also very demanding of the pilots who put ROLLING THUNDER in effect, as the North Vietnamese adapted quickly and often effectively to U.S. air efforts aimed at their territory.

ROLLING THUNDER Operations

ROLLING THUNDER was a complex military operation, which became more complex as North Vietnam worked to develop an integrated air defense system to thwart it. There is not space in this chapter to describe all the elements of the ROLLING THUNDER interdiction and pressure campaign. Instead, the focus will be on the air superiority aspects of ROLLING THUNDER. For example, before April 1965 there was no air superiority campaign because the only North Vietnamese defense was antiaircraft gunnery. The quality and intensity of North Vietnamese antiaircraft fire could and did complicate the air interdiction campaign, but antiaircraft guns never threatened U.S. control of North Vietnam's airspace. The war for the air began on April 3, 1965, when the small NVAF rose to combat U.S. strike aircraft. Though it began small (thirty MiG–15/17s in August 1964),[38] the NVAF rapidly grew, and it continued to challenge (though not necessarily to threaten) U.S. air superiority over North Vietnam through all the stages of the Vietnam War.

On April 4, 1965, four NVAF MiG–17s were maneuvered around a covering force of F–100s by North Vietnamese ground-control-intercept (GCI) radars to attack a strike force of F–105s. Two F–105s were lost to the MiGs over Thanh Hoa, seventy-six miles south of Hanoi. Without its bomb load, the F–105 was actually faster at all altitudes than the MiG–17, but the MiG was far more maneuverable, and North Vietnam's GCI radar net could place the MiGs in the path of incoming (and loaded) F–105s, forcing the USAF attack planes to either jettison their bombs prematurely or risk being shot down. (See Table 10–7) The F–100D was an inadequate escort for the F–105 for two reasons: it was not as maneuverable as the MiG–17 or as quick to climb. (See Table 10–8) The low wing loading of the MiG–17 gave it a tight turning circle, and its relatively high thrust/weight ratio gave it a quick acceleration which the heavier F–100D could not match. The Navy's F–8C had a thrust/weight ratio of .61 and good performance at higher altitudes, and, though not as nimble as the MiG–17, was able to employ its speed advantage when given sufficient room. The F–105D had been designed to carry tactical nuclear weapons; it was designed to approach targets at high speed and leave target areas at double the speed of sound. F–105 tactical doctrine against MiG–17s was simple—outrun them; "never try to out-turn or out-climb a MiG."[39]

To deal with the MiG–17s, the USAF 1) moved a detachment of EB–66 electronic warfare aircraft to Southeast Asia in April, 2) replaced the F–100Ds with F–4C Phantoms, and 3) in July, began flying patrols over the Gulf of Tonkin with EC–121 aerial early warning planes. The EB–66s carried radar jammers, which could mask the approach of U.S. strike forces and reduce the effectiveness of North Vietnamese GCI radars. The F–4C Phantoms were faster than the F–100Ds, quicker to accelerate, far faster in a climb, and equipped with their own air intercept radar. Though not as maneuverable as MiG–17s, the F–4Cs could use their treater power to determine when and how any air-to-air engagement would begin.

Phantoms also could carry AIM–7 Sparrow, AIM–9 Sidewinder, and AIM–4 Falcon air-to-air missiles. Sparrow was guided first by the Phantom's radar and then, in the proximity of its target, by its own radar seeker. Its range was twenty to thirty miles. Sidewinder could use infrared homing or be guided to tis target like Sparrow; its range as a radar-guided weapon was approximately ten miles.[40] With Sparrows and a shorter range missile, the F–4C did not need the maneuverability of a MiG–17 because it would

TABLE 10–7
F–100D, MiG–17F, F–105D and F–8C Comparison

Aircraft	Take-Off Weight (lbs)	Combat Radius (nm)	Maximum Speed (mph)	Armament
MiG–17F	13,000	500	710	three 23-mm guns
F–100D	39,750	460	860	four 20-mm guns
F–105D	52,500	570	1,300	one 20-mm gun
F–8C	27,550	520	1,000	four 20-mm guns, four Sidewinders

Note: Weights for F–100D and F–105D include standard bomb loads. Speed figures are approximate because measured speeds were given for each aircraft type at different altitudes.

Source: Jane's All the World's Aircraft, 1960–61 (London: Jane's, 1961), and *Encyclopedia of U.S. Air Force Aircraft and Missile Systems*, Vol I, M.S. Knaack (Washington: Office of Air Force Hisstory, 1978).

TABLE 10–8
Performance Characteristics: MiG–17F, F–105D, F–100D, and F–8C

Aircraft	Thrust/Weight Ratio	Wing Loading (weight/surface area)	Rate of Climb (ft per min)
MiG–17F	.57	50.1 lbs/sq ft.	10,500
F–100D	.42	103.2 lbs/sq ft.	4,100
F–105D	.50	136.4 lbs/sq ft.	34,000 (with afterburner)
F–8C	.61	7.35 lbs/sq ft.	8,700

Source: Jane's All the World's Aircraft, 1970–71 (London: Jane's, 1971)

527

never need to engage in a twisting, rolling dogfight. With its radar and guided weapons, the F–4C was meant to detect and destroy enemy aircraft before they came close. Over North Vietnam, however, the Rules of Engagement required U.S. aircraft to see those aircraft they attacked.

This requirement virtually negated the value of the Sparrow, which was designed to be used outside the range of the Phantom pilot's eyesight. Indeed, one advantage of F–4 series aircraft was that they carried two crew members—one to fly and one to monitor the plane's radar and engage targets beyond visual range. Over North Vietnam, however, a "target" might turn out to be a civilian airliner flying to Hanoi but outside the prescribed approach lanes, or—in 1965—a U.S. plane damaged and therefore straggling behind its parent formation. The areas of the Route Packages, VI A and VI B, north and east of Hanoi, that were open to attack were not that large, and, with Navy and Air Force attack groups striking adjacent sections, effective battle management was a challenge. A tight Rule of Engagement on air-to-air missile firings was one solution to that problem, but a negative consequence was the elimination of one of the advantages of the F–4's radar and air-to-air missile combination. In effect, the F–4Cs assigned to escort F–105s could use only Falcons and Sidewinders, and the Falcon was not available in 1965.

The key to dealing with the MiG threat, however, turned out to be the introduction of the EC–121 aerial early warning radar surveillance planes. With both endurance and radars of great range, these aircraft could detect MiGs taking off from airfields within North Vietnam's sanctuaries. This early warning proved to be decisive. The combat radius figures from Table 10–7 are the clue to why that was so. USAF strike forces flying from Thailand to the area near and north of Hanoi had to refuel inflight. Even with inflight refueling, however, the fuel margins for aircraft hitting targets in Route Package VI A were tight. The NVAF would attempt to hold its MiGs until the last possible launch time in order to give them a fuel advantage over the U.S. F–4s. If the F–4s could be alerted to the launch of MiGs as soon as the enemy planes were in the air, their usefulness as escorts would be much greater. The EC–121s, working under the code names BIG EYE and COLLEGE EYE, gave the Phantom escort flights the warning they needed to organize an effective defense. By the end of the second week of July 1965, the NVAF was compelled to withdraw from the aerial battle. The combination of EB–66s, F–4Cs, EC–121s, and Sidewinders had thwarted the threat of its MiG–17s.

On July 24, 1965, the North Vietnamese launched the first of thousands of SA–2 surface-to-air missiles against U.S. strike aircraft. The SA–2 was a radar beam-rider with a range of about 25 nm. When near its target, it was guided to an intercept by its own radar seeker. Before the SA–2s appeared, U.S. aircraft avoided much enemy ground fire by flying above it.[41] The SA–2s, most effective at altitudes near 20,000 feet, ruled out this tactic.

528

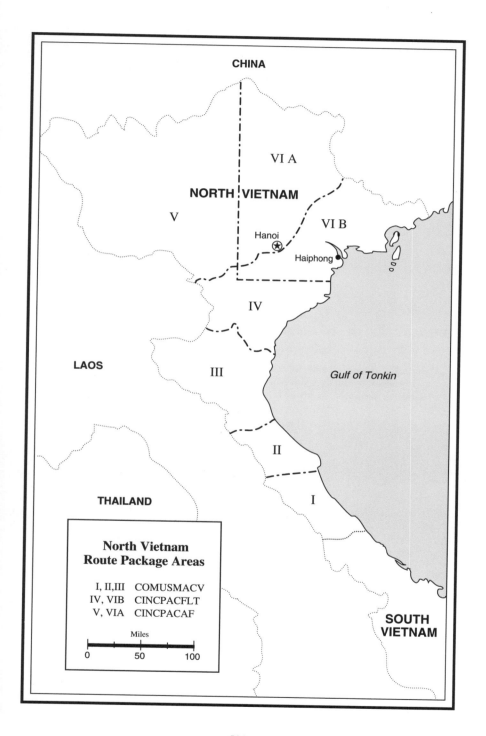

CHINA

VI A

NORTH VIETNAM

V

VI B

Hanoi

Haiphong

IV

LAOS

III

Gulf of Tonkin

II

THAILAND

I

**North Vietnam
Route Package Areas**

I, II, III   COMUSMACV
IV, VIB   CINCPACFLT
V, VIA   CINCPACAF

Miles

0   50   100

SOUTH
VIETNAM

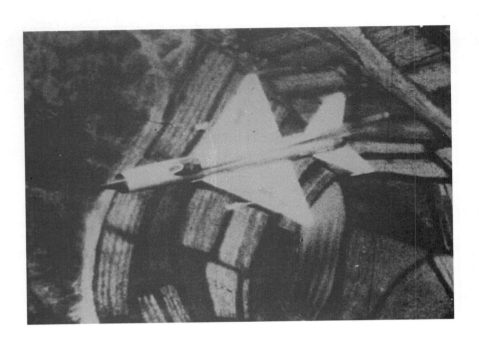

Above: The missile-armed, Soviet-built MiG–21 Fishbed contested the USAF for air superiority over North Vietnam; *below*: A Sparrow air-to-air missile mounted on an F–4C.

The SA–2, however, was not effective at low altitudes, before its flight path had stabilized, so it was possible to reduce its effectiveness by approaching and leaving target areas at low altitudes (under 5,000 feet). After August 1965, F–105 strike aircraft would penetrate an area protected by SAMs at 4,500 feet and then pop up to 10,000 feet in order to roll in on the target.[42] Unfortunately, this tactic drastically increased the effectiveness of North Vietnamese antiaircraft artillery. The introduction of the SA–2 also made flying escort or barrier missions to counter MiGs far more risky. Phantoms dared not prowl for MiGs at altitudes where U.S. pilots could see the farthest. Fortunately, the F–4 was a good climber (approximately 45,000 feet per minute for all models at combat weight with maximum power using afterburners for brief periods).[43] It could head off MiGs with its strong acceleration. The timing, however, had to be precise; otherwise, the F–4 would find itself tailed by several SAMs.

The SA–2 and its associated fire control radars were a major challenge to U.S. air superiority over North Vietnam. It was not that the missiles were unavoidable; U.S. pilots soon learned that the SA–2 could be out-maneuvered by a hard diving turn toward the missile's flight path followed by "an abrupt four-G rolling pull-up" at high speed.[44] The problem was that it was cheaper to operate the missile/radar system than it was the U.S. aircraft/jammer/aerial tanker/complex communications system opposed to it. SAMs were also a major threat to photoreconnaissance aircraft, which the North Vietnamese knew would always follow an attack by U.S. strike forces. When a strike was in progress, North Vietnamese SAM directors had to combat EB–66 jamming and allocate a limited number of SA–2s among a group of rapidly maneuvering targets. When photoreconnaissance planes made their passes, however, the targeting problem was simplified, and SAM barrages threatened to cut off the reconnaissance data which the Rules of Engagement required.

Three tactics were developed to reduce the SAM threat. The first was to employ several F–105s in each strike force to attack SAM sites before the bulk of the attacking planes showed over the target. This tactic failed because the North Vietnamese learned to turn off their S-band (2,000-4,000 MHz) SAM fire control radars until the strike aircraft neared, leaving insufficient time for the SAM-suppression aircraft to make their attack. The North Vietnamese also emplaced SAM batteries and their fire control radars in the sanctuaries around Hanoi and Haiphong, where they were immune to attack. Other SAM sites, outside the immune zones, were surrounded by a steadily increasing armory of light and medium-caliber antiaircraft guns, which served as a shield against U.S. SAM-suppression attacks. Finally, the SA–2 and its fire control radar were mobile, so attempts to roll back SAM batteries often expended ordnance on empty sites.[45]

The second anti-SAM technique was jamming. EB–66s acted in coor-

USAF EC–121 early warning radar surveillance aircraft in flight over South Vietnam.

dination with attack formations to mask the approach of U.S. aircraft. There were two types of jamming: spot jamming, in which a high level of noise at the bandwidth of the ground tracking radar was beamed back at it, and barrage jamming, in which the EB–66 sent out pulses across a range of radar energies in order to confuse several radars, any one of which might be operating. Spot jamming was employed where and when the frequency of the ground radar was known; where it was not, barrage jamming was used. The effect of jamming was to cloud the radarscope of the ground-based system, thereby covering the radar echoes marking the actual positions of U.S. planes. With effective jamming, the approach of U.S. strike formations could be disguised.[46] The EB–66s were capable of jamming both early warning and fire control radars, but the effectiveness of jamming fire control radars fell off with distance. Unfortunately, the threat of SAMs and MiG attack kept the unarmed EB–66s beyond the effective range for interfering with fire control radars, but the jamming planes were still employed against North Vietnam's early warning radars, which had relatively great range.

Because of its focused effect, spot jamming was more effective than barrage jamming. However, spot jamming depended on accurate intelligence concerning North Vietnamese radar frequencies. Where that was not available, the less effective barrage jamming was used. To obtain data on North Vietnamese early warning radars, EB–66s and even KC–135 tankers recorded North Vietnamese transmissions.[47] The North Vietnamese responded to jamming with a variety of countermeasures: overriding the jamming static with more powerful signals, switching radar broadcast frequencies, and working radars of different frequency in pairs, so that the second only broadcast when the first was jammed. More modern North Vietnamese radars measured the energy level of returning signals. Higher energy returns (the jamming signals produced by the EB–66) were filtered out, leaving the original signals unaffected. EB–66 crews countered this defense by matching the strength of their jammer signals to the echo or return of the signal broadcast by the enemy transmitter.[48]

Jamming was well worth the effort, but it was not possible to jam SA–2 fire control from strike aircraft in August 1965, and the EB–66s did not have the capability to operate in high threat areas over North Vietnam without an escort of F–4s. In addition, jamming could draw SAM fire, risking the jammer itself, as SA–2s guided along the jamming beam. On November 3, 1965, however, the base at Korat, Thailand, welcomed four F–100F "Wild Weasel I" Radar Homing and Warning Aircraft, and these specially equipped planes flew their first combat mission on December 3. The Wild Weasels carried receivers which could detect and discriminate among the GCI, early warning, and SAM fire control radars deployed in North Vietnam. The equipment on the special planes could also detect radar emissions from SA–2s and from any airborne-intercept radars that might be carried by NVAF MiGs. The F–100Fs also carried special cameras and recording devices to gather intelligence on SAM fire control radar.[49] With Wild Weasels in company, a strike formation would know when it was being tracked, when it was being "illuminated" by SAM fire control radars, and where the illuminating radars were located. Because their electronic equipment operated passively, as opposed to jammers, which were active, Wild Weasels did not attract SAMs. Moreover, they could direct SAM-suppression F–105s (christened "Iron Hand") to the area of SAM radar transmitters, making life hot for North Vietnamese radar operators. Together, Wild Weasel and Iron Hand were a major counter to the SA–2 fire control radar. Though the SA–2 could also be guided optically until its terminal phase, the continued use of Wild Weasel and Iron Hand drastically reduced SAM effectiveness.[50]

In April 1966, Wild Weasel F–100Fs were first equipped with AGM–45 Shrike radar homing missiles. With Shrike, the F–100Fs could effectively and quickly attack any SA–2 fire control radars that broadcast near them. SA–2 radar operators could avoid attack by turning off their sets, but then they could no longer target U.S. planes. SAM effectiveness dropped even more with Shrike use; in 1965, one U.S. aircraft was shot down for every thirteen SAMs fired; with Shrike, Wild Weasel strike escorts were more than doubling the number of missiles needed to down a U.S. plane.[51] In response, the NVAF, equipped by now with MiG–21s as well as MiG–17s, rose from its protected bases at Hoa Lac, Kep, and Kien Am to challenge U.S. strike forces. On April 23, two flights of MiG–7s under GCI radar control attacked a formation of USAF F–4Cs, and two of the attackers were destroyed with no loss to the F–4s. On April 25 and 26, MiG–21s attacked a single EB–66 orbiting over North Vietnam; F–4Cs intervened and downed one MiG.[52] After April, the North Vietnamese began using MiGs, SAMs, and antiaircraft guns together. The MiGs were directed toward the approach and departure routes of U.S. strike forces, while SAMs and guns covered the sky routes in the areas immediately adjacent to likely targets. The Seventh Air Force responded by increasing the number of F–4 escorts, and their greater number helped deter MiG attacks. Unfortunately, enlarging strike formations (which now included F–105s, Wild Weasels, Iron Hand F–105s, and escorting F–4s) made the formation harder to manage and provided more targets for SAMs and antiaircraft guns. Larger formations also complicated the tasks of air traffic controllers and air refueling squadrons.

In 1965 and early 1966, the 2d Air Division created several Tactical Air Control Centers to monitor and direct air operations in Route Packages V and VI A and over Laos. Subordinate centers were established in 1966 to coordinate Seventh Air Force traffic over friendly and enemy territory and to communicate with the Navy's radar picket ships in the Gulf of Tonkin. Charged with managing area air defense, area air transport, close air support of U.S. and South Vietnamese forces, search and rescue missions, and aerial refueling operations, the Tactical Air Control Centers at Tan Son Nhut, Udorn, and Monkey Mountain (Da Nang) faced a major air traffic problem.[53] As the size of USAF strike forces grew in 1966, for example, the need for an organized system of aerial refueling increased accordingly. Through its liaison office with the Seventh Air Force at Tan Son Nhut air base near Saigon, the Strategic Air Command developed a scheme to refuel 7th Air Force strike forces from KC–135 tankers. The basis for the plan was a set of refueling stations. The tankers met strike aircraft heading toward North Vietnam and then, again, on their way back. The trick was to place the tankers and the planes that needed refueling in the same area simultaneously, so as to make optimal use of the limited number of tankers and to preserve valuable F–105s, F–4s, and aircrews. It took all the skills of Tactical Air Control Center air controllers, using U.S. GCI radars, to keep order in the air refueling ovals. As a Strategic Air Command historian noted:

> ...as many as 54 aircraft often used the same refueling anchor at the same time. These would consist of three cells of tankers, each operating at different altitudes (usually with 500 feet altitude separation). Each cell consisted of three tankers and each tanker refueled five receivers. On...average, a single tanker sortie provided seven refuelings, offloading . . . 55,000 pounds of fuel.[54]

It was an impressive achievement, and it proved that routine aerial refueling operations for tactical aircraft were feasible.

Through the summer and fall of 1966, the air interdiction campaign

Above: Aerial view of the Monkey Mountain radar site overlooking Da Nang air base and the city's harbor; *below*: In-flight refueling of a B–52 by a KC–135 jet tanker.

continued. U.S. aircraft devastated North Vietnam's petroleum refining and storage facilities in June and July; in September, ROLLING THUNDER air strikes were directed against transportation routes. In Washington, the Central Intelligence Agency argued that the interdiction campaign was not achieving its objectives, the Joint Chiefs pressed for a more intensive bombing effort, and the President temporized.[55] In Southeast Asia, Seventh Air Force F–105s began receiving externally carried jamming pods at the end of October. The pods held barrage jammers. "If flight members maintained proper distances, the ECM pods denied the ground radars range, bearing, and altitude information."[56] The effect of the pods, combined with the proper formation of F–105s, was cumulative; when coupled with the spot jamming done by the EB–66s, the impact on North Vietnamese radars was dramatic.[57] The NVAF responded by aggressively attacking F–105s, particularly with MiG–21s, and that posed a problem for the F–4Cs escorting the F–105s. The MiG–21 had a higher service ceiling than the F–4C (42,000 feet versus 36,000 feet). Directed by GCI radars, MiG–21s attacked U.S. strike formations from above, making one diving pass, sometimes firing a heat-seeking missile, and then zooming away. In their dives, the MiG–21s did not give escorting F–4Cs time for a missile shot, and the Phantoms, because of the danger that MiG–17s might pounce on F–105s from below, dared not fly as a high-altitude screen between the F–105s and the MiG–21s. Yet the F–4 was faster than the MiG–21 and possessed a higher rate of acceleration. The trick was to free the F–4 from its escort role.

On January 2, 1967, 14 flights of F–4Cs, 6 flights of F–105 Iron Hand SAM suppressors, and 4 flights of F–104 covering fighters departed from Ubon (8th Tactical Fighter Wing) and Da Nang (366th Tactical Fighter Wing) and converged on Hanoi as part of Operation BOLO, a scheme to lure MiG–21s out of their sanctuaries and into the clutches of Seventh Air Force Phantoms. The F–4Cs (half from Ubon, half from Da Nang) mounted the jamming pods, which had been carried previously only by the F–105s. The plan was to have them imitate F–105s and so draw NVAF MiGs out for a dogfight. Though the force from Da Nang was forced to turn back because of poor weather, the "bait" from Ubon was challenged by MiGs from Phuc Yen, fifteen miles northwest of Hanoi. Three flights from the 8th Tactical Fighter Wing downed seven MiG–21s "within 12 minutes of combat."[58] Four days later, a second, smaller group of F–4Cs, disguised as a reconnaissance flight, attracted more MiG–21s and shot down two. Apparently reacting to such one-sided encounters, the North Vietnamese Air Force avoided USAF formations until February 1967.[59] BOLO showed that MiG–21s could be defeated by F–4Cs; unfortunately, in February and March Seventh Air Force units were ordered to attack new ground targets (steel manufacturing facilities) and there was no time to stage any repeats of the operation of January 2.

In April, the President authorized attacks on Hanoi's electric power system and on NVAF airfields. On April 24, F–105s and F–4s caught NVAF MiGs on the ground at Kep (thirty miles northeast of Hanoi), Hoa Lac, and Kien An, destroying nine.[60] The F–4Cs carried both jamming and 20-mm gun pods, for which they paid a performance penalty, but having guns solved one major problem. The goal of an attacking MiG was to maneuver into a three-dimensional "cone of vulnerability" which spread out from the rear of a Phantom; the Phantom would try to do the same to the MiG. What made dogfighting over North Vietnam so difficult in 1967 and later was that there were two cones of vulnerability—one for guns (MiG–21s carried two 30-mm) and another for heat-seeking missiles. The basic defense against an attack was to turn sharply into the attacking aircraft, in order to rotate the cone of vulnerability away from the attacker's weapons. But heat-seeking missiles had a greater range than guns, and turning to avoid the missiles reduced aircraft speed and increased the vulnerability of the turning aircraft to a gun attack staged by an attacker and his wingman. In a dogfight between aircraft armed with guns, two-plane elements tried to stay together, the leader pressing attacks while his wingman watched their cone of vulnerability. This tactic could be thwarted by a pair of attacking planes firing missiles first and then guns. If the attacking pair could stay together, they could separate their opponents and use guns to attack each separately. To counter this tactic, the defenders needed high speed and acceleration, lots of reserve altitude, and extremely close coordination. Before April 1967, MiG–21s could confront F–4Cs with both gun and missile threats; after April, the F–4Cs could do the same to the MiGs, and MiG–21 effectiveness declined.

May through July 1967 witnessed the confrontation of 2 integrated air superiority systems—the North Vietnamese combination of SAMs (over 200 sites, now all manned),[61] antiaircraft guns (about 7,500, or perhaps 5 times as many as U.S. planes faced over North Korea in 1952–53),[62] and MiGs (75 MiG–17s, MiG–19s, and MiG–21s)[63] against U.S. Wild Weasel, Iron Hand, Combat Air Patrol F–4s, KC–135 tankers, COLLEGE EYE aerial early warning aircraft, EB–66 jammers, and a communications and control network which linked surveillance aircraft, ground command centers, and F–105/F–4 strike formations. The goal of the North Vietnamese was air denial; U.S. forces had to maintain the freedom to strike all assigned targets. Despite the large numbers of U.S. planes and the growing sophistication of U.S. communications and electronic warfare techniques, the tactical advantage still lay with the North Vietnamese. They could achieve a major reduction in the interdiction campaign's intensity by simply forcing U.S. strike aircraft to jettison their ordnance before reaching their targets. On the other hand, to not destroy U.S. planes was simply to allow them to return again, rearmed and—as it developed—better prepared. By May 1967, for example, USAF F–4s and F–105s were carrying deception as well as barrage noise jammers.[64] Deception jammers did not broadcast a continuous signal; instead, they automatically responded to the signals of ground-based radars and sent out echoes of the same frequency in order to confuse enemy radar operators about the range of the jamming planes. Barrage jamming clouded radar screens; deception jamming produced many more returns than the enemy antiaircraft system could engage. As in the case of barrage jamming, there were accepted countermeasures which the North Vietnamese could and did employ, but the advantage in the electronic war lay with the U.S. From the end of April to the middle of August 1967, the jamming done by large formations (32–40 aircraft) of USAF planes was so effective that few SAMs were fired while the formations preserved their integrity.[65] With the SAM threat reduced, U.S. strike forces could attack their targets in larger formations, thereby holding down the time bombing aircraft were exposed to antiaircraft fire. The added freedom from ground fire (SAMs and guns) had another positive consequence for USAF units: it was easier to attack NVAF air bases that were outside the newly narrowed exclusion zones around Hanoi and Haiphong, and one official source estimated that such attacks reduced U.S. Air Force and Navy aircraft loss rates by two-thirds over Route Packages VI A and B.[66]

There were other reasons why the U.S. possessed an advantage in the air superiority war. One was the introduction of all-weather strike aircraft. The Navy began using all-weather A–6 bombers in the winter months of 1966–67, and these planes were a success against targets such as power plants because their special radars could distinguish large structures from surrounding features.[67] The USAF employed SAC-supplied radar bomb directors based in Laos to track and guide F–105s to targets near Hanoi; though accurate enough to crater enemy runways, the director system required the penetrating bomber to fly the last sixty miles of its run to the target "with speed and altitude held very precisely,"[68] and that was a prescription for trouble. Nevertheless, the radar-directed attacks showed what might be done, as the North Vietnamese were to learn in 1972. In a related area, the Navy gave the North Vietnamese another taste of the future when, in March 1967, Navy attack planes successfully employed the Walleye television-guided glide bomb.[69] Walleye was not an instant success because its warhead was small and it was too expensive to produce in numbers large enough to sustain the interdiction campaign. Walleye did portend the trend toward "smart" ordnance, however, and that trend meant that the amount of time U.S. aircraft would need to spend over heavily defended targets in order to hit them would decline drastically.

The North Vietnamese responded to improvements in U.S. electronic warfare equipment and tactics and to attacks on Hanoi during August 11–12 by employing their fighter aircraft more aggressively. On August 23,

MiG–21s tried a new tactic. Approaching USAF formations from behind at very low altitude, the MiGs zoomed to high altitude, arced over and plummeted down through the U.S. planes, firing two infrared-seeking missiles (similar to Sidewinder) each. Then the MiGs split up and headed for a sanctuary—either China or one of the North Vietnamese fields still immune to attack (Phuc Yen or Gia Lam). This tactic was temporarily successful. In September, more than double the expected number of USAF strike aircraft were forced to dump their bombs short of the target in order to avoid MiG–21 attacks.[70] SAM sites also fired barrages of missiles on initial optical guidance, and SAM fire control radars were kept off the air as long as possible in order to avoid attacks by Wild Weasel and Iron Hand. In response, President Johnson authorized attacks on Phuc Yen and Bac Mai airfields near Hanoi. By December, most NVAF MiGs had fled to China, but the NVAF remained active, with MiG–21s and MiG–17s staging coordinated attacks on U.S. forces.[71]

The first 3 months of 1968 showed how the air superiority war over North Vietnam had become a matter of combat between missile and gun-armed high performance jet fighters. From 1965 through March 1968, the ratio of SAMs fired to U.S. aircraft downed by them rose from 13 to 1 to 200 to 1. Over the same period, U.S. losses to NVAF fighters grew from 1 percent of all U.S. aircraft lost per year to 22 percent. On the other side, NVAF MiG losses rose from 2 in 1965 to 17 in 1966 and then 59 in 1967.[72] Electronic warfare pods for F–105s and F–4s, plus experience dealing with SAMs and the efforts of Wild Weasel and Iron Hand, steadily and drastically reduced the SAM threat. However, as the NVAF pilots received more training and better aircraft equipped with missiles, and as more of them survived encounters with U.S. planes, the NVAF MiG force—mostly based in China—grew more aggressive and effective. The North Vietnamese pilots did not wrest air superiority away from U.S. forces, but they challenged U.S. dominance even more severely than had the Chinese in Korea in the early 1950s.[73] They were able to do so because, first, they worked as part of an integrated system of air control and, second, U.S. rules of engagement gave them sanctuaries and the knowledge that USAF and USN strike forces would have to come to North Vietnam and struggle for air superiority on a day-to-day basis.

After President Johnson halted the interdiction campaign north of the 20th parallel at the end of March 1968, there were only two important developments in the air superiority war until North Vietnamese troops invaded South Vietnam in April 1972. First, North Vietnam attempted to extend its integrated and centrally directed air defense system south to the border with South Vietnam. And, second, the USAF and USN in Southeast Asia developed an integrated system of air battle management based on sophisticated systems of warning, communication, and coordination. The first development had its roots in an incident that occurred on May 23,

1968. U.S. planes were then restricted to raids on North Vietnamese supply routes south of the 20th parallel—that is, below Thanh Hoa. In an attempt to curtail those raids, the NVAF began dispatching individual MiGs south, beyond the area around Hanoi in which they normally operated. On May 23, one MiG raider was shot down by a long-range SAM fired by a U.S. Navy cruiser steaming in the Gulf of Tonkin.[74] MiGs lacked electronic countermeasure devices (such as jammers) that could defeat or decoy the Navy fire control and SAM intercept radars.[75] In effect, NVAF MiGs could not brave the kind of defense system which the North Vietnamese themselves constructed around Hanoi and Haiphong. As a result, the North Vietnamese strategy became one of extending the integrated air defense system established around Hanoi south, first to Thanh Hoa and then, later, to Vinh. Instead of sending MiGs south, the North Vietnamese opted to move their entire system (guns, missiles, radars, and MiGs) toward the border with South Vietnam. U.S. policy, however, permitted armed reconnaissance of the area below the 20th parallel; in order to carry out this policy, Seventh Air Force and Task Force 77 units were compelled to attack and destroy SAM sites in Route Packages I, II, and III. The Rules of Engagement which governed such raids prohibited U.S. planes from attacking SAM sites that had not yet launched a missile. However, the rules did not prohibit attacks on North Vietnamese radars, and Seventh Air Force Iron Hand F–105s conducted a series of hunter-killer operations against radar sites in Route Package I after April 1968 in order to keep North Vietnam from achieving its goal of constructing an integrated air defense system close to the border with South Vietnam.[76]

There were limits, however, on what such attacks could accomplish. First, the number of U.S. aircraft in Southeast Asia declined after the administration of President Richard Nixon announced a policy of "Vietnamization" in 1969. Efforts to offset the decline with more sophisticated weaponry, such as F–111 bombers, television-guided unpowered glide bombs (Walleye), and a system of radio-directed navigation for night-attacking F–4D Phantoms, were not entirely successful.[77] U.S. planes did receive improved flak suppression and radar-homing missiles, but these improvements were countered to some degree by a delay in deploying an improved F–4 model (the "E," with an integral 20-mm gun, more powerful engines, and improved fire control system) to the theater.[78] From 1968 through 1971, the most reliable means of countering North Vietnamese SAM site development was with F–105 Iron Hand daylight attacks supplemented and escorted by Phantoms. Yet, the frequency of such attacks was limited by Rules of Engagement and the number of available aircraft. A second problem was one that had concerned Air Force and Navy theater commanders since 1965. With their sanctuaries, NVAF MiGs were difficult to destroy. With the support of SAMs and antiaircraft guns, NVAF MiGs did not have to carry the burden of combat against U.S. air units.

What the North Vietnamese had constructed during the course of ROLLING THUNDER was a fine-tuned system of air defense. As U.S. forces countered one element—whether antiaircraft guns, fire control radars, or MiG–17s—the North Vietnamese simply added another or increased the action of some other, already existing, element. In March 1967, the Office of the Secretary of Defense completed a special study (entitled *Night Song*) of North Vietnam's air defense system. The study concluded that the North Vietnamese could, with Russian and Chinese assistance, match the U.S. step for step in an air war of attrition conducted over the North.[79] The only ways to defeat the North Vietnamese air defense system were 1) to cut off completely its outside sources of supply or 2) to develop an attacking system that could respond faster than the North Vietnamese defenses.

The key to North Vietnam's defensive system was its communications and intelligence network. To the degree that North Vietnamese defenders knew when, where, and in what strength U.S. air attacks were scheduled, the North Vietnamese could better mix their combination of guns, radars, SAMs, and MiGs. Where the North Vietnamese lacked intelligence and warning, U.S. aircraft losses were small and U.S. successes impressive. Operation BOLO showed what deception could produce. The issue was whether BOLO would remain an isolated, unique operation or become a precedent for routine U.S. air operations against North Vietnam's integrated air defense system. In short, could U.S. air units take advantage of North Vietnam's air defense command and control system even though they were not allowed to destroy it? If so, then air superiority over North Vietnam would be guaranteed.

Gradually, U.S. air forces in Southeast Asia put together a command, control, and intelligence network that was superior to that created by North Vietnam. The first steps were taken in 1965: the development of Navy and Air Force electronic surveillance and airborne early warning systems. As ROLLING THUNDER progressed, Navy and Air Force command centers and communications personnel achieved three additional advances: the encryption of more communications between ground command centers and planes in the air, the automation of information handling and display, and the integration of USAF and USN tactical communication networks. In 1965, for example, communications between the USAF Tactical Air Control Center at Da Nang and the Navy's Task Force 77 at Yankee Station were by voice radio and teletype. When the Navy deployed its new Naval Tactical Data System (NTDS) and associated airborne early warning aircraft to Yankee Station in November 1965, the Air Force Control Center at Da Nang could not receive signals directly from the Navy

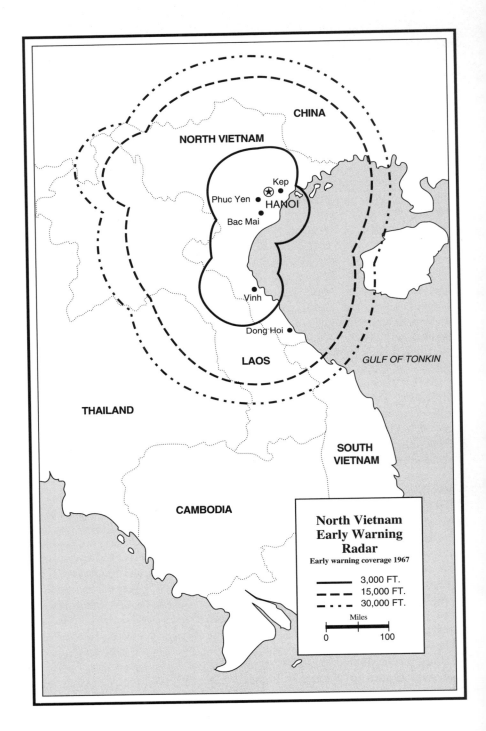

North Vietnam Early Warning Radar

Early warning coverage 1967

——————— 3,000 FT.
– – – – – 15,000 FT.
– · – · – · 30,000 FT.

Miles

0   100

system.[80] This problem was not overcome until March 1968, when Air Force data displays received signals from the Navy's NTDS through the Marine Corps Tactical Data System.[81] With this improvement, Air Force and Navy air controllers could see on their radarscopes what their respective surveillance and tracking radars were picking up. The Air Force itself also progressively modified its data display and communications systems. In late 1965, for example, data from aerial surveillance EC–121s was relayed by voice radio to USAF strike formations through tactical air control centers. By 1967, this data was apparently relayed and displayed automatically.[82]

As data-handling techniques improved, so too did the security of Air Force communications. When Seventh Air Force was created in April 1966, there was no secure voice link between its command center at Tan Son Nhut Air Base and subordinate control centers at Da Nang and Udorn, or between those centers and their airborne components.[83] Ultra High Frequency (UHF) links between strike forces over North Vietnam and radio relay planes orbiting over the Gulf of Tonkin were also "in the clear." Such unencrypted communications were a source of intelligence for the North Vietnamese. When U.S. jamming aircraft clouded North Vietnamese radars, enemy defenders used radio intercept and direction-finding techniques to gain advance warning of the direction and strength of U.S. attacks. In 1969, a special program (Seek Silence) finally gave Seventh Air Force a high degree of real-time signals security, thereby denying the North Vietnamese an important source of information.[84] By 1970, USAF armed reconnaissance sorties operating over Route Package I in North Vietnam were receiving up-to-the-minute reports on NVAF MiG movements over secure communications links. In 1965, USAF aircraft operating near Hanoi were beyond direct communication with tactical control centers in Thailand and South Vietnam. By 1970, the Seventh Air Force Directorate of Combat Operations had the capability to monitor both enemy and friendly air activity over Route Package I and to direct appropriate U.S. forces against enemy threats. In effect, the U.S. had constructed its own ground-control-intercept and early warning systems over enemy territory by combining aerial early warning aircraft, secure communications, and data display and analysis assets. The key to holding air superiority over North Vietnam in the face of an integrated, well coordinated defense was effective, real-time battle management, which gave strike and reconnaissance forces a comprehensive view of what was happening and then aided unit commanders in spreading their electronic warfare, SAM suppression, and MiG cover assets among enemy threats. (See Figure 10–2)

As ROLLING THUNDER progressed, the U.S. and North Vietnamese forces battling for control of the air improved their weapons and tactics.

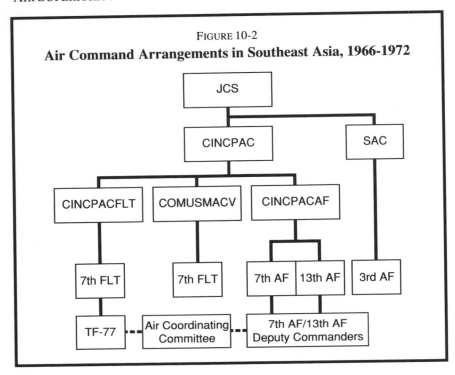

FIGURE 10-2

Air Command Arrangements in Southeast Asia, 1966-1972

> I always looked at air superiority as the ability to do with airpower what we wanted to do while the enemy couldn't do the same thing. With this perspective, there was no question that we could bomb North Vietnam at will while the [North Vietnamese] could not carry out similar operations.[85]

Indeed, by April 1968 the Seventh Air Force was on the way toward developing a system of air battle management far superior to that which had existed in 1965. As General Momyer, Seventh Air Force commander during most of ROLLING THUNDER, noted, the U.S. never lost air superiority over North Vietnam:

Notwithstanding the truth of this statement, ROLLING THUNDER did reveal some significant problems in the area of air superiority. The first was that the USAF lacked an air superiority fighter in the same category as the MiG–21. The second was that it took too long to develop and deploy a number of innovations important to air superiority tactics. The third problem was in the area of training: not enough time was spent preparing F–4 pilots for dogfights with MiGs. Finally, U.S. air-to-air missiles were not effective enough.

On the other hand, ROLLING THUNDER demonstrated that regular aerial refueling was suitable in tactical operations; indeed, the development of aerial refueling operations during ROLLING THUNDER (and, later, in the 1972 LINEBACKER operations) was an epic in itself, and its success illustrated the tremendous benefits gained from achieving air superiority. ROLLING THUNDER also proved that the F–4, designed as a fighter-bomber, could, if handled properly, hold its own in air-to-air combat with high performance aircraft. Finally, the continued but politically constrained air operations over North Vietnam revealed that tactical aircraft could operate within SAM envelopes and in the face of heavy antiaircraft fire.

The decision by North Vietnam to develop an integrated air defense system was both necessary and wise. Lacking an adequate air force and the resources to develop a large one, the North Vietnamese had no choice but to rely on missiles and antiaircraft fire. Yet as U.S. planes climbed to avoid ground fire, they grew more vulnerable to SAMs, and, if the aircraft reduced their approach and departure altitudes to get below the minimum SAM range, they increased their vulnerability to MiGs. This was a particularly serious problem for reconnaissance aircraft, which were required by the Rules of Engagement to fly missions after strikes at medium altitudes.[86] The North Vietnamese had a system of weapons whose functions were complementary.

Overcoming that combination of weapons was not easy. The most effective counter to it turned out to be an attack formation structured to fight effective electronic warfare. Each of these formations consisted of 8 or 10 flights of 4 aircraft, spread over about 25 square miles. Out in front were 2 flights of Iron Hand F–105s. Behind them were the strike flights of F–4s, equipped (by 1970) with noise and deception jamming pods; the strike aircraft were arranged so that their jammers covered enough of the formation's front to deny enemy radar operators a clear, reliable bearing and an accurate range of their position. Right behind the strike force was 1 or more photographic reconnaissance aircraft, and 2 or 3 nautical miles to the rear were 2 F–4s flying cover aginst MiG flights. When skies near the target were overcast, such formations flew at least 4,000 feet above the clouds in order not to be surprised by SAMs. Iron Hand flights fired Shrike or Standard Antiradiation Missiles (ARMs) to force enemy fire control radars off the air, and the first strike flights laid chaff clouds to confuse any radars which went back into operation once the actual bombing attack began. F–4s flying cover against MiGs did not have to maintain a high altitude because of the Phantom's ability to climb and accelerate rapidly. The trick was to hold formation integrity in order to maximize the benefits provided by the jammers and chaff clouds.[87] The only effective defense against such a formation was a diving hit-and-run attack by MiG–21s firing heat-seeking air-to-air missiles. However, holding such a large formation together was not easy; in addition, most missions flown after November 1968 did not require such a large strike force, which meant that many strike missions lacked indepth jamming and a heavy volume of chaff. Nevertheless, U.S. strike formations had the ability to penetrate the heaviest North Vietnamese defenses. They would use that ability to great advantage during operations LINEBACKER I and II.

LINEBACKER

In late 1971, North Vietnamese forces began massing for a possible invasion of South Vietnam across the Demilitarized Zone. Between December 26 and 30, 1971, Seventh Air Force responded accordingly, flying almost 1000 sorties against targets (many of them SAM sites or anti-aircraft gun positions) in Route Package I.[88] The actual invasion began on March 30, 1972. (See Table 10–9) Opposed to them were 93 MiG–21s, 33 MiG–19s, and 120 MiG–17s and –15s.[89] The Joint Chiefs of Staff had authorized a buildup of U.S. air strength in Southeast Asia as early as February, and the first USAF elements to move from U.S. bases after March 30 were Strategic Air Command B–52s and KC–135 tankers.[90] These aircraft were used to increase the number of sorties flown as part of the ARC LIGHT operations, an ongoing effort to apply the heavy bombload (108 500-lb. bombs) of the B–52 to enemy troop concentrations in South.[91] The bulk of ARC LIGHT strikes were flown over South Vietnam and Laos, but areas of North Vietnam adjacent to the Demilitarized Zone were targeted as part of the LINEBACKER program of halting the North Vietnamese invasion. Following the B–52s and KC–135s were additional tankers and a wave of tactical aircraft: F–105Gs and F–4Es. To add to the U.S. buildup, the Navy doubled its carrier strength in the Gulf of Tonkin during the first 2 weeks of April, and the Marine Corps shifted F–4 and attack squadrons to South Vietnam from Japan and Hawaii. By the end of June, USAF strength alone was 393 F–4s (D, E, and RF models), 30 F–105Gs (for Wild Weasel and Iron Hand operations), 19 EB–66s (for jamming), and 138 B–52s (at Andersen

---

TABLE 10–9

USAF Aircraft Available for Missions Over North Vietnam, March 1971

Aircraft Type	Da Nang	Ubon	Korat	Udorn	U-Tapao
F–4 (D & E & RF)	60	70	35	52	0
F–105 (G Models)	0	0	16	0	0
B–52	0	0	0	0	52

Source: Air War-Vietnam, Part II (New York, 1978), p. 112.

Air Force Base, Guam, and at U-Tapao).[92] Though the Seventh Air Force (now commanded by Gen. John W. Vogt, Jr.) had anticipated NVAF support for the ground invasion and had requested the new F–4E, with its improved search and sighting radar and nose-mounted 20-mm gun, as a primary reinforcement, NVAF aircraft did not attempt to thwart daylight USAF and USN air attacks on North Vietnamese tactical forces. Near the Demilitarized Zone, the NVAF conceded daytime air superiority to U.S. aircraft.[93]

The movement of F–4 and F–105 squadrons from U.S. bases to South Vietnam and Thailand was accomplished in record time largely because the Strategic Air Command sent along KC–135 tankers as escorts for the tactical aircraft. As Gen. Lucius D. Clay, Commander of Pacific Air Forces, observed,

> I think probably the most significant change in airpower over the last 25 years . . . is this *complete flexibility and our capacity to respond at a moment's notice*. If anybody had told me 25 years ago that you could take a fighter wing out of Holloman Air Force Base, New Mexico, and *have it overseas in less than a week and have it flying combat*, I'd have said "You're nuts!"[94]

In most cases, stateside squadrons were moved to bases already active. The wing of F–4Ds (the 49th) that left Holloman, however, had to reopen the airfield at Takhli, Thailand, which had been closed in 1971. The experience was not pleasant; the base had been stripped of nearly all facilities. As one pilot noted, "There was no hot water or air conditioning on the base. All water required testing for potability before we could drink it."[95] Despite this handicap, one of the 49th's squadrons was flying ground support missions within a day of its arrival. This ability to get into action quickly was largely a function of experience. In one of the 49th Wing's squadrons, for example, 24 of 25 aircraft commanders had flown "at least one previous tour in Southeast Asia; four men had two previous tours."[96] LINEBACKER was very much a veterans' campaign; even the B–52 pilots had been in action, and the past experience of the aerial refueling teams (ground air controllers and KC–135 crews) was essential in bringing the firepower of USAF units to bear on the North Vietnamese invasion forces.

The Strategic Air Command KC–135s were divided into 2 groups: those based in Thailand (114 of a total force of 172) supported tactical aircraft; the 58 remaining aircraft were flown from Kadena, Okinawa, in support of B–52 ARC LIGHT strikes mounted from Andersen AFB, Guam. By April 15, B–52s were flying 75 ARC LIGHT sorties per day; by June 21, the heavy bombers were flying over 100 sorties per day, and the demands on the tanker force were at record levels. In 1968, for example, KC–135s in Southeast Asia flew 32,000 sorties to support B–52s and tactical aircraft and to conduct radio relay and electronic reconnaissance missions. In 1972, with a late start, the SAC KC–135 force flew 34,728 such sorties, pumping over 1.4 million pounds of fuel.[97]

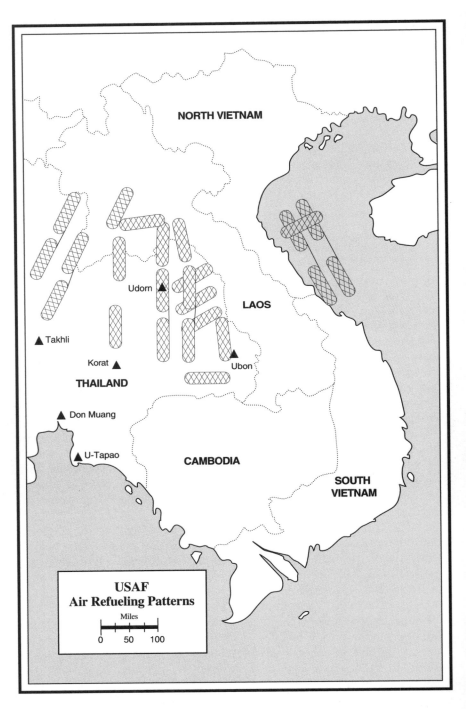

NORTH VIETNAM

LAOS

Udorn ▲

▲ Takhli

Korat ▲

THAILAND

Ubon ▲

▲ Don Muang

▲ U-Tapao

CAMBODIA

SOUTH
VIETNAM

**USAF
Air Refueling Patterns**

Miles

0   50   100

548

At the beginning of May, as U.S. air strength continued to build, and as the North Vietnamese offensive seemed to be having some success, President Nixon decided to mine Haiphong Harbor and to authorize air attacks across all of North Vietnam. From May 9 through October 22, Seventh Air Force flew interdiction sorties against Route Packages I, V, and VIA, while Navy carrier-based sorties struck the other route packages. The Nixon administration was determined both to halt the North Vietnamese invasion and to convince the government of North Vietnam that the United States was serious in its support of South Vietnam. There was—as at the end of ROLLING THUNDER—a 10-nm restricted zone around Hanoi and a 5-nm zone around Haiphong. But there were 3 important differences. First, all U.S. strike forces now carried effective laser-guided gravity bombs; compared with unguided ordnance, the accuracy of the new weapons was phenomenal. Second, SAC B–52s began attacking targets in North Vietnam below the 20th parallel, mostly at night. With the B–52s in action, USAF forces could place more ordnance on targets (1 B–52G could carry as much ordnance—more than 54,000 pounds—as 5 F–105s) and assault many targets around the clock. The heavy bombers carried a ground-scanning radar that could distinguish features such as airfields, bridges, and factories, and with F–4D and E escorts, the B–52s were relatively immune to MiG attack. The NVAF had constructed a number of airfields south of the 20th parallel before 1972, at Vinh, for example, and as far south as Dong Hoi, less than 50 nm from the Demilitarized Zone. Round-the-clock poundings closed these fields, and aggressive hunter-killer patrols by F–4Es destroyed a number of SAM radars and missile sites.[98] Finally, the USAF redeployed F–111A all-weather bombers to Thailand in September in order to supplement day bombing raids on North Vietnamese supply lines in Route Packages V and VIA.[99] This action gave the Seventh Air Force the capacity to strike major North Vietnamese targets at all times and under all weather conditions, an ability important not only to the interdiction campaign but also if and when U.S. forces gained the freedom to bomb all the NVAF's air bases.

To maintain air superiority in the areas near the major land battles, Seventh Air Force made the 432d Tactical Fighter Wing, based at Udorn, the primary theater counterair group. The veteran F–4 squadrons of the 432d were the 13th and 555th. Both had been at Udorn since early 1966. They were reinforced by three other squadrons transferred from the United States and the Philippines in April and July. Together, these squadrons were charged with shielding the extensive ground support operations flown by attack aircraft. During the day, the 432d's F–4Es flew barrier patrols in flights of four aircraft, using the "fluid four" formation first developed during the Korean War. The fluid four pattern spaced two elements of two aircraft each so that enemy fighters could not approach any element from behind without being detected and intercepted by the other element. At night, the wing's Phantoms escorted B–52s, EB–66s, and F–105s flying as

Wild Weasels in elements of two, weaving back and forth below and behind the bombers and their electronic countermeasures escorts to deter MiG attacks.[100] These tactics were quite effective.

Escorting strike missions over North Vietnam, however, was still difficult. The use of laser-guided bombs reduced the number of strike aircraft in raiding formations, allowing more planes to fly protection against MiGs. The use of newly developed chaff clouds—instead of bursts—also reduced the threat of North Vietnamese SAMs and antiaircraft guns. However, laser-guided bombs—though they could not be jammed as were radio-guided weapons in earlier wars—were not effective when the weather was poor. And chaff clouds, which formed protective lanes for U.S. strike aircraft, did not cover the F–4s which placed them, so that North Vietnamese antiaircraft forces quickly learned to target chaff-carrying aircraft before they dispersed their chaff loads.[101] The real counter to the U.S. interdiction effort that began in May, however, was the NVAF. From March through June, U.S. planes shot down twenty-four MiGs and lost eighteen of their own aircraft in air-to-air encounters. In June, however, MiG–21s began carrying four (as opposed to two) heat-seeking missiles, and MiG–17s and –19s began carrying such weapons for the first time.[102] U.S. planes found themselves dodging both ground-to-air and air-to-air missiles, and the

The Lang Giai railroad bridge (sixty-five miles from Hanoi) after an F–4 strike in May 1972.

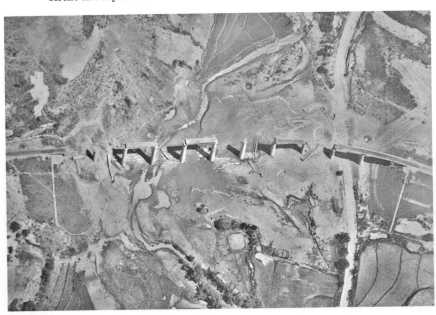

550

F–4 Phantom refueling in flight.

exchange ratio in air-to-air combat shifted from being in favor of the U.S. to one even for both sides. To regain the advantage, Seventh Air Force began eavesdropping on NVAF ground-control intercept transmissions. The goal was to increase the warning time of MiG attacks; the goal was achieved, and the MiG threat declined.[103]

In August, the U.S. and North Vietnam began serious negotiations aimed at ending the fighting in South Vietnam, halting U.S. bombing of North Vietnam, and returning U.S. prisoners of war held by North Vietnam. By November, U.S. air action was confined to raids on North Vietnam's transportation network and potentially dangerous NVAF bases. On December 13, however, North Vietnam's negotiators in Paris broke off all talks; in response, President Nixon ordered the Strategic Air Command to bomb Hanoi and Haiphong with conventional ordnance. The purpose of the new operation (called LINEBACKER II) was to impose a political settlement. In air superiority terms, the consequences were mixed. On the one hand, there were no more sanctuaries in North Vietnam for the NVAF. On the other, however, B–52s were subjected to a tremendous SAM barrage. It was a campaign for which the Joint Chiefs of Staff had pressed since 1965. It was also "reminiscent of another era, recalling a time when many of LINEBACKER II's participants had not yet been born."[104] According to the authors of an official Air Force account of LINEBACKER II, "the seemingly interminable lines of B–52s moving relentlessly into takeoff position recalled old photographs of a similar nature, showing desert-pink B–24s shimmering and dancing in the Libyan heat, or dull gray B–17s in the gloom of an English morning."[105] The operation began on December 18 and ended on the 29th. In that time, the B–52D and G models based at U-Tapao and at Andersen Air Force Base "flew 729 sorties against 34 targets in North Vietnam above the 20th parallel," dropping over 15,000 tons of bombs.[106] Of the total of 729 sorties, "498 penetrated the especially high threat zones immediately surrounding Hanoi and Haiphong."[107] Their bombing, accomplished at night, was amazingly accurate.

To accomplish this mission, both North Vietnam's MiG force and its SAMs had to be countered. Antiaircraft fire was of no threat to the high-flying B–52s. A greater threat was posed by the need to get as many bombers as possible over heavily defended targets in the shortest time. The B–52D models did not have powered controls. As one SAC officer put it, "flying the B–52D has been compared to driving an 18-wheel truck without power steering, air brakes, or automatic transmission in downtown Washington during the rush hour."[108] Yet precision flying was necessary to get the bombers over their targets so that they could take advantage of jamming, chaff drops, Iron Hand strikes, and F–4 escort flights. In short, the bombing was the product of an elaborately choreographed operation. B–52s flying from Guam had to rendezvous with tankers from Okinawa near the Philippines, fly to South Vietnam, turn north to Hanoi, and then rendezvous again with bombers flying from U-Tapao. The round trip from the Guam-based bombers was nearly 6,000 miles. Yet they accomplished their flights with precision. On December 28, for example, over 100 B–52s dropped bomb loads on Hanoi targets in just 15 minutes.[109] The approximately 150 tons of bombs dropped by just 6 B–52s in a matter of seconds covered an area 1/2 mile wide and 3 miles long.[110]

The NVAF was overwhelmed. B–52s plastered airfields such as Hoa Lac, Kep, and Phuc Yen, and F–4s from Seventh Air Force and Task Force 77 shielded the bombers. EB–66s and Navy and Marine EA–6 and EA–3 electronic warfare aircraft jammed North Vietnamese early warning and SAM fire control radars. F–105 and A–7E (USN) Iron Hand flights attacked SAM sites ahead of the bombers, while F–4s laid down chaff lanes. The NVAF withdrew to China; its MiG–21s, designed specifically to counter B–52s, were not a serious threat to LINEBACKER II operations. The only real threat was the SA-2, over 900 of which were fired against the B–52s during the 11 days of LINEBACKER II.[111] Only 15 bombers were lost to the missiles, however, largely because massive chaff drops had shielded them from SAM fire control radars.[112] Air superiority had been gained and held.

Conclusion

U.S. forces never lost air superiority during four years (1965–68, 1972) of intensive air action over North Vietnam. The campaign for air superiority, however, was often frustrating for those who waged it. One source of frustration has already been discussed—the Rules of Engagement which created sanctuaries for the NVAF and hazards for U.S. pilots. A second source of frustration was the relative ineffectiveness of U.S. air-to-air missiles. The F–4 was designed to carry missiles such as the AIM–4 Falcon, AIM–9 Sidewinder, and AIM–7 Sparrow. The Falcon proved to be inadequate and was eventually withdrawn. Sparrow was meant to be used against bombers at beyond visual range; the combination of Sparrow, an integral air search and targeting radar, and a weapons officer gave the F–4 great potential as an area air defense interceptor. Indeed, the Navy procured the F–4 so that it could extend its carrier task force air defenses against Russian bombers and make optimal use of its carrier fighter assets. The F–4 was also designed as a fighter-bomber; the Navy needed and wanted a multipurpose aircraft. In Vietnam, however, Sparrow's utility was usually offset by the need to visually identify enemy aircraft before attacking them. Sidewinder was a poor substitute, even at close range, because it was not designed for use against enemy fighters. MiGs pursued by F–4s could stay just beyond the effective threat envelope of Sidewinder, using maneuverability to overcome the high speed and acceleration of the F–4. It was a case of applying a weapon designed for one situation to a very different setting.[113]

F–4s also had a hard time with MiG–17s. The latter were highly maneuverable but slower than the Phantoms. However, the MiG–17 could and did cause serious problems if and when it once got among F–105s making a bombing run. The MiG–17 could easily slip onto the tail of an F–105 while the latter was still burdened by its bomb load, and escorting F–4s found it hard to drive off determined MiG–17s. The MiGs would pull into tight circles, sometimes to dodge Phantoms in order to get back to the F–105s and sometimes just for self-protection. This tactic (the Lufberry Circle) was developed during World War I. F–4s could make passes tangent to the circle, but they faced the prospect of being out-maneuvered if they entered it. The Phantom was not designed for dogfights where aircraft tailed and fired on one another at ranges of 1,000 feet or less; in such plane-on-plane combat, the MiG–17 had an advantage. The F–4, however, had great acceleration; its pilots had the option of accepting or declining combat. Once equipped with a gun (the F–4E), the Phantom was a formidable MiG–killer. (See Table 10–10) The MiG was more nimble, and its pilot was protected by armor, yet visibility from the MiG–21's cockpit was limited. F–4s could sneak up on MiG–21s and catch them by surprise. The MiG–21 was good at hit-and-run attacks against U.S. air formations because of its high-altitude

TABLE 10–10

Air-to-Air Weapon Success Rate, May 1972–Jan 1973

Weapon	Ratio of Kills to Firing Attempts	Ratio Expressed as a Percentage
AIMK–4 (Falcon)	0/5	0.0%
AIM–9 (Sidewinder)	10/100	10.0
AIM–7 (Sparrow)	23/216	10.6
20-mm gun	7/14	50.0
Total	40/335	11.9%

Source: Airpower in Three Wars, p. 157.

and very high-speed characteristics. Nonetheless, it was not the equal of the MiG–17 in a dogfight.

U.S. fighter performance against NVAF MiGs was the source of some controversy between the USAF and USN, spokesmen for the latter claiming that Navy training in air-to-air tactics prior to LINEBACKER was superior to that developed by the Air Force. This was not a minor issue. After ROLLING THUNDER, for example, the Air Force discovered that proper training had made a major difference in the airto-air combat performance of its fighter pilots.[114] In September 1968, the USN established the Fighter Weapons School, where F–4 pilots were matched against highly maneuverable F–5 aircraft flying like MiGs. The heart of the Navy's training program was an Air Combat Maneuvering Range, where engaged aircraft were monitored from the ground and their maneuvers recorded. After an exercise was completed, those involved went over it again by reviewing the recordings. The special range, with specially equipped aircraft, allowed USN fighter pilots to learn how best to deal with MiGs, especially the MiG–17.[115] The Air Force did not have such a range, even though the Aerospace Defense Command and the Tactical Air Command did have air combat tactics courses which matched F–4s against aircraft with different characteristics. The problem with the Air Force programs was that, in the legitimate interest of maintaining safety standards, air-to-air maneuvers were too constrained. However, it was not an easy task to down NVAF fighters, even when U.S. aircraft carried guns and could rely on accurate air warning. (See Table 10–10)

Critics of the air-to-air record of U.S. aircraft usually make the mistake of comparing the ratio of planes lost on both sides in Korea with similar ratios from the air engagements over North Vietnam. Korea and Vietnam, however, were not really comparable. Air-to-air combat over North Korea was more like that which took place over Europe in 1944 than that which developed over North Vietnam. In Korea, the opposing fighters approached each other at higher speeds than fighters had in World War II, and air-to-air encounters were completed in shorter time, but the aircraft themselves were easier to control. That is, trained, experienced pilots from World War II could transfer their skills from piston-engine fighters to jets. Moreover, the enemy in Korea had only one means of really challenging the United States in the air; it was the MiG or nothing. Finally, in Korea, enemy aircraft had to come to the U.S. fighters, and Chinese and North Korean pilots had to try to develop means to compensate for their inexperience with numbers.

These factors did not apply over North Vietnam. There, the conflict was between two systems, one of which was hampered by politically motivated constraints. In North Vietnam, the Vietnamese constructed a multi-faceted, mutually supporting system of air defense. The burden was on U.S. forces to penetrate it because they were never allowed to totally destroy it. When U.S. aircraft nullified one facet of the North Vietnamese defenses, the enemy system emphasized or developed another. Together, the MiGs, SAMs, guns, and radars were a formidable barrier. The duty of U.S. air units was to penetrate that barrier. Vietnam was not a conflict of fighter-on-fighter but of offensive systems against defensive systems. The measure of the success of the U.S. system was not the ratio of friendly to enemy planes lost, but whether the U.S. forces could achieve the goals set for them by the U.S. government—or in crude terms, whether the U.S. could afford the extravagance of waging an air war of attrition for four years under circumstances that were essentially self-defeating. Measured in these terms, the air superiority campaign was clearly successful.

In Vietnam, the USAF did not begin with a large cadre of veteran fighter pilots, as it had in Korea. More importantly, the use of SAMs in great numbers meant that previous air combat experience might actually be detrimental. Finally, the fighter and fighter-bomber missions were combined; indeed, the major improvements made to the F–4C (to produce the F–4D) were designed to improve the F–4's performance as a bomber.[116] In Korea, USAF F–86s had served as a barrier behind which an interdiction campaign took place. Over North Vietnam, U.S. forces had to fight their way through a variety of defenses to conduct interdiction bombing. In many instances, F–4s had MiG cover and interdiction responsibilities simultaneously. This is not to say that USAF pilots were adequately trained for air-to-air combat with missile-firing MiGs during LINEBACKER. Even the USAF's own air combat study, conducted in 1973, concluded that they were not.[117] The important point is that air-to-air combat with MiGs was never the primary mission of the majority of F–4 pilots. In terms of survival and mission performance, it was more important that they be able to avoid ground fire and SAMs, and deliver their ordnance on North Vietnamese targets.

The air war over North Vietnam was long, hazardous, and frustrating, particularly during 1966 and 1967. Pilot accounts suggest anger at having to continually repeat the same kind of restricted missions against an enemy who refused to fight in expected ways. The pressure on USAF and USN pilots to perform well in the face of seemingly pointless handicaps was great, yet neither they nor their superiors (including civilian officials in Washington) ever thought they would lose the air superiority campaign over North Vietnam. Some of this confidence was based on an appreciation of U.S. capabilities in areas like electronic warfare, which played such a strong role in the air war over the North. Some of it was based on an accurate assessment of the limitations of the NVAF. The remainder came from a sensible confidence—vindicated by events—in the skill and professionalism of U.S. military aviators.

Notes

1. *The Pentagon Papers (The Defense Department History of United States Decision-making on Vietnam)*, Gravel Ed, vol III (Boston, 1971), p 208.

2. *Ibid.*

3. *Ibid.*, p 210.

4. *Ibid.*, p 232.

5. *Ibid.*, p 318.

6. *Ibid.*

7. *The Pentagon Papers*, vol VI, p 1.

8. *Ibid.* Pages 2 through 17 of vol IV briefly chronicle the conflict between the Joint Chiefs and Admiral Sharp (CINCPAC), on the one hand, and the Office of the Secretary of Defense, on the other.

9. H. S. Wolk, "USAF Plans and Policies: Logistics and Base Construction in Southeast Asia, 1967" (Washington, 1968), p 7.

10. J. Van Staaveren, "USAF Deployment Planning for Southeast Asia, 1966" (Washington, 1968), p 3.

11. AFM 1–2, United States Air Force Basic Doctrine, Apr 1, 1955, reprinted in *Air Force*, Jan 1956, p 73.

12. H. S. Wolk, "USAF Plans and Policies: R&D for SEA, 1968" (Washington, Office of Air Force History, 1970), p 1.

13. Wolk, "USAF Plans and Policies: R&D for SEA, 1968," p 22; see also Townsend Hoopes, *The Limits of Intervention* (New York, 1970), and Intvw with Gen Earle E. Partridge, Apr 23–25, 1974, p 544, Office of Air Force History.

14. C. H. Hildreth, "USAF Counterinsurgency Doctrines and Capabilities, 1961–1962" (Washington, 1964), pp 4, 18, 19.

15. Gen W. W. Momyer, USAF, *Air Power in Three Wars* (Washington, 1978), p 119.

16. BDM Corporation, *A Study of Strategic Lessons in Vietnam* (McLean, Va, 1980), vol VI, *Conduct of the War*, Book 1, *Operational Analyses*, Table 6–4.

17. *Rules of Engagement, 1 January 1966–1 November 1969* (Project CHECO) (HQ PACAF, Hickam AFB, Hawaii, 1969).

18. R. F. Futrell, *et al*, *Aces and Aerial Victories: The United States Air Force in Southeast Asia, 1965–1973* (Washington, 1976), p 5.

19. Vice Adm M. W. Cagle, USN, "Task Force 77 in Action Off Vietnam," *U.S. Naval Institute Proceedings* (May, 1972), p 74.

20. *Rules of Engagement, 1 January 1966–1 November 1969*, p 14.

21. *Rules of Engagement, November 1969–September 1972* (Project CHECO) (HQ PACAF, Hickam AFB, Hawaii, 1973).

22. *Evolution of the Rules of Engagement for Southeast Asia, 1960–1965* (Project CHECO) (HQ PACAF, Hickam AFB, Hawaii, 1966).

23. Cagle, "Task Force 77 in Action Off Vietnam," p 94.

24. Momyer, *Air Power in Three Wars*, p 147.

25. J. J. Lane, Jr., *Command and Control and Communications Structures in Southeast Asia* [The Air War in Indochina, vol I, monograph 1] (Maxwell AFB, Ala., 1981), pp 40–60.

26. *Ibid.*, p 65; Momyer, *Air Power in Three Wars*, p 84; Intvw with Gen J. W. Vogt, Jr., Jan 31, 1986.

27. Lane, *Command and Control and Communications Structures in Southeast Asia*, pp 65–69; Vogt Intvw, Jan 31, 1986.

28. C. K. Hopkins "SAC Tanker Operations in the Southeast Asia War" (Headquarters, Strategic Air Command, 1979), pp 14, 90.

29. Futrell, *Aces and Aerial Victories*, p 4.

30. M. S. Knaack, *Encyclopedia of U.S. Air Force Aircraft and Missile Systems* Vol I: *Post-World War II Fighters* (Washington, 1978), p 168.

31. Futrell, *Aces and Aerial Victories*, p 4.

32. R. P. Fox, *Air Base Defense in the Republic of Vietnam, 1961–1973* (Washington, 1979), p 26.

33. *Ibid.*, p 27.

34. *Ibid.*, p 28.

35. *Ibid.*, pp 67–68.

36. H. S. Wolk, "USAF Logistic Plans and Policies in Southeast Asia, 1965" (Washington, 1966), pp 6, 25.

37. Wolk, "Logistics and Base Construction in Southeast Asia, 1967," p 1.

38. Futrell, *Aces and Aerial Victories*.

39. *Air-to-Air Encounters Over North Vietnam, 1 July 1967 – 31 December 1968*, (Project CHECO) (HQ PACAF, Hickam AFB, Hawaii, 1969), p 19.

40. Futrell, *Aces and Aerial Victories*, p 156.

41. Momyer, *Air Power in Three Wars*, p 121.

42. Comment by Gen. W. W. Momyer on an initial draft of this paper, April 1985.

43. Knaack, *Encyclopedia*, vol I, p 285.

44. Momyer, *Air Power in Three Wars*, p 127.

45. *Ibid.*, pp 133–36.

46. NAVEDTRA 10889–D, Fundamentals of Naval Intelligence 1975, Chap 11.

47. Hopkins, "SAC Tanker Operations in the Southeast Asia War."

48. J. A. Boyd, *et al.*, *Electronic Countermeasures* (Ann Arbor, Mich, 1961).

49. Knaack, *Encyclopedia*, vol I, pp 130–31.

50. *The USAF in Southeast Asia, 1965–1973*, Executive Summary, Part II (Project Corona Harvest) (HQ PACAF, Hickam AFB, Hawaii).

51. *Ibid.*, p II–11.

52. Futrell, *Aces and Aerial Victories*, pp 7–8.

53. Lane, *Command and Control and Communications Structures in Southeast Asia*, pp 76–77.

54. Hopkins, "SAC Tanker Operations in the Southeast Asia War," p 26.

55. *The Pentagon Papers*, Gravel Ed, vol IV.

56. P. Burbage, *et al.*, *The Battle for the Skies Over North Vietnam, 1964–1972* [USAF Southeast Asia Monograph Series, vol I, monograph 2] (Washington, 1976), p 145.

57. *Tactical Electronic Warfare Operations in Southeast Asia, 1962–1968* (Project CHECO) (HQ PACAF, Hickam AFB, Hawaii, 1969), p 40.

58. Futrell, *Aces and Aerial Victories*, p 11.

59. *Ibid.*

60. *Ibid.*, p 12.

61. *Air-to-Air Encounters Over North Vietnam, 1 July 1967–31 December 1968*, p 13.

62. *Tactical Electronic Warfare Operations in Southeast Asia, 1962–1968*, pp 3, 15.

63. *Air-to-Air Encounters Over North Vietnam, 1 July 1967–31 December 1968*, p 23.

64. *USAF Tactics Against Air and Ground Defenses in Southeast Asia, November 1968–May 1970* (Project CHECO)(HQ PACAF, Hickam AFB, Hawaii, 1970), p 42.

65. *The USAF in Southeast Asia, 1965–1973*, p II–9.

66. *Ibid.*, p II–15.

67. Cagle, "Task Force 77 in Action Off Vietnam."

68. Momyer, *Air Power in Three Wars*, pp 178–79.

69. Cagle, "Task Force 77 in Action Off Vietnam," p 97.

70. *Air-to-Air Encounters Over North Vietnam, 1 July 1967–31 December 1968*, p 11.

71. *Ibid.*, p 23.

72. Futrell, *Aces and Aerial Victories*, p 117.

73. *The USAF in Southeast Asia, 1965–1973, Executive Summary.*

74. Futrell, *Aces and Aerial Victories*, p 13.

75. *Air Tactics Against North Vietnam Air Ground Defenses, December 1966–1 November 1968* (Project CHECO) (HQ PACAF, Hickam AFB, Hawaii, 1969), p 39.

76. *Ibid.*, pp 37–38.

77. For data on Walleye, see Knaack, *Encyclopedia*, vol I, p 275, note 30; for details on the F–111, see Momyer, *Air Power in Three Wars*, p 181; more on the F–4D, and LORAN, is in the Knaack, *Encyclopedia*, vol I, p 274, note 28, and p 276, note 35.

78. Knaack, *Encyclopedia*, vol I, p 274, p 277–81.

79. Wolk, "USAF Plans and Policies: R&D for Southeast Asia, 1968," pp 24–25.

80. Cagle, "Task Force 77 in Action Off Vietnam," p 78; *Command and Control and Communications Structures in Southeast Asia*, p 77.

81. Lane, *Command and Control and Communications Structures in Southeast Asia*, p 93.

82. *Ibid.*, p 77.

83. *Ibid.*, p 141.

84. *Ibid.*, p 142.

85. Gen Momyer's comments on an initial draft of this paper, Apr 1985.

86. Hist, 7th Air Force, July 1–Dec 31, 1967, I, pp 20–60.

87. *USAF Tactics Against Air and Ground Defenses in Southeast Asia, November 1968–May 1970*, pp 41–49.

88. Momyer, *Air Power in Three Wars*, p 217.

89. Burbage, *The Battle for the Skies Over North Vietnam, 1964–1972*, pp 185–187.

90. Hopkins, "SAC Tanker Operations in the Southeast Asia War," p 84.

91. J. A. Doglione, *et al.*, "Airpower and the 1972 Spring Invasion," in *Air War–Vietnam* (New York, 1978), p 111.

92. *Ibid.*, p 125; *USAF Statistical Digest*, FY 1972 (Washington, HQ USAF), Table 9, pp 78–79.

93. *Air War–Vietnam*, p 122, note 2.

94. *Ibid.*, p 124.

95. *Ibid.*, p 123.

96. *Ibid.*

97. Hopkins, "SAC Tanker Operations in the Southeast Asia War," pp 91, 115.

98. *The USAF in Southeast Asia, 1965–1973, Executive Summary*, p II–6.

99. Knaack, *Encyclopedia*, vol I, pp 231–32.

100. Futrell, *Aces and Aerial Victories*, pp 14, 91.

101. Burbage, *The Battle for the Skies Over North Vietnam, 1964–1972*, p 177.

102. *The USAF in Southeast Asia, 1965–1973, Executive Summary*, p II–18.

103. R. H. Kohn and J. P. Harahan, eds, *Air Superiority in World War II and Korea* (Washington, 1983), p 86.

104. Brig Gen J. R. McCarthy, USAF, and Lt Col G. B. Allison, USAF, *Linebacker II: A View from the Rock* [USAF Southeast Asia Monograph Series, vol VI, monograph 8] (Maxwell AFB, Ala., 1979), p 5.

105. *Ibid.*

106. *Ibid.*, p 171.

107. *Ibid.*, p 172.

108. *Ibid.*, p 158.

109. Burbage, *The Battle for the Skies Over North Vietnam, 1964–1972*, pp 185–87.

110. *A Study of Strategic Lessons Learned in Vietnam*, vol VI, p 59.

111. *The USAF in Southeast Asia, 1954–1973, Executive Summary*, p II–1.

112. *Ibid.*

113. Futrell, *Aces and Aerial Victories*, p 10, 25.

114. Burbage, *The Battle for the Skies Over North Vietnam, 1964–1972*, p 120.

115. "Aerial Combat Tactics," *Interceptor*, May 1972, p 8.

116. Knaack, *Encyclopedia of U.S. Air Force Aircraft and Missile Systems*, vol I, p 273.

117. Burbage, *The Battle for the Skies Over North Vietnam, 1964–1972*, p 120.

Bibliographical Essay

Government Sources

Official records on the air war in Southeast Asia are held by the U.S. Air Force Historical Research Center at Maxwell Air Force Base, Alabama. The Center also has all the Project CHECO (Contemporary Historical Examination of Current Operations) reports. Project CHECO was created in 1962 by the Chief of Staff, USAF, and its work continued until June 30, 1975. The Office of Air Force History has prepared a guide to the available CHECO reports (entitled "Research Guide to the Published Project CHECO Reports"), but many of the more interesting studies remain classified. The classified and unclassified records from the war in Southeast Asia are very extensive. The Project CHECO studies, prepared by trained historians, pull together related pieces of the overall documents collection. Without the CHECO studies, the sheer size of the documentation available at Maxwell AFB would make any serious study of the Southeast Asia air war extremely time-consuming and difficult. The Historical Research Center is also custodian for the Project Corona Harvest studies.

Many of the documents stored at the Historical Research Center are also on microfilm at the Office of Air Force History, Bolling Air Force Base, Washington, D.C. The Office of Air Force History also has the *USAF Statistical Digest*, an annual compilation of data on USAF personnel and equipment. Finally, studies such as C. K. Hopkins' "SAC Tanker Operations in the Southeast Asia War" (Omaha, Nebr.: Headquarters, Strategic Air Command, 1979) are also available at the Office of Air Force History. Such studies are an excellent source of accurate data on USAF operations. Navy operational records are housed at the Navy's Classified Operational Archives in the Navy Yard, Washington, D.C. Most are still not open to researchers who lack a security clearance.

The story of the debate over the level of bombing of North Vietnam is contained in *The Pentagon Papers (The Defense Department History of United States Decisionmaking on Vietnam)*, Senator Gravel Edition (Boston, 1971), especially volumes III and IV. Though not a complete collection of the government's official papers on its war policy, the Pentagon Papers is an invaluable and completely unclassified source on the events in Washington which so strongly shaped the direction and intensity of the air war in Southeast Asia.

The Air Force has produced a number of studies and histories of operations in Southeast Asia. One of the best is *The U.S. Air Force in Southeast Asia, 1961–1973: An Illustrated Account*, edited by Carl Berger and published by the Office of Air Force History (revised edition, Washington, 1984). Besides a great number of excellent photographs, this book contains important maps, a 7th/13th Air Force organization chart, and interesting discussions of tanker operations (aerial refueling), air base defense, and communications. Far more than a collection of photographs, *The U.S. Air Force in Southeast Asia, 1961–1973* contains an appendix listing all the major USAF leaders who participated in the war in Southeast Asia. A useful companion volume is *Aces and Aerial Victories: The United States Air Force in Southeast Asia, 1965–1973*, by R. F. Futrell, *et al.* (Washington: Office of Air Force History, 1976). *Aces and Aerial Victories* provides a short summary of the air superiority campaign and contains dozens of first-hand accounts of action with North Vietnamese forces. Such accounts are indispensable to readers trying to understand what it meant to actually fight the air war. Other Air Force publications of value are the relevant monographs in the Southeast Asia and Air War in Indochina series. In the former series, there are four important titles: *The Tale of Two Bridges,* by Col. Delberth Corum, *et al.* (Monograph 1, Vol. I), and *The Battle for the Skies over North Vietnam* (Monograph 2, Vol. I), by Maj. Paul Burbage, *et al.* (both Washington: Office of Air Force History, 1976); *Air Power and the 1972 Spring Invasion,* by Col. John A. Doglione, *et al.* (Monograph 3, Vol. II) (Washington: Office of Air Force History, 1978); and *Linebacker II: A View from the Rock,* by Brig. Gen. J. R. McCarthy and Lt. Col. G. B. Allison (Monograph 8, Vol. II) (Maxwell AFB, Ala.: Air University, 1979). There is also Monograph 1, Vol. I, of the Air War in Indochina Series: *Command and Control and Communications Structures in Southeast Asia,* by Lt. Col. J. J. Lane, Jr. (Maxwell AFB, Ala.: Air University, 1981). Supplementing these is *Air Base Defense in the Republic of Vietnam, 1961–1973,* by R. P. Fox (Washington: Office of Air Force History, 1979), an excellent discussion of the many problems that hampered USAF efforts to construct and maintain secure bases for its units in South Vietnam.

Two other publications that deserve mention are *Air Power in Three Wars,* by Gen. W. W. Momyer (Washington: Office of Air Force History, 1978), and *Encyclopedia of U.S. Air Force Aircraft and Missile Systems,* Vol. I: *Post–World War II Fighters,* by M. S. Knaack (Washington: Office of Air Force History, 1978). Gen. Momyer was Commander, Seventh Air Force from July 1, 1966 through July 31, 1968, and his book contains a number of comparisons between air operations in World War II, Korea, and Southeast Asia. For General Momyer and for other USAF veterans of World War II, Army Air Corps operations over Germany in 1944 and 1945 served as the reference point when they evaluated USAF operations in Southeast Asia. What appeared to be heavy losses to the North Vietnamese air defense system during ROLLING THUNDER did not look that way at all to Air Force leaders who remembered the figures from air campaigns in Europe in World War II. This is a point that critics of ROLLING THUNDER often forgot. Often overlooked, too, is the fact that so much of the equipment used by the Air Force in Southeast Asia was designed for a European war. The *Encyclopedia of U.S. Air Force Aircraft and Missile Systems,* Vol. I, makes that point clearly. It also contains data on aircraft electronic warfare systems, aircraft costs, aircraft performance characteristics, and aircraft deployments. It is a most useful and detailed reference.

The general direction and evolution of the air war in Southeast Asia can be inferred from the unclassified Air Force publications discussed in the previous three paragraphs. Classified materials are more specific and describe activities in areas such as electronic warfare at a level of detail which is too close to operations to be revealed publicly. The important point is that so much can be found in the unclassified sources.

Nongovernmental Sources

There has been a virtual avalanche of unofficial, unclassified books and articles about the air war in Southeast Asia. Only those the author found most helpful will be cited here. For a longer list, consult *An Aerospace Bibliography,* compiled by S. D. Miller (Washington: Office of Air Force History, 1978). Also see the bibliographies at the end of two volumes of the Boston Publishing Company's series *The Vietnam Experience: Tools of War,* by E. C. Doleman, Jr. (Boston: 1984), and *Rain of Fire: Air War, 1969–1973,* by John Morrocco (Boston: 1985). The bibliographies of these two books are extensive and detailed.

The best nongovernment source for the air superiority campaign in Southeast Asia is *Rain of Fire,* by John Morrocco (Boston, 1985). *Rain of Fire* takes a very operational view of the air superiority fighting because it is based on oral histories stored at the Air Force Historical Research Center at Maxwell AFB, Alabama. The author of *Rain of Fire* has covered all the unclassified sources and woven a tightly knit narrative of the action over North Vietnam in the years when the North Vietnamese air defense system was at its best. A companion volume, *Tools of War*, by E. C. Doleman, Jr., discusses the technology employed in ground and air action in Southeast Asia. Though written for a lay audience, both books are accurate and interesting.

A nongovernment source still stands as the best account of Navy air activity during ROLLING THUNDER. Vice Adm. M. W. Cagle's "Task Force 77 in Action Off Vietnam," *U.S. Naval Institute Proceedings* 98 (May 1972), is the best unclassified description of Navy operations against North Vietnam's air defense system. Other articles and books dealing with Navy air action are listed in *A Select Bibliography of the U.S. Navy and the Southeast Asian Conflict, 1950–1975*, rev. ed., by E. J. Marolda and G. W. Pryce, III (Washington: Naval Historical Center, 1983).

Those interested in photographic collections should see *And Kill MiGs: Air to Air Combat in the Vietnam War*, by Lou Drendel (Carrollton, Tex.: Squadron/Signal Publications, 1984). For a personal view consult "How a Fighter Pilot Sees the Air War in Vietnam," by Maj. G. D. Larson, *Air Force*, July 1967, pp 45–49. The same edition of *Air Force* carries a one-page profile on Col. Robin Olds, Commander of the 8th Tactical Fighter Wing (September 1966–September 1967) based at Ubon, Thailand. The profile's description of Colonel Olds's career shows why USAF units in 1967 were superior to MiGs in actions such as Operation BOLO. USAF commanders had a wealth of experience from World War II and Korea which they passed down to younger pilots. As that reservoir of experience grew more dilute, both the Navy and the Air Force had to develop advanced air combat training schools.

There are several critical commentaries on the air war in Southeast Asia which deserve mention. In *Rolling Thunder: Understanding Policy and Program Failure* (Chapel Hill, NC: University of North Carolina Press, 1980), James C. Thompson argued that the effectiveness of the ROLLING THUNDER effort was not significantly reduced by political restrictions set in Washington. The official Air Force position is that the LINEBACKER II campaign refuted such arguments. The B–52 attacks against Hanoi and Haiphong were criticized by a former pilot (Dana Drenkowski) in *Armed Forces Journal International*, July 1977 ("The Tragedy of Operation Linebacker II," pp. 24–27). Drenkowski charged that the tactics set for the December 1972 attacks on Hanoi were inflexible and that Strategic Air Command Headquarters in Omaha refused to change those tactics, even after demands from pilots in Guam that something be done. In the September 1977 edition of *Armed Forces Journal International*, Adm. Thomas Moorer, former Chairman of the Joint Chiefs of Staff, bitterly refuted Drenkowski's charges (p. 8).

Finally, those interested in air combat tactics should consult *Fighter Combat, Tactics and Maneuvering*, by R. L. Shaw (Annapolis: United States Naval Institute Press, 1985). *Aces and Aerial Victories* contains a number of good drawings of fighter maneuvers to illustrate its accounts of NVAF/USAF encounters, but *Fighter Combat, Tactics and Maneuvering* explains why some tactics work and others do not, and why different tactics apply to missile engagements than to contests where the opposing fighters carry guns.

11

The Israeli Experience

Brereton Greenhous

"Air superiority in itself is not an aim. Its object is to enable airpower to be used correctly and wisely....Air superiority is a necessary evil.

–Maj. Gen. Mordechai Hod, commander of Chel Ha'Avir, (the Israeli Air Force), 1966–73.

Complex socio-geographic factors make the defense of Israel an extremely difficult problem, albeit one which perhaps receives less attention than it deserves from western minds because of past Israeli successes in solving it. Much of that success has been due to Israeli appreciation of air power and its importance in modern war. To Israel, a very, small enclave in a generally hostile and politically volatile Arab world, air power is vital.

Nevertheless, despite general recognition of its special position within the Israeli Defense Forces (*Zeva Haganah le-Israel,* or *Zahal*), the Israeli air arm (*Chel Ha'Avir*) has never enjoyed a formally independent status comparable to that of Great Britain's Royal Air Force (RAF) since 1918, or the United States Air Force (USAF) after 1947. The air arm remains technically subordinate to the General Staff, theoretically no more than *primus inter pares* with the Armor Branch or Infantry or Artillery. In practice, however, the highly specialized skills of Israeli airmen and the unquestionable importance of their role in the Israeli strategic scheme of things have given them a substantial degree of functional autonomy, perhaps comparable to that accorded the U.S. Army Air Forces during the Second World War.[1]

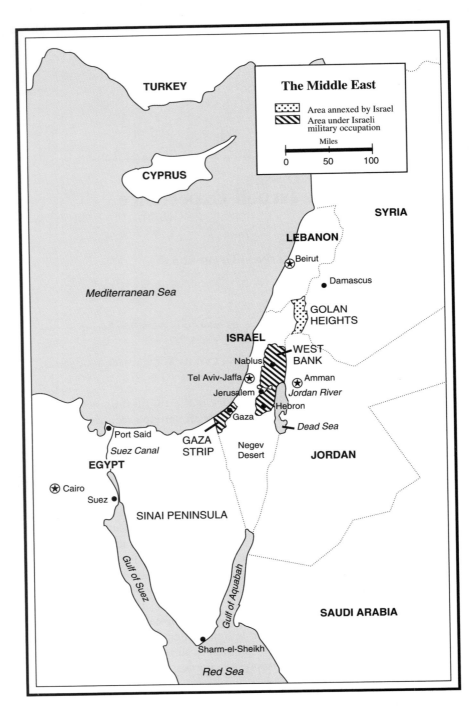

The Middle East

- Area annexed by Israel
- Area under Israeli military occupation

Miles

0   50   100

TURKEY

CYPRUS

Mediterranean Sea

SYRIA

LEBANON

Beirut

Damascus

GOLAN HEIGHTS

ISRAEL

WEST BANK

Nablus

Tel Aviv-Jaffa

Amman

Jerusalem

Jordan River

Hebron

Gaza

Dead Sea

GAZA STRIP

Port Said

Negev Desert

JORDAN

Suez Canal

EGYPT

Cairo

Suez

SINAI PENINSULA

Gulf of Suez

Gulf of Aquabah

SAUDI ARABIA

Sharm-el-Sheikh

Red Sea

Geo-Strategic Considerations

Twenty years ago, Israel consisted of little more than 8,000 square miles of territory along the eastern shore of the Mediterranean (an area less than that of Massachusetts), much of it, especially the triangular blade of the Negev in the south, a barren, desert waste. It stretched only 115 miles from north to south along the key maritime littoral where most of its population and all of its scientific and industrial resources were concentrated. The width of the country varied from 65 miles between the southern tip of the Dead Sea and the base of the Gaza Strip, down to a mere 12 miles just north of Tel Aviv.

With the Gaza Strip and all of the west bank of the Jordan in Israeli hands, the *de facto* area of the country has increased by nearly a third (making it comparable in size to Maryland). The length of the littoral has increased to 145 miles and the "neck" has thickened to 42 miles. Operational air speeds and heights have also increased and missiles have come into the picture, making the air defense of Israel more difficult than ever. An Israeli pilot put it perfectly in focus:

> At fifty thousand feet, in a supersonic Mirage, I can fly only north and south; otherwise, I'd be out of the country in a matter of seconds. You can see on one side Cyprus, Turkey—on the other, Iraq and Sharm-el-Sheikh. You have no trouble spotting the Suez Canal. But your own country is very difficult to see; it's under the belly of your plane. You have to turn around and look back to see it. You become very aware of its smallness.[2]

Despite their strategically precarious situation, the Israelis have always had to balance the demands of military preparedness against the social and economic necessities of creating a nation-state. With a population that has now grown to 4 million (3.37 million Jews) and outnumbered by surrounding Arabs 25- or 30-to-1, they cannot maintain the large standing armies espoused by many of their neighbors. Nor can the Israelis, with their delicately balanced, labor-intensive economy, afford to engage in a long war, either in terms of casualties in the field or socio-economic disruption at home. Mobilization means economic stagnation; mustering a citizen army of conscripts and reserves, trained by a small cadre of regulars, Israel must rely upon superior training and equipment, and the classic "force multipliers" of flexibility, mobility, and firepower, to win quickly. Lacking depth—geographically, demographically, and economically—Israeli strategists have always planned to take the offensive and fight short, decisive campaigns on foreign soil, a *blitzkrieg* concept in which air power is an essential element and air superiority the vital prerequisite.[3]

The Israelis have also had to guard against the possibility of a successful surprise by the enemy—one which might allow him to reach the heart of Israel before their reserves could be mobilized and deployed. Excellent intelligence minimizes this risk, but a key element in defensive planning is the need to achieve and maintain air superiority. *Chel Ha'Avir,** with a relatively large proportion of its aircrew and the necessary ground crew serving as regulars, must be ready to protect population centers, industrial resources, lines of communication, and ground troops initially engaged, from enemy air power. In particular, the air force must secure the mobilization process against interference by enemy air forces, so that the citizen army can reach its appointed battle stations quickly and in condition to fight.

At the same time, one of Israel's few strategic advantages is that its land borders adjoin vast, relatively uncluttered deserts or (in the north) mountain ranges. Axes of advance and adequate lines of communication for a substantial force are few and easily monitored, and the ability of an air arm to strike far afield—given air superiority—makes battlefield interdiction an especially effective weapon in principle. "In my time [1953–58] it had already become abundantly clear to us that the trick was to use the air force to destroy as much as you could of the enemy's air force...and for interdiction. Interdiction is God's gift to the Middle East," concluded Brig. Gen. Dan Tolkovsky, then the Commander of IAF.[4]

Altogether, these geo-strategic factors emphasize the military importance of air power to the Israelis throughout their relatively brief national history. Air power has also offered two inestimable advantages from their socio-economic perspective. The exercise of air power is relatively economical in human terms and, in the case of ground crew and the multiplicity of other supporting functions needed to keep aircraft serviceable and flying (which account for the vast majority of airmen), training and work environments tend to minimize military/civilian differences while the skills developed are equally applicable in both environments. In short, while air power is essential to Israeli strategy, the intrinsic nature of an air force meshes well with Israeli political needs.

The IAF Evolves

However, all this was not so obvious in 1948 when Israel was born. The embryonic air arm had not distinguished itself in the War of Independence ("the ground force was always disappointed with the air force" recalls Tolkovsky),[5] and in the immediate post-independence era the IAF case was not always put to best advantage in the debates that accompanied the establishment of the Israeli Defense Forces. The first Commander of the Air Force, Aharon Remez, had lost the confidence of the General Staff

---

**Chel Ha'Avir* has a very different philosophy and doctrine to English-speaking air forces and its personnel have a different motivation, but for the sake of reader comprehension, the service will be referred to as the Israeli Air Force or IAF in this paper.

during the war by "constantly selling futures that never happened," according to Tolkovsky. After the war, he pressed for "a truly independent air force . . . RAF-inspired, which simply couldn't have worked," and "got into awful rows with the Chief of Staff, [Yigael] Yadin."[6] "Aharon was no great organizer and not very systematic," wrote Ezer Weizman, who served as IAF's Commander in the 1960s. "Under his command the air force didn't exist in the day-to-day reality, rather it lived in the infinite. . . . Everyday questions like what kind of radar we needed and where it should be placed, what kind of plane we should prefer (taking into consideration the severe political restrictions that limited our purchasing ability) and how to train new pilots did not elicit clear answers from him."[7]

Remez resigned in 1950, to be succeeded very briefly by an infantryman turned naval officer, Shlomo Shamir, who was quite unfitted for the post. He was followed, within a year, by a brilliant and remarkable soldier, Chaim Laskov, who established the conceptual basis of Israeli air strategy.[8] Laskov later became head of the General Staff (Operations) Branch, 1955–56, and Chief of the General Staff from 1958 to 1960. His successor was Tolkovsky—like Remez, an ex-RAF pilot, but one who was more flexible and pragmatic in his approach to organization and doctrine. Tolkovsky rejected those British-inspired ideas that viewed air power in distinctly compartmented terms of strategic and tactical bombing, antisubmarine and maritime strike forces, air defense and tactical fighter operations. "I think I was probably in the happy position of being able to wed these things for the first time into a monolithic concept, which, of course, was the answer in this country."[9] The IAF was never going to be so diversified, or deployed over such large areas, that either functional or geographic commands would be appropriate.

Economics dictated that, in practice, this approach, which focused on the need for air superiority, required multi-purpose machines and the maximum possible degree of standardization. Bombers were out; so were pure interceptors and specialized ground support or reconnaissance airplanes. Israel could never afford the cost. All these functions were to be performed by one kind of machine, the most recent—and most expensive—acquisitions fulfilling the air superiority role as their primary mission, while older, perhaps obsolescent, aircraft concentrated on destroying enemy bases, interdicting his lines of communication, or attacking his forces in the field. Thus, when France became frustrated by Egyptian support of rebel Algerian nationalists (and the "nationalization" of the Suez Canal), and Israel found a willing purveyor of sophisticated new aircraft in 1955, Tolkovsky resisted pressure to buy the readily available Mystere II interceptors, preferring to wait for the Mystere IV, which had a multi-mission capability.[10] The price was significantly higher—"360,000 dollars and only one seat!" mourned Levi Eskhol, the Minister of Finance, when the first of them landed in Israel.[11] However, the Mystere IVs provided a foundation for building Tolkovsky's kind of air force.

Limited in his purchases by the decision in favor of quality rather than quantity, and constrained by the reluctance of the General Staff to go too far with an unproven concept, Tolkovsky needed to make the best possible use of what he had. He introduced pilot standards which were the stiffest in the world. Initial selection was (and is) unbelievably rigorous; and "washout" rates were (and are) in the region of 90 percent.[12] Tolkovsky's successor as Air Force Commander "once pinned pilot's wings on a single cadet, the only one who successfully completed the course," according to the British historian, Edgar O'Ballance.[13] Nor was the psychological aspect neglected. Ezer Weizman has recorded that when a pilot trainee

> reaches where he can fly at forty thousand feet, we send him up one night between nine and ten o'clock, tell him not to look down as he rises. He climbs to ten... twenty...thirty...forty thousand. Then we say, 'look down.' And what does he see? The whole of Israel a pearly blaze, humming with life, and around it the Arab states in glum darkness, with only here and there the barest glimmer of light. When he sees that, he becomes a Jewish pilot.[14]

Less romantically, Tolkovsky also started a program of modern radar acquisition, bringing in the first set shortly before the 1956 conflict. He set about maximizing his limited resources through improved aircraft service-ability rates (often, if not always, over 90 percent) and "skilled and devoted ground-crews, who refuel and rearm the plane at record speeds."[15] Still remaining was the matter of tactics—of how to get the maximum possible value from this increasingly finely tuned organization.

In Spain, during the late 1930s, the German Luftwaffe had developed a combat formation for fighters based on the *Rotte*, or pair, in which the wingman flew very slightly behind his leader, the latter initiating and car-rying through all attacks with the wingman's primary duty being to cover his leader's tail. Subsequently, in World War II, the British and Americans adopted this principle, generally using two such pairs in a "finger four" formation, so-called because the four aircraft flew in the same relationship to each other as the fingertips of an outstretched hand. The USAF contin-ued this tactical formation in Korea. However, the Luftwaffe had ended its war flying two machines abreast, so that by concentrating his search inward each pilot could watch the blind spots of his partner, behind and below him. Still, in an attack, the leader's business was with the chosen target, the wingman's mission essentially to hold his position and cover his usually more experienced leader. Thus, in either "finger four" or "line abreast," two aircraft formed a "welded wing,"[16] two machines flying as one in a shooter/cover relationship rather like that of a boxer who always leads with his left and uses his right to protect himself.

But good boxers hit with both hands and the best throw rapid combi-nations at their opponents from time to time. Occasionally, in World War II and Korea, experienced Allied pilots had rejected the tactical rigidity of the "welded wing" and flown their missions two abreast, covering each other and maneuvering independently in a coordinated, mutually supporting "fluid pair." This was the tactical concept embraced by Tolkovsky, a concept that effectively doubled his offensive fire power without any increase in the number of aircraft.

Two such pairs formed a "fluid four" or, in IAF's terms, a "two element combat formation," the Israelis evolving "their own special brand [of doctrine] mainly after 1953 when the first Meteor jets were acquired." According to former Commander of the IAF Maj. Gen. Benjamin Peled:

> Each fighter pilot must...bring to bear the maximum killing potential of his own expertise and his aircraft's weapons...to be orchestrated by the element leaders...within the environment of eyeball, radar, commint [communications intelligence] and elint [electronic intelligence] information within his group and from outside forces available to him. Each leader will decide on the spot the type of deployment he judges to be most conducive to achieve the maximum kills per engagement. This will also be the aim of each individual pilot...within the following constraint; [that] the order to initially engage and finally disengage is the leader's prerogative [and] a disabled member [of the group] will be escorted at all times."[17]

Operation KADESH

Tolkovsky's ideas were only budding into reality when they were required to meet their first test. During the latter part of 1955 the Soviet Union had begun delivering substantial quantities of modern weapons systems (including MiG–15 fighters) to Egypt, the most powerful of Israel's potential enemies. Then, in the spring of 1956 came the announcement that Egypt, Syria, and Jordan would each place their national forces under a single, unified command in the event of hostilities with Israel. There was every likelihood that Iraq would join them. The Suez Canal and the Strait of Tiran (leading into the Gulf of Aquaba) were both closed to Israeli shipping, and Egyptian forces began to concentrate in the Sinai.

The danger of coordinated attacks on several fronts was only too obvious, and the Israeli assessment was that actual hostilities only waited on Arab convenience. The Israeli decided to strike first and, conspiring with the British and French, who hoped to recover control of the canal, they launched Operation KADESH. They planned to smash the Egyptian forces in the Sinai, take the Gaza Strip—thus shortening their border somewhat—and, by seizing Sharm-el-Sheikh, at the southern tip of the Sinai, break the Arab blockade of the Gulf of Aquaba.[18] However, they would stop short of the Suez Canal, relying on the intervention there of British and French forces (in operations designed to reacquire the canal on the pretext that freedom of navigation was threatened by the Egyptian-Israeli conflict) to discourage the Arab alliance from escalating the campaign into a full-scale war.

Since their objectives were limited, the Israelis planned to restrict their military actions accordingly. In the air, this meant abandoning the most fundamental axiom of air superiority, first expounded by the Italian prophet, Giulio Douhet, that "it is easier and more effective to destroy the enemy's aerial power by destroying his nests and eggs on the ground than to hunt his flying birds in the air."[19] In Operation KADESH the task assigned to the IAF was simply "to support the ground forces and be prepared to counter enemy interference."[20] In an order analogous to the "Yalu River rule" of the Korean War, Israeli pilots were ordered to stay at least ten miles from the canal, even though all but one of the Egyptian airfields lay west of it. Although the appropriate contingency plans existed,[21] there would be no attempt to establish air superiority through a preemptive strike against the Egyptian Air Force [EAF] on the ground: that would be left to their British and French allies.

The IAF was outnumbered on paper by the EAF alone, all of whose combat aircraft were jets, and if the aircraft of Egypt's allies should become involved the apparent odds would become prohibitive. However, the picture was not as difficult as it appeared. In theory, the Egyptians could call on 156 combat machines, but only 84 of them (30 MiG–15s, 30 de Havilland Vampires, 12 Gloster Meteors, and 12 Il–28 light bombers) were operational.[22] The Israelis mustered 136 operational aircraft, of which 53 (16 Dassault Mystere IV As, 22 Dassault Ouragans, and 15 Meteors) were jets.[23] Only the Mysteres were seen as comparable to the MiG–15s although, as events were to show, the Ouragans, in the hands of superior pilots, were quite capable of matching them.

However, at the time it all seemed a great risk. "By the Air Staff's reckoning," wrote the noted military historian, S. L. A. Marshall, "its main decision, in conflict with what is elsewhere considered the controlling principle, came when its forces were committed full-scale to support of the land battle without first achieving air superiority or inflicting any material damage on the enemy Air Forces."[24] One might add, the commitment was made also without much radar capability; nor were their ground and air headquarters sited together—a handicap more significant in the realm of close air support than that of air superiority.[25]

The Israelis hedged their bets by persuading the French to station temporarily two interceptor squadrons from their L'Armeé de l'Air on Israeli soil, assigned to protect Israeli cities from Arab bombers,[26] but apparently they were never needed. High serviceability and phenomenally quick turn-arounds simply confirmed the advantages that superior pilot training and tactics already gave the Israelis. IAF claimed a sortie rate of better than four a day for their jets and about two-and-a-half a day for their propeller-driven machines, while the Egyptians averaged less than one a day even before the Anglo-French intervention.[27]

The first Israeli move was to drop a paratroop force near the Mitla Pass, about thirty miles east of the canal at 1700 hours on October 29, 1956.

The 16 C–47 transports were screened by Israeli fighters whose pilots could see MiGs being towed to dispersal areas on the airfields west of the canal. Obeying the ten-mile restriction, Israeli jets patrolled the whole length of the canal for an hour, but no Egyptian aircraft rose to challenge them. Only sporadic (and ineffective) antiaircraft fire indicated that the Egyptians knew they were there.[28]

It was after 0700 hours on the 30th when the EAF launched its first attacks against the paratroopers, while the balance of the Israeli airborne brigade (commanded by Col. Ariel Sharon) advanced overland from Kuntilla. The Egyptians did some damage, but four Vampires were caught by two Mysteres on their way back from strafing Sharon's men at El Thamade and all four were shot down.[29]

The Israelis maintained standing patrols of Mysteres along a line east of the canal, where they could hope to intercept Egyptian aircraft heading for the battlefield. Most air combat pitted 2 Mysteres, flying in a "fluid pair," against 4, 6 or 8 MiGs flying "welded wings." The speeds of the Mystere and MiG–15 in level flight at sea level were nearly identical, but the Mystere was more agile, with all its control surfaces power-assisted. The Mystere also provided a more stable gun platform for its two 30-mm DEFA cannon at high speeds. The MiG "was a simple lightweight fighter with no frills apart from a gyro gunsight. . . . It was heavily armed, with two 23-mm cannon, each with 80 rounds, and a 37-mm cannon with 40 rounds [but] . . . the slow firing Russian cannon had a low muzzle velocity."[30]

The biggest difference between the MiG and Mystere, however, was in the calibre of their pilots. "As to tactics, the Egyptians handled MiGs about the way they were used in Korea, flying in staggered formations at various heights and trying to break off engagements by climbing turns" which took advantage of the MiGs' better rate of climb. "Their pilots seemed to dislike to tighten these turns and Israel's air force got the impression that their shooting was not very good," reported S. L. A. Marshall.[31]

The Egyptian pilots' apparent distaste for tightening their climbing turns at high "Gs" may be explained by the absence of power-controls for the MiG–15's elevators and the need for the pilot to move his hand away from the "stick" in order to trim the aircraft. They were not unwilling to fight, explained Israeli Defense Forces Chief of Staff, Moshe Dayan, who had doubted IAF's capability to master the EAF before the fighting began. "But they were careful to appear in comparatively large formations of four to eight planes, and they sought to end an engagement quickly and steer clear of prolonged combat."[32] In other words, the Egyptians sensibly chose the "single-pass-and-away" tactic for which their MiGs (being designed as interceptors of bombers) and their training were best suited. The Israelis, no doubt, also preferred the kind of surprise attack that had traditionally accounted for four out of five air victories,[33] but, with their better flying and combat skills, they were perfectly willing to "dogfight" at close-quarters

Moshe Dayan, Israeli Defense
Forces Chief of Staff.

when the occasion arose. As it turned out, even the obsolescent Ouragans, in service with the French Air Force since the late 1940s, could hold their own in that kind of combat.[34]

During the evening of October 30, the British and French ambassadors presented identical ultimatums to the Egyptians and Israeli governments, calling for a cessation of hostilities, disengagement of forces, and an Anglo-French reoccupation of the Canal Zone in order to secure international freedom of navigation on that waterway. The Israelis, of course, accepted; the Egyptians—not appreciating the disaster about to fall upon them in Sinai—did not. Twenty-five hours later (and 13 hours after the ultimatum had expired), British bombers flying from Malta and Cyprus began to strike at Egyptian air bases. Bombing in darkness, Valiants and Canberras tried to hit the targets with 1,000-pound high-explosive bombs from altitudes of 30,000 to 40,000 feet.[35]

What Tolkovsky has rightly called "this awfully stupid attack . . . terribly inefficient . . . ,"[36] predictably did little damage. Nonetheless, the next morning British and French carrier-borne fighter-bombers and light bombers followed up with low-level attacks. By noon on November 1, the British and French were claiming that the EAF had lost 105 aircraft on the ground. More such sweeps on the 2d, 3d, and 4th (including the destruction of 20 Ilyushin Il–28 bombers at Luxor by French fighter-bombers operating from Israeli bases)[37] brought the total claim up to 260. Yet, the American military analyst and historian, Trevor Dupuy, has pointed out that the Egyptian Air Force was estimated to consist of only 255 aircraft at the start of these raids, and at least 40 planes escaped.[38] Moreover, one might add, 5 MiGs, 6 Vampires, and a Meteor had fallen victims to the IAF[39] before the British and French entered the conflict.*

Whatever the actual number destroyed on the ground in the course of the Anglo-French attacks, it was certainly true that the EAF was no longer able to fight by noon on November 1. Indeed, the Egyptians had apparently lost all will to fight by nightfall of the previous day, and the IAF was in undisputed control of the air over Sinai. "Actually, the Egyptian Air Force did send over [Israel] Il–28 bombers on two occasions, on the nights of the 30th and 31st, one bomber on each mission, but they dropped their bombs on open ground, far from city or village, without discrimination and without causing damage," according to General Dayan. No Israeli aircraft had been lost in air-to-air engagements, while "at least four MiGs and four Vampires were shot down by our pilots."[40]

The bulk of the Egyptian Air Force had been destroyed on the ground by the Anglo-French attacks, and air-to-air engagements between Israeli and Egyptian machines had been relatively few. The Israelis had achieved and retained air superiority more by Egyptian default than by their own efforts. Strategies on both sides had been unsophisticated, the Egyptians making no coherent attempt to establish air superiority even before the Anglo-French intervention, and the Israelis relying on standing patrols or the quick reaction times permitted by the comparatively short distances involved to get their aircraft to the right place at the right time. In that regard, the very smallness of their air force also worked to their advantage; other things being equal, small organizations normally have quicker reaction times than larger ones.

Tactically, however, Tolkovsky's ideas had proved extremely successful. Multi-purpose machines, flown by extremely well-trained pilots employing superior tactics, clearly could defeat larger numbers of specialized fighters flown by less skillful pilots using inferior tactics.

---

*This seems a good point at which to caution the reader against accepting any set of figures relating to Middle Eastern wars at face value, particularly those relating to strengths or casualties. The "fog of war" and, indeed, of peacetime tensions, is often inpenetrable; security on the one hand, and propaganda on the other, are both immensely important; and deceptoin is a way of life. "Official" figures are rarely available and, when they are, are not to be trusted. Accordingly, unofficial ones vary widely, even when proferrred by the most reputable authors. Those given in this essay are more likely to be generally right than specifically so; they represent the author's "educated guesses" from among the many alternative sets available.

Before the 1967 War, the Israeli combat aircraft inventory included
French-built Super-Mysteres (*above*) and Vautour II light bombers
(*below*).

The principles upon which the IAF had been built had now been tested in combat and not found wanting, and the broad directions that Israeli air power should take were now clearly perceived throughout the Israeli high command.

American and United Nations' pressure subsequently compelled Israel to surrender all its conquests in the Sinai, but a UN buffer zone kept Arab guerrillas from raiding into Israeli territory from the south, and the Strait of Tiran was opened to Israeli shipping. An uneasy truce extended over the next decade, marked by intermittent border clashes with Jordan and Syria. With the formation of the Palestine Liberation Organization in 1964 and the occurrence of a military coup in Syria, which put an even more extreme anti-Zionist government into power in Damascus early in 1966, the Egyptians were encouraged to close the Strait of Tiran again and give the United Nations Emergency Force, keeping peace in Sinai, its marching orders. Thus, the UN left and, with Arab armies massing along their southern and eastern borders, the Israelis in June 1967 decided on another preemptive attack against the strongest of their opponents.

Prelude to the 1967 War

This time they were outnumbered in every way. The core of the IAF's 245 combat aircraft consisted of 72 Dassault Mirage IIIs. Backing them up were 40 Super-Mysteres (half of them borrowed from the French) and 60 Mysteres. There were also 48 obsolete Ouragans and 25 Sud-Aviation Vautour II light bombers, and—for what they were worth, which was nothing in the air superiority context—76 Fouga Magister 2-seat jet trainers that carried a pair of machineguns and could be fitted with air-to-ground rockets. The Egyptians had about 450 operationally ready combat aircraft, including 120 MiG–21s, 80 MiG–19s, 150 MiG–17s and –15s, and 30 Su–7s, plus 70 Il–28 and Tu–16 bombers. If they intervened, the Syrians and Jordanians could add another 170 machines including 36 MiG–21s and 22 Hawker Hunters. There was also the possibility of the Iraqis adding some of their 100-plus MiGs, Hunters, and light bombers to the Arab total.[41]

Qualitatively, too, the Arabs had an apparent edge in equipment. Their newest fighter, the MiG–21, designed as a short-range interceptor, had an excellent thrust-to-weight ratio, which provided it with sparkling acceleration and a high rate of climb. Armed with two 30-mm cannons and two "Atoll" air-to-air, infra-red, homing missiles, "its only real weakness lay in its lack of structural strength that limited its speed at low altitudes."[42] Like the MiG–21, the Mirage III was comfortably supersonic, but its weight/thrust ratio was lower so that its acceleration and climb were slightly inferior to the MiG's. A low-wing loading gave it a good turning capability

575

despite its tailless, delta-wing configuration, and its two 30-mm DEFA cannon were admirable weapons complemented by two Israeli-designed and built Shafir air-to-air missiles.[43]

When it came to flying skills, the Israelis were still well ahead of the Egyptians, however. "MiG–21 pilots were limited to 5 hours [flying] training per month and the aircraft was not cleared for aerobatics," say the British historians Armitage and Mason. "MiG–19 pilots had similar restrictions on flying time but were also impeded by technical problems involving engine fires. The 2 MiG–17 squadrons were theoretically converted to the air-to-ground role, but realistic exercises were only practiced three times a year."[44] Presumably this last restriction also applied to the Su–7s, also supersonic but specifically designed for ground support, with two 23-mm cannon and a carrying capacity (at subsonic speeds) of over 1,000 kilograms of external ordnance.

Additionally, the Israelis had a precise assessment of the Arabs' best fighter. In August 1966, an Iraqi pilot had defected, bringing his MiG–21 with him, and the Israelis had been able to learn about its considerable capabilities and not insignificant weaknesses in practice dogfights.[45] Perhaps that experience helped to account for the results of a large-scale engagement over the southern Golan, on April 7, 1967, in which 6 Syrian MiGs were shot down without loss to the IAF's Mirages.[46]

From the Israeli perspective, the greatest threat was posed by the 30 Tu–16 bombers, subsonic but capable of 900 kilometers per hour at 36,000 feet, with a service ceiling of more than 46,000 feet and a combat radius of over 1,800 miles. The heavily armed Tupolevs, mounting six 23-mm guns in remotely controlled forward, dorsal, and ventral barbettes, 2 more guns in the tail controlled by automatic gun-ranging radar, and 1 fixed gun firing forward, could each carry over 19,000 pounds of bombs.[47]

O'Ballance reported that, in the event of war with Israel, the Egyptian air staff intended to use these machines as a strategic bombing force, striking at the relatively concentrated Israeli cities and industrial complexes.[48] If it came to a straight contest of bomber versus interceptor, the Israelis would be at a great disadvantage caused by the virtual impossibility of creating a radar network that could give a workable warning time of attack from the east in an era before the introduction of "look-down" airborne radar. The Tupolevs had the range to fly out from southern Egyptian bases, low over the Red Sea, then north over Saudi Arabia and Jordan, before turning west and climbing onto target vectors that would carry them to Tel Aviv or Haifa from positions beyond Israeli radar range in less than three minutes. Only standing patrols could hope to intercept them, and the IAF could hardly expect to maintain such patrols for prolonged periods. Moreover, this time the Israelis had no French fighters to help protect them nor British bombers to tackle Egyptian airfields. They did have a centralized, unified command-and-control system, now working out of a combined land/

air operations room in Tel Aviv known as "the Pit," but, when their own aircraft were not in the air and Arab bombers were, the Israelis could only defend themselves with two batteries of American HAWK surface-to-air missiles with a slant range of 21 miles, and a few obsolete antiaircraft guns of Second World War vintage.

However, it was the IAF's intention that that situation would not arise. The Israelis did have the considerable advantage of knowing how *not* to set about destroying their enemies' "nest and eggs" as a result of their careful study of the British attempt to carry out high-altitude night raids on Egyptian bases in 1956. They would neutralize the enemy "nests" by surprise attacks at low level, in daylight, with a bomb that would make runways unusable for a prolonged period, and then they would blow the enemy "eggs" to pieces on the ground. The basic idea was to be able to perform a fairly high speed, low-level, approach, yet have the bomb reach the ground with the terminal velocity of a dive-bombing attack. Yet to try and turn a fast-moving bomb from the lateral direction of flight it would have on leaving the aircraft to the vertical mode needed for it to penetrate a concrete runway, without losing the essential momentum required to drive it through the concrete, would create impossible "G" forces. The answer was to put a tube inside the bomb, along its axis, place a retro-rocket in the front to slow it down, then an automatic parachute to tilt it into the vertical, and, finally, insert an accelerator rocket in the rear to tear the parachute off and drive the bomb deep into the runway.[49]

The attack, when it was delivered, would have to be devastating. Anything less would leave the Israelis in a very awkward stance to meet a counterstrike, with nearly all their aircraft on the ground, refueling and rearming. And what about the Egyptians' allies? "I was torn between two alternatives," remembers the IAF's Commander, "Motti" Hod. "To do it simultaneously on the Egyptian and Syrian air force and have less punching power on both sides or to concentrate all our effort and have an effective blow on one, hoping I would have enough time to repeat it on the other side." He calculated it would take the Syrians "about two-and-a-half hours" to respond if the initial attack was launched against the stronger, Egyptian force, and if his assumption proved correct there would be time enough for a second strike in the north. "But this was very, very complicated to sell to the General Staff here, and to the Prime Minister—to the government—because they did not want to take the word of the Air Force that this could be done."[50]

The General Staff and the Prime Minister, however, agreed to the plan, and the decision was made to concentrate everything against the stronger opponent, and virtually every one of the principles of war was exemplified in the attack launched at 0745 hours (Israeli time, Egyptian time being one hour later) on June 5, 1967.

The Six-Day War

The Egyptian dawn alert was over, early patrols had landed, and most pilots and ground crews were breakfasting when the first Israeli planes screamed in at low level. Those coming across the Sinai to attack the airfields there and along the canal were screened until the last minute by the high ground east of the canal. Others, bound for bases in the Nile delta, around Cairo, and further south, outflanked the Egyptian radars by an indirect approach that took them far out over the Mediterranean. "Priorities were given, first, to bombers, second to airfields which were within range of attacking our bases in Israel, and thirdly, the air defense interceptors," according to General Hod.[51] Ground-based air defense systems (including nearly 1,000 antiaircraft guns, and about 160 SA–2 surface-to-air missiles deployed in 24 batteries)[52] were caught initially unaware as wave after wave of Israeli planes screamed overhead. The new "concrete dibber" bombs, some with time-delay fuses guaranteed to hamper repair efforts, drove into every runway, "regular" high-explosive bombs crashed into control towers and maintenance facilities, and finally the Israeli pilots turned their guns on aircraft lined up in neat rows, as if for a formal inspection. Then they raced back to Israel for another load of ordnance, their astonishing turnaround times providing a force multiplier that convinced the EAF there were at least 1,500 aircraft in action against it and persuaded Egypt's President Nasser that British and American aircraft were involved.[53] One Super-Mystere, "hit in the belly" by "tremendous antiaircraft fire," labored back to Israel with the pilot telling his wingman "that I might have to bail out and that he should make note of the spot. . . . Still, I managed to get back and land safely, and—listen to this—I took the same plane back to Syria an hour later—that's how good our mechanics are."[54]

In two hours and fifty minutes the EAF was crippled. All thirty of the feared Tu–16s were destroyed, along with a good proportion of the MiG–21s. Those that got off the ground were shot out of the sky. Two flights of four MiG–21s, on "stand-by," got airborne and managed to account for two Israeli machines before they were all shot down. Another twelve MiG–21s and eight MiG–19s, based at Hurghada on the Red Sea shore, flew north to engage sixteen Mirages over the canal. Four of them were shot down resulting in no Israeli losses, several more MiGs crashed while trying to land on damaged runways, and some which had landed were then destroyed by strafing.[55]

General Hod's concern about timing had been unjustified. It was nearly noon before the Syrians and Jordanians launched a few tentative strikes against targets in northern Israel. By then, the IAF was ready to turn on both. While the majority of its aircraft were busy totally destroying Jordan's Air Force and halving the Syrian combat strength, some Israeli machines were back over Egypt, this time knocking out key radar installations and ensuring that any enemy pilot who subsequently chose to fly over the Sinai would have to do so "blind" without knowing when or where he might meet Israeli fighters.[56] By nightfall, total Arab losses were estimated at 380 aircraft, while Israel admitted the loss of "19 pilots, of whom 8 were killed and 11 are missing. . . . Details of our planes lost are 4 Ouragons, 4 Mysteres, 4 Super-Mysteres, 2 Mirages, 1 Vautour and 4 Fouga Magisters."[57] The Fougas had all been lost while providing close air support for the Army, most of the others to ground fire; only 2 machines had been shot down in air-to-air engagements.[58]

About twenty Egyptian aircraft were destroyed in air combat, and something of the tactics employed can be gleaned from accounts of specific engagements. A Mirage pilot over the Sinai, credited with three victories in the war, "discovered four MiG–19s flying around below us. We came down on them. Number One stuck on to the tail of the last one and brought him down, then he took on the third and brought him down too," he reported. "Then he made room for me. Meanwhile, the two others had discovered us and turned around to fight us. I had a short battle with them. At a given moment I was sitting on the tail of the last one and gave him a short burst, but missed. Apparently my sights had gone wrong. I continued chasing him until I was in a convenient position for shooting, fired without using the sights, and hit him with one of my bursts.[59]

A Mirage might be expected to dispose of a MiG–19 without too much trouble but, by the same criteria, a MiG–21 should have been able to do the same to a Super-Mystere. Not so. "On the first day of the war we took off to attack a MiG–21 air base by the name of Teykel, located far in the mountainous area of northeastern Syria," recalls another pilot.

> When we reached the base we were surprised to see two MiG–21s circling above it. We had to switch from bombing to fighting. I ordered my No. 4 to draw the nearer MiG into a disadvantageous position. But the MiG was not decoyed easily. He went after No. 4 until he saw me coming at him. This sent him into a crazy pattern of aerobatics; he kept firing into the air like mad. I got him in my sights at about 150-200 meters and let go with two bursts. The first one hit his wing and sent him into a spiral dive. . . . In the meantime, Nos. 3 and 4 were engaging the other MiG. They got him in the wing tips. The MiG began to roll over quickly—the pilot had lost control of the plane—then crashed.[60]

From that account there seems little doubt that the MiGs were mishandled. The Super-Mysteres were far from home, with limited fuel, and the MiGs were faster, with that "sparkling acceleration" and better rates of climb. The Syrians should have gained height and then dived on the Israelis in "hit and run" passes designed to keep them from their homeward course even if they could avoid being shot down. Instead, the Syrians chose to dogfight at low altitude, engaging in a "crazy pattern of aerobatics" virtually guaranteed to topple their gyro gunsights, which lacked stability at high "Gs,"[61] a tactic which says more for their courage than their judgement.

As for Mirage *versus* MiG–21, "a real surprise awaited us at Gardaka air base, south of Sharm-el-Sheikh," according to a Mirage pilot.

> We suddenly discovered four MiGs trying to latch themselves on to our tail. There we were—four Mirages with limited firepower and just about enough fuel to get us back home, against four well-armed and fuelled MiGs above their own field. Well, the battle was at low altitude and lasted exactly two minutes. Three MiGs were shot down inside the base area . . . the fourth crashed while trying to land.[62]

Again, the MiGs should have declined to dogfight. Once they had been spotted, common sense dictated that they haul off and try another pass, the approach to combat usually taught by their Russian instructors, who "seemed content to just teach the single pass technique for air combat."[63] Courage they had in abundance, but they lacked "the high degree of our [Israeli] pilots' personal identification with their assignments, plus their handling of their craft and weapons [which] produces the combination that gets positive results."[64] There was also the unquantifiable psychological element explained by the Israeli flight leader who reported on the combat. "A good pilot," he said, "is not merely a mixture of skill, resourcefulness, discipline and good judgement, but also, even primarily, an outgrowth of the spiritual values and the cultural level which have nurtured him. Inside the fighter plane, all of your emotional forces are compressed into concentrating on your objective; everything else become secondary."[65] Or, as Napoleon put it, "the moral is to the physical as three is to one."

After the first 6 hours of the Six-Day War, Israeli air superiority was assured. The Jordanian Air Force had been totally destroyed on the ground, its 14 surviving fighter pilots being sent to help the neighboring Iraqis. The EAF had perhaps 150 combat airplanes fit to fight (and a surplus of pilots for them now) and the Syrians about 60. The Iraqi air arm—including 60 MiG–21s, 6 Tu–16s, and 50 Hawker Hunters—was still intact, but on the morning of the 7th one of those Tu–16s bombed Netanya, apparently mistaking it for Tel Aviv. It was shot down by ground fire, and the IAF retaliated with a strike against H–3, the desert airfield near Habbaniyah, which was the one Iraqi base it could reach. In what seems to have been the only air battle the Israelis have ever lost, their aircraft were "bounced" by 8 Hunters, some or all of them flown by the Jordanian pilots who had just arrived.

The Hunter was an extremely agile, lightweight machine, approaching obsolescence in 1967, but its success on this occasion may well have been due to the fact that the Israeli machines were operating at the very limit of their range and the Hunter pilots were clever enough to employ tactics designed to make the most of that fact. King Hussein claims that three of his pilots, "brought down nine enemy aircraft . . . including Mysteres and three Mirages. . . . One captain alone destroyed one Mirage, two Mysteres and a Vautour,"[66] and, although the Israelis said nothing about their losses, it was probably no coincidence that the IAF's commander noted "the Jordanians were the best our fliers engaged in the air."[67] Only two of the Israeli pilots survived, to be taken prisoner by the Iraqis.

However, the Israeli strike accounted for nine MiG–21s, four Hunters, and two transport planes destroyed on the ground.[68] The Iraqis, like the Syrians, decided that discretion was the better part of valor and made no more attempts to bomb Israel, while the remnants of the Egyptian Air Force kept bravely plugging away, flying their remaining MiGs and Su–7s in generally fruitless attempts to help their hard-pressed army in the Sinai. O'Ballance quotes Israeli sources as claiming that the Egyptians lost sixty-one aircraft and the other Arab forces lost sixteen in air-to-air engagements during the war.[69] A dozen or so Israeli aircraft may have been lost to airborne Arab fire; another thirty-plus fell to ground fire or were lost accidentally, according to a knowledgeable private Israeli source.[70]

If those figures are approximately correct, then the Israeli ratio of victories to losses in air combat during the 1967 war was in the region of six or seven to one. Bearing in mind the damage done to Arab morale (and to their command control system) by the preemptive, counterair strikes that opened the Israeli campaign, it is perhaps surprising that the ratio was not

French-built Mirage III fighters, faster and more capable than their MiG opponents.

higher. Would Israeli air superiority have been as great if it had had to fight for it against substantially larger Arab forces, better controlled and with their morale relatively intact? Probably not. In war there is an intricate relationship between quality and quantity (expressed mathematically in the Lanchester equations and his N-square Law),[71] which could have altered the balance significantly had the Arab air forces entered the battle more or less intact.

Escalation to the War of Attrition

The Israelis held their conquests after the 1967 cease-fire, giving themselves some "buffer" spaces, deep enough in the south to make a more orthodox strategy viable, but still relatively shallow on the west bank of the Jordan and the Golan Heights in the northeast. In the Sinai and on the Golan they were able to construct radar stations on high ground that significantly improved their early warning capability, and these were carefully tied in by landline and radio to the operations center at Tel Aviv.

There was every reason to do so. Their Arab enemies—at least the Egyptians and the Syrians—were intent on revenge. Armies and air forces were rebuilt with Russian support, while staff officers plotted new strategies around new technologies. The most important of these, from an airman's point of view, were the development of much more effective surface-to-air missiles, a quantum jump in the capability of low-level air defense artillery, and the integration of the two into a comprehensive air defense umbrella.

Meanwhile, Arab-Israeli borders were treated to a series of guerrilla skirmishes which the Egyptians finally escalated into the so-called "War of Attrition," involving artillery strikes and commando-type raids on both sides. The air arms eventually became committed, too, and on July 20, 1969, about forty Egyptian aircraft penetrated into Israeli airspace over the Sinai, strafing and bombing minor military installations. Israeli aircraft—probably Mirages and Super-Mysteres—rose to greet them. In the ensuing battle, the Israelis admitted losing two unidentified planes, but claimed to have downed two Su–7s, two MiG–17s, and one MiG–21. The Egyptians had a very different story, claiming *nineteen* Israeli planes for the loss of two of their own. They took a more moderate line on September 11 when, after another major clash, they claimed four victories while admitting two losses.[72] But, as the Egyptian Chief of Staff, Lt. Gen. Saad el Shazli, has remarked, although "frequently our pilots would swear they had shot down one or more of the enemy. . . . those kills somehow never fell on Egyptian soil."[73]

The Israelis were just beginning to convert to American warplanes. During the Six-Day War, the French, worried by the possibility of an Arab oil embargo against them, had shifted to a neutralist position and placed an embargo on the export of war materials to Israel. Unable (at that time) to build the most sophisticated weapons systems such as aircraft for themselves, the Israelis had to solicit help from the only practical alternative source, the United States. Backed by a powerful American Jewish lobby, their entreaties were rewarded and the Americans, at long last, were prepared to help. In April 1968, President Lyndon B. Johnson had authorized deliveries of the Douglas A–4 Skyhawk. Before the end of that year, agreement had also been reached for the sale of 40 McDonnell F–4 Phantoms over the next two years, the first of them arriving in September 1969.

Designated by the Americans as an "attack bomber," the little A–4 was well suited to the Israeli acquisition philosophy of multi-mission capability at two levels. A relatively cheap, subsonic single-seater, with two 30-mm cannon replacing the 20-mm ones that the Americans favored (and soon to be equipped with a Shafir air-to-air missile as well),[74] it was a maneuverable and extremely robust airplane. Used as an air superiority weapon, it could—and did—down the best Egyptian fighters on occasion, and it soon became the workhorse of the IAF. The F–4 was at the other end of the multi-mission spectrum in many respects. A big, ugly brute of a plane with all-weather capability, the twin-engine, two-seater Phantom could out-pace and out-range all Egyptian fighters *and* deliver some 12,000 pounds of external ordnance, which might include a variety of air-to-air and air-to- ground missiles.[75] Since the Russians appeared reluctant to reequip their Arab friends with the newest Soviet machines, the Israeli advantage was widening.

As the War of Attrition heated up—the kind of prolonged nibbling scuffle that the Israelis could not afford[76]—the IAF began to strike deeper into Egypt in a desperate effort to force the Egyptians to relinquish their strategy. That approach simply enabled President Nasser to pressure the Russians into becoming more involved. In April 1970, three squadrons of MiG–21Js, with Russian pilots and ground crews, arrived in Egypt. The –21J had improved on-board radar, a better stabilized gyro gunsight, and wingtip drop tanks, which gave it the range to reach Tel Aviv from airfields west of the canal.

The IAF promptly relinquished its deep strikes into the delta, but continued to attack military installations in the Canal Zone. The inevitable confrontation occurred on June 30, 1970, when eight Phantoms and eight Mirages tangled in a four-minute dogfight with sixteen MiG–21s piloted by Soviet airmen.[77] One of the Phantom pilots has given us the usual spartan account of what happened when the Soviets went into combat. "They came at us in pairs, and we let them pass in order not to be sandwiched between the pairs as they had anticipated we would. They passed as couples in a procession. We waited and got in behind."[78]

In other words, the Russians attacked with eight welded wings flying in trail or echelon. The intended "sandwich" maneuver was a basic tactic in which the welded wings formed the bread of the sandwich and the unfortunate victim or victims, the meat, contrasted with the more sophisticated "fluid pair" approach in which each slice of bread was represented by a single machine. Having "got in behind," the Israelis were in a perfect position to shoot and, no doubt, they did so.

The Mirages, flying top cover, now swooped down, turning the action into a classic *mêlée*, with:

> planes turning and twisting around and firing guns and rockets [missiles] at each other. Breaking hard, I succeeded in getting my sights on a MiG. He had guts and turned into the fight but I quickly realized he was inexperienced. He made elementary mistakes. Diving down to 2,000 m [6,561.68 feet.], I cut him off and soon locked on my radar—then we had time. It was clear that he could not get away. At a range of 1,000 m [three quarters of a mile] we fired a missile. The MiG exploded into a flaming ball.[79]

With the Phantom on his tail, the Russian had to turn into or out of the fight; sensibly he turned into it, where there was always the possibility of another MiG getting a shot at his pursuer. One of his mistakes may have

**The A–4 Skyhawk, the IAF's workhorse
during the War of Attrition.**

been a failure to appreciate that his opponent might fight in the vertical plane as well as the horizontal. The ability to turn tightly is a function of speed as well as wing loading. In a tight, level turn the drag of its delta wing would have bled off much of the MiG's speed, while the Phantom, with its heavier wing loading, would have had trouble turning with him and, if the turn was maintained, their positions might soon have been reversed. The Israeli's reference to "diving" offers a clue, however. Perhaps the latter pulled up sharply to lose speed, rolled over the top to cut the angle, and then dived inverted on the Russian in a maneuver sometimes known as the "high speed yo-yo."

Since the personal pronoun suddenly changes back from "I" to "we" when the missile was fired, it seems likely that the Israelis released a radar-homing Sparrow, which would have required the active participation of the man in the back seat. In any case, that 1970 engagement marks the first Israeli recognition of a victory by an air-to-air missile rather than by gunfire, although there very probably had been earlier successes. Their own Shafir I had been tested before the spring of 1963, although it was not yet considered a very satisfactory weapon. Until the end of the 1960s the Israelis felt that the minimum range of the air-to-air missile was too great, its maximum range too short, and the radar acquisition too weak. Not until the turn of the decade did they acquire sufficient confidence in it to consider it worthwhile, accepting the diminished flight performance that inevitably accompanied its external carriage.[80] And even then they kept their guns. Seven years later there was a range of such missiles in the Israeli inventory, but all Israeli aircraft still carried cannon as well.

The Egyptians had had rocket-powered, radar-guided SA–2 missiles in 1967, but, designed to combat speedy, high-flying, but unwielding strategic bombers, they had been ineffective against the nimble, low-flying Israeli fighters. The SA–2s were slow to accelerate, limited in the "Gs" they could pull and easily thwarted by a hard descending turn towards them. However, at the same time that they sent their own MiG squadrons, the Russians had started to bolster Egyptian defenses with improved SA–2A and SA–3 missiles. The Israelis had already begun to rely on American-supplied electronic countermeasures, but suddenly their ECM pods failed them.

In early August 1970, the War of Attrition was about to end as a result of American initiatives, when a sudden shift in the electronic balance resulted in the IAF losing five F–4s and their crews to Egyptian missiles. Several aircraft had already been lost in July, and Israeli defenses were obviously inadequate. They turned for help to the USAF, which had already met and mastered SA–2s in Vietnam. According to General Peled:

> We took advice from the experts of Vietnam because we had lost a couple of aircraft two weeks before that and we didn't like it. So there was a scramble to find out what is that magic called ECM pods. Everybody was begging the USAF to release some

.... They sent over pods and they sent over their operational experts to show us how these magical instruments could protect you from the wrath of the missiles—if only you flew the correct formation. You have a pod, it radiates, it spoofs, it jams, and if you're in the right relative positions to the missiles you're immune, like Superman. That's why we lost those five. It is the one thing we shouldn't have done—take recipes from another world, another situation where the USAF never had to face anything more complicated than SA–2As and Bs. We were faced with a mix of SA–2As and SA–3s and SA–2s improved. A cocktail.[81]

If Peled is to be believed, the IAF would soon have overcome "that foolish taking of advice" and taken its revenge, but it was frustrated by political *fiat*. The fighting concluded on August 7, 1970, with the Israelis claiming that, since the end of the Six Day War, the Egyptians (and Russians) had lost 110 aircraft while admitting that they themselves had lost 16.[82] Most of them, as we have seen, fell to missiles in the last 2 or 3 weeks of the conflict, a mishap illustrating a very important aspect of the electronic contest that was now an irrevocable part of the air war: a tendency for the advantage to swing very quickly from one protagonist to the other as an electronic advance was met with a countermeasure, to be matched in turn with a counter- countermeasure or another new electronic step, *ad infinitum*.[83]

The Russians, for reasons best known to themselves, were apparently reluctant to supply the Arab states with more modern aircraft when they began reequipping them after the Six-Day War and during the War of Attrition. But they were willing to bolster the ground-based Arab air defense with the latest missile systems and antiaircraft guns. The improved SA–2 and the SA–3 were retained, supplemented by the SA–6 and SA–7 and the four-barreled, radar-controlled and power-operated ZSU–23/4 antiaircraft cannon. These weapons, used in combination, provided a comprehensive air defense "umbrella" up to a height of some 72,000 feet and out to a slant range of about 31 miles.[84] The limitations of one—and they did all have limitations—were compensated for by the strengths of the others.

The radars and guidance systems of the Russian-built missiles worked on a wide spectrum of radio frequencies, and some of them could switch frequencies with bewildering rapidity, complicating the question of ECM and providing, *in toto*, an air defense far more sophisticated than that faced by the IAF in the War of Attrition. The weaknesses of the air defense system were its immobility and the interdependence of its component parts. Even with the key SA–6, which had all its missiles and radars mounted on tracked vehicles, setting up and recalibrating its instruments after a move took several hours.[85]

Even though the War of Attrition had been officially concluded in 1970, sporadic skirmishing continued at a rather lower level of intensity. However, it flared up to old heights on September 13, 1973, in a spectacular air battle apparently initiated by four Israeli fighters deliberately intruding into Syrian territory. The Syrians scrambled a force of MiGs to intercept them,

An Israeli Air Force F–4 Phantom, on display with its weaponry, 1971.

more Israeli fighters appeared, and the Egyptian Chief of Staff reported that "in the ensuing melee at least eight and possibly thirteen Syrians were shot down for the loss of one Israeli plane."[86] Edgar O'Ballance reports that "in this battle the Syrians had wanted to fire their SAMs, but the Soviet advisers held the vital fuses and would not allow the missiles to be used,"[87] a restriction that may well have played a major part in determining the course of events less than a month later.

The Yom Kippur War

On the eve of the 1973 Yom Kippur War, the Egyptians were estimated to have about 880 SAM launchers, including 80 SA–6s; the Syrians had 360 SAM launchers, including 60 SA–6s. There are no figures for the actual number of missiles held in stock. In addition, the Egyptians had about 2,000 SA–7s and 2,750 antiaircraft guns, including 150 ZSU–23/4s; the Syrians had half that number of SA–7s and about 1,900 guns, including 100 ZSU–23/4s. There were also nearly 600 Egyptian and 275 Syrian combat aircraft in their respective national inventories, of which 330 MiG–21s and

MiG–19s would play the major part in any struggle for air superiority.[88] The Jordanians were staying strictly neutral this time, but the Arab forces were bolstered by 2 Mirage squadrons from Libya, 3 MiG–21 squadrons from Iraq and 1 from Algeria, and an Iraqi squadron of Hunters, as well as several squadrons of MiG–17s and 1 of Su–7s.[89] However, none of them except the Libyan Mirage were a technological match for Israel's 140 Phantoms and 50 Mirages, even without taking pilot quality into account.

The debacles of 1956 and 1967 "had cost us few pilots but a near-total destruction of morale," in the opinion of General Saad el Shazli, the Egyptian Chief of Staff, "and in their many encounters since 1967 our men had frankly not matched the enemy's."[90] They might outnumber the Israelis by a margin of nearly three to one in aircraft but the Egyptians, at least, had no intention of fighting a conventional air-to-air battle for air superiority. "Throughout my planning, I was anxious not to bring our air force into direct conflict with the enemy's," wrote the Egyptian Chief of Staff. "From the start I adopted two main principles. First, to avoid chance air encounters. Second, to use our air force for sudden ground-attack strikes where enemy air cover was least likely. Primarily, I wanted the enemy's ground forces and ground targets to taste the psychological impact of our air force, while at the same time I wanted to preserve it from air combat."[91] The Syrians, on the other hand, "displayed a much greater commitment to battle from the start," in the opinion of an Indian commentator, Maj. Gen. D. K. Palit. "Syrian (and later Iraqi) MiGs were thrown into the fray with what seemed reckless abandon.... Furthermore, probably because of a lesser degree of SAM cover than in the Canal Zone, Syrian-based fighters remained in the air more often."[92]

The IAF appreciated the threat that the new missile technology posed, even if it overestimated its ability to deal with it. Had the Israeli government chosen to follow the precedents of 1956 and 1967 when it concluded that the Arabs were determined on war, then the missile screens would have been the first targets of a preemptive strike according to General Peled:

> We had well-made, sophisticated, complicated, well orchestrated operation plans to knock out the total missile force along the canal—106 batteries....You could equate it to a huge Cecil DeMille type of spectacle, or a huge backdrop, it had lighting, it had many other conditions to it. Had all the conditions existed to run the show it would have been a great success. Within half a day, there would have been no more missiles at all.[93]

However, for political reasons there could be no first strike this time. The Arabs must be seen as the aggressors for the sake of world public opinion, especially American opinion, since the United States was currently the Israelis' only external source of sophisticated weaponry. Even a precautionary mobilization on any scale would have to be delayed until the very last minute in order to avoid accusations of provoking an attack.

Very early on the morning of October 6, 1973—*Yom Kippur*, the Day of Atonement—Israeli intelligence reported that an attack would come, north and south, at 1800 hours. A partial mobilization of ground forces was ordered—the IAF had already been "placed on alert" on September 26—but, four hours earlier than predicted, the Egyptians crossed the canal and the Syrians struck simultaneously on the Golan Heights. In the Sinai the EAF attacked three air bases and airfields, ten HAWK SAM missile sites, three major command posts, and electronic jamming and monitoring centers as well as a number of radar stations.[94] The Egyptians admitted losing five aircraft from unspecified causes,[95] while the Israelis would claim a total of forty-two Egyptian planes downed before nightfall.[96]

The Egyptian Tu–16s destroyed in 1967 had been replaced, but they were now used simply as launching platforms for the Kelt air-to-ground missile with its 1,600-pound high-explosive warhead. The Egyptians apparently launched about 25 such missiles at targets deep inside the Sinai, mostly radar sites. The standard Kelt was, like the V-weapons of Second World War vintage, an unguided missile, but some of this particular batch may have been fitted with a radiation homing capability, for radars make singularly small targets in the vastness of the Sinai but at least 2 stations took direct hits.[97] One Kelt that allegedly went astray in the direction of Tel Aviv was intercepted by an Israeli fighter and promptly shot down.[98]

In the north, the Syrian Air Force "provided a considerable degree of close support to the ground forces attacking on the Golan Heights,"[99] attempting to break through the Israeli air defenses to bomb targets in the Huleh valley. "In the ensuing air battles, however, the Israelis had no difficulty in securing their own airspace, and the Syrian jets lost heavily against Mirages and Phantoms."[100] Shortly afterwards, when the Iraqis joined the fight, "it is reported that the only attempt to break through the Israeli air defense system was made by two Iraqi Tu–16 bombers. They did not succeed in reaching Tel Aviv; and one of the bombers was shot down," according to General Palit, who had close ties with the Syrian military authorities.[101] The Arab attacks had been well coordinated both in space and time despite the wide separation of their command systems, but the Israelis, fighting from interior lines over relatively short distances and with the advantage of a single, centralized control from "the Pit" in Tel Aviv, were able to thwart the enemy on each occasion.

When the Israelis turned to offensive action of their own during the afternoon of the 6th, however, they got a rude shock. Along the line of the Suez Canal a couple of hundred Israeli soldiers were in danger of being trapped in the fortified strongpoints of the Bar Lev Line and overwhelmed. The IAF's first ground support priority was to try and help them, but the Mirages and Phantoms assigned to provide protection for other Phantoms and Skyhawks attacking ground targets were quite unable to do so. The threat came from below, not above; from missiles, not MiGs.

589

All the missile batteries (and the ZSU–23s and ZSU–24s) were still west of the Canal, but the Israeli planes were well within range at some point in their passes, and there were already SA-7s on the east bank in the hands of Egyptian infantrymen. Their infra-red filters were not fooled by flares released by the Israelis, although their 3.3-pound warheads usually only damaged the tailpipes of their targets. By nightfall there would be lines of Skyhawks on each Israeli air base, waiting to have their tailpipe-sljrepaired or another 28 inches of pipe welded on to reduce the cone of radiation and minimize the effect of any further hits. The SA-2s and SA–3s were not very effective against the low-flying Israeli aircraft. Much more dangerous were the SA–6s. They were fast, using command frequencies outside the range of Israeli ECM, and "frequency hopping," as well as difficult to spot visually because their second-stage ramjet engine burned inside the tube of the first-stage rocket motor. They could be fired either singly, in a salvo of three, or sequentially in a "ripple" effect. If they were identified in time, then they might be avoided by a hard descending turn—which was liable to bring the aircraft into range of the lethal ZSU–23 and –24s.

The IAF paused for nearly two hours on the evening of that first day of war to reconsider its tactics. When attacks resumed, "the aircraft were forced to keep a safe distance from the missiles, rendering their bombing of the Egyptian forces imprecise and its impact marginal,"[102] admits one Israeli authority, although General Peled would certainly argue that their bombing did not suffer. While the Egyptians claimed thirteen Israeli aircraft downed on the 6th, an unofficial Israeli source has halved that figure, admitting to the loss of only six.[103] Official Israeli sources, as usual not specifying their own losses, reported thirty-seven Egyptian machines brought down, some by ground fire.[104]

The situation on the Golan Heights, in the north, was much more serious from a strategic perspective than that in the south. There was no broad stretch of uncluttered desert to absorb any enemy momentum. The Syrian "start line" was a meager ten to fifteen miles from the escarpment that overlooked much of northern Galilee. But when the Syrian attack was launched there was "evidence of some confusion at the outset . . . with inadequate measures for control and road discipline. (One observer has described the sight as something like a race of Damascus taxicabs). Strangely, there was at this time no Israeli air action against any of the vulnerable columns."[105]

If so, it was not for want of trying. "Motti" Hod, the newly retired Commander of the IAF from the 1967 campaign, had been appointed air adviser to the northern front commander, arriving on the Golan shortly after the Syrian artillery opened the assault. "From the first section of airplanes that appeared . . . I immediately saw that the tactics which we thought could be used there could not be used. And this was because, when the Skyhawks arrived, simultaneously we saw over fifty ground-to-air missiles in the air at one time. Over fifty on a very, very narrow strip of land!"[106]

Against this wall of missiles, the IAF could do little to hinder the Syrian advance, and during the night the enemy's armored spearheads began to gain momentum, with the few Israeli tanks unable to match the night-fighting effectiveness of superior Syrian equipment.[107] By morning, columns of Syrian armor were driving towards the escarpment that overlooked the Jordan and, in the south, one column was within fifteen kilometers of Lake Kinneret (the Sea of Galilee).

For "Benny" Peled, who planned to hit the Egyptian missile screen that morning, the priority had suddenly shifted to the Golan Heights: "The Defense Minister [Moshe Dayan] phoned me and said, 'Benny, leave Sinai, it's of no importance right now, its only sand, it's two hundred-odd kilometers from Israel. We have a problem right on our doorstep, so just drop everything.'"[108] So instead of attacking the SAM batteries which were, in effect, denying the Israelis their customary air superiority over the battlefield in the south, the Air Force was again required to emphasize close support on the Golan while the General Staff made desperate efforts to get more men and materiel into the battle there. It was an expensive way to work, but watching those masses of Syrian missiles had given "Motti" Hod an idea.

> The decision that I made, and employed there, was to try and draw out the maximum amount of missiles from their batteries, to drain them dry before air power could be implemented effectively. All the air force could have done—and did—through Sunday and Monday, to lunch time, was to drain dry the air defense system of the Syrians. And they were not clever enough to understand what we did. They kept on shooting and I kept on using tactics just to draw missiles.[109]

These tactics involved both fake and genuine attacks on the missile sites as well as on Syrian ground forces. Attacks were only pressed home under the most favorable circumstances, employing against the missile sites "mainly weapons which would create a lot of shrapnel . . . area weapons." The Syrians had ECM to confuse the Israelis' Shrike air-to-ground antiradiation missile, but the Shrikes "could be used as a surprise in certain cases."[110] Hanoch Bartov, the biographer of Israeli Chief of Staff David Elazar, says that twenty-seven of the thirty-six Syrian missile batteries on the Golan were "silenced" by nightfall on the 7th,[111] but General Hod remembers that "we did not silence them enough to give us freedom of action over the front...in the first two days."[112] In that time the Israelis had lost at least forty aircraft, virtually as many as they had lost in the whole of the Six Day War. Reputable scholars have argued that the figure was closer to eighty,[113] but that seems too high a total. As Armitage and Mason point out, even forty "may be represented either as approximately 3 percent of attack sorties flown, or 2 percent of all sorties flown or, rather more meaningfully, 40 percent of all losses throughout the war or 14 percent of the frontline combat strength of the IAF."[114]

In the south the Egyptians were more disciplined (although probably no less effective) in their expenditure of missiles. However, on the Golan Heights and along the road to Damascus the Syrians launched salvo after salvo at Israeli aircraft buzzing like wasps overhead until, "by noon on Monday they stopped shooting. We did some experiments. No more missiles."[115] The Syrians had used up all their stocks.

The Russians began to airlift replacement missiles to Syria, and the IAF turned briefly from close support to interdiction, bombing the airfield that the Russians were using. "They switched to another airfield and we bombed the second one. The first attack on the second base occurred when a Russian transport was on the ground already, and got hit there," reports General Hod. "We stopped the airlift for another 24 hours and by Wednesday afternoon and Thursday morning the situation had changed."[116]

The Egyptians, established on the east bank of the canal, seemed content to hold their ground under the protection of an unbroken missile umbrella. The Israeli Bar-Lev strongholds soon fell, and once they were lost there was no immediate requirement for air power in support of the ground forces since the Egyptians were still far short of the Israeli border. On the Golan, it was different. Although the Syrian offensive had been stopped and the attackers driven back to the old ceasefire line, the enemy was still very close to Israeli settlements. At the moment the Syrians had few, if any, missiles, and their air defenses were off balance. But the IAF was hurting, too. "Despite its heavy losses, the force will still be able to pack a considerable wallop in the north tomorrow, and in the south the day after," wrote Bartov. "But if another four to five days of erosion are allowed to pass before the counter-attack commences, the air force may reach its 'red line.' "[117]

Already it was clear that the IAF could not always give the ground forces that degree of support they were accustomed to when operating within reach of intact enemy missile screens.[118] References to the imminence of a "red line" suggest that *Zahal* was, by the 10th, at least considering the possibility that attrition would compel the Air Force to give up all offensive action in support of a ground offensive, saving its machines simply to protect Israeli airspace and drive off any Arab aircraft which attempted to attack Israeli troops. The Army, now that it was fully mobilized, could certainly hold off the enemy without help of air power, but whether it could advance successfully over any distance without air support and still avoid incurring excessive casualties was a questionable matter. And if it could not, the Israelis would be forced to choose between a short war and unbearable casualties on the one hand, or a long conflict and disastrous socio-economic attrition on the home front, on the other.

Consequently, the proposed combined air-ground assault took place the following morning, with the Syrian missile screen still in disarray and both Israeli aircraft and heavy artillery pounding missile sites in order to ensure that there would be no quick recovery. Israeli armor pushed forward, its axis of advance the road to Damascus. The IAF had no trouble with the Syrian Air Force either: aircraft on the ground were housed in hardened shelters—the Syrians had not failed to learn the lessons of 1967—but "most airfields were closed for long durations, due to accurate hits on their runways." Very few Syrian planes got into the air, and of those that did two were shot down in air-to-air engagements.[119] Interdiction and close air support missions were flown with minimal losses and considerable effect in a permissive environment, just as in the halcyon days of 1967.

On the southern front both Israeli and Egyptian air forces flew some close air support sorties, but neither could operate with the confidence and precision that accompanies assured air superiority and precedes effective air support. The airspace of the western Sinai was a no-man's-land of skirmishes and small-scale raids until October 14, when the Egyptians loyally answered a call to alleviate the pressure facing their Syrian allies—now being driven back on Saasa. They launched a second phase ground offensive designed to carry them to the high ridges another 9.3 miles east, though not all Egyptians agreed with the decision to attack. General el Shazly recalls telling his Minister for War that "the enemy air force is still too strong to be challenged by our own. And we do not have sufficient mobile SAMs to provide air cover. . . . The enemy air force can still cripple our ground forces as soon as they poke their noses beyond our SAM umbrella."[120]

El Shazly's predictions were accurate. The EAF made no great effort to challenge the IAF, although some of the Libyan Mirages flew their first sorties and two were shot down.[121] Consequently, Israeli airmen were able to fulfill their traditional close support role in disrupting the Egyptian assault.[122] Very untypically, the victors "did not pursue the battered Egyptian columns as they withdrew; the apparent failure was perhaps due to the inability of the IAF to carry its tactical air support into the SAM 'box,' and the unwillingness of the Israelis to expose themselves to Egyptian A[nti] T[ank] fire without such support."[123]

The worst problems with the missile screen seem to have been largely limited to Israeli aircraft engaged in close air support in which Egyptian targets were small and often mobile, and it was necessary to attack from low altitudes in order to be effective. From the 8th on, the IAF had been bombing the floating bridges that the Egyptians had thrown across the canal with relative impunity. "At about one pm—I don't remember exactly—the air force went for those fourteen bridges without a single missile battery being hurt," recalls Peled. "All in place, all in working order. But all the fourteen bridges were blown out of the water by four pm. We lost three aircraft. . . . We blew all the bridges out of the water . . . and we did it without touching [attacking] a single battery."[124]

At night the Egyptians put them back; pontoons are easily destroyed and just as easily replaced, and that sequence of events was followed several times over the next week. General Peled suggests that the attacks were successful solely because his air force knew "in real-time, where the target is, what it is, and how long it will be there."[125] Those factors, of course, permit attacks from relatively high altitude, giving the attackers more time to identify approaching missiles and a much better chance to thwart them electronically or avoid them tactically without coming within range of the low-level components of the screen.

The same premises can be applied to Israeli strategic raids deep into Egypt. More than half of the Egyptian SA–2 and SA–3 batteries were deployed in the Nile delta and around Cairo, but, says Peled, ". . . out of all the many missions we flew inside the well-protected Egyptian territory, against most sensitive targets, heavily defended, I can count only two aircraft that were lost."[126] Even these two may well have been victims of interceptors rather than missiles. On October 15 when "military targets in Egypt were massively attacked . . . seven Egyptian planes were downed in air battles."[127] We know too little about the tactics of these air-to-air engagements, which were almost certainly fought at higher altitudes and greater ranges than those typical of earlier campaigns. However, the performance of the MiG–21, now approaching obsolescence, was significantly less than that of the Phantom and Mirage (were the Libyan Mirages engaged?), while the differential in combat-flying skills between Arab and Israeli airmen must have been more marked than it had ever been before.

The combination of speed, numbers of aircraft, and sheer space requirement—since aircraft moving at supersonic speeds cannot turn tightly—means that the fighting probably occurred over an enormous cubic area. That last conclusion is supported by the fact that the Israelis used up a much higher proportion of their air-to-air missile stocks than their 30-mm cannon ammunition in the course of the war.[128] In addition, the American replacement airlift included more Sparrow missiles.[129] Missiles are longer range weapons than cannon, suggesting that the emphasis was changing from one of close-quarter dogfighting with the gun as the primary weapon, to one of more remote maneuver, using missiles.

Electronics and missiles were demonstrably changing the nature of war in many ways. The Egyptian ground offensive in the Sinai on the 14th, and the Israeli air attacks in the Nile delta, illustrated very well, however, the major limitation of ground-based attempts at achieving air superiority, at least in 1973. The tremendous complexity of an integrated, comprehensive missile screen, and its relative immobility, meant that 1) *all* base facilities and field formations, spread over a large geographic area, could not be adequately protected without applying a quite exorbitant proportion of available men and material exclusively to that task; and 2) any ground attack (offensive action being essential in winning a conventional war) relying on such a screen for protection against enemy air power must, of necessity, be unable to develop much momentum. After each tactical bound to the forward limit of missile protection, the advance must stop until all the elements of the missile screen can be reestablished on new ground.

To do that with the basic, long-range components of it, the SA–2s and SA–3s, was a major task—one the Arabs never got around to—involving considerable risk. Mutually supporting, so that if one was dismantled the security of another was threatened, the SA–2 and SA–3 sites consisted of buried concrete bunkers housing the appropriate radars (with only the antennas exposed). Either four or six launchers were carefully sited and dug-in in a precise symmetric relationship to the control center "because their parallax computer is very poor."[130] "Once installed, calibration was a major problem . . . which took some time to solve."

When a screen was firmly in place, with SA–6s, SA–7s, and ZSU–23/4s shifting about in the vicinity to complete it, there seemed little future in subjecting the screen to air attack, unless 1) a degree of tactical or technological surprise could be achieved that would permit a breach to be made without incurring inordinate losses, *and* 2) there was also a clear prospect of ground forces overrunning the area—or at least bringing it under fire—before it could be reconstructed. One wonders if General Peled's "huge Cecil DeMille type of spectacle" would have worked on October 7, even if it had been followed up by an immediate counterattack across the canal as originally planned.[131] It would seem unlikely that the Egyptians could have been tempted into squandering all their missile stocks, as the Syrians had.

The evidence suggests that the ground attack had to come first. When the missile screen was finally breached, the deed was done by the Israeli Army, not the Air Force. On the night of October 15–16, taking advantage of the confusion brought about by the failure of the Egyptian attack on the 14th, a carefully orchestrated counterattack secured an Israeli bridgehead on the west bank of the canal, near Deversoir, just north of the Great Bitter Lake and precisely at the junction of the Egyptian Second and Third Armies. Maj. Gen. Ariel Sharon, commanding the first troops to cross, claimed "he put four SAMs [batteries] out of action on the sixteenth, but seven or even more may have been an accurate figure."[132] By noon on the 16th, another authority recorded that "a battalion of 175mm guns had been ferried across [the canal] and was already firing its long-range cannon at Egyptian SAM sites."[133] Such heavy artillery would not normally be risked so far forward, least of all in a shallow and still precarious bridgehead, raising the distinct possibility that the Israeli Army had no confidence at all in the Air

Force's ability to suppress the missile batteries, or to provide tactical air support without their being suppressed. Otherwise, why risk those heavy guns so far forward?

Also by noon on the 16th, General el Shazly learned that "some of our SAM units, stationed almost ten miles behind the canal, began to report attacks by enemy tanks."[134] The armored reserve originally assigned to deal with a possible countercrossing at Deversoir had been dispatched to the east bank to be used in the ill-considered Egyptian offensive of the 14th,[135] and the only rapid deployment force available to the Egyptians now was the EAF. "Late on the afternoon of the 16th there was a substantial attack on the bridgehead forces by aircraft of the Egyptian Air Force," says Trevor Dupuy. "This led to a short air battle above the Canal, in which the Israelis claimed they destroyed ten MiG–17s without any loss to themselves, while the Egyptians claim ten Israeli planes were destroyed—six in air-to-air combat and four shot down by their SAM and ZSU–23/4 air defenses."[136]

In that account the Israeli aircraft are not identified by type, but the fact that all their victims were MiG–17s, obsolescent interceptors long since relegated to a ground support role, and that their mission was to contain the bridgehead, suggests that this was probably a low-level dogfight of the traditional kind, relying mainly, if not exclusively, on cannon fire.

The IAF had been gnawing at the periphery of the missile sites along the canal since the third day of the war, carefully drawing fire, experimenting with tactical and ECM combinations to use in the attack, and "beginning to make a dent in the SAM–2 and SAM–3 missile defenses," according to General Peled.

> Let me paint you a picture. You are the commander of an SA–6 site. It's mobile . . . so you come to a place, you set up, and spread out your cables so that your radar's working. Take into account that I'm seeing you all the time. I know when you get out of your little van to piss. . . . I know who's talking to you, and who you're talking to. I know what kind of information flows to you from the peripheral radars. I know everything about you. And then, after I know all that, I can cover you with 'chaff,' send decoys, madden you with jamming, spoofing, 'paint' all your things 'black,' give you false targets. And then I'll be coming at you with stand-off weapons that, once they lock on to your van, you're a goner![137]

Initially, the only stand-off air-launched weapon the Israelis had was Shrike, a rocket-powered, radar-homing missile that could be launched from a 10.6-mile distance. It had been in their inventory since the War of Attrition, when it had not been found very effective. "We expended about twenty missiles and we only got one-and-a-half hits, and we thought this weapon was not worth a bloody thing," says Peled. "Suddenly, during the Yom Kippur War, we found out (about a week later) that with about thirty Shrikes we had annihilated about eighteen batteries. Why? . . . Because everybody was dead scared—the picture was very confused."[138] It is surely worth remembering in assessing technological aspects of war, that the human element may still be decisive in intense struggles.

In the last week of the war, Israel acquired some additional "smart" weapons via the American "replacement" airlift. On October 18, General Elazar, Israeli Defense Forces' Chief of Staff, was complaining bitterly that the Air Force had chosen to attack missile sites at the northern end of the canal when all the action was further south, around the bridgehead.[139] No explanation had been offered for this aerial diversion, but in hindsight it seems possible that the airmen had gone north to try out their new acquisitions and adapt—or refine—their tactics to make the best use of them. Now there was Bullpup, another rocket-propelled, stand-off missile; Maverick, a TV-guided "lock on" missile; Walleye, another TV-guided but unpowered "glide" bomb; and Rockeye, a free-fall "area weapon" which contained a cluster of "bomblets."

More than one commentator has assigned Maverick a prominent role in defeating the missile threat, but General Peled is adamant that "we used experimentally a few Mavericks, in one case only, and that was in retaking the Mount Hermon stronghold."[140] The other weapons were used against missile sites with considerable effect, probably Rockeyes—lobbed in from 9,842 feet or more slant range—against SA–6s and vehicle-mounted –7s, and Walleyes against the heavier missiles. The IAF enjoyed considerable success with these new weapons in the last week of the war and gained knowledge and skills that were to prove invaluable almost a decade later.

Assessment of Yom Kippur

Statistically, what was the outcome of the Yom Kippur air war? Conservative figuring suggests that the Arabs lost about 400–410 fixed-wing combat aircraft in the course of 10,000–11,000 sorties for a loss rate of 4 percent. Better than 60 percent of these losses occurred in air-to-air engagements (which may have numbered 400), more than half of them the victims of air-launched missiles. Another 10–15 percent were accounted for by ground-based Israeli fire, split more or less evenly between HAWK missiles and guns, while perhaps the same percentage were victims of their own Arab ground-to-air missiles failing to distinguish between friend and foe. About 5 percent were destroyed on the ground, and the remaining losses must be assigned to accidental and "unknown" causes. Proportionately, in every case the Syrian losses were higher than those of the Egyptians.[141]

The Israelis appear to have lost 103 fixed-wing combat machines in about 10,000 sorties, for a loss rate of around 1.3 percent. General Peled, who should know, insists that "87 combat aircraft were lost to ground-to-air fire. Only 36 of them were lost to ground-to-air missiles of all kinds; out of those, only 10 were lost to SA–6s."[142] That leaves 16 aircraft either shot down or lost by accident. Even if we assume that all of them were shot down, the air combat ratio favors the Israelis over the Arabs by a margin of at least 15 to 1: the true figure was probably around 20 to 1.

The details General Peled gives concerning losses from ground-based fire are most interesting, attributing a rather smaller proportion of losses to missiles in general and SA–6s in particular than has generally been the case. However, the essence of the Arab defenses were their integrated, complementary nature, so that there is probably little to be gained by trying to quantify the success rate of individual weapon systems. Peled claims that the Arabs fired about 1,800 SA–2s, SA–3s and SA–6s, and about 12,000 "SA–7s and the like." If his figures are correct, then it took around 50 of the former and 336 of the latter to bring down one Israeli fighter. Other sources have suggested that the Israelis lost more aircraft to missiles and fewer to gunfire than Peled admits, a difference which would certainly alter the whole equation. However, Peled's figures seem more accurate.

Doctrinally, it is clear that a build up in air defense capabilities, based very largely on electronics, had seriously diminished the value of aircraft in some tactical environments. In the vicinity of well-sited and intact ground-based air defenses, air superiority over that area could not be easily attained even by an air force with the immense combat superiority that the IAF enjoyed. If close air support was essential—as it was on the Golan on October 7—then the price of it was high. The value of aircraft in the interdiction and strategic roles was also threatened as far as offensive operations were concerned. Wherever the enemy exercised enough control over the ground environment to establish securely a complex and massive aggregate of air defense weapons, the achievement of local air superiority was certain to be costly. Defensively, the airplane more than held its own in the Yom Kippur War; its traditional advantages of flexibility and mobility were as significant as ever in retaining air superiority over its own airspace when superior engine, airframe, weapons, and electronic technologies were allied with consummate flying skills, as in the Israeli case.

Israeli Drive into Lebanon

Nearly ten years after the Yom Kippur war had ended, the IAF went into action on a large scale once again. The occasion was an invasion of southern Lebanon intended to secure Israel's border areas against sporadic raids and indiscriminate artillery and missile strikes delivered by the Palestine Liberation Organization (PLO) from its bases on Lebanese territory. Starting on June 6, 1982, Israeli ground forces drove north along two roughly parallel axes, the coastal plain and the Bekaa Valley, with their usual speed. By the morning of the 8th, their armor was at Damour, within 16.5 miles of Beirut. That morning, according to a published account even more cryptic than usual, one Israeli pilot "providing cover for our forces" southeast of Beirut:

> received a message that two Syrian planes were closing in on us. Almost immediately I spotted them on my [radar] screen. Judging by the MiGs' speed and direction, it was clear they had taken off on an attack mission. . . . I attacked the MiG closest to me, while my partner . . . attacked the second MiG. I acted according to our combat doctrine, aware of the specific performance of my plane. I hit the MiG, it went into a spin, dropped and crashed. I did not see what happened to the pilots of the two MiGs, whether or not they managed to bail out after we hit their planes.[143]

Apparently the Israeli machines were single-seaters, but we are not even told whether the Syrians were downed by missiles or gunfire. Acting "according to our combat doctrine, aware of the specific performance of my plane," was a masterly piece of circumlocution, probably attributable to the combined efforts of a censor and a public relations writer rather than a pilot.

The Syrians had intervened in their own interests and to bolster their PLO allies. Syrian and Israeli ground forces met first in the Bekaa Valley. The eastern ridge of the valley bordered on Syrian territory, and the Syrians had set up a massive air defense barrier along their frontier, constructed essentially from the same missile elements as the 1973 screens (although, no doubt, there were electronic advances incorporated into all of them). Since the Israelis were forbidden to overfly Syrian territory with the exception of the actual battery position, "that basically gave us the possibility to come in only north/south or south/north."[144]

The first attack went in on June 9, 1982, backed by the sophisticated electronics of U.S.-supplied Hawkeye E-2Cs, small twin turbo-prop airborne command-and-control aircraft. Drones tempted the SAM batteries to fire, exposing their radars; improved Shrikes and Mavericks and laser-guided bombs then took out the radars while multi-frequency jamming devices protected the Israeli launch vehicles. "Within two hours they wiped out nineteen batteries and severely damaged four others, without any loss of their own aircraft," claims British military historian John Laffin, who was in Israel at the time and had access to local sources.[145]

His account implied that most of the Israeli success was due to superior technology—a shift in electronic advantage—but there were other elements in the IAF success, as General "Motti" Hod, has pointed out. He saw it as "a different kind of situation [from 1973]. Lebanon was . . . an isolated group of missiles in a very, very unfavorable geographic area, from the missile point of view, because of the mountains."[146] The Syrians, operating under political handicaps of their own, had their batteries on the high ground, along the eastern side of the Bekaa, with a very irregular topography all about them. Often flying below the missile sites, taking advantage of "dead" airspace, the Israelis "could plan and work like a pharmacy [laboratory?]. Very clean . . . and conclusions should not be drawn from what was done there to a massive battlefield defended area. It's a different story. . . ."[147]

The Syrian Air Force rose to try and protect the missile batteries as the Israeli attack developed. "The Israelis, in U.S.-built F–15s, F–16s, Phantoms and Skyhawks confronted Syrian pilots in Russian-made MiG–21s, MiG–23s and MiG–25s and Sukhoi 7s. So many planes—up to two hundred of them—were criss-crossing the sky above the Bekaa that the Syrian antiaircraft gunners had to hold their fire for fear of hitting their own planes," reports Laffin. Despite the density of aircraft that made Syrian gunners "hold their fire," Laffin thought that "many" Syrian machines were hit by Sidewinder missiles that were "not standard U.S. issue," but had been "adapted and improved in the light of experience gained . . . over Lebanon since 1976."[148]

The Israelis claimed twenty-three MiG–21s and –23s, out of "about one hundred . . . which swooped into the area, wave after wave."[149] Another anonymous pilot, quoted in the *IDF Journal,* recalled that:

> we were in the air at the climax of the large-scale attack on the missile batteries; the air was filled with tension, due to the large number of enemy aircraft flying about the area. We waited until we achieved positive identification of target while simultaneously approaching two enemy aircraft, painted brown and light yellow. We gave chase and when the aircraft reached a routine launch mode, I fired and was able to see the hit; immediately I turned to go for the other aircraft but I was too slow. My number two had already shot him down.[150]

The reference to "routine launch mode" makes it clear that the Israeli used a missile, but since he could distinguish the colors of the enemy aircraft, the range must have been relatively short. This time we are told nothing at all about the types of aircraft involved on either side, though whether through accident or design is hard to say.

On July 22 a combined air and ground assault on Syrian positions east of Joub Jannin and Mansoura, in the upper Bekaa, tempted the Syrians into another effort to establish an effective ground-based antiaircraft defense, and three SA–8 antiaircraft missile launching vehicles were brought up from Syria.[151] These were certainly the most sophisticated missile defenses yet battle-tested. The SA–8 was a fully mobile system with acquisition and tracking radars mounted on the launch vehicle, and it could engage more than one target simultaneously. There were four or six launchers on each vehicle. The missiles themselves were command-guided with semi-active radar or infra-red homing, and a range of 7.5 miles. *Jane's Weapon Systems* in 1983 suggested the design was "probably optimized for high acceleration, maximum speed and maneuverability rather than range."[152] However, "these most modern and sophisticated products of the Soviet arsenal were soon identified and destroyed by air attack on the afternoon of the 24th," according to Israeli authorities.[153] Some SA–6 batteries were also involved,

600

and one Phantom was lost to one of those older missiles. A second aircraft was lost to ground fire under unexplained circumstances.[154]

By the end of the Lebanon campaign, the IAF claimed an air-to-air kill ratio of 87:0 in aerial combat,[155] (a ratio which was astonishing, impossible to verify, but very likely correct) and reigned supreme over Lebanese skies. Good though Israeli airmen undoubtedly were, it was difficult to believe that they achieved such a spectacular, one-sided result simply through their exemplary flying skills allied with first-rate airframe, engine technology, and clever tactics. Apparently all the electronic advantage lay with them, too, weighing the air superiority equation more heavily in their favor than ever before.

It seemed unlikely that in the future the technological ascendency would always lie with the same protagonist to such a significant degree, however. The electronic edge, in particular, would change with bewildering rapidity, as it did briefly in 1973. In that campaign, while Egyptian missiles inhibited the "correct and wise" use of Israeli air power, the fighting on the ground dragged out over the first two weeks in exactly the fashion that Israel could least afford; but once the missile screen was broken and air superiority was achieved, air power could be employed freely, and the war once again was quickly brought to a conclusion.

All the more reason, then, for the IAF to maintain its emphasis on the human element, a field in which achieving excellence was, of necessity, a slow, long, drawn-out process, occurring over decades rather than years, but one which enabled the achiever to minimize the effects of any adverse swings in the technological balance. Meanwhile, air superiority—which was never as simple a matter as it might have appeared—became a vastly more complex problem all the time, but remains, for Israel, "a necessary evil."[156]

Notes

1. Gunther Rothenberg, *The Anatomy of the Israeli Army* (London, 1979), p 77.
2. Israeli pilot quoted in T. Berkman, *Sabra* (New York, 1969), p 15.
3. See Lt Col Amnon Gurion, "Israeli Military Strategy up to the Yom Kippur War," in *Air University Review,* Sept–Oct 1982, pp 52–57.
4. Intvw with Maj Gen Dan Tolkovsky, Tel Aviv, Jan 13, 1984.
5. *Ibid.*
6. *Ibid.*
7. Ezer Weizman, *On Eagle's Wings* (London, 1976), p 105.
8. Tolkovsky Intvw.
9. *Ibid.*
10. Weizman, *On Eagle's Wings,* pp 138–9.
11. *Ibid.,* p 142.
12. Edward Luttwak and Dan Horowitz, *The Israeli Army* (London, 1975), p 201.
13. Edgar O'Ballance, *No Victor, No Vanquished* (San Rafael, Calif, 1978), p 287.
14. Ezer Weizman quoted in Berkman, *Sabra* p 15.
15. Weizman, *On Eagle's Wings,* p 169.
16. M. Spick, *Fighter Pilot Tactics: The Techniques of Daylight Air Combat* (Cambridge, England, 1983), p 139.
17. Maj Gen B. Peled to author, Jul 30, 1984.
18. Maj Gen Moshe Dayan, *Diary of the Sinai Campaign* (New York, 1965), p 209.
19. Giulio Douhet, *The Command of the Air* [reprint] (Washington, Office of Air Force History, 1983), pp 53–4.
20. Robert Henriques, *One Hundred Hours to Suez* (London, 1957), p 201.
21. Intvw with Maj Gen Mordechai Hod, Tel Aviv, Jan 16, 1984.
22. Dayan, *Diary of the Sinai Campaign,* p 218.
23. *Ibid.,* p 221.
24. S. L. A. Marshall, *Sinai Victory* (New York, 1958), p 262.
25. Tolkovsky Intvw.
26. Hod Intvw.
27. Alfred Goldberg, "Air Operations in the Sinai Campaign," USAF Historical Division unpublished paper (Nov 1959), pp 23 and 39.
28. Marshall, *Sinai Victory,* p 258.
29. *Ibid.,* pp 45 and 259; Henriques, *One Hundred Hours to Suez,* p 199.
30. Spick, *Fighter Pilot Tactics,* p 124.
31. Marshall, *Sinai Victory,* p 261.
32. Dayan, *Diary of the Sinai Campaign,* p 109.
33. Spick, *Fighter Pilot Tactics,* p 14.
34. Henriques, *One Hundred Hours to Suez,* pp 195–6.
35. Goldberg, "Air Operations," p 24.
36. Tolkovksy Intvw.
37. R. Fullick and G. Powell, *Suez: The Double War* (London, 1979), pp 119–120.

38. Trevor Dupuy, *Elusive Victory: The Arab–Israeli Wars, 1947–1974* (New York, 1978), p 180.

39. Marshall, *Sinai Victory*, p 261.

40. Dayan, *Diary of the Sinai Campaign,* p 109.

41. Murray Rubinstein and Richard Goldman, *The Israeli Air Force Story* (London, 1979), pp 96–7.

42. Spick, *Fighter Pilot Tactics,* p 149.

43. *Ibid.*, pp 142 and 147; Bill Gunston, *An Illustrated Guide to the Israeli Air Force* (New York, 1982), pp 86–9.

44. M. J. Armitage and R. A. Mason, *Air Power in the Nuclear Age* (Urbana, Ill., 1983), p 269.

45. Dupuy, *Elusive Victory,* p 238.

46. Edgar O'Ballance, *The Third Arab-Israeli War, 1967* (Hamden, Conn, 1972).

47. See J. W. R. Taylor, *Combat Aircraft of the World* (New York, 1969).

48. O'Ballance, *Third Arab-Israeli War,* pp 57–8.

49. Intvw with Col Yoash Tsiddon-Chatto, Chief of Operational Planning and Requirements, 1963–66, taped in Tel Aviv, Jan 14, 1984. The concept was Israeli, the design and construction, French.

50. Hod Intvw.

51. *Ibid.*

52. *Ibid.*

53. Dupuy, *Exlusive Victory,* pp 265–69.

54. Quoted in R. Bondy, O. Zmorz and R. Bashan (eds), *Mission Survival* (New York, 1968), p 156.

55. R. S. Churchill and W. S. Churchill, *The Six Day War* (London, 1967), p 80.

56. *Ibid.*, p 81.

57. *Chel Ha'Avir* Press Conference, Jun 7, 1967, quoted in Bondy, Zmora and Bashan, *Misson Survival,* pp 157–58.

58. Avrihu Ben-Nun, "Three Hours in June," videotape at US Army Command and Staff College, Fort Leavenworth, Kansas, cited in Major C. E. Olschner, "The Air Superiority Battle in the Middle East, 1967–1973," Unpublished thesis at U.S. Army Command and Staff College, June 1978, p 17.

59. Bondy, Zmora and Bashan, *Mission Survival,* p 140.

60. *Ibid.*, pp 155–56.

61. Mark Lambert, "How Good is the MiG–21?" in *U.S. Naval Institute Proceedings,* Jan 1976, p 100.

62. Bondy, Zmora and Bashan, *Mission Survival,* p 142.

63. Lambert, "How Good is the MiG–21?"

64. Bondy, Zmora and Bashan, *Mission Survival,* p 142.

65. *Ibid.*

66. Hussein of Jordan, *My "War" With Israel,* (New York, 1969), p 74.

67. Bondy, Zmora and Bashan, *Mission Survival,* p 160.

68. *Aviation Week and Space Technology,* Jul 3, 1967, p 18.

69. O'Ballance, *Third Arab-Israeli War,* p 82.

70. Zeev Schiff, *October Earthquake: Yom Kippur 1973* (Tel Aviv, 1974), p 263.

71. See F. W. Lanchester, *Aircraft in Warfare: The Dawn of the Fourth Arm* (London, 1916), Chap V.

72. Edgar O'Ballance, *The Electronic War in the Middle East, 1968–1970* (Hamden, Conn, 1974), pp 69, 85.

73. Lt Gen Saad el Shazli, *The Crossing of the Suez* (San Francisco, 1980), p 20.

74. Tsiddon-Chatto intvw.

75. Taylor, *Combat Aircraft.*

76. Intvw with Maj Gen Benjamin Peled, commander of *Chel Ha'Avir* 1968–74, Tel Aviv, Jan 13, 1984.

77. Jacob Neufeld, "Israel builds an Air Force," May 1982, unpublished paper in Office of Air Force History, p 9.

78. Quoted in Spick, *Fighter Pilot Tactics,* p 147.

79. *Ibid.*, pp 147–48.

80. Tsiddon-Chatto Intvw.
81. Peled Intvw.
82. O'Ballance, *Electronic War*, p 127.
83. *Ibid.*, pp 102–10 and 135.
84. *Jane's Weapon Systems, 1983–4*.
85. Dupuy, *Elusive Victory*, pp 606 and 608.
86. El Shazly, *Crossing of the Suez*, p 277.
87. O'Ballance, *No Victory, No Vanquished*, p 282.
88. Dupuy, *Elusive Victory*, pp 606 and 608.
89. El Shazly, *Crossing of the Suez*, p 277.
90. *Ibid.*, p 19.
91. El Shazly, *Crossing of the Suez*, p 25.
92. Maj Gen D. K. Palit, *Return to Sinai: The Arab Offensive, 1973* (New Delhi, 1973), p 156.
93. Peled Intvw.
94. Maj Gens Hassan el Badry, Taha el Magdoub and Muhammed Dia el Din Zohdy, *The Ramadan War, 1973* (Dunn Loring, Va.), pp. 61–2.
95. El Shazli, *Crossing of the Suez*, p 63.
96. IAF Headquarters, *The Israeli Air Force in the Yom Kippur War* (Tel Aviv, 1975), p 15 [Hereafter, IAF HQ].
97. Dupuy, *Elusive Victory*, p 56.
98. Y. Ben-Porat, *et al, Kippur* (Tel Aviv, nd), p 40.
99. Palit, *Return to Sinai*, p 156.
100. *Ibid.*, p 97.
101. Palit, *Return to Sinai*, p 109.
102. Hanoch Bartov, *Dado: 48 Years and 20 Days* (Tel Aviv, 1981), p 310.
103. Schiff, *October Earthquake*, p 60.
104. IAF HQ, *Israeli Air Force*, p 8.
105. Dupuy, *Elusive Victory*, p 447.
106. Hod Intvw.
107. Dupuy, *Elusive Victory*, p 449.
108. Peled Intvw.
109. Hod Intvw.
110. *Ibid.*
111. Bartov, *Dado*.
112. Hod Intvw.
113. See, for example, P. Borgart, "The Vulnerability of the Manned Airborne Weapon System—Pt. 3, Influence on Tactics and Strategy," in *International Defense Review*, Dec 1977, p 1066; Palit, *Return to Sanai*, p 157, citing American Intelligence estimates.
114. Armitage and Mason, *Air Power in the Nuclear Age*, p 127.
115. Hod Intvw.
116. *Ibid.*
117. Bartov, *Dado*, p 143.
118. Maj Gen Avraham Adan, *On the Banks of the Suez* (San Rafael, 1980), p 119.
119. IAF HQ, *Israeli Air Force*, p 40.
120. El Shazly, *Crossing Of the Suez*, p 246.
121. O'Ballance, *No Victor, No Vanquished*, p 297.
122. Bartov, *Dado*, p 461.
123. Dupuy, *Elusive Victory*, p 489.
124. Peled Intvw.
125. *Ibid.*
126. *Ibid.*
127. IAF HQ, *Israeli Air Force*, p 73.
128. Peled Intvw.
129. O'Ballance, *No Victor, No Vanquished*, p 298.
130. Tsiddon-Chatto Intvw.
131. Bartov, *Dado*, p 310; Peled Intvw.
132. O'Ballance, *No Victor, No Vanquished*, p 298.

133. Dupuy, *Elusive Victory*, p 50.

134. El Shazly, *Crossing of the Suez*, p 253.

135. *Ibid.*

136. Dupuy, *Elusive Victory*, p 505.

137. Peled Intvw.

138. Peled Intvw.

139. Bartov, *Dado*, p 512.

140. Peled Intvw.

141. See Dupuy, *Elusive Victory*, Borgart, "Vulnerability," and IAF HQ, *Israeli Air Force;* J. Viksne, "The Yom Kippur War in Retrospect: Part II–Technology," *Army Journal,* May 1976; Oberst H. Topfer, "Zwei Jahre daonach: Der Nahost–Krieg 1973," in *Truppenpraxis,* Nov 1975; and Z Rendulic, "Pouke iz IV. arapskoizraelskog rata," *Glasnik RV i PVO* [Yugoslavian *Aviation and Air Defence Journal*], No. 4 (1975) for a variety of figures.

142. Peled Intvw.

143. Quoted by Capt Moshe Fogel, "Peace for Galilee: Combat Reports," in *IDF Journal,* Dec 1982, p 43.

144. Tsiddon-Chatto Intvw.

145. John Laffin, "The Desperate War," in *British Army Journal,* Apr 1983, p 9.

146. Hod Intvw.

147. *Ibid.*

148. Laffin, "Desperate War," pp 9–10.

149. Lt Col Mordechai Gichon, "Peace for Galilee: The Campaign," and Capt Moshe Fogel, "Peace for Galilee: Combat Reports," in *IDF Journal,* Dec 1982, pp 21 and 43.

150. *Ibid.,* p 43.

151. *Ibid.,* p 26.

152. *Jane's Weapons Systems,* 1983, p 99.

153. Gichon, *"Peace for Galilae,"* p 26.

154. Lt Col David Eshel, *The Lebanon War, 1982* (Hod HaSharon, 1982), p 47.

155. *IDF Journal,* Aug 1983, p 54.

156. Hod Intvw.

Bibliographical Essay

Security is an obsession in the Middle East. Israeli archives are doubtless full of fascinating documents in a language which few gentiles, other than biblical scholars and certain archeologists, can understand. Yet an inability to read them is surely no handicap, since every significant piece of paper generated on military matters since 1947 is still classified. Even such elementary statistics as the number of sorties flown remain secret.

However, the official record is one thing, and unofficial comments and criticisms are another. Since the broad essentials and sequence of events of each campaign are a matter of common knowledge and secrets do not exist in a vacuum, the blanket of official security which envelops everything often only serves to prevent confirmation of certain facts. No doubt there are genuine secrets still to be unearthed, but meanwhile senior Israeli officers are often willing to talk unofficially about many matters on which official sources are resolutely silent. It must be accepted that, consciously or unconsciously, these officers may not always be telling the truth, the whole truth, and nothing but the truth, but then, neither do contemporary documents in many cases. And after recording such discussions it is the historian's job to check their claims and criticisms against the contemporary public record and the statements of their peers in autobiographical publications and such magisterial secondary studies as Trevor N. Dupuy's *Elusive Victory: The Arab-Israeli Wars, 1947–1974* (New York: Harper & Row, 1978).

Dupuy's book is as near as one can get to an official history of the Arab-Israeli wars. There are no truly official histories, either in Hebrew or English (or in Arabic, for that matter), not even of the War of Independence which was fought nearly 40 years ago with Second World War materiel and tactics. The closest that the Israelis have come to such a publication is a 120-page public relations piece put out by Israeli Air Force Headquarters in February 1975 and entitled *The Air Force in the "Yom Kippur War"* (Israeli Ministry of Defence Publishing House), which is no more than a compendium of daily communiques.

Consequently, taped interviews and correspondence with three former commanders of the IAF—Dan Tolkovsky, Mordechai Hod, and Benjamin Peled—formed the basis of the study, and are deposited in the U.S. Air Force Historical Research Center, Maxwell Air Force Base, Alabama. A fourth former commander, Ezer Weizman, has published his memoirs; however, the flamboyant Weizman, a flyer to his fingertips, did not serve with the Air Force after he became chief of the Operations Branch of the Israeli General Staff in 1958. His *On Eagle's Wings* (London: Weidenfeld and Nicholson, 1976) is most valuable when he writes about the training of his pilots and the ethos he inculcated into them.

There are a number of other published first person accounts, beginning with then Maj. Gen. Moshe Dayan's *Diary of the Sinai Campaign* (New York: Harper & Row, 1965). Dayan, of course, was not an airman either, but as the Israeli Defense Forces Chief of Staff in 1956, the IAF came under his command, and he has much to say about its performance. He has also commented on air aspects of the 1967 and 1973 campaigns in *Moshe Dayan: Story of My Life* (New York: William Morrow and Company, Inc., 1976), but, understandably, there is little tactical detail. Nor is there much to be learned about air matters from Yitzhak Rabin's *The Rabin Memoirs* (Boston: Little, Brown and Company, 1979), although Rabin was the Chief of Staff during the 1967 war.

Maj. Gen. Avraham "Bren" Adan has given us his account of the 1973 campaign in *On The Banks of The Suez* (San Rafael, Calif.: Presidio Press, 1980). The emphasis is on his differences with the southern front commander, Lt. Gen. Shmuel Gonen, and with fellow divisional command Ariel Sharon, but because Adan's concern with applied airpower is peripheral to his main thesis his book is all the more valuable. It goes far towards clarifying the part played—and not played—by *Chel Ha'Avir* in breaching the Egyptian missile screen. In the same vein, Hanoch Bartov's biography of the late General David Elazar, *Dado: 48 Years and 20 Days* (Tel Aviv: Ma'ariv Book Guild, 1981) also looks at *Chel Ha'Avir* from an external perspective, illustrating almost in passing some of its warts as well as its beauty spots.

At a lower level, there are a number of first–person combat accounts in R. Bondy, O. Zmora and R. Bashan, eds., *Mission Survival* (New York: Sabra Books, 1968), a popular, public relations-oriented anthology which nevertheless has value.

On the "other side of the hill" we have nothing at all from the Syrians, but Lt. Gen. Saad el Shazly, who was the Egyptian Chief of Staff in 1973, has painted a painfully frank picture of his forces' problems prior to, and during, the Yom Kippur War in his *The Crossing of the Suez* (San Francisco: American Mideast Research, 1980). His criticisms of the Egyptian Air Force are harsh but can readily be reconciled with events. The same cannot be said of Maj. Gen. Hassan el Badri, Taha el Magdoub, and Mohammed Zia el Din Zohdy in, *The Ramadan War, 1973* (Dunn Loring, Va.: T. N. Dupuy Associates, Inc., 1974), who carefully ignore facts that do not suit their theories and very often expound too much traditional Arab propaganda to be convincing. All three Egyptian authors are soldiers, not airmen.

King Hussein of Jordan can claim to be soldier, airman, and head of state, giving him an unrivalled perspective from which to write *My "War" With Israel* (New York: William Morrow and Company, Inc., 1969), a transparently honest account of Jordanian participation in the 1967 campaign that emphasizes the fearful damage done to his army and air force by the IAF interdiction campaign.

The essential underpinnings of the Israeli air arm are to be found in Edward Luttwak and Dan Horowitz, *The Israeli Army* (London: Allen Lane, 1975) and Gunther Rothenberg, *The Anatomy of the Israeli Army* (London: B. T. Batsford Ltd., 1979). Luttwak and Horowitz concentrate on the political, strategic, and tactical debates which shaped Zahal doctrine; Rothenberg's is more concerned with structure and organization. Ze'ev Schiff's *A History of the Israeli Army (1870–1974)* (San Francisco: Straight Arrow Books, 1974) has an interesting chapter on pilot training. Murray Rubinstein and Richard Goldman's *The Israeli Air Force Story* (London: Arms and Armour Press, 1979) emphasizes technology, design, and procurement, as does Bill Gunston's *An Illustrated Guide to the Israeli Air Force* (New York: Salamander Books, 1982).

In addition to Dupuy's great single-volume study of the Arab-Israeli wars, the equally prolific British author, Edgar O'Ballance, has produced five separate, slimmer volumes recounting the flow of operations in five separate campaigns. *The Third Arab-Israeli War* (Hamden, Conn.: Archon Books, 1972) deals with the 1967 campaign, while the 1973 fighting is described in *No Victory, No Vanquished: the Yom Kippur War* (San Rafael, Calif.: Presidio Press, 1978). Each book provides a chapter on the air war. His account of *The Electronic War in the Middle East, 1968–70* (Hamden, Conn.: Archon Books, 1974) deals exclusively with the air aspects of the "War of Attrition" and is virtually the only work in its field outside of the periodical literature.

S. L. A. Marshall wrote perceptively about the 1956 war in *Sinai Victory* (New York: William Morrow & Co., 1958), paying appropriate attention to air aspects of the fighting. So did Robert Henriques, a British, non–Zionist Jew and a retired British Army officer of some distinction, in his *One Hundred Hours to Suez* (London: Collins, 1957). Henriques was certainly deceived by the Israelis on the political background to the war, but was more capable of judging for himself tactical air and ground matters.

Understandably, in view of the preemptive counterair strike, little has been written on air-to-air fighting in 1967, although Peter Young's *The Israeli Campaign 1967* (London: William Kimber, 1967) has a few interesting pages outlining the Egyptian Air Force's intentions, had it not been destroyed on the ground before it could act. Ze'ev Schiff's *October Earthquake: Yom Kippur, 1973* (Tel Aviv: University Publishing Projects, 1974) can be balanced off by D. K. Palit, *Return to Sinai: The Arab Offensive, 1973* (New Delhi: Palit and Palit, 1973), but neither of them emphasizes the air superiority aspects of the fighting. Palit is an Indian general who has many friends and contacts among the Egyptian and Syrian military and was on the scene soon after the fighting ended.

Putting the Middle Eastern experience of air power into a global context is M. J. Armitage and R. A. Mason, *Air Power in the Nuclear Age* (Urbana, Ill.: University of Illinois Press, 1983), an excellent survey of the field, while Israeli tactics are put into a wider and deeper perspective by Mike Spick's superb little book, *Fighter Pilot Tactics: The Techniques of Daylight Air Combat* (Cambridge, England: Patrick Stephens, 1983). Lastly, there are a multitude of articles in popular periodicals—*Time, Newsweek*, etc.—and technical journals such as *Aviation Week and Space Technology* and *International Defense Review*. There is much to be learned from a judicious study of the best of them, but they nearly all need to be read with an intensely critical eye. The paucity of precise information has often led authors to extrapolate from the known to the unknown, basing their aruguments on incestuous uses of each other's speculations, until the end product becomes "received knowledge" which is never questioned.

12

Some Concluding Insights

I. B. Holley, Jr.

The thoughtful individual who has read this volume will already have derived many insights from the foregoing chapters. The pages that follow offer a series of reminders for the reader and will also highlight some key points. Confronted with the need to attain air superiority, what should be done? What decisions can a commander reach that will make the task easier? What factors are within his power to affect? What actions can he initiate which will make a significant difference? It is of little value to assert that he must have superior aircraft, greater numbers than his enemy, and better trained crews. At this level of generalization, the need for more and better is commonplace. The thoughtful commander needs rather to know more explicitly *how* he can affect the attainment of these desired goals.

An obvious first step is to conceptualize the task at hand. Precisely what is meant by air superiority? The term air superiority most commonly conjures up visions of fighter aircraft engaged in dogfighting, but as the Italian theorist of air power, Giulio Douhet, suggested soon after World War I, it is more efficient to destroy enemy aircraft as they sit immobile on the ground. For many, this will bring to mind visions of World War II P–51 Mustangs or P–47 Thunderbolts swooping down on Luftwaffe airfields to strafe parked German aircraft. But why wait until the enemy is able to equip his air bases with combat-ready planes and pilots? Again, as Douhet suggested, why not destroy the enemy's capacity to fabricate aircraft in the first place? So one visualizes ever larger numbers of bombers streaming toward distant enemy production facilities, not only factories, but electric generating stations, refineries, transportation systems, and all the component elements that lie behind the industrial production that creates air power.

But fighters and bombers require highly skilled individuals to man them, and this means months or even years of rigorous training at a succession of specialized training bases. Trained manpower reminds one that not only crew members fly aircraft in combat but also those who direct them must be trained and, more importantly, *educated* in staff schools and war colleges. This specialized training and education are critical in order to achieve effective command and control, to insure that sound doctrine is formulated and disseminated, and to make certain that scarce resources are employed in ways leading to prompt victory with the least cost in lives and materiel. Command and control lead inescapably to the need for a network of rapid communications to knit the entire complex functioning.

Thus air superiority involves far more than finely honed fighter pilots courageously hurling their aircraft through body-wrenching maneuvers to bring their sights to bear on elusive enemy targets. Air *superiority* is indeed a seamless web involving the whole array of resources required to win that freedom for a nation's air forces to operate at will over chosen portions of enemy territory. Air *supremacy,* by contrast, is that situation in which a nation's air arm has achieved superiority virtually everywhere and is free to operate substantially unhindered by enemy air activity. From the fighter pilot at the cutting edge, back through the aircraft factory, and the whole research and development process, to the Congress which votes the appropriations, and even back to the voters and citizens whose collective will energizes the entire process, who can say that any element of this array is not essential in the struggle for air superiority?

The preceding chapters of this book have spelled out some of the vexing problems encountered over many years in the search for air superiority. This search, in a succession of historical contexts, reveals that while every episode was unique, there nonetheless were many common traits. This concluding chapter offers some insights of enough significance to inform a rising generation of air leaders, who may in their lifetimes confront anew the need to achieve air superiority in some future wars.

As the philosopher Santayana once said, "History can make a man wiser than he has any right to be on the basis of his own experience." By encountering the experience of others we may vicariously live it. But it would be a grave mistake to assume that one can derive "lessons" from the past, neat prescriptions on how to cope with the problems of the present and the unrolling future. Change is inexorable and the pace of change is rapid. Solutions valid yesterday might produce disaster tomorrow. What history offers is not lessons—not prescriptions or unchanging solutions— but insights. Reflecting upon a wide variety of historical episodes should, at best, suggest to those who will be in command tomorrow, not answers to the problems of tomorrow, but ways of approaching them. This will create an awareness of the inter-relationship of the many factors present in similar instances in the past, and some appreciation for the qualities of mind essential to the formulation of suitable solutions.

Given the large number of factors involved in the attainment of air superiority, the commander might focus his thinking around the principles of war, for as they relate to air superiority, they will almost certainly enhance his probability of success in battle. These principles embody the wisdom of many generations in dealing with war; reduced to a word or phrase the principles are easy to recall and in their variety stimulate reflection across a wide, though by no means all-embracing, spectrum of military concerns.

The first and most important is the principle of the *objective*. Although the Luftwaffe doctrinal manuals assigned first priority to winning air superiority, in September 1940 during the Battle of Britain, the Nazis abruptly switched their attacks from the RAF fighter bases, and their related radar installations, to strike at London in retaliation for British raids on Berlin (in themselves a response to accidental bombing of the British capital by the Luftwaffe). In doing this, the Germans ignored the fact that revenge is not one of the principles of war. This fatal neglect of the most important of the principles of war—the objective—offers another insight. It is not enough for military men to promulgate sound doctrine in their manuals. They must also see to it that the political leaders who make the decisions shaping strategy understand that doctrine. Manifestly, Hitler did not.

While it is easy to castigate the Nazi leaders for their abandonment of sound doctrine and the first principle of war, a more appropriate exercise might be to ask why Allied airmen did not see the significance of German experience for themselves, especially with regard to the importance of long-range fighters to accompany strategic bombers all the way to their distant targets and back. Here, too, a failure resulted from an intellectual or conceptual flaw in the thinking of those in command. By not subjecting the situation confronting them to an adequately rigorous and dispassionate analysis and by neglecting to study German experience as well as their own, the Allies delayed for more than two years the relatively simple technical solution to the problem of increasing the range of fighter aircraft.

While the academies, the staff schools, and the war colleges of the nation all teach the principles of war and stress the primacy of the *objective*, lapses in its application were certainly not limited to the era of World War II. Much the same might be said of the confusion over the objective in the more recent conflict in Vietnam. During the air war against North Vietnam, the objective was not clearly defined, and the United States did not undertake a comprehensive campaign to achieve air superiority.

The second principle, *mass* or concentration, also affects the quest for air superiority in a variety of ways, involving as it does such factors as the role of airlift and the capacity to build and operate air bases promptly and effectively in order to sustain a high sortie rate. In the invasion of Poland in 1939, the Luftwaffe almost immediately achieved air superiority. To be sure, the Polish air arm was woefully weak, but the Germans also skillfully applied the principle of concentration when employing their superiority both in numbers and aircraft performance. As soon as their ground forces overran a Polish airfield, the Luftwaffe flew in transports, Ju–52s, with maintenance crews and fuel. By such means their relatively short-legged fighters leapfrogged forward to sustain their superiority by concentrating their available aircraft over the battlefields where they were most needed.

When the U.S. forces moved into North Africa in November 1942, the initial failure to apply the principle of mass to the air arm led to serious losses. In the early air operations there, virtually all the available air assets were expended in providing air cover for the hard-pressed ground commanders whose troops suffered cruelly under repeated attacks by the Luftwaffe. Ground commanders, looking for continuous cover, argued that the best way to provide this was to assign specific air units to their commands. Given the scarcity of resources, continuous patrols aloft were out of the uestion, and even specifically assigned aircraft would have to return to their often distant bases to rearm and refuel.

The solution was not so much a formulation of new doctrine as a reassertion of a long-standing principle or its reaffirmation and recovery from the prevailing misapplication. The best way to serve the ground forces was to apply the principle of concentration. Spreading limited assets over the entire extended front was manifestly an impossible task, which left the airmen always outnumbered by the Luftwaffe wherever the Germans chose to concentrate. By going on the *offensive*, seizing the initiative, (applying yet another principle of war) and undertaking the maximum possible concentration, U.S. airmen were able to catch the enemy on the ground at his own bases. By shifting the pattern of attack from day to day they were able to keep the Germans perpetually off balance and achieve remarkable success.

Success in applying the principle of mass should not lead one to ignore an important factor in its implementation. The airmen had to sell the idea persuasively to the ground commanders. This they did. But to insure that the shift in practice was understood down through the whole chain of the command, key ground commanders such as Generals Bernard Law Montgomery and Harold Alexander had to be persuaded to support the shift with symbolic ostentation.

Two other principles of war, *economy of force* and *security*, the obverse of *mass*, must always be taken into consideration in any proposed concentration in the drive for air superiority. In order to concentrate, the commander must avoid dissipating his forces on secondary or less important objectives. At the same time, he must not "leave the back door open," as it were, by thinning down his covering forces so far as to expose his vital areas to enemy initiatives.

A good illustration of the principle of *security* may be seen in the deployment of the Luftwaffe during the German excursion into Czechoslovakia prior to World War II. By prompt neutralization of Czech air bases, the Luftwaffe not only immobilized the Czech air force and thus gained freedom of action for the *Wehrmacht* ground arms but at the same time made it virtually impossible for the Soviets to send assistance to the Czechs by air, the only way they could do so fast enough to avoid a *fait accompli* by the Germans.

Conversely, the Norwegians, in failing to deny the use of their airfields to the Germans, even if only temporarily with ill-trained and ill-equipped reservists, lost their best opportunity for delaying the arrival in their ports of the invader's seaborne troop transports. Even a brief delay in landing these vulnerable troop-laden ships would have given Great Britain's Royal Navy a better opportunity to catch them off shore without air cover. This was a most costly and disastrous lesson in the importance of the principle of *security*.

There are other dimensions to the principle of *security* beyond the business of allocating sufficient aircraft to counter enemy initiatives in areas apart from the main points of thrust. Security also involves decisions on what resources to expend in providing revetments and blast shelters and how far to disperse aircraft. Dispersal may minimize damage, but requires extensive taxiways which make concealment difficult and target identification easier.

Another aspect of *security* is the problem of air base defense. Here the painful experience encountered at Iwo Jima should not be forgotten. After the capture of the island, when the installation had become fully operational, Japanese survivors had hidden in caves on Mount Suribachi, crept out at night and attacked the base, killing forty-four and wounding twice that number. Although subsequent operations in Vietnam may have aroused somewhat more interest in air base defense, this has long been a neglected aspect of the air superiority equation in air arm thinking. Surely the perceptive commander will recognize from this that the quest for air superiority cannot rest entirely on warmed over doctrines from World War II; for want of adequate air base defense in Vietnam, the USAF lost more aircraft to guerrilla attacks on the ground than it did to surface-to-air missiles in the air.

While it is easy to visualize the idea of *economy of force* in terms of the way a commander allocates his available aircraft to objectives of varying importance or priority, the principle applies in other ways as well and often in relation to the principle of the *objective*. For example,

613

while the Germans have been criticized for attacking British bomber factories during the Battle of Britain in 1940 rather than concentrating on those facilities turning out fighters, surely the British were making an even greater mistake. Although RAF doctrine accorded first priority to air superiority, the British continued to produce obsolete bombers such as the Whitley and the Battle, which could not hope to dent the German aircraft industry, instead of devoting the productive resources to fabricating fighter components.

Whatever the doctrinal manual may have proclaimed about the priority of air superiority, RAF leaders were overwhelmingly bomber-minded. As Air Commodore L.E.O. Charlton put it, "air power is bombing capacity and nothing else."[1] This bomber orientation of the RAF was further reflected in the training program where Bomber Command had substantially more students in the training program than did Fighter Command. Certainly both fighters and bombers were necessary in the drive for air superiority, but during the Battle of Britain greater numbers of fighter pilots would have made more of a difference in the immediate outcome.

The principle of the *offensive,* sometimes described simply as retaining the initiative, is closely related to that other major principle, *surprise.* The dividends accruing to those who apply this principle are often spectacular. By a successful application of surprise in their opening assault on Russia in June of 1941, the Germans all but eliminated Soviet air power and achieved virtual air supremacy almost immediately. Had they then not lost sight of the *objective,* failing as they did to finish the job by destroying the major Russian aircraft factories before they could be transported to eastern sanctuaries beyond the range of German bombers, the outcome of the war might well have been far different. But there is no gainsaying the success of the initial resort to surprise.

The leaders of the Israeli Air Force have repeatedly demonstrated a high order of intellectual rigor in assessing the problems of national survival. Their operational plans seem to conform consistently to the principles of war. Heavily outnumbered as they are, it is little wonder they have resorted to the principle of *surprise* to achieve air superiority. In 1956 and again in 1967, they relied upon preemptive strikes to this end. But here a word of caution to the prudent commander is in order. The Israelis paid a price for the surprise they achieved; preemptive strikes cast a nation in the role of aggressor, no matter how great the provocation which induced the strike. So, in the Yom Kippur War of 1973, despite Israeli Air Force plans for knocking out enemy surface-to-air-missile (SAM) sites preemptively in an early bid for air superiority, the political authorities forced the abandonment of this tactic in a bow to world opinion.

The ability of the Luftwaffe to move rapidly into captured Polish airfields by air transport illustrates the principle of *mobility* as well as the principle of concentration or *mass*. Mobility, the capacity to maneuver effectively, is not just a function of the ability to move aircraft rapidly and flexibly over great distances. True mobility also involves the capacity to construct air bases promptly in forward areas. When the Allies invaded North Africa in 1942, for example, airfields were few and far between and seldom located where most needed. The engineer units sent to construct new bases were not only ill-equipped but lacking in sound doctrine. Eventually they hammered out specifications for minimal bases and constructed over a hundred. But the impressive achievements of the mature organization should not obscure the faulty conceptualization of the initial effort by those bent on attaining air superiority. To operate effectively in a hostile environment such as the sands of North Africa requires highly imaginative advance planning, balanced kits of spare parts, a wide range of ancillary equipment such as generators and fuel trucks, as well as the essential engineer equipment, all before tactical units could be successfully deployed.

The principle of *mobility* applies to retreat as well as advance. When the French and British squadrons in France retreated before the German onslaught in the spring of 1940 to less threatened air bases further south, their unpracticed withdrawals were hasty and disorganized. As a consequence they were less able to generate sorties even when they had the planes to do so—clear evidence that sortie rates offer a more useful index of air superiority than total number of aircraft on hand. Field artillerymen have long understood that their effectiveness hinged upon an ability to get into action promptly after displacing, whether advancing or retreating. French and British airmen, operating from sedentary bases in peacetime, seem to have forgotten the importance of portability.

Although the principle of *unity of command* has long been recognized, historically it has proved difficult to achieve. For example, British and American tactical units were sent out to North Africa in 1942 before the details of command had been settled. This virtually insured several months of confusion and conflict until a unified command structure could be hammered out. The solution finally agreed upon proved to be workable and durable. The nation providing the lion's share of resources gets to appoint the unified commander, but his principal subordinate must then be appointed by the other partner. This simple but practical arrangement set a precedent of great utility for Allied cooperation in other theaters as well as a guide for the long-range future in the quest for air superiority.

Whatever the doctrinal manuals may say about the necessity for *unity of command* (FM 100–20, *Command and Employment of Air Power*, published in July 1943, was certainly explicit on this point), any commander engaged in coalition warfare will find unity extraordinarily difficult to achieve. The compulsions and constraints of national sovereignty are not lightly put aside. Failure to achieve unity of command, however, exacts a high price, not least of which is permitting uncoordinated operations in the absence of an effective central planning authority. Here again the Allies may have been saved much in World War II because their enemy also suffered from a defective Luftwaffe command structure, providing little or no coordination below the level of Marshal Goering himself, a notoriously lax and undisciplined leader, who surrounded himself with a weak staff of cronies and sycophants.

For the commander bent on attaining air superiority, probably no principle has greater influence on his quest than the whole matter of *logistics*. Yet in no other areas is his power to influence most often indirect and limited. For example, while it is generally agreed that qualitative superiority favors victory, it is also true that transitioning to superior late model aircraft can impose a substantial degradation in combat readiness. Luftwaffe officers eagerly adopted the new and better models of high performance aircraft that became available from the German aircraft industry in the late 1930s. The new planes were, however, more difficult to fly, and even experienced pilots required extensive retraining. Moreover, new planes meant a new set of spares to be procured and distributed, and aircraft availability dropped sharply as maintenance crews struggled to master unfamiliar malfunctions. The Germans were fortunate because their major transition to a new generation of fighters came in 1938 when they were not at war. On the other hand, the French Air Force was in the midst of just such a change-over during the crisis of 1940. Some of the new models being introduced had outstanding performance characteristics, but with fewer than half their planes ready for combat at any one time, the French simply could not generate the sortie rate required to confront the Germans successfully. Clearly, *timing* is a critical principle in any such transitioning but not one over which a commander has much control because so many external factors such as the managerial skills of the aircraft industry are involved.

To illustrate the indirect character of a commander's authority, one has only to consider the problem of modifying aircraft that are already in production in order to improve their performance. In the struggle for air superiority, any technical change that will upgrade the performance of a given weapon—a significant increment of speed, range, climb, or the like—is avidly sought by the operational units. But so too are increases in the total number of planes produced. Therefore, the problem becomes a tradeoff of *more* versus *better*. The ideal, of course, is to get both, but this involves finding ways to inject modifications into the production line without slowing down the rate at which finished aircraft are delivered to the units in combat. Solving this problem is a challenge for the manufacturer, not the Air Force commander.

There are, however, numerous aspects of aircraft modification that are within the scope of Air Force commanders. Radical modifications mean diversity in spare parts. Unless Air Force decisionmakers exercise the most rigid control over the allocation and assignment of modified aircraft by block numbers, the spare parts problem out in the field can become a nightmare. What modifications are desired? While it is true that many modifications in production aircraft are initiated by the manufacturer's engineers in their continual drive to enhance performance, some modifications are devised in response to a need communicated from the operational units in reaction to encounters with the enemy. If the enemy tracking radars for AA guns and SAMs are turned off to outwit an incoming missile that has been homing in on their emissions, as happened in Vietnam, how rapidly and accurately does this tactical development get communicated back to the designers of electronic equipment, who are thus challenged to devise missiles with memories allowing them to continue firmly on course to their targets even when those targets are no longer emitting? Here the commander does indeed play a vital role; he must perfect his organization that deals with signals intelligence; he must discipline his pilots into developing their talent for turning out objective after-action reports; he must cultivate skillful debriefers and interrogators who can extract every possible shred of useful information from pilots returning from engagements with the enemy. Although there is a long chain of events between the pilot's reported observation and the introduction of a modification in the airplanes coming down the production line, this initial step is clearly a vital one for air superiority, and such steps are within the purview of the commander.

A single example will readily illustrate the need to perfect the system by which observations on the relationship between tactics and equipment are transmitted back from the engagement to the distant designer and aeronautical engineer. The RAF Spitfire with its float carburetor could not without momentary loss of power follow a Focke-Wulf 190 fighter when the Luftwaffe pilot undertook an evasive maneuver by an abrupt pushover. The inverted Focke-Wulf, with its fuel injection engine, continued at full power and therefore escaped, while the negative G-forces encountered in a pushover maneuver adversely affected the float carburetor of the Spitfire if the RAF pilot attempted to follow. Here was a "lesson" that could be passed on to neophyte Luftwaffe pilots on how to escape when hard pressed by a Spitfire on one's tail. But what of that "lesson" when the P–47 Thunderbolt with its Stromberg floatless carburetor appeared on the scene and the push-over maneuver no longer opened the way to survival? How long did it take for Nazi pilots to observe this change and communicate it to the German fighter force at large?

In any consideration of the principle of *logistics*, it is not enough to see the problem solely in terms of more and better. In the drive for "better," whether by innovations or by modifications in existing equipment, there is a natural tendency to press for an immediate fix to some threat, some

617

unexpected capability on the part of the enemy. Given a specific threat, the designers and engineers of the aeronautical industry can concentrate their energies on devising a solution. But the solutions developed, the items of equipment designed and installed, while individually effective, too often fail to form an integrated whole. This was especially true during fighting in Vietnam where the electronic equipment acquired by the USAF resulted from crash programs thrown together to come up with electronic replies to enemy innovations. The United States spent some thirty billion dollars on items for electronic warfare, much of it consisting of remarkably ingenious devices reflecting impressive skills on the part of the engineers involved. But there was far too little coordinated effort, too little attempt to unify the weapons systems as a whole. As a consequence, pilots began to complain that their fighters had so many specialized electronic warfare (EW) pods hanging under their wings that there were few pylons left free for armament. *Ad hoc* solutions also reduced inter-changeability and increased costs, but affected even more adversely the struggle for air superiority by increasing pilot tasking, sometimes near to the breaking point.

Reflecting upon the logistical principle inevitably brings the "more" versus "better" equation into focus. Because the United States has long enjoyed a marked superiority in the high technology area, it is easy to understate the importance of numbers in the struggle for air superiority. The Nazi and Soviet forces on the Eastern front in World War II illustrated this point.

An important factor in the ability of the Soviets to overcome their initial defeat resulting from Hitler's surprise assault in 1941 was the massive size of the Soviet Union and its resources—not only the immensity of the land itself and the depth of the stage, but also the staggering numbers of actors and the sheer scale of Russian armament. In the late 1930s when the U.S. Army Air Corps had fewer than 2,000 pilots including reservists and was struggling to enlarge its complement of 1,800 authorized aircraft to 2,230, the Soviets were already able to send 1,500 planes to aid the beleaguered Republicans in Spain without in the least stripping their home defenses. Clearly, Hitler forgot what Napoleon had learned the hard way and no future enemy of the Soviets should ever forget: superior strategy, tactics, morale, and the like, all are important, but numbers—sheer numbers of combat ready airplanes—even when manifestly inferior to those of the enemy, count suprisingly heavily in the balance.

Because the Air Force commander is understandably preoccupied with his primary weapons (the aircraft at his disposal), it is all too easy for him to devote inadequate attention to the infrastructure that supports his airplanes. Further, because a democratic government does not readily embrace the idea of a preemptive strike, the advantage of the initiative and surprise, at least in the opening stages of a war, will almost certainly lie with the enemy. Given the flexibility and ease with which aircraft can be moved over long distances to counter a surprise thrust by the enemy, it has repeatedly come about, that tactical units are deployed immediately to the threatened location while the infrastructure of support follows at a far more laggard pace.

The experience of the USAF in Korea afforded a painful example. At first the advantage lay with the North Koreans; the USAF infrastructure initially was largely lacking. The hard-won experience of World War II as to the critical importance of well-equipped engineer units ready to roll on call seemed to have been lost. The skills and equipment required by base-building engineer units manned by experienced reservists were not immediately available when the need arose in Korea.

Somewhat more comprehensible were the early shortages in such specialized categories as photo interpreters, aviation ordnance men and the like, despite the pool of talent developed in such fields as these during World War II. These kinds of shortages certainly highlight the importance of command support for a well trained reserve force in precisely those categories where lack of peacetime funding makes it impossible to sustain adequate strength in the active force.

In the battle for air superiority there are many dimensions to the matter of ancillary activities. Air-sea rescue presents a case in point. The long delay experienced by the British in developing a suitable rescue service at the onset of World War II cost the RAF many experienced pilots who had successfully parachuted into the sea from crippled aircraft. Despite this clear precedent, the USAF only belatedly perfected its air-sea rescue capabilities in Vietnam. To be sure, that organization, when mature, performed superbly, but in some future conflict the needless loss at sea of some of the most highly trained active force pilots in the initial stages of a conflict might well spell the difference between success and failure.

Yet another critical element in the logistical infrastructure is the capacity to effect prompt maintenance and repair, which sustains the high sortie rate so essential to air superiority. Here command decisions can have a direct impact. The relative merits of performing maintenance at the squadron level or in a consolidated facility at some higher echelon has long been debated. During peacetime, efficiency and economy seem to favor consolidation. But in wartime, the case for consolidation is by no means so positive. Where rapid repair of battle damage is a consideration, squadron level maintenance has much to be said for it. Whichever alternative is adopted, in wartime a fast and efficient maintenance and repair organization is a force multiplier.

The issue of battle damage repair for aircraft leads to air base survivability as a factor in air superiority. Here the experience of the RAF during the Battle of Britain is instructive. In peacetime, convenience and economy dictated a concentration of facilities adjacent to the runways. In wartime, enemy action prompted hasty dispersal and the need for revetments. The latter required bulldozers, the former additional vehicles for aircrews to reach their planes quickly in a scramble. Locating the operations room off base reduced its vulnerability but increased dependence upon telephone lines. Exposed lines could be made more secure by burying, but involved ditching machines.

Here again, for want of sufficient prewar thought on the wider ramifications of air superiority, many ancillary items of equipment, be they bicycles, telephones, bulldozers, or ditching machines, had scarcely been considered, even if funds were lacking to procure them. In a future conflict, the kinds of ancillary equipment required may well be entirely different, but the challenge to the imagination of the commander in anticipating such needs will be as acute as ever.

In the struggle for air superiority no aspect offers a greater challenge than command and control. These terms are so often glibly linked that they are easily assumed to be synonymous. *Command* is the obligation to make decisions, to give orders, to direct. *Control,* by contrast, is the process by which command is exercised; this involves the whole series of steps by which orders are communicated and the feedback on performance is monitored. Inexorably this involves the entire spectrum of communications, the technical terminology employed, the semantic adequacy of the message passed, and the means of communication used, electronic or otherwise.

Students of war have often observed that a good communications net is a force multiplier. Genghis Khan recognized this when he was at pains to see that at least some of the witnesses to his terror tactics were allowed to escape to the area he intended to assault next in order to demoralize the population so thoroughly as to insure him an easy victory. Whether the communication is by word of mouth or electronic, the principle remains the same. Certainly the RAF chain of radar stations and their associated communication links to the fighter control centers in the Battle of Britain demonstrated the validity of this contention. The Nazis also had radar sensors; what they had not yet perfected was the communications net, which make the findings of their radar available to the air defense commanders in a timely fashion. Similarly, in France during the crisis of May 1940, neither the French nor the British air forces had a well articulated communications net to facilitate command and control. As a consequence there were catastrophic delays in dispatching planes to where they were most needed.

Most recently, during the conflict in Southeast Asia, the importance of effective communications was again pointedly demonstrated. While the number of aircraft available for combat always seemed inadequate and the pace at which new equipment was being developed to counter enemy tactics too slow, the challenge confronting those in charge of the air war was to make the best possible use of the assets they did have. This involved orchestrating a succession of highly complex tactical moves. Fighters had to rendezvous with fighter-bombers or bombers on precise schedules even though the planes may have departed initially from different countries—from Thailand, South Vietnam and even Guam—as well as different air bases. Tankers had to be dispatched to rendezvous with fuel-lean strike aircraft returning with precariously narrow time windows from distant engagements. The last intelligence ferreted out by Wild Weasels or other means had to be digested and converted into specific instructions for the EW pods of outbound aircraft, all within a tight time frame. These and many similar tasks of coordination and direction imposed a heavy burden on the overworked communications net that had evolved all too slowly and only belatedly provided secure voice transmissions. The commander whose preoccupation with airplanes leads him to neglect communications courts disaster.

The problem of communications in the search for air superiority involves far more than the need to provide sufficient network capacity to carry the ever-mounting volume of traffic. Despite the need for close tactical coordination with naval vessels off the coast, in Vietnam it took nearly three years to establish a satisfactory system of common terminology and message format. And this delay occurred even though the same problems had surfaced in the effort to coordinate Air Force, Marine, and Navy air operations during the fighting in Korea more than ten years earlier. "Unification" within a single Department of Defense had left many facets of the job undone.

Because of the remarkable technical advances that have taken place in the field of electronics, it is all too easy to overlook the less sophisticated but effective means by which vital information may be made available. A case in point can be drawn from the experience of the AAF in the Pacific during World War II. While U.S. strategy called for the construction of island air bases moving ever closer to the Japanese heartland, it was painfully apparent that bases near enough to the Japanese for friendly fighters to accompany bomber attacks on the enemy installations were also near enough for the enemy to launch similar strikes in return. So American airmen had to devise doctrines which would take into account the existing conditions including the strengths and weaknesses of the equipment available to them. Since radar units were scarce and of limited performance early in the war, the obvious alternative was to rely upon coast watchers with clandestine radios at locations closer to the Japanese where they could give early warning of approaching enemy planes. Just because electronic sensing has subsequently become so effective, this is no reason to neglect such crude but workable alternatives as the coast watchers net.

From the foregoing discussion it is evident that the challenges confronting the commander in search of air superiority are formidable. There are so many factors to take into account that the prudent leader will welcome whatever assistance he can get from published doctrine. If it does nothing else, doctrine should alert him to what some of the probable variables will be and where to look for problems. Unfortunately, doctrine has a distressing tendency to harden into dogma. Solutions workable and helpful yesterday may be outdated or superseded by new conditions today.

As the late, great Justice Oliver Wendell Holmes once put it, "to rest upon a certainty is a slumber which, prolonged, means death." In the case of aerial combat, this is often literally true. Any tactical advance introduced by the enemy must be countered with a corresponding response, or the loss rate will soar. This puts a premium on the rigor with which the air arm's leadership improves the procedure for perfecting doctrine and the extent to which it encourages perceptive individuals to translate their observations into the raw materials of doctrine. An example from the Luftwaffe will illustrate this readily.

The experience of the Nazi Kondor Legion in the Spanish Civil War led to important improvements in Luftwaffe fighter tactics as a result of Werner Mölder's perceptive after-action reports. The reports analyzed the defects in the prevailing "vic" or three-plane formation and led to the substitution of the highly successful "finger four" formation with two units of two aircraft each. This gave the Germans a significant tactical advantage until it was belatedly adopted by most other air forces. In short, one observant individual who is capable of thinking the problem through and has a capacity for effective communication, can make a great deal of difference. But does the system for providing fighter pilots encourage such individuals? In an age when available technology presses hard on the physiological limits of man in the cockpit, the commander must make a special effort to identify, nourish, and develop those individual pilots who are capable of withstanding the physical demands of high performance aircraft and at the same time can reflect constructively on the ever-evolving character of their calling and successfully communicate their insights to those who formulate doctrine. Eddie Rickenbacker in World I made many of the same observations Mölders did and went on to become an ace, but his insights on aerial combat were not integrated into doctrine. In the struggle for air superiority, this marked a failure on the part of command.

A more common failure is the neglect of sound doctrine by those who give lip service to it. Here again an example from the Luftwaffe will illustrate the point. The manuals of the German Air Force, newly reconstituted by the Nazi government in the 1930s, clearly articulated the doctrine of air superiority: the priority objective was the enemy air force, whether it was to be found in the air, on the ground, or in the factory. But regardless of what the manuals said, Germany's geographical situation virtually dictated

622

that a major responsibility of the Luftwaffe was to support the Army that shielded the sources of German air power. This mission had a subtle impact upon Luftwaffe thinking. Just as in the United States, where the presence of ocean barriers led Air Corps officers to think of intercepting incoming bombers with aircraft rising from their local bases, so too did German Air Force officers tend to conceive their role as one of operating relatively short-range aircraft from interior lines and established bases in the defense of the fatherland. This left them ill-prepared to cope when called upon to fight in North Africa or deep within the Soviet Union. Nationalistic or geographical myopia can be a serious intellectual impediment.

At least on paper the RAF also accorded first priority to winning air superiority, but, as observed above, the service was overwhelmingly bomber-minded. Much the same attitude prevailed in the United States. In the era of "massive retaliation" during the 1950s, the Air Force poured the bulk of its funds into developing strategic bombers and fighter-bombers with nuclear capabilities to the neglect of aircraft suited to the more conventional air superiority role. This preoccupation with the potential for nuclear warfare extended well beyond airplanes to induce a substantial curtailment of interest in the development of doctrine and training for tactical air warfare. This concentration on nuclear capabilities was paralleled in the allocation of research and development finds, especially in the curtailment of funds for equipment used in electronic warfare. As a consequence, when the USAF first began to commit substantial numbers of operational units in Vietnam, it suffered from painfully high loss rates. In sum, the publication of sound doctrine is not enough; to be effective, air superiority doctrine must permeate the thinking of the service.

From the foregoing discussion it should be evident that a most important factor in attaining air superiority is the mind of the commander—at every echelon from the most junior squadron leader to the commanding general. His range of experience, whether direct personal experience or vicarious, indirect experience in the form of sound doctrine carefully studied and internalized, coupled with a lively imagination in deciding when to apply and when *not* to apply the valuable insight gleaned from the evidence of the past, can play a vital role in the quest for dominance in the air.

The growth of modern technology has had a decided impact on the quest for air superiority. By the late 1960s, U.S. experience in Vietnam and comparable developments in the Arab-Israeli wars began to drive home the realization that air warfare was undergoing a fundamental change. Missiles had certainly not replaced aircraft, but they were coming to play an increasingly larger role. As air-to-air missiles of greater range and accuracy succeeded one another in the inventory, the character of aerial engagements has changed. The classic dogfight of World Wars I and II was giving way to encounters with air-to-air missiles launched at targets barely in sight. No less unsettling has been the development of surface-to-air missiles—SAMS—of ever-increasing lethality.

In an age of missiles, the design, development, deployment, and operation of electronic gear also has become a factor in the fight for air superiority no less significant than the airplane itself. By 1982 the Israelis, whose geographic and demographic limitations have mandated reliance on superior wit and imagination, had developed an electronic countermeasure drone which managed to spoof the Syrian radars so successfully that the IAF was able to knock out nineteen SAM sites without suffering a single aircraft loss. In short, while superior aircraft and better trained pilots still give an edge on victory, the capacity for rapidly devising alternative tactics and upgrading electronic gear now may well hold the decisive vote.

In the race for dominance in the air, technological superiority is a critically important goal. Whether one speaks of aircraft or ancillary equipment, superior performance gives an edge on victory. But how is technological superiority to be defined? Modern weapons systems represent complex congeries of components. To excel in some features usually means a sacrifice in performance elsewhere. Ruggedness to survive high-G pullouts or snaprolls will almost certainly add weight and thus cut down on rate of climb; more munitions mean reduced range, and so on. In practice, then, technological superiority means that combination of tradeoffs that yield a weapon system with more advantages and fewer vulnerabilities than the weapons employed by the enemy. But how are such tradeoffs to be decided? This leads us to that imperative attribute, responsiveness.

Responsiveness means nothing more than the ability of a decisionmaker to react rapidly and soundly to significant changes in the tides of war. It requires accommodation or adaptability, an open-mindedness and receptivity, not merely openness to new ideas but an alertness or sensitivity to subtle indications of shifting trends before the direction of change becomes obvious to all. Responsiveness is a core requirement for effective command. It hinges upon perceptive observations followed by objective analysis leading to the formulation of a sound solution. Sometimes the solution will involve the formulation of a statement of requirements; for example, a specific guide to the weapons designer on precisely what modification in an existing weapon is needed to overcome an enemy threat. At other times the solution will involve the derivation of a new tactic. Since a change in tactics can be instituted faster than changes in hardware, it may provide a useful stopgap until a more far-reaching technological solution can be developed and deployed.

How, then, does an air force achieve air superiority? The answer in a nutshell is brain power—the ability of decisionmakers to use doctrine creatively, to make wise use of aviation history to remain open to innovation, yet searching in criticism and brutally objective in evaluation. All of which suggests that the cultivation of intellectual rigor in the officer corps may be the most promising, albeit one of the most difficult, actions to be exploited in the search for air superiority. No greater challenge exists for our service schools and colleges than to demand the level of intellectual rigor that will be required for success in the wars of the future.

Notes

1. L. E. O. Charlton, *The Menace of the Clouds* (London, 1937), p 28, quoted in Williamson Murray, "British and German Air Doctrine Between the Wars," *Air University Review* XXXI (Mar-Apr 1980), p 57.

Contributors

LEONARD BAKER was a journalist by profession before his death in 1984. Educated at the University of Pittsburgh, with a Master of Science in Journalism from Columbia University, Mr. Baker was a reporter for the St. Louis *Globe–Democrat,* and *Newsday.* He was also a freelance journalist in Washington, as well as Visiting Professor at the University of Louisville and Boston University. In addition to producing numerous government publications in the field of health, Baker authored many books including the Pulitzer Prize winning *Days of Sorrow and Pain—Leo Baeck and the Berlin Jews; John Marshall—A Life in Law; Roosevelt and Pearl Harbor; The Johnson Eclipse—A President's Vice Presidency;* and works on Louis Brandeis and Felix Frankfurter, as well as the Supreme Court.

BENJAMIN FRANKLIN COOLING served as Chief, Special Histories Branch and Senior Historian for Contract Programs, Office of Air Force History, Washington, D.C. He has previously been associated with the U.S. Army Center of Military History, and more recently, he served as Assistant Director for Historical Services, U.S. Army Military History Institute, Carlisle Barracks, Pennsylvania. A former National Park Historian and Assistant Professor at PMC Colleges, he has taught also at the University of Pennsylvania and the U.S. Army War College. He was a Naval War College Research Associate in 1973–74, and is currently a Fellow of the Company of Military Historians and Executive Director of the American Military Institute.

He holds a Master of Arts and Doctor of Philosophy in history from the University of Pennsylvania. He has written or edited numerous articles, volumes, and series in the field of military and naval history including *Benjamin Franklin Tracy: Father of the Modern American Fighting Navy;*

Symbol, Sword, and Shield, Defending Washington During the Civil War; War, Business, and American Society (editor); *New American State Papers, Military Affairs*–20 volumes (editor); *Gray Steel and Blue Water Navy, Formative Years of America's Military-Industrial Complex; War, Business, and International Military-Industrial Complex* (editor); *Combined Operations in Peace and War* (co-author); and *Forts Henry and Donelson: Key to the Southern Heartland,* which received the 1988 Douglas Southall Freeman prize for Civil War history. He also co–authored *Mr. Lincoln's Forts: A Guide to the Civil War Defenses of Washington,* a volume concerning the 1864 Confederate campaign against Washington, which was published in 1989.

ALVIN D. COOX holds a M.A. and a Ph.D. in history from Harvard University, is currently Professor of History and Director of the Japan Studies Institute at San Diego State University, and is also Adjunct Professor of Strategy and Policy at the U.S. Naval War College's San Diego Graduate Seminar Program. Among his awards are a Certificate of Commendation from the Institute of Technology of the Air University; a Citation for Outstanding Contributions in the Field of Aerospace Education from the San Diego Chapter of the Air Force Association; and a Writing Award from the U.S. Air Force Historical Foundation. He also has received the Samuel Eliot Morison Prize from the American Military Institute, and the California State University Trustees' Outstanding Professor Award for scholarly and teaching excellence. The author of numerous books and articles dealing with the prelude to and course of the Pacific War, he has in addition contributed to *The Historical Encyclopedia of World War II* (1980), the *Time/Life* book *Bombers Over Japan* (1982); and *The Cambridge History of Japan* (1989). His latest publication is the two-volume study of ground and air operations in limited war in the Far East, *Nomonhan: Japan Against Russia 1939* (1986).

BRERETON GREENHOUS is a historian with the Canadian Department of National Defence and has a special interest in the tactical aspects of the aircraft/armor interface. He was born in the United Kingdom in 1929 and has served in the British Army, with the Malayan Police, and in the Canadian Army between 1947 and 1965. Turning to an academic career, he earned a Bachelor of Arts at Carleton University, Ottawa, and a Master of Arts at Queen's University, Kingston. He taught at Lakehead University, Thunder Bay, Ontario, before taking his present post in 1971. He is the author of two regimental histories: *Dragoon: the Centennial History of the Royal Canadian Dragoons, 1883–1983;* and *Semper Paratus: the History of the Royal Hamilton Light Infantry, 1862–1977.* He is co–author of

Out of the Shadows: Canada in the Second World War and a contributing author to *Men At War: Politics, Technology and Innovation in the Twentieth Century.* He is also the editor of *A Rattle of Pebbles: The First World War Diaries of Two Canadian Airmen.* His articles on aspects of tactical air power have been required reading at West Point and the USAF Academy. He is the designated principal author of the forthcoming third volume of the Official History of the Royal Canadian Air Force (RCAF), which will deal with RCAF operations overseas during the Second World War.

ROBIN HIGHAM was born and educated both in Great Britain and the United States before joining the Royal Air Force as a pilot, 1943–47. After graduating cum laude from Harvard University in 1950 and earning a Master of Arts at the Claremont Graduate School in 1953, he returned to Harvard for his Ph.D. in Oceanic and British History. After teaching at the Universities of Massachusetts and North Carolina, he moved to Kansas State University in 1963. In 1968 he became Editor of *Military Affairs* and in 1970 of *Aerospace Historian,* journals well known in their fields. From 1975 to 1985 he served on the Publications Committee of the International Commission for Comparative Military History. In 1986 he was appointed a member of the State Aviation Advisory Committee of Kansas.

Higham's professional publications include such pioneering edited works as *Official Histories* with contributors from around the world; *A Guide to the Sources of British Military History; A Guide to the Sources of U.S. Military History* with Donald J. Mrozek; and with Jacob W. Kipp, the Garland series of international bibliographies in military history. He and Dr. Kipp also edited as well as contributed to *Soviet Aviation and Air Power.* Even more directly related to aviation have been his own monographs including *Britain's Imperial Air Routes, 1918–1939; The British Rigid Airship, 1908–1931: A Study in Weapons Policy; Armed Forces in Peacetime: Britain, 1918–1940; The Military Intellectuals in Britain; Air Power: A Concise History;* and *The Diary of a Disaster: British Aid to Greece, 1940–1941.* In addition he has published a wide range of articles, and for all these many contributions he was made the first recipient of the American Military Institute's Samuel Eliot Morison Prize for contributions to the field of military history in 1986.

I. B. HOLLEY, JR., is Professor of History at Duke University, Durham, North Carolina. Born in Connecticut, he received his B.A. from Amherst College in 1940, and his M.A. and Ph.D. in 1942 and 1947, respectively, from Yale University. He served for five years in the U.S. Army Air Forces during World War II and then joined the U.S. Air Force

Reserve, retiring as a Major General in 1981. His scholarly works include *Ideas and Weapons*, now in its third edition; *Buying Aircraft: Materiel Procurement for the Army Air Forces*, a volume in the official history series, *The United States Army in World War II;* and *General John M. Palmer, Citizen, Soldiers, and the Army of a Democracy*. Professor Holley has been Visiting Professor at the U.S. Military Academy, West Point, New York, and at the National Defense University in Washington, D.C. He is a regular lecturer at the Air University, Maxwell Air Force Base, Alabama; the Army War College, Carlisle Barracks, Pennsylvania; the Command and General Staff College, Fort Leavenworth, Kansas; and a number of other institutions. Many of his articles and chapters have been assigned as required reading at one or another of the military professional schools. Professor Holley is on the editorial advisory boards of several professional journals and a frequent contributor of book reviews.

THOMAS HONE received his Ph.D. in political science from the University of Wisconsin in 1973. More recently, he has served as a member of the Department of Defense Economics of the Naval War College, in Newport, Rhode Island. His special interest is how military units and organizations survive the stress of war and deal with constant changes in military technology. He has taught on the faculties of several universities, including the University of Wisconsin, Indiana University, Southern Illinois University (Carbondale), and Iowa State University, and has served briefly as a historian with the U.S. National Park Service, where his specialty was the Civil War. He has also worked for five years as as a consultant to the Department of Defense, specializing in planning, operations analysis, and program management. His research has focused on the development of the U.S. Navy in the period between World Wars I and II, particularly on how the Navy reacted to changes in the potential of air power during those years. His papers have appeared in the *Journal of Strategic Studies, Armed Forces and Society, Military Affairs*, the *Naval War College Review, Defense Analysis*, and the *U.S. Naval Institute Proceedings*. He is currently on leave from the Strategy Analysis Center of Booz, Allen, and Hamilton, serving as a member of the faculty of the Defense Systems Management College at Fort Belvoir, Virginia.

W. A. JACOBS is Professor of History at the University of Alaska, Anchorage, where he has taught Modern European History since 1973. He is a graduate of Wisconsin State University, Eau Claire, and holds an M.A. and a Ph.D. in history from the University of Oregon. Originally trained as a social and economic historian, he later turned to the history of warfare. His "Tactical Air Doctrine and AAF Close Air Support in the European

Theater, 1944–45," (*Aerospace Historian,* Spring 1980) and "Close Air Support for the British Army, 1939–45" (*Military Affairs,* Winter 1982) shed some light on tactical air organization, doctrine, and operations in the Second World War. His "Strategic Bombing and American National Strategy, 1941–43," (*Military Affairs,* Summer 1986) is an examination of the process by which an American strategic bombing offensive became part of Allied strategy. Jacobs's analysis of the organizational politics of Allied air command appeared in the *Journal of Strategic Studies* in March 1988. Jacobs is currently working on a comparative study of the operations of RAF Bomber Command and the American Eighth and Fifteenth Air Forces.

WILLIAMSON MURRAY is Associate Professor of History at Ohio State University. After active service in the United States Air Force, he received a Ph.D. from Yale University in 1975. He is the author of two books, *The Change in the European Balance of Power, 1938–1939: the Path to Ruin* and *Strategy for Defeat: The Luftwaffe, 1933–1945.* He has also authored numerous articles that have appeared in scholarly and military journals. Murray is co–editor with Professor Allan Millet of *On Military Effectiveness,* published by Allen and Unwin in 1988. Professor Murray has also been a research associate at the Air War College, and visiting professor at the United States Military Academy and at the Naval War College.

DAVID SYRETT was educated at Columbia University and the University of London. Professor Syrett has been a member of the History Department, Queens College, CUNY, since 1966. His major publications include *Shipping and the American War* and *The Siege and Capture of Havana, 1762; The Lost War: Letters from British Officers during the American Revolution; Neutral Rights and the War in the Narrow Seas, 1778–82.* His articles have appeared in *The William and Mary Quarterly, The Bulletin of the Institute of Historical Research, The Journal of the Society for Army Historical Research, New York History, The Mariner's Mirror, Military Review, U.S. Naval Institute Proceedings, Armed Forces and Society, The Naval War College Review, Military Intelligence, The American Neptune,* and *Marine-Rundschau.* During the academic year 1981–82 he was the John F. Morrison Professor of Military History at the U.S. Army Command and General Staff College, Fort Leavenworth, Kansas.

JOE GRAY TAYLOR was Dean of Liberal Arts at McNeese State University, Lake Charles, Louisiana, before his death in 1987. He received a M.A. (1948) and Ph.D. (1951) in history from Louisiana State University. During the Second World War, he flew seventy combat missions as a bombardier-navigator with the 81st Bomb Squadron, 12th Bomb Group, Tenth Air Force, in the China–Burma–India Theater. He is the author of five Air Force Historical Studies, including *Close Air Support in the War Against Japan* and *Air Supply in the Burma Campaigns*. He has published articles in *Air Force History* and *Military Affairs*. Among numerous works on non-military history, he has published *Louisiana: A Bicentennial History* and *Eating, Drinking, and Visiting in the South: An Informal History*.

KENNETH R. WHITING, retired Chief of the Documentary Research Division, Center of Aerospace Doctrine, Research and Education, at the Air University, is a renowned Sovietologist. He received his Ph.D. in Russian history from Harvard University in 1951 and has contributed numerous articles and studies on Soviet and Chinese affairs to a variety of publications. Among works of relevance to his essay in this volume are *The Chinese Communist Armed Forces; The Development of the Soviet Armed Forces, 1917–1972; Soviet Air Power, 1917–1976;* and "Soviet Aviation and Air Power under Stalin, 1928–1941," in Robin Higham and Jacob W. Kipp, editors, *Soviet Aviation and Air Power: A Historical View.*

Index

Soviets in: 183
as threat to Allied invasion in North
 Africa: 224, 228
Spanish Civil War: 124
 German experience in: 34-36, 53, 70,
  72-73, 622
 poses dilemma for USSR: 181
 and Soviet Aviation: 27-30, 42, 181,
  187, 618
 as testing ground for aviation: 18, 23
Sperrle, Hugo, commander *Luftflotte 2*:
 119, 124, 133
Spruance, Raymond A.: 391
 commander, Fifth Fleet: 400, 418
 comments on *kamikaze*: 421
Squadrons (British), 1st Carrier:
 431-432
Squadrons (Japanese), 3d: 428
Squadrons (RAF)
 85: 133
 92: 255
 114: 81
Squadrons (U.S.)
 13th Tactical Fighter Wing: 549
 58th Fighter: 240
 555th Tactical Fighter Wing: 549
 VMF-513: 482
Stalin, Josef
 on air superiority: 29-30
 builds aviation: 179-184, 212
 and effect of purges on aviation:
  27-29, 183
 as head of state: 185, 202
 and nonaggression pact with Germany:
  28
 purges of: 183
 at Yalta: 208
Stalingrad, USSR: 204, 206, 207
 airlift: 212
 battle for: 194, 199
 Soviet victory at: 196, 198
Stanmore, England, command
 headquarters at: 167
Stavanger, Sala airfield, seized by
 Germans: 79
State Committee for Defense (Soviet),
 replaces Council of People's
 Commissars: 184-185
Stavka. See High Command.
Stearley, Ralph F., participates in
 preparation of FM 100-20: 262
Stouffer, Samuel: 153
Strait of Tiran

closed to Israeli shipping: 569
opened to Israeli shipping: 575
Strategic Air Command. *See also*
 United States Air Force.
 deploys B-29s to Europe: 464-465
 ordered to bomb Hanoi and Haiphong:
  551
 refueling aircraft in Thailand: 520,
  534, 547
 reinforces FEAF: 464
Strategic bombardment: viii
 in Battle of Britain: 100
 command of, Northwest Africa: 139
 doctrine: 49, 51-53, 226, 325
 effects of, on German industry:
  202-203, 292, 310-311
 against Japan: 383, 396, 400-407,
  422-426, 430-432
 Japanese response to: 408-414,
  415-416
 and *Luftwaffe*: 31, 32, 65-66
 against North Korean airfields: 462,
  467, 477-480, 482, 484-486, 491,
  494
 in Operation POINTBLANK: 279-307
 plans for Korea: 461
 responsibility for, Korean War: 454
 Soviet views of: 187-188, 201, 211,
  212
 in Spanish Civil War: 27, 28, 181
 views
  in Air Corps Tactical School: 45
  in Air War College: 47
  in Britain: 165
  in RAF, 1934
  in World War II: 65
Strategic Offensive Against Germany:
 vii-viii
Strategical aviation in World War II: 6
Stratemeyer, George E.
 Chief of Air Staff: 262
 commander, FEAF: 459, 460-461, 465
 receives reinforcements: 465
 stricken with heart attack: 476
 supports separate command of air
  power: 262
Suez Canal: 590
 Allied forces at: 224
 Anglo-French reoccupation of: 572
 closed to Israeli shipping: 569
 Egyptian crossing of: 589
 IAF attacks on: 583
 nationalization of: 567